MW01492547

Writing Appalachia

WRITING APPALACHIA

An Anthology

Edited by Katherine Ledford
and Theresa Lloyd

Rebecca Stephens, Associate Editor

Richard Parmer, Permissions Manager

Support provided in part by Mary and Orme Wilson through the Thomas D. Clark Foundation.

Editorial and Sales Offices: The University Press of Kentucky
663 South Limestone Street, Lexington, Kentucky 40508-4008
www.kentuckypress.com

Cataloging-in-Publication data available from the Library of Congress

ISBN 978-0-8131-7879-0 (hardcover)
ISBN 978-0-8131-7881-3 (pdf)
ISBN 978-0-8131-7882-0 (epub)

This book is printed on acid-free paper meeting
the requirements of the American National Standard
for Permanence in Paper for Printed Library Materials.

Manufactured in the United States of America.

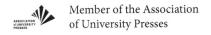
Member of the Association
of University Presses

Contents

A Note on the Selection of Texts

In choosing the copy-text for each entry, we have in most instances used the first published edition. When a writer has authorized a second published edition, as in, for example, a collection of poems or short stories, we have used that edition. In some instances, a writer has given us permission for yet another edition or has personally corrected a source text. In the bibliography and permissions section, we identify the edition from which the selection comes, the original publication date if it differs from that of the edition we used, and an author's request for emendations if one was made.

Introduction

Theresa Lloyd and Katherine Ledford

Appalachian literature is thriving. From the earliest oral traditions to print accounts of frontier exploration, from local color to modernism and postmodernism, from an exuberant flowering in the 1970s to its high popular and critical profile in the twenty-first century, Appalachian literature can boast a long tradition of delighting and provoking readers. Yet as anyone who enjoys reading or teaching this literature knows, finding an anthology that offers a representative selection of authors and texts from the earliest days to the present can be difficult. What you are now holding in your hands, or accessing through an electronic device, is the result of our efforts to assemble that book.

We are especially aware of the need to have a representative selection of Appalachian texts in one book because we teach Appalachian literature and have wished for such a book. The problem is not that the region's literature isn't available. Poems, short stories, and novels are available electronically from a myriad of websites; however, even today's computer-savvy readers and students can flounder when the material they seek is scattered to the four quarters of the internet.[1] Additionally, many specialized anthologies of Appalachian literature have appeared over the past few decades. Yet by their very nature, specialized anthologies cannot cover the full sweep of Appalachian literature and must be supplemented by other readings.[2]

Good older anthologies of Appalachian literature exist. Robert J. Higgs and Ambrose Manning's *Voices from the Hills: Selected Readings of Southern Appalachia* (1975) was an important, groundbreaking work that provided an excellent selection of Appalachian writings in one volume. But by the mid-1990s, changing ideas about Appalachia and literary theory, along with the remarkable number of fine authors whose works had appeared since the book's publication, made that collection feel incomplete. Aware of those gaps, Higgs and Manning, along with scholar and poet Jim Wayne Miller, published a two-volume sequel, *Appalachia Inside Out,* in 1995.

But to date, no one collection provides the historical depth and range of Appalachian literature, from Cherokee oral narratives to fiction and drama about mountaintop removal and prescription drug abuse, that contemporary readers and scholars seek. What is really needed, we feel, is a one-volume anthology of Appalachian literature that is comprehensive, reflects contemporary ideas about authorship and Appalachia, and brings readers well into the twenty-first century. That is what this book attempts to do.

In creating this anthology, we had a twofold task. Like all anthologists, we had to decide what principles would govern our selection of authors and, given those principles, what authors and texts we should include. But even before wrestling with those difficult decisions, we faced the conundrum that anyone working on our region confronts: just what do we mean when we say "Appalachia"? Geographically and conceptually, debate over this question runs high.

Merely determining the territory encompassed by the term "Appalachia" has been a matter of contention. Geographers' maps delineating the physiographic province of Appalachia, for example, outline a region stretching from central Alabama and Georgia northeast to the Atlantic Ocean off the coast of Labrador, and from the Piedmont through the western rim of the Cumberland Plateau as far as Ohio. However, late nineteenth- and early twentieth-century attempts to trace the region's boundaries, such as the map included in John C. Campbell's *The Southern Highlander and His Homeland* (1921), place the region within the borders of the slave-holding South with the Mason-Dixon Line demarcating the northern border, the Ohio and Mississippi Rivers marking off the western border, and elevation (the Blue Ridge) delimiting the eastern. The Appalachian Regional Commission's 1965 and subsequent maps of the region, guided by political and economic forces at play in the War on Poverty years, identify an area that incorporates portions of thirteen states, from the southern-tier counties of western New York to central Alabama and northeastern Mississippi, including significant parts of Ohio and a small chunk of the northwest South Carolina Piedmont. In sharp contrast to all of the above, folklorists and cultural geographers such as Henry Glassie and Terry Jordan-Bychkov insist that culturally, Southern and Central Appalachia are part of the Upland South, which runs from the eastern Piedmont of Virginia and the Carolinas west through Tennessee and Kentucky to include the Ozarks (Jordan-Bychkov argues that shared cultural traits extend the Upland South through East Texas); Northern Appalachia, they assert, is part of the mid-Atlantic and midwestern cultural regions.[3]

As with maps, the popular conception of the region has also been subject to vicissitudes and controversy. Prior to the mid-nineteenth century, the southern mountains were viewed as just that: southern, with a high elevation and a whiff of the backwater. Since the southern backwater had once lain as far east as the coastal plain, frontier rustication was not yet synonymous with mountain. Yet beginning in the mid-nineteenth century and flowering fully in the post–Civil War era, fueled by an enormous body of writing in the popular press, Appalachia became known as a land apart, home to what William Goodell Frost, president of Berea College, identified in 1899 as America's "contemporary ancestors." These curious creatures were alternately viewed either as a genetic and cultural reservoir of America's best (noble poor rural white people of northern European ancestry who spoke Elizabethan English and lived a lifestyle like that of the colonial era), or as a sad example of America's worst (degenerate poor rural white moonshiners and feudists who spoke substandard English).[4] Distorted though they may be, those two views of Appalachia are still present in the popular imagination, as best-seller lists and television shows indicate.[5]

That dichotomy—the romanticized and the degenerate—remained operative through the better part of the twentieth century, with few attempts at complicating it. (Horace Kephart, John C. Campbell, and Harry Caudill are notable exceptions.) Then, in the 1970s, under the influence of the civil rights movement and similar ideological initiatives among women, Native Americans, and other marginalized groups, Appalachian residents, together with activists and scholars, developed an Appalachian studies movement to challenge this distorted image of Appalachia and provide an accurate account of the region's history and contemporary situation.[6] This effort has produced outstanding writing, although in some quarters there has remained a tendency to continue romanticizing the region as a haven for old-time living and, as Ronald D Eller notes, "A flourishing minor industry has developed to fabricate such oddities as dulcimers, quilts, log cabins, and 'Hillbilly Chicken.'"[7] Some of the best statements on the conflicting narratives comprising the "invention" of Appalachia appear, of course, in the literature of the region and the scholarship on that literature.[8]

In navigating these turbulent waters, we also had to ask ourselves what story of the region we wanted to tell. In answering this question, we were influenced by current ideas about anthologies and the literary canon. Whereas most early- to mid-twentieth-century American anthologies attempted to produce a master narrative—a collection of canonical authors whose work and biographies support one particular vision of the nation, region, or group represented—contemporary critical theory's expanded ideas of authorship have challenged that approach, which tends to exclude writers who fail to conform to the master narrative, such as women or ethnic minorities.[9] Hence, anthologists today (ourselves included) tend to view their collections as dialogues or debates among sometimes conflicting voices.[10]

Indeed, in Appalachia, as in other regions, the culture, like the geographic configuration, can be seen as porous—that is, the boundaries are constantly changing. The result is that no one can definitively say what Appalachia is or is not, even though almost everyone seems to try. As Douglas Reichert Powell observes, "Regions are not so much places themselves but ways of describing relationships among places. These descriptions serve particular purposes for the people doing the describing."[11] It is precisely this unsettled definition and the controversies it continues to inspire that is the story we wish to tell in this anthology. Appalachia is complicated, and this rich complexity is worth celebrating and studying.

What is the traditional master narrative of Appalachian literature and scholarship? Higgs and Manning summarize it succinctly: "the mountaineer, [and] his struggles with himself, nature, and the outside world."[12] While it is undeniably true that this story of the (white male) mountaineer has been important throughout the region (and is represented in this anthology), many other stories have existed as well, and we do not want to leave them out—to perpetuate what Edward Cabbell calls black "invisibility" in Appalachia, for example, or to relegate women to "walk-ons in the third act," as Barbara Ellen Smith characterizes the region's historiography, or to deny the experiences of LGBTQ Appalachians.[13] Hence, diverse voices of gender, sexuality, ethnicity, and race speak throughout this anthology through authors such as Elias Boudinot, Frank X Walker, August Wilson, Dorothy Allison, Jeff Mann, and Blake Hausman.

In addition to correcting the obvious omission of a multitude of voices from the traditional Appalachian master narrative, we wanted to avoid miring this anthology in what Theresa Lloyd calls "mama and biscuits literature"—texts that for good or ill stereotype Appalachia as a land of simple agrarian folklife. Not that we fail to represent regional folklore—those looking for it will be pleased to find Jack tales, traditional songs, snake lore, and a great deal more. But along with an important agrarian heritage, our region has long had an urban and suburban dimension. Art historian Betsy White, for example, has demonstrated the presence of a thriving fine arts tradition fully reflective of international trends in western Virginia and East Tennessee towns along the Great Road, a heavily traveled trade route running along the contemporary I-81 corridor from Pennsylvania to Southern Appalachia.[14] In 1858, (West) Virginia artist and author David Hunter Strother confirmed this blend of backwoods and urbane, noting that in East Tennessee one could find both "the prints of the deer-skin moccasin and the French kid slipper," or "the mud-chinked cabin of the pioneer" beside "the elegant villa from a design by Downing or Vaux."[15] In the twentieth and twenty-first centuries, the region has felt the full effects of industrialization, modern transportation, consumerism, migration, the centralization of American agricultural production in agribusiness enterprises outside the region, suburbanization, the global connections of the internet, and the multiple genres of electronic media. These forces have virtually obliterated traditional agrarian Appalachia, although an interest in local foods in the region, part and parcel of a larger local foods movement in the United States, is fueling a return to home gardening and small-scale, specialized farming. This anthology includes not only the canonical texts that have constructed the idea of Appalachia as a rural, isolated folk society— such as work by Jesse Stuart and James Still—but also writings that challenge that stereotype by portraying the region as urban or suburban, and as fully engaged with the social, intellectual, economic, and political world beyond the mountains—as in texts by Thomas Wolfe, Lisa Alther, Jayne Anne Phillips, and many others.[16]

One non-agrarian facet of the Appalachian experience that has been fully documented in its literature is the effects of the extractive and manufacturing industries, such as coal and textiles. This anthology tells that story through both conventional and more radical texts. Represented are genres and authors such as fiction by Rebecca Harding Davis, Thomas Bell, and Denise Giardina; poetry by Don West, Irene McKinney, and Ron Rash; nonfiction by Mary Harris "Mother" Jones and Harry Caudill; protest songs by Aunt Molly Jackson and Ella May Wiggins; and a strike narrative collected from "Bloody" Harlan County in the 1930s.

Another story that we felt was important to tell was that of the Appalachian environment. Nowhere is human stewardship of the environment more pressing than in the region's coalfields, where people and nature suffer the effects of mining and mountaintop removal, as articulated here by Ann Pancake, Robert Gipe, and Wendell Berry. Yet nowhere more than in our mountains is the possibility of an intimate human-nature relationship as obvious, as witnessed by the writing of Harvey Broome, Harry Middleton, Marilou Awiakta, and bell hooks, among others. Presenting a new vision of agrarianism, Barbara Kingsolver argues the importance of local farming for Appalachia's people and environment, as Sandor Katz and Shannon Hayes encourage readers to relearn homemaking and fermentation skills as a form of activism.

Having explored the stories of Appalachia that we wanted this anthology to tell, we still faced a vexatious problem: who would get to tell those stories? That is, just who is an Appalachian author? The simple answer would be writers born in the region who write about regional topics—for example, Mildred Haun, Harriette Arnow, Wilma Dykeman, Robert Morgan, Fred Chappell, Lee Smith, Harry Caudill, and Jo Carson. However, that definition would have forced us to leave out important writings about the region by authors not born here, such as William Bartram, George Washington Harris, Mary Noailles Murfree, Horace Kephart, and others. It could also have led us to omit significant authors born here but whose writings are not obviously regional, such as Charles Wright. Ultimately, we decided to follow the lead of the Appalachian Writers Association in defining Appalachian authors: writers who were born in the region, adopted the region, or wrote about a significant experience in the region.

Nonetheless, decisions about whom to include were hard to make. We wanted to satisfy expectations by including authors who have a following among the region's readers and scholars, but we also wanted to break new ground by introducing authors who had been marginalized or ignored in the discourse of Appalachian literature. Furthermore, especially since the 1970s, that era of literary outpouring that some scholars identify as the Appalachian Renaissance, so many outstanding authors have been publishing that we were forced to omit many worthy candidates. (Our publisher wisely insisted that we keep the book to one reasonably sized volume.) We know that readers will lament the absence of one favorite author or another, but we hope that our suggestion of the range of Appalachian literature is broad enough to accommodate the region's multitudinous stories. We rely on the excellent specialized anthologies of Appalachian writing to flesh out the stories for those readers who seek more.

Another way that we wanted to break new ground was by including authors from Northern Appalachia. We acknowledge that there are strong arguments for not doing so and for focusing instead on what John Alexander Williams calls "core" Appalachia—that is, the southern mountains as defined by Campbell and others.[17] Aside from the precedent set by previous anthologies and collections of scholarship, along with the southern-focused expectations of readers who encounter the word "Appalachia," it is in writings from the southern highlands that one finds the "shared themes and narrated stances, . . . [the] repeated and revised tropes" that, according to Henry Louis Gates, are the hallmark of a literary movement.[18] But as Katherine Ledford notes, incorporating Northern Appalachian authors invites us to engage in comparative regional studies—for example, to examine the concept of the American frontier in the writings of New Yorker James Fenimore Cooper as well as in the southern account of Anne Newport Royall, or to study the effects of extractive-industrial economies in Jason Miller's Pennsylvania and Harry Caudill's Kentucky.

Scholars of the South may wonder how we distinguish Appalachian literature from its non-montane cousins of the Upland South. Hugh Holman raised the question in his 1976 review of *Voices from the Hills*, and it still has relevance.[19] There are, for example, obvious similarities between the poor mountain whites of Murfree and Fox, and their counterparts in the work of lowland southern authors Caldwell and O'Connor, who are not included in this Appalachian anthology.[20] But southern literary studies have tended to give short shrift to Appalachian authors, as Fred Chappell and Rodger Cunningham have noted, making the need for Appalachian literary studies of continuing relevance.[21] Even more important is the obvious fact of a demonstrable, self-conscious literary tradition in the southern highlands.

As for the genres we have included, they range from the traditional belles-lettres—fiction, poetry, and drama—to nonfiction, diaries, interviews, song lyrics, and oral literature. We have a preference for complete units—for example, short stories over selections from novels, essays over portions of nonfiction books or, when we simply could not ignore an important book, whole chapters or excerpts that provide a sense of completeness.

The difficulties of acquiring copyright permissions, the bane of the anthologist, vexed us as well. We had to make some hard choices when permissions trails went cold or when manageable deals could not be struck with copyright holders. Some writing we wished to include was off-limits to us due to copyright restrictions increasingly imposed by large commercial publishing houses. Within these restrictions, we have tried to construct an anthology that covers much ground and does so in a representative manner. We acknowledge that this anthology is only the beginning of the Appalachian story, and we encourage readers and instructors to supplement this anthology with a complete long work such as a novel or a collection of short stories or poems for a more sustained experience with an author and her or his craft.

As our story of creating this anthology suggests, we have been concerned with simultaneously representing, complicating, and furthering the discourse on the Appalachian region and its cultures. The complexity that we have struggled to understand and represent here speaks to the undeniable value of regional studies. Particularly since the rise of critical theory in the 1990s, some scholars have brushed off regional studies as a type of soft scholarship, inferior to studies of race, class, gender, sexuality, or the environment. The richness represented in these pages reveals that this assumption is simply not true.

This, then, is the vision of Appalachia and its literature represented in our anthology. Mountain and valley, rural and urban, folkloric and postmodern, traditional and au courant, northern and southern, white people and people of color, straight and gay, insiders and outsiders, sinners and saints—the dualisms multiply, endlessly and excitingly, and maybe, on some level, are not dualistic at all.

Notes

1. Websites for locating Appalachian writing include Documenting the American South (docsouth.unc.edu) and Making of America (quod.lib.umich.edu/m/moagrp/).

2. Outstanding specialized anthologies include W. K. McNeil, ed., *Appalachian Images in Folk and Popular Culture* (1995); Sandra L. Ballard and Patricia L Hudson, eds., *Listen Here: Women Writing in Appalachia* (2003); Felicia Mitchell, ed., *Her Word: Diverse Voices in Contemporary Appalachian Women's Poetry* (2003); Kevin E. O'Donnell and Helen Hollingsworth, eds., *Seekers of Scenery: Travel Writing from Southern Appalachia, 1840–1900* (2004); Mar-

ita Garin, ed., *Southern Appalachian Poetry: An Anthology of Works by Thirty-Seven Poets* (2008); Jessie Graves and William Wright, eds., *The Southern Poetry Anthology: Contemporary Appalachia* (2010); Chris Green, ed., *Coal: A Poetry Anthology* (2006); and *Anthology of Appalachian Writers* (a journal-like, serial publication of contemporary Appalachian writing published by Shepherd University).

3. John C. Campbell, *The Southern Highlander and His Homeland* (1921); Henry Glassie, *Pattern in the Material Folk Culture of the Eastern United States* (1968); Terry G. Jordan-Bychkov, *The Upland South: The Making of an American Folk Region and Landscape* (2003).

4. William Goodell Frost, "Our Contemporary Ancestors in the Southern Mountains," *Atlantic Monthly,* 1899. A recent controversial literary example that reinforces the degenerate-culture vision of Appalachia is J. D. Vance's *Hillbilly Elegy: A Memoir of a Family and Culture in Crisis* (2016). Vance's book has generated so much popular attention on the region that several Appalachian authors, including many of the authors featured in this anthology, decided to write back against Vance's portrayal of Appalachia in *Appalachian Reckoning: A Region Responds to "Hillbilly Elegy"* (2018). Examples of the degenerate-culture representation in the contemporary media include *The Wild and Wonderful Whites of West Virginia* (https://www. youtube.com/watch?v=AQBiXDNVeSA); *Buckwild* (http://www.mtv.com/ shows/ buckwild/ series.jhtml), *Squidbillies* (https://www.adultswim.com/search?q=squidbillies), and *Saturday Night Live*'s "Appalachian Emergency Room" (http://www.nbc.com/saturday-night-live/ video/appalachian-emergency-room/n12005/).

5. The contemporary popular media engage less in romanticization of Appalachians, although the trope abounds in the literature. Nothing seems to be filling the beloved shoes of *The Waltons* (serialized from 1972 to 1981 and made into television movies three times in the 1990s) or *Christy,* the 1994–1995 television series about a stoic young city girl teaching in the Tennessee mountains in 1912 who gently guides the mountain people away from their bad ways, bringing out their natural goodness. The character Kenneth Parcel, played by Jack McBrayer, on the television comedy *30 Rock* (2006–2013) may be the best example of contemporary media's embracing of the "good" qualities of Appalachian people, albeit couched within the all-too-familiar hillbilly stereotypes. Kenneth, from Stone Mountain, Georgia, is unfailingly cheerful, kind, and honest. He is also misogynistic and religiously narrow-minded. He rejects science and supports the Confederacy. References to incest abound when Kenneth is around.

6. Chad Berry, Philip J. Obermiller, and Shaunna L. Scott, eds, *Studying Appalachian Studies: Making the Path by Walking* (2015).

7. Eller, *Miners, Millhands, and Mountaineers: Industrialization of the Appalachian South, 1880–1930* (1982), xvii. For a discussion of the commodification and fetishization of Appalachia, see Allen W. Batteau, *The Invention of Appalachia* (1990).

8. Batteau, *The Invention of Appalachia.* See also Henry Shapiro, *Appalachia on Our Mind: The Southern Mountains and Mountaineers in the American Consciousness, 1870–1920* (1978).

9. For a discussion of master narratives in late nineteenth- and early twentieth-century anthologies of southern literature, see Susan Harrell Irons, "Southern Literary Reconstructionists: Shaping Southern Literary Identity, 1895–1915" (Ph.D diss., University of North Carolina, Chapel Hill, 2001).

10. William Andrews, preface to *The Literature of the American South: A Norton Anthology* (1998), xxii.

11. Douglas Reichert Powell, *Critical Regionalism: Connecting Politics and Culture in the American Landscape* (2007), 10.

12. Robert J. Higgs and Ambrose Manning, *Voices from the Hills: Selected Readings of Southern Appalachia* (1975), xvii.

13. Edward J. Cabbell, "Black Invisibility and Racism in Appalachia: An Informal Survey," in *Blacks in Appalachia*, ed. William H. Turner and Edward J. Cabbell (1985); Barbara Ellen Smith, "Walk-Ons in the Third Act: The Role of Women in Appalachian Historiography," *Journal of Appalachian Studies* (1998); Jeff Mann, *Loving Mountains, Loving Men* (2005).

14. Betsy K. White, *Great Road Style: The Decorative Arts Legacy of Southwest Virginia and Northeast Tennessee* (2006).

15. Strother, "A Winter in the South, Fifth Paper," *Harper's New Monthly Magazine* (1858), 721.

16. Rudy Abramson and Jean Haskell, eds., *The Encyclopedia of Appalachia* (2006), which emphasized the region's urban as well as rural dimensions, pioneered this multi-tiered approach to Appalachian studies. We follow this lead.

17. John Alexander Williams, *Appalachia: A History* (2002), 13.

18. Henry Louis Gates Jr., *The Signifying Monkey: A Theory of African-American Literary Criticism* (1988), 127.

19. C. Hugh Holman, "Appalachian Literature? Two Views," *Appalachian Journal* (1976), 79.

20. See, for example, Sylvia Jenkins Cook, *From Tobacco Road to Route 66: The Southern Poor White in Fiction* (1976).

21. Fred Chappell, "The Shape of Southern Literature to Come: An Interview with Will Hickson"; and Rodger Cunningham, "Writing on the Cusp: Double Alterity and Minority Discourse in Appalachia," in *The Future of Southern Letters,* ed. Jefferson Humphries and John Lowe (1996).

PART I
Early Appalachian Literature
Kevin E. O'Donnell

The texts collected here describe late eighteenth- and early nineteenth-century Appalachia as a geographical and political frontier. They also reveal how this borderland became a cultural, rhetorical, and mythical frontier.

Appalachia's first residents were Native Americans, who have occupied the region for at least eleven thousand years. In the eighteenth century, the dominant nations were the Cherokee, Creek, and Chickasaw in Southern Appalachia; the Shawnee in Central Appalachia; and the Iroquois (or Five Nations) in Northern Appalachia. According to King George's Proclamation of 1763, the lands west of the Blue Ridge were reserved for Native Americans and off-limits for white settlement.

The Proclamation of 1763 became a major grievance of the colonists on the eve of the American Revolution, since the Virginia gentry looked to land speculation in the trans-Allegheny region as a means of resolving their debts to English merchants. The defeat of the British in the Revolution was also the defeat of their Native American allies, resulting in the opening of the western lands. In many instances, the government gave vast tracts to those who had served in the Revolution.

Ethnically, Appalachia's white settlers were mostly Scots-Irish, German, and English. Migrants ranged from squatters to entrepreneurs and artisans, with many becoming tenants on large landholdings of the wealthy. Most African Americans came to the region as the slaves of white settlers or of assimilated Cherokee, with a few arriving as escaped slaves or free people. In many ways, Appalachia's settlement was typical of westward expansion throughout the United States.

The mythic history differs from the actual, however. James Fenimore Cooper's fictional frontier hero, Natty Bumppo, embodies a frontier myth already well established by the 1820s: he is a deliberate echo of Daniel Boone, a white who exhibits Native American traits and eschews Europeanized society. The historical Boone had been dead for only a few years by 1823, when Cooper first published *The Pioneers,* excerpted here.

Elias Boudinot (Gallegina "Buck" Watie), a Cherokee who had assimilated to white culture but still wanted to preserve the Cherokee Nation, represents another cultural hybrid that emerged in early nineteenth-century Appalachia. Boudinot helped found the *Cherokee Phoenix,* a bilingual English-Cherokee newspaper. His writings gave his nation a voice in regional and national politics in the dark days prior to the Cherokee's removal from their homeland. Initially a staunch opponent of the removal, he supported the policy only after he saw the tribe's options narrow. During the removal of 1838–1839, nearly a fourth of the nation died along the "Trail of Tears." Though Boudinot has been judged harshly, readers of his 1826 "An Address to the Whites," a fund-raising speech for a printing press, can see the impossible tensions he was attempting to negotiate as he tried to ensure his nation's survival.

A more traditionalist Cherokee voice emerges in the Cherokee myths collected by James Mooney at the end of the nineteenth century. That voice is clearly mediated: the myths were collected two generations after removal and transcribed by a young white American of Irish descent who was new to the Cherokee language. Nonetheless, the myths suggest one reason why the removal policy was so strongly opposed by most Cherokees—the culture was deeply and intimately connected to the landscape, including the flora and fauna, of Appalachia.

The selections here also include Enlightenment-era Euro-American views of Appalachia. Thomas Jefferson, in *Notes on the State of Virginia,* using grand and precise terms, describes Appalachian Virginia with a thinly veiled nationalist pride. William Bartram likewise deploys the language of the European Enlightenment to describe Appalachia—though Bartram's view is more intimate, botanically oriented, and infused with a poetic Romanticism. Bartram traveled into the mountains of what is now western North Carolina in the spring of 1775, around the onset of the American Revolution. It was a dangerous time to be on the frontier, yet the Indians refrained from killing him. He was the first to scientifically describe many of Southern Appalachia's most beautiful plant species, including the flame azalea, though other botanists preceded him in publication and thus secured the naming rights for themselves.

Sources: Annette Kolodny, *The Lay of the Land: Metaphor as Experience and History in American Life and Letters* (1975); Terry G. Jordan and Matti Kaups, *The American Backwoods Frontier: An Ethnic and Ecological Interpretation* (1989); Wilma Dunaway, *First American Frontier: Transition to Capitalism in Southern Appalachia, 1700–1860* (1996); Woody Holton, *Forced Founders: Indian, Debtors, Slaves & the Making of the American Revolution in Virginia* (1999); John Alexander Williams, *Appalachia: A History* (2002); Andrea Wulf, *Founding Gardeners: The Revolutionary Generation, Nature, and the Shaping of the American Nation* (2012).

Cherokee Narratives

Native American oral literature, such as that of the Cherokee, is Appalachia's earliest literary tradition. The Cherokee themselves date their arrival in southern Appalachia to several thousand years ago, and some Cherokee origination stories state that the people have always lived here. The Cherokee language is part of the Algonquian language family, which may explain the parallels between Cherokee creation accounts and those of the Iroquois and Ojibwe in the Northeast.

At the time of first contact with Europeans in the late 1500s, the Cherokee controlled a territory stretching from what is now Kentucky and Virginia south to the Carolinas, Georgia, and Alabama, with actual residence centered in the southern part of this area. The traditional economy included agriculture (the work of women) and hunting (the work of men). Socially, the Cherokee were matrilineal and matrifocal, with women holding important tribal leadership positions.

The Cherokee had a complex culture with highly developed sacred rituals and arts, including oral literature. Though the Cherokee developed a writing system in the nineteenth century, many of their traditional narratives, poems, and songs were transmitted orally.

James Mooney (1861–1921), a white ethnographer, collected the narratives included in this anthology from the Eastern Band Cherokee in the late nineteenth century. Eastern Band Cherokee are descended from removal-era traditionalists who eluded capture and expatriation, along with escapees from the Trail of Tears and others who returned to the mountains. With the help of white friends, these Cherokee were able to purchase tracts of their old lands in North Carolina, which form the current Cherokee homeland in the East.

How the World Was Made

The earth is a great island floating in a sea of water, and suspended at each of the four cardinal points by a cord hanging down from the sky vault, which is of solid rock. When the world grows old and worn out, the people will die and the cords will break and let the earth sink down into the ocean, and all will be water again. The Indians are afraid of this.

When all was water, the animals were above in Gălûñ'lătĭ, beyond the arch; but it was very much crowded, and they were wanting more room. They wondered what was below the water, and at last Dâyuni'sĭ, "Beaver's Grandchild," the little Water-beetle, offered to go and see if it could learn. It darted in every direction over the surface of the water, but could find no firm place to rest. Then it dived to the bottom and came up with some soft mud, which began to grow and spread on every side until it became the island which we call the earth. It was afterward fastened to the sky with four cords, but no one remembers who did this.

At first the earth was flat and very soft and wet. The animals were anxious to get down, and sent out different birds to see if it was yet dry, but they found no place to alight and came back again to Gălûñ′lătĭ. At last it seemed to be time, and they sent out the Buzzard and told him to go and make ready for them. This was the Great Buzzard, the father of all the buzzards we see now. He flew all over the earth, low down near the ground, and it was still soft. When he reached the Cherokee country, he was very tired, and his wings began to flap and strike the ground, and wherever they struck the earth there was a valley, and where they turned up again there was a mountain. When the animals above saw this, they were afraid that the whole world would be mountains, so they called him back, but the Cherokee country remains full of mountains to this day.

When the earth was dry and the animals came down, it was still dark, so they got the sun and set it in a track to go every day across the island from east to west, just overhead. It was too hot this way, and Tsiska′gĭlĭ′, the Red Crawfish, had his shell scorched a bright red, so that his meat was spoiled; and the Cherokee do not eat it. The conjurers put the sun another hand-breadth higher in the air, but it was still too hot. They raised it another time, and another, until it was seven handbreadths high and just under the sky arch. Then it was right, and they left it so. This is why the conjurers call the highest place Gûlkwâ′gine Di′gălûñ′lătiyûñ′, "the seventh height," because it is seven hand-breadths above the earth. Every day the sun goes along under this arch, and returns at night on the upper side to the starting place.

There is another world under this, and it is like ours in everything—animals, plants, and people—save that the seasons are different. The streams that come down from the mountains are the trails by which we reach this underworld, and the springs at their heads are the doorways by which we enter it, but to do this one must fast and go to water and have one of the underground people for a guide. We know that the seasons in the underworld are different from ours, because the water in the springs is always warmer in winter and cooler in summer than the outer air.

When the animals and plants were first made—we do not know by whom—they were told to watch and keep awake for seven nights, just as young men now fast and keep awake when they pray to their medicine. They tried to do this, and nearly all were awake through the first night, but the next night several dropped off to sleep, and the third night others were asleep, and then others, until, on the seventh night, of all the animals only the owl, the panther, and one or two more were still awake. To these were given the power to see and to go about in the dark, and to make prey of the birds and animals which must sleep at night. Of the trees only the cedar, the pine, the spruce, the holly, and the laurel were awake to the end, and to them it was given to be always green and to be greatest for medicine, but to the others it was said: "Because you have not endured to the end you shall lose your hair every winter."

Men came after the animals and plants. At first there were only a brother and sister until he struck her with a fish and told her to multiply, and so it was. In seven days a child was born to her, and thereafter every seven days another, and they increased very fast until there was danger that the world could not keep them. Then it was made that a woman should have only one child in a year, and it has been so ever since.

Origin of Strawberries

When the first man was created and a mate was given to him, they lived together very happily for a time, but then began to quarrel, until at last the woman left her husband and started off toward Nûñdâgûñ'yĭ, the Sun land, in the east. The man followed alone and grieving, but the woman kept on steadily ahead and never looked behind, until Une″lănûñ′hĭ, the great Apportioner (the Sun), took pity on him and asked him if he was still angry with his wife. He said he was not, and Une″lănûñ′hĭ then asked him if he would like to have her back again, to which he eagerly answered yes.

So Une″lănûñ′hĭ caused a patch of the finest ripe huckleberries to spring up along the path in front of the woman, but she passed by without paying any attention to them. Farther on he put a clump of blackberries, but these also she refused to notice. Other fruits, one, two, and three, and then some trees covered with beautiful red service berries, were placed beside the path to tempt her, but she still went on until suddenly she saw in front a patch of large ripe strawberries, the first ever known. She stooped to gather a few to eat, and as she picked them she chanced to turn her face to the west, and at once the memory of her husband came back to her and she found herself unable to go on. She sat down, but the longer she waited the stronger became her desire for her husband, and at last she gathered a bunch of the finest berries and started back along the path to give them to him. He met her kindly and they went home together.

The Ball Game of the Birds and Animals

Once the animals challenged the birds to a great ballplay, and the birds accepted. The leaders made the arrangements and fixed the day, and when the time came both parties met at the place for the ball dance, the animals on a smooth grassy bottom near the river and the birds in the treetops over by the ridge. The captain of the animals was the Bear, 'who was so strong and heavy' that he could pull down anyone who got in his way. All along the road to the ball ground he was tossing up great logs to show his strength and boasting of what he would do to the birds when the game began. The Terrapin, too—not the little one we have now, but the great original Terrapin—was with the animals. His shell was so hard that the heaviest blows could not hurt him, and he kept rising up on his hind legs and dropping heavily again to the ground, bragging that this was the way he would crush any bird that tried to take the ball from him. Then there was the Deer, who could outrun every other animal. Altogether it was a fine company.

The birds had the Eagle for their captain, with the Hawk and the great Tlă′nuwă, all swift and strong of flight, but still they were a little afraid of the animals. The dance was over and they were all pruning their feathers up in the trees and waiting for the captain to give the word when here came two little things hardly larger than field mice climbing up the tree in which sat perched the bird captain. At last they reached the top, and creeping along the limb to where the Eagle captain sat they asked to be allowed to join in the game. The captain looked at them, and seeing that they were four-footed, he asked why they did not go to the animals, where they belonged. The little things said that they had, but the animals had made fun of them and driven them off because they were so small. Then the bird captain pitied them and wanted to take them.

But how could they join the birds when they had no wings? The Eagle, the Hawk, and the others consulted, and at last it was decided to make some wings for the little fellows. They tried for a long time to think of something that might do, until someone happened to remember the drum they had used in the dance. The head was of ground-hog skin and maybe they could cut off a corner and make wings of it. So they took two pieces of leather from the drumhead and cut them into shape for wings, and stretched them with cane splints and fastened them on to the forelegs of one of the small animals, and in this way came *Tla'mehă,* the Bat. They threw the ball to him and told him to catch it, and by the way he dodged and circled about, keeping the ball always in the air and never letting it fall to the ground, the birds soon saw that he would be one of their best men.

Now they wanted to fix the other little animal, but they had used up all their leather to make wings for the Bat, and there was no time to send for more. Somebody said that they might do it by stretching his skin, so two large birds took hold from opposite sides with their strong bills, and by pulling at his fur for several minutes they managed to stretch the skin on each side between the fore and hind feet, until they had *Tewa,* the Flying Squirrel. To try him the bird captain threw up the ball, when the Flying Squirrel sprang off the limb after it, caught it in his teeth and carried it through the air to another tree nearly across the bottom.

When they were all ready the signal was given and the game began, but almost at the first toss the Flying Squirrel caught the ball and carried it up a tree, from which he threw it to the birds, who kept it in the air for some time until it dropped. The Bear rushed to get it, but the Martin darted after it and threw it to the Bat, who was flying near the ground, and by his dodging and doubling kept it out of the way of even the Deer, until he finally threw it in between the posts and won the game for the birds.

The Bear and the Terrapin, who had boasted so of what they would do, never got a chance even to touch the ball. For saving the ball when it dropped, the birds afterwards gave the Martin a gourd in which to build his nest, and he still has it.

The Rattlesnake's Vengeance

One day in the old times when we could still talk with other creatures, while some children were playing about the house, their mother inside heard them scream. Running out she found that a rattlesnake had crawled from the grass, and taking up a stick she killed it. The father was out hunting in the mountains, and that evening when coming home after dark through the gap he heard a strange wailing sound. Looking about he found that he had come into the midst of a whole company of rattlesnakes, which all had their mouths open and seemed to be crying. He asked them the reason of their trouble, and they told him that his own wife had that day killed their chief, the Yellow Rattlesnake, and they were just now about to send the Black Rattlesnake to take revenge.

The hunter said he was very sorry, but they told him that if he spoke the truth he must be ready to make satisfaction and give his wife as a sacrifice for the life of their chief. Not knowing what might happen otherwise, he consented. They then told him that the Black Rattlesnake would go home with him and coil up just outside the door in the dark. He must go inside, where he would find his wife awaiting him, and ask her to get him a drink of fresh water from the spring. That was all.

He went home and knew that the Black Rattlesnake was following. It was night when he arrived and very dark, but he found his wife waiting with his supper ready. He sat down and asked for a drink of water. She handed him a gourd full from the jar, but he said he wanted it fresh from the spring, so she took a bowl and went out of the door. The next moment he heard a cry, and going out he found that the Black Rattlesnake had bitten her and that she was already dying. He stayed with her until she was dead, when the Black Rattlesnake came out from the grass again and said his tribe was now satisfied. He then taught the hunter a prayer song, and said, "When you meet any of us hereafter sing this song and we will not hurt you; but if by accident one of us should bite one of your people then sing this song over him and he will recover." And the Cherokee have kept the song to this day.

The Hunter and Selu

A hunter had been tramping over the mountains all day long without finding any game and when the sun went down, he built a fire in a hollow stump, swallowed a few mouthfuls of corn gruel and lay down to sleep, tired out and completely discouraged. About the middle of the night he dreamed and seemed to hear the sound of beautiful singing, which continued until near daybreak and then appeared to die away into the upper air.

All next day he hunted with the same poor success, and at night made his lonely camp again in the woods. He slept and the strange dream came to him again, but so vividly that it seemed to him like an actual happening. Rousing himself before daylight, he still heard the song, and feeling sure now that it was real, he went in the direction of the sound and found that it came from a single green stalk of corn (*selu*). The plant spoke to him, and told him to cut off some of its roots and take them to his home in the settlement, and the next morning to chew them and "go to water" before anyone else was awake, and then to go out again into the woods, and he would kill many deer and from that time on would always be successful in the hunt. The corn plant continued to talk, teaching him hunting secrets and telling him always to be generous with the game he took, until it was noon and the sun was high, when it suddenly took the form of a woman and rose gracefully into the air and was gone from sight, leaving the hunter alone in the woods.

He returned home and told his story, and all the people knew that he had seen Selu, the wife of Kana'tĭ. He did as the spirit had directed, and from that time was noted as the most successful of all the hunters in the settlement.

Origin of the Bear: The Bear Songs

Long ago there was a Cherokee clan called the Ani'-Tsâ'gûhĭ, and in one family of this clan was a boy who used to leave home and be gone all day in the mountains.

After a while he went oftener and stayed longer, until at last he would not eat in the house at all, but started off at daybreak and did not come back until night. His parents scolded, but that did no good, and the boy still went every day until they noticed that long brown hair was beginning to grow out all over his body. Then they wondered and asked him why it was that he wanted to be so much in the woods that he would not even eat at home. Said the boy, "I find plenty to eat there, and it is better than the corn and beans we have in the settlements, and pretty soon I am going into the woods to stay all the time." His parents were worried and begged him not to leave them, but he said, "It is better there than here, and you see I am beginning to be different already, so that I can not live here any longer. If you will come with me, there is plenty for all of us and you will never have to work for it; but if you want to come you must first fast seven days."

The father and mother talked it over and then told the headmen of the clan. They held a council about the matter and after everything had been said they decided: "Here we must work hard and have not always enough. There he says there is always plenty without work. We will go with him." So they fasted seven days, and on the seventh morning all the Ani'-Tsâ'gûhĭ left the settlement and started for the mountains as the boy led the way.

When the people of the other towns heard of it they were very sorry and sent their headmen to persuade the Ani'-Tsâ'gûhĭ to stay at home and not go into the woods to live. The messengers found them already on the way, and were surprised to notice that their bodies were beginning to be covered with hair like that of animals, because for seven days they had not taken human food and their nature was changing. The Ani'-Tsâ'gûhĭ would not come back, but said, "We are going where there is always plenty to eat. Hereafter we shall be called *yânû* (bears), and when you yourselves are hungry come into the woods and call us and we shall come to give you our own flesh. You need not be afraid to kill us, for we shall live always." Then they taught the messengers the songs with which to call them, and the bear hunters have these songs still. When they had finished the songs the Ani'-Tsâ'gûhĭ started on again and the messengers turned back to the settlements, but after going a little way they looked back and saw a drove of bears going into the woods.

First Bear Song

> *He-e! Ani'-Tsâ'gûhi, Ani'-Tsâ'gûhi, akwandu'li e'lanti' ginûn'ti,*
> *Ani'-Tsâ'gûhi, Ani'-Tsâ'gûhi, akwandu'li e'lanti' ginûn'ti—Yû!*

> He-e! The Ani'-Tsâ'gûhi, the Ani'-Tsâ'gûhi, I want to lay them low on the ground,
> The Ani'-Tsâ'gûhi, the Ani'-Tsâ'gûhi, I want to lay them low on the ground—Yû!

The bear hunter starts out each morning fasting and does not eat until near evening. He sings this song as he leaves camp, and again the next morning, but never twice the same day.

Second Bear Song

This song also is sung by the bear hunter, in order to attract the bears, while on his way from the camp to the place where he expects to hunt during the day. The melody is simple and plaintive.

> *He-e! Hayuya'haniwă', hayuya'haniwă', hayuya'haniwă', hayuya'haniwă',*
> *Tsistuyi' nehandu'yanû', Tsistuyi' nehandu'yanû'—Yoho-o!*
> *He-e! Hayuya'haniwă', hayuya'haniwă', hayuya'haniwă', hayuya'haniwă',*
> *Kuwâhi' nehandu'yanû', Kuwâhi' nehandu'yanû'—Yoho-o!*
> *He-e! Hayuya'haniwă', hayuya'haniwă', hayuya'haniwă', hayuya'haniwă',*
> *Uyâhye' nehandu'yanû', Uyâhye' nehandu'yanû'—Yoho-o!*
> *He-e! Hayuya'haniwă', hayuya'haniwă', hayuya'haniwă', hayuya'haniwă',*
> *Gâtegwâ' nehandu'yanû', Gâtegwâ' nehandu'yanû'—Yoho-o!*
> (Recited) *Ûlĕ-'nû' asĕhĭ' tadeyâ'statakûhĭ' gûñ'năge astû' tsĭkĭ'.*

He! Hayuya'haniwă' (four times),
   In Tsistu'yĭ you were conceived (two times)—Yoho!
He! Hayuya'haniwă' (four times),
   In Kuwâ'hĭ you were conceived (two times)—Yoho!
He! Hayuya'haniwă' (four times),
   In Uyâ'hye you were conceived (two times)—Yoho!
He! Hayuya'haniwă' (four times),
   In Gâte'gwâ you were conceived (two times)—Yoho!
And now surely we and the good black things, the best of all, shall see each other.

Thomas Jefferson

1743–1826

Both as a private citizen living at the foot of the eastern slope of Virginia's Blue Ridge Mountains and as a public architect of nationhood, Thomas Jefferson witnessed and wrought extraordinary changes in a burgeoning nation.

In 1774, Jefferson purchased 157 acres of land in Virginia, including Natural Bridge, for 20 shillings. This private purchase demonstrated Jefferson's interest in protecting and utilizing the American landscape, echoed later in the public acquisition of the Louisiana Purchase, which Jefferson oversaw in 1803 as the third president of the United States. Jefferson's particular dedication to Virginia is further evidenced by Monticello, his lifelong home and farm; Poplar Forest, his private retreat; and the University of Virginia, which he established and designed.

Jefferson idealized independent farmers, distrusted cities and bankers, and believed in decentralized power, despite the fact that he often acted with authority. A plantation owner who sought self-sufficiency for his farming enterprises via the labor of enslaved people, Jefferson was frequently in debt. He was a founding father and principal author of the Declaration of Independence, but writer Andrea Wulf also calls Jefferson a "founding gardener" because of his interest in crop rotation and experiments with fertilizers and new plants.

When French diplomat François Barbé-Marbois asked Jefferson about Virginia, Jefferson answered his many questions in book format, complete with botanical descriptions, a history of Virginia, an explanation of politics, and a characterization of the Native people. In *Notes on the State of Virginia* (1787), the only book he ever published, Jefferson describes the natural resources of Virginia, including its mountains. In this selection, Jefferson attempts to identify the geologic forces that formed the Appalachian mountain range and to situate the mountains in the geography of the new nation, enticing his readers with descriptions of Virginia mountain scenery.

FROM Notes on the State of Virginia

QUERY IV. A NOTICE OF ITS MOUNTAINS?

For the particular geography of our mountains I must refer to Fry and Jefferson's map of Virginia; and to Evans' analysis of this map of America, for a more philosophical view of them than is to be found in any other work. It is worthy of notice, that our mountains are not solitary and scattered confusedly over the face of the country; but that they commence at about one hundred and fifty miles from the sea-coast, are disposed in ridges, one behind another, running nearly parallel with the sea-coast, though rather approaching it as they advance north-eastwardly. To the south-west, as the tract of country between the sea-coast and the Mississippi becomes narrower, the mountains converge into a single ridge, which, as it approaches the Gulf of Mexico, subsides into plain country, and gives rise to some of the waters of that gulf, and particularly to a river called the Apalachicola, probably from the Apalachies, an Indian nation formerly residing on it. Hence the mountains giving rise to that river, and seen from its various parts, were called the Apalachian mountains, being in fact the end or termination only of the great ridges passing through the continent. European geographers, however, extended the name northwardly as far as the mountains extended; some giving it, after their separation into different ridges, to the Blue Ridge, others to the North Mountain, others to the Alleghany, others to the Laurel Ridge, as may be seen by their different maps. But the fact I believe is, that none of these ridges were ever known by that name to the inhabitants, either native or emigrant, but as they saw them so called in European maps. In the same direction, generally, are the veins of limestone, coal, and other minerals hitherto discovered; and so range the falls of our great rivers. But the courses of the great rivers are at right angles with these. James and Potomac penetrate through all the ridges of mountains eastward of the Alleghany; that is, broken by no water course. It is in fact the spine of the country between the Atlantic on one side, and the Mississippi and St. Lawrence on the other. The passage of the Potomac through the Blue Ridge is, perhaps, one of the most stupendous scenes in nature. You stand on a very high point of land. On your right comes up the Shenandoah, having ranged along the foot of the mountain an hundred miles to seek a vent. On your left approaches the Potomac, in quest of a passage also. In the moment of their junction, they rush together against the mountain, rend it asunder, and pass off to the sea. The first glance of this scene hurries our senses into the opinion, that this earth has been created in time, that the mountains were formed first, that the rivers began to flow afterwards, that in this place, particularly, they have been dammed up by the Blue Ridge of mountains, and have formed an ocean which filled the whole valley; that continuing to rise they have at length broken over at this spot, and have torn the mountain down from its summit to its base. The piles of rock on each hand, but particularly on the Shenandoah, the evident marks of their disrupture and avulsion from their beds by the most powerful agents of nature, corroborate the impression. But the distant finishing which nature has given to the picture, is of a very different character. It is a true contrast to the foreground. It is as placid and delightful as that is wild and tremendous. For the mountain being cloven asunder, she presents to your eye, through the cleft, a small catch of smooth blue horizon, at an infinite distance in the plain country, inviting you, as it were, from the riot and tumult roaring around, to pass through the breach and participate of the calm below. Here the eye ultimately composes itself; and that way, too, the road happens actually to lead. You cross the Potomac above the junction, pass along its side through the base of the mountain for three miles, its terrible precipices hanging in fragments over you, and within about twenty miles reach Fredericktown, and the fine country round that. This scene is worth a voyage across the Atlantic. Yet here, as in the neighborhood of the Natural Bridge, are people who have passed their lives within half a dozen miles, and have never been to survey these monuments of a war between rivers and mountains, which must have shaken the earth itself to its centre.

The height of our mountains has not yet been estimated with any degree of exactness. The Alleghany being the great ridge which divides the waters of the Atlantic from those of the Mississippi, its summit is doubtless more elevated above the ocean than that of any other mountain. But its relative height, compared with the base on which it stands, is not so great as that of some others, the country rising behind the successive ridges like the steps of stairs. The mountains of the Blue Ridge, and of these the Peaks of Otter, are thought to be of a greater height, measured from their base, than any others in our country, and perhaps in North America. From data, which may found a tolerable conjecture, we suppose the highest peak to be about four thousand feet perpendicular, which is not a fifth part of the height of the mountains of South America, nor one-third of the height which would be necessary in our latitude to preserve ice in the open air unmelted through the year. The ridge of mountains next beyond the Blue Ridge, called by us the North mountain, is of the greatest extent; for which reason they were named by the Indians the endless mountains.

Query V. Its Cascades and Caverns?

The only remarkable cascade in this country is that of the Falling Spring in Augusta. It is a water of James' river where it is called Jackson's river, rising in the warm spring mountains about twenty miles southwest of the warm spring, and flowing into that valley. About three-quarters of a mile from its source it falls over a rock two hundred feet into the valley below. The sheet of water is broken in its breadth by the rock, in two or three places, but not at all in its height. Between the sheet and rock, at the bottom, you may walk across dry. This cataract will bear no comparison with that of Niagara as to the quantity of water composing it; the sheet being only twelve or fifteen feet wide above and somewhat more spread below; but it is half as high again, the latter being only one hundred and fifty-six feet, according to the mensuration made by order of M. Vaudreuil, Governor of Canada, and one hundred and thirty according to a more recent account.

In the lime-stone country there are many caverns of very considerable extent. The most noted is called Madison's Cave, and is on the north side of the Blue Ridge, near the intersection of the Rockingham and Augusta line with the south fork of the southern river of Shenandoah. It is in a hill of about two hundred feet perpendicular height, the ascent of which, on one side, is so steep that you may pitch a biscuit from its summit into the river which washes its base. The entrance of the cave is, in this side, about two-thirds of the way up. It extends into the earth about three hundred feet, branching into subordinate caverns, sometimes ascending a little, but more generally descending, and at length terminates, in two different places, at basons of water of unknown extent, and which I should judge to be nearly on a level with the water of the river; however, I do not think they are formed by refluent water from that, because they are never turbid; because they do not rise and fall in correspondence with that in times of flood or of drought; and because the water is always cool. It is probably one of the many reservoirs with which the interior parts of the earth are supposed to abound, and yield supplies to the fountains of water, distinguished from others only by being accessible. The vault of this cave is of solid lime-stone, from twenty to forty or fifty feet high; through which water is continually percolating. This, trickling down the sides of the cave, has incrusted them over in the form of elegant drapery; and dripping from the top of the vault generates on that and on the base below, stalactites of a conical form, some of which have met and formed massive columns.

Another of these caves is near the North mountain, in the county of Frederic, on the lands of Mr. Zane. The entrance into this is on the top of an extensive ridge. You descend thirty or forty feet, as into a well, from whence the cave extends, nearly horizontally, four hundred feet into the earth, preserving a breadth of from twenty to fifty feet, and a height of from five to twelve feet. After entering this cave a few feet, the mercury, which in the open air was 50°, rose to 57° of Fahrenheit's thermometer, answering to 11° of Reaumur's, and it continued at that to the remotest parts of the cave. The uniform temperature of the cellars of the observatory of Paris, which are ninety feet deep, and of all subterraneous cavities of any depth, where no chemical agencies may be supposed to produce a factitious heat, has been found to be 10° of Reaumur, equal to 54½° of Fahrenheit. The temperature of the cave above mentioned so nearly corresponds with this, that the difference may be ascribed to a difference of instruments.

At the Panther gap, in the ridge which divides the waters of the Crow and the Calf pasture, is what is called the *Blowing Cave*. It is in the side of a hill, is of about one hundred feet diameter, and emits constantly a current of air of such force as to keep the weeds prostrate to the distance of twenty yards before it. This current is strongest in dry, frosty weather, and in long spells of rain weakest. Regular inspirations and expirations of air, by caverns and fissures, have been probably enough accounted for by supposing them combined with intermitting fountains; as they must of course inhale air while their reservoirs are emptying themselves, and again emit it while they are filling. But a constant issue of air, only varying in its force as the weather is drier or damper, will require a new hypothesis. There is another blowing cave in the Cumberland mountain, about a mile from where it crosses the Carolina line. All we know of this is, that it is not constant, and that a fountain of water issues from it.

The *Natural Bridge,* the most sublime of nature's works, though not comprehended under the present head, must not be pretermitted. It is on the ascent of a hill, which seems to have been cloven through its length by some great convulsion. The fissure, just at the bridge, is, by some admeasurements, two hundred and seventy feet deep, by others only two hundred and five. It is about forty-five feet wide at the bottom and ninety feet at the top; this of course determines the length of the bridge, and its height from the water. Its breadth in the middle is about sixty feet, but more at the ends, and the thickness of the mass, at the summit of the arch, about forty feet. A part of this thickness is constituted by a coat of earth, which gives growth to many large trees. The residue, with the hill on both sides, is one solid rock of lime-stone. The arch approaches the semi-elliptical form; but the larger axis of the ellipsis, which would be the cord of the arch, is many times longer than the transverse. Though the sides of this bridge are provided in some parts with a parapet of fixed rocks, yet few men have resolution to walk to them, and look over into the abyss. You involuntarily fall on your hands and feet, creep to the parapet, and peep over it. Looking down from this height about a minute, gave me a violent head-ache. If the view from the top be painful and intolerable, that from below is delightful in an equal extreme. It is impossible for the emotions arising from the sublime to be felt beyond what they are here; so beautiful an arch, so elevated, so light, and springing as it were up to heaven! The rapture of the spectator is really indescribable! The fissure continuing narrow, deep, and straight, for a considerable distance above and below the bridge, opens a short but very pleasing view of the North mountain on one side and Blue Ridge on the other, at the distance each of them of about five miles. This bridge is in the county of Rockbridge, to which it has given name, and affords a public and commodious passage over a valley which cannot be crossed elsewhere for a considerable distance. The stream passing under it is called Cedar creek. It is a water of James' river, and sufficient in the driest seasons to turn a grist-mill, though its fountain is not more than two miles above.

William Bartram

1739–1823

Son of the self-taught and well-connected eighteenth-century botanist John Bartram, William Bartram became a naturalist, specializing in the flora and fauna of the southern backcountry during the colonial and early national periods. Born in Philadelphia, Bartram benefited from his father's professional and personal connections to European and American politicians, scientists, and wealthy citizens. Bartram's talent for drawing led him to his life's work after false starts in a number of professions, including time as a merchant and a disastrous stint as an indigo planter in Florida.

After accompanying his father on a botanical collecting expedition through Florida in 1765, Bartram journeyed on his own through the South from 1773 to 1777. *Travels* (1791), Bartram's best-known and most influential work, is an account of these journeys. Much of the book describes the physical features, plants, animals, and inhabitants of this region. The detailed descriptions and lush imagery influenced British poets such as Wordsworth and Coleridge, among others, in the Romantic literary movement.

In the excerpt below, Bartram narrates his travels among the Cherokee. Bartram's largely unbiased depiction of Native Americans is atypical for his era. Today, as during his time, Bartram's texts are read for insight into Native communities as well as for their exquisite descriptions of plants, animals, and landscapes.

FROM Travels through North and South Carolina, Georgia, East and West Florida, the Cherokee Country, etc.

FROM PART III, CHAPTER III

Next morning after breakfasting on excellent coffee, relished with bucanned venison, hot corn cakes, excellent butter and cheese, [I] sat forwards again for Cowe, which was about fifteen miles distance, keeping the trading path which coursed through the low lands between the hills and the river, now spacious and well beaten by travellers, but somewhat intricate to a stranger, from the frequent collateral roads falling into it from villages or towns over the hills. After riding about four miles, mostly through fields and plantations, the soil incredibly fertile, arrived at the town of Echoe, consisting of many good houses, well inhabited. I passed through, and continued three miles farther to Nucasse, and three miles more brought me to Whatoga. Riding through this large town, the road carried me winding about through their little plantations of Corn, Beans, &c. up to the council-house, which was a very large dome or rotunda, situated on the top of an ancient artificial mount, and here my road terminated. All before me and on every side, appeared little plantations of young

Corn, Beans, &c. divided from each other by narrow strips or borders of grass, which marked the bounds of each one's property, their habitation standing in the midst. Finding no common high road to lead me through the town, I was now at a stand how to proceed farther; when observing an Indian man at the door of his habitation, three or four hundred yards distance from me, beckoning me to come to him, I ventured to ride through their lots, being careful to do no injury to the young plants, the rising hopes of their labour and industry; crossed a little grassy vale watered by a silver stream, which gently undulated through; then ascended a green hill to the house, where I was cheerfully welcomed at the door and led in by the chief, giving the care of my horse to two handsome youths, his sons. During my continuance here, about half an hour, I experienced the most perfect and agreeable hospitality conferred on me by these happy people; I mean happy in their dispositions, in their apprehensions of rectitude with regard to our social or moral conduct. O divine simplicity and truth, friendship without fallacy or guile, hospitality disinterested, native, undefiled, unmodified by artificial refinements!

My venerable host gracefully and with an air of respect, led me into an airy, cool apartment; where being seated on cabins, his women brought in a refreshing repast, consisting of sodden venison, hot corn cakes, &c. with a pleasant cooling liquor made of hommony well boiled, mixed afterwards with milk; this is served up either before or after eating in a large bowl, with a very large spoon or ladle to sup it with.

After partaking of this simple but healthy and liberal collation, and the dishes cleared off, Tobacco and pipes were brought; and the chief filling one of them, whose stem, about four feet long, was sheathed in a beautiful speckled snake skin, and adorned with feathers and strings of wampum, lights it and smoaks a few whiffs, puffing the smoak first towards the sun, then to the four cardinal points, and lastly over my breast, hands it towards me, which I cheerfully received from him and smoaked; when we fell into conversation. He first enquired if I came from Charleston? if I knew John Stewart, Esq. how long since I left Charleston? &c. Having satisfied him in my answers in the best manner I could, he was greatly pleased; which I was convinced of by his attention to me, his cheerful manners, and his ordering my horse a plentiful bait of corn, which last instance of respect is conferred on those only to whom they manifest the highest esteem, saying that corn was given by the Great Spirit only for food to man. [. . .]

After leaving my princely friend, I travelled about five miles through old plantations, now under grass, but which appeared to have been planted the last season; the soil exceeding fertile, loose, black, deep and fat. I arrived at Cowe about noon. This settlement is esteemed the capital town: it is situated on the bases of the hills on both sides of the river, near to its bank, and here terminates the great vale of Cowe, exhibiting one of the most charming natural mountainous landscapes perhaps any where to be seen; ridges of hills rising grand and sublimely one above and beyond another, some boldly and majestically advancing into the verdant plain, their feet bathed with the silver flood of the Tanase, whilst others far distant, veiled in blue mists, sublimely mounting aloft, with yet greater majesty lift up their pompous crests and overlook vast regions.

The vale is closed at Cowe by a ridge of mighty hills, called the Jore mountain, said to be the highest land in the Cherokee country, which crosses the Tanase here.

On my arrival at this town I waited on the gentlemen to whom I was recommended by letter, and was received with respect and every demonstration of hospitality and friendship.

I took my residence with Mr. Galahan the chief trader here, an ancient respectable man, who had been many years a trader in this country, and is esteemed and beloved by the Indians for his humanity, probity and equitable dealings with them; which, to be just and candid I am obliged to observe (and blush for my countrymen at the recital) is somewhat of a prodigy; as it is a fact, I am afraid too true, that the white traders in their commerce with the Indians, get great and frequent occasions of complaint of their dishonesty and violence: but yet there are few exceptions, as in the conduct of this gentleman, who furnishes a living instance of the truth of the old proverb, that "Honesty is the best policy;" for this old honest Hibernian has often been protected by the Indians, when all others round about him have been ruined, their property seized and themselves driven out of the country or slain by the injured, provoked natives.

Next day after my arrival I crossed the river in a canoe, on a visit to a trader who resided amongst the habitations on the other shore.

After dinner, on his mentioning some curious scenes amongst the hills, some miles distance from the river, we agreed to spend the afternoon in observations on the mountains.

After riding near two miles through Indian plantations of Corn, which was well cultivated, kept clean of weeds, and was well advanced, being near eighteen inches in height, and the Beans planted at the Corn-hills were above ground; we left the fields on our right, turning towards the mountains, and ascending through a delightful green vale or lawn, which conducted us in amongst the pyramidal hills, and crossing a brisk flowing creek, meandering through the meads, which continued near two miles, dividing and branching in amongst the hills. We then mounted their steep ascents, rising gradually by ridges of steps one above another, frequently crossing narrow fertile dales as we ascended: the air felt cool and animating, being charged with the fragrant breath of the mountain beauties, the blooming mountain cluster Rose, blushing Rhododendron and fair Lilly of the valley. [. . .]

Proceeding on our return to town, [we] continued through part of this high forest skirting on the meadows: began to ascend the hills of a ridge which we were under the necessity of crossing; and having gained its summit, enjoyed a most enchanting view; a vast expanse of green meadows and strawberry fields; a meandering river gliding through, saluting in its various turnings the swelling, green, turfy knolls, embellished with parterres of flowers and fruitful strawberry beds; flocks of turkies strolling about them; herds of deer prancing in the meads or bounding over the hills; companies of young, innocent Cherokee virgins, some busy gathering the rich fragrant fruit, others having already filled their baskets, lay reclined under the shade of floriferous and fragrant native bowers of Magnolia, Azalea, Philadelphus, perfumed Calycanthus, sweet Yellow Jessamine and cerulean Glycine frutescens, disclosing their beauties to the fluttering breeze, and bathing their limbs in the cool fleeting streams; whilst other parties more gay and libertine, were yet collecting strawberries, or wantonly chasing their companions, tantalising them, staining their lips and cheeks with the rich fruit.

This sylvan scene of primitive innocence was enchanting, and perhaps too enticing for hearty young men long to continue idle spectators.

In fine, nature prevailing over reason, we wished at least to have a more active part in their delicious sports. Thus precipitately resolving, we cautiously made our approaches, yet undiscovered, almost to the joyous scene of action. Now, although we meant no other than an innocent frolic with this gay assembly of hamadryades, we shall leave it to the person of feeling and sensibility to form an idea to what lengths our passions might have hurried us, thus warmed and excited, had it not been for the vigilance and care of some envious matrons who lay in ambush, and espying us gave the alarm, time enough for the nymphs to rally and assemble together. We however pursued and gained ground on a group of them, who had incautiously strolled to a greater distance from their guardians, and finding their retreat now like to be cut off, took shelter under cover of a little grove; but on perceiving themselves to be discovered by us, kept their station, peeping through the bushes; when observing our approaches, they confidently discovered themselves, and decently advanced to meet us, half unveiling their blooming faces, incarnated with the modest maiden blush, and with native innocence and cheerfulness, presented their little baskets, merrily telling us their fruit was ripe and sound.

We accepted a basket, sat down and regaled ourselves on the delicious fruit, encircled by the whole assembly of the innocent jocose sylvan nymphs: by this time the several parties, under the conduct of the elder matrons, had disposed themselves in companies on the green, turfy banks.

My young companion, the trader, by concessions and suitable apologies for the bold intrusion, having compromised the matter with them, engaged them to bring their collections to his house at a stipulated price: we parted friendly. [. . .]

From part III, chapter IV

After waiting two days at Cowe expecting a guide and protector to the Overhill towns, and at last being disappointed, I resolved to pursue the journey alone, though against the advice of the traders; the Overhill Indians being in an ill humour with the whites, in consequence of some late skirmishes between them and the frontier Virginians, most of the Overhill traders having left the nation. [. . .]

I was left again wandering alone in the dreary mountains, not indeed totally pathless, nor in my present situation entirely agreeable, although such scenes of primitive unmodified nature always pleased me.

May we suppose that mankind feel in their hearts a predilection for the society of each other; or are we delighted with scenes of human arts and cultivation, where the passions are flattered and entertained with variety of objects for gratification?

I found myself unable, notwithstanding the attentive admonitions and persuasive arguments of reason, entirely to erase from my mind, those impressions which I had received from the society of the amiable and polite inhabitants of Charleston; and I could not help comparing my present situation in some degree to Nebuchadnezzar's, when expelled from the society of men, and constrained to roam in the mountains and wilderness, there to herd and feed with the wild beasts of the forest. [. . .]

Soon after crossing [a] large branch of the Tanase, I observed, descending the heights at some distance, a company of Indians, all well mounted on horse back; they came rapidly forward: on their nearer approach I observed a chief at the head of the carravan, and apprehending him to be the Little Carpenter, emperor or grand chief of the Cherokees, as they came up I turned off from the path to make way, in token of respect, which compliment was accepted, and gratefully and magnanimously returned; for his highness with a gracious and cheerful smile came up to me, and clapping his hand on his breast, offered it to me, saying, I am Ata-cul-culla; and heartily shook hands with me, and asked me if I knew it. I answered, that the Good Spirit who goes before me spoke to me, and said, that is the great Ata-cul-culla; and added, that I was of the tribe of white men, of Pennsylvania, who esteem themselves brothers and friends to the red men, but particularly so to the Cherokees, and that notwithstanding we dwelt at so great a distance, we were united in love and friendship, and that the name of Ata-cul-culla was dear to his white brothers of Pennsylvania.

After this compliment, which seemed to be acceptable, he inquired if I came lately from Charleston, and if John Stewart was well, saying that he was going to see him. I replied, that I came lately from Charleston on a friendly visit to the Cherokees; that I had the honour of a personal acquaintance with the superintendant, the beloved man, whom, I saw well but the day before I set off, and who, by letters to the principal white men in the nation, recommended me to the friendship and protection of the Cherokees. To which the great chief was pleased to answer very respectfully, that I was welcome in their country as a friend and brother; and then shaking hands heartily bid me farewell, and his retinue confirmed it by an united voice of assent. After giving my name to the chief, requesting my compliments to the superintendant, the emperor moved, continuing his journey for Charleston; and I, yet persisting in my intention of visiting the Overhill towns, continued on. Leaving the great forest I mounted the high hills, descending them again on the other side, and so on repeatedly for several miles, without observing any variation in the natural productions since passing the Jore: and perceiving the slow progress of vegetation in this mountainous, high country; and, upon serious consideration, it appearing very plainly that I could not, with entire safety, range the Overhill settlements until the treaty was over, which would not come on till late in June; I suddenly came to a resolution to defer these researches at this time, and leave them for the employment of another season and more favourable opportunity, and return to Dartmouth in Georgia, to be ready to join a company of adventurers who were to set off in July for Mobile in West Florida. The leader of this company had been recommended to me as a fit person to assist me on so long and hazardous a journey, through the vast territories of the Creeks.

Therefore next day I turned about on my return, proceeding moderately, being engaged in noting such objects as appeared to be of any moment, and collecting specimens; and in the evening of next day arrived again at Cowe.

Next morning Mr. Galahan conducted me to the chief of Cowe, who during my absence had returned from the chace. The remainder of this day I spent in observations in and about the town, reviewing my specimens, &c.

The town of Cowe consists of about one hundred dwellings, near the banks of the Tanase, on both sides of the river.

The Cherokees construct their habitations on a different plan from the Creeks; that is, but one oblong four square building, of one story high; the materials consisting of logs or trunks of trees, stripped of their bark, notched at their ends, fixed one upon another, and afterwards plaistered well, both inside and out, with clay well tempered with dry grass, and the whole covered or roofed with the bark of the chestnut tree or long broad shingles. This building is however partitioned transversely, forming three apartments, which communicate with each other by inside doors; each house or habitation has besides a little conical house covered with dirt, which is called the winter or hot-house; this stands a few yards distant from the mansion-house, opposite the front door.

The council or town-house is a large rotunda, capable of accommodating several hundred people: it stands on the top of an ancient artificial mount of earth, of about twenty feet perpendicular, and the rotunda on the top of it being above thirty feet more, gives the whole fabric an elevation of about sixty feet from the common surface of the ground. But it may be proper to observe, that this mount on which the rotunda stands, is of a much ancienter date than the building, and perhaps was raised for another purpose. The Cherokees themselves are as ignorant as we are, by what people or for what purpose these artificial hills were raised; they have various stories concerning them, the best of which amount to no more than mere conjecture, and leave us entirely in the dark; but they have a tradition common with the other nations of Indians, that they found them in much the same condition as they now appear, when their forefathers arrived from the West and possessed themselves of the country, after vanquishing the nations of red men who then inhabited it, who themselves found these mounts when they took possession of the country, the former possessors delivering the same story concerning them: perhaps they were designed and appropriated by the people who constructed them, to some religious purpose, as great altars and temples similar to the high places and sacred groves anciently amongst the Canaanites and other nations of Palestine and Judea. [. . .]

About the close of the evening I accompanied Mr. Galahan and other white traders to the rotunda, where was a grand festival, music and dancing. This assembly was held principally to rehearse the ball-play dance, this town being challenged to play against another the next day.

The people being assembled and seated in order, and the musicians having taken their station, the ball opens, first with a long harangue or oration, spoken by an aged chief, in commendation of the manly exercise of the ball-play, recounting the many and brilliant victories which the town of Cowe had gained over the other towns in the nation, not forgetting or neglecting to recite his own exploits, together with those of other aged men now present, coadjutors in the performance of these athletic games in their youthful days.

This oration was delivered with great spirit and eloquence, and was meant to influence the passions of the young men present, excite them to emulation, and inspire them with ambition.

This prologue being at an end, the musicians began, both vocal and instrumental; when presently a company of girls, hand in hand, dressed in clean white robes and ornamented with beads, bracelets and a profusion of gay ribbands, entering the door, immediately began to sing their responses in a gentle, low, and sweet voice, and formed themselves in a semicircular file or line, in two ranks, back to back, facing the spectators and musicians, moving slowly round and round. This continued about a quarter of an hour, when we were surprised by a sudden very loud and shrill whoop, uttered at once by a company of young fellows, who came in briskly after one another, with rackets or hurls in one hand. These champions likewise were well dressed, painted, and ornamented with silver bracelets, gorgets and wampum, neatly ornamented with moccasins and high waving plumes in their diadems: they immediately formed themselves in a semicircular rank, also in front of the girls, when these changed their order, and formed a single rank parallel to the men, raising their voices in responses to the tunes of the young champions, the semicircles continually moving round. There was something singular and diverting in their step and motions, and I imagine not to be learned to exactness but with great attention and perseverance. [. . .]

Next morning early I set off on my return, and meeting with no material occurrences on the road, in two days arrived safe at Keowe, where I tarried two or three days, employed in augmenting my collections of specimens, and waiting for Mr. Galahan, who was to call on me here, to accompany him to Sinica, where he and other traders were to meet Mr. Cameron, the deputy commissary, to hold a congress at that town, with the chiefs of the Lower Cherokees, to consult preliminaries introductory to a general congress and treaty with these Indians, which was to be convened next June, and held in the Overhill towns. [. . .]

I accompanied the traders to Sinica, where we found the commissary and the Indian chiefs convened in counsel: continued at Sinica sometime, employing myself in observations, and making collections of every thing worthy of notice: and finding the Indians to be yet unsettled in their determination, and not in a good humour, I abandoned the project of visiting the regions beyond the Cherokee mountains for this season; set off for my return to Fort James, Dartmouth, lodged this night in the forests near the banks of a delightful large creek, a branch of Keowe river, and next day arrived safe at Dartmouth.

James Fenimore Cooper

1789–1851

James Fenimore Cooper was reared in Cooperstown, a central New York State community founded by his father after a large land purchase in what was then the frontier. The area is now categorized as part of Northern Appalachia. Cooper is best known for the five novels in his "Leatherstocking Tales" series, which explore life on the American frontier.

Natty Bumppo, the protagonist of the Leatherstocking novels, was modeled in part on Daniel Boone, a frontiersman at home in the wilderness and among Native Americans. *The Pioneers* (1823), the first novel of the series, strikes a decidedly modern note in its emphasis on ecological balance. The chapter excerpted below condenses the novel's themes of development, conservation, stewardship, and morality.

Cooper's work was initially well received at home and widely read abroad. His relationship with American audiences became more hostile, however, as did his dealings with his Cooperstown neighbors, when his writing became more critical of the United States and he became entangled in a series of property litigations. Cooper's subsequent literary reputation has waxed and waned. Modern critics generally regard him as a product of his literary times and see his work, especially the Leatherstocking novels, as helping to articulate a national identity. Although Cooper's Native American characters rarely rise above negative stereotypes, Natty Bumppo is a significant contribution to the heroic construction of the frontiersman, one source for the southern mountaineer character type. Thus, Cooper's writing epitomizes the literary connection between Northern and Southern Appalachia.

FROM The Pioneers, or The Sources of the Susquehanna; a Descriptive Tale

VOLUME II, CHAPTER III

> "Men, boys, and girls
> Desert th' unpeopled village; and wild crowds
> Spread o'er the plain, by the sweet frenzy driven."
>
> *Somerville*

From this time to the close of April, the weather continued to be a succession of great and rapid changes. One day, the soft airs of spring would seem to be stealing along the valley, and, in unison with an invigorating sun, attempting, covertly, to rouse the dormant powers of the vegetable world; while on the next, the surly blasts from the north would sweep across the lake, and erase every impression left by their gentle adversaries. The snow, however, finally disappeared, and the green wheat fields were seen in every direction, spotted with the dark and charred stumps that had, the preceding season, supported some of the proudest trees of the forest. Ploughs were in motion, wherever those useful implements could be used, and the smokes of the sugar-camps were no longer seen issuing from the summits of the woods of maple. The lake had lost all the characteristic beauty of a field of ice, but still a dark and gloomy covering concealed its waters, for the absence of currents left them yet hid under a porous crust, which, saturated with the fluid, barely retained enough of its strength to preserve the contiguity of its parts. Large flocks of wild geese were seen passing over the country, which hovered, for a time, around the hidden sheet of water, apparently searching for an opening, where they might obtain a resting-place; and then, on finding themselves excluded by the chill covering, would soar away to the north, filling the air with their discordant screams, as if venting their complaints at the tardy operations of nature.

For a week, the dark covering of the Otsego was left to the undisturbed possession of two eagles, who alighted on the centre of its field, and sat proudly eyeing the extent of their undisputed territory. During the presence of these monarchs of the air, the flocks of migrating birds avoided crossing the plain of ice, by turning into the hills, apparently seeking the protection of the forests, while the white and bald heads of the tenants of the lake were turned upward, with a look of majestic contempt, as if penetrating to the very heavens with the acuteness of their vision. But the time had come, when even these kings of birds were to be dispossessed. An opening had been gradually increasing, at the lower extremity of the lake, and around the dark spot where the current of the river had prevented the formation of ice, during even the coldest weather; and the fresh southerly winds, that now breathed freely up the valley, obtained an impression on the waters. Mimic waves began to curl over the margin of the frozen field, which exhibited an outline of crystalizations that slowly receded towards the north. At each step the power of the winds and the waves increased, until, after a struggle of a few hours, the turbulent little billows succeeded in setting the whole field in an undulating motion, when it was driven beyond the reach of the eye, with a rapidity that was as magical as the change produced in the scene by this expulsion of the lingering remnant of winter. Just as the last sheet of agitated ice was disappearing in the distance, the eagles rose over the border of crystals, and soared with a wide sweep far above the clouds, while the waves tossed their little caps of snow into the air, as if rioting in their release from a thraldom of five months' duration.

The following morning Elizabeth was awakened by the exhilarating sounds of the martins, who were quarrelling and chattering around the little boxes that were suspended above her windows, and the cries of Richard, who was calling, in tones as animating as the signs of the season itself—

"Awake! awake! my lady fair! the gulls are hovering over the lake already, and the heavens are alive with the pigeons. You may look an hour before you can find a hole, through which, to get a peep at the sun. Awake! awake! lazy ones! Benjamin is overhauling the ammunition, and we only wait for our breakfasts, and away for the mountains and pigeon-shooting."

There was no resisting this animated appeal, and in a few minutes Miss Temple and her friend descended to the parlour. The doors of the hall were thrown open, and the mild, balmy air of a clear spring morning was ventilating the apartment, where the vigilance of the ex-steward had been so long maintaining an artificial heat, with such unremitted diligence. The gentlemen were impatiently waiting for their morning's repast, each being equipt in the garb of a sportsman. Mr. Jones made many visits to the southern door, and would cry—

"See, cousin Bess! see, 'duke, the pigeon-roosts of the south have broken up! They are growing more thick every instant. Here is a flock that the eye cannot see the end of. There is food enough in it to keep the army of Xerxes for a month, and feathers enough to make beds for the whole county. Xerxes, Mr. Edwards, was a Grecian king, who—no, he was a Turk, or a Persian, who wanted to conquer Greece, just the same as these rascals will overrun our wheat fields, when they come back in the fall.— Away! away! Bess; I long to pepper them from the mountain."

In this wish both Marmaduke and young Edwards seemed equally to participate, for the sight was most exhilarating to a sportsman; and the ladies soon dismissed the party, after a hasty breakfast.

If the heavens were alive with pigeons, the whole village seemed equally in motion, with men, women, and children. Every species of fire-arms, from the French ducking-gun, with its barrel of near six feet in length, to the common horseman's pistol, was to be seen in the hands of the men and boys; while bows and arrows, some made of the simple stick of a walnut sapling, and others in a rude imitation of the ancient cross-bows, were carried by many of the latter.

The houses and the signs of life apparent in the village, drove the alarmed birds from the direct line of their flight, towards the mountains, along the sides and near the bases of which they were glancing in dense masses, that were equally wonderful by the rapidity of their motion, as by their incredible numbers.

We have already said, that across the inclined plane which fell from the steep ascent of the mountain to the banks of the Susquehanna, ran the highway, on either side of which a clearing of many acres had been made, at a very early day. Over those clearings, and up the eastern mountain, and along the dangerous path that was cut into its side, the different individuals posted themselves, as suited their inclinations; and in a few moments the attack commenced.

Amongst the sportsmen was to be seen the tall, gaunt form of Leather-stocking, who was walking over the field, with his rifle hanging on his arm, his dogs following close at his heels, now scenting the dead or wounded birds, that were beginning to tumble from the flocks, and then crouching under the legs of their master, as if they participated in his feelings at this wasteful and unsportsmanlike execution.

The reports of the fire-arms became rapid, whole volleys rising from the plain, as flocks of more than ordinary numbers darted over the opening, covering the field with darkness, like an interposing cloud; and then the light smoke of a single piece would issue from among the leafless bushes on the mountain, as death was hurled on the retreat of the affrighted birds, who were rising from a volley, for many feet into the air, in a vain effort to escape the attacks of man. Arrows, and missiles of every kind, were seen in the midst of the flocks; and so numerous were the birds, and so low did they take their flight, that even long poles, in the hands of those on the sides of the mountain, were used to strike them to the earth.

During all this time, Mr. Jones, who disdained the humble and ordinary means of destruction used by his companions, was busily occupied, aided by Benjamin, in making arrangements for an assault of a more than ordinarily fatal character. Among the relics of the old military excursions, that occasionally are discovered through-out the different districts of the western part of New-York, there had been found in Templeton, at its settlement, a small swivel, which would carry a ball of a pound weight. It was thought to have been deserted by a war-party of the whites, in one of their inroads into the Indian settlements, when, perhaps their convenience or their necessities induced them to leave such an encumbrance behind them in the woods. This miniature cannon had been released from the rust, and being mounted on little wheels, was now in a state for actual service. For several years, it was the sole organ for extraordinary rejoicings that was used in those mountains. On the mornings of the Fourths of July, it would be heard, with its echoes ringing among the hills, and telling forth its sounds, for thirteen times, with all the dignity of a two-and-thirty pounder; and even Captain Hollister, who was the highest authority in that part of the country on all such occasions, affirmed that, considering its dimensions, it was no despicable gun for a salute. It was somewhat the worse for the service it had per-formed, it is true, there being but a trifling difference in size between the touch-hole and the muzzle. Still, the grand conceptions of Richard had suggested the impor-tance of such an instrument, in hurling death at his nimble enemies. The swivel was dragged by a horse into a part of the open space, that the Sheriff thought most eli-gible for planning a battery of the kind, and Mr. Pump proceeded to load it. Sev-eral handfuls of duck-shot were placed on top of the powder, and the Major-domo announced that his piece was ready for service.

The sight of such an implement collected all the idle spectators to the spot, who, being mostly boys, filled the air with their cries of exultation and delight. The gun was pointed on high, and Richard, holding a coal of fire in a pair of tongs, patiently took his seat on a stump, awaiting the appearance of a flock that was worthy of his notice.

So prodigious was the number of the birds, that the scattering fire of the guns, with the hurling of missiles, and the cries of the boys, had no other effect than to break off small flocks from the immense masses that continued to dart along the valley, as if the whole creation of the feathered tribe were pouring through that one pass. None pretended to collect the game, which lay scattered over the fields in such profusion as to cover the very ground with fluttering victims.

Leather-stocking was a silent, but uneasy spectator of all these proceedings, but was able to keep his sentiments to himself until he saw the introduction of the swivel into the sports.

"This comes of settling a country!" he said—"here have I known the pigeons to fly for forty long years, and, till you made your clearings, there was nobody to skear or to hurt them. I loved to see them come into the woods, for they were company to a body; hurting nothing; being, as it was, as harmless as a garter snake. But now it gives me sore thoughts when I hear the frighty things whizzing through the air, for I know it's only a motion to bring out all the brats in the village at them. Well! the Lord won't see the waste of his creaters for nothing, and right will be done to the pigeons, as well as others, by-and-by.—There's Mr. Oliver, as bad as the rest of them, firing into the flocks as if he was shooting down nothing but the Mingo warriors."

Among the sportsmen was Billy Kirby, who, armed with an old musket, was loading, and, without even looking into the air, was firing and shouting as his victims fell even on his own person. He heard the speech of Natty, and took upon himself to reply—

"What's that, old Leather-stocking!" he cried, "grumbling at the loss of a few pigeons! If you had to sow your wheat twice, and three times, as I have done, you wouldn't be so massyfully feeling'd to'ards the divils.—Hurrah, boys! scatter the feathers! This is better than shooting at a turkey's head and neck, old fellow."

"It's better for you, maybe, Billy Kirby," replied the indignant old hunter, "and all them as don't know how to put a ball down a rifle-barrel, or how to bring it up ag'in with a true aim; but it's wicked to be shooting into flocks in this wastey manner; and none do it, who know how to knock over a single bird. If a body has a craving for pigeon's flesh, why! it's made the same as all other creater's, for man's eating, but not to kill twenty and eat one. When I want such a thing, I go into the woods till I find one to my liking, and then I shoot him off the branches without touching a feather of another, though there might be a hundred on the same tree. But you couldn't do such a thing, Billy Kirby—you couldn't do it if you tried."

"What's that you say, you old, dried corn-stalk! you sapless stub!" cried the wood-chopper. "You've grown mighty boasting, sin' you killed the turkey; but if you're for a single shot, here goes at that bird which comes on by himself."

The fire from the distant part of the field had driven a single pigeon below the flock to which it had belonged, and, frightened with the constant reports of the muskets, it was approaching the spot where the disputants stood, darting first from one side, and then to the other, cutting the air with the swiftness of lightning, and making a noise with its wings, not unlike the rushing of a bullet. Unfortunately for the wood-chopper, notwithstanding his vaunt, he did not see his bird until it was too late for him to fire as it approached, and he pulled his trigger at the unlucky moment when it was darting immediately over his head. The bird continued its course with incredible velocity.

Natty lowered the rifle from his arm, when the challenge was made, and, waiting a moment, until the terrified victim had got in a line with his eye, and had dropped near the bank of the lake, he raised it again with uncommon rapidity, and fired. It might have been chance, or it might have been skill, that produced the result; it was probably a union of both; but the pigeon whirled over in the air, and fell into the lake, with a broken wing. At the sound of his rifle, both his dogs started from his feet, and in a few minutes the "slut" brought out the bird, still alive.

The wonderful exploit of Leather-stocking was noised through the field with great rapidity, and the sportsmen gathered in to learn the truth of the report.

"What," said young Edwards, "have you really killed a pigeon on the wing, Natty, with a single ball?"

"Haven't I killed loons before now, lad, that dive at the flash?" returned the hunter. "It's much better to kill only such as you want, without wasting your powder and lead, than to be firing into God's creaters in such a wicked manner. But I come out for a bird, and you know the reason why I like small game, Mr. Oliver, and now I have got one I will go home, for I don't relish to see these wasty ways that you are all practysing, as if the least thing wasn't made for use, and not to destroy."

"Thou sayest well, Leather-stocking," cried Marmaduke, "and I begin to think it time to put an end to this work of destruction."

"Put an ind, Judge, to your clearings. An't the woods his work as well as the pigeons? Use, but don't waste. Wasn't the woods made for the beasts and birds to harbour in? and when man wanted their flesh, their skins, or their feathers, there's the place to seek them. But I'll go to the hut with my own game, for I wouldn't touch one of the harmless things that kiver the ground here, looking up with their eyes on me, as if they only wanted tongues to say their thoughts."

With this sentiment in his mouth, Leather-stocking threw his rifle over his arm, and followed by his dogs, stepped across the clearing with great caution, taking care not to tread on one of the wounded birds that lay in his path. He soon entered the bushes on the margin of the lake, and was hid from view.

Whatever impression the morality of Natty made on the Judge, it was utterly lost on Richard. He availed himself of the gathering of the sportsmen, to lay a plan for one "fell swoop" of destruction. The musket-men were drawn up in battle array, in a line extending on each side of his artillery with orders to await the signal of firing from himself.

"Stand by, my lads," said Benjamin, who acted as an aid-de-camp on this momentous occasion, "stand by, my hearties, and when Squire Dickens heaves out the signal for to begin the firing, d'ye see, you may open upon them in a broadside. Take care and fire low, boys, and you'll be sure to hull the flock."

"Fire low!" shouted Kirby—"hear the old fool! If we fire low, we may hit the stumps, but not ruffle a pigeon."

"How should you know, you lubber?" cried Benjamin, with a very unbecoming heat for an officer on the eve of battle—"how should you know, you grampus? Haven't I sailed aboard of the Boadishy for five years? and wasn't it a standing order to fire low, and to hull your enemy? Keep silence at your guns, boys, and mind the order that is passed."

The loud laughs of the musket-men were silenced by the authoritative voice of Richard, who called to them for attention and obedience to his signals.

Some millions of pigeons were supposed to have already passed, that morning, over the valley of Templeton; but nothing like the flock that was now approaching had been seen before. It extended from mountain to mountain in one solid blue mass, and the eye looked in vain over the southern hills to find its termination. The front of this living column was distinctly marked by a line, but very slightly indented, so regular and even was the flight. Even Marmaduke forgot the morality of Leather-stocking as it approached, and, in common with the rest, brought his musket to his shoulder.

"Fire!" cried the Sheriff, clapping his coal to the priming of the cannon. As half of Benjamin's charge escaped through the touch-hole, the whole volley of the musketry preceded the report of the swivel. On receiving this united discharge of small-arms, the front of the flock darted upward, while, at the same instant, myriads of those in their rear rushed with amazing rapidity into their places, so that when the column of white smoke gushed from the mouth of the little cannon, an accumulated mass of objects was gliding over its point of direction. The roar of the gun echoed along the mountains, and died away to the north, like distant thunder, while the whole flock of alarmed birds seemed, for a moment, thrown into one disorderly and agitated mass. The air was filled with their irregular flights, layer rising above layer, far above the tops of the highest pines, none daring to advance beyond the dangerous pass; when, suddenly, some of the leaders of the feathered tribe shot across the valley, taking their flight directly over the village, and the hundreds of thousands in their rear followed their example, deserting the eastern side of the plain to their persecutors and the fallen.

"Victory!" shouted Richard, "victory! we have driven the enemy from the field."

"Not so, Dickon," said Marmaduke; "the field is covered with them; and, like the Leather-stocking, I see nothing but eyes, in every direction, as the innocent sufferers turn their heads in terror, to examine my movements. Full one half of those that have fallen are yet alive; and I think it is time to end the sport; if sport it be."

"Sport!" cried the Sheriff; "it is princely sport! There are some thousands of the blue-coated boys on the ground, so that every old woman in the village may have a pot-pie for the asking."

"Well, we have happily frightened the birds from this side of the valley," said Marmaduke, "and our carnage must of necessity end, for the present.—Boys, I will give you sixpence a hundred for the pigeons' heads only; so go to work, and bring them into the village, where I will pay you."

This expedient produced the desired effect, for every urchin on the ground went industriously to work to wring the necks of the wounded birds. Judge Temple retired towards his dwelling with that kind of feeling, that many a man has experienced before him, who discovers, after the excitement of the moment has passed, that he has purchased pleasure at the price of misery to others. Horses were loaded with the dead; and, after this first burst of sporting, the shooting of pigeons became a business, for the remainder of the season, more in proportion to the wants of the people. Richard, however, boasted for many a year, of his shot with the "cricket;" and Benjamin gravely asserted, that he thought they killed nearly as many pigeons on that day as there were Frenchmen destroyed on the memorable occasion of Rodney's victory.

Elias Boudinot
(Gallegina "Buck" Watie)
1804–1839

Born Gallegina "Buck" Watie to a prominent Cherokee family in 1804, Elias Boudinot was, like the Cherokee Nation itself, caught between the need to assimilate with encroaching colonists and the desire to maintain Cherokee sovereignty and identity. Educated through age seventeen in the Spring Place Moravian missionary school, Watie met a man named Elias Boudinot, president of the American Bible Society and former member of the Continental Congress, while en route to study at another mission school in Cornwall, Connecticut. Out of respect, Watie adopted Boudinot's name. While in Connecticut, Watie, now Boudinot, married a white woman, Harriet Gold, despite strong opposition.

Boudinot held important positions in the Cherokee Nation, including clerk of the Cherokee National Council, teacher at a missionary school, and editor of the *Cherokee Phoenix*. For years, Boudinot used his authority and position to strenuously argue against the proposal to remove all Cherokee from their homeland to reservation land in Oklahoma. Eventually, however, Boudinot shifted his allegiance to the pro-removal faction of the Cherokee after determining that further resistance was pointless, and in 1835 he was one of the signers of the Treaty of New Echota, which approved the removal.

The anti-removal Cherokee (the majority of the nation) took their protest against enforced removal to the Supreme Court, which eventually sided with them. Despite that ruling, the Cherokee were forced from their homeland in 1838, following a route that became known as the Trail of Tears. Many Cherokee felt that Boudinot and his colleagues had violated Cherokee law, which forbade selling tribal land, and in 1839, after their arrival in Oklahoma, Boudinot and other treaty signers were executed.

Boudinot delivered his "Address to the Whites," which stresses the need for assimilation, while touring to raise money for *Cherokee Phoenix* printing presses.

FROM An Address to the Whites Delivered in the First Presbyterian Church, on the 26th of May, 1826

Some there are, perhaps even in this enlightened assembly, who at the bare sight of an Indian, or at the mention of the name, would throw back their imaginations to ancient times, to the ravages of savage warfare, to the yells pronounced over the mangled bodies of women and children, thus creating an opinion, inapplicable and highly injurious to those for whose temporal interest and eternal welfare, I come to plead.

What is an Indian? Is he not formed of the same materials with yourself? For "of one blood God created all the nations that dwell on the face of the earth." Though it be true that he is ignorant, that he is a heathen, that he is a savage; yet he is no more than all others have been under similar circumstances. Eighteen centuries ago what were the inhabitants of Great Britain?

You here behold an *Indian,* my kindred are *Indians,* and my fathers sleeping in the wilderness grave—they too were *Indians.* But I am not as my fathers were—broader means and nobler influences have fallen upon me. Yet I was not born as thousands are, in a stately dome and amid the congratulations of the great, for on a little hill, in a lonely cabin, overspread by the forest oak, I first drew my breath; and in a language unknown to learned and polished nations, I learnt to lisp my fond mother's name. In after days, I have had greater advantages than most of my race; and I now stand before you delegated by my native country to seek her interest, to labour for her respectability, and by my public efforts to assist in raising her to an equal standing with other nations of the earth.

The time has arrived when speculations and conjectures as to the practicability of civilizing the Indians must forever cease. A period is fast approaching when the stale remark—"Do what you will, an Indian will still be an Indian," must be placed no more in speech. With whatever plausibility this popular objection may have heretofore been made, every candid mind must now be sensible that it can no longer be uttered, except by those who are uninformed with respect to us, who are strongly prejudiced against us, or who are filled with vindictive feelings towards us; for the present history of the Indians, particularly of that nation to which I belong, most incontrovertibly establishes the fallacy of this remark. I am aware of the difficulties which have ever existed to Indian civilization, I do not deny the almost insurmountable obstacles which we ourselves have thrown in the way of this improvement, nor do I say that difficulties no longer remain; but facts will permit me to declare that there are none which may not easily be overcome, by strong and continued exertions. [. . .] It needs only that the world should know what we have done in the few last years, to foresee what yet we may do with the assistance of our white brethren, and that of the common Parent of us all. [. . .]

The Cherokee nation lies within the charted limits of the states of Georgia, Tennessee, and Alabama. Its extent as defined by treaties is about 200 miles in length from East to West, and about 120 in breadth. This country which is supposed to contain about 10,000,000 of acres exhibits great varieties of surface, the most part being hilly and mountaneous, affording soil of no value. The vallies, however, are well watered and afford excellent land, in many parts particularly on the large streams, that of the first quality. The climate is temperate and healthy, indeed I would not be guilty of exaggeration were I to say, that the advantages which this country possesses to render it salubrious, are many and superior. Those lofty and barren mountains, defying the labour and ingenuity of man, and supposed by some as placed there only to exhibit omnipotence, contribute to the healthiness and beauty of the surrounding plains, and give to us that free air and pure water which distinguish our country. These advantages, calculated to make the inhabitants healthy, vigorous, and intelligent, cannot fail to cause this country to become interesting. And there can be no doubt that the Cherokee Nation, however obscure and trifling it may now appear, will finally become, if not under its present occupants, one of the Garden spots of America. And here, let me be indulged in the fond wish, that she may thus become under those who now possess her; and ever be fostered, regulated and protected by the generous government of the United States.

The population of the Cherokee Nation increased from the year 1810 to that of 1824, 2000 exclusive of those who emigrated in 1818 and 19 to the west of the Mississippi—of those who reside on the Arkansas the number is supposed to be about 5000.

The rise of these people in their movement toward civilization, may be traced as far back as the relinquishment of their towns; when game became incompetent to their support, by reason of the surrounding white population. They then betook themselves to the woods, commenced the opening of small clearings, and the raising of stock; still however following the chase. Game has since become so scarce that little dependence for subsistence can be placed upon it. They have gradually and I could almost say universally forsaken their ancient employment. In fact, there is not a single family in the nation, that can be said to subsist on the slender support which the wilderness would afford. The love and the practice of hunting are not now carried to a higher degree, than among all frontier people whether white or red. It cannot be doubted, however, that there are many who have commenced a life of agricultural labour from mere necessity, and if they could, would gladly resume their former course of living. But these are individual failings and ought to be passed over.

On the other hand it cannot be doubted that the nation is improving, rapidly improving in all those particulars which must finally constitute the inhabitants an industrious and intelligent people.

It is a matter of surprise to me, and must be to all those who are properly acquainted with the condition of the Aborigines of this country, that the Cherokees have advanced so far and so rapidly in civilization. But there are yet powerful obstacles, both within and without, to be surmounted in the march of improvement. The prejudices in regard to them in the general community are strong and lasting. The evil effects of their intercourse with their immediate white neighbours, who differ from them chiefly in name, are easily to be seen, and it is evident that from this intercourse proceed those demoralizing practices which in order to surmount, peculiar and unremitting efforts are necessary. In defiance, however, of these obstacles the Cherokees have improved and are still rapidly improving. To give you a further view of their condition, I will here repeat some of the articles of the two statistical tables taken at different periods.

In 1810 there were 19,500 cattle; 6,100 horses; 19,600 swine; 1,037 sheep; 467 looms; 1,600 spinning wheels; 30 waggons; 500 ploughs; 3 saw-mills; 13 grist-mills &c. At this time there are 22,000 cattle; 7,600 horses; 46,000 swine; 2,500 sheep; 762 looms; 2,488 spinning wheels; 172 waggons; 2,943 ploughs; 10 saw-mills; 31 grist-mills; 62 Blacksmith-shops; 8 cotton machines; 18 schools; 18 ferries; and a number of public roads. In one district there were, last winter, upwards of 0000 [*sic*] volumes of good books; and 11 different periodical papers both religious and political, which were taken and read. On the public roads there are many decent Inns, and few houses for convenience, &c., would disgrace any country. Most of the schools are under the care and tuition of christian missionaries, of different denominations, who have been of great service to the nation, by inculcating moral and religious principles into the minds of the rising generation. In many places the word of God is regularly preached and explained, both by missionaries and natives; and there are numbers who have publicly professed their belief and interest in the merits of the great Saviour of the world. It is worthy of remark, that in no ignorant country have the missionaries undergone less trouble and difficulty, in spreading a knowledge of the Bible, than in this. Here, they have been welcomed and encouraged by the proper authorities of the nation, their persons have been protected, and in very few instances have some individual vagabonds threatened violence to them. Indeed it may be said with truth, that among no heathen people has the faithful minister of God experienced greater success, greater reward for his labour, than in this. He is surrounded by attentive hearers, the words which flow from his lips are not spent in vain. The Cherokees have had no established religion of their own, and perhaps to this circumstance we may attribute, in part, the facilities with which missionaries have pursued their ends. They cannot be called idolators; for they never worshipped Images. They believed in a Supreme Being, the Creator of all, the God of the white, the red, and the black man. They also believed in the existence of an evil spirit who resided, as thought, in the setting sun, the future place of all who in their life time had done iniquitously. Their prayers were addressed alone to the Supreme Being, and which if written would fill a large volume, and display much sincerity, beauty and sublimity. When the ancient customs of the Cherokees were in their full force, no warrior thought himself secure, unless he had addressed his guardian angel; no hunter could hope for success, unless before the rising sun he had asked the assistance of his God, and on his return at eve he had offered his sacrifice to him.

There are three things of late occurrence, which must certainly place the Cherokee Nation in a fair light, and act as a powerful argument in favor of Indian improvement.

First. The invention of letters.

Second. The translation of the New Testament into Cherokee.

And third. The organization of a Government.

The Cherokee mode of writing lately invented by George Guest, who could not read any language nor speak any other than his own, consists of eighty-six characters, principally syllabic, the combinations of which form all the words of the language. Their terms may be greatly simplified, yet they answer all the purposes of writing, and already many natives use them.

The translation of the New Testament, together with Guest's mode of writing, has swept away that barrier which has long existed, and opened a spacious channel for the instruction of adult Cherokees. Persons of all ages and classes may now read the precepts of the Almighty in their own language. Before it is long, there will scarcely be an individual in the nation who can say, "I know not God neither understand

I what thou sayest," for all shall know him from the greatest to the least. The aged warrior over whom has rolled three score and ten years of savage life, will grace the temple of God with his hoary head; and the little child yet on the breast of its pious mother shall learn to lisp its Maker's name. [. . .]

The Government, though defective in many respects, is well suited to the condition of the inhabitants. As they rise in information and refinement, changes in it must follow, until they arrive at that state of advancement, when I trust they will be admitted into all the privileges of the American family.

The Cherokee Nation is divided into eight districts, in each of which are established courts of justice, where all disputed cases are decided by a Jury, under the direction of a circuit Judge, who has jurisdiction over two districts. Sheriffs and other publice officers are appointed to execute the decisions of the courts, collect debts, and arrest thieves and other criminals. Appeals may be taken to the Superior Court, held annually at the seat of Government. The Legislative authority is vested in a General Court, which consists of the National Committee and Council. The National Committee consists of thirteen members, who are generally men of sound sense and fine talents. The National Council consists of thirty-two members, beside the speaker, who act as the representatives of the people. Every bill passing these two bodies, becomes the law of the land. Clerks are appointed to do the writings, and record the proceedings of the Council. The executive power is vested in two principal chiefs, who hold their office during good behaviour, and sanction all the decisions of the legislative council. Many of the laws display some degree of civilization, and establish the respectability of the nation.

Polygamy is abolished. Female chastity and honor are protected by law. The Sabbath is respected by the Council during session. Mechanics are encouraged by law. The practice of putting aged persons to death for witchcraft is abolished and murder has now become a governmental crime.

From what I have said, you will form but a faint opinion of the true state and prospects of the Cherokees. You will, however, be convinced of three important truths.

First, that the means which have been employed for the christianization and civilization of this tribe, have been greatly blessed. Second, that the increase of these means will meet with final success. Third, that it has now become necessary, that efficient and more than ordinary means should be employed.

Sensible of this last point, and wishing to do something for themselves, the Cherokees have thought it advisable that there should be established, a Printing Press and a Seminary of respectable character; and for these purposes your aid and patronage are now solicited. They wish the types, as expressed in their resolution, to be composed of English letters and Cherokee characters. Those characters have now become extensively used in the nation; their religious songs are written in them; there is an astonishing eagerness in people of all classes and ages to acquire a knowledge of them; and the New Testament has been translated into their language. All this impresses on them the immediate necessity of procuring types. The most informed and judicious of our nation, believe that such a press would go further to remove ignorance, and her offspring superstition and prejudice, than all other means. The adult part of the nation will probably grovel on in ignorance and die in ignorance, without any fair trial upon them, unless the proposed means are carried into effect. The simplicity of this method of writing, and the eagerness to obtain a knowledge of it, are evinced by the astonishing rapidity with which it is acquired, and by the numbers who do so. It is about two years since its introduction, and already there are a great many who can read it. In the neighborhood in which I live, I do not recollect a male Cherokee, between the ages of fifteen and twenty five, who is ignorant of this mode of writing. But in connexion with those for Cherokee characters, it is necessary to have types for English letters. There are many who already speak and read the English language, and can appreciate the advantages which would result from the publication of their laws and transactions in a well conducted newspaper. Such a paper, comprising a summary of religious and political events, &c. on the one hand; and on the other, exhibiting the feelings, disposition, improvements, and prospects of the Indians; their traditions, their true character, as it once was and as it now is; the ways and means most likely to throw the mantle of civilization over all tribes; and such other matter as will tend to diffuse proper and correct impressions in regard to their condition—such a paper could not fail to create much interest in the American community, favourable to the aborigines, and to have a powerful influence on the advancement of the Indians themselves. How can the patriot or the philanthropist devise efficient means, without full and correct information as to the subjects of his labour. And I am inclined to think, after all that has been said of the aborigines, after all that has been written in narratives, professedly to elucidate the leading traits of their character, that the public knows little of that character. To obtain a correct and complete knowledge of these people, there must exist a vehicle of Indian intelligence, altogether different from those which have heretofore been employed. Will not a paper published in an Indian country, under proper and judicious regulations, have the desired effect? I do not say that Indians will produce learned and elaborate dissertations in explanation and vindication of their own character; but they may exhibit specimens of their intellectual efforts, of their eloquence, of their moral, civil and physical advancement, which will do quite as much to remove prejudice and to give profitable information.

The Cherokees wish to establish their Seminary, upon a footing which will insure to it all the advantages, that belong to such institutions in the states. Need I spend one moment in arguments, in favour of such, an institution; need I speak one word of the utility, of the necessity, of an institution of learning; need I do more than simply to ask the patronage of benevolent hearts, to obtain that patronage.

When before did a nation of Indians step forward and ask for the means of civilization? The Cherokee authorities have adopted the measures already stated, with a sincere desire to make their nation an intelligent and virtuous people, and with a full hope that those who have already pointed out to them the road of happiness, will now assist them to pursue it. With that assistance, what are the prospects of the Cherokees? Are they not indeed glorious, compared to that deep darkness in which the nobler qualities of their souls have slept. Yes, methinks I can view my native country, rising from the ashes of her degradation, wearing her purified and beautiful garments, and taking her seat with the nations of the earth. I can behold her sons bursting the fetters of ignorance and unshackling her from the vices of heathenism. She is at this instant, risen like the first morning sun, which grows brighter and brighter, until it reaches its fulness of glory.

She will become not a great, but a faithful ally of the United States. In times of peace she will plead the common liberties of America. In times of war her intrepid sons will sacrifice their lives in your defence. And because she will be useful to you in coming time, she asks you to assist her in her present struggles. She asks not for greatness; she seeks not wealth; she pleads only for assistance to become respectable as a nation, to enlighten and ennoble her sons, and to ornament her daughters with modesty and virtue. She pleads for this assistance, too, because on her destiny hangs that of many nations. If she complete her civilization—then may we hope that all our nations will—then, indeed, may true patriots be encouraged in their efforts to make this world of the West, one continuous abode of enlightened, free and happy people.

But if the Cherokee Nation fail in her struggle, if she die away, then all hopes are blasted, and falls the fabric of Indian civilization. Their fathers were born in darkness, and have fled in darkness; without your assistance so will their sons. You see, however, where the probability rests. Is there a soul whose narrowness will not permit the exercise of charity on such an occasion? Where is he that can hold his mite from an object so noble? Who can prefer a little of his silver and gold, to the welfare of nations of his fellow beings? [. . .]

There are, with regard to the Cherokees and other tribes, two alternatives; they must either become civilized and happy, or sharing the fate of many kindred nations, become extinct. [. . .]

There is, in Indian history, something very melancholy, and which seems to establish a mournful precedent for the future events of the few sons of the forest, now scattered over this vast continent. We have seen every where the poor aborigines melt away before the white population. I merely speak of the fact, without at all referring to the cause. We have seen, I say, one family after another, one tribe after another, nation after nation, pass away; until only a few solitary creatures are left to tell the sad story of extinction.

Shall this precedent be followed? I ask you, shall red men live, or shall they be swept from the earth? With you and this public at large, the decision chiefly rests. Must they perish? Must they all, like the unfortunate Creeks, (victims of the unchristian policy of certain persons,) go down in sorrow to their grave?

They hang upon your mercy as to a garment. Will you push them from you, or will you save them? Let humanity answer.

Anne Newport Royall

1769–1854

One of the most prominent and feared female journalists of her time, Anne Newport Royall was born near Baltimore, Maryland. She moved with her family to a log cabin on the western Pennsylvania frontier and then, with her widowed mother, settled in (West) Virginia. There she met and married William Royall, in whose household she and her mother worked as domestic servants. William Royall, a Revolutionary War veteran and a wealthy, well-educated gentleman farmer, had amassed one of the largest libraries in Virginia. Anne educated herself from this collection.

Following William Royall's death in 1812, Anne entered a lengthy court battle with William's relatives over his large estate, which he had left primarily to her. While the will was being contested, William's relatives froze the estate, and in 1819 his will was annulled, forcing Anne into poverty. In order to secure an income, she embarked on a writing career, documenting her travels in the South (in ten volumes) and reporting for newspapers in Washington, DC. Anne Newport Royall interviewed every sitting president from James Monroe to Franklin Pierce, an indication of her professional status.

Through her reporting, Royall became an advocate for truth-telling and clear-eyed assessment of power dynamics in the nation's capital. The exposés that she published from her Washington, DC, home in the newspapers *Paul Pry* and *The Huntress,* both of which she founded and edited, earned her powerful enemies. In 1829, Royall was arrested and convicted of being a common scold, akin to a charge of disturbing the peace in today's terms, though the charge of scold applied only to women. Nevertheless, she continued to publish her essays and editorials until her health declined.

FROM Sketches of History, Life, and Manners, in the United States, by a Traveller

Salt-works. [Kanawha County, (West) Virginia]—The salt-works in this county are [a] natural curiosity; they abound on both sides of the river, for the distance of twelve miles. This is another evidence of the providential care of the Deity. Here is a spot, that were it not for this article of commerce, and the facility with which it can be sent to market, would be destitute of almost every comfort and convenience of life. Immense quantities of salt are made here annually; upon an average about one million of bushels, which employ one thousand hands. This salt is sent down Kenhawa River in boats to every part of the western country, and exchanged for articles of consumption. It appears, however, notwithstanding this great bounty of nature, that very few of the proprietors have realized any solid advantage from it; owing, perhaps, to want of capital in the commencement, want of skill, or want of commercial integrity, or perhaps to all three.

The salt water is obtained from the bottom of the river by means of a gum,[1] which is from eighteen to twenty feet in length, and from four to five feet wide; these gums are from the sycamore tree. They are prepared by making a crow at one end, and a head to fit it tight. This being done, about twenty hands repair to the place where it is to be sunk, which is at the edge of low water, on the river; not any where, for the salt water is only found within certain limits. But to return, all hands proceed with provisions, and plenty to drink, to the place. The gum is first placed in the water on one end, (the one with the crow,) a man is then let down into it by a windlass, and digs round the edge with an instrument suited to the purpose; when he fills a bucket with the sand, gravel, or earth, which he meets in succession; the bucket is immediately drawn up, emptied, and let down again, and so on till the gum descends to a rock, which is uniformly at the same distance. As the man digs, the gum sinks; but no man can remain in it longer than twenty or thirty minutes, owing to the excessive cold that exists at the bottom; and another one is let down, and so on in rotation, till their task is performed. In the mean time a pump is placed in the gum to pump out the water as the men work, which otherwise would not only hinder, but drown them. This pump is kept continually at work; about eight or ten days and nights are consumed in this operation; the head is then put in, which effectually excludes the fresh water; and a man from a lofty scaffold commences boring through the rock, which takes some time, as the best hands will not bore more than two feet per day, and the depth is from one to two hundred and fifty, and in some instances three hundred feet, through a solid rock! The moment he is through, the salt water spouts up to a great height, and of stronger or weaker quality as it is near or remote from a certain point on the river, which is the place where salt water was first discovered. Their manner of boring is nothing more than an iron of great strength, and of considerable length, made very sharp at one end, while the other end is fixed into a shaft of wood, and a heavy lever fixed to this; the performer stands still on the scaffold and continues to ply the augur (as it is called) in a perpendicular direction. This part of the business is not so laborious as the other; nor does the performer require that relief which is indispensable in sinking the gum; but he must have some dozens of augurs continually going to and from the smith's shop. I saw several of these at work, and likewise those at the gum; it is impossible for any one to guess what a wretched appearance those poor creatures make when they are drawn out of this gum. They are unable to stand, and shiver as if they would shake to pieces; it can hardly be told whether they are black or white, their blood being so completely chilled. The trouble of making salt, after salt water is obtained, is trifling. When the man finishes boring, a tin tube is placed in the rock, and by means of a machine, which is worked by a horse, the water is thrown into cisterns, from which it is committed to the boilers. This water is so strong that they make

---

1. An American term for a hollow tree, after it is taken from the forests. [Royall's footnote]

it into salt twice in twenty-four hours! All their wood being consumed, they are now boiling with coal, which abounds in their mountains.

These salt-works have very recently been established. Some few years since, in the latter part of a very dry summer, the river being lower than it was ever known since it was settled by white people, the top of an old gum was discovered at the edge of low water, and salt water issuing out of it. In many places, where the fresh water had left it, it was incrusted into salt by the heat of the sun. It is supposed that the Indians, when they were in possession of the country, sunk the gum, and perhaps made some attempts at making salt. Col. David Ruffner, a very enterprising man, was the first that established salt-works in Kenhawa, at the place just mentioned; after him several others; but the old well, as it is called, that is, where the gum was discovered, is by far the strongest water, and it is weaker in proportion as it is distant from it, either up or down the river. Col. Ruffner invented a machine which forces the water up hill, to the distance of three miles, for which I understand he obtained a patent. The salt made here is not so fair as that made at King's works, in Washington county, but it is much stronger, and better for preserving meat. I saw this proved in Alabama; the meat (that is, bacon,) that was cured with the salt from King's works, spoiled, while that, which was salted with the Kenhawa salt, did not. Great quantities of it is consumed in Alabama; they take it in boats down the Ohio and up the Tennessee river. A great quantity is likewise taken up the Cumberland to Nashville. But what astonishes me, is, that they have to bore double the depth now to what they did at first; even at the old well, the water sunk, and they were compelled to pursue it by boring; this is the case with all of them.

These salt-works are dismal looking places; the sameness of the long low sheds; smoking boilers; men, the roughest that can be seen, half naked; hundreds of boatmen; horses and oxen, ill-used and beat by their drivers; the mournful screaking of the machinery, day and night; the bare, rugged, inhospitable looking mountain, from which all the timber has been cut, give to it a gloomy appearance.[2] Add to this the character of the inhabitants, which, from what I have seen myself, and heard from others, lack nothing to render them any thing but a respectable people. Here have settled people from the north, the east, and the west of the United States, and some from the nether end of the world.—However refined, however upright, however enlightened, crafty and wicked they might have been previous to their emigration, they have become assimulated, and mutually stand by each other, no matter what the case is, and wo be to the unwary stranger who happens to fall into their hands. I never saw or heard of any people but these, who gloried in a total disregard of shame, honour and justice, and an open avowal of their superlative skill in petty fraud; and yet they are hospitable to a fault, and many of them are genteel. I see men here whose manners and abilities would do honour to any community, and whilst I admired, I was equally surprised that people of their appearance should be content to live in a place which has become a byword. But their females in a great measure extenuate this hasty sketch. As nature compensates us in many respects for those

---

2. The river, which is extremely beautiful, is the only relief to the scenery. [Royall's footnote.]

advantages she denies us in others, and in all her works has mingled good with evil, you have a striking instance of this in the female part of the society of this place. In no part of the United States, at least where I have visited, are to be found females who surpass them in those virtues that adorn the sex. They possess the domestic virtues in an exemplary degree; they are modest, discreet, industrious and benevolent, and with all, they are fair and beautiful; albeit, I would be sorry to see one of those amiable females become a widow in this iron country, in which, however, for the honour of human nature be it remembered, there are a few noble exceptions amongst the other sex, which may justly be compared to diamonds shining in the dark. [. . .]

History [Greenbriar County, (West) Virginia]—Greenbriar river, which gives name to the county of that name, was discovered in the year 1749, by two enterprising hunters, by the name of Suel and Carver. [. . .]

The second year the whole settlement was cut off by the Shawanese, the whole being either killed or made prisoners. Mrs. Clendening, her three children, and her brother, were among the latter—though she escaped before she was taken far. The particulars of her capture, her escape, and her subsequent sufferings, are truly interesting, and might form the subject of a novel. I had the relation from her daughter, Mrs. Maiz, who now lives near this place, which is likewise confirmed by several others. Her relation begins as follows:—

"These settlers had been occasionally visited by the Shawanese, who inhabited the place where Chilicothe is now built. They were often among the whites, appeared friendly, and were received without suspicion. One day, however, they began the work of death on Muddy Creek: they killed Yokum and several others, captured the women and children, plundered the houses and burnt them to ashes. After this, they came to Clendening's, who had heard nothing of this hostility. When they came into the house, they asked for something to eat; but Mrs. Clendening was suspicious of them, from the circumstance of their being painted different from what she had ever seen them: she expressed her fears to her husband in a low voice, but he replied "No danger." Clendening employed much of his time in hunting. He killed great numbers of buffalo, deer, elk, &c: he would cut the meat from the bones and salt it away by itself. The bones, Mrs. Clendening would collect into a large kettle and boil them, for present use: this was done under a shed or scaffold, constructed near the house, for that purpose; and at that time she had a quantity of these bones boiling in the kettle. She therefore gave her infant to her husband, and taking a large pewter dish and flesh-fork in her hand, repaired thither to bring some for the Indians. But just as she turned the corner of the house, she heard Clendening exclaim "Lord have mercy on me." She dropped the dish and fork, and turning back, saw an Indian with the scalp of her husband in his hand; he held it by the long hair, and was shaking the blood from it. She rushed upon him, and in a fit of phrenzy, requested him to kill her, likewise, spitting in his face to provoke him to do so. He raised his tomahawk to kill her, when her brother, John Ewing, who was present, said to the Indian "Oh, never mind her, she is a foolish woman": "Yes," said the Indian, desisting, "she damn fool, too." They then plundered the house, set fire to it, and departed, taking Mrs. Clendening, her three children, and Ewing, with them. Ewing has since said that Clendening might have saved his life, had he not been encumbered with the child; he started to run, and was making an effort to cross a fence that was near the door, which separated the house from a field of Indian corn, which, had he gained, he would have eluded the pursuit of the Indians; it being in the month of June, the corn was high enough to have concealed him, but he was killed while in the act of rising the fence; he fell on one side and the child on the other. The Indians proceeded on to Muddy Creek and joined another party, who were guarding the prisoners captured the preceding day. As they passed by the settlement of Cea and Yokum, Mrs. Clendening discovered that they were likewise killed, and their wives and children among the prisoners.

On the following day, the Indians, except one old man, left them in camp, leaving this old man to guard them; they took Ewing with them. They were absent three days; during which, it came into Mrs. Clendening's head, that, if the other women would assist her, they might kill the old Indian and make their escape. But being narrowly watched by him, she had no opportunity to mention the subject without being overheard. She in the first place asked the Indian if he understood English, and he making no reply, she took it for granted that he did not; and consequently made the proposal to her sister prisoners, but they refused to aid her. Scarcely had they done speaking, when their ears were saluted with the whooping of an approaching party of Indians, a number of bells, and every token of a great number, both of horses and Indians. The old Indian sprung to his feet, and after listening some time attentively, exclaimed in good English, "g—d d—n good news." Mrs. C. now expected nothing but death for plotting his destruction; but she never heard any thing more of it. The Indians proved to be those who had left them, with another party, whom they went to meet, who were returning from Car's Creek, Rockbridge county, with a number of women and children, and a vast booty, disposed on the horses. Every horse had a bell, and every bell was open. Amongst the prisoners, was the lamented Mrs. Moore, who was afterwards cruelly burnt at their towns. They collected their prisoners and set out for their towns. Mrs. Clendening resolved, however, to effect her escape, at the risk of her life. Accordingly, when they arrived at the place called Keeny's Knobs, a favorable opportunity offered upon one of these; one of the Indians was carrying her child; the Indians were all in the van; the prisoners next to them; and the horses, with their bells ringing, behind; and one Indian behind all. When she, therefore, came to a very steep precipice on the side of the route, the Indians carelessly pursuing their way, she jumped down, and crept under a large rock. She lay still until she heard the last bell pass by: concluding they had not yet missed her, she began to hope. Sometime after the bells were out of hearing, she heard the footsteps of something approaching very heavily. It drew near the place where she was; she was leaning down on her hands and knees, with her head bent forward to the ground; and thus she awaited the fatal stroke! Already she felt the deadly axe on her head, in imagination; and for the first time feared death. She ventured, however, to raise her eyes to her foe; and behold, a large bear was standing over her. He gave a great snort, and ran off at full speed. The Indians missing her after some time, laid her child on the ground, would go off from it some distance, thinking its cries would induce her to return; they would torture and beat it, saying "make the calf bawl and the cow will come." At length they killed it, and went on without her. She remained under the rock till dark, when she sought her way back. She travelled all night, and concealed herself by day. The second night she reached her desolate habitation. When she came in sight of the farm, she heard (or thought she did) wild beasts, howling in every direction; she thought she heard voices of all sorts, and saw images of all shapes moving through the cornfield; in short, these sights and sounds so intimidated her, that she withdrew to a spring in the forest, and remained there till morning.[3] She then approached the place, and found the body of her husband with his eyes picked out, lying where it was when the Indians left him. She threw a buffalo hide over it, and vainly tried to cover it with earth; she procured a hoe for the purpose, but her strength was so much exhausted for want of food and sleep, that she found herself unequal to the task. She continued her route toward the settled part of the country, travelling at night only; in nine days she arrived at Dickinson's, on the Cowpasture river. During all this time, she eat nothing but a little salt, and an onion, which she found on a shelf, in a spring house, at some of the deserted places. She likewise found an Indian blanket, which proved a great friend to her in the end, as her clothes and skin were torn to pieces by the briers, she made leggings out of the blanket. When she got as far as Howard's Creek, not more than ten miles from where Lewisburg now is, she met several white men. These men had heard that every soul was killed, and were coming to drive away the cattle, and whatever else was left by the Indians. Among these men, was one, who was heir in-law of her family; he was much displeased that she had escaped. This wretch offered her no sort of consolation, nor any relief, whatever. Some of the men gave her a piece of bread and a cold duck, but her stomach loathing it, she put it in her petticoat, and pursued her journey, thinking to eat it when she felt an appetite; but unfortunately, she lost it, without ever tasting it. At the time her husband was killed, and herself taken, they had a negro man and woman, who happened to be at work in the field. The man made his escape with all possible speed, leaving the woman, who was his wife, to shift for herself. She also took to flight, but having a young child, and fearing its cries would betray her to the Indians, she picked up courage, and killed it. They both effected their escape, and got safe to Augusta; and it was from them that these people received the news of the whole family being slain. In the mean time Mrs. Clendening arrived safe, in her old neighborhood, and in the course of a few days married a Mr. Rogers, the father of Mrs. Maiz, (from whom I had this relation,) and moved to the same place where her first husband was killed—peace being restored; and on looking about the old premises, she found the dish and flesh-fork where she dropped it, on the day her husband was killed.

Meanwhile she had two children with the Indians, a little boy and girl. Her brother, by some means, returned before the general ransom of the prisoners. He informed her, that an old Indian man and woman, who had lost all their children, adopted her little son, and was very fond of it, the child likewise being fond of them.

---

3. The effect of a disordered imagination. [Royall's footnote]

But one day, the old man displeased with his wife, on some account, told the child, whom she was sending for water, not to go, if he did, he would kill him; the squaw said she would kill him if he did not. The child stood still, not knowing what to do; at length, the old man went out to the field, and the child, glad of an opportunity to please its mother, picked up the vessel and set off to the spring, but the old man seeing him from where he was, walked up behind him, and knocked out his brains. He related the circumstance himself, and would add, "I was obliged to approach him behind, that I might not see his face, for if I had, I could never have had the courage to kill him." The little girl was seven years with the Indians; when she was brought to her mother as her child, she disowned her, saying "it was not hers," and the child was returning, amongst various other children, who had not as yet been claimed by their parents, and friends. After the child had left her house some time, she called to mind a mark which was on some part of its body, and ran after it, with a view to be satisfied whether it was her's or not, and upon examination, found it to be her child; but it was long before she felt any attachment for it. The child grew up, and being a great heiress, rang loud in her day; many suitors came to woo her, and many were rejected. At length she gave her hand to a Mr. Davies, by whom she had several children, one of whom, a daughter, married Mr. Ballard Smith, late a member of Congress, and amongst the first lawyers in the western country. Mrs. Davies is still living. It is only seven years since her mother, Mrs. Rogers, died. This renowned female is represented to have been a woman of a great mind, unequalled fortitude, and invincible courage. Besides Mrs. Maiz, who is among the most sensible women I have seen, she has a son living near this place, of highly respectable standing.

The Crockett Almanac

Almanacs were a staple of American life in the nineteenth century when *The Crockett Almanac,* sometimes entitled *Davy Crockett's Almanack,* was published. Nineteenth-century almanacs contained calendars, moon phases, sunrise and sunset times, important dates, home remedies, and, most famously, weather prognostications. They also included jokes, light verse, and stories. Along with Benjamin Franklin's *Poor Richard's Almanack* (1732–1758) and the *Old Farmer's Almanac* (1792 to the present), *The Crockett Almanac* (1835–1856) is one of the best known and most influential iterations of this genre.

During the early years of *The Crockett Almanac,* the tales of Crockett's adventures and the accompanying woodcut illustrations were relatively realistic. In the 1840s, however, the tales moved steadily toward exaggeration, and, like a nineteenth-century superhero, Davy Crockett became sufficiently powerful to ride his pet crocodile up Niagara Falls and to capture a twenty-foot buffalo. Together with his fictional, and abundantly named, wife, Sally Ann Thunder Ann Whirlwind Crockett, the almanac's Davy Crockett brought a mountaineer frontier spirit to the national narrative of westward progress—brazen, sure-footed, and powerful. Other intriguing female characters, such as Judy Finx in the tale reprinted here, appear alongside Crockett or in extraordinary adventures of their own.

The actual Davy (David) Crockett, politician and soldier, was born in 1786 in eastern Tennessee in present-day Greene County near the Nolichucky River. In 1834, he published an autobiography, but he made no contributions to the Crockett almanacs, almost all of which were published after his death in 1836.

Whipping a Catamount

There war a gal named Judy Finx, that lived down to Mud creek. Every body has hearn on her, and every body has seen her, too, except them what her brother carries their eyes in his pocket. It's concluded that she takes the rag off quite, all along up and down the creek and something of a piece beyond. Judy went out one arternoon to a tea squall. As it war at a near neighbor's who lived only about five miles off, she did not take her rifle with her; she only put her butcher knife in her bosom; but she wore that as much for ornament as anything else. On the way home it war quite dark, and her neighbor where she had been let Judy have a tame bear to see her home, as there war no other beau present. They were going through a piece of woods together, when they heard a squalling like a woman's voice, and Judy knew it was a catamount right off. So she jumped on the bear's back, being intarmined that the varmint should have a chase before he got her. The bear knew what she wanted, and he set out at full speed. They had not gone fur before a great snake seized the bear by the hind leg and stopped his progress. The bear turned around and caught the snake by the neck with his teeth, and held on upon it. The snake thrashed about, and jest as the catamount came up, Judy caught the cretur by his long tail, and begun to chastise the catamount with it as if it had been a cowskin. The catamount squalled and grinned and snapped at the snake's tail whenever it came down upon his head and shoulders, and at last he caught it in his teeth. The bear then let go of the sarpent and he wheeled upon the catamount. The way them two made the leaves fly war a caution, and Judy did not stop to see which would gain the victory. She drove forward the bear and soon got home, safe and sound.

PART II
Slavery, the Civil War, and Reconstruction
Theresa Lloyd

The lives of African Americans in southern and central Appalachia during and after slavery, as well as the response of the region's whites to blacks, slavery, and the Civil War, have been obscured by myth and misunderstanding. Frederick Law Olmsted set the myth in motion with his widely read assertions about the relative mildness of slavery in the mountain South. Post–Civil War commentators continued the mythologizing, emphasizing the region's Union support and the supposed racial purity of white Appalachians to the extent that the presence of slavery and blacks in the region was obscured. Nonetheless, by 1860, slavery was present in almost every county in Appalachia below the Mason-Dixon Line. Although large concentrations of enslaved people existed on plantations in parts of the Shenandoah Valley, the Tennessee Valley, and northern Alabama, most enslaved African Americans lived on small farms with few others in bondage or labored in mines, businesses, and in some places, such as Asheville, North Carolina, the tourism industry. Slave auctions occurred in many southern Appalachian towns, and along drove roads, the sight of slave coffles was not uncommon. In fact, in the decades preceding the Civil War, owners in the Upper South, including Appalachia, often sold enslaved people to the markets in the Deep South, where workers in sugar and cotton fields were in high demand due to appalling disease and death rates.

One of the earliest Appalachian publications to address slavery was also among the first abolitionist newspapers in the United States. Elihu Embree, a white Quaker industrialist from East Tennessee, published two of the country's earliest abolitionist newspapers, *The Manumission Intelligencer* (1819) and its successor, *The Emancipator* (1820). During this time, there were abolitionist societies in East Tennessee. Shortly thereafter, however, hardening pro-slavery sentiments throughout the South silenced most southern mountain anti-slavery commentators.

In Northern Appalachia, Pittsburgh was an important abolitionist center, hosting several anti-slavery societies and serving as an Underground Railroad depot. Although African Americans did not enjoy full citizenship in Pennsylvania (they had lost the right to vote in the state in 1838), many of the city's abolitionists were blacks who had moved to the city from slaveholding regions of Appalachia. Martin Delany and Carter Woodson were from (West) Virginia, and John Peck originally lived in Hagerstown, Maryland. Delany published an anti-slavery newspaper, as did the white Pittsburgh abolitionist Jane Grey Swisshelm. In addition, Delany wrote several anti-slavery books, including *The Condition, Elevation, Emigration, and Destiny of the Colored People of the United States* (1852).

Responses to secession and the Civil War among southern mountain whites were complex. In some sections, loyalty to the Union ran high. Many East Tennesseans ardently opposed secession, obliging the Confederacy to send troops to quell incipient rebellion. In western Virginia, pro-Union sentiments were so strong that the area withdrew from Virginia to form the state of West Virginia. Some Appalachians, however, supported the Confederacy, western North Carolina being one of the strongholds (although even there Union support was powerful in some communities). Interestingly, pro- and anti-Union sentiments did not necessarily divide along lines of slave ownership; some slave owners were pro-Union, and some who did not own slaves supported the Confederacy. Whether they felt allegiance to the North or the South, however, Appalachians on the home front often suffered from the marauding of bushwhackers and of both Union and Confederate troops.

As during slavery days, life for African Americans in the post-Reconstruction Appalachian South was fraught with problems: lynchings occurred, and in some towns, whites expelled blacks en masse. Hence, whether voluntarily or by force, African Americans tended to migrate to cities inside and outside the region or to mining areas in Kentucky, Tennessee, Virginia, and West Virginia. In *Up from Slavery* (1901), Booker T. Washington describes his childhood in slavery on the eastern slope of the Blue Ridge (in Virginia) and his struggle to attain an education as a young freedman in the Kanawha Valley (West Virginia) salt mines; his account shows both the difficulty and the hope that emancipation brought to Appalachia's African American citizens.

Sources: Wilma Dunaway, *Slavery in the American Mountain South* (2003) and *The African-American Family in Slavery and Emancipation* (2003); John C. Inscoe, ed., *Appalachians and Race: The Mountain South from Slavery to Segregation* (2001) and *Mountain Masters: Slavery and Sectional Crisis in Western North Carolina* (1989); John C. Inscoe and Gordon B. McKinney, *The Heart of Confederate Appalachia: Western North Carolina in the Civil War* (2000).

Elihu Embree
1782–1820

Though most historians emphasize northern contributions to abolition efforts, one of the first solely anti-slavery newspapers in the United States, *The Emancipator,* was published by Elihu Embree and the Tennessee Manumission Society in Jonesborough, Tennessee, in 1820, twenty-one years prior to the publication of William Lloyd Garrison's *The Liberator.* Embree, who ran a successful ironworks business near Bumpass Cove with his brother, Elijah, became an abolitionist through the influence of his father, Thomas, a politically active abolitionist and Quaker minister. Thomas eventually moved with his family to Ohio to escape threats for his anti-slavery stance. Elihu remained in Tennessee and married Elizabeth Worley, who brought several slaves with her into the marriage. Though he sold the slaves in 1809, he bought them back in 1812 so that he could free them. Emancipating all his slaves proved costly, however, and he still owned one slave and her children at the time of his death.

The seven issues of *The Emancipator,* the successor to Embree's first newspaper effort, *The Manumission Intelligencer,* drew over two thousand subscribers, on par with large Tennessee newspapers of the time period. *The Emancipator* contained anti-slavery tracts, correspondence, abolitionist speeches, biographical sketches of activists, and the history of the abolition movement and slave trade. Though publication of *The Emancipator* ended after Embree unexpectedly died from fever at the age of thirty-eight, it exists as a testament to an influential anti-slavery movement in Appalachia prior to the Civil War.

FROM The Emancipator

ZEALOTS was a wealthy citizen, possessed of a wife & several sons & daughters, and had a considerable number of slaves, consisting of parents and children. ZEALOTS was raising up his children in great delicacy and tenderness, for he designed them to figure in the world, & to shine in wealth and honor amongst their contemporaries; hence, he was raising them without labour, and no pains or cost was spared in their education, especially his sons, whom he wished to be advanced to posts of honor and profit in the state; and as he had slaves to do the drudgery, and to wait upon them, they had nothing to do but to qualify themselves for the enjoyment of those stations in high life, for which their parent designed them. ZEALOTS was not one of those hard, or cruel masters to slaves; he always, as he said, gave them plenty to eat, and clothes to keep them warm; but he was possessed of the opinion that it was highly criminal in slaves to be idle, so that he never let them suffer for want of plenty of work to do. He seldom if ever beat them, excepting for real or imaginary faults; and was so particular in his tone of voice, when speaking to them, that he never lost his dignity as a master, but always spoke to them in the case absolute.

ZEALOTS was a very religious man, and exceedingly devout in all his devotional performances, he was orthodox in his creed, according to the popular religion of the times; regular in his devotions, both public and private; for his hours of prayer were seldom neglected, nor would he miss the Sunday service if he could possibly help it.

ZEALOTS considered the reading of the scriptures as a very great means of grace and salvation, and he would have taught his slaves to read, but for two reasons, the one was, he was afraid they would come to see that he was depriving them of the rights which God and nature had endowed them; and the other was, that he was unwilling to afford the time and expense. He seldom omitted calling in his slaves to evening prayers, when they had not too much business on hand; but it was with difficulty that he could get them to attend; and would often lament the vicious disposition of his negroes for refusing to join him in so holy an exercise. The truth of the matter was this: ignorant as he was keeping them, that eternal rule of justice which the Deity has implanted in man, taught them that their master was depriving them of one of heaven's best gifts to man, and that true religion and injustice can never dwell together in the same heart, and this was the cause of their not joining in his devotions, for they had no confidence in his religion!

ZEALOTS was one of those professors of religion that some men call enthusiasts, for he could tell you the very time when, and the place where his peace was made with his maker; and as I said, was very zealous in church services, and devotional exercises, but as to acts of humanity, public spiritedness and alms giving, he left them to be performed by those who had more time than he had to spare from the more important acts of devotion.

Much of the time that ZEALOTS was in his last sickness, his head was full of his religious flights of fanciful happiness, which he hoped shortly to enjoy, especially when such a state of felicity was spoken of in his hearing; but if any one happened to speak of doing justly, loving mercy, and relieving the oppressed, helping the needy, &c. he appeared uneasy at the recital, and would wave the discourse as soon as possible. When it was suggested to him by one of his friends, that he ought to liberate his slaves before his death, he groaned and said that slavery was indeed a dreadful thing, but as his slaves were his property, he could never think of throwing away his estate; & besides that he could not act so unjustly with his children, as to rob them of so valuable a possession as his slaves would be to them after his decease; and moreover, was he to free his slaves, his children would be reduced to the necessity of labouring for their support, which they had not been brought up to; and that his prospects of their future greatness would be frustrated, and they reduced to a level with the common citizens of the country.

It was completely in the power of ZEALOTS, even at that late period of his life, to have performed what eternal justice demanded of him, and is demanding of every person, that is in his circumstance, namely, "to undo the heavy burdens, and let the oppressed, go free!" But he chose rather to gratify his pride and avarice, and risk the fearful consequences of a future reckoning, than to perform an act which would have proved a lasting tranquility to his mind. How vague are all pretentions to religion, where justice, mercy and humanity, are not mixed with devotion.

ZEALOTS made good his determinations by formally, and with great exactness, dividing out his slaves amongst his heirs, whilst the distracted victims of his pride and covetousness, wrung their hands, & vented their sighs for the sorrowful separation which they saw must shortly take place amongst them. ZEALOTS breathed his last shortly after signing and sealing his last will and testament, and has gone to meet his God in Judgment, where we shall leave him, and return to another part of our subject.

❧

The following facts, and picture of the slave trade, as now carrying on by monsters in human shape, are at once sufficient to show the necessity of [a recent federal law outlawing the transatlantic slave trade], and to produce sentiments of sympathy for the poor victims, and indignation in the breast of every friend of humanity towards perpetrators of this once tolerated, but now detested outrage on human right.

We regret to find that the Royal Gazette of Sierra Leone contains authentic information of the shameful traffic in slaves, at the Galienas and the river Sheabor. [. . .]

On the 17th August, his Majesty's ship Pheasant, Capt. Kelly, returned to the harbor of Freetown, having made prize of the slave ship Novo Felicidade, which had on board 71 slaves. In his declaration, Capt. Kelly with true feelings of humanity, states:—

"I do further declare, that the state in which these unfortunate creatures were found, is shocking to every principle of humanity; seventeen men shackled together in pairs by the legs, and twenty boys were on the other side in the main hold, a space measuring eighteen feet in length, seven feet eight inches in main breadth, and one foot eight inches in height, and under them yams for their support.—One of these unfortunate creatures was in the last state of dysentry, whose natural evacuations ran involuntarily from him amongst those yams, creating an effluvia too shocking for description. On their being released from irons their appearance was most distressing, scarcely one of them could stand on his legs from cramp and evident starvation. The space allowed for the females, thirty-four in number was even more contracted than that for the men, measuring only nine feet four inches in length, 4 feet eight inches in main breadth, & two feet seven inches in height; but not being confined in irons, & perhaps allowed during the day to come on deck, they did not present so distressing an appearance as the men."

It is some gratification to find that many British cruisers have been active and successful in the cause of humanity, by seizing and confiscating numerous vessels engaged in this nefarious and disgusting commerce.

❧

"Oppression Maketh a Wise Man Mad"

—Solomon

A negro woman, a slave, who lived with, and belonged to a man who lives at or near Christianville Boatyard, Sullivan county, Ten. about 23 miles from this place; a few weeks ago being cruelly whipped by her mistress (which it is said was a common thing) on being let loose from her beating, ran to the bridge which crosses the north fork of Holston, and leaped off into the water and drowned before it was possible to get her out; thus ridding herself of a life which was rendered intolerable by being a slave to a cruel and unfeeling mistress.

If the condition of slaves is often rendered so wretched by their cruel owners as to make their lives so intolerable that they are induced to commit suicide, how unsafe are those who are their oppressors. Such creatures dread no consequences. How unwise and impolitic it is to raise up an inveterate and desperate enemy in our own houses, and about our farms, and in our towns and cities. Even the innocent is not safe where such policy is practiced; as they in many instances suffer with the guilty in this world. And if Solomon be correct that *"oppression maketh a wise man mad,"* which no doubt he is, why wonder at this uncultivated people, many of whom are little acquainted with the forgiving disposition which the gospel inculcates, and are very ignorant of the crime of suicide, or murder of their oppressors; why wonder that many desperate acts are committed by them. Nay I wonder that more mischief is not done by them, as the consequence attendant on the greatest crimes is but death, which is certain to overtake all sooner or later, but to these outcasts, neglected and tortured sons of Africa it is no terror, but a welcome release from a life which is rendered intolerable by the oppression of the boasted sons of *Liberty.*

Martin Robison Delany

1812–1885

Martin Delany emerged as a dynamic public speaker and advocate for the African American community during the turbulent years of the Fugitive Slave Act (1850), the Civil War (1861–1865), and Reconstruction (1863–1877). Born free in Charles Town, (West) Virginia, to a free mother and an enslaved father, Delany learned to read and write from his mother. He settled in Pittsburgh as a young man, pursuing a variety of careers before founding *The North Star* (1847–1849), an influential African American newspaper, with Frederick Douglass. Douglass's integrationist views differed sharply from Delany's more radical Black Nationalism, and Delany organized a national black emigrationist convention in 1854 in response to Douglass's 1853 convention that stressed integration.

Though Delany advocated for the right to full American citizenship for blacks in *The Condition, Elevation, Emigration, and Destiny of the Colored People of the United States* (1852), he also argued that select blacks should emigrate to Africa in order to fulfill their full potential. Throughout 1859 and 1861–1862, he serialized the novel *Blake; or, The Huts of America,* a response to Harriet Beecher Stowe's *Uncle Tom's Cabin.* Unlike the passive Uncle Tom, Blake, the novel's protagonist, is a charismatic and intelligent runaway slave who foments rebellion in Cuba and the American South.

Delany served in the Civil War as the first black major in the Union army, an honor that earned him a visit with Abraham Lincoln in 1865. He ran for lieutenant governor of South Carolina in 1874. Though he lost by only a small margin, Delany became disillusioned with the political process of Reconstruction. In 1879 he rededicated himself to helping blacks who wanted to emigrate to Liberia. Delany's controversial black nationalism, his impassioned and intelligent writing, and his multiple careers and honors during a time of severe oppression earned him an honored place in history.

FROM The Condition, Elevation, Emigration, and Destiny of the Colored People of the United States

It should be borne in mind, that Anti-Slavery took its rise among *colored men,* just at the time they were introducing their greatest projects for their own elevation, and that our Anti-Slavery brethren were converts of the colored men, in behalf of their elevation. Of course, it would be expected that being baptized into the new doctrines, their faith would induce them to embrace the principles therein contained, with the strictest possible adherence. [. . .]

It was expected that Anti-Slavery, according to its professions, would extend to colored persons, as far as in the power of its adherents, those advantages nowhere else to be obtained among white men. That colored boys would get situations in their shops and stores, and every other advantage tending to elevate them as far as possible, would be extended to them. At least, it was expected, that in Anti-Slavery establishments, colored men would have the preference. Because, there was no other ostensible object in view, in the commencement of the Anti-Slavery enterprise, than the *elevation* of the *colored man*, by facilitating his efforts in attaining to equality with the white man. It was urged, and it was true, that the colored people were susceptible of all that the whites were, and all that was required was to give them a fair opportunity, and they would prove their capacity. That it was unjust, wicked, and cruel, the result of an unnatural prejudice, that debarred them from places of respectability, and that public opinion could and should be corrected upon this subject. That it was only necessary to make a sacrifice of feeling, and an innovation on the customs of society, to establish a different order of things,—that as Anti-Slavery men, they were willing to make these sacrifices, and determined to take the colored man by the hand, making common cause with him in affliction, and bear a part of the odium heaped upon him. That his cause was the cause of God—that "In as much as ye did it not unto the least of these my little ones, ye did it not unto me," and that as Anti-Slavery men, they would "do right if the heavens fell." Thus, was the cause espoused, and thus did we expect much. But in all this, we were doomed to disappointment, sad, sad disappointment. Instead of realizing what we had hoped for, we find ourselves occupying the very same position in relation to our Anti-Slavery friends, as we do in relation to the pro-slavery part of the community—a mere secondary, underling position, in all our relations to them, and any thing more than this, is not a matter of course affair—it comes not by established anti-slavery custom or right, but like that which emanates from the pro-slavery portion of the community, by mere sufferance.

It is true, that the "Liberator" office, in Boston, has got Elijah Smith, a colored youth, at the cases—the "Standard," in New York, a young colored man, and the "Freeman," in Philadelphia, William Still, another, in the publication office, as "packing clerk"; yet these are but three out of the hosts that fill these offices in their various departments, all occupying places that could have been, and as we once thought, would have been, easily enough, occupied by colored men. Indeed, we can have no other idea about anti-slavery in this country, than that the legitimate persons to fill any and every position about an anti-slavery establishment are colored persons. Nor will it do to argue in extenuation, that white men are as justly entitled to them as colored men; because white men do not from *necessity* become anti-slavery men in order to get situations; they being white men, may occupy any position they are capable of filling—in a word, their chances are endless, every avenue in the country being opened to them. They do not therefore become abolitionists, for the sake of employment—at least, it is not the song that anti-slavery sung, in the first love of the new faith, proclaimed by its disciples.

And if it be urged that colored men are incapable as yet to fill these positions, all that we have to say is, that the cause has fallen far short; almost equivalent to a failure, of a tithe, of what it promised to do in half the period of its existence, to this time, if it have not as yet, now a period of twenty years, raised up colored men enough, to fill the offices within its patronage. We think it is not unkind to say, if it had been half as faithful to itself, as it should have been—its professed principles we mean; it could have reared and tutored from childhood, colored men enough by this time, for its own especial purpose. These we know could have been easily obtained, because colored people in general, are favorable to the anti-slavery cause, and wherever there is an adverse manifestation, it arises from sheer ignorance; and we have now but comparatively few such among us. There is one thing certain, that no colored person, except such as would reject education altogether, would be adverse to putting their child with an anti-slavery person, for educational advantages. This then could have been done. But it has not been done, and let the cause of it be whatever it may, and let whoever may be to blame, we are willing to let all that pass, and extend to our anti-slavery brethren the right-hand of fellowship, bidding them God-speed in the propagation of good and wholesome sentiments—for whether they are practically carried out or not, the professions are in themselves all right and good. Like Christianity, the principles are holy and of divine origin. And we believe, if ever a man started right, with pure and holy motives, Mr. Garrison did; and that, had he the power of making the cause what it should be, it would all be right, and there never would have been any cause for the remarks we have made, though in kindness, and with the purest of motives. We are nevertheless, still occupying a miserable position in the community, wherever we live; and what we most desire is, to draw the attention of our people to this fact, and point out what, in our opinion, we conceive to be a proper remedy. [. . .]

We believe in the universal equality of man, and believe in that declaration of God's word, in which it is there positively said, that "God has made of one blood all the nations that dwell on the face of the earth." Now of "the nations that dwell on the face of the earth," that is, all the people—there are one thousand millions of souls, and of this vast number of human beings, two-thirds are colored, from black, tending in complexion to the olive or that of the Chinese, with all the intermediate and admixtures of black and white, with the various "crosses" as they are physiologically, but erroneously termed, to white. We are thus explicit in stating these points, because we are determined to be understood by all. We have then, two colored to one white person throughout the earth, and yet, singular as it may appear, according to the present geographical and political history of the world, the white race predominates over the colored; or in other words, wherever there is one white person, that one rules and governs two colored persons. This is a living undeniable truth, to which we call the especial attention of the colored reader in particular. Now there is a cause for this, as there is no effect without a cause, a comprehensible remediable cause. We all believe in the justice of God, that he is impartial, "looking upon his children with an eye of care," dealing out to them all, the measure of his goodness; yet, how can we reconcile ourselves to the difference that exists between the colored and the white races, as they truthfully present themselves before our eyes? To solve this problem, is to know the remedy; and to know it, is but necessary, in order successfully to apply it. And we shall but take the colored people of the United States, as a fair sample of the colored races everywhere of the present age, as the arguments that apply to the one, will apply to the other, whether Christians, Mahomedans, or pagans. [. . .]

The argument that man must pray for what he receives, is a mistake, and one that is doing the colored people especially, incalculable injury. That man must pray in order to get to Heaven, every Christian will admit—but a great truth we have yet got to learn, that he can live on earth whether he is religious or not, so that he conforms to the great law of God, regulating the things of earth; the great physical laws. It is only necessary, in order to convince our people of their error and palpable mistake in this matter, to call their attention to the fact, that there are no people more religious in this Country, than the colored people, and none so poor and miserable as they. That prosperity and wealth, smiles upon the efforts of wicked white men, whom we know to utter the name of God with curses, instead of praises. That among the slaves, there are thousands of them religious, continually raising their voices, sending up their prayers to God, invoking His aid in their behalf, asking for a speedy deliverance; but they are still in chains, although they have thrice suffered out their three score years and ten. That "God sendeth rain upon the just and unjust," should be sufficient to convince us that our success in life, does not depend upon our religious character, but that the physical laws governing all earthly and temporary affairs, benefit equally the just and the unjust. Any other doctrine than this, is downright delusion, unworthy of a free people, and only intended for slaves. That all men and women, should be moral, upright, good and religious—we mean *Christians*— we would not utter a word against, and could only wish that it were so; but, what we here desire to do is, to correct the long standing error among a large body of the colored people in this country, that the cause of our oppression and degradation, is the displeasure of God towards us, because of our unfaithfulness to Him. This is not true; because if God is just—and he is—there could be no justice in prospering white men with his fostering care, for more than two thousand years, in all their wickedness, while dealing out to the colored people, the measure of his displeasure, for not half the wickedness as that of the whites. Here then is our mistake, and let it forever henceforth be corrected. We are no longer slaves, believing any interpretation that our oppressors may give the word of God, for the purpose of deluding us to the more easy subjugation; but freemen, comprising some of the first minds of intelligence and rudimental qualifications, in the country. What then is the remedy, for our degradation and oppression? This appears now to be the only remaining question—the means of successful elevation in this our own native land? This depends entirely upon the application of the means of Elevation. [. . .]

Moral theories have long been resorted to by us, as a means of effecting the redemption of our brethren in bonds, and the elevation of the free colored people in this country. Experience has taught us, that speculations are not enough; that the *practical* application of principles adduced, the thing carried out, is the only true and proper course to pursue. [. . .]

Cast our eyes about us and reflect for a moment, and what do we behold! every thing that presents to view gives evidence of the skill of the white man. Should we purchase a pound of groceries, a yard of linen, a vessel of crockery-ware, a piece of furniture, the very provisions that we eat,—all, all are the products of the white man, purchased by us from the white man, consequently, our earnings and means, are all given to the white man.

Pass along the avenues of any city or town, in which you live—behold the trading shops—the manufactories—see the operations of the various machinery—see the stage-coaches coming in, bringing the mails of intelligence—look at the railroads interlining every section, bearing upon them their mighty trains, flying with the velocity of the swallow, ushering in the hundreds of industrious, enterprising travellers. Cast again your eyes widespread over the ocean—see the vessels in every direction with their white sheets spread to the winds of heaven, freighted with the commerce, merchandise and wealth of many nations. Look as you pass along through the cities, at the great and massive buildings—the beautiful and extensive structures of architecture—behold the ten thousand cupolas, with their spires all reared up towards heaven, intersecting the territory of the clouds—all standing as mighty living monuments, of the industry, enterprise, and intelligence of the white man. And yet, with all these living truths, rebuking us with scorn, we strut about, place our hands akimbo, straighten up ourselves to our greatest height, and talk loudly about being "as good as any body." How do we compare with them? Our fathers are their coachmen, our brothers their cookmen, and ourselves their waiting-men. Our mothers their nurse-women, our sisters their scrub-women, our daughters their maid-women, and our wives their washer-women. Until colored men, attain to a position above permitting their mothers, sisters, wives, and daughters, to do the drudgery and menial offices of other men's wives and daughters; it is useless, it is nonsense, it is pitiable mockery, to talk about equality and elevation in society. The world is looking upon us, with feelings of commiseration, sorrow, and contempt. We scarcely deserve sympathy, if we peremptorily refuse advice, bearing upon our elevation.

We will suppose a case for argument: In this city reside, two colored families, of three sons and three daughters each. At the head of each family, there is an old father and mother. The opportunities of these families, may or may not be the same for educational advantages—be that as it may, the children of the one go to school, and become qualified for the duties of life. One daughter becomes school-teacher, another a mantua-maker, and a third a fancy shop-keeper; while one son becomes a farmer, another a merchant, and a third a mechanic. All enter into business with fine prospects, marry respectably, and settle down in domestic comfort—while the six sons and daughters of the other family, grow up without educational and business qualifications, and the highest aim they have, is to apply to the sons and daughters of the first named family, to hire for domestics! Would there be an equality here between the children of these two families? Certainly not. This, then, is precisely the position of the colored people generally in the United States, compared with the whites. What is necessary to be done, in order to attain an equality, is to change the condition, and the person is at once changed. If, as before stated, a knowledge of all the various business enterprises, trades, professions, and sciences, is necessary for the elevation of the white, a knowledge of them also is necessary for the elevation of the colored man; and he cannot be elevated without them.

White men are producers—we are consumers. They build houses, and we rent them. They raise produce, and we consume it. They manufacture clothes and wares, and we garnish ourselves with them. They build coaches, vessels, cars, hotels, saloons, and other vehicles and places of accommodation, and we deliberately wait until they have got them in readiness, then walk in, and contend with as much assurance for a "right," as though the whole thing was bought by, paid for, and belonged to us. By their literary attainments, they are the contributors to, authors and teachers of, literature, science, religion, law, medicine, and all other useful attainments that the world now makes use of. We have no reference to ancient times—we speak of modern things.

These are the means by which God intended man to succeed: and this discloses the secret of the white man's success with all of his wickedness, over the head of the colored man, with all of his religion. We have been pointed and plain, on this part of the subject, because we desire our readers to see persons and things in their true position. Until we are determined to change the condition of things, and raise ourselves above the position in which we are now prostrated, we must hang our heads in sorrow, and hide our faces in shame. It is enough to know that these things are so; the causes we care little about. Those we have been examining, complaining about, and moralizing over, all our life time. This we are weary of. What we desire to learn now is, how to effect a *remedy;* this we have endeavored to point out. Our elevation must be the result of *self-efforts,* and work of our *own hands.* No other human power can accomplish it. If we but determine it shall be so, it will be so. Let each one make the case his own, and endeavor to rival his neighbor, in honorable competition.

These are the proper and only means of elevating ourselves and attaining equality in this country or any other, and it is useless, utterly futile, to think about going any where, except we are determined to use these as the necessary means of developing our manhood. The means are at hand, within our reach. Are we willing to try them? Are we willing to raise ourselves superior to the condition of slaves, or continue the meanest underlings, subject to the beck and call of every creature bearing a pale complexion? If we are, we had as well remained in the South, as to have come to the North in search of more freedom. What was the object of our parents in leaving the south, if it were not for the purpose of attaining equality in common with others of their fellow citizens, by giving their children access to all the advantages enjoyed by others? Surely this was their object. They heard of liberty and equality here, and they hastened on to enjoy it, and no people are more astonished and disappointed than they, who for the first time, on beholding the position we occupy here in the free north—what is called, and what they expect to find, the free States. They at once tell us, that they have as much liberty in the south as we have in the north—that there as free people, they are protected in their rights—that we have nothing more—that in other respects they have the same opportunity, indeed the preferred opportunity, of being their maids, servants, cooks, waiters, and menials in general, there, as we have here—that had they known for a moment, before leaving, that such was to be the only position they occupied here, they would have remained where they were, and never left. Indeed, such is the disappointment in many cases, that they immediately return back again, completely insulted at the idea, of having us here at the north, assume ourselves to be their superiors. Indeed, if our superior advantages of the free States, do not induce and stimulate us to the higher attainments in life, what in the name of degraded humanity will do it? Nothing, surely nothing. If, in fine, the advantages of free schools in Massachusetts, New York, Pennsylvania, Ohio, Michigan, and wherever else we may have them, do not give us advantages and pursuits superior to our slave brethren, then are the unjust assertions of Messrs. Henry Clay, John C. Calhoun, Theodore Frelinghuysen, late Governor Poindexter of Mississippi, George McDuffy, Governor Hammond of South Carolina, Extra Billy (present Governor) Smith, of Virginia, and the host of our oppressors, slave-holders and others, true, that we are insusceptible and incapable of elevation to the more respectable, honorable, and higher attainments among white men. But this we do not believe— neither do you, although our whole life and course of policy in this country are such, that it would seem to prove otherwise. The degradation of the slave parent has been entailed upon the child, induced by the subtle policy of the oppressor, in regular succession handed down from father to son—a system of regular submission and servitude, menialism and dependence, until it has become almost a physiological function of our system, an actual condition of our nature. Let this no longer be so, but let us determine to equal the whites among whom we live, not by declarations and unexpressed self-opinion, for we have always had enough of that, but by actual proof in acting, doing, and carrying out practically, the measures of equality. Here is our nativity, and here have we the natural right to abide and be elevated through the measures of our own efforts.

James Adams
(birth and death dates unknown)

Our knowledge of James Adams, whose first-person account of slavery is printed below, comes solely from *A North-Side View of Slavery. The Refugee: or the Narratives of Fugitive Slaves in Canada. Related by Themselves, with an Account of the History and Condition of the Colored Population of Upper Canada* (1856), a collection of slave narratives published by Benjamin Drew, a white Boston abolitionist. Called the first truly American literary genre by the transcendentalist and abolitionist Theodore Parker, slave narratives are first-person accounts by African Americans who had escaped from bondage. The narratives were either penned by the ex-slaves themselves, such as the accounts of Frederick Douglass and Harriet Jacobs, or dictated to others, as with James Adams's account. These narratives were powerful tools in the abolitionist movement and indirectly gave voice to the many African Americans still held in bondage.

The Fugitive Slave Act of 1850 had increased black emigration to Canada, since the bill permitted the arrest of escaped slaves wherever found and required whites living in free states in the United States to help return escaped slaves to bondage. In 1855, Drew interviewed escaped slaves living in fourteen Canadian communities. Drew selected 114 of these accounts—including Adams's—for inclusion in his book. Drew's title—*A North-Side View of Slavery*—consciously echoed *A South-Side View of Slavery* (1856) in which a northern minister, Nehemiah Adams, had argued that the institution was mostly favorable and that slaves had little desire to change their situations. In contrast, Drew's narrators repeatedly insist on their desire for and right to freedom. *A North-Side View of Slavery* was published by John P. Jewett, the publishing house that had issued the famous anti-slavery novel *Uncle Tom's Cabin* in 1852.

James Adams was from present-day West Virginia. Comparison of the book's Appalachian and non-Appalachian narratives belies the popular misconception that mountain slavery was more benign than that of the lowlands.

FROM A North-Side View of Slavery. The Refugee: or the Narratives of Fugitive Slaves in Canada

I was raised in Virginia, about twenty miles above the mouth of the Big Kanawha. At the age of seventeen, I set out to seek freedom in company with Benjamin Harris, (who was a cousin of mine,) and a woman and four children. I was young, and they had not treated me very badly; but I had seen older men treated worse than a horse or a hog ought to be treated; so, seeing what I was coming to, I wished to get away. My father being overseer, I was not used so badly as some even younger than myself, who were kicked, cuffed, and whipped very badly for little or nothing. We started away at night, on the 12th of August, 1824. After we had crossed the river, alarm was given, and my father came down where we had crossed, and called to me to come back. I had not told my intention to either my father or mother. I made no answer at all, but we walked three miles back from the river, where we lay concealed in the woods four days. The nights we passed at the house of a white friend; a friend indeed. We set out on a Monday night, and on the night following, seven more of my fellow-servants started on the same race. They were overtaken on Wednesday night, while they were in a house on the Ohio side. One jumped from a window and broke his arm; he stayed in the woods some days, and then he returned. The other six, two women and four children, were carried back, and the man we stopped with told us that the two women were whipped to make them tell where we were, so they could come upon us. They told their master as near as they could. On Thursday five white men came to the house where we had been concealed, but we were then in the woods and mountains, three miles from the friend's house. Every evening, between three and four o'clock, he would come and bring us food. We had nothing to give him—it was the hand of Divine Providence made him do it. He and others on the river see so much abuse of colored people that they pity them, and so are ready to give them aid; at least it was so then. He told the white men he knew nothing about us, and nothing of the kind. They searched his premises, and then left, believing his story. He came to us and said, "Boys, we are betrayed, they are coming now round the hill after us." We picked up our bundles and started on a run; then he called us back, and said he did it to try our *spunk*. He then told us of those who were carried back, and of the searching of his premises. We lodged in his barn that night. On the morning of Friday, he took us twelve miles to a place where the woman would have to leave her children, because he could conceal her better without them. He pointed out a house occupied by a family of Methodists, where she could go and tell them she was going back, and so leave her children there. But when she reached the house the father and mother were absent, so she went at a venture to another house. As it was raining and dark, she was guided by a white boy, a stout lad, and a girl with a lantern. At this house, she slept on a pallet on the floor; and when all else were asleep, she put her baby, which she had all along kept in her arms, into her oldest boy's care, crept to the door and went out. We had bidden her good-by, not expecting to see her. When the boy and girl had come back from guiding her, I heard the boy say, "Now we shall get fifty dollars for giving her up, and she'll get a good fleecing into the bargain." The man where we had stopped intended to take her to his house after she had got rid of her children, and when opportunity offered, send her to Canada. We went to a fire which we saw burning in a clearing, and Ben slept while I kept watch. Presently the woman came towards us. I heard the cracking of sticks as she came, and awoke Ben. He raised a sort of tomahawk he had made, intending to strike the person approaching, supposing it was an enemy. Said she, "Oh Ben, don't strike me, it is I." This made me cry to think Ben was so near killing the woman. Then she begged us not to leave her until the man should come to find her. He not coming so soon as we expected, we all steered back the twelve miles through the woods. Towards night, we heard his cow-bells; we drove the cattle before us, knowing that they would go home. Just as they had guided us there, the man, who had also followed the bells, came up. He told us that the children had been carried back to their master. We supposed the boy—guide—had betrayed them, but do not know. We stayed in his barn all night, and left on Sunday morning, the woman remaining behind.

At about noon, we were near a village. He pointed out a haystack, where we were to rendezvous at night, to meet another man whom our friend was to send to take us further along on our way. At night we went to the haystack; a road ran by it. Instead of keeping watch by the stack, we were so jaded that we crossed the road and lay down to rest on the bare ground, where we fell asleep. The man, as we afterwards learned from him, came as agreed upon, whistled and made signals, but failed to wake us up. Thinking we had been pursued away, he went back without us. The next morning, when we awoke, the sun was rising red, right on the public road. We saw a man at his door some two hundred yards from us. I went to ask him how the roads ran; Harris told me to inquire the way to Carr's Run, near home, so we would go the contrary. By the time I got back, Ben, who had watched, saw the man leave his house with his gun, and take a circle round to come down on us; but before he could head us, we were past him in the road running. We ran and walked about four miles barefoot; then we took courage to put on our shoes, which we had not dared stop long enough to do before, for fear the man with the gun would get ahead of us.

We were now on the top of a high hill. On our right was a path leading into the woods. In this path we descended, and after walking a few minutes, we arrived at a house by the main road. We went in to ask for a drink of buttermilk. Only the woman of the house was at home. Said she, "Boys, you are the very ones my husband was looking for last night." We denied it, being right on the road, and afraid. She insisted, "for," said she, "the man who came to tell my husband, said there was a big one and a little one." I was the little one. She gave us crackers, cheese, and onions. Against her advice, we left the house and moved on. Presently we came to a toll-gate, about which there were standing several white men. We walked up boldly to the gate; one of the men then asked us, "Where are you going?" Ben answered, "We are going to Chillicothe to see our friends there." Then he made answer and said, "You can't go any further, you must go back with me, you are the very boys I was looking for last night." We told him we wanted to go on, but he said, "There are so many buckskin Yankees in these parts that you will be taken before you get half through the town." We then went back to his house, but we did not stop more than ten minutes, because it would be dangerous for him as well as for us if we were caught on his premises. He stuck up a pole close to his house and tied a white cloth on it; then he led us up to the top of the hill (this was Monday, quite early in the morning), and showed us a rough place of bushes and rocks where we could lie concealed quite pleasantly, and so high up that we could see the main road, and the toll-gate, and the house, and the white flag. Said he, "If there's any danger, I'll send a child out to throw down the white flag; and if you get scared away from here, come back at night and I'll protect you." Soon after he left us, we saw five white men come to his house on horseback;

they were the five who had carried back the others that tried to escape. Two of them went into the house; then we saw a little girl come out and climb up on the fence, as if she were playing about, and she knocked down the flag-pole,—which meant that we were to look out for ourselves. But we did not feel that there was any immediate danger, and so we kept close under cover. Pretty soon the two came out of the house, and they all rode forward very fast, passed the toll-gate, and were soon out of sight. I suppose they thought to overtake us every minute, but luckily I have never seen them since. In the evening the man came and conducted us to his house, where we found the men we had seen at the toll-gate in the morning. They were mostly armed with pistols and guns. They guided us to a solitary house three miles back among the mountains, in the neighborhood of which we remained three days. We were told to go up on the mountain very high, where was an Indian cave in the rocks. From this cave we could look a great distance around and see people, and we felt afraid they would see us. So instead of staying there, we went down the mountain to a creek where trees had been cut down and branches thrown over the bank; we went under the branches and bushes where the sand was dry, and there we would sit all day. We all the time talked to each other about how we would get away, and what we should do if the white folks tackled us; that was all our discourse.

We stayed there until Friday, when our friends gave us knapsacks full of cakes and dried venison, and a little bundle of provision besides, and flints and steel, and spunk, and a pocket-compass to travel through the woods by. We knew the north-star, but did not travel nights for nearly a week. So on Friday morning we set out, the men all bidding us good-by, and the man of the flag-staff went with us half a day to teach us the use of the compass; we had never seen one before. Once in a while he would put it on a log to show us how to travel by it. When he was leaving us, he took his knife and marked on the compass, so that we should steer a little west of north.

During the six days succeeding, we traversed an unbroken wilderness of hills and mountains, seeing neither man nor habitation. At night we made a fire to sit by. We saw deer on our way; we were not annoyed by wild animals, and saw but one snake, a garter-snake. The first sign of man we met with was a newly-made road; this was on the seventh day from the time we left the house in the mountains. Our provisions held out well, and we had found water enough. After crossing the road, we came out from the mountains to a level cleared place of farms and houses. Then we were afraid, and put ourselves on our guard, resolving to travel by night. We laid by until starlight, then we made for a road leading to the north. We would follow a road until it bent away from the north; then we would leave it and go by the compass. This caused us to meet many rivers and streams where there were no bridges; some we could wade over, and some we crossed by swimming. After reaching the clearings, we scarcely dared build a fire. Once or twice we took some green corn from the fields, and made a brush fire to roast it. After lighting the fire, we would retire from it, as far almost as we could see it, and then watch whether anybody might come to it. When the fire had gone out, the corn would be about done.

Our feet were now sore with long travelling. One night we came to a river; it was rather foggy, but I could see a ferry-scow on the other side. I was afraid of alligators, but I swam over, and poled the scow back and ferried Ben across,—his ancle was so sore, that he did not like to put his foot in the water if he could help it. We soon reached an old stable in the edge of a little town; we entered it and slept alternately one keeping watch, as we always managed while in the neighborhood of settlements. We did not do this in the wilderness,—*there* we slept safely, and were quite *reconciled*. At cock-crowing in the morning we set out and went into the woods, which were very near; there we stayed through the day.

At night we started on and presently came into a road running north-west. Coming to a vine patch we filled our knapsacks with cucumbers; we then met a white man, who asked us, "Which way are you travelling?" My cousin told him "To Cleveland, to help a man drive a drove of cattle." He then said, "I know you must be runaways,—but you needn't be afraid of me,—I don't want to hurt you." He then told us something that we knew before—that the last spring five fugitives were overtaken at his house by my master and two other men; that the fugitives took through his wheat-field,—one of them, a little fellow, could not run so fast as the rest, and master called to him to stop, or he'd shoot him. His answer was, "shoot and be d——d!" The man further told us, that he took through the wheat-field as if he would assist in catching the slaves, but that when he got near enough, he told them to "push on!" Ben and I knew about the pursuit, and what the little fellow had said; for it got round among the servants, after master got back. That little fellow's widow is now my wife. We went to the man's house, and partook of a good luncheon. He told us to hurry, and try to get through Newark before daylight. We hurried accordingly, but it was daybreak when we crossed the bridge. We found the little toll-gate open and we went through—there were lights in a tavern window at the left of the gate, and the windows had no curtains. Just as we were stepping off the bridge, a plank rattled,—then up started after us a little black dog, making a great noise. We walked smartly along, but did not run until we came to a street leading to the right,—then we ran fast until we came to a left hand turn, which led to the main road at the other side of the town. Before sunrise, we hid in a thicket of briars, close by the road, where we lay all day, seeing the teams, and every thing that passed by.

At dark we went on again, passed through Mount Vernon in the night, and kept on until daylight. Again we halted in concealment until night, then we went on again through Wooster. After leaving Wooster, we saw no more settlements, except one little village, which we passed through in broad day. We entered a store here, but were asked no questions. Here we learned the way to Cleveland. In the middle of the afternoon we stopped for a little rest. Just before night we moved forward again and travelled all night. We then stopped to rest until four in the afternoon, meanwhile roasting some corn as before. At about four, we met a preacher, who was just come from Cleveland. He asked us if we were making our escape,—we told him "No." He said, "You need not be afraid of me,—I am the friend of all who travel from the South to the North." He told us not to go into Cleveland, as we would be taken up. He then described a house which was on our way, where, he said, we might mention our meeting him, and we would find friends who would put us on board a boat. We hid until dark,—then we went to the house, which we recognized readily from the preacher's description. We knocked at the door, and were invited in. My cousin told them what the minister had said. The man of the house hid us in his barn two nights and three days. He was a shoe-maker. The next night after we got there, he went to Cleveland himself to get a berth for us aboard some boat for Canada. When he returned, he said he had found a passage for us with Capt. B., who was to sail the next Thursday at 10, P. M. At that hour we embarked, having a free passage in a schooner for Buffalo. On board this boat, we met with an Englishman whom we had often seen on a steamboat at the plantation. He knew us, and told us a reward of one hundred dollars was offered for each of us, and he showed us several handbills to that effect. He said they had been given him to put up along the road, but he had preferred to keep them in his pocket. Capt. B. took away our knives and Ben's tomahawk, for fear of mischief.

We reached Buffalo at 4, P. M. The captain said, that if there was any danger in the town, he would take us in his yawl and put us across. He walked through the town to see if there were any bills up. Finding no danger, he took us out of the hatchway,—he walked with us as far as Black Rock Ferry, giving us good advice all the way, how we should conduct ourselves through life in Canada, and we have never departed from his directions,—his counsel was good, and I have kept it.

I am now buying this place. My family are with me,—we live well, and enjoy ourselves. I worship in the Methodist church. What religious instruction I received on plantation, was from my mother.

I look upon slavery as the most disgusting system a man can live under. I would not be a slave again, except that I could not put an end to my own existence, through fear of the punishment of the future.

Men who have never seen or felt slavery cannot realize it for the thing it is. If those who say that fugitives had better go back, were to go to the South and see slavery, they would never wish any slave to go back.

I have seen separations by sales, of husbands from wives, of parents from children,—if a man threatens to run away, he is sure to be sold. Ben's mother was sold down South—to New Orleans—when he was about twenty years old.

I arrived in Canada on the 13th September, 1824.

Fannie A. Fain

1834–1903

Born in the northeastern Tennessee town of Blountville, Fannie Rhea was educated in nearby Jonesborough and Rogersville. She taught school in Blountville before her marriage to John Fain. Although the Fains were slaveholders and Fannie's brothers fought for the Confederacy, Mr. Fain refused to join the army, and during the first Confederate conscription, he hired a substitute. When the practice of hiring substitutes was abolished, Mr. Fain left home and hid for fifteen months rather than be drafted. While Mr. Fain was in hiding, Fannie was left to manage the farmwork as well as her numerous household chores alone. After the war, the Fains moved to Jonesborough, where Mr. Fain ran a dry goods store.

Fannie Fain's Civil War diary provides a gripping firsthand account of the struggle to survive on the home front in southern Appalachia. Unlike the genre today, nineteenth-century diaries were records of public life rather than personal documents. Fain writes as family and community historian; her vivid descriptions make the Civil War in East Tennessee come alive in all its complexity and also record a homemaker's work in the nineteenth century. Her audience is herself and her family; there is no indication that she contemplated publication.

Entries in the manuscript are not in chronological order, perhaps the result of Fain's copying of an original text no longer extant. For the sake of narrative continuity, we have rearranged the entries chronologically. We have also corrected Fain's occasional irregularities in spelling and grammar and for clarity have written out some words that she abbreviated. Fannie Fain refers to her husband as "Mr. Fain," the common practice for married people in her era; the text's "Johns" are a brother and an uncle.

FROM Civil War Diary

Sabbath night, Nov. 15th 1863

Several months have elapsed since I last opened my book to record any of the transpiring events of the day and equally as many changes have taken place (if not more) as months passed. Since then we have had wars & rumors of wars, fighting and bloodshed in our own little quiet town. During the months of June, July and August nothing special took place, we all were then busily engaged in trying to make & put away things for winter use. Mr. Fain was farming some, working his corn, potatoes, garden, etc. until harvest set in, then he was cutting, hauling, cleaning & putting it away, after which we worked at fruit. I canned a good deal, knowing everything would be scarce and hard to get this winter. We had just gotten through with these things when lo & behold, a very sudden & unexpected Yankee Raid was made through our town on Saturday, Sept 19th, a little after sun-up.

From that time to this we have had nothing but war troubles and soldiers in our town all the time. They went to Bristol, had a little skirmish with the Confederates, burnt commissary stores & a small Bridge beyond Bristol, fell back here that night, camped on field belonging to John at the head of town, burnt rails & threw down fencing. They arrested several persons in Bristol, guarded them in the Court house that night. Next morning they started off early to Zollicoffer to take it, having first arrested several persons here. Among others they took Brother John, but [he] was soon released through the influence of Friends. On their way to Zollicoffer they had a fight, found they could not succeed in hills, so they retreated, went back to Jones-boro & Greeneville, Mr. Easley, Mr. John [Snapp] & William Snapp joining them here, many others from the surrounding towns. Soon after here came the Confeder-ates in hot pursuit. All day Monday they were coming and going.

All the while both Armies were stealing horses. Our mare was taken twice by the Federals but returned, once sent after the Confederates, but not taken. On Monday night [the Confederates] camped on the same field of John's. Tuesday the 22nd, 1863, they hastened on hunting the Yankees, found them at the river near Bachman. Had a skirmish there, kept it up until [the Yankees] drove the Confederates back, and they reached the East end of town, planted cannon and there formed a regular line of battle. All the morning Mr. Fain & John were out trying to get back Father's horses which were stolen the night before. Here were all the soldiers, the street full, but they had not come. [. . .]

[W]e concluded to go to the cellar, with our family, Mr. Bailey's & Mrs. Easley's all here waiting; but after studying a little, they all concluded for us to leave. So we fastened up, left all & took out through the meadow for Shrite's. On the way there we met nothing but pickets & soldiers throwing fences in every direction, preparing for fighting, & the fight did come. Before we got there the cannonading commenced, and continued for some time. When they commenced the musketry, this we did not hear. We remained these two or three hours, then the news reached us that a line of battle was being formed out near there, so we all took up the line of march toward Jane Tipton's. [. . .] To add still more sorrow to our troubles, while we were at Shrite's, Mr. Fain and others went to the top of the hill & there beheld another house & Father's & all below them in flames, Mather's being the first to catch, caught from a shell. This was the saddest of all events, and moreover we thought probably some if not all our friends were consumed amid the flames, as they were in the cellars. Fortunately, the fire spread no higher up than the Courthouse & Mr. James' house, though we all expected the whole town to burn. We travelled on to Brother George's over the hills & reached there between eight & nine o'clock, rather wearied, each one had a child to carry, and remained there until Friday when all things were again quiet, except Mr. Fain, who came in the next morning to hear what had become of our friends. He learned of their whereabouts, and all were well. Father's family, hav-ing made their escape through the fire, wound their way to Crawford Fain's. [When] Mother's family went out, the house was burning, but before she left, she tried to save some of her things. Jeny & Nace pulled out many things, but a great many were destroyed. She & John came & stayed with us, the other children went to Uncle Bob's, [and] were here some.

We all tried to gather up things and set in again. We had not more than got fairly straightened up when another fight was anticipated here, the Confederate force being below, and fighting at Blue Spring, near Rheatown on Sunday the 11th of Oct. The Confederates fell back to Carter's Station, the Federals pursued, fought here the 14th on the hills and around the graveyard. Our family, Brother Hugh, Mother & Mary, the black ones, with a wagon of plunder, started off again for Brother George's, [and] reached there about twelve, Mr. Fain still in town. He retired to the hills east of town during the fight, then came in, found our kitchen had been opened & some things taken out. [. . .]

We have had no fighting since, but the Confederate Army all the time consuming & destroying everything in the country. Many of the houses were plundered and robbed after the fights. How many were killed and wounded on either side in the two fights has not been ascertained certainly. The object of the last fight was I suppose to give the Confederates an opportunity for moving off everything from Zollicoffer, as they intended to evacuate the place, and fall back to Abingdon. The Federals pursued within six miles of that place then fell back destroying the Rail-road & bridges, to Watauger river. Last Friday week the Confederates made an excursion into Hawkins C[oun]ty and captured 800, killed 15, wounded 20, took 60 wagons & a number of horses, so reported. The prisoners passed through here the following Sabbath on way to Richmond, some were deserters, & some shot to death.—Mr. Briscoe preached to-day from Matt, the parable of the sower being his subject. Very few were out, the day being unpleasant. In the afternoon I was down at Mother's two or three hours, spent part of the time singing.

Wednesday, [Nov.] 18th. [1863]

This morning we rose tolerably early. Mr. Fain & the black boys killed and cleaned four five [*sic*] hogs, brought them to the smoke house, cut them up, but did not salt. I ground and put away four crocks of sausage. Burr packed up a large box of sweet potatoes to-night. John was up and sit a short time. Crawford Fain & Fult Hall are with us, having drove in about eight o'clock on way from Bristol.

The latest dispatch seems to be that the Confederates have retaken Knoxville, but it is not confirmed.

Our children have all been well so far this winter. Martha Ellen says a lesson occasionally, Jonnie says almost anything he wishes now. James Rhea, now 5½ mo. old, sits in his chair much of the time.

Jan. 1, 1864

New Year's day we spent at Mother's. Brainerd & Bob both came home to spend New Year. I have been busy making up some winter clothing for the past two weeks, and preparing some for Mr. Fain in case he should have to leave home, which I trust he will not have to do. To-day Mr. Briscoe preached. Very few out. The weather has been extremely cold for the past three days, somewhat moderated to-day. The thermometer stood within two degrees of zero two mornings, New Year's morning & the next. Yesterday Mr. Fain went to Bristol & bought several articles, one bunch of bale cotton, some snuff, soda, a pistol, etc., had a cold ride.

Sabbath January 31st. [1864]

The last record which I made was Jan. 1st, Sabbath. Now the month is passed and we see upon the last day, it closes sadly with me, and has been spent mostly in dread and uneasiness, and the very thing which I so much dreaded did come upon me, my dear husband was forced to leave me and his little ones. To me it was the hardest trial ever yet befell me. This is one of the sad features in this wicked, unholy war. He left Thursday about dark Jan. 28th, 1864, in company with several others. It was to him a great trial, and the danger of the trip was another great circumstance, and now I know not where he is and can neither hear from him nor write to him. I have tried to make a perfect and entire consecration of him, my little ones & myself, all we have and are, to the Lord, to him who gave us all. I trust he may be spared, his life & health and soon be brought back to us in great mercy. [. . .] The time to me will be long, sad & lonely, but I pray we may be preserved and all we have.

April [?] 1864

Father and I went out to Sister Ruth's to get Cousin Rachel to do some coloring [dying yarn] for me, and to attend to the weaving. The day was cloudy and threatening. Friday Mother spent the day with us, the first time she has been up for some time. A small company of cavalry came in that morning, hunting up deserters or rather stragglers who were committing depredations, and the first thing we knew they had their horses, twenty head, on our meadow; kept them there that day, then left. That morning George & I went out, planted some corn & beans, tomatoes, cucumbers, bunch beans, etc. Rained on us all the time while out. Yesterday Brainerd left, has gone to North Carolina with Vaughn. He hated to go very much. I trust he may be spared & brought back to us. I hope this week to hear something from Mr. Fain.

Sabbath, Sept. 11th, 1864

This has been a real fall day, quite cool all day unless it was an hour or two at mid-day. Another w[ee]k has passed & still no change in things & no news. Can hear nothing from the seat of war at any point. No stir or excitement during the past week of consequence, except the news from Atlanta last Tuesday the 6th, which was that the Federals had the place & the Confederates were 90 miles from there.

Monday, Tuesday & Wednesday of last week we had rain. Friday & Saturday we were working with fruit. Yesterday we put away 1 bushel of corn in brine, the first I ever tried. I have not canned any fruit yet, will as soon as I can get some good. Jimmy was quite sick all last week, worse on Wednesday & Thursday. Wednesday he threw up two very large worms, was quite sick all day at his stomach & continued so all next day. In the evening on Thursday, I got John to call Nat in. He lanced his gum for his last stomach tooth, & left him some powders for his stomach. He has been improving since. To-day he seems quite well, but weak. He is wormy & teething. Bond's Camp meeting is now in progress, just a basket-meeting. John went down today on Pet, also Brainerd. We have a sacramental meeting in contemplation for the last of the week. Should things keep quiet, I hope I may be on hand to enjoy it.

Sunday, Oct. 2nd, 1864.

I have not recorded anything in my diary for three weeks past. Some changes have taken place since then. [. . .]

All last week we had very exciting times. On Monday we heard a heavy force of Federals were coming upon the Saltworks, some of the Confederates were ordered up there. On Tuesday we heard they were coming up the country. Thursday we heard the rebel pickets were driven three miles below Jonesboro on Wednesday evening. Thursday the Federals came up to Carter's Station, fell back & were fortifying six miles this side of Jonesboro. Friday they came up & skirmished most of the day. Saturday the fight began early in the day & continued until about twelve when they began evacuating, Vaughn having been ordered to Abingdon to defend the Salt Works. We heard 10,000 Federals were coming in through Pound Gap. We had exciting times here yesterday evening, the refugees getting away. Many men went out. John, Mr. Rutledge, Mr. Cate are all the men left in our part of the town. The day so far has been unusually quiet. The Federals have been looked for all day.

Sunday 15th, 1865.

Last Sunday night Phebe [a slave] had child born. Friday night about nine o'clock died. They are now just about fixing to bury. It suffered a good deal the night & day before it died. [. . .]

Tuesday night I wrote to Mr. Fain. Sent it off by a Mrs. Caldwell who was going within 15 miles of Knoxville. Her husband was captured on the last raid, his Father & family are all Union & in Federal lines. Brother Jim came home on Wednesday evening. He is suffering with his old wound. I fear that wound is to be his ruin unless he gets out of the Army & has it attended to. I had a letter from Mr. Fain on Thursday. He is only in tolerable health, he writes. I trust his life and health may be spared for years to come and we be soon reunited. On Wednesday Brother H. butchered eight hogs. We had a time getting all put away. No one to do it but Sister H. and myself.

Feb. 19th, 1865.

Today I attended church, heard Mr. Alexander, a chaplain in the [Confederate] Army, preach. He has preached here once before. I was then much pleased with his sermon. He is a refugee from New Market. He prayed a most excellent prayer to-day,

& I had prepared myself to listen to a good sermon, but I must confess I was much disappointed. When it came, it was nothing but heaping abuses, railed out against the North & Northern people. He took for his text, "Lord, what will thou have me to do," Acts 9 & 6, but did not touch his text [and] grossly wandered from it.

I wish I could write out the whole synopsis, word for word. He started out by saying that the war now going on was not only affecting the country in a political point, but the church of God was being greatly affected. He said this revolution had been brewing for the thirty years past, that Henry W. Beecher said at the beginning of the war that he wanted the next generation to be haters of the South & now we see the influence of his theology. This war, [Mr. Alexander] said, was brought on by the fanatics & abolitionists of the North. Then he spoke of Slavery, how it had been written & preached upon in the North, that there they called for an Anti-Slavery Bible, that if [the] Bible recognizes Slavery, then [they] will reject it. They wanted an Anti-Slavery Government and an Anti-Slavery people, that fanaticism & infidelity were the ruling principles of the North, and all kinds of other kinds of "isms" thrown in, Universalism, Unitarianism, Woman Rightism, etc. Then he spoke of the way the Sacramental meetings were conducted, of one in Troy, New York, where the table of the Lord was spread & the United States flag was hoisted, which they said represented a piece of space snatched from the ethereal regions, and bestudded with stars. Then at the close of the services the Star Spangled Banner was sung, as was also in some Baptist Associations and Methodist Conferences.

Then he went on to say that the North would not be satisfied with the blood and lives of the men, but that the women & children had to suffer in this war on the part of the South, that their lives would be required. Then he spoke of Beast Butler, as he is called, how he treated them in New Orleans, called those nice and virtuous ladies "Base women" & told his soldiers to just let themselves loose upon them. Then he said as this Evil returned to the Northern cities, in place of [Butler's] being censured and condemned as he ought to have been for his base, vile conduct upon these women, he & his men received applause & cheers throughout the North & his power was extended. Then he said that General Sherman told a good & pious lady in Memphis last year in his blasphemous manner that God Almighty had not room enough in his house.

Now all this was on the part of the North, & the South, [Mr. Alexander] seemed to think comparatively speaking was faultless, & just such a state of affairs our church would have when Governor Brownlow & the military authorities took possession of it, that the Federal authorities had gone so far as to enquire of the condition of churches in some places where they held sway, & when they found a disloyal preacher, he was abandoned & someone of their own selection was placed for the congregation. Then he alluded to a certain little Yankee manner, trying to pry into the condition of our church, whether we had regular supplies & good salary, etc. This I knew about, the latter was from Mr. Sawyer at K. to Mr. Briscoe. I heard the letter read.

Now this was to me a strange sermon, & coming from a man of Theology acquired at the Northern Seminaries. It once was that our best preachers & teachers in the South hailed from the North, but now it seems that nothing too bad or too unchristian can be said of them by their brethren in Christ's ministry. Oh! this vile, wicked war, what a division it has made, what wickedness & unkindness it has brought about. Enough of this kind of preaching for me.

Sabbath night, Feb. 26th. [1865]

This morning I attended Sabbath School with all the children. I never had Jimmie there before. He behaved tolerably well. I had a Bible Class to-day. Wish I could have it every Sabbath. Find it very interesting & the best way for studying the Bible. It was the first class I ever had in Sabbath School, but since I have been married & could not attend regularly, I gave it up to others, but they still seem to have partiality for me and still wish me for a teacher.

Sabbath, Apr 2nd. [1865]

For the past two weeks we have had report after report daily about the Federal Forces but not half of them true. They were retracted in Jonesboro; Carter's Station, etc, but at first they were false, but 'tis said today they are certainly at those two points; 25,000 at Bull's Gap, a heavy force building up the railroad working night & day. Some think they are on to Lynchburg. . . . Mr. Brisco preached today, while in church Col. Toole [?] with his scout came through hollering, considerably. The male portion thought they were Yankees and started off. 'Tis said Sherman is badly whipped in North Carolina (lost 75 pieces of artilery, & 20,000 of his men; it may not be true).

Sunday, Apr. 9th. [1865]

No Federals made their appearance as yet, though expected at any time & have been for the past two weeks. We cannot hear certainly of any being any nearer than Jonesboro. There they are said to be in heavy force. This morning 'twas rumored they were in Abingdon in force, though that may be false. Their movements seem to be a mystery to everyone. This country is entirely evacuated, and why they do not come on and take possession is a little strange. All are ready and waiting. We hear to-day of the bush-whackers having robbed Cousin Eliza Fain, extensively, but can't tell as to the truth. This day so far has been unusually quiet, none moving about scarcely. . . .

We had a letter from Brainerd dated Mar 18th. He was then very well but tired of his imprisonment. He gave me the latest news from Mr. Fain, said he had received a letter from him some time during the first of March, at Cincinatti. His plan then was to bring goods to Knoxville, move his family through the lines, but this move up the country has somewhat confused things. Willy was at home two or three days this week, left on Wednesday, may be 'twill be the last time for a long while. Jimmy left this evening two weeks ago & has not been back. Poor boys, what will become of them, I pray their lives may be spared, until this wicked war is over.

Sunday, [April] 23rd. [1865]

'Tis two weeks today since I made any record in my book. During the first five days we had many Confederate victories reported, which were usually false. When the truth came they were entirely on the Federal side. Some very great changes have taken place in this country which I trust will be for our benefit. The day I last made a record was the day when General Lee surrendered his Army & evacuated Richmond & Petersburg; consequently, the States of Virginia & Tennessee were given up. This news reached us the last of that week, Friday, 14th. This news produced utter confusion & despair upon the rebels, despair seemed depicted upon their countenances. Then in a few days we hear the [US] Army had succeeded in North Carolina, & that State given up so we then concluded the fighting was done in this part of the country. Some of the soldiers have been passing on their way home & coming every day. The boys will soon all be at home, that is, my brothers, if their lives are still spared. Brainerd is still a prisoner so far as we know. I am thankful to my Heavenly Father that this war has wound up as it has. My husband who has been from his family & home for 15 months can return & all my friends. I have looked for Mr. Fain every day for a week. He will surely come soon.

Rebecca Harding Davis
1831–1910

Rebecca Harding Davis, born Rebecca Blaine Harding in Washington, Pennsylvania, was the oldest of five children. When Rebecca was five years old, the Harding family moved to Wheeling, Virginia (now West Virginia), then a burgeoning industrial center straddling the North and South. At fourteen, she returned to Washington, Pennsylvania, enrolling in a girls' school.

At thirty, having earned a college degree despite the hostility of her family to female education and despite being primarily housebound through her domestic responsibilities caring for her father and younger siblings, Davis published *Life in the Iron Mills* (1861) in the *Atlantic Monthly*. The novella immediately gained her recognition in literary circles. She was invited to spend time with well-known New England authors such as Nathaniel Hawthorne, Ralph Waldo Emerson, and the Alcotts. After marrying an admirer of her writing and having three children, Davis carved out a life as a working mother, an uncommon role for a woman of her class and time. Davis published over five hundred pieces, including short stories set in the North Carolina mountains, where she sometimes vacationed.

Davis's concern with social justice, first evinced in *Life in the Iron Mills,* is present throughout her writings. Her evenhanded depiction of southern mountaineers is unusual for her era. "The Yares of the Black Mountains," published in 1875, presents northern post–Civil War attitudes toward the southern mountains and their residents, as well as internal divisions about secession and war that still lingered among Appalachians a decade later.

The Yares of the Black Mountains: A True Story

"OLD FORT!"

The shackly little train jolted into the middle of an unploughed field and stopped. The railway was at an end. A group of Northern summer-tourists, with satchels and water-proofs in shawl-straps, came out of the car and looked about them. It was but a few years after the war, and the South was unexplored ground to them. They had fallen together at Richmond, and by the time they had reached this out-of-the-way corner of North Carolina were the best of boon companions, and wondered why they had never found each other out in the world before. Yet, according to American habit, it was a mere chance whether the acquaintance strengthened into lifelong friendship or ended with a nod in the next five minutes.

It bade fair just now to take the latter turn.

Nesbitt, who had been in consultation with one or two men ploughing at the side of the station, came hurrying up: "Civilization stops here, it appears. Thirty miles' staging to Asheville, and after that carts and mules. The mails come, like the weather, at the will of Providence. I think I shall explore no farther. When does your train go back, conductor?"

"The scenery disappoints me," said Miss Cook, bridging her nose with her eye-glasses. "It lacks the element of grandeur."

"You'll find it lacking in more than that beyond," said a Detroit man who had come down to speculate in lumber. "Nothing but mountains, and balsam timber as spongy as punk. A snake couldn't get his living out of ten acres of it."

Across the field was a two-roomed wooden house, over which a huge board was mounted whereon was scrawled with tar, "Dinner and BAR-ROOM." They all went, stumbling over the lumpy meadow, toward it. Miss Cook, who was always good-humored except on aesthetic questions, carried the baby's satchel with her own.

"Shall you go on?" she asked the baby's mother. "The conductor says the mountains are inaccessible to women."

"Of course. Why, he has slept every night since we came on to high land."

"I doubt very much whether the cloud-effects will be as good as in the White Mountains. The sky is too warm." This was said thoughtfully.

"He has one stomach-tooth almost through. The balsam-air will be such a tonic! We'll go up if it is on foot, won't we, Charley?" And she buried her face in the roll of blanket.

There was a fine odor of burnt beans and whisky in the hot little parlor of the house, with its ragged horsehair chairs and a fly-blown print of the "Death of Robert E. Lee" on the wall. On the other side of the hall was the bar-room, where a couple of red-faced Majors in homespun trousers and shirts were treating the conductor. It was a domestic-looking bar-room after all, in spite of red noses and whisky: there were one or two geraniums in the window, and a big gray cat lay asleep beside them on the sill.

One of the Majors came to Baby's mother in the parlor. "There is a rocking-chair in the the—the opposite apartment," he said, "and the air will be better there for the child. A very fine child, madam! very fine, indeed!"

She said yes, it was, and followed him. He gave Baby a sprig of geranium, bowed and went out, while the other men began to discuss a Methodist camp-meeting, and the barkeeper shoved a newspaper over his bottles and worked anxiously at his day-book. The other passengers all went to dinner, but Nesbitt was back at her side in five minutes.

"I'm glad you stayed here," he said. "There is a bare wooden table set in a shed out yonder, and a stove alongside where the cooking goes on. You would not have wanted to taste food for a month if you had seen the fat pork and cornbread which they are shoveling down with iron forks. Now, if I thought—if we were going to rough it in the mountains—camp-fire, venison, trout cooked by ourselves, and all that sort of thing, I'd be with you. But this civilized beastliness I don't like—never did. I'll take this train back, and strike the trunk-line at Charlotte, and try Texas for my summer holiday. I must be off at once."

"Good-bye, then, Mr. Nesbitt. I am sorry you are not going: you've been so kind to Charley."

"Not at all. Good-bye. God bless you, little chap!" stopping to put his finger in the baby's thin hand. He was quite sure the little woman in black would never bring her child back from the mountains.

"I'm glad he's gone," said Miss Cook, coming in from the shed. "It's absurd, the row American men make about their eating away from home. They want Delmonico's table set at every railway-station."

"You will go on up the mountain, then?"

"Yes. I've only three weeks' vacation, and I can get farther from my usual rut, both as to scenery and people, here than anywhere else. I've been writing on political economy lately, and my brain needs complete change of idea. You know how it is yourself."

"No, I—" She unlocked her satchel, and as she took out Baby's powder looked furtively at Miss Cook. This tight little person, buckled snugly into a waterproof suit, her delicate face set off by a brown hat and feather, talking political economy and slang in a breath, was a new specimen of human nature to her.

She gave the powder, and then the two women went out and deposited themselves and their wraps in a red stage which waited at the door. A fat, jolly-faced woman, proprietor of the shed and cooking-stove, ran out with a bottle of warm milk for the child, the Carolinian majors and barkeeper took off their hats, the Detroit man nodded with his on his head, and with a crack of the whip the stage rolled away with them. It lurched on its leather springs, and luffed and righted precisely like a ship in a chopping sea, and threw them forward against each other and back into dusty depths of curled hair, until even the baby laughed aloud.

Miss Cook took out her notebook and pencil, but found it impossible to write. "There is nothing to make note of, either," she said after an hour or two. "It is the loneliest entrance to a mountain-region I ever saw. These glassless huts we see now and then, and the ruins of cabins, make it all the more forlorn. I saw a woman ploughing with an ox just now on the hillside, where it was so steep I thought woman, plough, and ox would roll down together.—Is there no business, no stir of any sort, in this country?" she called sharply to the driver, who had got down and looked in at the window at that minute.

"I don't know," he said leisurely. "Come to think on't, it's powerful quiet ginerally."

"No mining—mills?"

"Thar war mica-mines. But ther given over. An' thar war a railroad. But that's given over too. I was a-goin' to ask you ladies ef you'd wish to git out an' see whar the traveller was murdered last May, up the stream a bit. I kin show you jest whar the blood is yet; which, they do say, was discovered by the wild dogs a-gnawin' at the ground."

The baby's mother held it closer, with her lips unusually pale. "No, thank you," she said cheerfully. "Probably we can see it as we come back."

"Well, jest as *you* please," he replied, gathering up the reins with a discontented air. "Thar's been no murder in the mountings for five years, an' 'tisn't likely there'll be another."

A few miles farther on he stopped to water his horses at a hill-spring. "Thar's a house yonder, ef you ladies like to rest an hour," he said, nodding benignantly.

"But the mail?—you carry the mail?"

"Oh, the mail won't trouble itself," taking out his pipe and filling it. "That thar child needs rest, I reckon."

The two women hurried up the stony field to the large log hut, where the mistress and a dozen black-haired children stood waiting for them.

"Something to eat?" cried Miss Cook. "Yes, indeed, my good soul; and the sooner the better. Finely-cut face, that," sketching it rapidly while the hostess hurried in and out. "Gallic. These mountaineers were all originally either French Huguenots or Germans. It would be picturesque, dirt and all, under a Norman peasant's coif and red umbrella, but in a dirty calico wrapper—bah!"

The house also was dirty and bare, but the table was set with fried chicken, rice, honey, and delicious butter.

"And how—how much are we to pay for all this?" said Miss Cook before sitting down.

"If ten cents each would not be too much?" hesitated the woman.

Miss Cook nodded: her very portemonnaie gave a click of delight in her pocket. "I heard that these people were miserably poor!" she muttered rapturously. "Don't look so shocked. If you earned your bread by your brains, as I do, you'd want as much bread for a penny as possible."

The sky began to darken before they rose from the table, and, looking out through the cut in the wall which served for a window, they saw that the rain was already falling heavily. A girl of sixteen, who had been spinning in the corner, drew her wheel in front of the window: the square of light threw her delicately lined face and heavy yellow hair into relief. She watched the baby with friendly smiles as she spun, giving it a bit of white wool to hold.

"What a queer tribe we have fallen among!" said Miss Cook in scarcely lowered tones. "I never saw a spinning-wheel before, except Gretchen's in Faust, and there is a great hand-loom. Why, it was only Tuesday I crossed Desbrosses Ferry, and I am already two centuries back from New York. Very incurious, too, do you observe? The women don't even glance at the shape of our hats, and nobody has asked us a question as to our business here. People who live in the mountains or by the sea generally lack the vulgar curiosity of the ordinary country farmer."

"Do they? I did not know. These are the kindest people *I* ever met," said the little woman in black with unwonted emphasis.

"Oh, they expect to make something out of you. Travellers are the rarest of game in this region, I imagine," observed Miss Cook carelessly, and then stopped abruptly with a qualm of conscience, remarking for the first time the widow's cap which her companion wore. These people had perhaps been quicker than she in guessing the story of the little woman—that the child, dying as it seemed, was all that was left to her, and that this journey to the balsam mountains was the last desperate hope for its life.

She looked with a fresh interest at the thin, anxious face, the shabby black clothes, and then out of the window to where the high peaks of the Black Range were dimly visible like cones of sepia on the gray horizon. She had read a paper in some magazine on the inhospitable region yonder, walled by the clouds. It was "almost unexplored, although so near the seaboard cities"; the "haunt of beasts of prey"; the natives were "but little raised above the condition of Digger Indians." All this had whetted Miss Cook's appetite. She was tired of New York and New Yorkers, and of the daily grinding them up into newspaper correspondence wherewith to earn her bread. To become an explorer, to adventure into the lairs of bears and wolves, at so cheap a cost as an excursion ticket over the Air-line Railroad, was a rare chance for her. As it rained now, she gathered her feet and skirts up from the dirty floor and confided some of these thoughts to her companion, who only said absently, "She did not know. Doctor Beasly—perhaps Miss Cook had heard of Doctor Beasly?—had said Charley must have mountain air, and that the balsams were tonics in themselves. She did not suppose the Diggers or animals would hurt *her.*"

The truth was, the little woman had been fighting Death long and vainly over a sick-bed. She knew his terrors there well enough: she had learned to follow his creeping, remorseless fingers on clammy skin and wasted body, and to hear his coming footsteps in the flagging beats of a pulse. She had that dry, sapless, submissive look which a woman gains in long nursing—a woman that nurses a patient who holds part of her own life and is carrying it with him, step by step, into the grave. The grave had closed over this woman's dead, and all that he had taken with him from her: even to herself she did not dare to speak of him as yet. The puny little boy on her arms was the only real thing in life to her. There was a chance in these mountains of keeping him—a bare chance. As for wild beasts or wild people, she had thought of them no more than the shadows on the road which passed with every wind.

The rain beat more heavily on the roof: the driver presented himself at the door, dripping. "Ef we don't go on, night'll catch us before we make Alexander's," he said. "Give me that little feller under my coat. I'll kerry him to the stage."

Miss Cook shivered in the chilly wind that rushed through the open door. "Who would believe that the streets in New York were broiling at 105° this minute?"

"That baby's not wrapped warm enough for a night like this," said the woman of the house, and forthwith dragged out of a wooden box a red flannel petticoat, ragged but clean, and pinned it snugly about him.

"She'll charge you a pretty price for it," whispered Miss Cook; "and it's only a rag."

"No, no," laughed the woman, when the widow drew out her portemonnaie. "Joe kin bring it back some day. That's all right."

"You seem as touched by that as though it were some great sacrifice," said Miss Cook tartly after they were settled again in the stage.

"It was all she had." Adding after a pause, "I have been living in New York for five years. My baby was born there, and—and I had trouble. But we came strangers, and were always strangers. I knew nobody but the doctor. I came to look upon the milkman and baker who stopped at the door as friends. People are in such a hurry there. They have no time to be friendly."

The stage tossed and jolted, the rain pelted against the windows. Miss Cook snored and wakened with jumps, and the baby slept tranquilly. There was a certain purity in the cold damp air that eased his breathing, and the red petticoat was snug and warm. The touch of it seemed to warm his mother too. The kind little act of giving it was something new to her. It seemed as if in the North she too had been in a driving hurry of pain and work since her birth, and had never had time to be friendly. If life here was barbarous, it was at ease, unmoving, kindly. She could take time to breathe.

It was late in the night when the stage began to rattle over the cobble-stoned streets of the little hill-village of Asheville. It drew up in front of an inn with wooden porches sheltered by great trees: there were lights burning inside, and glimpses of supper waiting, and a steam of frying chicken and coffee pervading the storm. One or two men hurried out from the office with umbrellas, and a pretty white-aproned young girl welcomed them at the door.

"Supper is ready," she said. "Yours shall be sent to your room, madam. We have had a fire kindled there on account of the baby."

"Why, how *could* you know Charley was coming?" cried the widow breathlessly.

"Oh, a week ago, madam. While you stopped at Morganton. The conductor of the Salisbury train sent on a note, and afterward the clergyman at Linville. We have been warned to take good care of you," smiling brightly.

The baby's mother said nothing until she was seated in her room before a wood-fire which crackled and blazed cheerfully. The baby lay on her lap, its face red with heat and comfort.

"Since I left Richmond one conductor has passed me on to another," she said solemnly to Miss Cook. "The baby was ill at Linville, and the train was stopped for an hour, and the ladies of the village came to help me. And now these people. It is just as though I were coming among old friends."

"Pshaw! They think you have money. These Southerners are impoverished by the war, and they have an idea that every Northern traveller is overloaded with wealth, and is fair game."

"The war? I had forgotten that. One would forgive them if they were churlish and bitter."

The woman was a weak creature evidently, and inclined to drivel. Miss Cook went off to bed, first jotting down in her notebook some of the young girl's queer mistakes in accent, and a joke on her yellow dress and red ribbons. They would be useful hereafter in summing up her estimate of the people. The girl and the widow meantime had grown into good friends in undressing the boy together. When his mother lay down at last beside him the firelight threw a bright glow over the bed, and the pretty young face came again to the door to nod goodnight.

It was only an inn, and outside a strange country and strange people surrounded her. But she could not rid herself of the impression that she had come home to her own friends.

The sun rose in a blue dappled sky, but before he was fairly above the bank of wet clouds Miss Cook was out, notebook in hand. She had sketched the outline of the mountains that walled in the table-land on which the village stood; had felt the tears rise to her eyes as the purple shadow about Mount Pisgah flamed into sudden splendor (for her tears and emotions responded quickly to a beautiful sight or sound); she had discovered the grassy public square in which a cow grazed and a woman was leisurely driving a steer that drew a cart; she had visited four emporiums of trade—little low-ceilinged rooms which fronted on the square, walled with calicoes and barrels of sugar, and hung overhead with brown crockery and tin cups; she had helped two mountaineers trade their bag of flour for shoes; had talked to the negro women milking in the sheds, to a gallant Confederate colonel hoeing his corn in a field, to a hunter bringing in a late lot of peltry from the Smoky Range. As they talked she portioned out the facts as material for a letter in the *Herald*. The quaint decaying houses, the swarming blacks, the whole drowsy life of the village set high in the chilled sunshine and bound by its glittering belt of rivers and rampart of misty mountain-heights, were sketched in a sharp, effective bit of word-painting in her mind.

She trotted back to the Eagle Hotel to put it on paper; then to breakfast; then off again to look up schools, churches, and editors.

Late in the afternoon, tramping along a steep hill-path, she caught sight of two women in a skiff on a lonely stream below. It was the baby's mother and the pretty girl from the inn. No human being was in sight; the low sunlight struck luminous bars of light between the trunks of the hemlocks into the water beneath the boat as it swung lazily in the current; long tangled vines of sweetbrier and the red trumpet-creeper hung from the trees into the water; the baby lay sound asleep on a heap of shawls at his mother's feet, while she dipped the oars gently now and then to keep in the middle of the stream.

"How lazy you look!" called Miss Cook. "You might have been made out of the earth of these sleepy hills. Here, come ashore. D'ye see the work I've done?" fluttering a sheaf of notes. "I've just been at the jail. A den! an outrage on the civilization of the nineteenth century! Men have been branded here since the war. Criminals in this State are actually secured in iron cages like wild beasts! I shall use that fact effectively in my book on the 'Causes of the Decadence of the South': one chapter shall be given to 'The Social and Moral Condition of North Carolina.'"

"You will need so many facts!" ejaculated the little woman, awestruck, yet pityingly. "It will take all your summer's holiday to gather them up."

Miss Cook laughed with cool superiority: "Why, child, I have them all now—got them this morning. Oh, I can evolve the whole state of society from half a dozen items. I have the faculty of generalizing, you see. No," folding up her papers decisively, "I've done the mountains and mountaineers. Between slavery and want of railroads, humanity has reached its extremest conditions here. I should not learn that fact any better if I stayed a week."

"You are not going back?"

"Back? Emphatically, yes. I go to Georgia to-morrow morning. This orange I have sucked dry."

Miss Cook posted to the inn and passed the night in making sketches to illustrate her article from a bundle of photographic views which she found in possession of the landlady.

Looking out of the parlor-window next morning, she saw half the inmates of the house gathered about a cart drawn by two oxen in which sat the widow and Charley. A couple of sacks of flour lay at her feet, and a middle-aged man, a giant as to height and build, dressed in butternut homespun, cracked his long whip at the flies.

"Where can she be going?" asked Miss Cook of a young woman from Georgia whom she had been pumping dry of facts all the morning. The Georgian wore a yellow dress with a coarse frill about her swarthy neck: she sat at the piano and played "Love's Chidings."

The man, she said, was Jonathan Yare, a hunter in the Black Mountains. Her brother had told her his terrible history. Her brother had once penetrated into the mountains as far as the hut where the Yares lived, some thirty miles from here. Beyond that there were no human beings: the mountains were given up to wild beasts. As for these Yares, they had lived in the wilderness for three generations, and, by all accounts, like the beasts.

Miss Cook rushed out: political economist and author though she might be, she had a gossip's keen enjoyment in a piece of bad news. "Do you know these hunters?" she whispered. "They have a terrible history: they live like wild beasts."

The little woman's color left her. Her head filled instantly with visions of the Ku-Klux. "I never asked what they were," she gasped. "I only wanted to take Charley among the balsams."

The man looked back at this moment, and seeing that the valise and box and baby's bottle of milk were in the cart, cracked his long whip over the near ox, and the next moment the widow and her baby were jolting up the rocky hill-street.

She felt a spasm of fear. When Death laid his hand on her child she had taken him up and fled to these mountains without a second thought, as the women in the times of the apostles carried their dead and dying to be cured by miraculous aid. But she was a woman like the rest of us, used to jog along the conventional paths to church, to market, to the shops; her only quarrels with the departed David had been about his unorthodox habits in business and politics; and she never could be easy until she was sure that her neighbors liked her new bonnet. What would her neighbors—any neighbor—David himself, have said at seeing her in league with this desperate character, going into frightful solitudes?

The man spoke to her once or twice, but she answered with an inaudible little chirp, after which he fell into silence, neither whistling nor speaking to his oxen, as she noticed.

She could not help observing how unusually clear the light about her was from the thinness of the air, although the sun was out of sight in a covered, foreboding sky, and black, ragged fragments of cloud from some approaching thunderstorm were driven now and then across the horizon. The road, if road you chose to call it, crept along beside the little crystal-clear Swannanoa River, and persisted in staying beside it, sliding over hills of boulders, fording rushing mountain-streams and dank, snaky swamps, digging its way along the side of sheer precipices, rather than desert its companion. The baby's mother suddenly became conscious that the river was a companion to whom she had been talking and listening for an hour or two. It was narrow, deep, and clear as the air above it: it flowed with a low soothing sound in which there came to her somehow an assurance of security and goodwill.

Multitudes of trailing vines hedged in the river; they covered the banks, and threw long, clutching branches into the water: they crept out on projecting trees on either side and leaped across the stream, ridging it with arches of wreaths and floating tendrils. There were the dark, waving plumes of the American ivy, the red cornucopias of the trumpet-creeper, morning-glories with great white blossoms, the passion-flower trailing its mysterious purple emblems through the mud beneath the oxen's feet,—all creeping or turning in some way toward the river.

Surely there were some airy affections, some subtle friendlinesses, among these dumb living creatures! They all seemed alive to her, though she was a prosaic woman, who had read little beyond her cookery-book and Bible. It was as though she had come unbidden into Nature's household and interrupted the inmates talking together. The Carolina rose stretched in masses for miles along the road—the very earth seemed to blush with it: here and there a late rhododendron hung out its scarlet banner. The tupelo thrust its white fingers out of the shadow like a maiden's hand, and threw out into the air the very fragrance of the lilies-of-the-valley which used to grow in the garden she made when she was a little girl. The silence was absolute, except when a pheasant rose with a whirr or a mocking-bird sounded its melancholy defiant call in the depths of the forest. Long habit of grief had left her heart tender and its senses keen: these things, which were but game or specimens for the naturalist, were God's creatures to her, and came close to her. Charley woke, and looking up saw her smiling down on him with warm cheeks. She did not know the name of a plant or tree or bird, but she felt the friendliness and welcome of the hills, just as she used to be comforted and lifted nearer to God by distant church music, although she could not hear a word of the hymn.

Leaving the road, they entered deep silent gorges, and followed the bed of mountain-streams cañons walled in by gray frowning rocks, over which the sky bent more darkly each moment. At last there was a break in the gorge. About her was a world of gigantic mountains. There was no sign of human habitation—nothing but interminable forests that climbed the heights, and, failing half-way, left them bare to pierce the clouds.

She had started on this journey with a vague notion of reaching some higher land where balsam trees grew, the air about which would be wholesome for Charley. She had penetrated to the highest summits of the Appalachian Range, the nursery or breeding-place from which descend the Blue Ridge, the Alleghanies, the Nantahela—all the great mountain-bulwarks that wall the continent on its eastern coast. The mighty peaks rose into the sky beyond her sight, while the gathering storm-clouds clung to their sides, surging and eddying with the wind. How petty and short-lived was wind or storm! She looked up at those fixed, awful heights, forgetting even the child on her knee. It was as if God had taken her into one of the secret places where He dwelt apart.

She came to herself suddenly, finding that the cart had stopped and the driver was standing beside examining the baby's milk.

"I reckon," he said, "it's sour, and the little chap's hungry. I'll get some fresh, an' you kin look at the mountings."

He went into the laurel, and with a peculiar whistle brought some of the wild cattle to him, and proceeded to milk one of the cows, returning with a cupful of foaming warm milk. Now, one of the Ku-Klux would hardly go to milking cows, she thought; and there was something in the man's steady grave eyes that looked as if he too understood the meaning of the "mountings." They jogged on in silence.

Half an hour later the clouds closed about them and the rain fell heavily. The cart was dragged through the bed of a mountain-stream, and then stopped in front of a low log house built into a ledge of the mountain. A room on either side opened into a passage, through which a wagon might be driven, and where the rain and wind swept unchecked. An old woman stood in it looking up the stream. Her gray hair hung about her sallow face, her dress was a dirty calico, her feet were bare. Behind her was the kitchen, a large forlorn space scarcely enclosed by the log and mud walls. A pig ran unnoticed past her into it. Another woman, tall and gaunt, was fording the stream: she was dripping wet, and carried a spade. Surely, thought the baby's mother, human nature could reach no lower depths of squalor and ignorance than these.

"Mother," said Jonathan Yare, "here is a friend that has come with her baby to stay with us a while."

The old woman turned and instantly held out her arms for the child. "Come in— come to the fire," she said cordially. "I am glad Jonathan brought you to us."

If a princess had been so taken by surprise, her courtly breeding could not have stood her in better stead.

She took the baby and its mother into a snug boarded room with half a dozen pictures from the illustrated papers on the walls, and a fire of great logs smouldering on the hearth. When they were warmed and dry they went into the kitchen. Supper was ready, and two or three six-foot mountaineers stood by the table.

"We are waiting for father," said the woman who had carried the spade. Both men and women had peculiar low voices. One could never grow used to hearing such gentle tones from such great sons of Anak. At the same moment an old man of eighty, whose gigantic build dwarfed all of his sons, came into the doorway. His eyes were closed, and he groped with his staff. The widow, as soon as she saw his face, went directly up to him and took his hand.

"My name is Denby," she said. "I brought my baby here to be cured. He is all I have, sir."

"You did right to come." She guided his hand to Charley's, and he felt his skin, muscles, and pulse, asking questions with shrewder insight than any physician had done. Then he led her to the table. "Boys, Mistress Denby will like to sit beside me, I think," he said.

She had an odd feeling that she had been adopted by some ancient knight, although the old man beside her wore patched trousers that left his hairy ankles and feet bare. Before the meal was over another strange impression deepened on her. She saw that these people were clothed and fed as the very poorest poor; she doubted whether one of them could read or write; they talked little, and only of the corn, or the ox that had gone lame; but she could not rid herself of the conviction that she had now, as never in her life, come into the best of good company. Nature does not always ennoble her familiars. Country people usually are just as uneasy and vulgar in their cheap and ignorant efforts at display or fashion as townsmen. But these mountaineers were absolutely unconscious that such things were. A man was a man to them—a woman, a woman. They had never perhaps heard either estimated by their money or house or clothes. The Yares were, in fact, a family born with exceptionally strong intellects and clean, fine instincts: they had been left to develop both in utter solitude and without education, and the result as to manner was the grave self-control of Indians and a truthful directness of thought and speech which seemed to grow out of and express the great calm Nature about them as did the trees or the flowing water.

These were the first human beings whom the widow had ever met between whom and herself there came absolutely no bar of accident—no circumstance of social position or clothes or education: they were the first who could go straight to something in her beneath all these things. She soon forgot (what they had never known) how poor they were in all these accidents.

After that Charley and his mother were adopted into the family. At night, when the child was asleep, the old hunter always sat with her and his wife beside the fire, telling stories of bear-hunts, of fights with panthers, of the mysterious Rattlesnake Valley, near which no hunter ventures. He had been born in this house, and passed the whole of his eighty years in the mountains of the Black Range. One night, noticing the scars which his encounters with bears had left on him, she said, "It is no wonder that the townspeople in Asheville talked to me of the 'terrible history of the Yares.'"

The old man smiled quietly, but did not answer. When he had gone to bed his wife said with great feeling, "It was not their fights with wolves and bears that turned the people at Asheville agen the name of my boys and their father. They were the ony men anigh hyar that stood out fur the Union from first to last. They couldn't turn agen the old flag, you see, Mistress Denby."

"They should have gone into the Federal army and helped to free the slaves," cried the widow with rising color, for she had been a violent abolitionist in her day.

"Waal, we never put much vally on the blacks, that's the truth. We couldn't argy or jedge whether slavery war wholesomest for them or not. It was out of our sight. My lads, bein' known as extraordinar' strong men an' powerful bear-fighters, hed two or three offers to join Kirk's Loyal Rangers in Tennessee. But they couldn't shed the blood of their old neighbors."

"Then they fought on neither side? Their old neighbors most probably called them cowards."

"Nobody would say that of the Yares," the woman said simply. "But when they wouldn't go into the Confederit army, they was driv out—four of them, Jonathan first—from under this roof, an' for five years they lay out on the mounting. It began this a-way: Some of the Union troops, they came up to the Unaka Range, and found the house whar the Grangers lived—hunters like us. The soldiers followed the two Granger lads who was in the rebel army, an' had slipped home on furlough to see their mother. Waal, they shot the lads, catchin' them out in the barnyard, which was to be expected, p'raps; an' when their ole father came runnin' out they killed him too. His wife, seein' that, hid the baby (as they called him, though he was nigh onto eight year old) under a loose board of the floor. But he, gettin' scart, runs out and calls, 'Gentlemen, I surrender,' jest like a man. He fell with nine bullets in his breast. His mother sees it all. There never was a woman so interrupted as that pore woman that day. She comes up to us, travelin' night an' day, talkin' continual under her breath of the lads and her ole man's gray hair lyin' in a pool of blood. She's never hed her right mind sence. When Jonathan heard that from her, he said, 'Mother, not even for the Union will I join in sech work as this agen my friends.' He knowed ony the few folks on the mountings, but he keered for them as if they war his brothers. Yet they turned agen him at the warnin' of a day, and hunted him as if he was a wild beast. He's forgot that now. But his sister, she's never forgot it for him agen them. Jonathan's trouble made a different woman of Nancy."

But Mrs. Denby had felt but little interest in the gaunt, silent Nancy.

"You say they hunted your sons through the mountains?"

"Jest as if they war wolves. But the boys knowed the mountings. Thars hundreds of caves and gullies thar whar no man ever ventered but them. Three times a week Nancy went—she war a young girl then: she went up into Old Craggy and the Black miles and miles to app'inted places to kerry pervisions. I've seen her git out of her bed to go (fur she hed her aches and pains like other wimmen), and take that pack on her back, when the gorges war sheeted with snow and ice, an' ef she missed her footin' no man on arth could know whar she died."

"But five years of idleness for your sons—"

The old woman's high features flushed. "You don't understan', Mistress Denby," she said calmly. "My sons' work in them years was to pertect an' guide the rebel deserters home through the mountings—people at the North don't know, likely, what crowds of them thar war—an' to bring the Union prisoners escaped from Salisbury and Andersonville safe to the Federal lines in Tennessee. One of the boys would be to Salisbury in disguise, an' the others would take them from him and run them into the mountings, an' keep 'em thar, bringin' them hyar when they could at night fur a meal's good victuals. About midnight they used to come. Nancy an' me, we'd hear a stone flung into the river yonder—seemed es ef I'd never stop listenin' fur that stone—an' we'd find them pore starved critters standin' in the dark outside with Jonathan. In ten minutes we'd have supper ready—keepin' the fire up every night—an' they'd eat an' sleep, an' be off before dawn. Hundreds of them hev slep' in this very room, sayin' it was as ef they'd come back to their homes out of hell. They looked as ef they'd been thar, raally."

"In *this* room?" Mrs. Denby stood up trembling. Her husband had been in Salisbury at the same time as Albert Richardson, and had escaped. He might have slept in this very bed where his child lay. These people might have saved him from death. But Mrs. Yare did not notice her agitation.

"Thar was one winter when Major Gee sent guards from Salisbury to watch the mounting-passes, 'specially about this house, knowin' my boys' work. Then they couldn't come anigh: thar was nigh a year I couldn't hear from them ef they were alive or dead. I'd hear shots, an the guards 'ud tell me it was 'another damned refugee gone'—p'raps one of my boys. I'd set by that door all night, lookin' up to the clouds coverin' the mounting, wonderin' ef my lads was safe an' well up thar or lyin' dead an' unburied. I'd think ef I could ony see one of my lads for jest once—jest once!" The firelight flashed up over her tall, erect figure. She was standing, and held her arm over her bony breast as if the old pain was intolerable even now.

She said quietly after a while, "But I didn't begrudge them to their work. One night—the soldiers were jest yonder: you could see the campfire in the fog—thar war the stone knockin' in the stream. I says, 'Nancy, which is it?' She says, 'It's Charley's throw. Someut ails Jonathan.' An' Charley hed come to say his brother war dyin' in a cave two mile up: they'd kerried him thar. I found my lad thar, worn to a shadder, an' with some disease no yerbs could tech. Wall, fur a week we came an' went to him, past the guard who war sent to shoot him down when found like a dog; an' thar he was lyin' within call, an' the snow an' sleet driftin' about him. One day Nancy was dumb all day—not a word. I said to father, 'Let her alone: she's a-studyin' powerful. Let her alone.' 'Mother,' she says at night, 'I've been thinkin' about Jonathan. He must hev a house to cover him, or he'll die.' 'Yes, Nancy, but what house?' 'I'll show you,' says she. 'You bide hyar quiet with father. The guard is used to seein' me come an' go with the cattle.' She took an axe an' went out, an didn't come home till mornin'. In three days she hed cut down logs an' built a hut, six feet by ten, among the laurels yonder, haulin' an' liftin' them logs herself, an floored it, an' kivered it with brush, an' brought him to it; an' thar she stayed an' nursed him. The snow fell heavy an' hid it. Yes, it seems onpossible for a woman. But not many's got my Nancy's build," proudly. "One day, when Jonathan was growin' better, Colonel Barker rode up: he war a Confederit. 'Mrs. Yare,' says he, 'thar's word come your boys hev been seen hyarbouts, an' the home guard's on its way up.' An' then he tuk to talkin' cattle an' the like with father, an' turned his back on me. An' I went out an' give the signal. An' in ten minutes Nancy came in with the milk-pail as the guard rode up. I knowed the boys war safe. Waal, they sarched the laurel for hours, an' late in the afternoon they came in. 'Colonel,' says they, 'look a-here!' So we went out, an' thar war the house. 'Who built this?' says he. 'I did,' says Nancy, thinkin' the ownin' to it was death. The tears stood in his eyes. 'God help us all!' says he. 'Men, don't touch a log of it.' But they tore it to the ground when he was gone, an' took Nancy down to Asheville, an' kep her in the jail thar for a month, threatenin' to send her to Salisbury ef she'd not tell whar the boys war. They might hev hung her: of course she'd not hev told. But it wore her—it wore her. She'd be a prettier girl now," thoughtfully, "ony for what she's gone through for her brothers. Then they arrested father an' took him to Richmond, to Libby Prison. As soon as Nancy heard that, she sent for the commandant of the post.

"'Give me,' she says, 'a written agreement that my father shall be released when his four sons come into Richmond, and let me go.' So they did it."

"And the boys went?"

"Of course. They reported themselves at Asheville, hopin' that would release their father sooner. But they hed to be forwarded to Salisbury, an' held thar until he was brought on."

"They were in that prison, there?"

"Yes. But they was well treated, bein' wanted for soldiers. It was in the last year, when the men war desertin' and the drafts war of no use. On the fourth day the lads war brought into the guard-house before the officers.

"'Mr. Yare,' says the major very pleasantly, 'I believe you an' yor brothers are reputed to be onusually daring men.'

"'That I don't know,' says Jonathan.

"'You hev certainly mistaken the object of the war and your duty. At any rate, you hev incurred ten times more risk an' danger in fighting for refugees than you would have done in the army. We have determined to overlook all the offences of your family, and to permit you to bear arms in our service.'

"'I will never bear arms in the Confederit service,' says Jonathan quietly. You know he's a quiet man, an' slow.

"A little man, a young captain, standing by, says in a heat, 'Bah! Why do you waste words with such fellows? The best use to make of the whole lot is to order them out to be shot.'

"'I agree with you, Mac,' says the colonel. 'It's poor policy, at this stage of the game, to tax the commissariat and put arms into the hands of unwilling soldiers.— But'—then he stopped for a minute—'you have no right to answer for your brothers, Yare,' he said. 'I give you half an hour,' taking out his watch. 'You can consult together. Such of you as are willing to go into the ranks can do so at once: the others—shall be dealt with as Captain McIntyre suggests.'

"They took the lads back into the inside room. When the half hour was up, all but five minutes, they saw a company drawn up in a hollow square outside. They were led out thar, facin' them, an' thar war the officers. It was a sunshiny, clar day, an' Jonathan said he couldn't help but think of the mountings an' his father an' me.

"Charley, he spoke first. 'Jonathan is the oldest,' he says. 'He will answer for us all.'

"'You will go into the service?' says the major.

"'No, said Jonathan, 'we never will.'

"The major made a sign. My lads walked down and the soldiers presented arms. The major was lookin' curiously at Jonathan. 'This is not cowardice,' said he. 'Why will you not go into the ranks? I believe, in my soul, you are a Union man!'

"Jonathan says he looked quick at the guns leveled at him, and couldn't keep his breath from comin' hard.

"'Yes,' he says out loud. 'By God, I am a Union man!'

"Captain McIntyre pushed his sword down with a clatter and turned away. 'I never saw pluck like that before,' he said.

"'Corporal,' said the major, 'take these men back to jail.'

"Two weeks after that Lee surrendered, an' my lads came home."

The women talked often in this way. Mrs. Denby urged them again and again to come out of their solitude to the North. "There are hundreds of men there," she said, "of influence and distinction whose lives your sons have saved at the peril of their own. Here they will always pass their days in hard drudgery and surrounded by danger."

The mother shook her head, but it was Nancy who answered in her gentle, pathetic voice: "The Yares hev lived on the Old Black for four generations, Mistress Denby. It wouldn't do to kerry us down into towns. It must be powerful lonesome in them flat countries, with nothing but people about you. The mountings is always company, you see."

The little townswoman tried to picture to herself these mountaineers actually in the houses of the men whom they had rescued from death—these slow-speaking giants clad in cheap Bowery clothes, ignorant of art, music, books, bric-a-brac, politics. She understood that they would be lonesome, and that the mountains and they were company for each other.

She lived in their hut all summer. Her baby grew strong and rosy, and the mountains gave to her also their good-will and comfort.

Booker T. Washington

1856–1915

Booker T. Washington was born into slavery on a farm in the Blue Ridge Mountains of Virginia. The son of an enslaved woman named Jane, Washington did not know his father, who was probably white. After emancipation, Jane moved with her children to Malden, West Virginia, where her husband, Washington's stepfather, was employed in the salt works. As a child, Washington worked in the salt furnaces and the coal mines. In 1872, he entered Hampton Normal and Agricultural Institute and later matriculated at Wayland Seminary. Washington became the founding leader of Tuskegee Institute in Alabama in 1881.

The opening chapters of Washington's popular but controversial autobiography *Up from Slavery* (1901), one of which is excerpted below, provide a detailed account of Appalachian slaves' lives and the lives of Appalachian freed people. Washington portrays himself as an African American Horatio Alger who, despite humble beginnings, achieves success through hard work and dedication to education.

The excerpt also documents a controversial aspect of Washington's approach to race relations. Because of the hostility toward freed blacks in Alabama during the post-Reconstruction era, Washington believed it was critical to rally support from moderate whites through a publicly conciliatory message. Though Washington's message of self-reliance and responsibility was well received in the white community, especially among northern capitalists, many influential leaders in the black community, notably W. E. B. DuBois, founder of the NAACP, criticized Washington's accommodationist philosophy. Nonetheless, Washington was one of the most influential African American leaders of the post-Reconstruction era.

FROM Up from Slavery: An Autobiography

FROM CHAPTER 2: BOYHOOD DAYS

After the coming of freedom there were two points upon which practically all the people on our place were agreed, and I find that this was generally true throughout the South: that they must change their names, and that they must leave the old plantation for at least a few days or weeks in order that they might really feel sure that they were free.

In some way a feeling got among the coloured people that it was far from proper for them to bear the surname of their former owners, and a great many of them took other surnames. This was one of the first signs of freedom. When they were slaves, a coloured person was simply called "John" or "Susan." There was seldom occasion for more than the use of the one name. If "John" or "Susan" belonged to a white man by the name of "Hatcher," sometimes he was called "John Hatcher," or as often "Hatch-er's John." But there was a feeling that "John Hatcher" or "Hatcher's John" was not the proper title by which to denote a freeman; and so in many cases "John Hatcher" was changed to "John S. Lincoln" or "John S. Sherman," the initial "S" standing for no name, it being simply a part of what the coloured man proudly called his "entitles."

As I have stated, most of the coloured people left the old plantation for a short while at least, so as to be sure, it seemed, that they could leave and try their freedom on to see how it felt. After they had remained away for a time, many of the older slaves, especially, returned to their old homes and made some kind of contract with their former owners by which they remained on the estate.

My mother's husband, who was the stepfather of my brother John and myself, did not belong to the same owners as did my mother. In fact, he seldom came to our plantation. I remember seeing him there perhaps once a year, that being about Christmas time. In some way, during the war, by running away and following the Federal soldiers, it seems, he found his way into the new state of West Virginia. As soon as freedom was declared, he sent for my mother to come to the Kanawha Valley, in West Virginia. At that time a journey from Virginia over the mountains to West Virginia was rather a tedious and in some cases a painful undertaking. What little clothing and few household goods we had were placed in a cart, but the children walked the greater portion of the distance, which was several hundred miles. [. . .]

At that time salt-mining was the great industry in that part of West Virginia, and the little town of Malden was right in the midst of the salt-furnaces. My stepfather had already secured a job at a salt-furnace, and he had also secured a little cabin for us to live in. Our new house was no better than the one we had left on the old planta-tion in Virginia. In fact, in one respect it was worse. Notwithstanding the poor con-dition of our plantation cabin, we were at all times sure of pure air. Our new home was in the midst of a cluster of cabins crowded closely together, and as there were no sanitary regulations, the filth about the cabins was often intolerable. Some of our neighbours were coloured people, and some were the poorest and most ignorant and degraded white people. It was a motley mixture. Drinking, gambling, quarrels, fights, and shockingly immoral practices were frequent. All who lived in the little town were in one way or another connected with the salt business. Though I was a mere child, my stepfather put me and my brother at work in one of the furnaces. Often I began work as early as four o'clock in the morning.

The first thing I ever learned in the way of book knowledge was while working in this salt-furnace. Each salt-packer had his barrels marked with a certain number. The number allotted to my stepfather was "18." At the close of the day's work the boss of the packers would come around and put "18" on each of our barrels, and I soon learned to recognize that figure wherever I saw it, and after a while got to the point where I could make that figure, though I knew nothing about any other figures or letters.

From the time that I can remember having any thoughts about anything, I recall that I had an intense longing to learn to read. I determined, when quite a small child, that, if I accomplished nothing else in life, I would in some way get enough education to enable me to read common books and newspapers. Soon after we got settled in some manner in our new cabin in West Virginia, I induced my mother to get hold of a book for me. How or where she got it I do not know, but in some way she procured an old copy of Webster's "blue-back" spelling-book, which contained the alphabet, followed by such meaningless words as "ab," "ba," "ca," "da." I began at once to devour this book, and I think that it was the first one I ever had in my hands. I had learned from somebody that the way to begin to read was to learn the alphabet, so I tried in all the ways I could think of to learn it,—all of course without a teacher, for I could find no one to teach me. At that time there was not a single member of my race anywhere near us who could read, and I was too timid to approach any of the white people. In some way, within a few weeks, I mastered the greater portion of the alphabet. In all my efforts to learn to read my mother shared fully my ambition, and sympathized with me and aided me in every way that she could. Though she was totally ignorant, so far as mere book knowledge was concerned, she had high ambitions for her children and a large fund of good, hard, common sense which seemed to enable her to meet and master every situation. If I have done anything in life worth attention, I feel sure that I inherited the disposition from my mother,

In the midst of my struggles and longing for an education, a young coloured boy who had learned to read in the state of Ohio came to Malden. As soon as the coloured people found out that he could read, a newspaper was secured, and at the close of nearly every day's work this young man would be surrounded by a group of men and women who were anxious to hear him read the news contained in the papers. How I used to envy this man! He seemed to me to be the one young man in all the world who ought to be satisfied with his attainments.

About this time the question of having some kind of a school opened for the coloured children in the village began to be discussed by members of the race. As it would be the first school for Negro children that had ever been opened in that part of Virginia, it was, of course, to be a great event, and the discussion excited the widest interest. The most perplexing question was where to find a teacher. The young man from Ohio who had learned to read the papers was considered, but his age was against him. In the midst of the discussion about a teacher, another young coloured man from Ohio, who had been a soldier, in some way found his way into town. It was soon learned that he possessed considerable education, and he was engaged by the coloured people to teach their first school. As yet no free schools had been started for coloured people in that section, hence each family agreed to pay a certain amount per month, with the understanding that the teacher was to "board 'round"—that is, spend a day with each family. This was not bad for the teacher, for each family tried to provide the very best on the day the teacher was to be its guest. I recall that I looked forward with an anxious appetite to the "teacher's day" at our little cabin.

This experience of a whole race beginning to go to school for the first time, presents one of the most interesting studies that has ever occurred in connection with the development of any race. Few people who were not right in the midst of the scenes can form any exact idea of the intense desire which the people of my race showed for an education. As I have stated, it was a whole race trying to go to school. Few were too young, and none too old, to make the attempt to learn. As fast as any kind of teachers could be secured, not only were day-schools filled, but night-schools as well. The great ambition of the older people was to try to learn to read the Bible before they died. With this end in view, men and women who were fifty or seventy-five years old would often be found in the night-school. Sunday-schools were formed soon after freedom, but the principal book studied in the Sunday-school was the spelling-book. Day-school, night-school, Sunday-school, were always crowded, and often many had to be turned away for want of room.

The opening of the school in the Kanawha Valley, however, brought to me one of the keenest disappointments that I ever experienced. I had been working in a salt-furnace for several months, and my stepfather had discovered that I had a financial value, and so, when the school opened, he decided that he could not spare me from my work. This decision seemed to cloud my every ambition. The disappointment was made all the more severe by reason of the fact that my place of work was where I could see the happy children passing to and from school, mornings and afternoons. Despite this disappointment, however, I determined that I would learn something, anyway. I applied myself with greater earnestness than ever to the mastering of what was in the "blue-back" speller.

My mother sympathized with me in my disappointment, and sought to comfort me in all the ways she could, and to help me find a way to learn. After a while I succeeded in making arrangements with the teacher to give me some lessons at night, after the day's work was done. These night lessons were so welcome that I think I learned more at night than the other children did during the day. My own experiences in the night-school gave me faith in the night-school idea, with which, in after years, I had to do both at Hampton and Tuskegee. But my boyish heart was still set upon going to the day-school, and I let no opportunity slip to push my case. Finally I won, and was permitted to go to the school in the day for a few months with the understanding that I was to rise early in the morning and work in the furnace till nine o'clock and return immediately after school closed in the afternoon for at least two more hours of work.

The schoolhouse was some distance from the furnace, and as I had to work till nine o'clock, and the school opened at nine, I found myself in a difficulty. School would always be begun before I reached it, and sometimes my class had recited. To get around this difficulty I yielded to a temptation for which most people, I suppose, will condemn me; but since it is a fact, I might as well state it. I have great faith in the power and influence of facts. It is seldom that anything is permanently gained by holding back a fact. There was a large clock in a little office in the furnace. This clock, of course, all the hundred or more workmen depended upon to regulate their hours of beginning and ending the day's work. I got the idea that the way for me to reach school on time was to move the clock hands from half-past eight up to the nine o'clock mark. This I found myself doing morning after morning, till the furnace "boss" discovered that something was wrong, and locked the clock in a case. I did not mean to inconvenience anybody. I simply meant to reach that schoolhouse in time.

When, however, I found myself at the school for the first time, I also found myself confronted with two other difficulties. In the first place, I found that all of the other children wore hats or caps on their heads, and I had neither hat nor cap. In fact, I do not remember that up to the time of going to school I had ever worn any kind of covering upon my head, nor do I recall that either I or anybody else had even thought anything about the need of covering for my head. But, of course, when I saw how all the other boys were dressed, I began to feel quite uncomfortable. As usual, I put the case before my mother, and she explained to me that she had no money with which to buy a "store hat," which was a rather new institution at that time among the members of my race and was considered quite the thing for young and old to own, but that she would find a way to help me out of the difficulty. She accordingly got two pieces of "homespun" (jeans) and sewed them together, and I was soon the proud possessor of my first cap. [. . .]

My second difficulty was with regard to my name, or rather *a* name. From the time when I could remember anything, I had been called simply "Booker." Before going to school it had never occurred to me that it was needful or appropriate to have an additional name. When I heard the school-roll called, I noticed that all of the children had at least two names, and some of them indulged in what seemed to me the extravagance of having three. I was in deep perplexity, because I knew that the teacher would demand of me at least two names, and I had only one. By the time the occasion came for the enrolling of my name, an idea occurred to me which I thought would make me equal to the situation; and so, when the teacher asked me what my full name was, I calmly told him "Booker Washington," as if I had been called by that name all my life; and by that name I have since been known. Later in my life I found that my mother had given me the name of "Booker Taliaferro" soon after I was born, but in some way that part of my name seemed to disappear, and for a long while was forgotten, but as soon as I found out about it I revived it, and made my full name "Booker Taliaferro Washington." I think there are not many men in our country who have had the privilege of naming themselves in the way that I have.

More than once I have tried to picture myself in the position of a boy or man with an honoured and distinguished ancestry which I could trace back through a period of hundreds of years, and who had not only inherited a name, but fortune and a proud family homestead; and yet I have sometimes had the feeling that if I had inherited these, and had been a member of a more popular race, I should have been inclined to yield to the temptation of depending upon my ancestry and my colour to do that for me which I should do for myself. Years ago I resolved that because I had no ancestry myself I would leave a record of which my children would be proud, and which might encourage them to still higher effort.

The world should not pass judgment upon the Negro, and especially the Negro youth, too quickly or too harshly. The Negro boy has obstacles, discouragements, and temptations to battle with that are little known to those not situated as he is. When a white boy undertakes a task, it is taken for granted that he will succeed. On the other hand, people are usually surprised if the Negro boy does not fail. In a word, the Negro youth starts out with the presumption against him.

The influence of ancestry, however, is important in helping forward any individual or race, if too much reliance is not placed upon it. Those who constantly direct attention to the Negro youth's moral weaknesses, and compare his advancement with that of white youths, do not consider the influence of the memories which cling about the old family homesteads. I have no idea, as I have stated elsewhere, who my grandmother was. I have, or have had, uncles and aunts and cousins, but I have no knowledge as to where most of them are. My case will illustrate that of hundreds of thousands of black people in every part of our country. The very fact that the white boy is conscious that, if he fails in life, he will disgrace the whole family record, extending back through many generations, is of tremendous value in helping him to resist temptations. The fact that the individual has behind and surrounding him proud family history and connection serves as a stimulus to help him to overcome obstacles when striving for success.

The time that I was permitted to attend school during the day was short, and my attendance was irregular. It was not long before I had to stop attending day-school altogether, and devote all of my time again to work. I resorted to the night-school again. In fact, the greater part of the education I secured in my boyhood was gathered through the night-school after my day's work was done. I had difficulty often in securing a satisfactory teacher. Sometimes, after I had secured someone to teach me at night, I would find, much to my disappointment, that the teacher knew but little more than I did. Often I would have to walk several miles at night in order to recite my night-school lessons. There was never a time in my youth, no matter how dark and discouraging the days might be, when one resolve did not continually remain with me, and that was a determination to secure an education at any cost. [. . .]

After I had worked in the salt-furnace for some time, work was secured for me in a coal-mine which was operated mainly for the purpose of securing fuel for the salt-furnace. Work in the coal-mine I always dreaded. One reason for this was that anyone who worked in a coal-mine was always unclean, at least while at work, and it was a very hard job to get one's skin clean after the day's work was over. Then it was fully a mile from the opening of the coal-mine to the face of the coal, and all, of course, was in the blackest darkness. I do not believe that one ever experiences anywhere else such darkness as he does in a coal mine. The mine was divided into a large number of different "rooms" or departments, and as I never was able to learn the location of all these "rooms," I many times found myself lost in the mine. To add to the horror of being lost, sometimes my light would go out, and then, if I did not happen to have a match, I would wander about in the darkness until by chance I found someone to give me a light. The work was not only hard, but it was dangerous. There was always the danger of being blown to pieces by a premature explosion of powder or of being crushed by falling slate. Accidents from one or the other of these causes were frequently occurring, and this kept me in constant fear. Many children of the tenderest years were compelled then, as is now true I fear, in most coal-mining districts, to spend a large part of their lives in these coal-mines, with little opportunity to get an education; and, what is worse, I have often noted that, as a rule, young boys who begin life in a coal-mine are often physically and mentally dwarfed. They soon lose ambition to do anything else than to continue as a coal-miner.

In those days, and later as a young man, I used to try to picture in my imagination the feelings and ambitions of a white boy with absolutely no limit placed upon his aspirations and activities. I used to envy the white boy who had no obstacles placed in the way of his becoming a Congressman, Governor, Bishop, or President by reason of the accident of his birth or race. I used to picture the way that I would act under such circumstances; how I would begin at the bottom and keep rising until I reached the highest round of success.

In later years, I confess that I do not envy the white boy as I once did. I have learned that success is to be measured not so much by the position that one has reached in life as by the obstacles which he has overcome while trying to succeed. Looked at from this standpoint, I almost reach the conclusion that often the Negro boy's birth and connection with an unpopular race is an advantage, so far as real life is concerned. With few exceptions, the Negro youth must work harder and must perform his task even better than a white youth in order to secure recognition. But out of the hard and unusual struggle through which he is compelled to pass, he gets a strength, a confidence, that one misses whose pathway is comparatively smooth by reason of birth and race.

From any point of view, I had rather be what I am, a member of the Negro race, than be able to claim membership with the most favoured of any other race. I have always been made sad when I have heard members of any race claiming rights and privileges, or certain badges of distinction, on the ground simply that they were members of this or that race, regardless of their own individual worth or attainments. I have been made to feel sad for such persons because I am conscious of the fact that mere connection with what is known as a superior race will not permanently carry an individual forward unless he has individual worth, and mere connection with what is regarded as an inferior race will not finally hold an individual back if he possesses intrinsic, individual merit. Every persecuted individual and race should get much consolation out of the great human law, which is universal and eternal, that merit, no matter under what skin found, is in the long run, recognized and rewarded. This I have said here, not to call attention to myself as an individual, but to the race to which I am proud to belong.

Part III

Regionalism, Local Color, and the Settlement Schools

Theresa Lloyd

The writings in this section, which date from the mid-nineteenth to the early twentieth centuries, demonstrate the development of the erroneous idea of Appalachia as a stunted frontier isolated from the rest of the United States and inhabited by mountaineers whose pioneer lifestyle was frozen in time.

Like many myths, the notion of Appalachia as perpetual frontier has its roots in truth. To residents of the East Coast in the eighteenth and early nineteenth centuries, the southern and northern backcountry *were* the frontier, and life on the frontier was raw; individualism and a certain disregard for governmental oversight were almost required for people willing to strike out for the backwoods.

Capturing the spirit of life on the frontier (or perhaps appealing to eastern readers' expectations of it) was the literary genre that we now call Old Southwest Humor. Although the genre was far from uniquely Appalachian, the palme d'or of the genre goes to East Tennessee author George Washington Harris for his Sut Lovingood character, a "nat'ral born durn'd fool."

As Reconstruction came to an end in the 1870s, northern interest in southern Appalachia increased for several reasons, not all of which were especially laudable. With new populations of southern and eastern Europeans immigrating to the United States, observers worried about the country's supposed "racial purity" imagined that Appalachia was a reservoir of unadulterated Anglo-Saxon, Teutonic, or Celtic genetic stock. To others, Appalachia seemed still to exemplify the rural past for which rapidly urbanizing and industrializing Americans were nostalgic. Ironically, industrialization was rapidly coming to Appalachia, too, in the form of the timber and mineral industries, driven by advancements in railroad technology. Expanding rail transportation brought to the mountains recreational travelers eager for colorful, exotic sights.

One literary genre that furthered the idea of Appalachia as an exotic destination was local color fiction. Local color writers such as Mary Noailles Murfree and John Fox Jr. attempted to provide a strong sense of place through descriptions of locations, customs, and characters and to replicate regional speech by employing dialect features such as phonetic spelling and nonstandard grammar. A local color vision of Appalachia also featured prominently in the travel writing that was a staple of the era's magazines, and in book-length nonfiction studies of the region such as Horace Kephart's influential *Our Southern Highlanders* (1913, 1922). Emma Bell Miles, in

The Spirit of the Mountains (1905), presented a more balanced vision of the region than Kephart.

Another group of people who flocked to the southern mountains were social reformers, whose most widespread intervention was the establishment of settlement and industrial schools. Appalachian settlement schools, like their urban counterparts, provided basic schooling along with instruction in domestic life, hygiene, and the arts. Industrial schools in Appalachia, like the primarily African American industrial institutions such as Tuskegee, also provided vocational training. Some settlement schools—and, more directly, nursing services—emphasized medical care, which late nineteenth- and early twentieth-century Appalachians living in remote areas were often lacking, as was true throughout the rural United States.

Social reformers such as William Goodell Frost and Frances Goodrich successfully promoted the home production of handmade crafts as a way to stimulate economic development in the mountains. Ironically, craft production in southern Appalachia was dying out by this time because store-bought goods were ubiquitous; to teach crafts production, revivalists relied on older mountain crafts workers and outside teachers.

Despite the notion of Appalachia as a monolithically white frontier, other voices have always been present in the region, as the poetry of eastern Kentucky author Effie Waller Smith demonstrates. An African American, Smith wrote of the natural beauty of the mountains, her race, and her ambitions as a woman.

The legacy of this era, then, is mixed. The era's local color fiction and nonfiction too often relied on quaintness, stereotype, and sentimentality; that Appalachian people were (and are) frozen in time is a literary conceit. By foisting unfamiliar values onto mountaineers, social reformers attempted to change the very culture that they claimed to be preserving. But the era was pivotal for female authors and educators, who did important work in Appalachia. Furthermore, rural populations did exist in Appalachia, as they did throughout America; many of them faced poor schools, lack of healthcare, and scant cash income.

Sources: Allen W. Batteau, *The Invention of Appalachia* (1990); John C. Inscoe, ed., *Appalachians and Race: The Mountain South from Slavery to Segregation* (2001); Kevin E. O'Donnell and Helen Hollingsworth, eds., *Seekers of Scenery: Travel Writing from Southern Appalachia, 1840–1900* (2004); Mary Beth Pudup, Dwight B. Billings, and Altina L. Waller, eds., *Appalachia in the Making: The Mountain South in the Nineteenth Century* (1995); Jess Stoddard, *Challenge and Change in Appalachia: The Story of the Hindman School* (2002); David Whisnant, *All That Is Native and Fine: The Politics of Culture in an American Region* (1983).

George Washington Harris
1814–1869

Southwestern humor was one of the nineteenth century's most popular types of writing, and George Washington Harris's Sut Lovingood tales are masterpieces of the genre. Harris was born in Allegheny City, Pennsylvania, and reared in Knoxville, Tennessee, where he spent his adult life. Harris worked as a railroad conductor, steamboat captain, sawmill manager, and jeweler and was also involved in politics. His earliest writings were polemical pieces for Knoxville newspapers. An ardent secessionist, he penned satirical sketches blasting Lincoln and the Unionists.

The Sut Lovingood tales first appeared in 1854. Harris published eight of them separately before they appeared in the book *Sut Lovingood: Yarns Spun by a "Nat'ral Born Durn'd Fool"* (1867), from which "Parson John Bullen's Lizards" comes. Harris died under mysterious circumstances in 1869 when coming home from Virginia; his last words suggested that he might have been poisoned. At the time of his death, he was said to have had a manuscript of further Sut tales. If so, it remains missing.

Harris's Sut Lovingood is the archetypal fool—crude, poor, and a drunkard; a great player of practical jokes; suspicious of authority and eager to expose its hypocrisy; and transgressive to the point of amorality. Sut is rhetorically characterized by an almost incomprehensible, colorful mountain dialect; braggadocio; and the telling of tall tales. Interpreting this rapscallion for a middle-class audience is a genteel frame narrator, George, who is separated from Sut by his educated speech and his urbanity.

Today's readers can be exasperated by Harris's heavy use of phonetic spelling, nonstandard grammar, cacography, and eye dialect. Read Sut's words aloud, however, and the wonderful humor comes alive.

Parson John Bullen's Lizards

AIT ($8) DULLARS REW-ARD.

'TENSHUN BELEVERS AND KONSTABLES! KETCH 'IM! KETCH 'IM!

THIS kash wil be pade in korn, ur uther projuce, tu be kolected at ur about nex camp-meetin, *ur thararter,* by eny wun what ketches him, fur the karkus ove a sartin, wun SUT LOVINGOOD, dead ur alive, ur ailin, an' safely giv over tu the purtectin care ove Parson John Bullin, ur lef' well tied, at Squire Mackjunkins, fur the raisin ove the devil pussonely, an' permiskusly discumfurtin the wimen very powerful, an' skeerin ove folks generly a heap, an' bustin up a promisin, big warm meetin, an' a makin the wickid larf, an' wus, an' wus, insultin ove the passun orful.

Test,   JEHU WETHERO.
                    Sined by me,
                JOHN BULLEN, the passun.

I found written copies of the above highly intelligible and vindictive proclamation, stuck up on every blacksmith shop, doggery, and store door, in the Frog Mountain Range. Its blood-thirsty spirit, its style, and above all, its chirography, interested me to the extent of taking one down from a tree for preservation.

In a few days I found Sut in a good crowd in front of Capehart's Doggery, and as he seemed to be about in good tune, I read it to him.

"Yas, George, that ar dockymint am in dead yearnist sartin. Them hard shells over thar dus want me the wus kine, powerful bad. *But,* I spect ait dullers won't fetch me, nither wud ait hundred, bekase thar's nun ove 'em fas' enuf to ketch me, nither is thar hosses by the livin jingo! Say, George, much talk 'bout this fuss up whar yu're been?" For the sake of a joke I said yes, a great deal.

"Jis' es I 'spected, durn 'em, all git drunk, an' skeer thar fool sefs ni ontu deth, an' then lay hit ontu me, a poor innersent youf, an' es soun' a belever es they is. Lite, lite, ole feller an' let that roan ove yourn blow a litil, an' I'll 'splain this cussed misfortnit affar: hit hes ruinated my karacter es a pius pusson in the s'ciety roun' yere, an' is a spreadin faster nur meazils. When ever yu hear eny on 'em a spreadin hit, gin hit the dam lie squar, will yu? I haint dun nuffin tu one ove 'em. Hits true, I did sorter frustrate a few lizzards a littil, but they haint members, es I knows on.

"You see, las' year I went tu the big meetin at Rattlesnake Springs, an' wer a sittin in a nice shady place convarsin wif a frien' ove mine, intu the huckil berry thickit, jis' duin nuffin tu nobody an' makin no fuss, when, the fust thing I remembers, I woke up frum a trance what I hed been knocked inter by a four-year old hickory-stick, hilt in the paw ove ole Passun Bullin, durn his alligater hide; an' he wer standin a striddil ove me, a foamin at the mouf, a-chompin his teeth—gesterin wif the hickory club— an' a-preachin tu me so you cud a-hearn him a mile, about a sartin sins gineraly, an' my wickedness pussonely an' mensunin the name ove my frien' loud enuf tu be hearn tu the meetin 'ous. My poor innersent frien' wer dun gone an' I wer glad ove hit, fur I tho't he ment tu kill me rite whar I lay, an' I didn't want her tu see me die."

"Who was she, the friend you speak of Sut?" Sut opened his eyes wide.

"Hu the devil, an' durnashun tole *yu* that hit wer a she?"

"Why, you did, Sut"—

"I *didn't,* durn ef I did. Ole Bullin dun hit, an' I'll hev tu kill him yet, the cussed, infernel ole talebarer!"—

"Well, well, Sut, who was she?"

"Nun ove y-u-r-e b-i-s-n-i-s-s, durn yure littil ankshus picter! I *sees yu* a lickin ove yure lips. I *will* tell you one thing, George; that night, a neighbor gal got a allfired, overhandid stroppin frum her mam, wif a stirrup leather, an' ole Passun Bullin, hed et supper thar, an what's wus nur all, that poor innersent, skeer'd gal hed dun her levil bes' a cookin hit fur 'im. She begged him, a trimblin, an' a-cryin not tu tell on her. He et her cookin, he promised her he'd keep dark—an' then went strait an' tole her mam. Warnt that rale low down, wolf mean? The durnd infunel, hiperkritikal, pot-bellied, scaley-hided, whisky-wastin, stinkin ole groun'-hog. He'd a heap better a stole sum *man's* hoss; I'd a tho't more ove 'im. But I paid him plum up fur hit, an' I means tu keep a payin him, ontil one ur tuther, ove our toes pints up tu the roots ove the grass.

"Well, yere's the way I lifted that note ove han'. At the nex big meetin at Rattil-snaik—las' week hit wer—I wer on han' es solemn es a ole hat kivver on collection day. I hed my face draw'd out intu the shape an' perporshun ove a taylwer's sleeve-board, pint down. I hed put on the convicted sinner so pufeckly that an' ole obsarvin she pillar ove the church sed tu a ole he pillar, es I walked up tu my bainch:

"'Law sakes alive, ef thar ain't that *orful* sinner, Sut Lovingood, pearced plum thru; hu's nex?'

"Yu see, by golly, George, I *hed* tu promis the ole tub ove soap-greas tu cum an' hev myself converted, jis' tu keep him frum killin me. An' es I know'd hit wudn't interfare wif the relashun I bore tu the still housis roun' thar, I didn't keer a durn. I jis' wanted tu git *ni* ole Bullin, onst onsuspected, an' this wer the bes' way tu du hit. I tuk a seat on the side steps ove the pulpit, an' kivvered es much ove my straitch'd face es I could wif my han's, tu prove I wer in yearnis. Hit tuck powerful—fur I hearn a sorter thankful kine ove buzzin all over the congregashun. Ole Bullin hissef looked down at me, over his ole copper specks, an' hit sed jis' es plain es a look cud say hit: 'Yu am thar, ar you—durn yu, hits well fur yu that yu cum.' I tho't sorter diffrent frum that. I tho't hit wud a been well fur *yu*, ef I hadent a-cum, but I didn't say hit jis then. Thar wer a monstrus crowd in that grove, fur the weather wer fine, an' b'levers wer plenty roun' about Rattilsnaik Springs. Ole Bullin gin out, an' they sung that hyme, yu know:

> 'Thar will be mournin, mournin yere, an' mournin thar,
> On that dredful day tu cum.'

"Thinks I, ole hoss, kin hit be possibil enybody hes tole yu what's a gwine tu hap-pin; an' then I tho't that nobody know'd hit but me, and I wer cumforted. He nex tuck hisself a tex pow'fly mixed wif brimstone, an' trim'd wif blue flames, an' then he open'd. He cummenced ontu the sinners; he threaten'd 'em orful, tried tu skeer 'em wif all the wust varmints he cud think ove, an' arter a while he got ontu the idear ove Hell-sarpints, and he dwelt on it sum. He tole 'em how the ole Hell-sarpints wud sarve em if they didn't repent; how cold they'd crawl over thar nakid bodys, an' how like ontu pitch they'd stick tu 'em es they crawled; how they'd rap thar tails roun' thar naiks chokin clost, poke thar tungs up thar noses, an' hiss intu thar years. This wer the way they wer tu sarve men folks. Then he turned ontu the wimmen: tole 'em how they'd quile intu thar buzzims, an' how they *wud* crawl down onder thar frock-strings, no odds how tite they tied 'em, an' how sum ove the oldes' an' was ones wud crawl up thar laigs, an' travil *onder* thar garters, no odds how tight they tied *them*, an' when the two armys ove Hell-sarpents met, then—That las' remark *fotch 'em*. Ove all the screamin, an' hollerin, an' loud cryin, I ever hearn, begun all at onst, all over the hole groun' jis' es he hollered out that word 'then.' He kep on a bellerin, but I got so buisy jis' then, that I didn't listen tu him much, fur I saw that my time fur ack-shun hed cum. Now yu see, George, I'd cotch seven ur eight big pot-bellied lizzards, an' hed 'em in a littil narrer bag, what I had made a-purpus. Thar tails all at the bot-tim, an' so crowdid fur room that they cudent turn roun'. So when he wer a-ravin ontu his tip-toes, an' a-poundin the pulpit wif his fis'—onbenowenst tu enybody, I ontied my bag ove reptiles, put the mouf ove hit onder the bottim ove his britch-es-laig, an' sot intu pinchin thar tails. Quick es gunpowder they all tuck up his bar laig, makin a nise like squirrils a-climbin a shell-bark hickory. He stop't preachin rite in the middil ove the word 'damnation,' an' looked fur a moment like he wer a listen fur sumthin—sorter like a ole sow dus, when she hears yu a-whistlin fur the dorgs. The tarifick shape ove his feeters stopp't the shoutin an' screamin; instantly yu cud hearn a cricket chirp, I gin a long groan, an' hilt my head a-twixt my knees. He gin hisself sum orful open-handed slaps wif fust one han' an' then tuther, about the place whar yu cut the bes' steak outen a beef. Then he'd fetch a vigrus ruff rub whar a hosses tail sprouts; then he'd stomp one foot, then tuther, then bof at onst. Then he run his han' atween his waisbun an' his shut an' reach'd way down, an' roun' wif hit; then he spread his big laigs, an' gin his back a good rattlin rub agin the pulpit, like a hog scratches hisself agin a stump, leanin tu hit pow'ful, an' twitchin, an' squirmin all over, es ef he'd slept in a dorg bed, ur ontu a pisant hill. About this time, one ove my lizzards scared an' hurt by all this poundin' an' feelin, an' scratchin, popp'd out his head frum the passun's shut collar, an' his ole brown naik, an' wer a-surveyin the crowd, when ole Bullin struck at 'im, jis' too late, fur he'd dodged back agin. The hell desarvin ole raskil's speech now cum tu 'im, an' sez he, 'Pray fur me brethren an' sisteren, fur I is a-rastilin wif the great inimy rite now!' an' his voice wer the mos' pitiful, trimblin thing I ever hearn. Sum ove the wimmen fotch a painter yell, an' a young docter, wif ramrod laigs, lean'd toward me monstrus knowin like, an' sez he, 'Clar case ove Delishus Tremenjus.' I nodded my head, an' sez I, 'Yas, spechuly the tremenjus part, an' Ise feard hit haint at hits worst.' Ole Bullin's eyes wer a-stickin out like ontu two buckeyes flung agin a mud wall, an' he wer a-cuttin up more shines nor a cockroach in a hot skillet. Off went the clamhammer coat, an' he flung hit ahine 'im like he wer a-gwine intu a fight; he hed no jackid tu take off, so he unbuttond his galluses, an' vigrusly flung the ainds back over his head. He fotch his shut over-handed a durnd site faster nor I got outen my pasted one, an' then flung hit strait up in the air, like he jis' wanted hit tu keep on up furever; but hit lodged ontu a black-jack, an' I sed one ove my lizzards wif his tail up, a-racin about all over the ole dirty shut, skared too bad tu jump. Then he gin a sorter shake, an' a stompin kine ove twis', an' he cum outer his britches. He tuck 'em by the bottim ove the laigs, an' swung 'em roun' his head a time ur two, an' then fotch 'em down cherall-up over the frunt ove the pulpit. You cud a hearn the smash a quarter ove a mile! Ni ontu fifteen shorten'd biskits, a boiled chicken, wif hits laigs crossed, a big dubbil-bladed knife, a hunk ove terbacker, a cob-pipe, sum copper ore, lots ove broken glass, a cork, a sprinkil ove whisky, a squirt, an' three lizzards flew permiskusly all over that meetin-groun', outen the upper aind ove them big flax britches. One ove the smartes' ove my lizzards lit head-fust intu the buzzim ove a fat 'oman, es big es a skin'd hoss, an' ni onto es ugly, who sot thuty yards off, a fannin hersef wif a tucky-tail. Smart tu the las', by golly, he imejuntly commenced runnin down the centre ove her breas'-bone, an' kep on, I speck. She wer jis' boun' tu faint; an' she did hit fust rate—flung the tucky-tail up in the air, grabbed the lap ove her gown, gin hit a big histin an' fallin shake, rolled down the hill, tangled her laigs an' garters in the top ove a huckilberry bush, wif her head in the branch an' jis' lay still. She wer interestin, she wer, ontil a serious-lookin, pale-faced 'oman hung a nankeen ridin skirt over the huckilberry bush. That wer all that wer dun to'ards bringin her too, that I seed. Now ole Bullin hed nuffin left ontu 'im but a par ove heavy, low quarter'd shoes, short woolen socks, an' eel-skin garters tu keep off the cramp. His skeer hed druv him plum crazy, fur he felt roun' in the air, abuv his head, like he wer huntin sumthin in the dark, an' he beller'd out, 'Brethren, brethren, take keer ove yerselves, the Hell-sarpints *hes got me!*' When this cum out, yu cud a-hearn the screams tu Halifax. He jis' spit in his han's, an' loped over the frunt ove the pulpid *kerdiff!* He lit on top ove, an' rite amung the mos' pius part ove the congregashun. Ole Misses Chaneyberry sot wif her back tu the pulpit, sorter stoopin forrid. He lit astradil ove her long naik, a shuttin her up wif a snap, her head atwix her knees, like shuttin up a jack-knife, an' he sot intu gittin away his levil durndest; he went in a heavy lumberin gallop, like a ole fat waggon hoss, skared at a locomotive. When he jumpt a bainch he shook the yeath. The bonnets, an' fans clar'd the way an' jerked most ove the children wif em, an' the rest he scrunched. He open'd a purfeckly clar track tu the woods, ove every livin thing. He weighed ni ontu three hundred, hed a black stripe down his back, like ontu a ole bridil rein, an' his belly wer 'bout the size, an' color ove a beef paunch, an' hit a-swingin out frum side tu side; he leand back frum hit, like a littil feller a-totin a big drum, at a muster, an' I hearn hit plum tu whar I wer. Thar wer cramp-knots on his laigs es big es walnuts, an' mottled splotches on his shins; an' takin him all over, he minded ove a durnd crazy ole elephant, pussessed ove the devil, rared up on hits hind aind, an' jis' *gittin* frum sum imijut danger ur tribulashun. He did the loudest, an' skariest, an' fussiest runnin I ever seed, tu be no faster nur hit wer, since dad tried tu outrun the ho'nets.

"Well, he disapear'd in the thicket jis' bustin—an' ove all the noises yu ever hearn, wer made thar on that camp groun': sum wimen screamin—they wer the skeery ones; sum larfin—they wer the wicked ones; sum cryin—they wer the fool ones, (sorter my stripe yu know;) sum tryin to git away wif thar faces red—they wer the modest ones; sum lookin arter ole Bullin—they wer the curious ones; sum hangin clost tu thar sweethearts—they wer the sweet ones; sum on thar knees wif thar eyes shot, but facin the way the ole mud turtil wer a-runnin—they wer the 'saitful ones; sum duin nuthin—they wer the waitin ones; an' the mos' dangerus ove all ove em by a durnd long site.

"I tuck a big skeer mysef arter a few rocks, an' sich like fruit, spattered ontu the pulpit ni ontu my head; an' es the Lovingoods, durn em! knows nuffin but tu run, when they gits skeerd, I jis' put out fur the swamp on the krick. As I started, a black bottil ove bald-face smashed agin a tree furninst me, arter missin the top ove my head 'bout a inch. Sum durn'd fool professor dun this, who hed more zeal or sence; fur I say that eny man who wud waste a quart ove even mean sperrits, fur the chance ove knockin a poor ornary devil like me down wif the bottil, is a bigger fool nor ole Squire Mackmullen, an' he tried tu shoot hissef wif a onloaded hoe-handle."

"Did they catch you, Sut?"

"Ketch thunder! *No sir!* jis' look at these yere laigs! Skeer me, hoss, jis' skeer me, an' then watch me while I stay in site, an' yu'll never ax that fool question agin. Why, durn it, man, that's what the ait dullers am fur.

"Ole Barbelly Bullin, es they calls 'im now, never preached ontil yesterday, an' he hadn't the fust durn'd 'oman tu hear 'im, *they hev seed too much ove 'im.* Passuns ginerly hev a pow'ful strong holt on wimen; but, hoss, I tell yu thar ain't meny ove em kin run start nakid over an' thru a crowd ove three hundred wimen an' not injure thar karacters *sum.* Enyhow, hits a kind ove show they'd ruther see one at a time, an' pick the passun at that. His tex' wer, 'Nakid I cum intu the world, an' nakid I'm a gwine outen hit, ef I'm spard ontil then.' He sed nakidness warnt much ove a sin, purtickerly ove dark nights. That he wer a weak, frail wum ove the dus', an' a heap more sich truck. Then he totch ontu me; sed I wer a livin proof ove the hell-desarvin nater ove man, an' that thar warnt grace enuf in the whole 'sociation tu saften my outside rind; that I wer 'a lost ball' forty years afore I wer born'd, an' the bes' thing they cud du fur the church, wer tu turn out, an' still hunt fur me ontil I wer shot. An' he never said Hell-sarpints onst in the hole preach. I b'leve, George, the durnd fools am at hit.

"Now, I wants yu tu tell ole Barbelly this fur me, ef he'll let me an' Sall alone, I'll let him alone—a-while; an' ef he don't, ef I don't lizzard him agin, I jis' wish I may be dod durnd! *Skeer him if yu ken.*

"Let's go tu the spring an' take a ho'n."

"Say George, didn't that ar Hell-sarpint sermon ove his'n, hev sumthin like a Hell-sarpint aplicashun? Hit looks sorter so tu me."

Mary Noailles Murfree
(Charles Egbert Craddock)
1850–1922

The best-known author of local color fiction about the southern mountains, Mary Noailles Murfree was born in Murfreesboro into a prominent Middle Tennessee family and was reared and educated in Nashville. During the Civil War, her family's plantation house in Murfreesboro was burned, her father's fortune was ruined, and she began writing for financial gain.

Murfree's earliest pieces have a Middle Tennessee setting, but she began to write about the mountains by the late 1870s. Although Murfree claimed to have chosen a mountain setting haphazardly, the mountains were a popular topic in magazine writing of the post–Civil War era. She had published a few stories in the *Atlantic* before her 1884 collection *In the Tennessee Mountains* appeared, bringing her instant fame. Murfree published her earliest mountain tales under the pseudonym Charles Egbert Craddock.

Attempting to capitalize on the success of her first collection, Murfree wrote twenty-eight short stories and eight novels with mountain settings. In her later years, her popularity and that of local color generally were on the wane, and she died in destitute circumstances.

Murfree admitted that she derived her "knowledge" of mountain life from vacationing at Beersheba Springs, Tennessee, a fashionable watering hole on the Cumberland Plateau located well west of the mountains. Although some of her mountain characters complete heroic actions, her reliance on broadly drawn character types, along with her insider/outsider plots, romantic descriptions, and use of dialect to paint mountain people as uneducated, helped to cement stereotypes of Appalachia. Consequently, her fiction is controversial among today's readers.

FROM The Star in the Valley

It was near dusk, on a dull, cold evening, when Chevis dismounted before the door of the blacksmith's little log-cabin. The chestnut-tree hung desolate and bare on the eaves of the forge; the stream rushed by in swift gray whirlpools under a sullen gray sky; the gigantic wall of broken rocks loomed gloomy and sinister on the opposite side of the road,—not so much as a withered leaf of all their vines clung to their rugged surfaces. The mountains had changed color: the nearest ranges were black with the myriads of the grim black branches of the denuded forest; far away they stretched in parallel lines, rising tier above tier, and showing numberless gradations of a dreary, neutral tint, which grew ever fainter in the distance, till merged in the uniform tone of the sombre sky.

Indoors it was certainly more cheerful. A hickory fire dispensed alike warmth and light. The musical whir of a spinning-wheel added its unique charm. From the rafters depended numberless strings of bright red pepper-pods and ears of popcorn; hanks of woolen and cotton yarn; bunches of medicinal herbs; brown gourds and little bags of seeds. On rude shelves against the wall were ranged cooking utensils, drinking vessels, etc., all distinguished by that scrupulous cleanliness which is a marked feature of the poor hovels of these mountaineers, and in striking contrast to the poor hovels of lowlanders. The rush-bottomed chairs, drawn in a semicircle before the rough, ill-adjusted stones which did duty as hearth, were occupied by several men, who seemed to be making the blacksmith a prolonged visit; various members of the family were humbly seated on sundry inverted domestic articles, such as wash-tubs, and splint-baskets made of white oak. There was circulating among Jerry Shaw's friends a flat bottle, facetiously denominated "tickler," readily emptied, but as readily replenished from a keg in the corner. Like the widow's cruse of oil, that keg was miraculously never empty. The fact of a still near by in the wild ravine might suggest a reason for its perennial flow. It was a good strong article of apple-brandy, and its effects were beginning to be distinctly visible.

Truly the ethereal woodland flower [Celia] seemed strangely incongruous with these brutal and uncouth conditions of her life, as she stood at a little distance from this group, spinning at her wheel. Chevis felt a sudden sharp pang of pity for her when he glanced toward her; the next instant he had forgotten it in his interest in her work. It was altogether at variance with the ideas which he had hitherto entertained concerning that humble handicraft. There came across him a vague recollection from his city life that the peasant girls of art galleries and of the lyric stage were wont to sit at the wheel. "But perhaps they were spinning flax," he reflected. This spinning was a matter of walking back and forth with smooth, measured steps and graceful, undulatory motion; a matter, too, of much pretty gesticulation,—the thread in one hand, the other regulating the whirl of the wheel. He thought he had never seen attitudes so charming.

Jerry Shaw hastened to abdicate and offer one of the rush-bottomed chairs with the eager hospitality characteristic of these mountaineers,—a hospitality that meets a stranger on the threshold of every hut, presses upon him, ungrudgingly, its best, and follows him on his departure with protestations of regret out to the rickety fence. Chevis was more or less known to all of the visitors, and after a little, under the sense of familiarity and the impetus of the apple-brandy, the talk flowed on as freely as before his entrance. It was wilder and more antagonistic to his principles and prejudices than anything he had hitherto heard among these people, and he looked on and listened, interested in this new development of a phase of life which he had thought he had sounded from its lowest note to the top of its compass. He was glad to remain; the scene had impressed his cultivated perceptions as an interior by Teniers might have done, and the vehemence and lawlessness of the conversation and the threats of violence had little reality for him; if he thought about the subject under discussion at all, it was with a reassuring conviction that before the plans could be carried out the already intoxicated mountaineers would be helplessly drunk. Nevertheless, he glanced ever and anon at the young girl, loath that she should hear it, lest its virulent, angry bitterness should startle her. She was evidently listening, too, but her fair face was as calm and untroubled as one of the pure white faces of those flower-stars of his early stay in the mountains.

"Them Peels ought n't ter be let live!" exclaimed Elijah Burr, a gigantic fellow, arrayed in brown jeans, with the accompaniments of knife, powder-horn, etc., usual with the hunters of the range; his gun stood, with those of the other guests, against the wall in a corner of the room. "They ought n't ter be let live, an' I'd top off all three of 'em fur the skin an' horns of a deer."

"That thar is a true word," assented Jerry Shaw. "They oughter be run down an' kilt,—all three o' them Peels."

Chevis could not forbear a question. Always on the alert to add to his stock of knowledge of men and minds, always analyzing his own inner life and the inner life of those about him, he said, turning to his intoxicated host, "Who are the Peels, Mr. Shaw,—if I may ask?"

"Who air the Peels?" repeated Jerry Shaw, making a point of seizing the question. "They air the meanest men in these hyar mountings. Ye might hunt from Copperhead Ridge ter Clinch River, an' the whole spread o' the valley, an' never hear tell o' no sech no 'count critters."

"They ought n't ter be let live!" again urged Elijah Burr. "No man ez treats his wife like that dad-burned scoundrel Ike Peel do oughter be let live. That thar woman is my sister an' Jerry Shaw's cousin,—an' I shot him down in his own door year afore las'. I shot him ter kill; but somehow 'nother I war that shaky, an' the cussed gun hung fire a-fust, an' that thar pore wife o' his'n screamed an' hollered so, that I never done nuthin' arter all but lay him up for four month an' better for that thar pore critter ter nuss. He'll see a mighty differ nex' time I gits my chance. An' 't ain't fur off," he added threateningly.

"Wouldn't it be better to persuade her to leave him?" suggested Chevis pacifically, without, however, any wild idea of playing peacemaker between fire and tow.

Burr growled a fierce oath, and then was silent.

A slow fellow on the opposite side of the fireplace explained: "Thar's whar all the trouble kem from. She would n't leave him, fur all he treated her awful. She said ez how he war mighty good ter her when he war n't drunk. So 'Lijah shot him."

This way of cutting the Gordian knot of domestic difficulties might have proved efficacious but for the shakiness induced by the thrill of fraternal sentiment, the infusion of apple-brandy, the protest of the bone of contention, and the hanging fire of the treacherous gun. Elijah Burr could remember no other failure of aim for twenty years.

"He won't git shet of me that easy agin!" Burr declared, with another pull at the flat tickler. "But ef it hed n't hev been fur what happened las' week, I mought hev let him off fur awhile," he continued, evidently actuated by some curiously distorted sense of duty in the premises. "I oughter hev kilt him afore. But now the cussed critter is a gone coon. Dad-burn the whole tribe!"

Chevis was desirous of knowing what had happened last week. He did not, however, feel justified in asking more questions. But apple-brandy is a potent tongue-loosener, and the unwonted communicativeness of the stolid and silent mountaineers attested its strength in this regard. Jerry Shaw, without inquiry, enlightened him.

"Ye see," he said, turning to Chevis, "'Lijah he thought ez how ef he could git that fool woman ter come ter his house, he could shoot Ike fur his meanness 'thout botherin' of her, an' things would all git easy agin. Waal, he went thar one day when all them Peels, the whole lay-out, war gone down ter the Settlemint ter hear the rider preach, an' he jes' run away with two of the brats,—the littlest ones, ye onderstand,—a-thinkin' he mought tole her off from Ike that thar way. We hearn ez how the pore critter war nigh on ter distracted 'bout 'em, but Ike never let her come arter 'em. Leastways, she never kem. Las' week Ike kem fur 'em hisself,—him an' them two cussed brothers o' his'n. All 'Lijah's folks war out 'n the way; him an' his boys war off a-huntin', an' his wife hed gone down ter the spring, a haffen mile an' better, a-washin' clothes; nobody war ter the house 'ceptin' them two chillen o' Ike's. An' Ike an' his brothers jes' tuk the chillen away, an' set fire ter the house; an' time 'Lijah's wife got thar, 't war nuthin' but a pile o' ashes. So we've determinated ter go up yander ter Laurel Notch, twenty mile along the ridge of the mounting, ter-night, an' wipe out them Peels,—'kase they air a-goin' ter move away. That thar wife o' Ike's, what made all the trouble, hev fretted an' fretted at Ike till he hev determinated ter break up an' wagon across the range ter Kaintucky, whar his uncle lives in the hills thar. Ike hev gin his cornsent ter go jes' ter pleasure her, 'kase she air mos' crazed ter git Ike away whar 'Lijah can't kill him. Ike's brothers is a-goin', too. I hearn ez how they'll make a start at noon ter-morrer."

"They'll never start ter Kaintucky ter-morrer," said Burr, grimly. "They'll git off, afore that, fur hell, stiddier Kaintucky. I hev been a-tryin' ter make out ter shoot that thar man ever since that thar gal war married ter him, seven year ago,—seven year an' better. But what with her a-foolin' round, an' a-talkin', an' a-goin' on like she war distracted—she run right 'twixt him an' the muzzle of my gun wunst, or I would hev hed him that time fur sure—an' somehow 'nother that critter makes me so shaky with her ways of goin' on that I feel like I hain't got good sense, an' can't git no good aim at nuthin'. Nex' time, though, thar'll be a differ. She ain't a-goin' ter Kaintucky along of him ter be beat fur nuthin' when he's drunk."

It was a pitiable picture presented to Chevis's open-eyed imagination,—this woman standing for years between the two men she loved: holding back her brother from his vengeance of her wrongs by that subtle influence that shook his aim; and going into exile with her brute of a husband when that influence had waned and failed, and her wrongs were supplemented by deep and irreparable injuries to her brother. And the curious moral attitude of the man: the strong fraternal feeling that alternately nerved and weakened his revengeful hand.

"We air goin' thar 'bout two o'clock ternight," said Jerry Shaw, "and wipe out all three o' them Peels,—Ike an' his two brothers."

"They ought n't ter be let live," reiterated Elijah Burr, moodily. Did he speak to his faintly stirring conscience, or to a woful premonition of his sister's grief?

"They'll all three be stiff an' stark afore daybreak," resumed Jerry Shaw. "We air all kin ter 'Lijah, an' we air goin' ter holp him top off them Peels. Thar's ten of us an' three o' them, an' we won't hev no trouble 'bout it. An' we'll bring that pore critter, Ike's wife, an' her chillen hyar ter stay. She's welcome ter live along of us till 'Lijah kin fix some sort 'n place fur her an' the little chillen. Thar won't be no trouble a-gittin' rid of the men folks, ez thar is ten of us an' three o' them, an' we air goin' ter take 'em in the night."

There was a protest from an unexpected quarter. The whir of the spinning-wheel was abruptly silenced. "I don't see no sense," said Celia Shaw, her singing monotone vibrating in the sudden lull,—"I don't see no sense in shootin' folks down like they war nuthin' better nor bear, nor deer, nor suthin' wild. I don't see no sense in it. An' I never did see none."

There was an astonished pause.

"Shet up, Cely! Shet up!" exclaimed Jerry Shaw, in mingled anger and surprise. "Them folks ain't no better nor bear, nor sech. They hain't got no right ter live,—them Peels."

"No, that they hain't!" said Burr.

"They is powerful no 'count critters, I know," replied the little woodland flower, the firelight bright in her opaline eyes and on the flakes of burnished gold gleaming in the dark masses of her hair. "They is always a-hangin' round the still an' a-gittin' drunk; but I don't see no sense in a-huntin' 'em down an' a-killin' 'em off. 'Pears ter me like they air better nor the dumb ones. I don't see no sense in shootin' 'em."

"Shet up, Cely! Shet up!" reiterated Shaw.

Celia said no more. Reginald Chevis was pleased with this indication of her sensibility; the other women—her mother and grandmother—had heard the whole recital with the utmost indifference, as they sat by the fire monotonously carding cotton. She was beyond her station in sentiment, he thought. However, he was disposed to recant this favorable estimate of her higher nature when, twice afterward, she stopped her work, and, filling the bottle from the keg, pressed it upon her father, despite her unfavorable criticism of the hangers-on of stills. Nay, she insisted. "Drink some more," she said. "Ye hain't got half enough yit." Had the girl no pity for the already drunken creature? She seemed systematically trying to make him even more helpless than he was.

He had fallen into a deep sleep before Chevis left the house, and the bottle was circulating among the other men with a rapidity that boded little harm to the unconscious Ike Peel and his brothers at Laurel Notch, twenty miles away. As Chevis mounted Strathspey he saw the horses of Jerry Shaw's friends standing partly within and partly without the blacksmith's shop. They would stand there all night, he thought. It was darker when he commenced the ascent of the mountain than he had anticipated. And what was this driving against his face,—rain? No, it was snow. He had not started a moment too soon. But Strathspey, by reason of frequent travel, knew every foot of the way, and perhaps there would only be a flurry. And so he went on steadily up and up the wild, winding road among the great, bare, black trees and the grim heights and chasms. The snow fell fast,—so fast and so silently, before he was half-way to the summit he had lost the vague companionship of the sound of his horse's hoofs, now muffled in the thick carpet so suddenly flung upon the ground. Still the snow fell, and when he had reached the mountain's brow the ground was deeply covered, and the whole aspect of the scene was strange. But though obscured by the fast-flying flakes, he knew that down in the bosom of the white valley there glittered still that changeless star.

"Still spinning, I suppose," he said to himself, as he looked toward it and thought of the interior of the log-cabin below. And then he turned into the tent to enjoy his cigar, his aesthetic reveries, and a bottle of wine.

But the wheel was no longer awhirl. Both music and musician were gone. Toiling along the snow-filled mountain ways; struggling with the fierce gusts of wind as they buffeted and hindered her, and fluttered derisively among her thin, worn, old garments; shivering as the driving flakes came full into the pale, calm face, and fell in heavier and heavier wreaths upon the dappled calico sun-bonnet; threading her way through unfrequented woodland paths, that she might shorten the distance; now deftly on the verge of a precipice, whence a false step of those coarse, rough shoes would fling her into unimaginable abysses below; now on the sides of steep ravines, falling sometimes with the treacherous, sliding snow, but never faltering; tearing her hands on the shrubs and vines she clutched to help her forward, and bruised and bleeding, but still going on; trembling more than with the cold, but never turning back, when a sudden noise in the terrible loneliness of the sheeted woods suggested the close proximity of a wild beast, or perhaps, to her ignorant, superstitious mind, a supernatural presence,—thus she journeyed on her errand of deliverance.

Her fluttering breath came and went in quick gasps; her failing limbs wearily dragged through the deep drifts; the cruel winds untiringly lashed her; the snow soaked through the faded green cotton dress to the chilled white skin,—it seemed even to the dull blood coursing feebly through her freezing veins. But she had small thought for herself during those long, slow hours of endurance and painful effort. Her pale lips moved now and then with muttered speculations: how the time went by; whether they had discovered her absence at home; and whether the fleeter horsemen were even now ploughing their way through the longer, winding mountain road. Her only hope was to outstrip their speed. Her prayer—this untaught being!—she had no prayer, except perhaps her life, the life she was so ready to imperil. She had no high, cultured sensibilities to sustain her. There was no instinct stirring within her that might have nerved her to save her father's, or her brother's, or a benefactor's life. She held the creatures that she would have died to warn in low estimation, and spoke of them with reprobation and contempt. She had known no religious training, holding up forever the sublimest ideal. The measureless mountain wilds were not more infinite to her than that great mystery. Perhaps, without any philosophy, she stood upon the basis of a common humanity.

When the silent horsemen, sobered by the chill night air and the cold snow, made their cautious approach to the little porch of Ike Peel's log-hut at Laurel Notch, there was a thrill of dismayed surprise among them to discover the door standing half open, the house empty of its scanty furniture and goods, its owners fled, and the very dogs disappeared; only, on the rough stones before the dying fire, Celia Shaw, falling asleep and waking by fitful starts.

"Jerry Shaw swore ez how he would hev shot that thar gal o' his'n,—that thar Cely," Hi Bates said to Chevis and Varney the next day, when he recounted the incident, "only he didn't think she hed her right mind; a-walkin' through this hyar deep snow full fifteen mile,—it's fifteen mile by the short cut ter Laurel Notch,—ter git Ike Peel's folks off 'fore 'Lijah an' her dad could come up an' settle Ike an' his brothers. Leastways, 'Lijah an' the t'others, fur Jerry hed got so drunk he could n't go; he war dead asleep till ter-day, when they kem back a-fotchin' the gal with 'em. That thar Cely Shaw never did look ter me like she hed good sense, nohow. Always looked like she war queer an' teched in the head."

There was a furtive gleam of speculation on the dull face of the mountaineer when his two listeners broke into enthusiastic commendation of the girl's high heroism and courage. The man of ledgers swore that he had never heard of anything so fine, and that he himself would walk through fifteen miles of snow and midnight wilderness for the honor of shaking hands with her. There was that keen thrill about their hearts sometimes felt in crowded theatres, responsive to the cleverly simulated heroism of the boards; or in listening to a poet's mid-air song; or in looking upon some grand and ennobling phase of life translated on a great painter's canvas.

Hi Bates thought that perhaps they too were a little "teched in the head."

There had fallen upon Chevis a sense of deep humiliation. Celia Shaw had heard no more of that momentous conversation than he; a wide contrast was suggested. He began to have a glimmering perception that despite all his culture, his sensibility, his yearnings toward humanity, he was not so high a thing in the scale of being; that he had placed a false estimate upon himself. He had looked down on her with a mingled pity for her dense ignorance, her coarse surroundings, her low station, and a dilettante's delight in picturesque effects, and with no recognition of the moral splendors of that star in the valley. A realization, too, was upon him that fine feelings are of most avail as the motive power of fine deeds.

He and his friend went down together to the little log-cabin. There had been only jeers and taunts and reproaches for Celia Shaw from her own people. These she had expected, and she had stolidly borne them. But she listened to the fine speeches of the city-bred men with a vague wonderment on her flower-like face,—whiter than ever to-day.

"It was a splendid—a noble thing to do," said Varney, warmly.

"I shall never forget it," said Chevis, "it will always be like a sermon to me."

There was something more that Reginald Chevis never forgot: the look on her face as he turned and left her forever; for he was on his way back to his former life, so far removed from her and all her ideas and imaginings. He pondered long upon that look in her inscrutable eyes,—was it suffering, some keen pang of despair?—as he rode down and down the valley, all unconscious of the heart-break he left behind him. He thought of it often afterward; he never penetrated its mystery.

He heard of her only once again. On the eve of a famous day, when visiting the outposts of a gallant corps, Reginald Chevis happened to recognize in one of the pickets the gawky mountaineer who had been his guide through those autumnal woods so far away. Hi Bates was afterward sought out and honored with an interview in the general's tent; for the accidental encounter had evoked many pleasant reminiscences in Chevis's mind, and among other questions he wished to ask was what had become of Jerry Shaw's daughter.

"She's dead,—long ago," answered Hi Bates. "She died afore the winter war over the year ez ye war a-huntin' thar. She never hed good sense ter my way o' thinkin', nohow, an' one night she run away, an' walked 'bout fifteen mile through a big snowstorm. Some say it settled on her chist. Anyhow, she jes' sorter fell away like afterward, an' never held up her head good no more. She always war a slim little critter, an' looked like she war teched in the head."

There are many things that suffer unheeded in those mountains: the birds that freeze on the trees; the wounded deer that leaves its cruel kind to die alone; the despairing, flying fox with its pursuing train of savage dogs and men. And the jutting crag whence had shone the camp-fire she had so often watched—her star, set forever—looked far over the valley beneath, where in one of those sad little rural graveyards she had been laid so long ago.

But Reginald Chevis has never forgotten her. Whenever he sees the earliest star spring into the evening sky, he remembers the answering red gleam of that star in the valley.

William Goodell Frost

1854–1938

William Goodell Frost was born into a New York reformist family who offered their home as a station on the Underground Railroad. Additionally, his aunt, Lavinia Goodell, was the first woman to practice law before the Wisconsin Supreme Court. In 1876, Frost received an AB at the progressive Oberlin College, where he later returned to teach Greek. While teaching at Oberlin, Frost became interested in Appalachia, and his interest deepened when he became the president of Berea College in Berea, Kentucky, in 1893. Berea College was founded in 1855 by Kentucky abolitionist John G. Fee as an interracial institution; its supporters, both black and white, also championed black colleges such as Howard and Fisk. In the years after Kentucky's 1904 legislation outlawing interracial education, Berea kept its white students at the Berea campus and founded Lincoln Institute in Louisville to educate African Americans. Frost implemented programs at Berea that he felt were suited to white mountain students.

Frost's essay "Our Contemporary Ancestors in the Southern Mountains" is one of the most famous (and, today, controversial) pieces ever written about Appalachia. The essay appeared in 1899 in an *Atlantic Monthly* series on multiculturalism in the United States; the series also included a piece by African American scholar W. E. B. Du Bois. Frost's motivation in the piece is to champion mountaineers, yet his compliments reinforce stereotypes of Appalachia as a romantic but backward culture, and his vision of mountaineers as a reservoir of American cultural purity grows out of the anti-immigration sentiments of his era.

FROM Our Contemporary Ancestors in the Southern Mountains

At the close of the Revolutionary War there were about two and one half million people in the American colonies. To-day there are in the Southern mountains approximately the same number of people—Americans for four and five generations—who are living to all intents and purposes in the conditions of the colonial times! These people form an element unaccounted for by the census, unreckoned with in all our inventories of national resources. And their remoteness is by no means measured by the mere distance in miles. It is a longer journey from northern Ohio to eastern Kentucky than from America to Europe; for one day's ride brings us into the eighteenth century. Naturally, then, these eighteenth-century neighbors and fellow countrymen of ours are in need of a friendly interpreter; for modern life has little patience with those who are "behind the times." [. . .]

In this vast inland and upland realm may be found a contemporary survival of that pioneer life which has been such a striking feature in American history. Beginning with the survivals in matters external, we are at once introduced to the first type of American architecture,—the log cabin. The blind or windowless one-room cabin is replaced in the broader valleys by the double log cabin,—two cabins side by side, with a roofed space between serving for dining-room most of the year; in county towns even a second story with balcony is sometimes developed. In the Carolinas "stick chimneys" prevail, but in Tennessee and Kentucky substantial stone chimneys are the rule, aesthetically placed upon the outside of the wall. The great characteristic in the log-cabin stage of life is the absence of "conveniences." For a camping party this is very interesting, though sometimes embarrassing. To the mountain people, as to our pioneer ancestors, it is a matter of course. The writer recalls an early experience when enjoying the hospitality of a mountain home. His feminine companion thought of a possible return of hospitalities, wondering whether her hostess ever came to Berea, fifteen miles away, for shopping.

"When you cannot get what you need at this little store down by the creek, where do you go?"

The mountain woman answered with a frank smile, "I go without."

And it appeared that she had never been to any town or city in her life! It is brought home to a visitor in this region that the number of things which people can go without is very great. We expected to find our sylvan hosts without electric lights, but it did strike us as barbarous for them to burn kerosene lamps without chimneys. Still, it is a delicate matter to carry a lamp chimney safely over twenty miles of mountain road, on horseback. Possibly if we lived where they do we should live somewhat as they do!

One of our college women, in a "university extension" tour, desired to starch her waist [blouse], and asked her wondering hostess for a little wheat flour.

"Oh yes," was the reply, "we've got some wheat flour." And then followed the search. No storeroom, flour bin, or even flour barrel or flour bag appeared. The woman's eyes were cast among the rafters whence depended numerous bags and bunches.

"Oh yes, we've got some wheat flour." And at last it came forth from a cleft between the logs, a scant pint of flour "wrapped up in a napkin." The dreariness of this destitution is greatly relieved by what are to us the novel resources of sylvan life. If these primitive folk cannot step to the telephone and by a supernatural fiat "order" whatever may be desired, they can step into the forest and find or fashion some rude substitute. (Though in truth the handmade product is not a substitute, but an archetype.) Is the lamp chimney lacking? The mountain potteries are still making flambeaux, lamps of almost classic pattern in which grease is burned with a floating wick. Is the sawmill remote? In the high mountains where streams are small and mills impracticable the whipsaw is brought into use, and two men will get out three or four hundred feet of boards from the logs in a day. Handmills for grinding can still be constructed by well-brought-up mountain men, and in some places they have not yet lost the tradition of the fashioning of the old English crossbow! And who does not have a feeling akin to reverence in the presence of a hand loom? When a mountain maid speaks of her "wheel" she does not refer to a bicycle, but to the spinning-wheel of our ancestors, her use of which here in our mountains calls to mind the sudden and entire disappearance of cloth-making from the list of household industries. Not a single member of the Sorosis could card, spin, dye, or weave. Their mothers, for the most part, had forgotten these arts, yet their grandmothers, and their foremothers for a hundred generations, have been spinners. Spinning, in fact, has helped to form the character of our race, and it is pleasant to find that here in Appalachian America it is still contributing to the health and grace and skill of womankind.

Along with these Saxon arts we shall find startling survivals of Saxon speech. The rude dialect of the mountains is far less a degradation than a survival. The Saxon pronoun "hit" holds its place almost universally. Strong past tenses, "holp" for helped, "drug" for dragged, and the like, are heard constantly; and the syllabic plural is retained in words in -st and others. The greeting as we ride up to a cabin is "Howdy, strangers. 'Light and hitch yer beasties." Quite a vocabulary of Chaucer's words which have been dropped by polite lips, but which linger in these solitudes, has been made out by some of our students. "Pack" for carry, "gorm" for muss, "feisty" for full of life, impertinent, are examples. [. . .]

Two other pioneer reminders are large families and a scarcity of money. Barter is carried on at every store, where the tall gaunt figure and immobile face, so well described by Miss Murfree, and proverbially characteristic of Americans in the pioneer stage of development, still predominate at every counter.

A little sympathy and patience are necessary if we would recognize these marks of our contemporary ancestors through the exterior which is, at first sight, somewhat rude and repellent. The characteristics thus far noted are only on the surface; it will require still more insight and imagination to really know the heart of a mountain man. As in external matters the great characteristic is "going without things," so in the realm of ideas we are first impressed by the immense blank spaces. Can you divest your mind of those wonderful ideas which have been born since the Revolution, and have expanded and filled the modern world—evolution and the rest? Appalachian America may be useful as furnishing a fixed point which enables us to measure the progress of the moving world! And yet to set down the mountain people with the scornful verdict "behind the times" would be almost brutal. There is a reason for their belated condition, and they have large claims upon our interest and our consideration.

Subtract the ideas which have been born since the Revolution, and we come back to some very distinct and interesting notions. To begin with, we have the Revolutionary patriotism. Mr. Henry Cabot Lodge has recently told anew the story of the battle of King's Mountain, in which the backwoodsmen of Appalachian America annihilated a British army. Cedar kegs used as canteens, and other accoutrements which saw service in that enterprise, may still be found in mountain cabins. As Appalachian America has received no foreign immigration, it now contains a larger proportion of "Sons" and "Daughters" of the Revolution than any other part of our country.

The feeling of toleration and justification of slavery, with all the subtleties of state rights and "South against North," which grew up after the Revolution did not penetrate the mountains. The result was that when the civil war came there was a great surprise for both the North and the South. Appalachian America clave to the old flag. It was this old-fashioned loyalty which held Kentucky in the Union, made West Virginia "secede from secession," and performed prodigies of valor in east Tennessee, and even in the western Carolinas. The writer was describing this loyalty to a woman's club in a border city when a fine old Southern lady, with entire good nature but much spirit, exclaimed, "Ah, sir, if those mountain folks had been educated they would have gone with their states!" Probably she was right. [. . .]

If the mountaineer's patriotism is old-fashioned, his literary sustenance, if such it may be called, is simply archaic. His music is in a weird minor key, and like that of Chaucer's Prioress, "entuned in hire nose full swetely." The hymns which are lined out and sung in unison in very slow time are usually quite doleful. The banjo, as well as most secular music, is commonly accounted wicked. Yet not a few old English ballads, familiar in Percy's Reliques, have been handed down from mother to daughter, with interesting variants like those of the Homeric lays. For example, the mountain minstrel represents the hero of Barbara Allen as coming not "out of the west countree," but (for all the world!) out of the Western States! And besides these transmissions there is a certain mass of stock phrases, anecdotes always related in the same words, standing illustrations, and the like, which are of the nature of literature, and might be called the literature of the illiterate. As an instance of this we recently jotted down the following apothegm of a mountain preacher. "Yeou cayn't help a-havin' bad thoughts come inter yer heads, but yeou hain't no necessity fer ter set 'em a cheer." The saying was repeated in a gathering of ministers in the East, and an aged man who was born in England said that he had heard the same thing from an unlearned country preacher when he was a boy. Doubtless that saying has been passed from mouth to mouth for generations. With these literary treasures may be mentioned the examples of slow Saxon wit exhibited in the names of places in the mountains. The post-office department has pruned away many expressive names like "Hell-fer-sartin" and "Stand-around" (why not as classic as Tarrytown?), but has spared many imaginative and picturesque designations, as Fair Play, Wide-Awake, Cutshin, Quality Valley, Saddler, Amity, Troublesome, Stamping Ground, and Nonesuch.

In examining social life, and its variations in the mountains, we discover a new kind of isolation, a higher potency of loneliness. The people are not only isolated from the great centres and thoroughfares of the world, but also isolated from one another. The families who live along one valley form a community by themselves, and the children grow up with almost no examples or analogies of life outside these petty bounds. As we need a fresh air fund for the little ones of the city, we need a fresh idea fund for these sons and daughters of solitude. The very words by which a stranger is directed are suggestive of this isolation of each locality. In place of the street and number of a city, or the "range" and "section" of the west, we are directed by the watercourses. We are told to follow the middle fork of the Kentucky River, go up such a creek, and turn off on such a branch. The mountain world is mapped out by "forks," "creeks," and "branches." This double isolation produces many marked variations in social conditions. It may happen, for example, that one or two leading families on the "branch"—the pillars of the narrow society—die out, or move out, and the social state, left unsupported, collapses. The tales of awful degradation in the mountains may be true. But such tales are not to be taken as representative. The very next valley may be filled with homes where homespun linen tablecloths, and texts and hymns handed down by tradition, witness to a self-respect and character that are unmistakable. [. . .]

The ancestry of the mountain folk is for the most part creditable. As has been indicated already it is almost wholly Revolutionary and British. In Kentucky a majority of the families may be traced back to rural England, both by distinct English traits and by the common English names like Chrisman, Baker, Allen, and Hazelwood. In other parts of the mountains the Scotch-Irish strain predominates, with corresponding names, including all the Macs. The impression has been made that some of the early settlers in the Southern colonies were "convicts," but it must be remembered that many of them were only convicted of having belonged to Cromwell's army, or of persisting in attending religious meetings conducted by "dissenters." But, whatever their origin, the "leading families" of the mountains are clearly sharers in the gracious influences which formed the English and Scottish people, and when a mountain lad registers by the name of Campbell or Harrison we have learned to expect that he will not prove unworthy of his clan. [. . .]

The reverse side of family affection is the blood feud, which still survives in full vigor. Thoroughly to trace the origin, motives, and code of the blood feud in the mountains would require an article by itself. As an institution it has its roots deep in Old World traditions. Yet it seems to have been decadent when the confusions of the civil war gave it a new life. It is made possible by the simple fact that the people of this region have not yet grasped the decidedly modern notion of the sacredness of life. Mountain homicides are not committed for purposes of robbery. They are almost universally performed in the spirit of an Homeric chieftain, and the motive is some "point of honor."

Among the social virtues of the mountaineer hospitality has a high place. This virtue is to be found in solitary places the world over. Its two blending motives are compassion for a stranger, and curiosity to learn whatever news he may bring; and both motives are creditable.

While we cannot here trace all the social codes of mountain life, it is important to note that there are social codes and moral standards which are most strictly observed. Herein the "mountain white" shows his genus. It is his social standards and his independent spirit that prove his worth, or at least his promise. He is not a degraded being, although, to tell the truth, he has not yet been graded up! The "poor whites" were degraded by actual competition with slave labor. The "mountain whites" had little contact with slavery, and retained that independent spirit which everywhere belongs to the owners of land. Mr. John Fox, Jr., is responsible for the statement that when a man was sent with a sum of money to relieve distress in a plague-stricken district in the mountains of Kentucky, he could find none who would confess their need, and rode for days without being able to execute his commission. The mountaineer is not a suppliant for old clothes. When Mr. Fox gave a reading from his Cumberland tales in Berea, the mountain boys were ready to mob him. They had no comprehension of the nature of fiction. Mr. Fox's stories were either true or false. If they were true, then he was "no gentleman" for telling all the family affairs of people who had entertained him with their best. If they were not true, then, of course, they were libelous upon the mountain people! Such an attitude may remind us of the general condemnation of fiction by the "unco' gude" a generation ago. [. . .]

Though the points of resemblance between these lonely people of the hills and our forefathers on the bleak New England shore are numerous and striking, there are one or two points of contrast which place them very far apart. Judged by modern standards, the early settlers in the New World were rude of speech, and stinted in all material resources. More than this, they were but babes in all scientific conceptions, and strangers to many of the ideas with which every modern child is familiar. They were crude, poor, narrow, *but they were at the head of the procession.* They shared the best thought of their time, and were consciously in motion. They were inspired by the great task of nation building. The mountain folk, on the contrary, the best of them, are consciously stranded. They are behind relatively as well as absolutely, and their pride is all the more vehement because conscious of an insecure foundation. Shy, sensitive, undemonstrative, the mountain man and woman are pathetically belated. The generations of scorn from the surrounding lowlands have almost convinced them, inwardly, that "what is, must be," and they are but feebly struggling with destiny.

Such people are so far out of touch with modern life that they surprise and disappoint some who, without intimate acquaintance, try to give them assistance. Few teachers can really begin simply enough, and condescend to teach the things which "we always knew." I recall a breezy mountain top, and a young hunter—a Doryphorus rather than an Apollo—whose woodcraft had won my admiration. Delicately I touched upon the question of education.

"Can you write numbers?"

The answer came slow and guarded.

"Reckon I can write some numbers."

Then on a piece of bark I drew the nine digits. He read them all. Next came the combination of figures, and I included the date 1897.

"I don't guess I can tell that thar."

I explained it. And then a new test occurred to me.

"Do you know what 1897 means?"

"Hit's the year, hain't hit?"

"But why is this year called 1897? It is 1897 years since what?"

"I never heard tell."

Another instance came to light through the distribution of reading matter. When I was young in the mountains I distributed a barrel of copies of the New York Independent, and had great satisfaction in observing the eagerness with which they were taken. A little later I discovered that these simple folk could not comprehend the high themes discussed in that excellent periodical, and that their eagerness was only to secure paper for the walls of their cabins! Yet in many places a mere scrap of printed paper will be cherished. More than once one of our extension lecturers has been intercepted in attempting to throw into the fire the paper which had been wrapped around some toilet article.

"Don't burn thet thar, stranger, hit mought have some news on hit." [. . .]

How the mountains are to be enlightened, however, is a double problem; first as to the means, and secondly as to the method. The first question is one of philanthropy, and the second question is one of pedagogics. There could not be a clearer call for the intervention of intelligent, patriotic assistance. We are sometimes remonstrated with for breaking in upon this Arcadian simplicity, and we have had our own misgivings. But it must be remembered that ruthless change is knocking at the door of every mountain cabin. The jackals of civilization have already abused the confidence of many a highland home. The lumber, coal, and mineral wealth of the mountains is to be possessed, and the unprincipled vanguard of commercialism can easily debauch a simple people. The question is whether the mountain people can be enlightened and guided so that they can have a part in the development of their own country, or whether they must give place to foreigners and melt away like so many Indians.

The means for extending this saving aid must be furnished by the patriotic people of the nation. It cannot be left to the states concerned; for these are all poor Southern states, inexperienced in popular education. Appalachian America is a ward of the nation, such a ward as we have never had before. The mountain man is not to be compared with the negro, except in the basal fact of need. Nor can he be compared with the Western pioneer, for the Western frontier had always a certain proportion of educated leaders, and it was closely knit by family and commercial ties with the older and richer parts of the land. But Appalachian America is a frontier without any related back tier, and must be dealt with accordingly.

The question of the method by which these contemporary ancestors of ours are to be put in step with the world is an educational one. I wish only to bring forward two suggestions. In the first place, the aim should be to make them intelligent without making them sophisticated. As a matter both of taste and of common sense, we should not try to make them conform to the regulation type of Americans; they should be encouraged to retain all that is characteristic and wholesome in their present life. Let us not set them agog to rush into the competition of cities, but show them how to get the blessings of culture where they are. Let them not be taught to despise the log cabin, but to adorn it. So, too, the whole aim of our aid should be to make them able to help themselves. Industrial education, instruction in the care of their forests, rotation of crops, and similar elementary matters will make them sharers in the gifts of science. Normal instruction will help them to get some benefit from the newly organized and very inadequate public schools. Publications adapted to their present needs, and university extension lectures upon such elementary themes as hygiene, United States history, and settling quarrels without bloodshed, are in order.

John Fox Jr.
1862–1919

John Fox Jr. was born in the central Kentucky Bluegrass county of Bourbon, where his father ran a well-respected co-educational school. At the age of sixteen, Fox entered Harvard on a scholarship funded by Bourbon County's Garth Fund for Poor Boys. After graduating, he lived in New York, where he wrote for various newspapers and magazines. In 1885 he returned to eastern Kentucky to work in the office of a coal mine in which one of his nine brothers had interests.

In 1895, shortly after Fox moved to Big Stone Gap, Virginia, the first of his sizeable body of mountain novels and short stories was published. Fox's fiction met with immediate and continuing success. Fox was also well known throughout the United States and Europe for his lectures on mountain life, which included demonstrations of mountain speech and banjo playing.

Fox's reputation today is mixed. Much of his fiction remains in print, and Big Stone Gap capitalizes on its association with Fox through its John Fox, Jr. Museum and its annual staging of a theatrical adaptation of *The Trail of the Lonesome Pine* (1908), one of Fox's most popular novels, which the state of Virginia designated as its state play. Although Fox claimed that his depictions of mountain life were accurate, that assertion has been challenged, as has his belief that geographic isolation led to a retardation of mountain culture. His reliance on mountain stereotypes leads some critics to categorize his work as belonging to the local color literary movement while others emphasize his connections with realism in American fiction.

The Pardon of Becky Day

The missionary was young and she was from the North. Her brows were straight, her nose was rather high, and her eyes were clear and gray. The upper lip of her little mouth was so short that the teeth just under it were never quite concealed. It was the mouth of a child and it gave the face, with all its strength and high purpose, a peculiar pathos that no soul in that little mountain town had the power to see or feel. A yellow mule was hitched to the rickety fence in front of her and she stood on the stoop of a little white frame-house with an elm switch between her teeth and gloves on her hands, which were white and looked strong. The mule wore a man's saddle, but no matter—the streets were full of yellow pools, the mud was ankle-deep, and she was on her way to the sick-bed of Becky Day.

There was a flood that morning. All the preceding day the rains had drenched the high slopes unceasingly. That night, the rain-clear forks of the Kentucky got yellow and rose high, and now they crashed together around the town and, after a heaving conflict, started the river on one quivering, majestic sweep to the sea.

Nobody gave heed that the girl rode a mule or that the saddle was not her own, and both facts she herself quickly forgot. This half log, half frame house on a corner had stood a siege once. She could yet see bullet holes about the door. Through this window, a revenue officer from the Blue Grass had got a bullet in the shoulder from a garden in the rear. Standing in the post-office door only just one month before, she herself had seen children scurrying like rabbits through the back-yard fences, men running silently here and there, men dodging into doorways, fire flashing in the street and from every house—and not a sound but the crack of pistol and Winchester; for the mountain men deal death in all the terrible silence of death. And now a preacher with a long scar across his forehead had come to the one little church in the place and the fervor of religion was struggling with feudal hate for possession of the town. To the girl, who saw a symbol in every mood of the earth, the passions of these primitive people were like the treacherous streams of the uplands—now quiet as sunny skies and now clashing together with but little less fury and with much more noise. And the roar of the flood above the wind that late afternoon was the wrath of the Father, that with the peace of the Son so long on earth, such things still could be. Once more trouble was threatening and that day even she knew that trouble might come, but she rode without fear, for she went when and where she pleased as any woman can, throughout the Cumberland, without insult or harm.

At the end of the street were two houses that seemed to front each other with unmistakable enmity. In them were two men who had wounded each other only the day before, and who that day would lead the factions, if the old feud broke loose again. One house was close to the frothing hem of the flood—a log-hut with a shed of rough boards for a kitchen—the home of Becky Day.

The other was across the way and was framed and smartly painted. On the steps sat a woman with her head bare and her hands under her apron—widow of the Marcum whose death from a bullet one month before had broken the long truce of the feud. A groaning curse was growled from the window as the girl drew near, and she knew it came from a wounded Marcum who had lately come back from the West to avenge his brother's death.

"Why don't you go over to see your neighbor?" The girl's clear eyes gave no hint that she knew—as she well did—the trouble between the houses, and the widow stared in sheer amazement, for mountaineers do not talk with strangers of the quarrels between them.

"I have nothin' to do with such as her," she said, sullenly; "she ain't the kind—"

"Don't!" said the girl, with a flush, "she's dying."

"*Dyin'?*"

"Yes." With the word the girl sprang from the mule and threw the reins over the pale of the fence in front of the log-hut across the way. In the doorway she turned as though she would speak to the woman on the steps again, but a tall man with a black beard appeared in the low door of the kitchen-shed.

"How is your—how is Mrs. Day?"

"Mighty puny this mornin'—Becky is."

The girl slipped into the dark room. On a disordered, pillowless bed lay a white face with eyes closed and mouth slightly open. Near the bed was a low wood fire. On the hearth were several thick cups filled with herbs and heavy fluids and covered with tarpaulin, for Becky's "man" was a teamster. With a few touches of the girl's quick hands, the covers of the bed were smooth, and the woman's eyes rested on the girl's own cloak. With her own handkerchief she brushed the death-damp from the forehead that already seemed growing cold. At her first touch, the woman's eyelids opened and dropped together again. Her lips moved, but no sound came from them.

In a moment the ashes disappeared, the hearth was clean and the fire was blazing. Every time the girl passed the window she saw the widow across the way staring hard at the hut. When she took the ashes into the street, the woman spoke to her.

"I can't go to see Becky—she hates me."

"With good reason."

The answer came with a clear sharpness that made the widow start and redden angrily; but the girl walked straight to the gate, her eyes ablaze with all the courage that the mountain woman knew and yet with another courage to which the primitive creature was a stranger—a courage that made the widow lower her own eyes and twist her hands under her apron.

"I want you to come and ask Becky to forgive you."

The woman stared and laughed.

"Forgive me? Becky forgive me? She wouldn't—an' I don't want her—" She could not look up into the girl's eyes; but she pulled a pipe from under the apron, laid it down with a trembling hand and began to rock slightly.

The girl leaned across the gate.

"Look at me!" she said, sharply. The woman raised her eyes, swerved them once, and then in spite of herself, held them steady.

"Listen! Do you want a dying woman's curse?"

It was a straight thrust to the core of a superstitious heart and a spasm of terror crossed the woman's face. She began to wring her hands.

"Come on!" said the girl, sternly, and turned, without looking back, until she reached the door of the hut, where she beckoned and stood waiting, while the woman started slowly and helplessly from the steps, still wringing her hands. Inside, behind her, the wounded Marcum, who had been listening, raised himself on one elbow and looked after her through the window.

"She can't come in—not while I'm in here."

The girl turned quickly. It was Dave Day, the teamster, in the kitchen door, and his face looked blacker than his beard.

"Oh!" she said, simply, as though hurt, and then with a dignity that surprised her, the teamster turned and strode towards the back door.

"But I can git out, I reckon," he said, and he never looked at the widow who had stopped, frightened, at the gate.

"Oh, I can't—I *can't!*" she said, and her voice broke; but the girl gently pushed her to the door, where she stopped again, leaning against the lintel. Across the way, the wounded Marcum, with a scowl of wonder, crawled out of his bed and started painfully to the door. The girl saw him and her heart beat fast.

Inside, Becky lay with closed eyes. She stirred uneasily, as though she felt some hated presence, but her eyes stayed fast, for the presence of Death in the room was stronger still.

"Becky!" At the broken cry, Becky's eyes flashed wide and fire broke through the haze that had gathered in them.

"I want ye ter fergive me, Becky."

The eyes burned steadily for a long time. For two days she had not spoken, but her voice came now, as though from the grave.

"You!" she said, and, again, with torturing scorn, "You!" And then she smiled, for she knew why her enemy was there, and her hour of triumph was come. The girl moved swiftly to the window—she could see the wounded Marcum slowly crossing the street, pistol in hand.

"What'd I ever do to you?"

"Nothin', Becky, nothin'."

Becky laughed harshly. "You can tell the truth—can't ye—to a dyin' woman?"

"Fergive me, Becky!"

A scowling face, tortured with pain, was thrust into the window.

"Sh-h!" whispered the girl, imperiously, and the man lifted his heavy eyes, dropped one elbow on the window-sill and waited.

"You tuk Jim from me!"

The widow covered her face with her hands, and the Marcum at the window—brother to Jim, who was dead—lowered at her, listening keenly.

"An' you got him by lyin' 'bout me. You tuk him by lyin' 'bout me—didn't ye? Didn't ye?" she repeated, fiercely, and her voice would have wrung the truth from a stone.

"Yes—Becky—yes!"

"You hear?" cried Becky, turning her eyes to the girl.

"You made him believe an' made ever'body, you could, believe that I was—was *bad.*" Her breath got short but the terrible arraignment went on.

"You started this war. My brother wouldn't 'a' shot Jim Marcum if it hadn't been fer you. You killed Jim—your own husband—an' you killed *me.* An' now you want me to fergive you—you!" She raised her right hand as though with it she would hurl the curse behind her lips, and the widow, with a cry, sprang for the bony fingers, catching them in her own hand and falling over on her knees at the bedside.

"Don't, Becky, don't—don't—*don't!*"

There was a slight rustle at the back window. At the other, a pistol flashed into sight and dropped again below the sill. Turning, the girl saw Dave's bushy black head—he, too, with one elbow on the sill and the other hand out of sight.

"Shame!" she said, looking from one to the other of the two men, who had learned, at last, the bottom truth of the feud; and then she caught the sick woman's other hand and spoke quickly:

"Hush, Becky," she said; and at the touch of her hand and the sound of her voice, Becky looked confusedly at her and let her upraised hand sink back to the bed. The widow stared swiftly from Jim's brother, at one window, to Dave Day at the other, and hid her face on her arms.

"Remember, Becky—how can you expect forgiveness in another world, unless you forgive in this?"

The woman's brow knitted and she lay quiet. Like the widow who held her hand, the dying woman believed, with never the shadow of a doubt, that somewhere above the stars, a living God reigned in a heaven of never-ending happiness; that somewhere beneath the earth a personal devil gloated over souls in eternal torture; that whether she went above, or below, hung solely on her last hour of contrition; and that in heaven or hell she would know those whom she might meet as surely as she had known them on earth. By and by her face softened and she drew a long breath.

"Jim was a good man," she said. And then after a moment:

"An' I was a good woman"—she turned her eyes towards the girl—"until Jim married *her*. I didn't keer after that." Then she got calm, and while she spoke to the widow, she looked at the girl.

"Will you git up in church an' say before ever'body that you knew I was *good* when you said I was bad—that you lied about me?"

"Yes—yes." Still Becky looked at the girl, who stooped again.

"She will, Becky, I know she will. Won't you forgive her and leave peace behind you? Dave and Jim's brother are here—make them shake hands. Won't you—won't you?" she asked, turning from one to the other.

Both men were silent.

"Won't you?" she repeated, looking at Jim's brother.

"I've got nothin' agin Dave. I always thought that she"—he did not call his brother's wife by name—"caused all this trouble. I've nothin' agin Dave."

The girl turned. "Won't you, Dave?"

"I'm waitin' to hear whut Becky says."

Becky was listening, though her eyes were closed. Her brows knitted painfully. It was a hard compromise that she was asked to make between mortal hate and a love that was more than mortal, but the Plea that has stood between them for nearly twenty centuries prevailed, and the girl knew that the end of the feud was nigh.

Becky nodded.

"Yes, I fergive her, an' I want 'em to shake hands."

But not once did she turn her eyes to the woman whom she forgave, and the hand that the widow held gave back no answering pressure. The faces at the windows disappeared, and she motioned for the girl to take her weeping enemy away.

She did not open her eyes when the girl came back, but her lips moved and the girl bent above her.

"I know whar Jim is."

From somewhere outside came Dave's cough, and the dying woman turned her head as though she were reminded of something she had quite forgotten. Then, straightway, she forgot again.

The voice of the flood had deepened. A smile came to Becky's lips—a faint, terrible smile of triumph. The girl bent low and, with a startled face, shrank back.

"*An' I'll—git—thar—first.*"

With that whisper went Becky's last breath, but the smile was there, even when her lips were cold.

Effie Waller Smith

1879–1960

Much of the biographical information about poet Effie Waller Smith comes from oral history. Smith's parents were born into slavery. After their marriage, they settled in Pike County, Kentucky, in a racially mixed community. Effie's family became financially secure, and she and her two siblings attended local segregated schools before progressing to the Kentucky Normal School for Colored Persons in Frankfort. All three became teachers.

From 1901 until 1916, Effie Waller Smith taught school in Kentucky and East Tennessee. In Pike County, she became known as "the singing poet of the Cumberlands" who sometimes dismissed school early and spent the afternoon exploring nature with her students. Smith enjoyed hiking in the rugged Breaks region along the Kentucky-Virginia border, finding inspiration in nature for her writing. Smith's first publications were in local newspapers. With the encouragement and possible financial support of white readers in Pikeville, Kentucky, she published her first book of poetry, *Songs of the Months* (1904). In 1909, she published two more books of poetry: *Rhymes from the Cumberlands* and *Rosemary and Pansies*. Smith's short stories and poems also appeared in national publications such as *Putnam's Monthly*.

Answer to Verses Addressed to Me by Peter Clay

Backward down the stream of time
   My wandering mind now floats,
When I a hoyden country lass,
   In homespun petticoats

That reached down to my ankles bare,
   Ankles bare and brown, too;
Not browned by summer suns, for birth
   Had giv'n to them that hue.

I think now of those days when hills
   And vales with music rang,
Of which in crude, uneven,
   Yet rhythmic, words, I sang.

And I'm thinking, poet friend,
   How you have, oftentimes,

Admired with pure unselfishness
   Those simple, homely rhymes.

For 'tis the genius of the soul
   (Though underneath a skin
Of dusky hue its fire may burn)
   Your unfeigned praises win.

Oh, that earth had more of beings
   With generous minds like yours,
Who alike, true worth and honor
   To the black and white secures.

Accept, dear poet, then, my thanks
   For your glowing words of praise,
For the simple, homely, faulty rhymes
   Of my early girlhood days.

The "Bachelor Girl"

She's no "old maid," she's not afraid
   To let you know she's her own "boss,"
She's easy pleased, she's not diseased,
   She is not nervous, is not cross.

She's no desire whatever for
   Mrs. to precede her name,
The blessedness of singleness
   She all her life will proudly claim.

She does not sit around and knit
   On baby caps and mittens,
She does not play her time away
   With puggy dogs and kittens.

And if a mouse about the house
   She sees, she will not jump and scream;
Of handsome beaux and billet doux
   The "bachelor girl" does never dream.

She does not puff and frizz and fluff
   Her hair, nor squeeze and pad her form.

With painted face, affected grace,
    The "bachelor girl" ne'er seeks to charm.

She reads history, biography,
    Tales of adventure far and near,
On sea or land, but poetry and
    Love stories rarely interest her.

She's lots of wit, and uses it,
    Of "horse sense," too, she has a store;
The latest news she always knows
    She scans the daily papers o'er.

Of politics and all the tricks
    And schemes that politicians use,
She knows full well and she can tell
    With eloquence of them her views.

An athlete that's hard to beat
    The "bachelor girl" surely is,
When playing games she makes good aims
    And always strictly minds her "biz."

Amid the hurry and the flurry
    Of this life she goes alone,
No matter where you may see her
    She seldom has a chaperon.

But when you meet her on the street
    At night she has a "32,"
And she can shoot you, bet your boots,
    When necessity demands her to.

Her heart is kind and you will find
    Her often scattering sunshine bright
Among the poor, and she is sure
    To always advocate the right.

On her *pater* and her *mater*
    For her support she does not lean,
She talks and writes of "Woman's Rights"
    In language forceful and clean.

She does not shirk, but does her work,
  Amid the world's fast hustling whirl,
And come what may, she's here to stay,
  The self-supporting "bachelor girl."

Emma Bell Miles
1879–1919

Emma Bell Miles was born in Evansville, Indiana. Her parents were teachers, and in 1890, to improve Emma's faltering health, the family moved from the Cincinnati area to Walden's Ridge (now Signal Mountain) near Chattanooga, Tennessee. There, Miles grew up with her feet in two worlds—the rural mountain culture of Walden's Ridge and the world of art and books represented by her parents and the wealthy Chattanoogans vacationing nearby.

Miles evinced considerable artistic talent as a child, and in 1899, her parents sent her to the St. Louis School of Art in Missouri, which had one of the best art programs for women in the United States. In 1901, she married Frank Miles, a native of Walden's Ridge. The marriage was difficult; among other challenges, Frank was unable to hold a job, forcing the frail Emma to generate an income by selling her artwork and lecturing to Chattanooga's thriving arts community. Emma contemplated ending the marriage but was unable to make a permanent break.

Emma Bell Miles said that as a young girl she was educated by reading *Harper's Monthly*. Her own poetry and prose began appearing in the magazine in 1904. *The Spirit of the Mountains* (1905) joined an outpouring of magazine articles and books about southern mountain life that appeared in the late nineteenth and early twentieth centuries. As opposed to stock depictions of mountaineers as quaint, isolated, or violent, Miles's descriptions, although somewhat romanticized, present a nuanced portrait of Southern Appalachian people and folkways. The book was based on direct observation and employs rhetorical techniques of nonfiction; however, Miles did fictionalize neighbors, relatives, and places connected with Walden's Ridge. The book had limited sales, but its influence was considerable. Horace Kephart quoted extensively from it in *Our Southern Highlanders* (1913).

FROM The Spirit of the Mountains

FROM CHAPTER III: GRANDMOTHERS AND SONS

"There's more marries than keeps cold meat."

The best society in the mountains—that is to say, the most interesting—is that of the young married men and that of the older women. The young people are so shy that they can hardly be said to form a part of society at all. They are hedged with conventions and meet almost as formally as young Japanese. For example, on entering church the men are expected to turn to the left and seat themselves, and the women to the right. It is permitted a young fellow who is avowedly out courting to sit beside his "gal," but I cannot imagine what would happen if a young woman were to place herself on the men's side of the house.

After marriage something of the young man's shyness wears off; he gradually loses his awe of the opposite sex, and even within the conventions he finds room for intelligent conversation. Then he begins to be interesting, for his twenty-odd years of outdoor experience have really taught him much. As for the woman, it is not until she has seen her own boys grown to be men that she loses entirely the bashfulness of her girlhood, and the innate beauty and dignity of her nature shines forth in help-fulness and counsel.

I have learned to enjoy the company of these old prophetesses almost more than any other. The range of their experience is wonderful; they are, moreover, reposito-ries of tribal lore—tradition and song, medical and religious learning. They are the nurses, the teachers of practical arts, the priestesses, and their wisdom commands the respect of all. An old woman has usually more authority over the bad boys of a household than all the strength of man. A similar reverence may have been accorded to the mothers of ancient Israel, as it is given by all peoples to those of superior holi-ness—to priests, teachers, nuns; it is not the result of affection, still less of fear.

It was Lute Purvine—"Clodpoll"—who brought me word that Aunt Genevy Rog-ers was about to put a coverlet into her loom. As I had often expressed a wish to see a really fine web in the process of making, she invited me to come and watch the very beginning of the work. [. . .]

Another visitor arrived in a few moments, a bare-footed woman, clad in a single faded calico garment. I learned that she was Mary Burns, and that her husband was helping with the logs. She sat on the edge of the porch, refusing a chair, as if accus-tomed to dropping down anywhere. In spite of approaching maternity, to which she was evidently quite near, she was almost beautiful. I say almost, because she was hardly clean and her hair had not been combed in weeks—perhaps not thoroughly dressed since she was married.

"Air ye feelin' any better to-day, Mary?" inquired Aunt Genevy. "Law, I know jist how ye feel. Hit shore is miser'ble. The winter John was born we didn't have no tur-nips, nor 'taters, nor nothin'; the fence was so bad the hogs had broke in and eat 'em about all—and Zach he was away might' near all his time a-huntin' and cyard-playin' with a passel o' fool boys, and I had all o' my firewood to git, with jist what help sister Lou could give me—and Lou was jist a little gal then that I didn't dast hardly let go to the spring by herself."

The woman replied in a monotone slower and sweeter even than Aunt Genevy's: "I'm glad hit's hot enough so'st I ain't needin' any wood. I git chips over thar where Gid's a-workin' to cook his meals; but hit shore gits away with me a-packin' water up the hill from the spring."

She looked up with a smile such as I have rarely seen on any but a baby's face, showing teeth as white and small as a child's.

"Yes, I know how that is, too," said the old woman. "When Lizzie was crawlin'— she was my second baby, the one that died—I'd take her and the bucket and start, and when I got to the top o' the hill I'd set her on the ground and go down to the spring, and git her as I come back. I always did think, though, hit was settin' in them damp bushes that started her to bein' sick all the time. Of course, I had to git water on rainy days the same as any others, and I was afeared to leave her in the house with the fire. I've knowed of two babies bein' burnt to death while their mothers was out a-workin' . . . Law, I know all about children, Mary, and work, too. Mine was never more'n two year apart. Don't you lose heart, Mary; there's better days a-comin' for ye whenever this is over."

She meant, as I discovered later, more than she said in the last sentence. It was known in the neighborhood that Gideon Burns, although not a pronounced drunkard or villain, was cruel to his wife beyond what is usual to mountain men. He never struck her, or, if he did, it was not known; and Mary rarely complained. But the sympathy of the neighbor women was with her, and the more experienced hoped that the coming of the child would work a change.

Uncle Zach and the boys came in presently, and we all sat down to dinner round the table in the open entry. Rilley's three children ate with us, and some others I did not know, who had been playing about all morning. During the meal I noticed that Mary Burns was particularly urged to take her time and eat a portion of everything before her.

"Why, do you like them pickles?" said Aunt Genevy, as if surprised. "We're all tired of 'em; I put 'em on the table and they ain't tetched." This was not quite true. "I'll jist put the rest into a bowl for ye whenever ye git ready to go home. Now, Rilley, don't ye let me forget 'em. But don't you be in a hurry, Mary. I'm a-fixin' to put in some chain a'ter dinner, and you can stay and talk to me or Rilley, jist as you please." [. . .]

"Hit's gittin' hot," [Mary] complained; and presently said: "Mis' Rogers, I hate to be so much trouble to you'ns, but my head's achin' so bad. I'd like to git your comb a while to comb my hair. I had a tuckin'-comb a while back—hit ust to be mammy's— but them hounds o' Gid's chawed hit up last week."

Aunt Genevy told her where she might find the comb, and Mary brought it and let down her hair. What a web, what a cloak it spread over her shoulders! So matted was it that at first one could not be sure of its texture. But its color was chestnut, glinting gold, and its length and weight were extraordinary. I soon saw that she could never untangle it alone, and went to her assistance. Her pain must have been excruciating; in spite of care, handfuls came away by the roots. But she did not complain, and by patient persistence we straightened out the mouse-nests and witch-bridles lock by lock, until at last the whole mass flowed smoothly, waving around her beautiful face. [. . .]

And with all her beauty she had not even the mountain woman's poor best of cheap calico to wear! I tried to imagine her dressed in a white dimity such as young girls wear in more favored regions, but even this seemed incongruous, although she could not have been more than seventeen years old. As we coiled and fastened her hair I asked if she were going to the feet-washing, knowing how dear to the mountaineer heart is the privilege of attending every form of religious service.

"I reckon not," she answered, in her sweet, hushed, nun-like tones. "I ain't been to church sence my shoes wore out, some time last March." So she had trodden the freezing mud of early April with bare feet! It would never have occurred to her to hide her poverty or her present physical distress; she hardly realized that in this respect, also, she was ill-used by her husband. [. . .]

Next morning a commotion in the road brought me to the window. A man on a mule, riding without bridle or saddle, was scaring all the pigs and chickens round the barn gate. He had a tin bucket in his hands, and was thumping it to frighten the mule, that sidled and reared, only to be gripped into submission by the rider's strong legs. The fellow was ragged enough, but splendidly built and tall, with a strong, good-humored, rather sensual face.

That was all I had time to notice. He galloped on to the barn, somehow caused the beast to come to a stop with a plunge, and then sent a curious call or whoop ringing all over the farm. Seldom have I seen in a grown man such a display of sheer boyish spirits. Uncle Zach went to the barn and took charge of the mule, that, it appeared, had been caught straying near Burns' cabin, and the man strode away with his bucket. I heard him yodeling musically away through the woods.

"That's a sight of a feller, that Gid Burns," was the old man's comment as he came in to breakfast. "Said he 'lowed to git a bucket o' water as he went back by the spring. Fust thing I ever knowed him to do for that woman o' hisn." [. . .]

There was to be preaching Sunday morning at the church, and we all made ready to go, Rilley and John and the old folks, the two younger boys and I. Mary Burns was sitting on her doorstep as we passed, and looked up with her smile.

"Has she no kinfolks at all?" I inquired. She had, it appeared, a father, and married brothers and sisters, living at some distance in the other valley; but she did not know how to write to send them a letter. They were honest people, said Uncle Zach. The oldest brother, a stone-cutter, was well-to-do. Her father lived on his own farm. I knew better than to interfere by so much as a word, or I should have advised the poor child to make her way back to her father's house, where, by all the traditions of the land, she should have been well and tactfully received. But I do not think she would have wished to go.

Gid Burns was at church. He sat with the younger men of the congregation—that is, near the door, on the left. His elders and the pillars of the church, with a visiting preacher or two and the man who was expected to lead the singing, occupied the front seats and the "amen corner." Aunt Genevy walked straight up to the front. Rilley and her children sat a little way behind her. The boys did not come in at all, preferring to remain with their fellows outside until the last bell rang, when they would slip quietly into the rearmost seats. Thus is precedence managed in the mountains.

Burns added a rich and powerful untrained tenor voice to "Some Have Mothers in the Promised Land," and seemed very attentive to the sermon. When meeting was out he was invited to a seat in our wagon, and accepted courteously and promptly. He and Uncle Zach exchanged views on the preacher's doctrine, and, although neither could read, they quoted a number of texts with tolerable accuracy, while we women and Rilley's children remained meekly and decorously silent. [. . .]

In the same abstract way Gid prated on of righteousness, temperance and judgment to come, without a thought of his own selfishness, since the victim of it was only a woman, and his wife at that. The adolescent male of the human species has, even under civilization, an inborn contempt for girls. And this feeling in the mountaineer's maturity is superseded by a sort of wondering, half-amused pity. In Gideon's mind the pity had not yet arrived.

His strong teeth flashed, his eyes gleamed as he talked. There was undeniably a certain charm about him. He was simply a young savage with an overabundance of energy.

As we neared his hut a smoke of cooking rose from its chimney. Gid leaped over the revolving wheel, inviting us all in to dinner, as part of a habit of hospitality. I do not think he realized that acceptance was out of the question. Through the door I saw poor Mary, stooping painfully over her fire of gathered chips, sick, overheated, and probably suffering in ways of which we did not know. A few hours later she sent a little neighbor girl in haste to Aunt Genevy.

I would have accompanied Aunt Genevy to the hut across the fields, but was required to stay and set up supper for Uncle Zach and the boys, who wished to go back to the feet-washing that night.

At last, when the night-work was done and the table cleared—the boys helping me far more than they were wont to help their mother—I was free to take my way through the soft dusk to Burns' cabin. I was ready to cry with anxiety. Aunt Genevy opened the door for me, and as she drank the hot coffee I had brought I heard the faint mewing of a new little voice. She and Mary had got through the awful hour quite alone—Gid had not put in an appearance since dinner—and she had just completed the dressing of the baby with such old flour-sacks as lay at hand. There was no light save a lantern that was used for 'possum-hunting in 'possum-time. The new mother moaned bitterly on her wretched pallet. A kettle of steaming water sat on the stones which served the purpose of fire-irons, and this I was bidden to replenish. Next I took charge of the little one, while Aunt Genevy, herself weary almost unto death, lessened the woman's discomfort as far as was possible.

At ten o'clock or thereabouts she told me I might go. "And send down Zach or Luther with some things you'll find tied up in a bundle under the head of my bed— jist as soon as they git home. I was aimin' to fetch 'em, but I forgot."

"Can't I bring them and stay with you?" I asked.

"You'd best git the boys and Zach some breakfast in the morning, if ye will," answered this old mountain woman, ever mindful of her man's comfort, although her own loss of food and sleep might be making her faint. And so I left, promising to bring her and Mary some breakfast before sunrise.

Gideon, having been informed by Uncle Zach at church of what was probably taking place at his house, did not return that night. But he was there before me in the morning. The breakfast I had carried across the field was not more than enough for two, but he accepted a portion when it was offered him, Aunt Genevy declaring that she had slept several hours and was able to go home for her breakfast by-and-by.

"You hain't never looked at this big, fine boy yit," she said, with a little diffidence, and threw the door wide open for the sake of light as Burns, awkwardly and reluctantly, tiptoed to the bed. Mary raised the blanket, and the man peered down at the brown-velvet skull and red, wrinkled forehead which alone were visible.

"Hello, Buster!" he said, clearing his throat huskily. "Git up and go with pappy to ketch a 'possum!" Then he let down the ragged blanket gingerly and inquired: "Ain't he liable to smother?" And then: "Hain't ye got nary dress that'll fit him?"

"I ain't got nothin' to make one out of," answered his wife, with the indifference of weakness and, I thought, despair.

Indeed, I felt my own sensibilities numbed by his lack of concern in the matter. He meandered about the room a little, evidently ill at ease, and suddenly broke out: "Well, I expect I'll have to go to the store."

And then I could have boxed his ears.

But he went on, still with the same unconcern of manner and immobility of countenance: "I'll git this big man a suit o' clothes. Anything you want from thar, Mary?"

The woman's lids flew wide and a sudden radiance dispelled the weariness on her face. I wondered anew how the man could fail to be charmed by her beauty. I should have known that the first bond established between the primitive mother and her baby is that of being alike temporarily repulsive to their lord and master, and so companions in crime. She answered, quicker than I had ever heard her speak: "Yes, Gid; I want me a tuckin'-comb and some crackers and—and—a pair o' shoes."

She need not have faltered over the latter request. Gideon merely extracted a handful of small change from his clothes, counted his two dollars and odd cents deliberately, and said: "Well, I expect this'll git 'em, and some dinner besides. Much obleeged to you'ns. I'll git back ag'in dinner-time." And he shut the door behind him.

"Praise God!" muttered the old woman.

I looked at Mary Burns. Her face had taken the expression of a happy child's, and she was gazing at the little elevation of the blanket beside her. Then, because it was imperative I should go home that morning, I left them there together, the old woman and the young; the one with her hardships and suffering like a lesson learned and mastered, the other with her eyes just opened on its meaning.

I have never seen Gideon Burns nor his wife since that hour. But I have seen hundreds like them in the mountains, hundreds robbed of life's sweetest gift by the continual failure of well-meant efforts to bridge the gulf fixed by the mountaineers between woman and man.

At twenty the mountain woman is old in all that makes a woman old—toil, sorrow, child-bearing, loneliness and pitiful want. She knows the weight not only of her own years; she has dwelt since childhood in the shadow of centuries gone. The house she lives in is nearly always old—that is to say, a house with a history, a house thronged with memories of other lives. Her new carpet even, so gay on the rude puncheons, was made of old clothes and scraps of cloth. Who wove the cloth? It was woven on her grandmother's loom. Yes, and she knows who built the loom. The marks of his simple tools are on its timbers still. Into her pretty patchwork she puts her babies' outgrown frocks, mingling their bright hues with the garments of a dead mother or sister, setting the pattern together finally with the white in which she was married, or the calico she wore to play-parties when a girl. Perhaps she keeps her butter in a cedar keeler or piggin that her grandfather made. At all events she churns it in a home-made churn. Her door swings on huge wooden hinges. Who made them? In what fray was the oak latch dented and split, and who mended it with a scrap of iron? How many feet have worn down the middle of the doorstep-stone! How many hearth-fires have sent their smoke in blue acrid puffs to darken the rafters! How many storms have beaten the hand-cleft shingles of the roof and strained at the mortised joints of its timbers!

Thus it comes that early in childhood she grows into dim consciousness of the vastness of human experience and the nobility of it. She learns to look upon the common human lot as a high calling. She gains the courage of the fatalist; the surety that nothing can happen which has not happened before; that, whatever she may be called upon to endure, she will yet know that others have undergone its like over and over again. Her lot is inevitably one of service and of suffering, and refines only as it is meekly and sweetly borne. For this reason she is never quite commonplace. To her mind nothing is trivial, all things being great with a meaning of divine purpose. And if as a corollary of this belief she is given to an absurd faith in petty signs and omens, who is to laugh at her?

Is it sickness? How many have lain in agony unto death on her old four-poster bed! Has her husband ill-treated her? She can endure without answering back. She has heard her elders tell of so many young husbands! Her dead babe? So many born here have slept and laughed for a time beside that hearth and dropped from the current of life!

She has heard the stories of everything in the house, from the brown and cracked old cups and bowls to the roof-beams themselves, until they have become her literature. From them she borrows a sublime silent courage and patience in the hour of trial. From their tragedies she learns, too, a sense of the immanent supernatural. It is almost as if they were haunted by audible and visible ghosts. Who would not fear to sit alone with old furniture that bears marks of blows, stains of blood and tears? They are friendly, too. They stand about her with the sympathy of like experience in times of distress and grief. This is one of the reasons why a mountain woman usually shows a disproportionate reluctance to selling her spinning-wheel or four-poster, even though the price offered be a bribe beyond imagination to one who sees whole dollars every day.

Few of these things become part of the man's life. Men do not live in the house. They commonly come in to eat and sleep, but their life is outdoors, foot-loose in the new forest or on the farm that renews itself crop by crop. His is the high daring and merciless recklessness of youth and the characteristic grim humor of the American, these though he live to be a hundred. Heartily, then, he conquers his chosen bit of wilderness, and heartily begets and rules his tribe, fighting and praying alike fearlessly and exultantly. Let the woman's part be to preserve tradition. His are the adventures of which future ballads will be sung. He is tempted to eagle flights across the valleys. For him is the excitement of fighting and journeying, trading, drinking and hunting, of wild rides and nights of danger. To the woman, in place of these, are long nights of anxious watching by the sick, or of waiting in dreary discomfort the uncertain result of an expedition in search of provender or game. The man bears his occasional days of pain with fortitude such as a brave lad might display, but he never learns the meaning of resignation. The woman belongs to the race, to the *old people*. He is a part of the *young nation*. His first songs are yodels. Then he learns dance tunes, and songs of hunting and fighting and drinking, and couplets of terse, quaint fun. It is over the loom and the knitting that old ballads are dreamily, endlessly crooned. . . .

Thus a rift is set between the sexes at babyhood that widens with the passing of the years, a rift that is never closed even by the daily interdependence of a poor man's partnership with his wife. Rare is a separation of a married couple in the mountains; the bond of perfect sympathy is rarer. The difference is one of mental training and standpoint rather than the more serious one of unlike character, or marriage would be impossible. But difference there certainly is. Man and woman, although they be twenty years married—although in twenty years there has been not one hour in which one has not been immediately necessary to the welfare of the other—still must needs regard each other wonderingly, with a prejudice that takes the form of a mild, half-amused contempt for one another's opinions and desires. The pathos of the situation is none the less terrible because unconscious. They are so silent. They know so pathetically little of each other's lives.

Of course, the woman's experience is the deeper; the man's gain is in the breadth of outlook. His ambition leads him to make drain after drain on the strength of his silent, wingless mate. Her position means sacrifice, sacrifice and ever sacrifice, for her man first, and then for her sons.

Olive Dame Campbell
1882–1954

Educator and folk song collector Olive Dame Campbell was born in Medford, Massachusetts, in 1882. She graduated from Tufts College in 1903 and married John C. Campbell in 1907. An Indiana native educated in New England, John had already been working as an educator in the southern mountains for over a decade.

When John died in 1919, Olive continued his work. She assumed his position as executive secretary of the Southern Mountain Worker's Conference (later the Council of the Southern Mountains), which John had helped found. Olive also edited John's papers into the book *The Southern Highlander and His Homeland* (1921), portions of which she wrote herself. Expanding on John's interest in applying the Danish folk school model of adult education to the mountains, Olive Campbell visited Denmark in 1922; co-founded the John C. Campbell Folk School in Brasstown, North Carolina, with Marguerite Butler in 1925; and published *The Danish Folk School* in 1928. Campbell served as director of the school until 1946, when she retired to Nantucket.

The following selection comes from the diary that Campbell kept when she and John traveled through the southern mountains in 1908–1909 investigating the region's church and missionary schools. The diary indicates the conflicted responses that northerners had toward southern mountain culture and the differing attitudes toward schools manifested by the people of the region.

FROM Appalachian Travels: The Diary of Olive Dame Campbell

October 6th [1908], Tuesday, Knoxville: A wait of two nights here in order to get at Dr. Claxton and Dr. Duncan, both of whom were out of town, after all our Sunday hustle. The city (the business part of it) has a suggestion of Springfield, though on an inferior scale. The soft-coal smoke is spoiling it too. I have not taken such a fancy to this country. I do not think it nearly so pretty as Virginia, and our car ride to Fountain City today did not show us pretty suburbs. John says that Maryville is not so pretty as Virginia nor nearly as fine as the Asheville region. I shall be interested to see the Blue Ridge and Murphy section tomorrow.

We had a tiring ride here from Bristol though it was interesting too in showing the people. Nothing could have been more different from New England—the towns were small and straggling—unattractive mostly, and the men unkempt. At one place we took the whole town aboard, old soldiers, mountaineer loafers, everybody—and in a body they left at Jonesboro—where it appeared there was court to be held that day. We had a number of girls aboard, each one dressed in her best; even those, apparently well acquainted, took separate seats, where they could look out of the window and wave to acquaintances at every station. Some Washington College boys who were on the train, got off at every station to yell to some acquaintance. They were like children—and chewing gum! Every one chews—the men tobacco, I suppose—but the women and children gum. I suppose I ought to be thankful it was not tobacco or snuff. I became quite worn watching a little baby, in front of me chew and chew and chew—rolling the gum inside and outside, winding her finger in it, etc. It is not an alluring performance. Such conditions must make a woman of Miss de Graffenreid's culture sigh for her poor South. [. . .]

October 8th: I found the other side of Knoxville much more attractive and the views going toward Maryville grew prettier when we finally struck the Blueridge line. Saw plenty of small frightened pigs and in one place a man with a gun sitting on the R.R. platform and holding a live possum by the tail. At Blueridge we held a conference with the hotel keeper and Colonel Bass and decided to go through to Murphy. The scenery continued pretty and the grade up—although it did not equal the beauty of the ride in the morning round the mountain and along the Hiawassee River. We did, however, have three very drunk young fellows roaring and whooping on the back platform (only one coach to the train and one freight car—the coach divided into smoking and non-smoking compartments). They drank white-moonshine copiously, and were watched by three train officials who finally shipped them safely at a small station. There were some Young-Harris students (unattractive) aboard who advised us not to try to go through that night, and as it turned out, we couldn't leave Murphy anyway, as all the horses were busy, it being horse-swapping day. Ten or more of us—with baggage, crammed into a crazy old hack which creaked in a dangerous way up a steep hill to the Dickey Hotel—alluringly known as the Drummer's Home. It proved to be very comfortable, as well as picturesque, and the food was excellent—heaps of fried chicken, hot biscuit, meat etc, etc. John trotted off first thing to the horse swapping convention—ostensibly to make arrangements for morrow with the livery keeper. I stayed at home as women do not go (to the swappings here.) I had fun, however, watching the groups pass the house. There were all sorts and conditions of mounts as well as cattle. John came back much amused, and had also had a talk with County Commissioner Norval. He said [there were] fruit, cattle raising possibilities in the mountains. Can't let the church schools go yet—doing good work. Mountain people do not want an education unless they can get it for nothing. (He was under criticism for spending too much on schools and felt sore.) In North Carolina they get appropriation from general State fund. County can tax itself for high school. District can also tax itself. [. . .]

October 8th, Continued: Up before light—we boasted an electric light in our room—a small one but real—and off again on the road. We had a most dilapidated surrey and the horses were not "right peart" in appearance. They went however very well and covered the rough twenty miles to Young-Harris before 12 noon. These were the worst roads I have struck yet—great ledges of rock jerking up in the middle or side of the road indifferently; up and down hill with a rising grade and many times a steep drop off on the side. We had to keep turning out and out, for we met fifty odd men, horses, mules, teams, oxen, etc. on the road, most of them bound, I suppose, to the horse swapping convention which lasts three days. There was the sorriest collection of animals on parade—to be swapped, but also we met many smart mounts, mules and otherwise. In one place—passing a team of steers, our surrey had to be half-lifted—quite exciting. I would also add that we passed plenty of pigs and hens galore.

The country all along was of the prettiest and glorious with color. I never saw such gorgeous reds as there in the black gums, sourwood and dogwood. There were maples too and woodbine and oak in rich color. Especially along the first half of our way the road was massed with laurel (ivy) and rhododendron (not the "big laurel"). It must be beautiful in June, and even now the rich green was in handsome contrast with the autumn color. Now one would be riding along in a valley, fording a creek or branch, now high on a mountain side, looking parallel into the branches of a tree whose trunk was hidden. We saw some nice farms—quite prosperous in appearance, bottom land and other scraggly corn fields high up, that did not look as if they would yield more than five bushels an acre. Our driver, Charlie Lance (I called him Spear), a rather good looking mountain lad with a heart trouble which I lay to indigestion, said some acres would yield 50 bushels and they got about $1.00 per bushel.

The cabins looked very attractive tucked in along the roadside, though I can't help thinking that in spite of their picturesqueness and the beauty of their position backed by blue mountains—they must be desperately lonely in winter when these roads are well-nigh impassible. Hard on the women and children. It is very pretty now. We passed a sorghum mill where the cane was heaped high and the horse was going around the tread mill. There were lots of children about and there was an air of festivity and cheer. John called a little boy to bring us a piece of cane—and he came running across the field and through the branch with two great long pieces. We broke and chewed some—a sweet rather acid pleasant flavor.

At another place where the road was high, we looked down into a hollow by a creek to a mill, where children were playing. On the opposite side, alone under the bushes, one little girl sat solemnly fishing. I wonder how much schooling she gets a year. [. . .]

October 9th: Had a good night but woke to find it still raining after a showery night. Charlie was cheerful and we resolved to go ahead. I heard a screech as I was finishing dressing, and John prophesied a chicken for breakfast. We had it sure enough—an improvement on the pork of the night before. These mountain people spread their tables most bountifully, chicken, rice, biscuit and corn bread (Charlie ate enormously of the former which were strong of soda—poor weak heart!) dried peach sauce, sweet potatoes, some breakfast food and various odd things which are spread out at angles all along the tables. You pick and choose.

This day's drive was the best yet—in spite of the showers ending in a heavy downpour as we arrived at Nacoochee about 2:15 P.M. All along the clouds shifted over the top of the mountains alternating with flashes of sunshine. For half the way the road mounted steadily till we reached the highest point in Indian Grave Gap. Fortunately the roads had not softened and we made fine time. From there on Charlie let the horses go and we galloped cheerfully down the mountain side passing Mr. Glenn and his grandson who had camped there that night after chestnuts—by three nut wagons (nearly tipped over in a mad rush by the 3rd which did not move aside) and down amid a pour to the Chattahoochee. Made a mistake at the cross roads and went 4 miles out but finally got in safely. We passed such a funny old sow with a crowd of little squeaking pigs which ran under our wagon. [. . .]

Charlie a thrifty lad, had earned $1.50 a day logging—very hard work. Had $150 in the bank and had just bought a farm of good bottomland for $350. Owned saddle horse. Now earning $20 a month and board—at livery stable driving, but preferred it to logging as it was not so hard. Drove the horses hard—saw everything—no remarks or details lost. Told me instantly names of all trees which were used for tan bark etc. Described a farm of ginseng owned by his uncle—1/4 acre now—valued at $3000. Would sell none until he had an acre. Seeds worth a lot apiece. A beautiful plant with red berries—required a lot of care and shade—900 berries on one plant. [. . .]

October 30th to November 3rd, Rome, Georgia:

Miss Berry's School:

Arrived at 8:00 P.M. and were met by Henry Gaines, one of the boys, and quite a character—loquacious if nothing else, who drove us four miles out in the country to the school. Were met by Miss Berry and several teachers and conducted to a charming model log cabin which serves as a center for the school, a home for some of the teachers, and a place to put visitors. There was a red lantern on the porch, which dimly showed logs, vines and rustic furniture, and when we pulled the old-fashioned latchstring we found a large room, with a cozy fire in the grate, a big carved four-poster, old fashioned bureau and wardrobe—latticed windows. We left our grips and sat down before a huge open fire in the main room, while they got dinner ready for us. The teachers generally meal with the boys but there is a nice little kitchen in the cabin where they can cook for visitors or themselves if they feel so inclined. One of the boys wipes dishes, cleans up, sweeps, dusts, etc., every day. Miss Berry sat down with us and Miss Neal who is one of her secretaries. A delicious supper of fried chicken, toast, tea and jelly—gelatin with real cream and nice tea. A fire also in that room. Then we adjourned to the front room, met several teachers and talked.

Miss Berry is a Southern woman in the region of forty—dark and rather heavily built with sweet voice and vivacious animated manner. She belongs to an aristocratic old family, was brought up with nursery maids and governesses, lived abroad and had a busy society life. Her sisters are now in the run of fashion. One has married an Italian nobleman and lives out of Rome. None understand her interest in the work. Her mother we met twice—a little erect old lady, with sparkling dark eyes, a dignified manner and deep voice. She ran the whole plantation during the war—a mere girl—her husband being 20 years older. The work started from a cabin on the old place (Miss Berry has given her share of the estate to the school), where she saw children playing in the woods, gradually found their need and ignorance, started a chain of Sunday Schools and finally this school—from the first on a working agricultural basis. There is no endowment or regular income except [a small annual amount] given by the town. She has to raise it all herself by speaking, writing, etc. She will have nothing but the very best teachers she can find—and they are a splendid corps—all absorbed in the work and devoted personally to her. She is a woman of great personal power—a leader.

No boys are taken from the town or from districts where there are more than 5 months' schooling—none except the needy and these from rural places—lowland and highland. All are obliged to work two hours a day at the rate of 6 cents. They have an academy (?) training and instruction in farming—building—dairy work (they make their own butter which is delicious and this last summer sold $100 worth a month of cream and butter to the town). They have a steam laundry where the boys do their own washing and pressing, their own power house, a shop and open work shed, a barn and poultry yard, where they also raise pigeons. There are several small houses—5–6—which are used as dormitories—one of them a charming old Southern mansion which they hope to eventually become Miss Berry's home, they hope. At present she has no regular abiding place—but lives in her trunk between school and home (her mother is alone). There are about 150 boys, all fine looking. They have musical training and make an excellent impression in church with their quiet manners and good singing. They also sing well our old Northern college songs. We heard them after supper Saturday night around the old tinny piano.

They tell most amusing stories of the place. Miss Neal gave me an account of how they got their bathroom in the log cabin. A fussy old lady who complained of every draft and pointed out every crack, took up Miss Berry's offer of a bath. Miss Berry sent to her old home for an old zinc tub. Mr. McLean brought it in the cold pale dawn—and the young teachers got up and scrubbed it on the porch of Brewster Hall (there being no water at the cabin). Then they warmed the water and lugged it over. This old lady had given a scholarship of $50 but no more. A demure little charity worker staying at the same time left $300 as she wanted to "help toward a bathroom which seemed their greatest need."

The school is beset with foreign missionaries—one spoke Sunday after John finished—urging all to enlist and quite looking down on those who stayed on the farm—just opposed to Miss Berry's idea and training.

They have had amusing mission barrels—among donations a whole black Bishop's coat. It went to a big fellow who came in a grass green shirt and coat almost up to his elbows. He looked well though odd in it, especially when he danced a clog dance, as he could inimitably. Another donation was a good tuxedo coat, and another fine white coat. They had had two installments of out-of-style Rogers Peet's—the first all of one bright tan color! One came full of bonnets and another of children's clothes in spite of repeated statements that the school was for boys. Old theological books of course and old text books of no use—express paid by the school.

John told his story of the pretty child and plain father, the child naively remarking "God is doing better work now." The boys—to our amusement—applied it to John and me. They all clustered about John on Sunday and listened absorbed to Alabama tales. They had a Y.M.C.A. testimony meeting—all sitting on cushions on the floor in front of the big cabin dining room fireplace. Miss Berry has the boys there for a special talk every Sunday night. Then singing after supper at the table—the evening service is a pleasant feature. The boys also work in the kitchen—cook and wash under direction of a Mrs. Grawther (?), and wait on table. There are 17 teachers, including Mr. Berry, practical farmer, Mrs. Berry nurse, etc.; Miss Brewster (who has been here since the beginning and is specially close to Miss Berry) in English; Miss Neal in office; Miss Brooks in music; Mr. Adams head of school academy; Mr. McLane general superintendent of grounds, buildings, etc.

Miss Berry believes in waking a boy up by taking him from his old environment into a new atmosphere. Better school in Rome than among mountains. Wants same for girls on cottage plan.

Lucy Furman

1869–1958

Born in the western Kentucky town of Henderson but reared in Indiana by her maternal aunt after her parents' deaths, Lucy Furman was educated at Sayre Institute in Lexington, Kentucky. At Sayre, she was a classmate of Katherine Pettit, who co-founded, with May Stone, Hindman Settlement School in Knott County in eastern Kentucky in 1902. Furman arrived at Hindman in 1907 for what was intended to be a short visit for her health. Once at the school, she decided to stay—for seventeen years. Initially she worked as a music teacher and volunteered for outdoor work, eventually taking on the role of superintendent of the grounds, gardens, and dairy. Her delight in her students led her to become the boys' housemother.

Furman wrote a humorous, fictionalized account of her work at Hindman in her first novel, *Mothering on Perilous* [*Creek*] (1913). The novel was a success and motivated readers to donate to the school. She continued to find Hindman and rural southeastern Kentucky a source of artistic inspiration, publishing *Sight to the Blind* in 1914, with an introduction by the muckraking journalist Ida Tarbell. Eliminating trachoma, an eye disease, the subject of the narrative, was a primary goal of Hindman. Furman continued her focus on the school and the surrounding communities in *The Quare Women* (1923), *The Glass Window* (1924), and *The Lonesome Road* (1927). In 1924, Furman built a house for herself on Hindman's grounds where she lived briefly before leaving the school due to bad health. She lived the rest of her life outside the mountains.

FROM Sight to the Blind: A Story

One morning in early September, Miss Shippen, the trained nurse at the Settlement School on Perilous, set off for a day of district-visiting over on Clinch, accompanied by Miss Loring, another of the workers. After riding up Perilous Creek a short distance, they crossed Tudor Mountain, and then followed the headwaters of Clinch down to Skain's Fork, where in a forlorn little district-school-house the trained nurse gave a talk on the causes and prevention of tuberculosis, the spitting of tobacco-juice over the floor by teacher and pupils abating somewhat as she proceeded. Two miles farther on she stopped at the Chilton home for a talk to half a dozen assembled mothers on the nursing and prevention of typhoid, of which there had been a severe epidemic along Clinch during the summer.

Afterward the school-women were invited to dinner by one of the visiting mothers. Mrs. Chilton at first objected to their going, but finally said:

"That's right; take 'em along with you, Marthy. I allow it'll pyeerten Aunt Dalmanuthy up to hear some new thing. She were powerful' low in her sperrits the last I seed."

"Pore maw!" sighed Marthy, her soft voice vibrant with sympathy. "It looks like things is harder for her all the time. Something new to ruminate on seems to lift her up a spell and make her forget her blindness. She has heared tell of you school-women and your quare doings, and is sort of curious."

"She is blind?" inquired the nurse.

"Blind as a bat these twelve year," replied Mrs. Chilton; "it fell on her as a judgment for rebelling when Evy, her onliest little gal, was took. She died of the breast-complaint; some calls it the galloping consumpt."

"I allus allowed if Uncle Joshuay and them other preachers had a-helt off and let maw alone a while in her grief," broke in Marthy's gentle voice, "she never would have gone so far. But Uncle Joshuay in especial were possessed to pester her, and inquire were she yet riconciled to the will of God, and warn her of judgment if she refused."

"Doubtless Uncle Joshuay's high talk did agg her on," said Mrs. Chilton, impartially, "but she need n't to have blasphemed like she done at Evy's funeral occasion."

Marthy covered her face with her hands.

"Oh, that day!" she exclaimed, shuddering. "Will I ever forget it? John and me had got married just a month before Evy died in October, and gone to live up the hollow a small piece from maw, and even then she were complaining of a leetle scum over her eyes. Losing Evy, and rebelling like she done atterward, and Uncle Joshuay's talk, holp it along fast, and it were plain to all before winter were over that he had prophesied right, and her sight were a-going. I would come down the branch of a morning and beg her to let me milk the cow and feed the property and red up the house and the like, but she would refuse in anger, and stumble round over chairs and table and bean-pot and wash-kittle, and maintain all spring and summer her sight were as good as ever. Never till that day of the funeral occasion, one year atter Evy died, did she ever give in."

Here Marthy again covered her face with her hands, and Mrs. Chilton took up the tale:

"I can see her now, up thar on the hill-shoulder, betwixt you and John on the front log, by Evy's grave-house, and Uncle Joshuay a-hollering and weeping and denouncing like he does, and her setting through it like a rock. Then finally Uncle Joshuay he thundered at her the third time, 'Hain't it the truth, Sister Dalmanuthy, that the judgment and the curse of God has fell on you for your rebelliousness, like I prophesied, and that you hain't able to see John thar or Marthy thar or the hand thar before your face thar?' when Aunt Dalmanuthy riz up sudden, and clinched her hands, and says slow and fierce: 'Man, it *is* the truth you speak. The curse *has* fell; and I hain't able to see John here or Marthy here or the hand here before my face here. But listen what I got to say about it. I'm able to hate and to curse as good as God. And I do! I hate and curse the Hand that, after taking all else I loved, snatched from my bosom the one little yoe lamb I treasured thar; I hate and curse Him that expected me to set down tame and quiet under such cruelty and onjestice; I hate and curse and defy the Power that hated and spited me enough, atter darkening the light of my life, to put out the sight of my eyes! Now,' she says, 'you lay claim to being mighty familiar with the Lord; take that message to Him!' she says." [. . .]

After a somewhat protracted silence, Marthy's gentle voice resumed:

"And from that day to this John and me hain't left her sence. We shet up our house and moved down to hern; and she tuck to setting by the fire or out on the porch, allus a-knitting, and seldom speaking a word in all them years about Evy or her sorrow or her curse. When my first little gal come along, I named it Evy, thinking to give her some easement or pleasure; but small notice has she ever showed. 'Pears like my young uns don't do much but bother her, her hearing and scent being so powerful' keen. I have allus allowed if she could git her feelings turnt loose one time, and bile over good and strong, it might benefit her; but thar she sets, day in, day out, proud and restless, a-bottling it all up inside."

"She biles over a right smart on you, Marthy, I should say," remarked the hostess.

"No, now, Susan, she don't, neither, considering her provocations. She were the smartest, most managing woman in these parts, and I never did have no faculty, and don't run her house like I ought; and John is a puny man and not able to do all her bidding; and the young uns they gits terrible noisy and feisty at times, all but Evy."

"The women" rode with Marthy a mile farther, stopping before a lonely log-house, with corn-fields climbing to meet the timber half-way up the mountain in the rear. Marthy ushered her guests into the porch with the words, "Here's the fotch-on women, Maw."

The tall, gaunt, forbidding-looking old woman sitting there turned sightless eyes toward them, putting forth a strong hand.

"Howdy, women," she said grimly. "Git cheers for 'em, Evy."

They seated themselves, and Aunt Dalmanutha resumed her knitting, swiftly and fiercely, all the pent-up force of a strong nature thrown into the simple act. Instead of the repose that characterizes the faces of the blind, her eaglelike countenance bore the marks of fretful, sullen, caged, almost savage energy.

"Go quick and take a look that 'ere pot of beans, Marthy," she ordered. "Evy declar's they hain't scorching, but my nose informs me different'. Take the women's bonnets, Evy, and lay 'em on my 'stead; and round up all the young uns back in the corn-crib, so 's I can git the benefit of the talk. Now, women," she continued peremptorily, "I been hearing a whole passel about your doings and goings and comings these four or five year' gone, and I'm right smart curious to know what it's all about. What air you in these parts for, anyhow, and how come you to come?"

"We are here," began Miss Shippen, quietly, "first and foremost because we want to educate the children who have never had the chance they deserve—"

"That's so; they hain't, more shame to the State," interrupted Aunt Dalmanutha. "Take me, now; I were raised forty-five mile' from a school-house or church-house, and never had no chance to l'arn 'a' from 'izard.' And these few pindling present-day district-schools scattered here and yan they only spiles the young uns for work, and hain't no improvement on nothing."

"Next," proceeded the trained nurse, "we want to be friendly and helpful to the grown-up people who need it, especially to the sick and suffering."

"I heared of the nursing you done in these parts in the typhoid last summer," said Aunt Dalmanutha, "and certainly it sounded good. But, women, one more question I crave to put to you. Do you mix in religion and preachifying as you go along?"

"We do not preach at all," replied Miss Shippen; "we let our deeds speak for us."

Aunt Dalmanutha extended a swift hand. "I am proud to make your acquaintance then," she said. "I have had my 'nough of religion and preachifying, but of plain human friendliness not, because there is little of it on the ramble."

"My special work," continued the trained nurse, "is of course with the sick, nursing and teaching how to nurse, and how to prevent as well as to cure illness, and sending cases I cannot help down to the level country for proper treatment. I see, Aunt Dalmanutha, that you are blind. Have you any objection to letting me take a close look at your eyes?"

"Look all you want," was the grim reply; "I am used to being a' object and a spectacle."

The nurse took from her satchel a glass with which she carefully examined the dulled and lifeless eyes, sitting down afterward without a word.

"And not only a' object and a spectacle," continued Aunt Dalmanutha, bitterly, "but a laughing-stock and a byword for the preachers in especial to mock and flout at. Yes, I that were once the workingest and most capablest woman up and down Clinch; I that not only could weave my fourteen yard', or hoe my acre of corn, or clear my man's stint of new ground, a day, but likewise had such faculty in my headpiece that I were able to manage and contrive and bring to pass; I that rejoiced in the work of my hands and the pyeertness of my mind and the fruits of my industry, and when my man died were able to run the farm and take keer of the children as good as before—I am sot down here in the midst of rack and ruin, with the roof a-leaking over me, the chimbly sagging out, the fence rotten and the hogs in the corn, the property eatin' their heads off, and the young uns lacking warm coats and kivers, John and Marthy being so mortal doless; I am sot here bound hand and foot, my strength brought to naught, my ambition squenched, my faculty onusable, a living monument to the hate and revenge and onjestice of God!" [. . .]

Miss Shippen waited a full minute before answering quietly and slowly: "It *was* cruel, it was unjust, it was horrible, it was wicked, that you should have been made to suffer so; above all, Aunt Dalmanutha, it was unnecessary. With a little knowledge, and proper food and fresh air, your daughter's life could have been saved; with knowledge and proper treatment your sons need not have died of dysentery or typhoid or even diphtheria; with knowledge your blindness itself, which is no curse, but would as surely have come upon you had you never lost Evy and never rebelled in your heart, need have lasted only a few months. For these are cataracts that you have on your eyes, and nothing would have been simpler and easier than their removal."

Amazement, incredulity, almost horror were written upon Aunt Dalmanutha's countenance as she heard these quiet words.

"Where do you get your authority over preachers, woman?" she demanded, leaning fiercely forward.

"I get my authority," replied the trained nurse, firmly, "from my knowledge of modern medicine and surgery; I get my authority from things seen with my eyes and heard with my ears during days and nights of duty on the battle-line between life and death; I get my authority," she continued more solemnly, "from Him whose spirit of freedom and tolerance has made possible the advances in modern science; who is the source of the rising tide of helpfulness manifest in human hearts everywhere; who, when he was on earth, went about doing good, and proclaiming not the hate, the vengeance, the cruelty of God, but His mercy, His kindness, His pity, His fatherly love."

The blind woman sat as though turned to stone, except that the veins in her neck and temples throbbed violently.

"Do you mean to tell me God never wanted to take my loved ones from me?" she asked at length from a dry throat.

"I do. I mean that their deaths, so far from being the will of God, were the fruit alone of ignorance and of evil conditions."

"You mean to say that the hand of vengeance wa' n't never lifted ag'in' me, and I hain't never sot under no curse?"

"I do."

"And that the preachers has lied to me?" she said through clenched jaws.

"They were simply mistaken; they knew no better."

Aunt Dalmanutha lifted a shaking arm. "Woe to them if ever they cross my path ag'in!" she cried hoarsely.

"Don't think about them," said the nurse; "the thing for you to do at once is to go down to Lexington, in the Blue Grass country, to a doctor I know there who does great things for eyes, and who, if it is not too late, will remove those cataracts and restore you to sight and usefulness and strength, as God intends. I will write at once to the hospital, and make the arrangements; you should start within a week. The trip," she added, "need cost you nothing, if you are unable to pay your way."

Aunt Dalmanutha drew herself up proudly.

"I hain't a' object of charity," she said. "If I go, I'll pay my way. I got something laid by still from my weaving days. But it has come on me too sudden'; I feel all lost; I will have to study a heap before I can make up my mind." She moved her hands about before her in a dazed, helpless way. [. . .]

One week later there was a call from the road in front of the school hospital, and Miss Shippen was pleased and relieved to see Aunt Dalmanutha mounted on a nag behind John. [. . .]

"I have pondered your words," she said to Miss Shippen, "and have made up my mind to foller them. With naught but them to swing out on, I am setting forth into the unknown. I that hain't never so much as rid in a wagon, am about to dare the perils of the railroad; that hain't been twenty mile' from home in all my days, am journeying into a far and absent country, from which the liabilities are I won't never return. Far'well, if far'well it be!"

On the last day of October, Miss Shippen had just dismissed her seventh-grade class in home-nursing, and was standing in the hospital porch drinking in the unspeakable autumnal glory of the mountains, when a wagon, rumbling and groaning along the road and filled with people, stopped with a lurch at the gate. Advancing, the nurse was at first puzzled as to the identity of the people; then she recognized the faces of John and Marthy Holt and of little Evy. But for several seconds she gazed without recognition at the striking figure on the front seat beside John. This figure wore a remarkable hat, bristling with red, yellow, and green flowers, and a plaid silk waist [blouse] in which every color of the rainbow fought with every other. Her bright and piercing dark eyes traveled hungrily and searchingly over the countenance of the trained nurse; her lips opened gradually over teeth of dazzling whiteness and newness. Then, leaning swiftly from the wagon, she gathered the nurse into a powerful, bear-like hug, exclaiming, with solemn joy:

"You air the woman! I know you by your favorance to your talk. I allowed you would look that fair and tender. Here air the woman, John and Marthy, that restored unto me my sight, and brung me up out of the Valley of the Shadow. She tolt me what to do, and I follered it, and, lo! the meracle was performed; wonderful things was done unto me!" Here Aunt Dalmanutha—for it was she—supplemented the embrace with kisses rained upon the head and brow of the trained nurse. [. . .]

Embarrassed by the open-mouthed family gaze, and by the additional presence of several teachers, who stopped to see and listen, Miss Shippen said:

"Tell me all about your trip, Aunt Dalmanutha."

"Tell about it? Tell that which ten thousand tongues could scarce relate? God knows my stumbling speech hain't equal to the occasion; but I'll do my best. You last seed me a-taking my fearsome way to the railroad; and what were the sinking of my heart when John left me thar on the cyar, words will never do jestice to; seemed like I were turnt a-loose in space, rushing I knowed not whither. The first ground I toch was when I heared the voice of that 'ere doctor you writ to inquiring for me at the far eend. He said he allowed I would be skeered and lonesome, so he come hisself to fetch me to the hospital. Woman, it were the deed of a saint, and holp me up wonderful'. Then I were put to bed a spell, and soft-footed women waited on me. Then one morning he tolt me he were aiming to peel them 'ere ingun-skins off my eyes, and for me to have no fears, but trust in him; that he believed them eye-nerves, shet back thar in the dark, was still alive and able to do business. And though my heart shuck like a ager, I laid down on that table same as a soldier. When I got up, I were blind as ever, with rags tied thick around my eyes. And I sot there patient day after day, and the doctor, he'd drap in and cheer me up. 'Aunt Dally,' he would say— he claimed he never had no time to git out the Dalmanuthy—'in just a leetle while you'll be a-trotting around the Blue Grass here worse'n a race-hoss; but you got to git your training gradual.' Then he'd thin the bandages more and more, till a sort of gray twilight come a-sifting through. 'And don't think,' he would say, 'that I am aiming to let you lope back to them mountains till I git you plumb made over. Fust thing is a new set of teeth,—you done gummed yourself into dyspepsy and gineral cantankerousness,—and then I'm sot on taking you to my house to visit a month and eat good victuals and git your stummick opened up whar it done growed together, and your mind unj'inted, and your sperrits limbered similar.' And straightway he sont for a tooth-dentist, that tuck a pictur' of my gums in wax then and thar. Then come the great day when I looked my fust on a human countenance ag'in. I axed that it be the doctor's, and I seed him only through black glasses darkly; but, O God! what a sight it were none but the blind can ever tell! Then for quite a spell I looked out through them dark glasses at the comings and goings and people there in the hospital. Then one day the doctor he run in and says, 'Time for you to look on the sunlight, Aunt Dally. Keep on them glasses, and wrop a shawl round you, and come with me. I'm aiming to show you the prettiest country God ever made.' Then he holp me into a chariot that run purely by the might of its own manoeuvers, and I seed tall houses and chimblys whiz by dimlike, and then atter a while he retch over and lifted my glasses.

"Women, the tongue of seraphim hain't competent to tell what I seed then! That country hain't rugged and on-eend like this here, but is spread out smooth and soft and keerful, with nary ragged corner nowhar', and just enough roll to tole the eye along. [. . .]

"But it were not till I sot in the railroad cyars ag'in, and the level country had crinkled up into hills, and the hills had riz up into mountains, all a-blazin' out majestical' in the joy of yaller and scarlet and green and crimson, that I raley got my sight and knowed I had it. Yes, the Blue Grass is fine and pretty and smooth and heavenly fair; but the mountains is my nateral and everlastin' element. [. . .]

"Then when I stepped off the train, thar was the living human faces of my own blood, John and Marthy, and the eight young uns whose countenances I had never beheld. And as I gazed, women, more scales drapped from my long-blind eyes. In the face of John here, the boy I had allus abused for no-git-up and shiftless, I beheld loving-kindness and onselfishness writ large and fair; looking on little Evy, I seed love divine in her tender eyes, and light raying out from her yaller hair and from the other seven smaller head' bunched around her like cherubim'. And Marthy! Right here, women, I ax your pardon if I stop a spell, for of a truth words fails me and tears squenches me. What did I see in that kind, gentle, patient face of hern? Women, it were the very living sperrit of Christ hisself I seed thar—the sperrit that returned love for hate, mercy for revilement, joy and life for curses and death. Yes, when them eyes of hers was turnt on me so full of love, right thar my heart broke. I had bemeaned and berated and faulted her so continual', and helt her up as a pore, doless creetur', without no backbone or ambition; and now I knowed that if thar ever were a tender, ginuwine, angel daughter on this here earth, it were her to me. Women, when she tuck me to her bosom, I just slid right down thar on my unworthy knees thar on the ground at her feet thar, and with bitter tears beseeched of her to forgive and forgit my hard-heartedness and stone-blindness and dog-meanness, which of course, being Marthy, she had already done allus-ago. [. . .]

"And now, fellow-sisters, you see before you a ree-surrected woman. I hain't only got the sight of my eyes; I got mind-sight, heart-sight, soul-sight. I hain't only got these fine store-teeth and a tamed and biddable stummick; but the innard power to chaw and digest speritual truth. I hain't only wearing these gayly, boughten clothes,

I'm a-fla'nting the robes of joy and the gyarments of praise. I know the Lord don't hate me and never did; I know I am free, restored, and saved; I know my Redeemer liveth, and has fotch me up out of the blackness of darkness on to the top-most peaks of joy and peace and thanksgiving.

"And don't think, women,—don't never, *never* think I hain't aiming to let my light shine! I aim to use my faculty not for worldly betterment alone, but to turn it loose likewise in the line of religion and preachifying. Yes, every night this enduring winter will see me a-s'arching the Scriptur'; and what I can't read I can ricollect; and come August, when the craps is laid by and the funeral occasions sets in, I will be ready for 'em. There won't be one in twenty mile' that won't see me a-coming, and a-taking my stand by the grave-houses in these resurrection gyarments, for to norate the wonders of my experience, and to shame and confound and drownd out Uncle Joshuay and t'other blind leaders of the blind wherever they dare raise their gray heads and hoary lies, and gin'rally to publish abroad, world-without-eend, the ons'archable riches and glory and power of the love of God."

Horace Kephart

1862–1931

Horace Kephart was born in Pennsylvania's Allegheny Mountains. After graduation from Cornell University, he secured a position cataloguing a private book collection in Italy and then worked at the Yale University Library. Later, he served as director of the St. Louis Mercantile Library.

Kephart had a lifelong fascination with the pioneer lifestyle. In his early forties, disenchanted with urban, domestic life, he began seeking respite through camping trips in the Ozarks. In 1904, following separation from his wife and children, Kephart settled in Hazel Creek, North Carolina, then a remote mountain community sixteen miles from the nearest railroad station. During his three years at Hazel Creek, Kephart integrated himself into mountaineer culture and kept twenty-seven journals of his observations.

Displeased with caricatures of Southern Appalachian people as gun-toting moonshiners, Kephart sought to document the reality of life in Southern Appalachia. Ironically, he often reinforced the popular images of mountaineers as isolated and uncivilized, as the following selection indicates. Nonetheless, Kephart's *Our Southern Highlanders: A Narrative of Adventure in the Southern Appalachians and a Study of Life among the Mountaineers* (originally published in 1913 and reprinted in 1922) has served as an inspiration for research in and literature about Southern Appalachia. Linguists, for example, have utilized Kephart's representations of mountain speech.

Kephart wrote about the extensive and devastating changes that the powerful timber industry wrought on the mountains and their residents. Because he felt indebted to the land and people for his own renewal, Kephart, along with his friend George Masa, a Japanese American photographer living in Asheville, tirelessly advocated for the formation of the Great Smoky Mountain National Park, a dream that became a reality a year after Kephart's untimely death in an automobile accident.

FROM Our Southern Highlanders: A Narrative of Adventure in the Southern Appalachians and a Study of Life among the Mountaineers

FROM CHAPTER XV: HOME FOLKS AND NEIGHBOR PEOPLE

The saddest spectacle in the mountains is the tiny burial-ground, without a headstone or headboard in it, all overgrown with weeds, and perhaps unfenced, with cattle grazing over the low mounds or sunken graves. The spot seems never to be visited between interments. I have remarked elsewhere that most mountaineers are singularly callous in the presence of serious injury or death. They show a no less remarkable lack of reverence for the dead. Nothing on earth can be more poignantly lonesome than one of these mountain burial-places, nothing so mutely evident of neglect.

Funeral services are extremely simple. In the backwoods, where lumber is scarce, a coffin will be knocked together from rough planks taken from someone's loft, or out of puncheons hewn from the green trees. It is slung on poles and carried like a litter. The only exercises at the grave are singing and praying; and sometimes even those are omitted, as in case no preacher can be summoned in time.

In all back settlements that I have visited, from Kentucky southward, there is a strange custom as to the funeral sermon, that seems to have no analogue elsewhere. It is not preached until long after the interment, maybe a year or several years. In some districts the practice is to hold joint services, at the same time and place, for all in the neighborhood who died within the year. The time chosen will be after the crops are gathered, so that everybody can attend. In other places a husband's funeral sermon is postponed until his wife dies, or *vice versa*, though the interval may be many years. These collective funeral services last two or three days, and are attended by hundreds of people, like a camp-meeting.

Strange scenes sometimes are witnessed at the graveside, prompted perhaps by weird superstitions. At one of our burials, which was attended by more than the usual retinue of kinsfolk, there were present two mothers who bore each other the deadliest hate that women know. Each had a child at her breast. When the clods fell, they silently exchanged babies long enough for each to suckle her rival's child. Was it a reconciliation cemented by the very life of their blood? Or was it a charm to keep off evil spirits? No one could (or would) explain it to me.

Weddings never are celebrated in church, but at the home of the bride, and are jolly occasions, of course. Often the young men, stimulated with more or less "moonshine," add the literally stunning compliment of a shivaree.

The mountaineers have a native fondness for music and dancing, which, with the shouting-spells of their revivals, are the only outlets for those powerful emotions which otherwise they studiously conceal. The harmony of "part singing" is unknown in the back districts, where men and women both sing in a jerky treble. Most of their music is in the weird, plaintive minor key that seems spontaneous with primitive people throughout the world. Not only the tone, but the sentiment of their hymns and ballads is usually of a melancholy nature, expressing the wrath of God and the doom of sinners, or the luckless adventures of wild blades and of maidens all forlorn. A highlander might well say, with the clown in *A Winter's Tale,* "I love a ballad but even too well; if it be doleful matter, merrily set down, or a very pleasant thing indeed, and sung lamentably."

But where banjo and fiddle enter, the vapors vanish. Up strike The Fox Chase, Shady Grove, Gamblin' Man, Sourwood Mountain, and knees are limbered, and merry voices rise.—

> Call up your dog, O call up your dog!
> Call up your dog!

Call up your dog!
Let's a-go huntin' to ketch a groundhog.
Rang tang a-whaddle linky day!

Wherever the church has not put its ban on "twistifications" the country dance is the chief amusement of young and old. [. . .]

In homes where dancing is not permitted, and often in others, "play-parties" are held, at which social games are practiced with childlike abandon: Roll the Platter, Weavilly Wheat, Needle's Eye, We Fish Who Bite, Grin an' Go 'Foot, Swing the Cymblin, Skip t' m' Lou (pronounced "Skip-tum a-loo") and many others of a rollicking, half-dancing nature. [. . .]

A substitute for the church fair is the "poke-supper," at which dainty pokes (bags) of cake and other home-made delicacies are auctioned off to the highest bidder. Whoever bids-in a poke is entitled to eat with the girl who prepared it, and escort her home. The rivalry excited among the mountain swains by such artful lures may be judged from the fact that, in a neighborhood where a man's work brings only a dollar a day, a pretty girl's poke may be bid up to ten, twenty, or even fifty dollars.

As a rule, the only holidays observed in the mountains, outside the towns, are Christmas and New Year's. Christmas is celebrated after the southern fashion, which seems bizarre indeed to one witnessing it for the first time. The boys and men, having no firecrackers (which they would disdain, anyway), go about shooting revolvers and drinking to the limit of capacity or supply. Blank cartridges are never used in this uproarious jollification, and the courses of the bullets are left to chance, so that discreet people keep their noses indoors. Christmas is a day of license, of general indulgence, it being tacitly assumed that punishment is remitted for any ordinary sins of the flesh that may be committed on that day. There is no church festivity, nor are Christmas trees ever set up. Few mountain children hang up their stockings, and many have never heard of Santa Claus.

New Year's Day is celebrated with whatever effervescence remains from Christmas, and in the same manner; but generally it is a feeble reminder, as the liquid stimulus has run short and there are many sore heads in the neighborhood.

Most of the mountain preachers nowadays denounce dances and "play-parties" as sinful diversions, though their real objection seems to be that such gatherings are counter-attractions that thin out the religious ones. Be that as it may, they certainly have put a damper on frolics, so that in very many mountain settlements "goin' to meetin'" is recognized primarily as a social function and affords almost the only chance for recreation in which family can join family without restraint.

Meetings are held in the log schoolhouse. The congregation ranges itself, men on one side, women on the other, on rude benches that sometimes have no backs. Everybody goes. If one judged from attendance he would rate our highlanders as the most religious people in America. This impression is strengthened, in a stranger, by the grave and astoundingly patient attention that is given an illiterate or nearly illiterate minister while he holds forth for two or three mortal hours on the beauties of predestination, free-will, foreordination, immersion, foot-washing, or on the delinquencies of "them acorn-fed critters that has gone New Light over in Cope's Cove."

After an *al fresco* lunch, everybody doggedly returns to hear another circuit-rider expound and denounce at the top of his voice until late afternoon—as long as "the spirit lasts" and he has "good wind." When he warms up, he throws in a gasping *ah* or *uh* at short intervals, which constitutes the "holy tone." Doctor MacClintock gives this example: "Oh, brethren, repent ye, and repent ye of your sins, ah; fer if ye don't, ah, the Lord, ah, he will grab yer by the seat of yer pants, ah, and held yer over hell fire till ye holler like a coon!"

During these services there is a good deal of running in and out by the men and boys, most of whom gradually congregate on the outside to whittle, gossip, drive bargains, and debate among themselves some point of dogma that is too good to keep still about.

Nearly all of our highlanders, from youth upward, show an amazing fondness for theological dispute. This consists mainly in capping texts, instead of reasoning, with the single-minded purpose of confusing or downing an opponent. Into this battle of memories rather than of wits the most worthless scapegrace will enter with keen gusto and perfect seriousness. I have known two or three hundred mountain lumber-jacks, hard-swearing and hard-drinking tough-as-they-make-'ems, to be whetted to a fighting edge over the rocky problem "Was Saul damned?" (Can a suicide enter the kingdom of heaven?)

The mountaineers are intensely, universally Protestant. You will seldom find a backwoodsman who knows what a Roman Catholic is. As John Fox says, "He is the only man in the world whom the Catholic Church has made little or no effort to proselyte. Dislike of Episcopalianism is still strong among people who do not know, or pretend not to know, what the word means. 'Any Episcopalians around here?' asked a clergyman at a mountain cabin. 'I don't know,' said the old woman. 'Jim's got the skins of a lot o' varmints up in the loft. Mebbe you can find one up thar.'"

The first settlers of Appalachia mainly were Presbyterians, as became Scotch-Irishmen, but they fell away from that faith, partly because the wilderness was too poor to support a regular ministry, and partly because it was too democratic for Calvinism with its supreme authority of the clergy. This much of seventeenth century Calvinism the mountaineer retains: a passion for hair-splitting argument over points of doctrine, and the cocksure intolerance of John Knox; but the ancestral creed itself has been forgotten.

The circuit-rider, whether Methodist or Baptist, found here a field ripe for his harvest. Being himself self-supporting and unassuming, he won easily the confidence of the people. He preached a highly emotional religion that worked his audience into the ecstasy that all primitive people love. And he introduced a mighty agent of evangelization among outdoor folk when he started the camp-meeting.

The season for camp-meetings is from mid-August to October. The festival may last a week in one place. It is a jubilee-week to the work-worn and home-chained women, their only diversion from a year of unspeakably monotonous toil. And for the young folks, it is their theater, their circus, their county fair. (I say this with no disrespect: "big-meetin' time" is a gala week, if there be any such thing at all in the mountains—its attractiveness is full as much secular as spiritual to the great body of the people.)

It is a camp by day only, or up to closing time. No mountaineer owns a tent. Preachers and exhorters are housed nearby, and visitors from all the country scatter about with their friends, or sleep in the open, cooking their meals by the wayside.

In these backwoods revival meetings we can witness to-day the weird phenomena of ungovernable shouting, ecstasy, bodily contortions, trance, catalepsy, and other results of hypnotic suggestion and the contagious one-mindedness of an overwrought crowd. This is called "taking a big through," and is regarded as the madness of supernatural joy. It is a mild form of that extraordinary frenzy which swept the Kentucky settlements in 1800, when thousands of men and women at the camp-meetings fell victims to "the jerks," "barking exercises," erotic vagaries, physical wreckage, or insanity, to which the frenzy led.

Many mountaineers are easily carried away by new doctrines extravagantly presented. Religious mania is taken for inspiration by the superstitious who are looking for "signs and wonders." At one time Mormon prophets lured women from the backwoods of western Carolina and eastern Tennessee. Later there was a similar exodus of people to the Castellites, a sect of whom it was commonly remarked that "everybody who joins the Castellites goes crazy." In our day the same may be said of the Holy Rollers and Holiness People.

In a feud town of eastern Kentucky, not long ago, I saw two Holiness exhorters prancing before a solemnly attentive crowd in the courthouse square, one of them shouting and exhibiting the "holy laugh," while the other pointed to the Cumberland River and cried, "I don't say *if* I had the faith, I say I *have* the faith, to walk over that river dry-shod!" I scanned the crowd, and saw nothing but belief, or willingness to believe, on any countenance. Of course, most mountaineers are more intelligent than that; but few of them are free from superstitions of one kind or other. There are to-day many believers in witchcraft among them (though none own it to any but their intimates) and nearly everybody in the hills has faith in portents.

The mountain clergy, as a general rule, are hostile to "book larnin'," for "there ain't no Holy Ghost in it." One of them who had spent three months at a theological school told President Frost, "Yes, the seminary is a good place ter go and git rested up, but 'tain't worth while fer me ter go thar no more 's long as I've got good wind."

It used to amuse me to explain how I knew that the earth was a sphere; but one day, when I was busy, a tiresome old preacher put the everlasting question to me: "Do you believe the yearth is round?" An impish perversity seized me and I answered, "No—all blamed humbug!" "Amen!" cried my delighted catechist, "I knowed in reason you had more sense."

In general the religion of the mountaineers has little influence on every-day behavior, little to do with the moral law. Salvation is by faith alone, and not by works. Sometimes a man is "churched" for breaking the Sabbath, "cussin'," "tale-bearin'"; but sins of the flesh are rarely punished, being regarded as amiable frailties of mankind. It should be understood that the mountaineer's morals are "all tail-first," like those of Alan Breck in Stevenson's *Kidnapped.*

One of our old-timers nonchalantly admitted in court that he and a preacher had marked a false corner-tree which figured in an important land suit. On cross-examination he was asked:

"You admit that you and Preacher X— forged that corner-tree? Didn't you give Preacher X—a good character, in your testimony? Do you consider it consistent with his profession as a minister of the Gospel to forge corner-trees?"

"Aw," replied the witness, "religion ain't got nothin' to do with corner-trees!"

John Fox relates that, "A feud leader who had about exterminated the opposing faction, and had made a good fortune for a mountaineer while doing it, for he kept his men busy getting out timber when they weren't fighting, said to me in all seriousness:

"'I have triumphed agin my enemies time and time agin. The Lord's on my side, and I gits a better and better Christian ever' year.'

"A preacher, riding down a ravine, came upon an old mountaineer hiding in the bushes with his rifle.

"'What are you doing there, my friend?'

"'Ride on, stranger,' was the easy answer. 'I'm a-waitin' fer Jim Johnson, and with the help of the Lawd I'm goin' to blow his damn head off.'"

But let us never lose sight of the fact that these people, intellectually, are not living in our age. To judge them fairly we must go back and get a medieval point of view, which, by the way, persisted in Europe and America until well into the Georgian period. If history be too dry, read Stevenson's *Kidnapped,* and especially its sequel *David Balfour,* to learn what that viewpoint was. The parallel is so close—eighteenth century Britain and twentieth century Appalachia—that here we walk the same paths with Alan and David, the Edinboro' law-sharks, Katriona and Lady Allardyce. The only difference of moment is that we have no aristocracy.

As for the morals of our highlanders, they are precisely what any well-read person would expect after taking their belatedness into consideration. In speech and conduct, when at ease among themselves, they are frank, old-fashioned Englishmen and Scots, such as Fielding and Smollet and Pepys and Burns have shown us to the life. Their manners are boorish, of course, judged by a feminized modern standard, and their home conversation is as coarse as the mixed-company speeches in Shakespeare's comedies or the offhand pleasantries of Good Queen Bess.

But what is refinement? What is morality?

"I don't mind," said the Belovéd Vagabond, "I don't mind the frank dungheap outside a German peasant's kitchen window; but what I loathe and abominate is the dungheap hidden beneath Hedwige's draper papa's parlor floor." And we do well to consider that fine remark by Sir Oliver Lodge: "Vice is reversion to a lower type *after perception of a higher.*"

I have seen the worst as well as the best of Appalachia. There *are* "places on Sand Mountain"—scores of them—where unspeakable orgies prevail at times. But I know that between these two extremes the great mass of the mountain people are very like persons of similar station elsewhere, just human, with human frailties, only a little more honest, I think, in owning them. And even in the tenebra of far-back coves, where conditions exist as gross as anything to be found in the wynds and closes of our great cities, there is this blessed difference: that these half-wild creatures have not been hopelessly submerged, have not been driven into desperate war against society. The worst of them still have good traits, strong characters, something responsive to decent treatment. They are kind-hearted, loyal to their friends, quick to help anyone in distress. They know nothing of civilization. They are simply *the unstarted*—and their thews are sound.

Frances Louisa Goodrich

1856–1944

A leader of the crafts revival in the southern mountains, Frances Goodrich was born in Binghamton, New York, and reared in Cleveland, Ohio. Her father, a Presbyterian minister, was active in Cleveland's strong abolitionist community; after the Civil War, his church engaged in urban social reform.

In 1876, two years after Goodrich's father's death, the family moved to New Haven, Connecticut, where Frances studied art at Yale for three years. In 1890, she traveled to Asheville, North Carolina, to visit a friend who was teaching at the Asheville Home Industrial School for girls. Goodrich secured a position at a nearby mission school. By 1909, she had helped found seven more such schools.

Goodrich, concerned about the perceived isolation of mountain women in remote homes, held meetings where they could socialize as they sewed and studied the Bible. In 1894 or 1895, a woman brought a handmade coverlet to a meeting. In later years, Goodrich cited this coverlet as the inspiration for her idea of encouraging mountain women to earn money by weaving.

In 1931, Goodrich, who had recently helped found the Southern Highland Handicraft Guild, published *Mountain Homespun*, which includes seven fictionalized sketches depicting the encounters of a non-Appalachian female teacher with Appalachian women. These sketches are clearly indebted to the conventions of the local color literary movement, yet Goodrich eschews the standard negative stereotypes of the genre and instead, in an empathetic narrative voice, presents Appalachian women as wise repositories of community strength.

The Three Gray Women

Lois Rice was teaching for the second year the Middle-Lonesome School. It was fodder-pulling time and according to an ancient custom and by general consent the school was closed for a week. The children were in the fields, stripping off the lower leaves of the corn for "blade fodder" while the larger boys and the men were "topping" the stalks; cutting the "top fodder" with a quick, dexterous slash of the knife. Both kinds of fodder would make "roughness" on which the cattle would feed during the winter.

On Tuesday evening Esther Chalmers came to Lois with a message: "Maw wants you should go with her tomorrow to her aunts' in Tennessy. She's heard that Aunt Lizzie is kindly bad off, and she's took a notion to strike out and go over the mountain soon in the morning."

Lois accepted the summons gladly. Soon after sunrise she was on her way to the Chalmers to join Martha.

The night had been still, with a heavy frost, the first "killing frost" of the season. As Lois neared the big black walnut tree in the lane, where the children lingered after school to crack and eat the nuts, she saw that on the ground beneath it the leaves lay like a carpet, almost like a designed decoration; light, sharp green, toning up the brownish green grass and the brown earth around them. Above, the branches were almost bare. The flowers in the Chalmers yard, so gay the day before, were black, save for the chrysanthemums, bronze and yellow, that had withstood the cold.

Martha was ready and together she and Lois "took the mountain," thus cutting off many miles of travel by wagon road. At first they followed a logging road that wound in and out of the mountain side by easy grades. As they rounded an open slope, Lois saw a figure approaching them, in silhouette against the sky, tall and lank and sunbonneted.

"Yonder comes Serinthy Whissenbee," exclaimed Martha, "going to her brother's in the Holly Bottoms."

"How can she recognize a sunbonnet at this distance," thought Lois, to whom this headgear seemed a leveler and a disguise.

After greetings and polite inquiries after health, the two women sat down on a bank and engaged in the exchange of news. Lois watched with interest the movements of the two bonnets so close together, as they expressed the feelings of the speakers. She heard that Aunt Lizzie was on the mend though she had been "aiming to die."

"They plumb give her up," said Serinthy, "but Doc Burns come by and he fotched her out of it. They tell me he can cure mighty nigh anything that's a workin' on a body."

The mounting sun warned the wayfarers to be moving on so the last words were exchanged and Martha and Lois climbed on while Serinthy descended toward the Holly Bottoms with her budget of news.

When the crest of the mountain was gained, the travelers followed an obscure trail along a ridge and soon saw far below them Peachtree Cove, widening out into the flatwoods beyond, and far away they could dimly descry a town. Almost at their feet, in a fold of the hill above the Cove, lay the little homestead which was their goal.

A short descent through open woods and pasture brought them to the barns and to the house. There a scene of activity presented itself. What was being done was to Lois a mystery, no less so after Martha had exclaimed: "If they ain't right now a warpin' 'em a chain."

Against the house, a low structure of logs covered with weatherboarding, leaned a heavy wooden frame. On the ground in front of this stood a small upright frame, holding large spools filled with cotton yarn. Between the two moved an erect old woman, her hands filled with threads. These came from the spools and were being laid over and under pegs on the larger frame.

At the approach of the visitors, the warper, fastening her threads securely around a peg, stepped forward to greet her niece and then to make welcome the teacher. Aunt Elvira was the oldest of three sisters and Lois soon found that she had qualities lacking in the others. Her features, strong and rugged, were only relieved from ugliness by their expression. There was in her face not merely good will, but radiance that won Lois' heart.

Aunt Lizzie was sitting in a low "rocky chair," that had been brought out onto the grass before the house that she might watch "the doin's." She had a mouse-like face, with mouth drawn in, not only from loss of teeth, but from a shrewd suspicion of things in general and unwillingness to be committed to anything. Her neck was bound up with surgeon's plaster and she was not loath to tell how bad off she had been before Doc Burns had come.

"It warn't jest a plain risin', it war a kee-ar-bunkle," she explained with dignity. "I wor ne'er a one for much doctrine, but I mighty nigh faith Doc Burns."

Aunt Hannah was large, like her sister Elvira and like her was a master hand at the loom. Her specialty, a rare one, was the weaving of white counterpanes. The warp they were preparing was for her loom. Aunt Elvira, it was explained, wove coverlets, while Aunt Lizzie, when well, carded and spun and filled the quills for the others.

"They are like the Three Fates," thought Lois, "who spun and wove."

When Aunt Hannah began to tell her great trouble and would not cease telling it, about the loss of the one lens that had been left in her spectacles, without which she could not see to thread up her loom, and when she was joined in her lament by both of her sisters, Lois thought also of the Three Gray Women in the Wonder Book who lost the one eye they had between them.

Still lamenting, Aunt Hannah set about getting dinner, while Aunt Elvira went on with the warping. Lois watched the process closely and with some explanation from Martha began to understand the method in what had looked to her quite aimless. The pegs had been set into the warping bars in a definite pattern. The purpose of the warping was to prepare a set of warp threads for winding upon the big back beam of the loom, so that they could be drawn forward, each thread in its own order, and each crossed with its neighbor threads. It is only so that the warp can be made to run smoothly and with even tension through the "gears," that is, the harness eyes, and through the reed to the front or cloth beam and be rolled on this as the web progresses. All this Lois comprehended but vaguely even when Elvira let her "pick the cross" at the end of a "bout," crossing each thread with the one next it and laying them all on the pegs so as to "hold the cross" until the warping was done and the crosses could be tied.

It was all interesting to Lois, but the prettiest sight came at the end, when Martha, tall and buxom, took the warp from the bars, looping the cream-white bunch of threads into itself, and laying this chain of great links over her shoulder as it lengthened. It was clear to anyone seeing this why the warp was, in common speech, the chain.

At the bountiful dinner the talk was all of the big meeting going on down in the settlement, four miles away.

"They do say it's the awfullest meetin' ever heard of. It's a regular tare-up of a meetin'," said Hannah, keen for excitement.

"Does seem like the people's takin' a interest," said Aunt Lizzie. "When the mourners get to takin' on and the others go to shoutin', you can't hear nothin'."

"Poor sister ain't fit to go anywheres till that neck of hers gets swaged down, but I'm aimin' to go and see for myself, come Sunday," said Hannah.

"This poke-stalk religion ain't worth much, to my way of thinkin'," said Elvira, and seeing the puzzled look on Lois' face, she added, "Laws, child, ain't you seen pokeweed a growin' up so biggity in the summer time and then in winter, nothin' left of it but a gray rag you couldn't kinnle a fire with?"

Lois laughed as she recognized the aptness of the simile.

Early in the "evening" (a part of the day that begins at 12 [noon]), Martha prepared to start, for the days were shortening and she must be home by sundown. What was to be done about the missing lens? How could the web be drawn in? If Martha could stay, her eyes would suffice, but she had made no arrangement to be gone overnight. Timidly, Lois offered her services, and after some consultation it was decided that since she was a school-teacher she would be able to learn from Hannah to thread the harness. Outside of the help she might give, the three sisters were overjoyed to have the company for even one night and day of one they termed "a plumb sweet thing." Martha was uneasy at the thought of Lois "taking the mountain" alone the next day, fearing she might lose the trail, so blind in places. She bethought her that her "old man" was aiming to take his wheat around by road to the mill in the settlement below, and whenever he did so he could "come up by to fetch Miss Lois."

"Ef 'tain't tomorrow it'll be the next day."

So it was settled, and furthermore Shadrach could get a new pair of glasses at Bart's store on the way. "You can get them there," she said, "as low as ten cents."

This was most satisfactory, but Aunt Hannah gave one parting injunction for Shad to be "mighty perticklar to get specs, not glasses. Them that clinch the nose, I despise 'em."

Around the fire that evening there was comfort and good cheer. Lois told the three ancient dames about her home and her family in answer to their eager questions, and then heard from them of old times on the mountain; exciting tales of adventure with bear and wildcat and lynx; of deer hunts, of one when two of them as girls chased a stag over the mountains with their dogs a whole day and killed him at the Old Stand in North Carolina.

Then the subject of old songs came up; "love ballets," and ballad after ballad was sung. Elvira and Hannah had been famous singers in their day. "The False Knight upon the Road," "The Maid Freed from the Gallows," "The Silk Merchant's Daughter," "The Seven Bretheren," and others. Some of them Lois had heard before, but others, centuries old, were new to her.

The last song, "Ellender and the Brown Girl," was sung alone by Hannah. She sat with head thrown back, eyes looking off as if she saw the things of which she sang acted out before her. Her voice, still strong and clear, intoned rather than sang the ancient tune with its gapped scale.

Go dig my grave both wide and deep
And paint my coffin black,

And bury fair Ellender in my arms,
The brown girl at my back.

They dug his grave both wide and deep
And painted his coffin black,
They buried fair Ellender in his arms,
The brown girl at his back.

At the end, Hannah said solemnly, "My mother taught me that and I *aim to not forget it.*"

Lois woke early the next morning and taking a bucket ran to the spring for water over grass glistening with hoarfrost. A red dawn was in the eastern sky and high up, where the rose melted into gray-blue, a planet still shone. Looking toward the house she saw Elvira gazing at the beauty with her old face transfigured. "She sees it and feels it, too," said Lois softly.

Breakfast dispatched, the beaming of the web began. One end of the "chain" was fastened along the big beam and then laid over the "rake" whose teeth spread the threads apart. While one of the women turned the beam slowly, the others held the warp taut, paying it out as needed and watching that no thread caught in its progress. When all but a yard or two was thus rolled onto the big beam at the back of the loom, the ends of the threads were brought forward into position to be passed through the harness, a task requiring good eyesight.

Hannah went to a little chest under one of the beds and brought out the draft, rolled up and tied with black thread. When opened out, the long strip of yellowed paper showed a series of figures and crisscross lines in faded ink. Along the top was written: "Hannah McRae her County-Pin Draft." "A preacher drawed that off for me nigh on to fifty year ago," said Hannah. "Of all the county-pin drafts I've wove or seen wove, this is my favorite."

Lois felt horribly uncertain whether she could ever master the meaning of this mysterious paper, but her reputation as a teacher, and "high-larnt," was at stake, and make good she must. She took the place assigned her and listened intently to the instructions. There were before her four wooden frames, each holding many doubled threads, about eight inches long, and in the center of each pair was a loop or eye. The point was to get the right thread through the right eye. Hannah numbered the frames for her: one, two, three, and four.

"We'll commence with the selvedge," said she. "That ain't in the draft. You take these first two threads, here, and pass them through the first eye in the first harness. Yes, that's right. It'll go quicker once you've done it a spell. Now this next thread goes into the first eye in the second harness, the next 'un in the first on the third, and the next into that 'un on the fourth. Now one in the first harness, one in the second, and so on. It takes nine threads to make a plime-blank good edge for this kind of weaving. There's some that never learn that."

After the selvedge was successfully drawn in, they began with the draft. Lois soon found how this corresponded with the harness sets and harness eyes and the battle was won.

"I knew in reason she'd catch on to it," said Hannah, "but she's learnt the quickest ever."

"It takes more'n good sense," said Elvira, "she's been learned to put her thoughts on a thing and not let 'em squander all over creation."

Aunt Lizzie rocked to and fro in satisfaction, saying, "I just love to set and watch them pretty hands a flyin' about so spry. They're the *least* hands ever I see, on a woman."

With encouragement of this sort, Lois worked steadily and carefully at her self-imposed task. Though tiring, the novelty and importance of it kept it from becoming tiresome.

The last threads were drawn in by noon. As the four women sat down to dinner, Lois, weary but triumphant, heard the sound of wheels and the gee and haw of the mule driver. With the weird cry used in the mountains to stop the mules, Shadrach drew up before the house. After the "howdies" had been said the bridles were loosened and the bundles of "roughness" brought for the animals were thrown down before them. Shad, after a great splashing of hands and face in the basin on the porch rail, came in smiling benignly.

"He is always so joval," Aunt Hannah had said that morning, and jovial he looked with his clustering black locks and beard, as he opened his wallet and brought out, not one, but three pairs of spectacles of the desired sort.

The excitement though undemonstrative was intense, and the pleasure of each of the sisters as she found she could distinguish near objects with these new aids was good to witness.

In parting from Lois, both Aunt Hannah and Aunt Lizzie threw their old arms about her, "loving her neck," a sign of approval distinctly rare from them.

Elvira looked into her eyes and said, "I wish you well."

For Lois' comfort, Shad had brought on top of the load of wheat left at the mill, a splint-bottomed chair. On this, behind the driver's seat of rough board, she balanced herself in the moving wagon bed.

As the wheels half rolled, half slid down the steep road into the valley, she spoke thus with herself: "They are not one bit like Hawthorne's Gray Women except for the lost eye. His were quarrelsome and grasping, and these are generous and kind. Their religion isn't the poke-stalk kind. If ever I'm old and poor I want to be like Elvira. She *has something* I'll need then. I reckon I'd better begin to get it now."

PART IV
Prose, Poetry, and Songs of Labor
Theresa Lloyd

It is tempting to view Appalachia as having been a classless agrarian society prior to the development of the extractive industries, timber and mining, in the late nineteenth and early twentieth centuries. However, absentee land ownership, tenancy, and class division were present in varying degrees from the early days of white settlement in Appalachia. Furthermore, small-scale coal mining, along with extensive iron and salt works, were present before the Civil War. Nonetheless, mountain society changed dramatically with rapid post–Civil War industrialization, which laid the groundwork for the region's wide-scale poverty and dependency.

Serious industrial development in Southern and Central Appalachia accompanied the extension of railroads into the region. Between 1865 and 1890, land speculators and railroad owners acquired vast landholdings through legal and quasi-legal means. Timbering the old-growth forests that covered these lands was the first large-scale extractive endeavor. The earlier timber harvest had been small and often judicious compared to the rampant cutting that denuded much of the region from around 1890 to 1920, resulting in severe and persistent flooding. Along with this environmental alteration came social change. Logging jobs lured farmers out of the fields, and logging camps and sawmill towns to house them and their families sprang up. But by 1920, the logging boom was drawing to a close; left behind were scarred, barren mountainsides and unemployed loggers.

A boom-and-bust employment cycle, company towns, and environmental destruction were also features of Appalachia's coal industry. Extensive coal mining started in northeastern Pennsylvania's anthracite region around 1820. Development of bituminous coalfields began in western Pennsylvania in the 1850s and exploded in Central and Southern Appalachia from the 1870s through the early 1900s with the penetration of railroads into the mountainous terrain. Mountain farmers displaced by absentee—and often dishonest—land acquisition, and those looking for cash income flocked to the mines, where the need for labor was so great that companies also recruited African Americans from throughout the South, as well as immigrants from southern and eastern Europe. Dangerous working conditions, low wages, and oppressive policies in company towns were endemic in the coalfields. Among the many mining disasters was one at Fraterville, Tennessee, where 216 miners were killed in an explosion in 1902. Oppressive practices in company towns included the issuance of scrip rather than money, price gouging and usury at the company store, inadequate and dangerous housing conditions, political corruption, and strict discipline enforced by private or public police.

Conflict between workers and operators followed hot on the heels of the opening of coalfields. Pennsylvania's anthracite miners first struck in 1842 and made their initial attempts at unionization in 1848. Labor unrest in West Virginia included the Paint Creek–Cabin Creek strike of 1912–1913 and Battle of Blair Mountain in 1921.

Appalachians also worked in the mills that arose in the region to take advantage of the natural resources (such as iron, second-growth timber, and waterpower for operating machines) and the cheap labor. Many mountaineers migrated to the Piedmont to work in that region's numerous textile and furniture mills. Unlike in the timber and coal industries, women made up a large percentage of the workforce in textile mills. Additionally, these mills, like coal mines, utilized child labor and paid poorly.

The hardships of work and oppressive living conditions in newly industrialized Appalachia gave birth to a rich and important body of literature, which includes fiction, poetry, drama, and songs. The development of Appalachia's literature of protest paralleled the rise of social justice and workers' literature internationally.

In the decades following World War II, under the influence of New Criticism, interest in social justice literature waned. The rise of critical theory in the 1970s and 1980s opened readers' eyes to a variety of marginalized literary traditions, and today the literary and cultural merits of this body of work are again fully appreciated.

Sources: Ronald D Eller, *Miners, Millhands, and Mountaineers: Industrialization of the Appalachian South, 1880–1930* (1982); Ronald L. Lewis, *Transformation of the Appalachian Countryside: Railroads, Deforestation, and Social Change in West Virginia, 1880–1920* (1998); Wilma Dunaway, *The First American Frontier: Transition to Capitalism in Southern Appalachia, 1700–1860* (1996); Cary Nelson, *Revolutionary Memory: Recovering the Poetry of the American Left* (2001).

Mary Harris "Mother" Jones

1837–1930

Born in Cork, Ireland, and reared in Toronto, Canada, Mary Harris trained as a dressmaker and teacher before she moved in 1861 to Memphis, Tennessee, where she met and married George Jones, an iron molder and member of the International Iron Molders Union. After the death of her husband and their four children in a yellow fever epidemic in 1867, she worked as a dressmaker in Chicago. There she became interested in the plight of the working class and began attending Knights of Labor meetings. After 1877, she devoted her life to improving the lot of working people, earning a reputation as a skilled and passionate orator.

During the late nineteenth and early twentieth centuries, Jones worked as a union organizer throughout the United States, including the Appalachian coalfields. Despite her age, she chose to live and strike as the miners did, often navigating difficult terrain, going without food, and sleeping outdoors. Though Mother Jones was dedicated to human rights, she did not have a unified philosophy about how to achieve this worthy goal. At times she advocated violence, as in the Paint Creek–Cabin Creek (West Virginia) strike of 1912–1913, while at other times she endorsed civil disobedience. She also organized miners' wives and encouraged them on the strike lines, although she opposed women's suffrage.

When the well-loved organizer died, more than fifteen thousand working people attended her funeral, and thirty thousand attended a subsequent memorial service held in her honor.

FROM Autobiography of Mother Jones

FROM CHAPTER XVIII: VICTORY IN WEST VIRGINIA

One morning when I was west, working for the Southern Pacific machinists, I read in the paper that the Paint Creek Coal Company would not settle with their men and had driven them out into the mountains. I knew that Paint Creek country. I had helped the miners organize that district in 1904 and now the battle had to be fought all over again. [. . .]

From the brakemen and the conductor of the train I picked up the story of the strike. It had started on the other side of the Kanawha hills in a frightful district called "Russia,"—Cabin Creek. Here the miners had been peons for years, kept in slavery by the guns of the coal company, and by the system of paying in scrip so that a miner never had any money should he wish to leave the district. He was cheated of his wages when his coal was weighed, cheated in the company store where he was forced to purchase his food, charged an exorbitant rent for his kennel in which he lived and bred, docked for school tax and burial tax and physician and for "protection," which meant the gunmen who shot him back into the mines if he rebelled or so much as murmured against his outrageous exploitation. No one was allowed in the Cabin Creek district without explaining his reason for being there to the gunmen who patrolled the roads, all of which belonged to the coal company. The miners finally struck—it was a strike of desperation.

The strike of Cabin Creek spread to Paint Creek, where the operators decided to throw their fate in with the operators of Cabin Creek. Immediately all civil and constitutional rights were suspended. The miners were told to quit their houses, and told at the point of a gun. They established a tent colony in Holly Grove and Mossey. But they were not safe here from the assaults of the gunmen, recruited in the big cities from the bums and criminals.

To protect their women and children, who were being shot with poisoned bullets, whose houses were entered and rough-housed, the miners armed themselves as did the early settlers against the attacks of wild Indians.

"Mother, it will be sure death for you to go into the Creeks," the brakeman told me. "Not an organizer dares go in there now. They have machine guns on the highway, and those gunmen don't care whom they kill."

The train stopped at Paint Creek Junction and I got off. There were a lot of gunmen, armed to the teeth, lolling about. [. . .]

I stood for a moment looking up at the everlasting hills when suddenly a little boy ran screaming up to me, crying, "Oh Mother Jones! Mother Jones! Did you come to stay with us?" He was crying and rubbing his eyes with his dirty little fist.

"Yes, my lad, I've come to stay," said I.

A guard was listening.

"You have?" says he.

"I have!" says I.

The little fellow threw his arms around my knees and held me tight.

"Oh Mother, Mother," said he, "they drove my papa away and we don't know where he is, and they threw my mama and all the kids out of the house and they beat my mama and they beat me."

He started to cry again and I led him away up the creek. All the way he sobbed out his sorrows, sorrows no little child should ever know; told of brutalities no child should ever witness.

"See, Mother, I'm all sore where the gunmen hit me," and he pulled down his cotton shirt and showed me his shoulders which were black and blue.

"The gunmen did that?"

"Yes, and my mama's worse'n that!" Suddenly he began screaming, "The gunmen! The gunmen! Mother, when I'm a man I'm going to kill twenty gunmen for hurting my mama! I'm going to kill them dead—all dead!"

I went up to the miners' camp in Holly Grove where all through the winter, through snow and ice and blizzard, men and women and little children had shuddered in canvas tents that America might be a better country to live in. I listened to their stories. I talked to Mrs. Sevilla whose unborn child had been kicked dead by gunmen while her husband was out looking for work. I talked with widows, whose husbands had been shot by the gunmen; with children whose frightened faces talked more effectively than their baby tongues. I learned how the scabs had been recruited in the cities, locked in boxcars, and delivered to the mines like so much pork.

"I think the strike is lost, Mother," said an old miner whose son had been killed.

"Lost! Not until your souls are lost!" said I. [. . .]

One night in July, a young man, Frank Keeney, came to me. "Mother," he said, "I have been up to Charleston trying to get some one to go up to Cabin Creek, and I can't get anyone to go. The national officers say they don't want to get killed. Boswell told me you were over here in the Paint Creek and that perhaps you might come over into the Cabin Creek district. "

"I'll come up," said I. "I've been thinking of invading that place for some time."

I knew all about Cabin Creek—old Russia. Labor organizer after organizer had been beaten into insensibility, thrown into the creek, tossed into some desolate ravine. The creek ran with the blood of brave men, of workers who had tried to escape their bondage. [. . .]

Monday night, a fellow by the name of Ben Morris, a national board member came to me and said, "Mother, I understand you are going up to Cabin Creek tomorrow. Do you think that is wise?"

"It's not wise," said I, "but necessary."

"Well, if you go, I'll go," said he.

"No, I think it is better for me to go alone. You represent the National office. I don't. I'm not responsible to anyone. If anything happens and you are there, the operators might sue the Union for damages. I go as a private citizen. All they can do to me is to put me in jail. I'm used to that."

He left me and went directly to the governor and told him to send a company of the militia up to Cabin Creek as I was going up there. Then he got the sheriff to give him a body guard and he sneaked up behind me. At any rate I did not see him or the militia on the train nor did I see them when I got off. [. . .]

That night we held a meeting. When I got up to speak I saw the militia that the national organizer had had the governor send. The board member was there. He had made arrangements with the local chairman to introduce him. He began speaking to the men about being good and patient and trusting to the justice of their cause.

I rose. "Stop that silly trash," said I. I motioned him to a chair. The men hollered, "sit down! sit down!"

He sat. Then I spoke.

"You men have come over the mountains," said I, " twelve, sixteen miles. Your clothes are thin. Your shoes are out at the toes. Your wives and little ones are cold and hungry! You have been robbed and enslaved for years! And now Billy Sunday comes to you and tells you to be good and patient and trust to justice! What silly trash to tell to men whose goodness and patience has cried out to a deaf world."

I could see the tears in the eyes of those poor fellows. They looked up into my face as much as to say, "My God, Mother, have you brought us a ray of hope?"

Some one screamed, "Organize us, Mother!"

Then they all began shouting . . . "Organize us! Organize us!"

"March over to that dark church on the corner and I will give you the obligation," said I.

The men started marching. In the dark the spies could not identify them.

"You can't organize those men," said the board member, "because you haven't the ritual."

"The ritual, hell," said I. "I'll make one up!"

"They have to pay fifteen dollars for a charter," said he.

"I will get them their charter," said I. "Why these poor wretches haven't fifteen cents for a sandwich. All you care about is your salary regardless of the destiny of these men."

On the steps of the darkened church, I organized those men. They raised their hands and took the obligation to the Union.

"Go home from this meeting," said I. "Say nothing about being a union man. Put on your overalls in the morning, take your dinner buckets and go to work in the mines, and get the other men out."

They went to work. Every man who had attended the meeting was discharged. That caused the strike, a long, bitter, cruel strike. Bullpens came. Flags came. The militia came. More hungry, more cold, more starving, more ragged than Washington's army that fought against tyranny were the miners of the Kanawha Mountains. And just as grim. Just as heroic. Men died in those hills that others might be free.

One day a group of men came down to Eksdale from Red Warrior Camp to ask me to come up there and speak to them. Thirty-six men came down in their shirt sleeves. They brought a mule and a buggy for me to drive in with a little miner's lad for a driver. I was to drive in the creek bed as that was the only public road and I could be arrested for trespass if I took any other. The men took the shorter and easier way along the C. and O. tracks which paralleled the creek a little way above it.

Suddenly as we were bumping along I heard a wild scream. I looked up at the tracks along which the miners were walking. I saw the men running, screaming as they went. I heard the whistle of bullets. I jumped out of the buggy and started to run up to the track. One of the boys screamed, "God! God! Mother, don't come. They'll kill . . ."

"Stand still," I called. "Stand where you are. I'm coming!"

When I climbed up onto the tracks I saw the boys huddled together, and around a little bend of the tracks, a machine gun and a group of gunmen.

"Oh Mother, don't come," they cried. "Let them kill us; not you!"

"I'm coming and no one is going to get killed," said I.

I walked up to the gunmen and put my hand over the muzzle of the gun. Then I just looked at those gunmen, very quiet, and said nothing. I nodded my head for the miners to pass.

"Take your hands off that gun, you hellcat!" yelled a fellow called Mayfield, crouching like a tiger to spring at me.

I kept my hand on the muzzle of the gun. "Sir," said I, "my class goes into the mines. They bring out the metal that makes this gun. This is my gun! My class melt the minerals in furnaces and roll the steel. They dig the coal that feeds furnaces. My class is not fighting you, not you. They are fighting with bare fists and empty stomachs the men who rob them and deprive their children of childhood. It is the hard-earned pay of the working class that your pay comes from. They aren't fighting you."

Several of the gunmen dropped their eyes but one fellow, this Mayfield, said, "I don't care a damn! I'm going to kill every one of them, and you, too!"

I looked him full in the face. "Young man," said I, "I want to tell you that if you shoot one bullet out of this gun at those men, if you touch one of my white hairs, that creek will run with blood, and yours will be the first to crimson it. I do not want to hear the screams of these men, nor to see the tears, nor feel the heartache of wives and little children. These boys have no guns! Let them pass!"

"So our blood is going to crimson the creek, is it!" snarled this Mayfield.

I pointed to the high hills. "Up there in the mountain I have five hundred miners. They are marching armed to the meeting I am going to address. If you start the shooting, they will finish the game."

Mayfield's lips quivered like a tiger's deprived of its flesh.

"Advance!" he said to the miners.

They came forward. I kept my hand on the gun. The miners were searched. There were no guns on them. They were allowed to pass.

I went down the side of the hill to my buggy. The mule was chewing grass and the little lad was making a willow whistle. I drove on. That night I held my meeting.

But there weren't any five hundred armed men in the mountains. Just a few jack rabbits, perhaps, but I had scared that gang of cold blooded, hired murderers and Red Warrior camp was organized. [. . .]

The struggle went on with increasing bitterness. The militia disarmed both gunmen and miners but they were of course, on the side of the grand dukes of the region. They forbade all meetings. They suspended every civil right. They became despotic. They arrested scores of miners, tried them in military court, without jury, sentenced them to ten, fifteen years in the Moundsville prison.

I decided to call the attention of the national government to conditions in West Virginia. I borrowed one hundred dollars and went out and billed meetings in Cincinnati, Columbus, Cleveland, and from these cities I came to Washington, D.C. I had already written to Congressman W. B. Wilson, to get up a protest meeting.

The meeting was held in the armory and it was packed: senators, congressmen, secretaries, citizens. It is usual to have star orators at such meetings, who use parlor phrases. Congressman Wilson told the audience that he hoped they would not get out of patience with me, for I might use some language which Washington was not accustomed to hear.

I told the audience what things were happening in West Virginia, proceedings that were un-American. I told them about the suspension of civil liberty by the military. Of the wholesale arrests and military sentences.

"This is the seat of a great republican form of government. If such crimes against the citizens of the state of West Virginia go unrebuked by the government, I suggest that we take down the flag that stands for constitutional government, and run up a banner, saying, 'This is the flag of the money oligarchy of America.'"

The next day by twelve o'clock all the military prisoners but two were called down to the prison office and signed their own release.

From Washington I went to West Virginia to carry on my work. The day before I arrived, an operator named Quinn Morton, the sheriff of Kanawha County, Bonner Hill, deputies and guards drove an armored train with gatling guns through Holly Grove, the tent colony of the miners, while they were sleeping. Into the quiet tents of the workers the guns were fired, killing and wounding the sleepers. A man by the name of Epstaw rose and picked up a couple of children and told them to run for their lives. His feet were shot off. Women were wounded. Children screamed with terror.

No one was arrested.

Three days later, a mine guard, Fred Bobbett, was killed in an altercation. Fifty strikers and their organizers were immediately arrested, and without warrant. [. . .]

We took the train for Charleston. I thought it better for the delegates to interview the governor without me, so after cautioning them to keep cool, I went over to the hotel where they were to meet me after their interview.

As I was going along the street, a big elephant, called Dan Cunningham, grabbed me by the arm and said, "I want you!" He took me to the Roughner Hotel, and sent for a warrant for my arrest. [. . .]

After many weeks we were taken before the judge advocate. The court had sent two lawyers to my bullpen to defend me but I had refused to let them defend me in that military court. I refused to recognize the jurisdiction of the court, to recognize the suspension of the civil courts. My arrest and trial were unconstitutional. I told the judge advocate that this was my position. I refused to enter a plea.

I was tried for murder. Along with the others I was sentenced to serve twenty years in the state penitentiary. I was not sent to prison immediately but held for five weeks in the military camp. I did not know what they were going to do with me. My guards were nice young men, respectful and courteous with the exception of a fellow called Lafferty, and another sewer rat whose name I have not taxed my mind with.

Then from California came aid. The great, lion-hearted editor of the San Francisco Bulletin, Fremont Older, sent his wife across the continent to Washington. She had a talk with Senator Kearns. From Washington she came to see me. She got all the facts in regard to the situation from the beginning of the strike to my unconstitutional arrest and imprisonment. She wrote the story for Collier's Magazine. She reported conditions to Senator Kearns, who immediately demanded a thorough congressional inquiry.

Some one dropped a Cincinnati Post through my prison window. It contained a story of Wall Street's efforts to hush up the inquiry. "If Wall Street gets away with this," I thought, "and the strike is broken, it means industrial bondage for long years to come in the West Virginia mines."

I decided to send a telegram, via my underground railway, to Senator Kearns. There was a hole in the floor of my prison-cabin. A rug covered the hole. I lifted the rug and rang two beer bottles against one another. A soldier who was my friend came crawling under the house to see "what was up." He had slipped me little things before, and I had given him what little I had to give—an apple, a magazine. So I gave him the telegram and told him to take it three miles up the road to another office. He said he would. "It's fine stuff, Mother," he said.

That night when he was off duty he trudged three miles up the road with the telegram. He sent it.

The next day in Washington, the matter of a congressional inquiry in the West Virginia mines came up for discussion in the Senate.

Senator Goff from Clarksburg, who had stock in the coal mines of West Virginia, got up on the floor and said that West Virginia was a place of peace until the agitators came in. "And the grandmother of agitators in this country," he went on, "is that old Mother Jones! I learn from the governor that she is not in prison at all but is only detained in a very pleasant boarding house!"

Senator Kearns rose. "I have a telegram from this old woman of eighty-four in this very pleasant boarding house," said he. "I will read it."

To the astonishment of the senators and the press he then read my telegram. They had supposed the old woman's voice was in prison with her body.

"From out the military prison walls of Pratt, West Virginia, where I have walked over my eighty-fourth milestone in history, I send you the groans and tears and heartaches of men, women and children as I have heard them in this state. From out these prison walls, I plead with you for the honor of the nation, to push that investigation, and the children yet unborn will rise and call you blessed."

Then the senate took action. A senatorial commission was appointed to investigate conditions. [. . .]

Shortly after the miner's convention, Governor Hatfield set aside all the military sentences, freeing all of the prisoners but eight. The operators recognized the union and many abuses were corrected.

The working men had much to thank Senator Kearns for. He was a great man, standing for justice and the square deal. Yet, to the shame of the workers of Indiana, when he came up for re-election they elected a man named Watson, a deadly foe of progress. I felt his defeat keenly, felt the ingratitude of the workers. It was through his influence that prison doors had opened, that unspeakable conditions were brought to light. I have felt that the disappointment of his defeat brought on his illness and ended the brave, heroic life of one of labor's few friends.

One day when I was in Washington, a man came to see me who said General Elliott had sent him to me. General Elliott was the military man who had charge of the prisoners sentenced to the penitentiary in the court martial during the strike. Never would I forget that scene on the station platform of Pratt when the men were being taken to Moundsville; the wives screaming frantically; the little children not allowed to kiss or caress their fathers. Neither the screams nor the sobs touched the stone heart of General Elliott.

And now General Elliott had sent a friend to me to ask me to give him a letter endorsing him for Congress.

"And did General Elliott send you?"

"Yes."

"Then tell the general that nothing would give me more pleasure than to give you a letter, but it would be a letter to go to hell and not to Congress!"

Members of the National Committee for the Defense of Political Prisoners (Dreiser Committee)

In 1931, the National Committee for the Defense of Political Prisoners, comprised of well-known writers Theodore Dreiser, John Dos Passos, Sherwood Anderson, and others, sponsored hearings in the Kentucky coalfields. The committee (known as the Dreiser Committee) also had a presence in Harlan to promote the Communist-oriented National Miners Union.

At the time of the investigations, Harlan County was in a state of turmoil so extreme that it was dubbed "Bloody Harlan." By 1929, coal production had fallen precipitously, accompanied by a sharp drop in work and wages. In the spring of 1931, eleven thousand workers struck after miners who had joined the United Mine Workers were fired. The strikers were evicted from their homes in company housing, and they moved to Evarts, a non-company town. Violence ensued, food became scarce, and although the governor sent in relief and ordered the mines to rehire union miners, county sheriff J. H. Blair, who worked on behalf of the coal operators, refused to relent. Police denied access to the press, harassed reporters, and prohibited the circulation of pro-union newspapers.

In 1932, the Dreiser Committee issued *Harlan Miners Speak: Report on Terrorism in the Kentucky Coal Fields,* which consists of vivid, firsthand accounts from residents of Harlan County and commentary by committee members. Despite this report and efforts in Harlan, miners did not win the right to organize until 1937.

FROM Harlan Miners Speak: Report on Terrorism in the Kentucky Coal Fields

Affidavit of Debs Moreland [. . .]

DEBS MORELAND, *being duly sworn, says:*

I am a resident of the town of Panzy, Harlan County, Kentucky. I was born in Birmingham, Alabama, and lived there until 1925 when I came to Panzy where I have since resided, being employed during such time by the Perkin Harlan Coal Company, in the capacity of miner.

On April 7, 1931, the employees of the Perkin Harlan Coal Company went out on strike. I was among them. From that date until the present time, although the mine has resumed periodic operation I have not been reemployed there, or elsewhere. On or about the beginning of August I was placed in charge of the Panzy Relief Kitchen which was being operated by the National Miners Union: This Relief Kitchen furnished food for about 100 families of striking miners. Food was furnished at the

Kitchen and was also provided for families of miners who were unable to come to the Kitchen.

I was arrested on or about August 24th and placed in jail where I was held on a trumped-up charge of Criminal Syndicalism until September 26th, when I was released without having been brought to trial. Judge D. C. Jones called me into his office that night about 6 P.M. and asked me to leave the State of Kentucky. He said, "I will release you on condition you do not go back and resume work which you have been doing." He asked me whether I belonged to the National Miners Union. I replied in the affirmative. He said he proposed to do away with the National Miners Union on the ground that it was a Communist organization and inquired whether I was aware of the fact that the National Miners Union was a branch of the Communist Party's affiliated bodies. I replied that I had not been aware of it, but that if conditions in Harlan County would be improved by the Communists or anyone else, I would throw my lot in with them. At that point, he showed me the door and as I emerged from his office he told the Deputy Sheriff in the anteroom to turn me loose. During this conversation, Judge Jones also stated there would not be a chance of my getting work in Harlan County, intimating that I was to be black-listed. I returned home and on or about the first of October, I resumed work at the Relief Kitchen.

On October 15th, at about 11 P.M., four of John Henry Blair's imported deputy sheriffs knocked on my door, called me by my name, and when I opened the door rushed by me into the house. I recognized these as the same men who had come to my house time and again and searched it, claiming to have search warrants. They organized raiding parties which went through house after house on regular trips and which broke up meetings whenever the miners attempted to hold them. These were a part of a group who were lodged in the Harlan Hotel and were not local police officials but were strangers to Harlan County but working hand in hand with the officials and the mine owners. They said they wanted to know if I lived there. I said, "Yes." They said, "We have a warrant against you for banding and confederating." I asked to see the warrant. One of them held out a paper. I reached for it. Another one grabbed it and said, "You don't have to see this. You are the man we want." I said, "It's mighty funny you have a warrant for me for banding and confederating. I have not been in any trouble." They said, "You know how it is. We have to do our duty. We have the warrant and we have to take you in. You can tell that to the judge."

I was hustled into their auto. They drove through Harlan (where the jail was located), through Cumberland, through Lynch, into Virginia, up at the top of Big Black Mountain, altogether a distance of about 60 miles. When we reached a point about a half mile beyond the top of Big Black Mountain, in a section uninhabited for miles about, in the midst of a thick forest, the car stopped. On one side of the road was a steep embankment, almost perpendicular, which fell to a depth of about 40 feet; on the other side was a sheer precipice at the top of which was an impenetrable forest. It was then about 1:30 in the morning, and a dark, moonless night. Three of these hired thugs got out of the car. The fourth sought to obtain information from me as to the number of organizers there were for the National Miners Union in the county, how many guns we had, and where our guns were. I said I had no knowledge of these matters. He said, "You are nothing but a thoroughbred red, and we haven't any use for you. And we intend to break it up." At that point he said, "Unload." And followed me out of the car.

I emerged from the car and they formed a circle about me. I asked what they intended to do, beat me up? One answered, "No, you son of a bitch, we are not going to beat you up. We are going to kill you. We are damned tired of being bothered with you reds." At that time I was given a terrific blow from behind on the back of my neck which felled me. When I arose, another one hit me on the cheek and knocked me down again. They pulled me to my feet, tearing at my clothes. I saw that my only hope was to make a dash, so I tore loose and made a lunge over the embankment. I slid and rolled down the embankment about 30 feet, tearing my clothes more and being bruised by the stones and shrubs until I was stopped by a large rock. I lay there half stunned, just conscious of their flash lights playing about and the whiz of bullets flying all around me. About 25 shots were fired. Then I heard them say, "That's one red son of a bitch we are rid of." I saw the reflection of the head lights of their car rounding the curve as they drove away.

I was unable to move and lay there until about 5:30 A.M. Then after numerous attempts I succeeded in reaching the top of the bank At about six o'clock a car came along and at my request consented to take me along to Big Stone Gap, a town about 10 miles further into Virginia. At the moment I left this car at Big Stone Gap, two cars crowded with Harlan thugs drove by, probably coming from the place where my death had been planned to see whether the job had been satisfactorily done. I darted into a hallway when I saw them, and in this way probably saved my life for the second time. I got a lift in a truck out of Big Stone Gap and slept on the side of the road that night. In the morning I got another ride in Middleboro. From there, I made my way to Chattanooga, Tenn., then to Lexington, Ky., then to New York.

It was not until a week after I had been kidnaped from my home for the purpose of murder that I was able to communicate with my wife and child in Panzy. I received a letter from my wife thereafter that Blair denies having issued any warrant for me at any time.

Protest Songs from the
Textile Mills and Coalfields

Protest songs have sustained strikers on picket lines, memorialized disasters, galvanized support for unions, sparked folk revivals, and established Appalachia in the national consciousness as a site of labor struggle. In *Coal Dust on the Fiddle* (1943), a collection of songs from the bituminous coal mines, George Korson explains that the folk songs of immigrant miners, traditional ballads of the Southern Appalachians, and African American spirituals combined in music that documented and commemorated life in the mines.

In 1931, protest singers Aunt Molly Jackson and her siblings came to the attention of the Dreiser Committee, which had come to eastern Kentucky to investigate the oppression of striking coal miners. When Theodore Dreiser took Jackson to New York, her plaintive tone and direct manner captivated influential folk song collectors, including Pete Seeger, who adapted many of Jackson's songs and helped start a musical movement that reached its height in the folk festivals of the 1960s.

Less well known than the music of coal, protest songs from the textile mills played an important role in the labor strife of the 1920s. Millhand and union member Ella May Wiggins, born in Sevierville, Tennessee, and killed en route to a union rally, composed "The Mill Mother's Song" in 1929.

In workshops at the Highlander Folk School during the 1960s and 1970s, Guy and Candie Carawan recast these compositions as "freedom songs," the most famous of which was "We Shall Overcome." With the current movement to ban mountain-top-removal coal mining, the music of protest is undergoing yet another transition as people employ it in support of the cause.

The Mill Mother's Song

ELLA MAY WIGGINS

We leave our home in the morning,
We kiss our children good-bye,
While we slave for the bosses,
Our children scream and cry.

And when we draw our money,
Our grocery bills to pay,
Not a cent to spend for clothing,
Not a cent to lay away.

And on that very evening,
Our little son will say,
"I need some shoes dear mother,
And so does sister May."

How it grieves the heart of a mother
You every one must know,
But we can't buy for our children,
Our wages are too low.

Now listen to me, Workers,
Both women and men,
We are sure to win our union,
If all would enter in.

I hope this will be a warning,
I hope you will understand,
And help us win our victory,
And lend to us a hand.

It is for our dear children
That seem to us so dear,
But for us nor them, dear workers,
The bosses do not care.

But understand all workers,
Our union they do fear,
Let's stand together, workers,
And have a union here.

Hard Times in Coleman's Mine

AUNT MOLLY JACKSON

You sit down for breakfast and all you have to eat
Is cornbread and bulldog gravy without a bite of meat.
It's a hard time in old Coleman's mines,
A hard time, poor boys.

In the summertime, you live on cornbread and wild greens,
In the winter time, you live on cornbread and pinto beans.
It's a hard time in old Coleman's mines,
A hard time, poor boys.

You go in the mine and work all day without a bite to eat,
Without a pair of pants to wear, no shoes on your feet.
It's a hard time in old Coleman's mines,
A hard time, poor boys.

When you're asked about leaving, this is what you say:
We're so darn poor and ragged, we can never get away.
It's a hard time in old Coleman's mines,
A hard time, poor boys.

You're all ragged and hungry, worried and blue,
And I'm so disgusted that I don't know what to do.
It's a hard time in old Coleman's mines,
A hard time, poor boys.

Well I will do the best I can and do, you do as you like,
But you better all get together, boys, and come out on a strike.
It's a hard time in Coleman's mines,
A hard time, poor boys.

Strike for union conditions, boys, that's seventy cents a ton,
Get together like big brothers, boys, till a victory you have won.
It's a hard time in these old mines,
A hard time, I know.

Which Side Are You On?

FLORENCE REECE

Come all you good workers,
Good news to you I'll tell,
Of how that good old union,
Has come in here to dwell.

Chorus:
Which side are you on, boys?
Which side are you on?
Which side are you on, boys?
Which side are you on?

My daddy was a miner,
And I'm a miner's son,
And I'll stick with the union,
Till every battle's won.

They say in Harlan County,
There are no neutrals there.
You'll either be a union man,
Or a thug for J. H. Blair.

Oh workers can you stand it?
Oh tell me how you can!
Will you be a lousy scab,
Or will you be a man?

Don't scab for the bosses,
Don't listen to their lies.
Poor folks ain't got a chance,
Unless they organize.
(*Chorus*)

The L&N Don't Stop Here Anymore

Jean Ritchie

Oh, when I was a curly headed baby,
My daddy sat me down on his knee.
He said, "Son, go to school and learn your letters,
Don't you be no dusty miner, boy, like me."

Chorus: (repeat after each verse)
For, I was born and raised
At the mouth of Hazard Holler,
Coal cars rolled and rumbled past my door.
Now they stand in a rusty row all empty,
And the L&N don't stop here anymore.

I used to think my daddy was a black man
With scrip enough to buy the company store.
But now he goes downtown with empty pockets
And his face is white as a February snow.

Last night I dreamed I went down to the office
To get my payday like I done before.
Them ol' kudzu vines had covered up the doorway,
And there was trees and grass, well, growin' right through the floor.

I never thought I'd live to love this coal dust,
Never thought I'd pray to hear the tipple's roar.

But Lord, how I wish that grass would turn to money,
And those greenbacks filled my pocket once more.

They Can't Put It Back

BILLY EDD WHEELER

Down in the valley 'bout a mile from me
Where the crows no longer cry
There's a great big earth moving monster machine
Stands ten stories high
The ground he can eat is a sight
Takes a hundred tons at a bite
He can dig up the grass, it's a fact
But he can't put it back

They come and tell me I got to move
To make way for the big machine
But I ain't a movin' unless they kill me
Like they kill the fish in my stream
But look at the big machine go
Took that shady grove
A long time to grow
He can rip it out with one whack
But he can't put it back

I never was one to carry signs, oh no
Picket with placards, walk in lines
Maybe, I'm behind the times

You can bet your sweet life
They're gonna hear from me
I ain't gonna take it layin' down
'Cause I'm gettin' tired of seeing rocks that bleed
On the bare guts of the ground
I ain't gonna sell my soul
So they can strip out another little tiny vein o' coal
I ain't a-movin' outta' my tracks
'Cause they can't put it back
They can't put it back
They can't put it back

Muriel Rukeyser

1913–1980

Born to a wealthy family in New York City, poet and essayist Muriel Rukeyser sought to make sense of the discrepancies she saw between the privileges of her youth, the loss of her family's money in the Great Depression, and the difficulties faced by other families around her. Her prolific career began at the age of twenty-two when poet Stephen Vincent Benét chose her first poetry collection, *Theory of Flight* (1935), for publication in the Yale Younger Poets series. After attending Vassar College in the 1930s, Rukeyser wrote for magazines such as *New Masses* and *Daily Worker*.

Rukeyser investigated the case of injustice at the Hawk's Nest Tunnel, still deemed the worst intentional industrial disaster in American history: over seven hundred workers died from silicosis contracted while drilling the tunnel in the early 1930s. The lung disease, which even at the time was preventable, resulted from ineptitude and negligence on the part of Union Carbide, the company in charge of the project.

In "Absalom," Rukeyser writes in the voice of a mother of three sons who died from silicosis because of their work at Hawk's Nest. The mother's individual voice for her sons becomes a universal voice seeking justice for all. Rukeyser's writing style is experimental. In *The Book of the Dead*, published in her poetry collection *U.S. 1*, from which "Absalom" is taken, Rukeyser interweaves sources such as trial transcriptions with passages from the Egyptian *Book of the Dead*.

Absalom

I first discovered what was killing these men.
I had three sons who worked with their father in the tunnel:
Cecil, aged 23, Owen, aged 21, Shirley, aged 17.
They used to work in a coal mine, not steady work
for the mines were not going much of the time.
A power Co. foreman learned that we made home brew,
he formed a habit of dropping in evenings to drink,
persuading the boys and my husband—
give up their jobs and take this other work.
It would pay them better.
Shirley was my youngest son; the boy.
He went into the tunnel.

> *My heart   my mother   my heart   my mother*
> *My heart   my coming into being.*

My husband is not able to work.
He has it, according to the doctor.
We have been having a very hard time making a living since
    this trouble came to us.
I saw the dust in the bottom of the tub.
The boy worked there about eighteen months,
came home one evening with a shortness of breath.
He said, "Mother, I cannot get my breath."
Shirley was sick about three months.
I would carry him from his bed to the table,
from his bed to the porch, in my arms.

    My heart is mine in the place of hearts,
    They gave me back my heart, it lies in me.

When they took sick, right at the start, I saw a doctor.
I tried to get Dr. Harless to X-ray the boys.
He was the only man I had any confidence in,
the company doctor in the Kopper's mine,
but he would not see Shirley.
He did not know where his money was coming from.
I promised him half if he'd work to get compensation,
but even then he would not do anything.
I went on the road and begged the X-ray money,
the Charleston hospital made the lung pictures,
he took the case after the pictures were made.
And two or three doctors said the same thing.
The youngest boy did not get to go down there with me,
he lay and said, "Mother, when I die,
I want you to have them open me up and
see if that dust killed me.
Try to get compensation,
you will not have any way of making your living
when we are gone,
and the rest are going too."

    I have gained mastery over my heart
    I have gained mastery over my two hands
    I have gained mastery over the waters
    I have gained mastery over the river.

The case of my son was the first of the line of lawsuits.
They sent the lawyers down and the doctors down;
they closed the electric sockets in the camps.

There was Shirley, and Cecil, Jeffrey and Oren,
Raymond Johnson, Clev and Oscar Anders,
Frank Lynch, Henry Palf, Mr. Pitch, a foreman;
a slim fellow who carried steel with my boys,
his name was Darnell, I believe. There were many others,
the towns of Glen Ferris, Alloy, where the white rock lies,
six miles away; Vanetta, Gauley Bridge,
Gamoca, Lockwood, the gullies,
the whole valley is witness.
I hitchhike eighteen miles, they make checks out.
They asked me how I keep the cow on $2.
I said one week, feed for the cow, one week, the children's flour.
The oldest son was twenty-three.
The next son was twenty-one.
The youngest son was eighteen.
They called it pneumonia at first.
They would pronounce it fever.
Shirley asked that we try to find out.
That's how they learned what the trouble was.

> *I open out a way, they have covered my sky with crystal*
> *I come forth by day, I am born a second time,*
> *I force a way through, and I know the gate*
> *I shall journey over the earth among the living.*

He shall not be diminished, never;
I shall give a mouth to my son.

Don West
1906–1992

Born into a family of north Georgia sharecroppers, Don West became a poet, educator, activist, and organizer who celebrated, questioned, and defended the people and the land from which he came. While an undergraduate at Lincoln Memorial University, West befriended two fellow students, James Still and Jesse Stuart; all three became important writers. Stuart and West eventually parted ways because of ideological differences. Whereas Stuart romanticized the mountaineer by celebrating the agrarian ideal and avoided political engagement, West believed poetry should be politically committed and address the common person's struggles.

West became increasingly politicized as he witnessed the cruel effects of the Great Depression on the already impoverished Appalachian coalfields and small farms. After receiving a grant to tour the Danish folk schools popularized by John C. and Olive Dame Campbell, West decided to adapt that model of adult education to create a center for training leaders in social justice movements. On his return, he met Myles Horton, himself an educator and activist raising money for a similar school. Working together, they co-founded the Highlander Folk School in Tennessee in 1932.

Because of his pro-union and anti-segregation stance, West was targeted by conservative politicians and Ku Klux Klan members. West, however, never lost his belief in the Social Gospel and veneration for the image of "Jesus the Toiler" who required people to take action on behalf of the poor and oppressed.

What Shall a Poet Sing?

What is a poet saying
Down by a Georgia pine
Where a broken body's swaying
Hung to a cotton line . . . ?

With his folk all burdened down,
Pinched by hunger's pang,
Whether he's white or brown,
What shall a poet sing . . . ?

Symbols

They were symbols,
The preacher said—

The bread and wine
In memory of him,
Of Jesus the Toiler . . .

I see other symbols.
Hungry and cold
They tramp America
Like ghosts passing by—
In the coal camps,
Dirty with dust,
Begging a crust,
A nickel, a dime,
Or an old coat
For winter time.

Toiler's children,
Gaunt and tired,
With rickets and flux—
These are symbols I see . . .

Toil and Hunger

Toil and hunger
Took him away—
My old Dad.
While he ripped up
The sad red earth
His life dripped down
In the furrow,
And Georgia's clay hills
Sucked it up.

Plum trees blossom
From sweat-salted earth
And sorrow climbs up
Through the leaves
To scent the flowers
On the blooming trees.

Toil and hunger
Attended his birth,
And bury him now
In the sad red earth!

No Lonesome Road

For Byron Reece

Once I too said that all men walk
A solitary road
And that each one must grope alone
And drag his little load.

I thought that I must walk forlorn
Upon that lonesome street
All hedged about the granite walls
Of pride and self-conceit.

But now I've learned that all can trudge
Upon a common way
Thru moonlit night and stumbling dark
Or in the flaming day.

And men cry out in word and name
As they are passing by
To those whose faith and fortitude
Have shoved them near the sky

Like Galileo at the stake,
Jesus nailed to a tree.
Cold bleeding feet at Valley Forge
Are on that road with me.
And I would not forget the men
Who dig and plow the soil
And those who fight that all shall live
With simple lives of toil.

It is no lonesome road we tread
Though so the cynics say.
The poet, farmer, working man
Must walk a common way.

Thomas Bell
1903–1961

Born Adalbert Thomas in Braddock, Pennsylvania, to Slovak immigrant parents, Thomas Bell was intimately familiar with the plight of immigrant laborers in the steel mills. Bell published six novels, one of which was made into a film, *From This Day Forward* (1946), and one into a Broadway play, *Till I Come Back to You* (1943), but *Out of This Furnace* (1941) is his most enduring work.

Covering the lives of three generations (from the 1880s to 1937) of a working-class Slovak family that immigrated to Braddock, the novel depicts the machinations of both the steel industry and the steelworkers' union. *Out of This Furnace* is in part autobiographical. Bell's precise portrayal of many aspects of life in Braddock, from the names of the alleys to the detailed description of mill housing, points to his intimate knowledge of this community. Bell, however, changed some family history to make it less dramatic in its fictional form and therefore more believable. Bell said that he wrote the novel after he witnessed the oppression of Slovak immigrants. Though the novel focuses on a long list of injustices, it ends on an optimistic tone as the union wins rights for steel mill workers.

Bell changes his narrative style with each of the three generations, demonstrating how successive generations found a distinct voice as they shaped their cultural and political identities. Dobie, the narrator of the chapter excerpted here, reflects that he was forged in the furnace of adversity to become a strong union man who believed in freedom and the rights of the worker.

FROM Out of This Furnace

[CHAPTER] 17

He came home on the day before Christmas. After Washington's marbled vistas Braddock looked mean and soiled; after the hotel's splendors,—its rugs, its carefully assembled furnishings, its Niagaras of hot water,—the house seemed cramped and a little shabby, Julie's modest attempts at elegance more heart-warming than successful. "The party's over," he reflected, conscious of a letdown. He lunched on scrambled eggs and wondered if he still had a job. Without Julie the house felt empty.

He was going to join her in Donora for Christmas with her family. On the way to the union office he phoned the grocery store near her mother's house. Their conversation was brief. "I couldn't talk with those people just dying to hear what I was saying," she explained later. Her voice over the phone took him back to the days when they were going together. "I bet you don't remember the last time I called you up."

"You called me? When?"

"The day we were married."

"Was that the last time? My goodness!" She paused, and Dobie could hear the store's doorbell tinkle as someone entered or departed. "Well, get here as soon as you can. Unless you'd rather have me come home."

"No, you stay right where you are. I'll be up on that train gets to Webster around seven."

"Can't you come any sooner?"

"No trains. Besides, I have to pick up my pay, missus. And I want to stop down the union."

"Well, all right. But don't be too late."

The house, he assured her, was undisturbed, and the Cassidys seemed to be taking care of the dog and the chickens satisfactorily.

As he entered the union office the organizer let his heels drop to the floor with a thump. "Well, it's about time! I was wondering when you'd show up." He shook hands as though he hadn't seen Dobie for months. "Where's Hagerty?"

"I left him in Pittsburgh. They wanted to have a talk with him about that spy business."

"I read about that." The organizer cocked an eyebrow. "It sounded a little fishy to me."

"Oh, I guess it was on the level all right. After all, he was under oath. I think Murray and the rest of them were sore, though. Because he didn't let them in on it beforehand."

"He didn't? Hell, I don't blame them. But it's just the kind of thing he'd do. He gets an idea and says it or does it without thinking and then he wonders why somebody's always jumping on him. He can't get it into his head that working with an organization isn't the same as being on your own."

He glanced at his watch. "Were you going anywhere right away?"

"I want to pick up my pay. Yesterday was payday, wasn't it?"

"Sure. Well listen. They're having a special meeting around ha' past-three. They figured you and Hagerty might show up in time and tell them all about it."

Dobie shifted Julie's Christmas present—a silver-boxed, tissue-wrapped nightgown that had cost him five dollars in Washington—under his arm and fumbled for his tobacco and papers.

"Think the cop will let me in?"

"Why the hell not?"

"You know what Todd said before I left."

"I wouldn't let that worry me."

"No, but it won't be a hell of a merry Christmas for us if I find out he meant it."

"Your envelope ought to tell you."

"Yeah, I thought of that. Well, I may as well go down."

"If Hagerty shows up I'll send him right along."

"Okay."

Braddock Avenue was lively with Christmas crowds under a heavy, sunless sky. He was stopped twice by men who said they'd read about him in the papers and asked questions about Washington. At the general office building the guard on duty in the hall nodded as he came through the door. He said the meeting hadn't started yet but a couple of the boys were downstairs. Dobie went first to the cashier's window. The cashier nodded too and after the usual delay pushed an envelope toward him. Dobie glanced at the figures in one corner. They were for his regular two weeks' wages.

Feeling better, he went downstairs. The meeting room was a bare, cheerless place, plainly furnished with a battered table, chairs that didn't match and a ceiling radiator which periodically sprayed Employee and Management Representatives alike with boiling water. The view from the windows—the concrete retaining wall set into the railroad embankment back of the building—was uninspiring. Several men were already there and others kept coming; after the quitting whistle blew a whole group arrived in work clothes.

He told them about Washington.

Gralji said, "I hear you met Lewis."

"That's right. They took us to his office the first day."

"What kind of a guy is he?"

"He looks just like his pictures, if that's what you mean. He shook hands and talked for a while and then we went to the Labor Board."

"What did he have to say?"

"Oh, I don't remember. He asked us about the trip and how things were in the mills and stuff like that."

"Big bastard, ain't he?"

"He's big, all right."

They wanted to know about Hagerty and he told them what he knew. Opinion was divided. "What he should've done," someone said, "was like that fella in Clairton or Duquesne or wherever it was. The one that told the Swock"—he pronounced S.W.O.C. like a word—"about being offered a spy job and they said all right, take it, and he deposited the money he got with the Swock and made out phony reports."

"I'm only telling you what I know," Dobie said. "I didn't get much chance to talk to him. You'll have to wait till he gets here."

"We tried to get Carnegie Hall to hold a big meeting where you guys could make a report but they wouldn't let us have it. We're pretty sure that's some of Flack's work."

"I wouldn't be surprised. How's he been taking it?"

Gralji shrugged. Burke grinned. "I heard he's ordered another clock and is buying them pills of his by the barrel."

"He don't look so good and that's a fact."

Dobie rolled a cigarette. "Anybody heard anything about me and Hagerty getting fired?"

Nobody had.

"I just got my envelope and there's only my regular pay in it."

"If you were fired they would've paid you off."

"Yeah, but I'd like to know for sure. I won't enjoy my Christmas much if I have to keep wondering whether I still have a job."

"They won't fire you. They're in enough trouble now."

"The only way to make sure is go in and start to work. You'll have to wait till Monday, though. The mill shuts down tonight."

"Why don't you ask Flack?" Gralji suggested. "Just ask him straight out are you fired or ain't you?"

"Yeah, I could do that. Wonder if he's in."

He was saved the trip upstairs. The door opened and Flack strode in. Someone murmured, "Oh-oh! Fireworks," and then the room fell silent. Flack glanced around, his head moving jerkily. He barked, "Where's Hagerty?"

Dobie was sitting with one leg over a corner of the table, his foot swinging. It seemed to be up to him to reply. "I don't know, Mr. Flack. I haven't seen him since this morning."

Flack's spectacles caught the light and gave his expression a blank, cold stare. "Expect him here today?"

"He didn't say anything to me about coming."

Flack advanced farther into the room until he stood a few feet from Dobie. He was dressed in his usual dark suit, black necktie and pearl stickpin—a well-dressed, impressively neat man. And a thoroughly angry one. Anger radiated from him in waves that were almost visible. Dobie hadn't seen him so nearly beside himself since the day the defiant representatives had refused to sign the sliding scale agreement. "What the hell's eating him?" he wondered. Flack had been mentioned more than once in the Washington testimony and seldom flatteringly, but so had a dozen other Superintendents.

He stood slightly bowed, his hands twitching, his wrath all but lifting his heels off the floor. "I wanted to have a little heart-to-heart talk with Hagerty," he said. "With both of you." His speech was clipped and harsh. "I suppose you bastards are pretty proud of what you did down in Washington."

"I certainly ain't ashamed of it, Mr. Flack."

"Oh, you *ain't!*"

Dobie took a deep breath. "And I don't like to be called a bastard."

"I don't care whether you like it or not! Who in hell do you think you are?" His hand flew up. "I'll do the talking here! You're not in Washington now. Why did you lie about me?"

"I didn't lie about you."

"You're a God-damn' liar! You dragged my name through sweat and shit down there and by God I'll break you if it's the last thing I do! I'll show you!"

Dobie's lip curled. "You'll show me nothing. If you didn't like what was said about you in Washington that's too bad, but I didn't say anything that wasn't the truth. I was under oath and I didn't feel like going to jail for perjury."

Flack's sneer was monumental. "You've learned a lot since you've been hanging around with those Government bastards, haven't you?"

"I know I don't have to take this kind of crap from you or anybody else. You asked me who I thought I was. Well who the hell do you think you are, God? Listen, Mr. Flack: I don't like to be called names and I'm telling you for the last time I didn't lie about you; and if you keep saying I did I'll sue you for criminal libel, by Jesus I will!"

Flack turned purple. "Sue me? You'll sue me? Why you dumb Hunky son of a bitch I ought to ram this down your dirty throat!" His fist was six inches from Dobie's face.

Dobie slipped off the table. "Try it. Try it, you pot-bellied old bastard, and I'll knock you right through that door!"

The others surged between them, their voices a babble in Dobie's ears. He heard himself saying, "Oh, for Christ's sake let me go. I won't hurt the old bastard." The door opened and a guard stuck his head in. "What's going on in here?" he asked. Someone infected with the general belligerence snapped, "Nothing! Beat it!" and the guard withdrew his head in sheer astonishment. Flack was mopping his face, his hand shaking. Dobie glanced at Gralji. "Well, I guess that did it."

Then resentment stirred within him. "No, by God. I've been getting pushed around till I'm God-damn good and sick of it. We'll get this straightened out right now."

Men fell back as he approached Flack. The Superintendent looked up and for a moment there was something close to alarm in his eyes.

Dobie felt himself scowling. "We may as well finish this thing right now. Before I left Todd told me I'd be out of a job if I went to Washington. I want to know if that still goes." He paused. "I'm speaking as a representative, and as far as I'm concerned you can call in the stenographer and make it official."

Flack didn't reply. He kept mopping his face and it was hard to say whether he had understood.

"If I'm fired, all I want from you is a pass to get my tools and stuff out of the shop. If I ain't—well, that'll suit me fine."

Still Flack didn't reply. Dobie put one hand into his trousers' pocket. "I'll tell you this much, Mr. Flack. If you fire me that won't be the end of it. I ain't saying that to be tough or start an argument. It's just the plain fact."

Flack said hoarsely, "I think there has been too much arguing and trouble-making already." He cleared his throat. "We'd all be better off if we concentrated on doing our work as well as we could."

It was Dobie's turn to be silent.

Flack put his handkerchief away. When he spoke again his face was completely expressionless. "As to your—the matter you mentioned," he said, "there has never been any question of discharging anyone for activities outside working hours, and there won't be as long as I'm in charge here." His eyes swept the faces around him. "I want that clearly understood."

"That means I ain't fired, right?"

"I know of no reason why you shouldn't go to work as usual on Monday morning."

"Okay. That's fine. That's all I wanted to know."

Behind Dobie there was an approving murmur that made Flack lift his head. He couldn't have misunderstood it but perhaps he had been a steel mill Superintendent too long to value it. Imperceptibly he had resumed his usual manner. Now he stood erect and in the gaze he directed at Dobie there was most of the old arrogance, the cold impersonality of long-established authority.

"I should like to say this," he said, "speaking not as the Superintendent of this plant but personally. It has not been pleasant for myself or my family to have things published in the newspapers without being given an opportunity to reply. Not that I expect either your sympathy or your understanding. As for what happened here this afternoon, we were both excited and angry and may have said things we didn't really mean. I think the best thing we could all do is forget it."

Their eyes met. Dobie thought, "You meant every word of it, you bastard. And I don't forget that easy." And perhaps Flack's thoughts were not dissimilar. Aloud, Dobie said with a faint shrug, "That's okay with me, Mr. Flack."

For a second he wondered if Flack meant to offer his hand. He didn't; the movement of his hand was a gesture for room to pass. The circle of men broke.

No one spoke until the door had closed.

"What the hell did you guys say about him down there?" Burke demanded. "I didn't read anything in the papers that should've made him so sore."

Dobie shrugged. "I guess it was more the idea of having it said right out in court like that."

"You know what I think?" Gralji said. "I bet the big shots in New York and Pittsburgh never realized what was really going on and they've been raising hell with the Superintendents."

Dobie was getting into his coat. "Don't kid yourself. They knew, all right. If they're sore at him it's because he let it get as far as Washington."

Someone chuckled. "He sure was mad, wasn't he? Jesus, for a minute there I thought he'd bust. Especially when you started talking about suing him."

"Mad or not," Gralji said, "he didn't have any right to say some of the things he did."

"Dobie didn't do so bad himself, if you ask me."

"Where's my package? I don't want to lose that; it's my wife's Christmas present." He found it under a pile of coats, its silver bow somewhat discouraged. He slipped it under his arm and faced the others. His voice was edged with a sort of good-humored truculence. "Listen," he said: "I may be a Hunky but I ain't dumb and I ain't nobody's son of a bitch. Flack's just finding it out, that's all. Well, I got to catch a train. See you guys next week."

"Merry Christmas."

He paused at the door. "You're telling me. That's all I could think of, what a lousy Christmas we'd have if I was fired."

"How do you feel now?"

"Swell."

"Don't get into any more arguments."

He grinned. "Not me. I love peace. Well, so long."

"So long."

The guard looked his way as he came up the stairs; at the sound of his footsteps in the tiled hall faces were lifted from desk tops and the cashier's head swiveled slowly on his neck like some absurd puppet in a cage. He marched past them with an amused glint in his eyes. The guard wished him a merry Christmas and opened the door for him.

It was already dark outside. He halted for a moment on the steps, breathing in the cold, smoke-scented air. Someone came out of the gate across the way, moving up out of the darkness in the mill, passing briefly under the light swinging above the gate and then disappearing into the shadows of Thirteenth Street. People waited for a Dooker's Hollow bus on the corner. The windows of the automobile salesroom on the other corner—Dobie could remember when it was a car barn—were squares of bright light. Beyond them Braddock Avenue curved out of sight, its trolley tracks squeezed between lines of parked cars, its dreary buildings shabby even in the pink fog of its countless beer signs. He stood and contemplated it all, a lean, silent figure, his coat collar up, hands thrust in pockets, the frivolous package under his arm. And he felt good. The story of what had happened back there would be all over the mill in a week, and the farther it went the better it would get. It shouldn't do the membership campaign any harm, he reflected. But it wasn't of the union or even of Flack that he thought now.

He lifted his eyes to the dark sky. "We've come a long way, hey Pop?"

Then he went to join Julie.

PART V

Appalachian Folklore

Theresa Lloyd

The terms "folklore," "folklife," and "folkways" refer to cultural practices transmitted orally among members of a group. The literature represented in this section is an example of verbal folklore, more specifically folk narrative and folk song. These readings demonstrate both the bounty of folklore in Appalachia and the way that the region's folklore has been deployed to support cultural-political agendas.

Appalachian folklore provides a record of the ethnic history of the region. The Cherokee origin stories and tales presented in the first section of this anthology are a reminder of the Native American presence. Blues songs sung by both black and white Appalachians originated in the African American community. From the Scots-Irish, English, and Germans came secular and sacred songs, folktales, legends, and religious practices. With the rapid development of the coalfields and heavy industry in the region, immigrants from southern and eastern Europe arrived in Northern and Central Appalachia bringing folk traditions with them; although much of their verbal lore was lost as they adopted the English language, some of their folkways have continued.

Vernacular oral traditions are important in Appalachia's religious history and in some instances contemporary practice, especially among the Old Baptist, Holiness, Pentecostal, and independent congregations. These traditions are transmitted not in seminary but face-to-face in the oral tradition: hence their inclusion as folklore.

The idea of Southern Appalachia as a folk culture has cultural-political dimensions. For example, throughout the late nineteenth and early twentieth centuries, the presence of (supposedly) British folkways in Appalachia underpinned a portrait of the region as a rural Anglo-Saxon antidote to industrialism and immigration. Post–World War II developers capitalized on the image of picturesque folk residing in a scenic mountainous landscape as a marketing tool to attract tourists, at a time when in reality most Appalachian people themselves were as media savvy as their counterparts in the rest of the United States. In fact, as Appalachians adopted the latest fashions and technologies and substituted radio, film, and television for local storytelling and music, the number of active tradition-bearers in the region dwindled precipitously.

Written literature has also furthered the idea that Appalachia is a folk culture. Descriptions of material folk culture and quaint customs were a staple of Old Southwest Humor and local color. An excessively free hand with folkways has often bedeviled the region's literature up to the present, reinforcing stereotypes. Nowhere has Appalachian literature's reliance on folklore been more obvious than in the use of literary dialect—that is, attempting to replicate vernacular speech through phonetic spelling, nonstandard grammar, and a colorful vocabulary often identified as "Elizabethan" or "Chaucerian." Admittedly, Appalachian residents have spoken regional dialects; however, Appalachians have never spoken the English of Shakespeare or Chaucer.

Yet the uses of Appalachian folklore have more often been positive. Self-conscious collecting of folk material by local residents in the late twentieth century, such as for the *Foxfire* books or for deposition in Appalachian archives, has bolstered the regional pride of interviewers and interviewees. Late twentieth-century authors such as Fred Chappell and Lee Smith have incorporated folklore into their writing in a way that goes beyond window dressing to offer sensitive insight into Appalachian culture.

Thus, although it would be erroneous to see Appalachia purely as a folk culture, folklore continues to thrive in the region. Native Americans make conscious attempts to preserve tales, dance, music, and language. Small towns hold local foodways festivals. Bluegrass and old-time music jam sessions take place at community stores. New Hispanic immigrants compose songs about "Norte Carolina."

Since folklore is by definition a group endeavor and the original author of many folktales and folksongs is often unknown, we have organized this section by genre rather than by individual writer.

Sources: John B. Rehder, *Appalachian Folkways* (2004); Terry Jordan-Bychkov, *The Upland South: The Making of an American Folk Region and Landscape* (2003); Michael B. Montgomery and Joseph S. Hall, *Dictionary of Smoky Mountain English* (2004); Ted Olson, *Blue Ridge Folklife* (1998); Michael Ann Williams, *Great Smoky Mountains Folklife* (1995).

A Constellation of Folk Narratives

Appalachia boasts a rich assortment of myths, folktales, legends, and vernacular sacred narratives, all of which are represented in this anthology.

Myths are a culture's sacred texts; every culture has them, be they oral or written. The sacred texts of Appalachia's Euro-American settlers have long been inscribed in the Hebrew and Christian Bibles. Lacking writing until contact with whites, Native Americans conveyed their sacred teachings orally. When the Cherokee devised a written language, they began to inscribe their sacred texts in writing. The first section of this anthology opens with Cherokee texts collected orally from members of the Eastern Band.

The folk narratives for which Southern Appalachia is probably best known are folktales. Folktales are fictional; sometimes they are called "fairy tales," even though the tales rarely depict fairies. The most famous folktales from Southern Appalachia are the Jack tales (although not all Appalachian folktales deal with a character named Jack, and not all Jack tales are from Southern Appalachia). Jack tales contain motifs that can be found throughout European folktales. The most immediate source of the Appalachian Jack tales is the British tradition familiar to most readers from stories such as "Jack and the Beanstalk." We include a Jack tale told by Northern Appalachian storyteller Bonelyn Lugg Kyofski from Pennsylvania.

The most extensive genre of Appalachian storytelling is legend. Hardin Taliaferro drew on a tall-tale tradition from his birthplace, Surry County, North Carolina, when he wrote his account of Uncle Davy Lane in *Fisher's River (North Carolina) Scenes and Characters* (1859). In "Mat Layson," one of many legends collected by Leonard Roberts from the Kentucky brothers Dave and Jim Couch (pseudonyms), Jim Couch recounts a supernatural tale of witchcraft performed by his great-great-uncle. Animal and hunting legends in Appalachia (and elsewhere in the United States) sometimes become tall tales.

The setting for and purpose of telling tales varies. Among Euro-Americans in Appalachia, folktales were often told within the family or in other settings when children were present; the purpose was to entertain the children (or adults) and/or to keep them busy at a task. Many Appalachian children, like children throughout the United States, encountered folktales by hearing them read from a book (Richard Chase's Jack tales were favorites, along with conventional "fairy tale" collections). Supernatural and pioneering stories were recounted in the family or at neighborhood gatherings; a gifted teller could gain status in the community. Tall tales were more often swapped by men than by women. Stories were told on front porches, in front of the hearth, while lounging at a country store, during a hunt, or—in more recent times—in the break room at work. A relatively new venue for telling tales is the storytelling festival featuring professional tale-tellers. The storytelling revival began in the East Tennessee town of Jonesborough in 1973, and was the brainchild of Jimmy Neil Smith. Jonesborough annually hosts the renowned International Storytelling Festival.

Appalachia's religious traditions include some vernacular forms. In "spirit preaching," for example, common among the Old Baptists, Holiness, and Pentecostal churches, preachers chant their sermon rhythmically, punctuating each line with a vocalization such as "haah," which is shown in Howard Dorgan's transcription of a sermon by Elder Earl Sexton below. Another religious vernacular narrative tradition is that of the conversion narrative, delivered either publicly in sermons or testimonials, or privately in personal settings. We include two nineteenth-century Primitive Baptist conversion narratives.

Uncle Davy Lane

Hardin E. Taliaferro

I must not forget, in these random sketches, my old friend and neighbor Uncle Davy Lane. Some men make an early and decided impression upon you—features, actions, habits, all the entire man, real and artificial. "Uncle Davy" was that kind of man.

I will mention a few things that make me remember him. His looks were peculiar. He was tall, dark, and rough-skinned; lymphatic, dull, and don't-care-looking in his whole physiognomy. He had lazy looks and movements. Nothing could move him out of a slow, horse-mill gait but snakes, of which "creeturs he was monstrous 'fraid." The reader shall soon have abundant evidence of the truth of this admission in his numerous and rapid flights from "sarpunts."

Uncle Davy was a gunsmith, and, as an evidence of the fact, he carried about with him the last gun he ever made. His gun, a rifle, was characteristic of its maker and owner—rough and unfinished outside, but good within. It was put in an old, worm-eaten half-stock which he had picked up somewhere, and the barrel had never been dressed nor ground outside. He would visit a neighbor early in the morning, sit down with it across his knees, in "too great a hurry" to set it aside, would stay all day, would lay it by only at meals, which he seldom refused, but "never was a-hongry."

He had a great fund of long-winded stories and incidents, mostly manufactured by himself—some few he had "hearn"—and would bore you or edify you, as it might turn out, from sun to sun, interspersing them now and then with a dull, guttural, lazy laugh.

He became quite a proverb in the line of big story-telling. True, he had many obstinate competitors, but he distanced them all farther than he did the numerous snakes that "run arter him." He had given his ambitious competitors fair warning thus:

"Ef any on 'um beats me, I'll sell out my deadnin' and hustle off to other deadnin's."

In sheer justice to Uncle Davy, however, and with pleasure, I record the fact, that he reformed his life, became a Christian, I hope, as well as a Baptist, and died a penitent man.

As stated, he was never known to get out of a snail's gallop only when in contact with snakes; and the reader shall now have, in Uncle Davy's own style, an account of his flight from a coachwhip snake.

The Chase.

"I had a hog claim over beyant Moor's Fork, and I concluded I'd take old Bucks-masher (his rifle), and go inter the big huckleberry patch, on Round Hill, in sarch for 'um. Off I trolloped, and toddled about for some time, but couldn't find head nur tail uv 'um. But while I was moseyin' about, I cum right chug upon one uv the big-gest, longest, outdaciousest coachwhip snakes I uver laid my peepers on. He rared right straight up, like a May-pole, licked out his tarnacious tongue, and good as said, 'Here's at you, sir. What bizness have you on my grit?' Now I'd hearn folks say ef you'd look a vinimus animil right plump in the eyes he wouldn't hurt you. Now I tried that good, just like I war trying to look through a mill-stone. But, bless you, honey! he had no more respect fur a man's face and eyes than he had fur a huckleberry, sure's gun's iron. So I seed clearly that I'd have to try my trotters.

"I dashed down old Bucksmasher, jumped 'bout ten steps the fust leap, and on I went wusser nur an old buck fur 'bout a quarter, and turned my noggin round to look fur the critter. Jehu Nimshi! thar he were right dab at my heels, head up, tongue out, and red as a nail-rod, and his eyes like two balls uv fire, red as chain lightnin'. I 'creased my verlocity, jumped logs twenty foot high, clarin' thick bushes, and bush-heaps, deep gullies, and branches. Again I looked back, thinkin' I had sartinly left it a long gap behind. And what do you think? By jingo! he'd hardly begun to run—jist gittin' his hand in. So I jist put flatly down again faster than uver. 'Twasn't long afore I run out'n my shot-bag, I went so fast, then out'n my shirt, then out'n my britches—luther britches at that—then away went my drawers. Thus I run clean out'n all my linnen a half a mile afore I got home; and, thinks I, surely the tarnul sarpunt are distanced now.

"But what do you think now? Nebuchadnezzar! Thar he were, fresh as a mount-ing buck jist scared up. I soon seed that wouldn't do, so I jumped about thirty-five foot, screamed like a wildcat, and 'creased my verlocity at a monstrous rate. Jist then I begun to feel my skin split, and, thinks I, it's no use to run out'n my skin, like I hev out'n my linnen, as huming skin are scarce, so I tuck in a leetle.

"But by this time I'd run clean beyant my house, right smack through my yard, scaring Molly and the childering, dogs, cats, chickens—uvry thing—half to death. But, you see, I got shet uv my inimy, the sarpunt, for it had respect fur my house, ef it hadn't fur my face and eyes in the woods. I puffed, and blowed, and sweated 'bout half an hour afore I had wind to tell Molly and the childering what war the matter.

"Poor old Bucksmasher staid several days in the woods afore I could hev the pluck to go arter him."

When Uncle Davy told one snake story, he must needs exhaust his stock, big and little. After breathing a little from telling his coachwhip story, which always excited him, he would introduce and tell the story of his adventure with

The Horn-Snake.

"Fur some time arter I were chased by that sassy coachwhip, I were desput 'fraid uv snakes. My har would stand on eend, stiff as hog's bristles, at the noise uv uvry lizzard that ran through the leaves, and my flesh would jerk like a dead beef's.

"But at last I ventured to go into the face uv the Round Peak one day a-huntin'. I were skinnin' my eyes fur old bucks, with my head up, not thinkin' about sarpunts, when, by Zucks! I cum right plum upon one uv the curiousest snakes I uver seen in all my borned days.

"Fur a spell I war spellbound in three foot uv it. There it lay on the side uv a steep presserpis, at full length, ten foot long, its tail strait out, right up the presserpis, head big as a sasser, right toards me, eyes red as forked lightnin', lickin' out his forked tongue, and I could no more move than the Ball Rock on Fisher's Peak. But when I seen the stinger in his tail, six inches long and sharp as a needle, stickin' out like a cock's spur, I thought I'd a drapped in my tracks. I'd ruther a had uvry coachwhip on Round Hill arter me en full chase than to a bin in that drefful siteation.

"Thar I stood, petterfied with relarm—couldn't budge a peg—couldn't even take old Bucksmasher off uv my shoulder to shoot the infarnul thing. Nyther uv us moved nur bolted 'ur eyes fur fifteen minits.

"At last, as good luck would hev it, a rabbit run close by, and the snake turned its eyes to look what it were, and that broke the charm, and I jumped forty foot down the mounting, and dashed behind a big white oak, five foot in diamatur. The snake he cotched the eend uv his tail in his mouth, he did, and come rollin' down the mounting arter me jist like a hoop, and jist as I landed behind the tree he struck t'other side with his stinger, and stuv it up, clean to his tail, smack in the tree. He were fast.

"Of all the hissin' and blowin' that uver you hearn sense you seen daylight, it tuck the lead. Ef there'd been forty-nine forges all a-blowin' at once, it couldn't a beat it. He rared and charged, lapped round the tree, spread his mouf and grinned at me orful, puked and spit quarts an' quarts of green pizen at me, an' made the ar stink with his nasty breath.

"I seen thar war no time to lose; I cotched up old Bucksmasher from whar I'd dashed him down, and tried to shoot the tarnil thing; but he kep' sich a movin' about and sich a splutteration that I couldn't git a bead at his head, for I know'd it warn't wuth while to shoot him any whar else. So I kep' my distunce tell he wore hisself out, then I put a ball right between his eyes, and he gin up the ghost.

"Soon as he war dead I happened to look up inter the tree, and what do you think? Why, sir, it were dead as a herrin'; all the leaves war wilted like a fire had gone through its branches.

"I left the old feller with his stinger in the tree, thinkin' it war the best place fur him, and moseyed home, 'tarmined not to go out agin soon.

"Now folks may talk as they please 'bout there bein' no sich things as horn-snakes, but what I've seen I've seen, and what I've jist norated is true as the third uv Mathy.

"I mout add that I passed that tree three weeks arterwards, and the leaves and the whole tree was dead as a door-nail."

Mat Layson

JIM COUCH

"I am going to tell you a whole string of witchcrafts," Jim said as he settled down to recording, "that happened up and down Cutshin and Greasy creeks, and most of them I saw with my own eyes.

"One of my great-great-uncles was named Mat Layson [fictitious], and he was a witch. His brother had a boy named Henry, and he told me this happened to him. Old Mat taken him out one time to train him to be a witch. Well, Henry said he took him out one morning just as the sun was rising over the hill. Said he set a silver plate he had down on the ground behind him. He cursed the Lord and blessed the Devil and then shot at the sunball. Said he farred three shots, and every time he would shoot, a drop of clear blood would fall in that silver plate behind him.

"He told Henry, 'Now put your hand on top of your head and the other'n at the bottom of your feet. Now swear that you'll give all between those hands to the Devil to do with you just as he pleases.' Henry, being a boy, did what he told him. Old Mat said, 'Now we'll go right over to the old lick and kill us a deer.'

"Well, Henry said he went on over to the old lick with him, and he told him to be quiet. Said Mat said some kind of ceremony and made some kind of noise, and the deer was coming through there just like a gang of sheep. He ra'red up and said, 'Lord how mercy!' and when he said that, they just vanished and were gone. The old man cussed him out and told him never to say that again. He told him he wouldn't.

"They went on up to the top of another ridge, and old Mat said, 'Now we are going to kill us a turkey.' He said his ceremony again and some talking, and he said forty or fifty big turkeys flew in there and flopped right down and lit all over the ground around them. He said he just ra'red up again and said, 'Lord how mercy!' He said when he said that, all the turkeys disappeared.

"He said old Mat told him, 'For a little I'd kill you right here. You don't know how to be a witch.' Uncle Henry said he was afraid to tell that for a long time after, afraid he would die.

"Weren't long after that old Mat went to Henry Shepherd's father's house to try and get some milk. And they told him they didn't have milk to spare. Just enough for the fambly. Well, in a little while it got so their cows wouldn't give no milk. They'd just run into the gap a-bawling and bawling and cutting a shine. They wouldn't give no milk. They got to inquiring about it, and they found an old feller over there who was a kind of witch doctor, and he told Henry's mother that a man would come there between this time and tomor' night. Says, 'Don't you let him have a thing offen this place. Don't even let him have a drink of water.' He said, 'If you don't, your cows will be all right and never be bothered again.' Well, the next day she looked out and saw the old man Mat a-coming. Said he come over and set around a few minutes, and he asked her to let him borrey some salt. She told him that she didn't have it. And he asked her to let him borrey some coffee, and she said she didn't have that. Everything he would ask for, she would tell him she didn't have it. He said, 'I believe I want a drink of water.' And she said, 'They hain't a drop of water in the house.' He went out and got that water bucket and took the dipper and turned it up and drained the water bucket enough to get him a swaller of water before he left there.

"Another time old Mat showed his witchcrafts. Back in Leatherwood in Perry County it was awful thin settled in there and in Greasy and along the Harlan County line. An old man there by the name of Ransom Turner nearly allas kept a bunch of dogs. And they would get over on Big Laurel Creek and in that section and jump a deer and bring it over to Leatherwood, and then they would lose it in the creek where old Mat lived.

"Uncle Henry said one time he heared the dogs coming down the old House Branch of Leatherwood and said his daddy jumped on a horse and took down the creek lickety-split to see what they's after. They was a big waterhole there on Leatherwood. The deers when they got run in there they would generally run in that waterhole for protection from the dogs. He rode his horse like a ball of far [fire] down there. Got purty close to the place, and he saw the deer come in across the road. And all at once the dogs turned right back the other way, just bawling every breath in their back tracks. Said he rode a few paces further where a hornbean bush growed right next to the small creek. He stopped and saw old Mat right in the top of that hornbean bush just a-wringing and twisting and a-tying them limbs in knots, and them dogs every one turning on the back track. He said the ugliest word he ever heared his daddy say in his life he said right then. He said he looked up at old Mat and said, 'Mat, if they was no hell and if I had a gun, damned if I didn't kill you, you old turkey cock.'

"His daddy went to the waterhole and shot him a deer anyway. You see, old Mat witched the dogs and turned them on their back tracks toward home soon as the deer run off in there, so's he could get the deer. But they had seen the dogs after them and saw the deer run to the waterhole this time and got their deer."

Grandma Hess's Story about Jack, Bill, and Tom

TOLD BY BONELYN LUGG KYOFSKI

Well, this is a story about Jack, Bill, and Tom, who lived with their widowed mother up on the mountainside. Up on the mountainside, and they were loggers. (It wasn't very far from here.) But they were good loggers.

Bill was the oldest of those brothers, and he was a great big strapping guy, and he was one of the best loggers anywhere around. When Bill would larrup into a tree, you really knew that tree had been hit. He'd haul off with that ax, and everything would just shake when he hit that tree.

Tom was bigger than Bill [Jack], too. Now Tom wasn't quite as big and strong. But Tom had a little bit of flair to him. Everybody liked to watch Tom when he was cuttin' down a tree, because he'd come out, and he'd swing around the ax a couple of times, you know. He'd lick his thumb, run it along the blade—eeeeep—to make sure it was sharp enough, and t-h-e-n he would swing into the tree with a whole lot of style about him. Everybody liked to watch Tom.

But of course, Jack was a pretty good, pretty good wood chopper himself. But he was the littlest one, you know, so people just didn't pay too much attention.

But something very, very important happened one day in the lives of Jack, Bill, and Tom. Word went out from the king. The king says, "Oh, I've got myself a terrible problem. And any man that can come and chop down this great big tree that's giving me troubles, well, he can marry my daughter, and have half my kingdom."

Well, both Bill and Tom decided that's what they had to do. They were gonna take right off, and they were going to chop down that tree just as fast as they could. And both of them were going to have half the kingdom, and both of them were going to marry the king's girl. How were they gonna do that?

[*Audience:* Don't know.]

I don't know either, but they were plannin' on doin' it.

And Jack says, "I'm gonna go, too." And the boys said to him, "Jack, you can't go." What'd they say?

[*Audience:* "You're too little."]

"You're too little. You've gotta' stay home with Mom." That was exactly what they said. But Jack just waited until they'd gone on down the road, and he went to his Mom, and he says, "Mom, I've got to go." And she says, "I know you've gotta go, Jack. A man's gotta do what a man's gotta do. You go off there. And you—you have my blessing. You also have a gift. I have a very special thing for you." And so she gave him this little pouch, this little stretchy pouch to put around his neck, on a leather thong. And she gave him a kiss, and she said, "You have my blessing, Jack! You go off and do it!"

And so Jack went off down the road just as happy as you could please, on a beautiful day like today, and he was whistling along, having a wonderful time, swinging along, and having just the best time in the world, when all at once . . . he stopped for a minute and he heard a very strange noise:

[*Italicized words on a higher pitch, here and throughout.*]

Chop, *chop.* Chop-chop-*chop.*

Chop, *chop.* Chop-chop-*chop.*

He said, "My, that's a strange noise. Well, I'm not in very much of a hurry. I think I'll go and investigate that." And so he went off the road, and went off into the woods, and followed the noise, and he heard it getting louder:

Chop, *chop.* Chop-chop-*chop.*

Chop, *chop.* Chop-chop-*chop.*

And the first thing you knew, he came to this beautiful clearing. And in that beautiful clearing was an ax all by itself. That ax was just going all over the place. It was going

Chop, *chop.* Chop-chop-*chop.*

And it was chopping down trees just as fast as you please. And it was lining them up into two-by-fours, and timbers, and all sorts of firewood and kindling, just as nice as you please. And Jack looked at that ax, and he said, "My, but that would be a handy thing for a man to have. I wonder how you'd get your hands on something like that."

Well, he reached out like this, and that ax handle came right over into his hand like this, and he had that ax. So naturally, he just opens up his little pouch, and sticks the ax down there, and pulls it shut, and goes on down the road.

And he's swinging along having a wonderful time because it's a beautiful day. And he said, "Well, well, it's such a beautiful day," stopped for a minute, and heard this very strange noise:

Dig, *dig*. Dig-dig-*dig*.
Dig, *dig*. Dig-dig-*dig*.
"My, a shovel, you say!"

Well, he had to investigate; he just couldn't take anybody's word for it. So he went, sure enough, out through the woods, and he looked, until all at once he came to a hearing—to a clearing, and sure enough, he found—what did he find?

[*Audience:* A shovel.]

A shovel! A magical shovel, and it was just digging by itself. It was going

Dig, *dig*. Dig-dig-*dig*.
Dig, *dig*. Dig-dig-*dig*.
Dig, *dig*. Dig-dig-*dig*.

And it was digging trenches, and it was digging holes, and it was digging all sorts of things, all by itself. And Jack says, "My, but that would be a handy thing for a man to have. I wonder how you'd get your hand on something like that?" And so he reached out his hand, like that, and sure enough, the handle of that shovel came right over into his hand, and he opens up his pouch, sticks the shovel down there, pulls it shut, and goes back to the road, and goes on swinging down the road, whistling away.

But it's such a beautiful day, all at once he stops, and takes a deep, deep breath, and he hears a very strange sound:

Gurgle, *gurgle*. Gurgle-gurgle-*gurgle*.
Gurgle, *gurgle*. Gurgle-gurgle-*gurgle*.

"My, that's a strange sound," says Jack. "I think I'm gonna go investigate that and see what that's all about. I'm not in any very much of a hurry."

And so Jack wanders off through the woods until he hears

Gurgle, *gurgle*. Gurgle-gurgle-*gurgle*,

much louder. He was getting closer. Pretty soon, he comes out to a side hill, where he sees the most beautiful cascade of water, just tumbling right down from the side of the hill. He said, "My, that's the strangest looking waterfall I've ever seen. It's coming from a little tiny spot, way up there on the hill. I think maybe I'll go investigate that." So sure enough, Jack climbs up the hill till he comes to that little spot, and he looks, and that wonderful cascade of water is coming out of a little tiny hickory nut. Not any bigger than that. "My," he says, "I think that'd be a handy thing for a man to have. I wonder how you'd get your hands on something like that." Well, good old Jack always has his knife right here beside him, you know—he's a woodsman—so he takes a piece of wood and whittles himself out a little plug, and sticks it right in that hickory nut, like that, really good and tight, and then he puts that hickory nut down in his little pouch, goes back down to the road again, and wanders on off down towards the king's place.

Well, by this time he's getting very, very close to that castle. In fact, he can look out there at that castle and he can see all the problems the king is having. There's this great big tree that's growing and growing and growing and growing. This tree is knocking down the wall of the castle, for pity's sake.

"Well," Jack says, "somebody ought to do something about that." And then he looked and he saw a whole line-up of men. There had to be at least four hundred and twenty-nine men lined up there, waiting to chop down that tree because *they* wanted to marry the king's girl and get half the kingdom too.

W-e-l-l, when Jack got a little closer he saw not only was there a great big tree there, but right—beside—that—tree—was—one—of—the—strangest—things—he—had—ever—seen.

It was a stump.

A great big stump.

And there on the stump . . . was b-l-o-o-d.

All this red stuff coming down over the edge.

And beside that stump was an ax.

And on that ax was all this red runny stuff, too, blood all over that ax.

Well, beside the stump was the strangest thing he *had* ever seen.

Ears.

Left ears.

The problem about this was, if you tried to chop down that tree and you failed, you had to go over there and put your head down on that block, and they'd take an ax and go *thawaak!* and take off your left ear.

There were all these men running around with hands stuck up against their heads [!!!!] with blood oozing out around the fingers. Ooohs.

Anyway, Jack saw that, and he said, "Well, a man's gotta do what a man's gotta do."

You know, Jack had taken his own good time about this, and Bill and Tom were right up at the head of the line. It was Bill's turn. So Bill gets up there and he takes his ax, and he chops an enormous chunk out of this tree—you know, that first great big chip they take to make sure which way the tree's going to fall down. Well, Bill whacked out an enormous chunk, and it looked just fine until all at once, *zip.* Would you believe that that chunk just grew right back again. Every time anybody took a chip out of that tree, why the tree would grow right back.

Well, Bill was a really big strong logger. He chopped and he chopped and he chopped and he chopped. He went on for eight hours, just chopping away. And, sure enough, he'd take chunks right out of the tree, and the minute he'd take the chunks out, they'd grow back again. Well, didn't take very long. Eight hours was just about enough and Bill says, "Just can't do it any more." So Bill goes over and puts his head down on the chopping block, and sure enough, they take the ax and *thwakk!* There go one of the family ears! [!!!!]

Well, Jack felt pretty bad, you know. Tom—Bill gave him a bad time some of the time, but he was really pretty fond of Bill, and the boys only had six ears among them, you know, and . . . there went one of them.

Well, Bill was standing there with the blood oozing around his hands, and it was Tom's turn. And Tom was no coward, you know. He had to go on and do the same thing. And so sure enough, Tom comes up, and in his usual way, takes his ax and he does his swirls with it, comes up and licks his finger, goes *eeeep!* across the ax to make sure it was sharp enough—it was very, very sharp—and hauls off and with his usual flair, larrups into that tree. Takes the first chunk out, and guess what?

[*Audience:* It grows right back.]

It grows right back. Right you are. Yes. And, anyway, that's what happened. It grew right back, and he chopped and he chopped. Now Tom wasn't quite as big and strong as Bill. Didn't take him quite as long. Probably about six hours, and that was as much as he could do. And so, anyway, poor old Tom has to go over and put his head down on the block. And *chop!* Oooh! There goes another one of the family ears. And there he is.

By this time both Tom and Bill have seen Jack there. And they're really concerned. They come over to him. And you know what they say to him?

[*Audience:* "You're going to get your ears chopped off."]

Yes: "You don't think you can chop down anything that Bill and Tom—Bill and I can't chop down, do you? You're too little. You should have stayed home with Mother. Why didn't you stay home? Don't you do this."

And Jack said, "A man's gotta do what a man's gotta do." And, so he stood right there in line.

Well now there were some other people in line who were all at once beginning to realize that maybe it wouldn't be such a good idea to be chopping that tree down after all. Or trying to. Because, after all, they'd been in lots of competitions with Bill and Tom before. And some of them were saying, "Well, if Bill and Tom can't do it, I don't reckon I can do it." Well, there was something to that, all right. But, this time most of the men just decided that they would turn around and leave.

And it was Jack's turn. He was right there in front. And so, Jack turned his back to the audience, just a little bit, and he whips out his wonderful ax. And that ax just started on that tree. And it went

Chop, *chop.* Chop-chop-*chop.*

Chop, *chop.* Chop-chop-*chop.*

The first thing you knew, that tree was down. It was chopped into timbers, it was chopped into kindling wood, two-by-fours, firewood, the whole business, right there, stacked up alongside the castle wall.

Well, Jack was very proud of himself. And he went over to the king. Bowed. And he was all ready for the king to say, "Good job, Jack. You can have half my kingdom and marry my girl."

But you know how kings are. This king looked at him, and says, "Well, now, Jack, that's a pretty good job. But I don't think, somehow, it's quite worth half a kingdom and marrying my girl. Now I've got this other problem, Jack, that might be pretty important." He says, "We've got a terrible drought in the kingdom. Hasn't rained in so long. Now you make it rain, Jack, and then, then, we'll see about your getting half the kingdom and marrying my girl."

Jack thinks, "Gee, I can't make it rain, but you know, maybe I could fix him a little river." So Jack goes up the side of the hill, and he takes out his shovel. And the shovel starts:

Dig, *dig*. Dig-dig-*dig*.

Dig, *dig*. Dig-dig-*dig*.

Dig, *dig*. Dig-dig-*dig*.

First thing you know, he's got this wonderful riverbed that's just sweeping down, up through the pasture, and down past the castle, down into the meadow. And Jack goes up to the top again, and takes out his little hickory nut, hauls the plug out of it, puts it up at the top of that river, and

Gurgle, *gurgle*. Gurgle, *gurgle*.

Gurgle-gurgle-*gurgle*.

Well, the first thing you know, there's this wonderful river, that's just sweeping down through the pasture. You can just see the grass getting greener. You can see all of the cattle just coming as fast as they can to get a drink of water and get some of that nice green grass. Well, anyway, it was a wonderful river, and Jack was very proud of himself.

So he goes down to the king, and, uh, very pleased, he says, "OK."

He says, uh, "Yes, sir!"

The king, uhhmm, said, "Well,"—you know how kings are. The king says, "Well, that's, that's pretty good, Jack. But it doesn't seem to me to be quite worth half the kingdom and marrying the king's girl."

Uh-oh! Jack was just remembering. He doesn't have anything left in that little bag of tricks of his.

Empty!

And so the king says, "But I've got a real problem." He says, "It's a giant."

"A giant?" says Jack.

"A giant!" says the king. Says, "This giant is stealin' my cattle. He's always into my steers." He says, "Every time I turn around I'm finding that I'm losin' 'em. They're just goin', and that giant is eating them. I've got to do something about it. Now, Jack, you take care of that giant, then you can marry my girl and have half my kingdom."

So old Jack says, "Well, a man's gotta do what a man's gotta do."

So, sure enough, he trots up to the edge of the forest. Gets up there, and takes a d-e-e-p breath. The minute he takes that deep breath he smells the most wonderful aroma. [*Sniff, sniff.*] Barbecue! He can smell the steaks from here. And so he starts wandering into the forest, and he hasn't gone very far before, sure enough, he sees this wonderful clearing. And here in the middle of the clearing is a barbecue pit. It is such a big barbecue pit, well, it's probably about as big as this porch. And on it are seven cows. They're on spits, and they're just turning around and around. They're about medium rare, about now, and Jack has never smelled anything so good in his entire life.

And so, just as he's looking at these cows, he turns around and he sees two calves, right here [*indicating eye level*], with knees on top of them, and the rest of the giant goes on up from there. It's the biggest fellow that Jack's ever seen. He has to be fifty or sixty feet high. And he says to Jack, "And who might you be?"

Jack says there's nothin' to it, and turns around and says, "My name's Jack."

The giant says, "Can you give me any good reason why I shouldn't eat you right now?"

Jack looked up and he says, "Well, . . . I reckon I can eat more than you can eat."

The giant laughed and laughed. He said, "You? You little squirt? You can eat more than I can eat? That's a good one! Now, I'll tell you what we're going to do. We're going to sit down and we are going to eat, and when we are finished eating, and you've eaten as much as you can eat, I'm—going—to—have—you—for—dessert!"

Mmm!

So Jack and the giant sat down beside all of those wonderful spinning cows, and each of 'em hanks off a quarter and starts to chew.

Well, they ate and ate—of course, Jack was starved. He hadn't eaten since he left his mother's place, and the giant was pretty good at eating, too. Well, the giant just ate and ate and ate. And Jack ate as much as he needed, and then, he started just spitting his, his meat right into his little pouch. So the more he ate and the more the giant ate, the less Jack was feeling it because the pouch was filling up and filling up and filling up, and he kept right on eating. And he yanked off another quarter and he kept right on eating. The giant couldn't believe it. He took another quarter and kept on eating.

Well, by the time they'd gone through two-and-a-half cows, the giant said, "Jack, you eat more than any little guy I've ever seen in my whole life. Aren't you getting full?"

And Jack says, "Oh, no." He says, "I don't have much trouble when I start gettin' full—I like to eat, you know." He pulls out his knife and sticks it into that little pouch that his mother had given him, rips it open and dumps the meat out on the ground, settles it around him again, and takes another big bite of beef.

The giant looked at him and he says, "Well, you little shrimp. Anything you can do, I can do!" Grabs his knife, and sticks it in his stomach, and goes *rrrip*. [!!!!!!]

And so, Jack went off on down the mountain, and said hello to the king, and the king said, "Good job, Jack. I think maybe you can marry my daughter *and* have half my kingdom." And he lived happily ever after, of course.

[*Applause.*]

(Oh, thank you.)

Two Conversion Narratives

R. H. PITTMAN

Webb, Elder Daniel Smith, of Hillsville, Va., son of Elder Isaac and Malesia Jane Webb, was born in Carroll County, Va., March 5, 1855. The second Sunday morning in June, 1867, he was riding along horseback thinking that some day he would be a rich man, and at a very old age would get religion. Suddenly a very dark object appeared coming directly at him, with a glittering sharp point in front of it, and like lightning it thrust through him and a voice said, "Already too late." He began to pray, was deeply convicted of sin and for five years lamented his condition, and sought the mercy of God, in tears and with groanings which cannot be uttered. One night in June, 1872, while on his bed death seized him. He tried to call his father but could not speak, and felt doomed to the dark pit of destruction. With his last breath he prayed. "Lord, save me." He heard the sweetest sound of music and looking up saw a white cord letting down from heaven and a bud on the end just ready to open. The bud entered into his bosom and took him out of the world. He saw the world a black ball and God fanned it out of existence with one fan of his hand. He then said, "Surely, God can be just and forgive sins for He with one fan of his hand can blot this earth out, and now, O Lord, may I return to my body, that I may tell to others what a dear Saviour I have found." In this vision he returned to his body and felt free from sin and that he would never have any more sorrow. In September, 1873, he married Miss Mary Ellen Edwards, a God-given companion, and in 1875 both joined the Primitive Baptist Church. One night he dreamed he was under a white cloud and a white hand and arm put through and the neck of a phial protruded out of the palm of the hand and anointed him to go and preach, and his wife dreamed the same thing. Later he dreamed of preaching and baptizing the young and old, the rich and poor and hearing the Lord's people shouting, and his wife dreamed the same thing at the same time. Again he dreamed that ten elders met at Harmony Church and ordained him to preach, and said, "Go, and as you go, preach." And he sprang out of bed and exclaimed, "Lord, I'll go," and his wife saw the same vision and told it to him. Confirmed of the heavenly calling, he began preaching in 1886, was ordained in 1887, by the same ten elders that he and his wife saw in the dream four years before. He has often times been warned in dreams of dangers coming to the church, and many times has dreamed of ingatherings at certain churches, and of certain noble people joining, and has lived to see these dreams fulfilled. Elder Webb's service in the ministry has been blessed of the Lord. He has baptized about seven hundred persons into the fellowship of the Baptist Church and in the evening of life writes: "Faith in God is my only staff, hope in Christ my greatest riches and the fellowship of the brethren my sweetest pleasure." His good wife died February 6, 1908, leaving himself, eight sons and three daughters as sorrowing members of the broken family.

Hardy, Mrs. Temesia Ann (1822–1904), of North Carolina, was one of the most industrious and faithful women of her day and generation. She was a daughter of Elder Parrott Mewborn and the oldest of a family of ten children, was convicted of sin and killed to the love of it and the fashions of the world, while sitting at a loom weaving a fine dress for herself, and so sudden, deep and lasting was the impression made on her mind that she left her work immediately, took off the ornaments from her dresses, and the remainder of her life plain and neat dresses, and a meek and quiet spirit were her adornings. Being blessed of the Lord with a good hope through grace she was baptized by her father into the fellowship of Bear Creek Church in the twenty-fourth year of her age, and ever afterwards proved her faith by her works. She was twice married, first to Lemuel M. Hardy and after his death to his brother Benj. G. Hardy, both deacons and clerks of the church at Mewborns; and, into the duties of her husbands, as deacons, she fully entered and was, perhaps, as much as any one of her day, a spiritual deaconess. Her zeal was wonderful, her constitution and capacity for labor remarkable, her faith strong and unwavering, and her feeling of unworthiness and thankfulness to God for innumerable blessings were constantly being manifested. As an example of her gratitude it is said she did not wish to eat a meal without thanks being returned to God in a public way, and if no gentleman was present to do so she herself would. Sister Hardy was the mother of five children—Elder L. H. Hardy of Reidsville, N. C., being one and to whom she was very much attached.

FROM But Thank God That Light: A Sermon

ELDER EARL SEXTON

But thank God that light (haah)[1]
has shined down into our hearts, (haah)
that guiding morning star (haah)
that Jesus said He was (haah)
there in the Book of Revelations. (haah)
Read that "I am the bright and Morning Star." (haah)
And again He said, "To him that overcometh (haah)
will I give the Morning Star." (haah)
Thank God for that Morning Star today! (haah)
We read of wearied and down, (haah)
in a world of darkness. (haah)
And things are getting darker every day. (haah)
But praise God this morning, (haah)
amid all this darkness, (haah)
any child of God (with rising inflection and warbled on "any")
that can see the Morning Star (haah)
because it's a-shining in your heart . . . (haah)
But thank God this morning (haah)
the Morning Star is shining. (haah)
And we come on up to the time (haah)
when Jesus built the church here in the world, (haah)
He went away for a period of time, (haah)
He's not come back yet. (haah)
But He's coming one of these days, (haah)
He told the disciples when He gathered them there, (haah)
just before He went to the Father, (haah)
He said, "Let not your heart be troubled. (rising inflection and warbled on "let")
Ye believe in God. (with rising and falling inflection)
Believe also in me. (with rising and falling inflection)
In my Father's house there are many mansions. (haah)

---

1. Sermons in some mountain churches are delivered in a chanting style; the end of each line is marked with a vocalization, such as "haah." This vocalization, along with other information about the delivery style, is given in parentheses at the end of each line of this text.

If it were not so I would have told you. (haah)
I go and prepare a place for you. (with rising and falling inflection)
And if I go I come again (rising inflection and warbled on "And")
and receive you unto myself, (haah)
that where I am (haah)
there you may be also." (haah)

A Constellation of Folk Songs

This anthology features three types of folk songs important in Appalachia: ballads, the blues, and sacred songs. Historically, these genres illustrate the qualities that folklorists ascribe to all types of folk songs: they circulate orally within a group and exist in traditional variants. Although some of these songs have been adopted by commercially popular singing groups, the versions that we present were either collected in the field or recorded by traditional musicians.

Late nineteenth-century visitors to the southern mountains were excited to discover people singing ballads brought by settlers from the British Isles, where the songs had nearly disappeared. Ballads, which are narrative songs performed a cappella, date from at least the Middle Ages and were sung throughout America wherever English, Lowland Scots, and Scots-Irish settled. The tradition lingered in semi-isolated, rural areas such as the southern mountains, the Ozarks, and New England long after it had died out in urban settings. By the 1920s, the tradition had mostly become inactive, even in Appalachia, except among a few families that maintained traditional folkways.

The association of ballads almost exclusively with Southern Appalachia is a reflection of the zeal with which they were collected in the region. Olive Dame Campbell collected ballads in the mountains, but she had trouble publishing her manuscript until it came to the attention of the eminent English ethnomusicologist Cecil B. Sharp, who with his assistant Maude Karpeles made several collecting trips to the region from 1916 to 1918. In subject matter, the British ballads sung in the southern mountains focused primarily on family tragedy and love and were sometimes known as "love songs."

Non-British ballads were also popular, such as songs about murder and executions commemorating sensational local cases. "The Ballad of Frankie Silver" depicts the murder and dismemberment of Charlie Silver by his wife, Frankie, in Kona, North Carolina, in 1831, and the execution of Frankie in Morganton in 1833. Although authorship of an execution ballad was sometimes attributed to the murderer and broadsides of the song were circulated at his or her public hanging, the Frankie Silver ballad was composed by a Kentuckian and based on a similar ballad from his home state.

Secular music from the African American community includes work-related songs and the blues. For example, "John Henry" details the death of a railroad worker in West Virginia. The blues arose in the cultural flowering of the black community in the 1890s, the same era in which black musicians developed jazz and ragtime; its roots were in complex African American field hollers. The subject matter of the blues was the collective hard times that the black community faced in the segregated South. Grievances were typically couched in a description of love gone bad, but other disasters were recounted as well. Bessie Smith, born in Chattanooga, Tennessee, sang classic blues in the 1920s; classic blues featured a female singer backed by a band. In contrast, the musical idiom of Brownie McGhee, who was born in Knoxville and reared in Kingsport, Tennessee, reflects a Piedmont guitar style of syncopation and finger-picking analogous to ragtime piano.

This anthology includes two examples of sacred music. Lloyd Chandler's "Remember and Do Pray for Me" is an example of the conversation-with-death song; Chandler stated that the song was given to him by the Lord in 1915. The gospel song "What a Time We're Living In" was composed by revival preacher Robert Akers in the 1970s.

Labor and protest songs were so vital to the evolution of organized labor in southern Appalachia that we dedicate an entire section of part IV to this genre.

The Two Sisters

There lived an old lord by the northern sea,
Bow down,
There lived an old lord by the northern sea,
The boughs they bent to me.
There lived an old lord by the northern sea,
And he had daughters one, two, three.
That will be true, true to my love,
Love and my love will be true to me.

A young man came a-courting there,
He took choice of the youngest there.

He gave this girl a beaver hat,
The oldest she thought much of that.

O sister, O sister, let's we walk out
To see the ships a-sailing about.

As they walked down the salty brim,
The oldest pushed the youngest in.

O sister, O sister, lend me your hand,
And I will give you my house and land.

I'll neither lend you my hand or glove,
But I will have your own true love.

Down she sank and away she swam,
And into the miller's fish pond she ran.

The miller came out with his fish hook

And fished the fair maid out of the brook.

And it's off her finger took five gold rings,
And into the brook he pushed her again.

The miller was hung at his mill gate
For drowning of my sister Kate.

The Daemon Lover

Well met, well met, my old true love,
Well met, well met, says he,
I've just returned from the salt water sea
And it's all for the sake of thee.

We've met, we've met, my old true love,
We've met, we've met, says she,
I have just married a house-carpenter,
A nice young man is he.

If you'll forsake your house-carpenter
And go along with me,
I'll take you where the grass grows green
On the banks of sweet Tennessee.

She picked up her tender little babe
And kisses give it three.
Stay here, stay here, my tender, little babe,
And keep your pa company.

They hadn't been a-sailing but about two weeks,
I'm sure it was not three,
Till this fair damsel began for to weep,
She wept most bitterly.

What are you weeping for, my love?
Is it for my gold or store?
Or is it for your house-carpenter,
Whose face you'll see no more?

I'm neither weeping for your gold,
Nor neither for your store,
But I'm weeping for my tender little babe
Whose face I'll see no more.

What banks, what banks before us now
As white as any snow?
It's the banks of Heaven, my love, she replied,
Where all good people go.

What banks, what banks before us now
As black as any crow?
It's the banks of hell, my love, he replied,
Where I and you must go.

They hadn't been sailing but about three weeks,
I'm sure it was not four,
Till that fair ship begin for to sink,
She sank and riz' no more.

Father Grumble

There was an old man who lived in the woods,
    As you shall plainly see,
Who thought he could do more work in a day
    Than his wife could do in three.

"With all my heart!" the good dame said,
    "And if you will allow,
You shall stay at home to-day,
    And I'll go follow the plow.

"But you must milk the tiny cow,
    Lest she should go quite dry;
And you must feed the little pigs
    That are within the sty.

"And you must watch the speckled hen,
    Lest she might go astray;
And not forget the spool of yarn
    That I spin every day."

The old woman took the stick in her hand
    And went to follow the plow;
And the old man took the pail on his head
    And went to milk the cow.

But Tiny she winked, and Tiny she blinked,
    And Tiny she tossed her nose;

And Tiny she gave him a kick on the shins
    Till the blood ran down to his toes.

And a "Ho, Tiny!" and a "So, Tiny!
    Pretty little cow, stand still!
If ever I milk you again," he said,
    "It will be against my will."

And then he went to feed the pigs
    That were within the sty;
And knocked his head against the shed
    And caused the blood to fly.

And then he watched the speckled hen,
    Lest she might lay astray;
But he quite forgot the spool of yarn
    That his wife spun every day.

And when the old woman came home at night,
    He said he could plainly see
That his wife could do more work in a day
    Than he could do in three;

And when he saw how well she plowed,
    And made the furrows even,
He said his wife could do more work in a day
    Than he could do in seven.

Frankie Silver

This dreadful, dark and dismal day
Has swept all my glories away.
My sun goes down, my days are past,
And I must leave this world at last.

Oh, Lord, what will become of me?
I am condemned, you all now see.
To heaven or hell my soul must fly,
All in a moment when I die.

Judge Daniels has my sentence passed,
These prison walls I leave at last.
Nothing to cheer my drooping head
Until I am numbered with the dead.

But oh! that Dreadful Judge I fear.
Shall I that awful sentence hear?
"Depart you cursed down to hell
And forever there to dwell."

I know that frightful ghosts I'll see
Gnawing their flesh in misery,
And then and there attended be
For murder in the first degree.

There shall I meet the mournful face
Whose blood I spilled upon this place.
With flaming eyes to me he'll say,
"Why did you take my life away?"

His feeble hands fell gentle down,
His chattering tongue soon lost its sound.
To see his soul and body part
It strikes terror to my heart.

I took his blooming days away,
Left him no time to God to pray,
And if sins fall upon his head
Must I bear them in his stead?

The jealous thought that first gave strife
To make me take my husband's life.
For months and days I spent my time
Thinking how to commit this crime.

And on a dark and doleful night
I put this body out of sight;
With flames I tried to consume
But time would not admit it done.

You all see me and on me gaze.
Be careful how you spend your days,
And never commit this awful crime,
But try to serve your God in time.

My mind on solemn subjects roll.
My little child, God bless its soul.
All you that are of Adam's race,
Let not my faults this child disgrace.

Farewell, good people. You all now see
What my bad conduct's brought on me,
To die of shame and of disgrace
Before this world of human race.

Awful indeed to think on death,
In perfect health to lose my breath.
Farewell, my friend, I bid adieu.
Vengeance on me must now pursue.

Great God, how shall I be forgiven?
Not fit for earth, not fit for heaven;
But little time to pray to God,
For now I try that awful road.

John Henry

John Henry was a steel-driving man,
You could hear his hammer half a mile.
But, alas, one day he couldn't go down.
He laid down his hammer and he cried,
He laid down his hammer and he cried.

When John Henry was a little babe
A-sitting on his mamma's knee,
He looked up in his papa's face:
"A hammer'll be the death of me,
A hammer'll be the death of me."

John Henry had a little wo-man,
Her name was Polly Ann.
When John Henry lay there on his bed:
"Polly, do the best you can."

John Henry had a little wo-man
And he kept her all dressed in blue.
She would talk out through the old tunnel
And said, "John Henry, I've been true to you,"
And said, "John Henry, I've been true to you."

John Henry had one only son;
He could sit in the palm of your hand.
He awarded this lot to his lonesome cries:

"Son, don't be a steel-driving man,
Son, don't be a steel-driving man."

John Henry had a little hammer,
The handle was made of bone;
Every time he hit the steel on the head
You could hear the hammer moan,
You could hear the hammer moan.

John Henry told his shaker,
Said, "Boy, you'd better pray.
For if I should miss this piece of steel
Tomorrow would be your burying day,
Tomorrow would be your burying day."

They took John Henry to the White House
And laid him on the stand.
A man from the east and a lady from the west
Come to see the old steel-driving man,
Come to see the old steel-driving man.

Pawn Shop

Brownie McGhee

I was walking down the street this morning, heard someone call my name,
    I could not stop,
Hey-hey, someone called me and I could not stop,
Well friends you know I was broke and hungry, on my way to that old pawn
    shop.

Well I went to the pawn shop, with my last suit in my hand,
Yeah-hey, my last suit in my hand,
Well I said why don't you give me a loan, well and help me Mr. Pawn Shop
    Man.

Well I went to the pawn shop, lawd I carried my old radio,
Yeah-hey, carried my old radio,
Well he said Brownie you ain't got a TV, we don't take radios in no more.

I said I have lost my job, big man come and took my car,
Say-hey, man had come and took my car,
Well you know I'm going to the pawn shop, see if I can get a loan on my
    old guitar.

Play the blues for me now.
Yeah.

I asked the pawn shop man what was those three balls doing on the wall,
Hey-yeah, what are those three balls doing on the wall,
Said, well I'm betting you two to one, buddy, you won't get your stuff out of
    here at all.

Remember and Do Pray for Me
(A Conversation with Death)

LLOYD CHANDLER

"Oh, what is this I cannot see,
With icy hands gets a hold on me?"
"Oh I am Death, none can excel
I open the doors of heaven and hell."

"O Death, O Death, how can it be
That I must come and go with thee?
O Death, O Death, how can it be?
I'm unprepared for eternity."

"Yes, I have come for to get your soul,
To leave your body and leave it cold,
To drop the flesh from off your frame;
The earth and worm both have their claim."

"O Death, O Death, if this be true,
Please give me time to reason with you."
"From time to time you heard and saw,
I'll close your eyes, I'll lock your jaw.

"I'll lock your jaw so you can't talk.
I'll fix your feet so you can't walk.
I'll close your eyes so you can't see.
This very hour come and go with me."

"O Death, O Death, consider my age
And do not take me at this stage.
My wealth is all at your command
If you will move your icy hand."

"The old, the young, the rich, the poor,

Alike with me will have to go.
No age, no wealth, no silver nor gold:
Nothing satisfies me but your poor soul."

"O Death, O Death, please let me see,
If Christ has turned his back on me."
"When you were called and asked to bow,
You wouldn't take heed and it's too late now."

"O Death, O Death, please give me time,
To fix my heart and change my mind."
"Your heart is fixed, your mind is bound
I have the shackles to drag you down.

"Too late, too late, to all farewell
Your soul is doomed, you're summonsed to hell;
As long as God in heaven shall dwell
Your soul, your soul shall scream in hell."

What a Time We're Living In

Robert Akers

CHORUS:
Well, what a time, what a time, we're living in,
What a time, what a time, we're living in,
There is hate on every hand, not many love their fellow man.
What a time, what a time, we're living in.

Now this earth, this old earth's going to pass away,
This old old earth, this old earth's going to pass away,
This old earth's going to pass away, all the works of
    men shall decay,
This old earth, this old earth's going to pass away.

Now you going to kneel, you going for kneel after while,
You going to kneel, you going to kneel after while
Every knee will bow, every tongue confess, when God
    calls his children to rest,
You going to kneel, you going to kneel after while.

CHORUS

Play it for me boys.
I like this next verse.

Well, I'm going to leave, I'm going to leave after while,
Oh, I'm going to leave, I'm going to leave after while,
Soon that trumpet it will sound and my feet's going
    to leave the ground,
I'm going to leave, I'm going to leave after while.

CHORUS

Oh, there'll be peace, there'll be peace after while,
There'll be peace, there'll be peace after while,
Lion'll lay down by the lamb, we shall be led by a child,
There'll be peace, there'll be peace after while.

CHORUS

Play it one more time, boys.
Oh, there'll be joy, there'll be joy after while,
There'll be joy, there'll be joy after while,
All the saints shouting around God's throne and the
    faithful are welcomed home,
There'll be joy, there'll be joy after while.

CHORUS

Amen.

PART VI

Modernism in Appalachian Literature

Katie Hoffman

A movement that began in Europe in the late nineteenth century, modernism made its way to the United States in the early twentieth century and flourished during the interwar period, having significant influence for at least two decades beyond that.

American modernism played itself out in two different strands. Some American modernists—especially those outside of Appalachia, such as Ezra Pound, Gertrude Stein, Wallace Stevens, and T. S. Eliot—experimented with literary innovations such as abandoning the strictures of classical forms, eschewing rhymes in their poetry, celebrating textual structure over emotional content, privileging the urban over the rural, abandoning linear narrative for stream-of-consciousness, and creating literature that was not readily accessible by the everyday reader due to its numerous literary allusions and its frequent use of esoteric language. Modernists of this stripe sometimes suggested that focusing on rural, pastoral places or on the interdependence of human beings was as undesirable as writing in a classical or traditional form. The modernist movement freed these writers to create fresh new forms of literature, focusing on the text as the primary concern rather than its context.

A second strand of modernism—a regional or ethnic variety, which included Appalachian modernism—was somewhat different. Regional or ethnic modernists maintained a focus on history—especially community history—and wrote about rural, regional, or ethnic cultures. One group of regional modernists, centered at Vanderbilt University and known as the Fugitives or Agrarians, valorized the rural, agrarian life of the traditional South. (Unfortunately, the Agrarians tended to be insensitive to the racism, classism, and sexism of the Old South.) Non-Appalachian regional or ethnic American modernists include William Faulkner, Jean Toomer, and Langston Hughes. Although some regional modernists experimented with literary style, among the Appalachian modernists literary experimentation tends to be subtle, as can been seen in the work of Jesse Stuart and Louise McNeill, represented in this section.

Regional modernists differed in their response to the urban/rural divide, as evidenced in the fiction of the Appalachian writers Thomas Wolfe and Harriette Arnow. Although Wolfe's characters may chafe against the limitations of their hometown, they do not long for a rural life. In contrast, Gertie Nevels, protagonist of Arnow's *The Dollmaker* (1954), a Kentucky outmigrant whose husband has moved the family to Detroit as he searches for work, is alienated by her dreary, crowded, and grinding urban life and longs to return to the self-sufficiency, beauty, and community of her rural Appalachian home.

Appalachian modernists found themselves wrestling with issues of cultural representation. Many of these writers, such as Mildred Haun and Jesse Stuart, emerged from within mountain culture to explain rather than exploit it; both Haun and Stuart grew up in families from the Appalachian Mountains, and their writing reflects their close, complex relationships with their native rural traditions. Like other modernists, Haun and Stuart write against the romanticism of the previous era, but theirs is a specific reaction to the tradition of nineteenth-century travel and local color writing in which mountain culture had been misrepresented at worst and sugarcoated by sympathetic intermediaries at best. Other Appalachian modernists, including those whose works appear in this section of the anthology, also write about their rural culture and traditions because it was what they knew—and what they also knew to be misunderstood.

The works included here reflect a richness of voice among Appalachian writers who published during the first half of the twentieth century. When reading them side by side, readers are afforded the opportunity to consider these authors in context together. Doing so allows for the recovery of a number of valuable works and authors whose focus on regional subjects is sometimes neglected in literary studies.

Sources: Sylvia Jenkins Cook, *From Tobacco Road to Route 66: The Southern Poor White in Fiction* (1976); Charles H. Daughaday, "The Changing Poetic Canon: The Case of Jesse Stuart and Ezra Pound" (2005); Parks Lanier, *The Poetics of Appalachian Space* (1991); George Brosi, *The Literature of the Appalachian South* (1992); Danny L. Miller, Sharon Hatfield, and Gurney Norman, eds., *An American Vein: Critical Readings in Appalachian Literature* (2005); Ted Olson and Kathy H. Olson, eds. *James Still: Critical Essays on the Dean of Appalachian Literature* (2007).

Thomas Wolfe

1900–1938

Both critically acclaimed and widely popular during his lifetime, Thomas Wolfe provided readers in the 1930s and 1940s with a vision of urban southern mountain life markedly different from the rural- and wilderness-based Appalachia depicted by local color writers in the last decades of the nineteenth century. Today, Wolfe is most remembered for his semi-autobiographical novel *Look Homeward, Angel: A Story of the Buried Life* (1929).

Born the youngest of eight children, Wolfe grew up in a downtown Asheville boarding house owned and operated by his mother, Julia Westall Wolfe. His father, William Oliver Wolfe, a stonecutter from Pennsylvania, operated a successful tombstone business in Asheville. At fifteen, Wolfe entered the University of North Carolina at Chapel Hill. He continued his study of playwriting at Harvard University, earning a master's degree in English in 1922.

Look Homeward, Angel recounts the experiences of Eugene Gant and his family, fictionalized versions of Thomas Wolfe and the Wolfe family. The novel's thinly veiled fictionalized portraits of Asheville residents engendered a community backlash that led the author into a self-imposed exile following the book's publication.

Wolfe died from tubercular meningitis in 1938. Today he is embraced by Asheville.

The Lost Boy features members of the Gant family. Wolfe published a somewhat different version of the novella in 1937; that version was included in *The Hills Beyond* (1941).

FROM The Lost Boy: A Novella

Grover stood there, looking scornfully. "Old stingy Crocker—afraid that she might give a crumb away."

He grunted scornfully and again he turned to go. But now another fact caught his attention. Just as he turned to go, Mr. Crocker came out from the little place behind the little partitioned place where they made all their candy, bearing a tray of fresh-made candy in his skinny hands. Old man Crocker rocked along the counter to the front and put it down. He really rocked along. He was a cripple. And like his wife, he was a wrenny, wizened little creature, with thin lips, a pinched and meager face. One leg was inches shorter than another, and on this leg there was an enormous thick soled boot, and to this boot there was attached a kind of wooden, rocker-like arrangement, six inches high at least, to make up for the deficiency of his game right leg. And on this wooden cradle Mr. Crocker rocked along. That was the only way you could describe it. A little, pinched and skinny figure of a man with bony hands and meager features, and when he walked he really rocked along, with a kind of prim and apprehensive little smile, as if he was afraid he was going to lose something.

"Old stingy Crocker," muttered Grover. "Humph! he wouldn't give you anything, would he?"

And yet he did not go away. He hung there curiously, peering through the window, with his dark and quiet eyes, with his dark and gentle face now focussed and intent, alert and curious, flattening his nose against the glass. Unconsciously he scratched the thick-ribbed fabric of one stockinged leg with the scruffed and worn toe of his old shoe. The fresh warm odor of the new-made fudge had reached him. It was delicious. It was a little maddening. Half consciously, still looking through the window with his nose pressed to the glass, he began to fumble in one trouser pocket and pulled out his purse, a shabby worn old black one with a twisted clasp. He opened it and prowled about inside.

What he found was not inspiring—a nickel and two pennies and—he had forgotten them!—the stamps. He took the stamps out and unfolded them. There were five twos, eight ones, all that remained of the dollar-sixty-cents worth which Reed, the pharmacist, had given him for running errands a week or two before.

"Old Crocker," Grover thought, and looked somberly at the grotesque little form as it rocked back into the shop again, around the counter, and up the other side.

"Well—" again he looked indefinitely at the stamps in his hand—"He's had all the rest of them. He might as well take these."

So, soothing conscience with this sop of scorn, he opened the door and went into the shop and stood a moment looking at the trays in the glass case and finally decided. Pointing with slightly grimy finger at the fresh-made tray of chocolate fudge, he said, "I'll take fifteen cents worth of this, Mr. Crocker."

He paused a moment, fighting with embarrassment, then he lifted his dark face and said quietly, "And please, I'll have to give you stamps again."

Mr. Crocker made no answer. He did not look at Grover. He pressed his lips together primly. He went rocking away and got the candy scoop, came back, slid open the door of the glass case, put fudge into the scoop and, rocking to the scales, began to weigh the candy out. Grover watched him quietly. He watched him as he peered and squinted, he watched him purse and press his lips together, he saw him take a piece of fudge and break it in two parts. And then old Crocker broke two parts in two. He weighed, he squinted and he hovered, until it seemed to Grover that by calling Mrs. Crocker stingy he had been guilty of a rank injustice. Compared to her frugal mate, the boy reflected, she was a very cornucopia of abundance, a goddess of rich plenty. But finally, to his vast relief, the job was over, the scales hung there suspended, quivering apprehensively, upon the very hair-line of nervous balance, as if even the scales were afraid that one more move from Old Man Crocker and the scales would be undone.

Mr. Crocker took the candy then and dumped it in a paper bag and, rocking back along the counter towards the boy, he dryly said: "Where are the stamps?" Grover gave them to him. Mr. Crocker relinquished his claw-like hold upon the bag and set it down upon the counter. Grover took the bag and dropped it in his canvas sack, and then remembered. "Mr. Crocker—" again he felt the old embarrassment that was almost like strong pain—"I gave you too much," Grover said. "There were eighteen cents in stamps.—You—you can just give me three ones back."

Mr. Crocker did not answer for a moment. He was busy with his bony little hands, unfolding the stamps and flattening them out on top of the glass counter. When he had done so, he peered at them sharply, harshly, for a moment, thrusting his scrawny neck forward and running his eye up and down, as a bookkeeper who totes up rows of figures.

When he had finished, he did not look at Grover. He said tartly: "I don't like this kind of business. If you want candy, you should have the money for it. I'm not in the stamp business. I'm not the post office. I don't like this kind of business. The next time you come in here and want anything, you'll have to pay me money for it."

Hot anger rose in Grover's throat. His olive face suffused with angry color. His tarry eyes got black and bright. The hot words rose unbidden to his lips. For a moment he was on the verge of saying: "Then why did you take my other stamps? Why do you tell me now, when you have taken all the stamps I had, that you don't want them?"

But he was a boy, a boy of eleven years, a quiet, gentle, gravely thoughtful boy, and he had learned good manners, he had been taught how to respect his elders. So he just stood there looking with his tar-black eyes. Old Man Crocker, prim-lipped, pursing at the mouth a little, without meeting Grover's gaze, took the stamps up in his thin, parched fingers and, turning, rocked away with them down to the till.

He took the twos and folded them and laid them in one rounded scallop, then took the ones and folded them and put them in the one next to it. Then he closed the till and started to rock off, down towards the other end. Grover, his face now quiet and grave, kept looking at him, but Mr. Crocker did not look at Grover. Instead he began to take some [stamped] cardboard [shapes] and fold them into boxes.

In a moment Grover said, "Mr. Crocker, will you give me the three ones, please?"

Mr. Crocker did not answer. He kept folding boxes, he compressed his thin lips quickly as he did so. But Mrs. Crocker, back turned to her spouse, also folding boxes with her parsley hands, muttered tartly: "Hm! *I'd* give him nothing!"

Mr. Crocker looked up, looked at Grover, said, "What are you waiting for?"

"Will you give me the three ones, please?" Grover said.

"I'll give you nothing," Mr. Crocker said.

He left his work and came rocking forward along the counter. "Now you get out of here! Don't you come in here with any more of those stamps—" said Mr. Crocker.

"I should like to know where he gets them—that's what *I* should like to know," said Mrs. Crocker.

She did not look up as she said these words. She inclined her head, a little to the side, in Mr. Crocker's direction, and she continued to fold the boxes with her parsley fingers.

"You get out of here," said Mr. Crocker, "and don't you come back here with any stamps . . . Where did you get those stamps?" he said.

"That's just what *I've* been thinking," Mrs. Crocker said. "*I've* been thinking all along."

"You've been coming in here for the last two weeks with those stamps," said Mr. Crocker, "I don't like the look of it. Where did you get those stamps?" he said.

"That's what *I've* been thinking," said Mrs. Crocker, for a second time.

Grover had got white underneath his olive skin. His eyes had lost their luster. They looked like dull, stunned balls of tar. "From Mr. Reed," he said—"I got the stamps from Mr. Reed," said Grover. He burst out desperately, "Mr. Crocker,—Mr. Reed will tell you how I got the stamps. You ask Mr. Reed. I did some work for Mr. Reed, he gave me those stamps two weeks ago."

"Mr. Reed," said Mrs. Crocker acidly. She did not turn her head. "I call it mighty funny," Mrs. Crocker said.

"Mr. Crocker," Grover said, "if you'll just let me have three ones—"

"You get out of here," cried Mr. Crocker, and he began rocking forward towards Grover. "Now don't you come in here again, boy! There's something funny about this whole business! I don't like the look of it. I don't want your trade," said Mr. Crocker, "if you can't pay as other people do, then I don't want your trade."

"Mr. Crocker," Grover said again, and underneath the olive skin his face was gray, "if you'll just let me have those three—"

"You get out of here," Mr. Crocker cried, and began to rock down towards the counter's end. "If you don't get out, boy—"

"*I'd* call a policeman, that's what *I'd* do," Mrs. Crocker said.

Mr. Crocker rocked around the lower end of the counter. He came rocking up towards Grover. "You get out," he said.

He took the boy and pushed him with his bony little hands, and Grover was sick and gray down to the hollow pit of his stomach.

"You've got to give me those three ones," he said.

"You get out of here!" shrilled Mr. Crocker. He seized the screen door, pulled it open, and pushed Grover out. "Don't you come back in here," he said, pausing for a moment, working thinly at the lips. He turned and rocked back in the shop again. The screen door slammed behind him. Grover stood there on the pavement. And light came and went and came again into the square.

The boy stood there a moment, and a wagon rattled past. There were some people passing by. The driver of the Garrett wagon came out with grocery-laden box and put it in the wagon and slammed up the lid. But Grover did not notice them, and later he could not remember them. He stood there blindly, gray beneath the olive, in the watches of the sun, feeling this was Time, this was the Square, this was the center of the universe, the granite core of changelessness, and feeling, this is Grover, this the Square, this is Now.

But something had gone out of day. He felt the overwhelming, the soul-sickening guilt that all the children, all the good men of the earth have felt since time began. And even anger had died down, had been drowned out, in this swelling and soul-sickening tide of guilt, and "This the Square"—thought Grover as before—"This is Now. There is my father's shop. And all of it is as it has always been—save I."

And the square reeled drunkenly around him, light went in blind gray motes before his eyes, the fountain sheeted out to rainbow iridescence and returned to its proud, pulsing plume again. But all the brightness had gone out of day, and "Here the Square, and here is permanence and here is time—and all of it the same as it has always been, save I."

The scuffed boots of the lost boy moved and stumbled blindly over. The numb feet crossed the pavement—reached the sidewalk, reached the plotted central square—the grass plots, and the flower beds, so soon with red and packed geraniums.

"I want to be alone," thought Grover, "where I can not go near him—oh God, I hope he never hears, that no one ever tells him—"

The plume blew out, the iridescent sheet of spray blew over him. He passed through, found the other side and crossed the street and—"Oh God, if papa ever hears,"—thought Grover, as his numb feet started up the steps into his father's shop.

He found and felt the steps—the width and thickness of old lumber twenty feet in length—the draymen sprawled out on the other end, the whips long, snaking on the sidewalk, the square down-slanted to a funnel here, the cobbles, rude and strong, the side stairs going up into the calaboose; below, the market's arch of three o'clock, the slanting place for draymen and the country wagons, the dip and rise, [. . .] the shacks and houses, and beyond, the rim of hill, immensely near, just greening into April.

He saw it all—the iron columns on his father's porch, just shabby, painted with the dull anomalous black-green that all such columns in this land and weather come to; two angels, fly-specked, and the waiting stones; the fly-specked window of the jeweler, his window platform, his screwed eyeglass, and within, the little wooden fence around him, his great brow, his yellow wrinkled features, and a safe, great dust, much yellowed newspaper.

Beyond and all round, in the stonecutter's shop, cold shapes of white and marble, rounded stone, the base, the languid angel with strong marble hands of love.

The partition of his father's office was behind his shop. He went on down the aisle, the white shapes stood around him. He went on to the back of the workroom. This he knew—the little cast-iron stove in left-hand corner, caked, brown, heat-blistered, and the elbow of the long stack running out across the shop, the high, the dirty window, looking down across the market square [. . .], the rude old shelves, plank-boarded, thick, the wood not smooth but pulpy, like the strong hair of an animal; upon the shelves the chisels of all sizes and a layer of stone dust; an emery wheel with pump tread, and a door that let out on the alleyway, yet the alleyway twelve feet below; a tin urinal, encrusted, copperous, stinking, and a wooden frame or screen of torn cotton that enclosed it. Here in the room, two trestles of this coarse spiked wood upon which rested gravestones, and at one, a man at work.

The boy looked, saw the name was Creasman: the carved analysis of John, the symmetry of S, the fine sentiment of Creasman, November—Nineteen—Three;—with much coarseness, much brown stubble, many pine trees, much red clay about and over him.

The man looked up. He was a man of fifty-three, gaunt-visaged, mustache cropped, immensely long and tall and gaunt. He must have been six feet and four, or more. He wore good clothes, good dark clothes—heavy, massive,—save he had no coat. He worked in shirt sleeves with his vest on, a strong watch chain stretching cross his vest, wing collar and black tie, Adam's apple, bony forehead, bony nose, light eyes, gray-green, undeep and cold, and, somehow, lonely-looking, a striped apron going up around his shoulder, and starched cuffs. And in his hand, the wooden mallet, not a hammer, but a tremendous rounded wooden mallet like a butcher's bole; and in his other hand, a strong cold chisel tool.

"How are you, son?"

He did not look up as he spoke. He spoke quietly, absently. He worked upon the chisel and the wooden mallet, as a jeweler might work on your watch, except that in the man and in the wooden mallet there was power too.

"What is it, son?" he said.

He moved around the table from the head, started up on J once again.

"Papa, I never stole the stamps," Grover said.

The man put down the mallet, laid the chisel down. He came around the trestle. "What?" he said.

And Grover winked his tar-black eyes, they brightened, the hot tears shot out. "I never stole the stamps," he said.

"Hey? What is this?" the man said. "What stamps?"

"That Mr. Reed gave to me when the other boy was sick and I worked there for three days. And Old Man Crocker," Grover said, "he took all the stamps. And he took all the rest of them from me today. And I told him Mr. Reed had given them to me. And now he owes me three ones—and Old Man Crocker says he don't believe that they were mine—he says—I must have got them somewhere," Grover said.

"The stamps that Reed gave to you—hey?" the stonecutter said. "The stamps you had—" He wet his thumb upon his lips, he walked from his workshop out into the storeroom and cleared his throat and cried "Jannadeau—" But now Jannadeau, the jeweler, was not there.

The man came back, he cleared his throat, and as he passed the old gray painted board-partition of his office, he cleared his throat and wet his thumb, and said, "Now, I tell you—"

Then he turned and strode up towards the front again and, passing Jannadeau's little, fenced-in, grimy square, he cleared his throat and said, "I tell you now—" And coming back, along the aisle between the rows of marshalled gravestones, he said underneath his breath, "By God, now—"

He took Grover by the hand across the square. They went out flying. They went down along the aisle by all the gravestones, marble porch, the fly-specked angels waiting among the gravestones, the wooden steps, the draymen and the cobbled slant, the sidesteps of the calaboose, the city hall, the market, the four sides, not quite symmetric, of the square, the architectures and the brick,—across the whole thing, but they did not notice it.

And the fountain pulsed, the plume blew out in sheeted iridescence, and it swept across them, and an old gray horse, with torn lips, with a kind of peaceful look about his torn lips, swucked up the cool, the flowing and the mountain water from the trough as Grover and his father went across the square.

The man took the hand—the hand of his small son—the boy's hand was imprisoned, caught, in the stonecutter's hand and they strode down through the aisle, past the cold marbles, across the porch, where the two angels were, and down the steps, and by the draymen sitting on the step.

They went across the square through the sheeted iridescence of the spray and to the other side and to the candy shop. The man was dressed in his long apron still. He had not paused to change the long striped apron, he was still holding Grover by the hand. He opened the screen door and stepped inside. "Give him the stamps," he said. Mr. Crocker came rocking forward behind the counter, with the prim and careful look that now was somewhat like a smile. "It was just. . . ." he said.

"Give him the stamps," the man said, and threw some coins down on the counter.

Mr. Crocker rocked away and got the stamps. He came rocking back. "I just didn't know—" he said.

The stonecutter took the stamps and gave them to the boy. And Mr. Crocker took the coins.

"It was just that—" Mr. Crocker said, and smiled.

The man in the apron cleared his throat:—"You never were a father," the man said, "you never knew the feeling of a father, or understood the feeling of a child; and that is why you acted as you did. But a judgement is upon you. God has cursed you. He has afflicted you. He has made you lame and childless as you are—and lame and childless, miserable as you are, you will go to your grave and be forgotten."

And Crocker's wife kept kneading her bony little hands and said, imploringly, "Oh, no—oh don't say that, please don't say that."

The stonecutter, the breath still hoarse in him, left the store. Light came again into the day.

"Well, son," he said, and laid his hand on the boy's back, and "Well, son," he said, "now don't you mind."

They walked across the square, the sheeted spray of iridescent light swept out on them, the horse swizzled at the water-trough, and "Well, son," the stonecutter said.

And the old horse sloped down—ringing with his hoofs upon the cobblestones.

"Well, son," said the stonecutter once again, "be a good boy."

And he trod his own steps then with his great stride and went back again into his shop.

The lost boy stood upon the square, hard by the porches of his father's shop.

"This is Time," thought Grover, "This is Grover, this is Time—"

A [street] car curved out into the square, upon the bill-board of the car-end was a poster and it said St. Louis and Excursion and The Fair.

And light came and went into the Square, and Grover stood there thinking quietly: "Here the Square and here is Grover, here is my father's shop, and here am I."

Jesse Stuart

1906–1984

Jesse Stuart was born in northeastern Kentucky's Greenup County. His parents, hard-working tenant farmers, instilled in him and his four siblings a drive for education, a poignant emphasis given his father's illiteracy and his mother's second-grade education. Stuart graduated from Lincoln Memorial University with a BA in 1929, making friends while there with Don West and James Still. At Vanderbilt University, where he attended graduate school in 1931–1932, Stuart studied with influential southern writers and critics such as Donald Davidson, who also taught Appalachian authors Mildred Haun and Jim Wayne Miller. After graduate school, Stuart returned to Greenup to work as an educator and author.

During the mid-twentieth century, Jesse Stuart was one of the most widely read Appalachian writers; his direct, approachable style and his careful portraits of self-reliant northeastern Kentucky individuals and communities resonated with readers. Stuart said that *Man with a Bull-Tongue Plow* (1934), his first poetry collection, was inspired by his own time behind a plow on his father's farm. His fiction, such as the short story "Men of the Mountains," which appeared in a collection with the same name, provides detailed depictions of rural Appalachia. A champion of public education, Stuart served as a public schoolteacher, principal, and superintendent, experiences recounted in his nationally influential autobiography *The Thread That Runs So True* (1949).

406

I love the smell of dead leaves in the rain.
I love the clean-sweet smell of rain-washed woods.
I love black sticks a-lying in the rain.
I love rain-dripping ferns in solitudes.
I think the blacksnakes love the April showers,
They wake from freezing sleep and shed their skins,
I think they love Spring rains and thunder showers.
Spring is the time for them new life begins.
I think the terrapin would love Spring rain.
It's buried now beneath the hardened ground.
Rain melts the earth and it will rise again.
The terrapins awaken to the sound
Of April thunder and downpours of rain.
The terrapins, blacksnakes and men love rain.

Men of the Mountains

Behind the sun and before the sun in misty rays of light are the hills eternal where mortal men are laid—the trees mark their resting places now and the briars—the mountains are their tombs eternal. Men wrought of mountain clay and stone and roots of mountain trees—eat plants from the mountain earth and hear the music of mountain wind and water—men live among the mountains, curse the mountains, love the mountains, plant corn among them and lift the rocks and cut the timber—have seasons to fail and see the dry hard rocks point to the skies—men of the mountains unafraid of the cruel mountains, the homey mountains that give them scanty food and take them home in the end to sleep a while.

"Flem was always a good worker," says Pa, "and a good man. I hate to hear that—poor old Flem—digging his own grave and him just fifty-six years old. W'y he's the same age I am and I'm not ready to leave this old world yet. Much as we talk about being unafraid to die when we go to getting up in years then's the time we want to live. We watch each precious day. Poor old Flem. We got to get over there and see if we can help him any. Do that much for a good neighbor."

Pa puts on his little gray hat. He walks out of the house, pulls out a package of red-horse and puts his brown fingers in at the head of the half-opened package of sweet scrap tobacco. He brings a wad of brown cut-up in the tips of his fingers to his mouth, shoves the scrap in, shoves it back properly. Then he takes a twist of home-made from his pocket so strong that it smells in the July heat. He twists off the end and shoves that into his mouth with his thumb and index finger, tamps it in like you tamp a fence post.

"Got to take a little sweet terbacker with the home-made any more," says Pa. "My ticker ain't good as it used to be. That's what the years bring a man. That's one way I know I'm not the man I used to be. Can't take my terbacker like I ust to could take it. W'y I chawed home-made—the strongest taste-bud that we could grow and I never thought a thing about it. Look at me now. Have to buy sweet terbacker and do a lot of mixing."

The July sun is hot—hot as a roasted potato. The wind, in dry burning sheets, moves slowly over the land and rubs the dry bellies of the poplar leaves—their green throats rattle. Pa walks slowly down the path, a dry line of dirt, a cow path where there is no grass at all.

"A awful drouth," says Pa. "Don't know what the poor people are going to do this winter for bread corn and feed for their stock. God Almighty only knows about a season anymore. We never know—I've spent my life here among these hills and the older I get the less I trust the seasons. Can't get seasons any more like we used to get. Used to just go out and plant the corn and work it a couple of times—awfullest corn crops you ever saw popped out'n the ground. Land was a lot better then—but we had a season.

"Lord, look at these brown acres—look at the corn. By-the-grace-of-God I'm ashamed for a man to go through my field. Bumble-bee corn—a bumble-bee can't suck the tassels without his starn-end rubbing the ground! Look at the hills—once the land of plenty—the land of good crops—bone-dry—kick this dust with your toe and see how hard it is for yourself. It's going to be awful hard on poor old Flem to dig his grave through such hard dirt."

The dust is flying from where Pa is kicking with the toe of his shoe. I can smell the dust. I would rather smell wilted horse-weeds—that pig-pen smell they have—any old day as to smell July dust from a Kentucky mountain road—dust that has settled on the blackberry briars and sassafras sprouts—the red-mouse-eared sassafras sprouts that are coloring in the drouth. Lean cattle on the hill—seven cows to forty acres of grassed hillside and cows lean as rails. Buzzards sailing up over wilted trees—buzzards looking down on pastures and old rail-piles. Buzzards always know when the fires run through the mountains and burn terrapins to death, the lizards, the frogs, the snakes. Their crisp bodies turned to the sun, around them the black ashes flying in the wind. Buzzards high above in the blue heavens, high in the winds, coasting with wings spread, coasting, coasting, and peering. They know when the drouth comes to the high bony hills where life is hard for man and beast.

"That hill over there," says Pa, pointing to a sag of corn that fits into a lap between two hills, "w'y old Flem cleaned that up for me when you was just a boy. Old Flem took his three boys in there—just little shavers then—and dogged if he didn't clear that land. He'd take them little boys and clear land all through these hills. That Flem was a worker. What I mean he was a worker. Great big raw-boned man, so deef he couldn't hear the wind blow. That's all I didn't like about him. Had to get right up close and holler in his ear. Then he had that eye where some man back in Carter County hit him with a rock and his eye stays open all the time. Can't get the lid down. It looks right funny to see that eye standing wide open like a snake's eye. That's what a man gets for fighting with rocks. Mountains full of rocks, and men fit with them before they ever fit with guns. Look at poor old Flem—old at fifty-six. Just my age. I get around just fine—if I just had a new ticker—"

Buzzards search the mountains—circle low down to the wilted trees. Snake marks are across our paths—long trailer-marks in the sand. Birds fly about and chirrup with a disconsolate wail.

"Poor birds are hunting water," says Pa, "poor birds. I'd rather see a man in trouble. He can help hisself more."

Pa swishes the sweat from his red forehead with his index finger and it drops in a straight line of fast-shooting white beads as he slings his hand. It hits the dry sand and sprinkles it—water to the dry earth—the bitterness of sweat to the parching lips of the earth. "Whoo-ee-ain't it hot," says Pa. "Never saw anything like this in my life. Hottest time I ever saw. Drouth. Birds dying and them buzzards up there just waiting for us all to die."

We leave the hollow road and turn to the right. We walk up this avenue of wilted weeds, of wilted trees, of brown corn-field rocks gleaming in the sun and lazy wilted corn—starving to death for water—standing in the dust down between two sweeps of hills—slanting back against the sun-scorched buff-colored clouds. We smell the burning weeds, the dying corn, the wilted sweeps of saw-briared hills and gloomy arms of scorched pine trees, the weeping fingers of the sourwoods. When we have reached the head of this little hollow, we cross the gap and go down the neck of the next hollow where Flem lives—right on the old John Kaut farm where all that big timber used to stand.

"We'll soon find out about this grave-digging," says Pa. "Son, that kindly bluffs me. When it comes to digging graves—it ain't very long. I've seen too much of it happen. These old men get the warning—they nearly always know—never hear of one missing it. But just to think of old Flem being the one called—who'd a ever thought about that? Just can't tell where the tree is going to fall, but where the tree does fall there is where the tree is going to lie—"

Flem's house is in sight—a house made from the rough oak planks and slabs from where the saw-mill used to set when it cut the giant oaks into slivers—a house there in the sun—the July Kentucky sun high in the burnt-up clouds. Windows in the house like burnt holes in a brown quilt, the color of seasoned-out lumber, brown against the wind—sweltering in the sun—the resin running from the pine knot-holes—smelly, tasty, bee-colored in the sun. Smoke coming from the rough-stone flue—smoke, thin smoke and light-blue against the wind, fat puffs of smoke with big bellies in the sun—going out with the wind—in all directions over the hot dog-tongued earth. Palings around the garden with fruit jars sunning—stone jars and glass jars and rag-rugs out on the palings to sun. Hoes with their goosenecks hung over the palings, a scythe, an oat cradle with one broken finger. Wilted corn on the mountain slopes above the house—a whole mountain of wilted corn—each stalk of corn crying for water. And the wilted arms of the corn—whispering—whispering—to the hot wind.

"Look in the garden," says Pa, "look at Flem's garden. Burnt up alive just like our garden. Look at them little tater vines. Bet you can gravel down there at them tater roots and you won't find taters bigger than a marble. Look at them cabbages. Looks for the world like wilted pusley to me. Look up that mountain—look at Flem's lean cows—and them buzzards. See them! There they are—always right around where the milk cows are trying to find grass to eat—right above the cows they snoop aroun' in the air. Why don't a buzzard wait for a buzzard to die?"

We walk in at the gate—a lean-to gate that we open and it shuts itself, weighted with a chain and plow-points—and up to the house. We smell the resin on the pine boards—scent of pine. We love the smell of pines in the spring, but the smell of pine on a hot day, the smell of pine, molted pine, wormy wood—we have to hold our noses. Around the house in the blistering heat—the smell of the wilted ragweeds—the poor wilted lady's finger and forget-me-nots drooping—the scent of pinks and iron-weeds in August.

"Hello," says Pa, "how are you, Flem." Flem does not hear. Pa goes up and he hollers in Flem's ear: "Hello, Flem. How are you!"

Flem laughs and he says: "I'm so deef can't hear nothing no more. Ain't heard the wind blow for years. The only way I can tell when the wind blows is to see the brush moving and the corn moving. It's awful to be deef. You'll never know till you get that way. When did you come over, Mick?"

"Just come," says Pa, getting up and hollering in Flem's ear. "Just come over through the hot sun and the whole air is filled with buzzards."

"Filled with buzzards," says Flem. "I'll be dogged. Sign of dead stock. Sign of deaths. Don't get me though. I got the hole dug to catch me. I'm looking for this thing."

Flem laughs. One of his eyes squints, the other eye can't, for the lid is stiff—stands open like a snake's eye—he never takes that eye off you. Flem is a big man, has a belly big as a nailkeg, doesn't have on any drawers—you can see a big white patch of his belly where his blue shirt has worked up from his overalls. When Flem laughs his belly bobs up and down—up like a hand under dough lifting it up—down like a hand over dough beating it down. His hair is gray and stiff as wires in a brush—hair that won't lie down nor sit up nor do anything. It has a little crown in it—a twisted place in the bristled stuff. He has heavy eyebrows like ferns on the edge of a rock cliff.

"Wear number ten shoes," says Flem. "I see you got a mighty little foundation, Mick." Flem laughs and his belly works up and down. I see Flem's little pipe-stem hairy legs with the big feet to hold them down.

Pa says, "I got little feet. I wear eights." Pa laughs and pulls out his tobacco. He tamps it into his mouth, the sweet with the bitter, then reaches some to Flem.

"Thank you," Flem says, "I don't chaw my terbacker. I smoke it." Flem takes out a leaf of home-made tobacco, crumbles it in a little red corn-cob pipe, strikes a match on his pants leg, and wheezes as he sucks the long dry stem. Long streams of thin smoke come from Flem's mouth—thinner than the air and bluer.

"My ticker ain't good as it used to be," says Pa, hollering in Flem's ear, "that's why I got to take a little sweet with the bitter any more. Can't take it like I used to take it. Getting younger every day, too."

Flem says: "Huh—yes—ahh. Huh."

"God," says Pa, "he's the deefest man I ever tried to talk to. He's about got me winded. You try to talk with him a while. Let's get him to show us his grave."

Hodd is Flem's boy, twenty-two now, with two rows of black broken teeth, freckles on his face, patches of unshaved beard growing here and there, a straw hat on his head, a blue shirt on his back with two dark blue stripes on the back where his overall suspenders have not let the sun fade the blue out, overalls torn at the cuffs into ravelling ruffles.

"Hello, Hodd," Pa says, "will you talk to your Pa a little for us?"

"I'll do my best," says Hodd. "Pa's deef as a rock in this hot weather and deef ain't no name for it. Just sets around—can't do nothing—can't talk to nobody. He's got his grave dug—guess you know about that."

"Heard about it," says Pa.

"Well, he has," says Hodd, "and he's got Ma's grave dug with his. Right beside his. Ma's taken a cry every day since he's done it. She says it's the sure sign when a Simpson digs a grave. He's not much longer for this world."

Flem just sits on his rocking chair and rocks. Life doesn't have any noises for him, he can't hear the jingle of the harness any more nor the sound of the hoe and ax nor the barking of fox-hounds.

"Tell Flem," says Pa, "that I want to go back there where he has got them graves dug. Tell him I want to see them." And Hodd hollers in Flem's ear.

"All right, we'll go," says Flem. "About three miles back there. But we'll go."

Flem leads the way up the path. Pa walks second. Hodd is third and Ott comes out. He says: "Where you going, Hodd?" And Hodd says: "We're going to Pa's graves out here on the hill. Come along with us."

Ott comes up the hill. He is tall, thin at the hips, with twisted legs and a hairy chest, unbuttoned shirt, a partly bald head with hair thin as timber on a hill where the fire has run over it year after year. His lips turn down at the corners like the curve of a horse-shoe. He says: "Uhuh—ahh—"

And he walks up the path, his legs working strong and fast. We move on toward the graves, the sun high on the mountain above us among the burned-copper clouds. Flem is easily winded, walks with a stick. He gets his breath like a snoring hog sleeping in the sun. Sweat drips from Pa's face. He slings it with his forefinger from his forehead, and he wipes among his scattered wire-stubbled beard with his red handkerchief.

"Ma is worried plum sick," says Ott, "the way Pa has done. He tried to get me and Hodd to come back here and help him with the graves. We wouldn't do it. Me to dig my father's grave and my mother's grave. No. I just couldn't bear it. W'y he's been coming back here and working one hour at a time for the past five weeks. He brings that crazy boy of Mort Flannigan's back here. He comes with Pa. He laid down and had Mort's boy to mark him off—right back yander on the Remines pint."

Lazy July wind seeps out of the brush. It is soft and hot. It runs fast then slow. The scent of the corn—corn sweltering in the heat on the slope to our right—corn ready to tassel—corn so small and twisted. The mountain path is slow and twisting and the wilted leaves hang in pods in the July sunlight. Sweat runs from my face, from Pa's face, from Hodd's, Ott's, and Flem's faces. Flem is in the lead, setting the walking pace. It is slow as the slow smelly wind that comes out of the brush. The buzzards are above the mountain tops, flying in circles over the pasture slope where the lean cows pick the brown grass, grass that would burn quick if Flem would throw down a lighted match-stem.

"Ma's been just crying her eyes out," says Ott, "about Pa. Corn in the ground for another year. Pa is going to die. We know he's going to die. Nothing we can do about it. He says he's going to die. Ain't worked none this summer. Ma says she hates to die and leave little Effie, the baby girl you know, just twelve now. Just us three left at home. All safe, Ma says, but Effie and she says there's so much weakedness in the world she hates to die and leave her."

It seems like we are climbing to the sun, the sun that crosses the earth, in the region of the hill man's destiny—great backbones of ridges where the crow flies, where cows wither on the bone on the dry summer grass and where buzzards circle low. Men of the mountains growing old. Pa growing old at fifty-six—mixing sweet tobacco with strong. Flem Simpson growing old and his autumn not here. His grave is dug.

"W'y," says Pa, "Flem ain't but from March to June older than I am. I am still getting around and I've worked as hard in my day as any man."

"Yes," says Hodd, "but you wasn't hit in the head with a rock like Pa. That's what got Pa. You know about that fight. He's been a peaceful man ever since. He communes with the Lord often—gets out at night and communes with the Lord."

"Lord, I'm hot," says Pa, wiping the sweat from his face.

"No hotter than I am," says Hodd. "Look at Pa, though, he's still wiggling like a young weaned calf—big in the middle and little on both ends. . . . Soon be at the top of the mountain."

The sun is high in the sky—high among the mountains, the color of a red sandrock—floating—floating—heat below is dancing to the tune of grasshopper in the weeds. Heat on the fields of wilted corn on the mountains where the earth is baked in a big brown pone. If rain was to hit the baked earth, rain wouldn't soak down for a while—it would go up in steam. Great brown sheets of earth—wilted mountains of leaves—green clouds of leaves—clouds, wilted and drooping.

"Let the old men get their wind," says Hodd, as we top the mountain. "Won't be so bad now—it's about all going down the hill now."

Pa wipes the sweat from his face and moves faster and faster as the road on the mountain ridge goes down a knoll and up another knoll to the Remines point.

"Coming in sight of where I'm going to be laid out to rest, boys," says Flem, "just right over the pint here in these chestnut oaks. Nice quiet place out here away from the houses—back like the woods was when I was a boy."

We walk over the hill—here are the graves—two graves dug under the chestnut-oaks—twin graves—side by side. "Here they are, boys," says Flem. "Will show you this one is a fit for me. The other one is a fit for my wife. Prudy just comes to my shoulder you know. So when I laid down to measure her grave I had to make allowances. I measured from my shoulders down. But I just laid down here and had Mort's boy to measure me on the ground. He was a little scared, but he helped me here with these graves with tears in his eyes."

"God," says Pa. "Hodd, ask your Pa what made him do this. I didn't believe he had any graves out here when he told me. I thought he was just a funning me a little. . . . Poor old Flem."

Pa sheds some tears. He remembers Uncle Fonse Tillman and the strange way he knew about his approaching death—now another one of Pa's comrades passing away and acting the same way about it. "A funny thing," says Pa. "I believe Flem knows what he's doing. Flem is a goner from these mountains. Gone to sleep among them forever and that before the winds of falltime blow."

"I just fit—see, boys," says Flem as he gets down in his grave and lies down, "a little wide here in the middle but it won't be when my oak-board coffin fits in here. Most people dig a hole to fit the coffin and order the coffin to fit the man. I'm making my coffin to fit me and digging the hole first." Flem's head is against the earth and he says, "How do I look down here, boys?"

He looks up at us and laughs, his belly shaking. Then he looks through the wilted leaves of the chestnut-oaks above his grave at the molten copper clouds that halfway secure the sun—hot clouds—clouds without rain. His one eye, the snake-eye, looks glassy from down in the grave. The other eye is squinted.

"Good place to be when a man is tired," says Flem, "no more worry about bread, land to tend, and pasture for the cattle. No more worry—out here where the fox-horns will blow and maybe I can hear them then. All troubles will be over, Prudy by my side, and we'll sleep here till resurrection day. A good place to sleep—right here on the mountain-top."

It touches Pa to hear Flem say this. Pa says to Ott: "Guess you'll have to run the farm when your Pa dies. Sure did pick a good place to be buried. I'd hate to dig my grave. Don't believe I could. Even if it is cool away from all the heat we been having. I just wouldn't like it."

Flem is still down in his grave. "Come on out of your grave, Pa," says Hodd. Flem can see Hodd's lips working but he can't tell what he is saying.

"Say it louder," says Flem, "like Gabriel is going to do when he blows his trumpet."

Hodd hollers as loudly as he can, down into the grave: "Come on out of your grave, Pa."

"That's more like it," says Flem, "more like the trumpet I'm going to hear on resurrection morning, when time shall be no more, and these fifty-six years ain't going to be a drop in the bucket. Help me out of my grave, boys."

Pa gets him by one hand and Hodd gets him by the other.

"I want to live where there's not any time. Then I can farm and lift rocks and cut sprouts the way I want to with a strong set of arms and a strong set of legs. We'll have seasons and crops. That's what I want and not this awful sun to burn up the crops—"

Flem comes from the grave and starts to get down in Prudy's grave to show us the length of it. "Oh, God," says Hodd, "don't get down in Ma's grave. No need of that—I don't want to think about Ma coming to this lonely place when she's always liked to go to town on Saturdays where she could see people. Ma don't like fox-horns. Has to be buried way out in these lonely woods."

"I'm ready to go," says Flem. "Can't farm any more. Don't have the legs—don't have the arms. Can't see as well. Can't talk to people. I'm in the way. Can't trade like I used to trade. Country is changing. Government telling me what to do—how to plant the mountains. Tell me I can only raise so many hogs and a lot of stuff like that. It's getting time for us old men who ain't used to that to die, Mick. God Almighty sent this drouth on such people as that. Won't let us plant—won't let us have what we want—we've always had that—even under a Republican, much as I hate that Party. I tell you, I'm tired and ready to sleep. I told the Master I was ready and I'd like to bring the old woman along with me, too. I told the Master she was ready—she'd been with me all through life and I wanted to be by the side of her in death."

Tears come in Pa's eyes. Hodd looks to the waters of the Little Sandy and keeps his eyes away from his father. Ott looks at me and I look at Ott and then at Pa. The Little Sandy River winds slowly down among the hills, down among the wilted clouds of leaves—a brown muddy river—curled like a snake crawling through the briars. Giant oaks tremble in the wind. Leaves flutter in the hot July wind.

"Great place to be buried," says Pa, "here among these mighty hills. They'll get me in the end. Oak roots will go in to old Flem. He'll go back to the mountains and only a tree some day will mark where he is buried."

Flem says: "Come down here a minute, boys. Got something I want to show you." We follow Flem down under the hill—just a little way down under the rim of the hill to a rock cliff—where lichen is bluish-gray and dying—the sourwoods lean over and twist their slender bodies groping for the light.

"Come in here," says Flem. "Look here, see these barrels of salt—seven of them— four for me and three for the old woman. The children can take care of themselves. I'm going to have four barrels of salt dumped in on my oakboard box—and three dumped in on the old woman's. We're going to keep like a jar of apples till the judgment. Going to keep right here on this mountain till resurrection day, looking fresh as two lilies. We're not going to be a couple of skeletons coming out of the grave. We're going to come out of there—the whole of us just like we went in. Salt around us and oakboards from our hills—buried on our mountain-top where only the fox-horns blow and the wind and the hound-dogs bark—w'y we'll keep forever."

"We got to get home and feed," says Pa, "got to be going. Come over, Hodd, you and Ott—come over when you can. Come over, Flem," says Pa, hollering in his ear. "Come over and see me before you change worlds. After you get out of here you won't be at a place where we can neighbor like we used to neighbor."

"I want to get around to your place and Hankas's place before September and see all you boys once more," says Flem, "then I'm ready for my rest. No drouths then, no crop failures, and people telling me what to raise and how to raise it. I'll still be a Democrat, though. You can't change a mountain Democrat or a mountain Republican."

"That's right," says Pa, "you know me. I'll be a Republican in Heaven or in Hell. But I like you Flem because you are what you are and a good neighbor. I hope we get to neighbor again in other mountains."

We walk up the hill—we take the near cut across the spur home. The path is dry and white as a crooked dog-bone. Pa walks in front. Pa's shirt is wet with sweat as a dish-rag—sweat has come through the crown of his hat in places. We see the sun sinking—we look back at the vast hills, timber-covered, the great green clouds of wilted leaves that dry-rustle in the wind, and the houses down in the valley. "A good neighbor," says Pa, "a good neighbor if I ever had one on this earth."

James Still

1906–2001

Many people are surprised to learn that James Still was not a native of eastern Kentucky but of central Alabama, for his name has become synonymous with Appalachian literature. Many of his short stories and poems as well as his novel *River of Earth* (1940) are set in Knott County, Kentucky, where he worked at the Hindman School and lived for almost all of his adult life. Still's work delves deeply into the lives of people and communities in one corner of Appalachia but simultaneously speaks to experiences in rural places and small towns everywhere. His writing also explores nature and the individual's relationship to it.

Although Still enjoyed a private, self-reliant life in a cabin built in 1837, he traveled regularly to Central America and Europe, served as an assistant professor of English at Morehead State University for nearly a decade, and lectured widely on college campuses. An enthusiastic participant in local community events, Still also cultivated widespread professional relationships, meeting Carson McCullers, Katherine Anne Porter, and other influential authors.

Still's writing career was marked by two periods of primary activity—in the 1930s and early 1940s and again in the 1970s and 1980s, his works of the latter time fueled in part by the rise of the Appalachian studies movement and the growing interest in Appalachian writers that it engendered. A defining moment between these two periods of activity was Still's military service in North Africa and the Middle East from 1942 to 1945.

Still is regarded as one of the most accomplished and influential Appalachian writers.

Rain on the Cumberlands

Through the stricken air, through the buttonwood balls
Suspended on twig-strings, the rain fog circles and swallows,
Climbs the shallow plates of bark, the grooved trunks,
And wind-pellets go hurrying through the leaves.
Down, down the rain; down in plunging streaks
Of watered grey.

Rain in the beechwood trees. Rain upon the wanderer
Whose breath lies cold upon the mountainside,
Caught up with broken horns within the nettled grass,
With hoofs relinquished on the breathing stones
Eaten with rain-strokes.

Rain has buried her seed and her dead.
They spring together in this fertile air
Loud with thunder.

Spring

Not all of us were warm, not all of us.
We are winter-lean, our faces are sharp with cold
And there is the smell of wood smoke in our clothes;
Not all of us were warm, though we hugged the fire
Through the long chilled nights.

                                    We have come out
Into the sun again, we have untied our knot
Of flesh: We are no thinner than a hound or mare,
Or an unleaved poplar. We have come through
To the grass, to the cows calving in the lot.

Wolfpen Creek

How it was in that place, how light hung in a bright pool
Of air like water, in an eddy of cloud and sky,
I will long remember. I will long recall
The maples blossoming wings, the oaks proud with rule,
The spiders deep in silk, the squirrels fat on mast,
The fields and draws and coves where quail and peewees call.
Earth loved more than any earth, stand firm, hold fast;
Trees burdened with leaf and bird, root deep, grow tall.

Of the Wild Man

It will take a little while to find him.
He may be in some unlikely place
Lying beneath a haw, lost in leafy sleep,
Or atop a high field digging his keep.
He is somewhere around. Go and look.

It will take a little while to find him,
For hunger drives no wild man home.
Dark bays no hasting to a will like his.
He may dine on berries, abide where he is.
He is somewhere around. Go and look.

The Nest

Nezzie Hargis rested on a clump of broomsage and rubbed her numb hands. Her cheeks smarted and her feet had become a burden. Wind flowed with the sound of water through trees high on the ridge and the sun appeared caught in the leafless branches. Cow paths wound the slope, a puzzle of trails going nowhere. She thought, "If ever I could see a smoke or hear an ax ring, I'd know the way."

Her father had said, "Nezzie, go stay a night with your Aunt Clissa"; and Mam, the woman her father had brought to live with them after her mother went away, explained, "We'd take you along except it's your ailing grandpaw we're to visit. Young 'uns get underfoot around the sick." But it had not been the wish to see her grandfather that choked her throat and dampened her eyes—it was leaving the baby. Her father had reminded, "You're over six years old, half past six by the calendar clock. Now, be a little woman." Buttoned into a linsey coat, a bonnet tied on her head, she had looked at the baby wrapped in its cocoon of quilts. She would have touched its foot had they not been lost in the bundle.

Resting on the broomsage she tried to smile, but her cheeks were too tight and her teeth chattered. She recollected once kissing the baby, her lips against its mouth, its bright face pucked. Mam had scolded, "Don't paw the child. It's onhealthy." Her father had said, "Womenfolk are always slobbering. Why, smack him on the foot." She had put her chin against the baby's heel and spied between its toes. Mam had cried, "Go tend the chickens." Mam was forever crying, "Go tend the chickens." Nezzie hated grown fowls—pecking hens and flogging roosters, clucking and crowing, dirtying everywhere.

Her father had promised, "If you'll go willing to your Aunt Clissa's, I'll bring you a pretty. Just name a thing you want, something your heart is set on." Her head had felt empty. She had not been able to think what she wanted most.

She had set off, her father calling after, "Follow the path to the cattle gap, the way we've been going. And when we're home tomorrow, I'll blow the fox horn and come fetch you." But there were many trails upon the slope. The path had divided and split again, and the route had not been found after hours of searching. Beyond the ridge the path would wind to Aunt Clissa's, the chimney rising to view, the hounds barking and hurrying to meet her, and Uncle Barlow shouting, "Hold there, Digger!" and, "Stay, Merry!" and they would not, rushing to lick her hands and face.

She thought to turn back, knowing the hearth would be cold, the doors locked. She thought of the brooder house where diddles were sheltered, and where they might creep. Still across the ridge Uncle Barlow's fireplace would be roaring, a smoke lifting. She would go to the top of the ridge and the smoke would lead her down.

She began to climb and as she mounted her fingers and toes ached the more. Briers picked at the linsey coat and tugged at the bonnet. How near the crest seemed, still ever fleeing farther. Now more than half of the distance had been covered when the sun dropped behind the ridge and was gone. The cold quickened, an occasional flake of snow fell. High on the ridge the wind cried, "O-oo-o."

Getting out of breath she had to rest again. Beneath a haw where leaves were drifted she drew her coat tight about her shoulders and closed her eyes. Her father's words rang in her ears:

"Just name a thing you want. . . . I'll bring you a pretty."

Her memory spun in a haste like pages off a thumb. She saw herself yesterday hiding in the brooder house to play with newly hatched diddles, the brooder warm and tight, barely fitting her, and the diddles moist from the egg, scrambling to her lap, walking her spread palms, beaks chirping, "Peep, peep." Mam's voice had intruded even there: "Nezzie! Nezzie! Crack up a piece of broken dish for the hens. They need shell makings." She had kept quiet, feeling snug and contented, and almost as happy as before her mother went away.

Nezzie opened her eyes. Down the slope she saw the cow paths fading. Too late to return home, to go meeting the dark. She spoke aloud for comfort, "I ought to be a-hurrying." The words came hoarsely out of her throat. She climbed on, and a shoe became untied. She couldn't lace it anew with fingers turned clumsy and had to let the strings flare.

And she paused, yearning to turn back. She said to herself, "Let me hear a heifer bawl or a cowbell, and I will. I'll go fast." The wind moaned bitterly, drafting from the ridge into the pasture. A spring freezing among the rocks mumbled, "Gutty, gutty, gutty." She was thirsty but couldn't find it. She discovered a rabbit's bed in a tuft of grass, a handful of pills steaming beside it. The iron ground bore no tracks.

Up and up she clambered, hands on knees, now paying the trails no mind. She came to the pasture fence and attempted to mount. Her hands could not grasp, her feet would not obey. She slipped, and where she fell she rested. She drew her skirts over her leaden feet. She shut her eyes and the warmth of the lids burned. She heard the baby say, "Gub."

The baby said, "Gub," and she smiled. She heard her father ask again, "You know what 'gub' means? Means, get a move on, you slowpokes, and feed me."

She must not tarry. Searching along the panels she found a rail out of catch and she squeezed into the hole. Her dress tore, a foot became bare. She recovered the shoe. The string was frozen stiff.

A stretch of sassafras and locust and sumac began the other side of the fence. She shielded her face with her arms and compelled her legs. Sometimes she had to crawl. Bind-vines hindered, sawbriers punished her garments. She dodged and twisted and wriggled a passage. The thicket gave onto a fairly level bench, clean as a barn lot, where the wind blew in fits and rushes. Beyond it the ground ascended steeply to the top.

Dusk lay among the trees when she reached the crest of the ridge. Bending against the wind she ran across the bit of plateau to where the ridge fell away north. No light broke the darkness below, no dog barked. And there was no path going down. She called amid the thresh of boughs: "Aunt Clissa! Uncle Barlow! It's Nezzie."

Her voice sounded unfamiliar. She cupped her hands about her mouth: "Nezzie a-calling!" Her tongue was dry and felt a great weariness. Her head dizzied. She leaned against a tree and stamped her icy feet. Tears threatened, but she did not weep. "Be a little woman," her father had said.

A thought stirred in her mind. She must keep moving. She must find the way while there was light enough, and quickly, for the wind could not be long endured. As she hurried the narrow flat the cold found the rents in the linsey coat and pierced her bonnet. Her ears twinged, her teeth rattled together. She stopped time and again and called. The wind answered, skittering the fallen leaves and making moan the trees. Dusk thickened. Not a star showed. And presently the flat ended against a wall of rock.

How thirsty she was, how hungry. In her head she saw Aunt Clissa's table—biscuits smoking, ham fussing in grease, apple cake rising. She heard Uncle Barlow's invitation: "Battle out your faces and stick your heels under the table; keep your sleeves out of the gravy and eat till you split." Then she saw the saucer of water she had left the diddles in the brooder. Her thirst was larger than her hunger.

She cowered by the wall of rock and her knees buckled. She sank to the ground and huddled there, working at the bow of her bonnet strings. Loosening the strings she chafed her ears. And she heard her father say: "A master boy, this little 'un is. Aye, he's going somewhere in the world, I'd bet my thumb."

Mam's sharp voice replied, "Young 'uns don't climb much above their raising. He'll follow his pappy in the log woods, my opinion."

"If that be the case, when he comes sixteen I'll say, 'Here,' and reach him the broadax. He'll make chips fly bigger'n bucket lids."

"Nowadays young 'uns won't tip hard work. Have to be prized out of bed mornings. He'll not differ."

"I figure he'll do better in life than hoist an ax. A master boy, smart as a wasper. Make his living and not raise a sweat. He'll amount to something, I tell you."

Nezzie glimpsed the baby, its grave eyes staring. They fetched her up. She would go and spend the night in the brooder and be home the moment of its return. And she would drink the water in the diddles' saucer. She retraced her steps, walking stiffly as upon johnny-walkers, holding her hands before her. The ground had vanished, the trees more recollected than seen. Overhead the boughs groaned in windy torment.

Yet she did not start down directly, for the pitch of the slope was too fearful. She tramped the flat, going back the way she had come, and farther still. She went calling and listening. No spark broke the gloom. The dogs were mute. She was chilled to the bone when she squatted at the edge of the flat and ventured to descend. She fell in a moment, fell and rolled as a ball rolls. A clump of bushes checked her.

From there to the bench she progressed backward like a crawdabber, lowering herself by elbows and knees, sparing her hands and feet. She traveled with many a pause to thresh her arms and legs and rub her ears. It seemed forever. When she reached the bench snow was spitting.

She plodded across the bench and it had the width of the world. She walked with eyes tight to shun the sting of snowflakes. She went on, sustained by her father's voice:

"Let this chub grow up and he'll be somebody. Old woman, you can paint yore toenails and hang 'em over the banisters, for there'll be hired girls to do the work. Aye, he'll see we're tuk care of."

"He'll grow to manhood, and be gone. That's about the size of it. Nowadays . . ."

Sitting on a tuft she blew her nose upon her dress tail. Then she eased herself upon the ground with her head downhill. She began squirming left and right, gaining a few inches at each effort. She wallowed a way through briery canes, stands of sumac, thorny locusts. She bumped against rocks. Her coat snagged, her breath came in gasps. When snow started falling in earnest she was barely aware of it. And after a long struggle she pressed upon the rail fence. She groped the length of two panels in search of a hole before her strength failed.

Crouched against the fence she drew herself small into her coat. She pulled the ruffle of her bonnet close about her neck and strove against sleep. The night must be waited out. "Tomorrow," she told herself, "Pap will blow the fox horn and come for me. He will ride me on his head as he did upon an occasion." In her mind she saw the horn above the mantelpiece, polished and brass-tipped; she saw herself perched on her father's head like a topknot.

"What, now, is Pap doing?" She fancied him sitting by the hearth in her grandfather's house. "What is Grandpaw up to?" He was stretched gaunt and pale on a featherbed, his eyes keen with tricks. Once he had made a trap of his shaky hands, and had urged, "Nez', stick a finger in and feed the squirrel." In had gone her finger and got pinched. "'T'was the squirrel bit you," he had laughed. And seeing her grandfather she thought of his years, and she thought suddenly of the baby growing old, time perishing its cheeks, hands withering and palsying. The hateful wisdom caught at her heart and choked her throat. She clenched her jaws, trying to forget. She thought of the water in the diddles' saucer. She dozed.

"Nezzie Hargis!"

She started, eyes wide to the dark.

"I'll bring you a pretty. . . . Just name a thing you want."

She trembled and her teeth chattered. She saw herself sitting the baby on her lap. It lay with its fair head against her breast.

"Name a thing . . . something your heart is set on."

Her memory danced. She heard her father singing to quiet the baby's fret. "Up, little horse, let's hie to mill." She roved in vision, beyond her father, beyond the baby, to one whose countenance was seen as through a mist. It was her mother's face, cherished as a good dream is cherished—she who had held her in the warm, safe nest of her arms. Nezzie slept at last, laboring in sleep toward waking.

She waked to morning and her sight reached dimly across the snow. An ax hewed somewhere, the sound coming to her ears without meaning. She lifted an arm and glimpsed the gray of her hand and the bloodless fingers; she drew herself up by the fence and nodded to free her bonnet of snow. She felt no pain, only languor and thirst. The gap was three panels distant and she hobbled toward it. She fell. Lying on the ground she crammed snow into her mouth. Then she arose and passed under the bars, hardly needing to tilt her head.

Nezzie came down the slope. She lost a shoe and walked hippity-hop, one shoe on, one shoe off. The pasture was as feathery as a pillow. A bush plucked her bonnet, snatching it away; the bush wore the bonnet on a limb. Nezzie laughed. She was laughing when the cows climbed by, heads wreathed in a fog of breath, and when a fox horn blew afar. Her drowsiness increased. It grew until it could no longer be borne. She parted a clump of broomsage and crept inside. She clasped her knees, rounding the grass with her body. It was like a rabbit's bed. It was a nest.

Anne Wetzell Armstrong

1872–1958

Born in Grand Rapids, Michigan, Anne Wetzell Armstrong moved as a young girl to Knoxville, Tennessee, where her father served as a broker for a British mineral and timber company. For the rest of her life, Armstrong claimed East Tennessee as her home. Though she enjoyed a youth of great wealth and privilege, a railway accident in 1889, just as she was leaving for college, seriously injured her father, and the family's fortunes declined. Armstrong managed to attend Mount Holyoke College for two years, but left school to marry Leonard Waldrop. They divorced in 1894, and Armstrong supported her infant son and her parents by teaching school in Knoxville.

In 1902, Anne married Robert Franklin Armstrong. With his encouragement, she began to write fiction, publishing her first novel, *The Seas of God,* in 1915. In 1918, she became an executive for a Wall Street bank and then a manager for Eastman Kodak Company in Rochester, New York. When she was transferred by Eastman Kodak to East Tennessee, she and Robert built a cabin on land that was later inundated by the Tennessee Valley Authority (TVA). Her second novel, *This Day and Time* (1930), is told from the point of view of a mountain woman whose home is about to be taken by the TVA lake system. In contrast, "The Branner House," excerpted below, evokes the mood of early twentieth-century Knoxville as it explores urban Appalachian themes of wealth and social class.

FROM The Branner House

It stood rather high above the street, a roomy ramshackle house, its dilapidation partly concealed by the dense foliage of two enormous magnolia trees. Across the front ran a gallery, as we used to call it, and on either side, above and below, hung little balconies, sagging under their weight of overgrown honeysuckle vines and jasmine. The house, though somewhat pretentious, had probably never been considered handsome, but from the time I first knew it, it had fallen into an almost hopeless state of decay. Just the same, what with the life that went on in it, the Branner house remained for me throughout my youth the most enchanting of human abodes.

My mother, though, did not like the Branners at all. She had come south too late in her life ever to amalgamate with people so radically different, and the Branners stood to her, I think, for everything in the South which she mistrusted, and more or less disapproved. Coming as a child, with me, it was different.

My own special friend among the Branners was Belle, a harum-scarum weed of a girl, who looked, with her cropped black curls—her hair had been cut after typhoid—like a handsome Neapolitan boy. Enticed by Belle, who had stopped school at fourteen, to take up French and music—pursuits which left her plenty of leisure—I played hooky, I remember, a few times, though luckily my mother never found out, as Professor Woggs at the high school accepted without question the notes of excuse which Belle had written in an excellent imitation of my mother's refined handwriting.

When I was about sixteen, I suppose it was, I used to long to spend every evening at the Branner house, but my mother never consented willingly to my going there. Instead, I would sit on our own porch, silently, through the black breathless summer evenings, while peal after peal of laughter would come from the Branners, across the street on the corner below. Then I would hear the jingling of their piano, and out into the night would float Belle's rich voice in a melodramatic quaver:

In the gloaming, oh, my darling.

Again peals, shrieks, of laughter. It was the meeting place of all the young people in our end of town. Even after I had gone upstairs for the night, I could still hear sounds of wild merriment coming from the Branners. I would lie awake, tossing under the mosquito canopy, thinking miserably: "If she won't let me have fun while I'm young, I might just as well never have been born."

Occasionally, Mrs. Branner would come over and sit with my mother for a while in the evening. It would be late, but still too hot—and there would still be too much din at her own house—to go to bed. One of these times, hearing a murmur from the porch below, and then distinguishing Mrs. Branner's high honeyed tones alternating with the lower-pitched, more incisive accents of my mother's voice, I crept down in my nightgown, stood on the stairs in the unlighted hall—dark, to keep the moths and beetles out—and listened shamelessly.

"I've just finished some dresses for the brats." Mrs. Branner always designated her children in this fashion.

"I thought I heard your sewing machine," my mother said, rather severely.

Mrs. Branner laughed. "They wanted 'em for tomorrow."

"But *sewing*—a night like this!"

"They're only young once," Mrs. Branner defended herself. "Law, when I remember the times *I* had"—and she started recounting the triumphs of her youth when as "Pet" Knox, the daughter of General Knox, she had been, according to all accounts, a belle of belles.

Through the darkness, I could feel my mother stiffening. She considered it extremely bad taste for a woman to boast of her youthful popularity, of the "sweethearts" she had had.

"When I remember—aye, Lord!" Mrs. Branner sighed with satisfaction. "Old women like you and me," she went on, "are through with *our* good times—we've got to see that the brats have theirs."

My mother was silent. "You're making a great mistake," she said finally.

"Oh I don't know"—

"You're making selfish children."

"They'll do the same when *they* have brats. And you and I don't want anything now—only to see *them* happy. Let 'em have a good time while they can." Her talk ran on. She was saying now that it was time they were letting Belle and me go to the dances (cotillions at the Sans Souci Club). "They're old enough, you know, and we can fix 'em up some little evenin' dresses that won't cost much. There ain't one of my girls a beauty, but I make 'em *look* like beauties. You know what men are—a girl's got to look pretty, or she won't have sweethearts."

I could catch the impatient swish of my mother's palm-leaf fan. "Angie," she said at last, and her voice trembled slightly, "has never given a thought to beaux."

"Oh, *hasn't* she?" I said to myself, in the darkness.

Mrs. Branner laughed outright, but softly. "Yes? Well, I don't want *my* girls to be old maids!"

It was not, I imagine, very long after this that one evening my mother sat on the porch as usual, plying her palm-leaf fan. It was still early, not yet completely dark. I can never forget that evening. It is as if it were yesterday.

Rushing out the front door, I swept by my mother like a whirlwind. "Going to Belle's," I called back, when I was almost at the gate.

My mother (this was so unlike me!) leaned forward quickly, her fan brought to a complete stop. "You're not to stay"—she began in an authoritative, though subdued and startled, voice.

But already I was half-way across the street. "Pooh!" I thought, "it wasn't so hard. I ought to have started long ago. If a girl of *my* age can't run across to a neighbor's without asking permission, when's she going to?" I fled down the block. But all the time my heart was pounding. I felt as if my mother were following as I ran up a flight of stone steps from the street, tripping on my skirt, and then up a longer flight, tripping again, to the Branners' front door. It was a double door, and one side stood open. The gas burned dimly in the hall, in a single jet, under a red glass globe. Against one wall was a decrepit mahogany sofa, its springs broken and sticking up through the leather. Above the sofa hung a rusty sword flanked by engravings of General Stonewall Jackson and General Robert E. Lee, while the table opposite held an unused silver water pitcher and goblets, a tray heaped with dusty visiting cards, and a bowl filled with magnolia blossoms that had evidently been picked some time; their petals were brown and falling off.

I knocked lightly. I could never overcome a slight feeling of timidity when I stood at the Branners' door. But Belle had insisted I should come.

I rapped again. A good deal of noise, sounds of people talking and running about, came down from upstairs, and I could catch glimpses, through a door at the back, of Lou, the Branners' house girl, moving back and forth, apparently waiting on someone at supper.

Lou thrust her head, wound with a white cloth, out the dining-room door: "Law, it's Miss Angie!"

She came slopping good-naturedly through the hall, pieces of shoes tied with rags on her big bare feet. The buttons had all burst off the elaborate lace-trimmed lawn dress that had once been Kate Branner's, and it was straining at its pins.

"Come in, Miss Angie." From the foot of the stairs, she called: "Miss Belle!" A pause. "*Oh,* Miss Belle!" Then, after another pause: "Jes' go 'long up, Miss Angie."

Looking down as I climbed the stairs, I could see into the library, make out dimly the high bookcases with their glass doors and rows and rows of old calf-bound volumes that no one had ever opened since Mr. Branner died. Through the dining-room door, Knox Branner was visible now, eating alone at one end of the long table. He always got home late. Behind him, on the massive dingy sideboard, some pieces of a tarnished silver tea set shone dully, amidst a clutter of other things, and there were faint gleams from the stoppers of two whisky decanters.

"Good evenin', Miss Angie!" He waved his hand and smiled, with a graceful movement half rising from his chair, holding his napkin against him. "How are *you?*" he called out, with the most enheartening emphasis on "you."

He had dark wavy hair, a curling moustache, and gleaming teeth. I thought that "Mr. Knox" was the handsomest, the most polite, altogether the most charming, young man in the world. He had graduated from the university with honors and had intended to practise law, but then his father had died—it might be years before he could make even the barest living at the law, and there were his sisters—they must have their chance. So he took anything he could get, clerked in a shoe store, fitting a pair of shoes, so I had heard someone say, as he might have handed a duchess down to dinner—and contributed every cent that he could to the family purse.

There was a loud outcry from one of the bedrooms above: "Mary Jo, let that sash alone! Your hands are filthy! Mama, come here!"—presumably to settle Mary Jo, eleven, and the youngest of the Branners.

There was always this same noisy excitement at the Branners, always these half laughing, half crying, appeals to "Mama."

And there was always this smell through the house, here on the stairs, everywhere—an all-pervasive smell of fried things, fried chicken, fried ham, fried beefsteak, generations of fried dishes, together with odors of mould, of soot, of dust, a whiff of stale flowers, in short, all the odors that might very naturally accumulate in the course of time in a warm, moist, highly-favoring climate. [. . .] But what could she do? "Five girls to marry off!"

The smell, so far as I was concerned, was entrancing.

Louise McNeill

1911–1993

Louise McNeill was born in Pocahontas County, West Virginia, on the farm where her family had lived since 1769. After studying at Middlebury College with Robert Frost and attending the Iowa Writers' Workshop, McNeill received her doctorate from West Virginia University. During her thirty-year tenure as a professor of English and history, she also became an active opponent of strip mining and participated in the first Earth Day in 1970. Governor Jay Rockefeller appointed McNeill West Virginia's poet laureate in 1979, a position that she held until her death in 1993.

McNeill's oeuvre is small but its importance is great, and many Appalachian poets acknowledge her as an inspiration. McNeill published her first book of poems, *Gauley Mountain,* in 1939. The book was highly regarded in the literary world; it was also well received by general readers despite a small print run. As in *Spoon River Anthology* (1915)—Edgar Lee Master's influential collection of poems—many of the *Gauley Mountain* poems are small biographies of their subjects, including the acquisitive Verner family, featured here.

McNeill was also deeply involved in contemporary global issues. In her 1972 volume of poetry, *Paradox Hill: From Appalachia to Lunar Shore,* McNeill reflects on the implications of the scientific frontier in Appalachia and elsewhere.

Katchie Verner's Harvest

It pleasures her to gather
A hoard when autumn comes:
Of grapes in scroll-worked silver,
Red-streaked-with-amber plums,
Winesaps and seek-no-farthers,
Green peppers, russet pears,
White roastin'-ears for drying
On frames above the stairs,
Queer handled gourds for dishes
And dippers at the spring,
Long butternuts, fat pumpkins,
Cream-colored beans to string,
Wild meats to jerk and pickle,
Brown chestnuts tipped with cold,
Cranberries from the marshes,
Tree honey dripping gold.

In barrels and crocks and suggins,
In pokes upon the floor
And hanging from the rafters
Is Katchie Verner's store
Against the mountain winter
When sleet-hard drifts will freeze
The deep loam of her garden
And gird her orchard trees.

Oil Field

A crawling, black transgressor
Old Verner never feared
Has undermined the meadow
Which he surveyed and cleared.
A pipe of soldered metal
That runs with yellow oil
Glides down a hidden furrow
Beneath his fallow soil.
And round that lengthened sky line
The steel-ribbed derricks stand
Like windmill ghosts arisen
To haunt Old Verner's land.

Of Fitness to Survive

If the firefly and the glow worm
By their burning are in tune
With the structure of the atom
And are rendered thus immune,
In that light which follows darkness
But on which no darkness falls,
Then the *two* will feast and flourish,
Creeping down the embered halls—
Eating of the fire-egg burning
In the fire-hawk's flaming nest;
Sucking of the fire-milk flowing—
Lava from the fire-hag's breast.

Potherbs

(*Of the edible wild plants my granny taught me.*)

With fire to the eastward and fire to the west,
Then I may go hunting, with hunger possessed,
To break the harsh nettle, the blade of the sedge,

The fern and the toadflax, the flag on the edge
Of gullies, the crowfoot, the wild heron's bill;
I will hunt for the pokeweed upon that burnt hill—
Burnt hill of the atom, hot dust of the cloud—
If goose-grass is living, I will not be proud.

The New Corbies

If trees remain and carrion crows
Still gather on the oak,
That morning when the green wind blows
And carries off the smoke,
The crows will find below them there,
All blooming from the ground,
As flowered and as fat a feast
As crows have ever found.

Of scarlet red and bloated white,
And flowered full in bloom
Those tropic blossoms all will burst
To waft their sweet perfume.

And floating from the oak tree's limb,
Like hunger, then the crows
Will taste of man and savor him—
The richest fruit that grows,
When from the forehead of his dream
Exudes the atom rose.

Cassandra

I sat by the window and trod my loom,
And I saw the shape of a gaunt mushroom
Grow up the iceberg and spread the sky;
And I wove in my cloth that the world would die.

Genesis

God upon the firmament
Walking to creation went,
Thought of light and let it be
MC^2 to equal E.

Mildred Haun

1911–1966

Mildred Haun's literary output was small but outstanding. Haun was born near the Great Smoky Mountains in rural Hamblen County, Tennessee, and was reared in Cocke County. At the age of ten, she stopped attending school. Following the death of her father, a farmer, when she was eleven, she moved in with an aunt and uncle south of Nashville in Franklin, Tennessee; there, she entered high school at the age of sixteen. She studied at Vanderbilt University, receiving a BA in 1935 and an MA in 1937.

Vanderbilt was at this time the center of a dynamic group of writers and scholars called the Fugitives (later they evolved into the Agrarians). Like Appalachian authors Jesse Stuart and James Still, who also attended Vanderbilt, Haun studied with Fugitive professors. While in the class of Fugitive author John Crowe Ransom, Haun began to write the short stories that she later collected into her one published book, *The Hawk's Done Gone* (1940). Donald Davidson, also a Fugitive, supervised her thesis on the folklore of Cocke County. From 1944 to 1946, Haun worked as an assistant to another Fugitive, Allen Tate, editor of the *Sewanee Review*. When Haun accused Tate of sexual impropriety, however, she lost the support of her literary mentors. She spent most of the remainder of her life working as a technical writer.

"The Piece of Silver," not a part of *The Hawk's Done Gone* and unpublished until the 1968 edition of Haun's work, was written early in her career. The story explores issues of intrafamilial violence, prejudice, folk belief, class, and women. One of the characters in this story is Melungeon, a member of a multiracial group centered in Hancock County, Tennessee. Melungeons historically experienced discrimination, as Haun's story suggests.

The Piece of Silver

Pa told folks George went back to the mine up in Virginia after Cathey Hancock died. When anybody asked him, that is what he said. But Ma, she never did say anything save that she didn't know. "I just don't know," she would say. And then say it another time to herself, "I don't rightly know." Even when I took the piece of silver to her she didn't say much. She just looked at it and said, nigh like she was saying it to herself and I wasn't there to hear her say it: "Hit is back in the shape of the neckpiece," and she took it, handling it gentle-like, as if it was a baby, and put it in the washstand drawer where George had kept it. The next day she asked me, in a low voice and anxious seeming, if that deer I seed looked fat and healthy.

George, he was three years older than me. And him and Cathey Hancock played together more than me and him did, for she was tomboyish and rough, and tough as a pine knot, always. With this withered right side of mine, and one leg shorter than tother, I wasn't given to playing as hard as they did. They played a heap over there in the old hollow oak that shaded the big spring. Cathey liked it there, and George did too. He liked to set in the hollow of it and come out smelling of the doty wood and to hear Cathey brag on him for being a real woods man. That's why I went there looking. I recollected them spread-out limbs of the tree and the picture of George and Cathey in the clear water. I thought about it in the daytime and at night time I dreampt about it. And it come into my head to go look there for George.

Cathey did the climbing, the biggest part of it, she did, when they was playing. She would holler back to George from limb to limb. "Look how high up I am," she would say, for she was ever a better climber than George. And a better runner. She would climb, easy as a squirrel, to the topmost limb of the tree and sing back down to George, for he nigh always crawled into the hollow trunk and set—just set and looked at her like he would give his right hand to be like her, maybe. I would scramble up on the stump on the bluff close by and watch them and listen to them and wonder in my mind at Cathey's ways.

> Possum up a simmon tree
> Raccoon on the ground
> Raccoon says to the possum
> O, shake them simmons down.

That's what Cathey would sing. And she would shake the spread-out limbs of the oak and George would crawl around the tree ducking his head down to make like he was picking up persimmons to eat them. I had seed him around the tree and in the trunk of it so much, when he was little, ducking his head up and down and leaping on his all fours, that it nigh seemed natural that morning when I thought I seed his eyes a-shining. But somehow a queer feeling took holt of me and I stopped. Stopped and whistled when I got in good sight of it. And the buck jumped out. Jumped out of the trunk and looked at me and nigh started toward me. But then went running off up the hollow. I couldn't help but note the eyes—they were so gentle seeming, and almost spoke. I stood awhile. Then went on to the tree.

George set a heap a store by Cathey. From the day she was born, he did. Ma named it often. "He just dotes on her," she would say and sometimes seem sad when she said it and hold her hands tight in her lap. Cathey's pa and ma lived on our place, off up the hollow there in the little log house, and Ma was granny-woman to Old Lady Hancock when Cathey was born. There wasn't anybody else to be. Pa was out in the field when Old Man Hancock come for Ma, so she, of course, couldn't leave George at the house by himself and had to take him with her. And he seed Cathey soon after she was born. He was two year old then and cried like a weaned calf to hold her in his arms. And always afterwards wanted to hold her in his arms, Ma said. She sometimes said it, and Pa laughed and jested George about it.

As soon as they was big enough, George and Cathey took to playing together. Cathey would come down here soon of a morning and stay the day—the whole day long. And always she had her own way about what they should play. Or shouldn't.

She made George set in the playhouse with her, and he would do it, no matter how much Pa teased him and called him girlified and threatened to make him wear dresses. He would make cornstalk dolls when she told him to make them and would rock them to sleep in his arms and try to sing the songs she told him to sing. Or he would help her stick thorns into the heads and hearts of them to kill them dead so they could have big funerals and buryings for them.

But she liked most of all to play with that old iron kittle—the one that had a crack nigh the top of it from the water freezing in it. She would put two forked sticks into the ground and put the kittel on a stick that retch from one fork to tothern. She would fill the kittel to the crack with muddy water and splunge chips and leaves down deep into it with her hands and watch it close till she said it was done enough to eat. Then she would play that she was eating. She would tell George to eat some too, and he would dip and blow and sup and make out he was putting victuals into his mouth and maw. Cathey would say, sometimes, "Hyear, George, you stir the stew whiles I run to the woodpile to fetch the wood. Now say the rhyme. Say it nine times and the stew will be done." And she would hand him the stirring stick.

George, he would stir the muddy water round and round in easy motion and say the rhyme and stir and keep on saying it some more.

> Onery doury dickory day
> Halibone crackle bone tenderlay
> Whiskey brandy American thyme
> Humble bumble twenty-nine
> Oory ary ockery ann
> Mulberry wax and tarry tan.

That's what he would say nine times. Then Cathey, she would take the stew off and they would set the table, with them pieces of broke dishes that Cathey brought, and they would make like they was eating.

Sometimes, in the springtime and in the summer, they would play over in the first hollow of the cow field, amongst the clover and the persimmon bushes, and George would stand still as a stone and watch Cathey catch the honeybees from off the white clover blossoms. "They won't sting," she would say, "if you will hold your breath, or if you will charm them—like this." And she would hold her breath and catch a bee that wouldn't ever sting her. Then she would catch anothern, just walk up to the clover blossom it was lighted on and say out loud, as she wove her finger round and round it in circles,

> Johnnie jizzer jacket
> You can make your racket
> But you can't no more sting me
> Than the devil can count sixpence.

And George, he would look at her and seem pleasured at her ways. But he wouldn't ever offer to touch a bee hisself.

Sometimes they would ask me to play with them when they were playing and twice I did—before the time I got afeared of Cathey. I never had set much a store by her nor cared much for her ways, but I never had feared her till that day I seed her running. Her and George had been carrying on in the playhouse all the day long, till they were tired and wore out from gathering wood and making stews and washing dishes. And so they took to running. They run a race down the road. Cathey made the mark in the dust to start from and said the rhyme, "One for the money, two for the show, three to make ready, and here we go." And they started. But before they got halfway to the first apple tree George stopped and stood still as a post and watched Cathey. I watched her too and took note that she wasn't ever hitting the ground with her feet—nigher flying than running, it was. She went all the way to the mark and turned and come all the way back to where George was standing without stopping. And she wasn't panting. George didn't name the running to her but he took to begging her to sing and kept on a-begging, saying to her a blue million times or more, "Sing 'Tam Lin,' Cathey, about the Queen of Fairyland."

"I don't care to," Cathey said.

"You sing better than a mocking bird, you do," he said and kept a-begging. But Cathey just shook her head and laughed nigh fit to kill and kept shaking her head, her hair a-flying wild in the wind.

"I know what let's do," she said. "Let's play cat."

"Play cat?"

"Play like we're turning into cats."

"I don't know how," George said. "Sing 'Tam Lin' for me."

"This away," Cathey said. And she got down on her all fours and took to meowing. It sounded for all the world like a real cat. I looked at her and thought her ears stuck up and I kept on a-looking. I took note of her eyes too. And her mouth. Seemed like—to me it did, I didn't name it to George—they got littler and rounder. And I took holt of George's hand and helt it tight, for I somehow felt afeared of Cathey.

"I don't want to play cat," George said.

"You're lazy as a cow bird," Cathey said, and shook her head and looked sullen. "I'll get my bonnet and go home." But she didn't go, for George begged her not to then. He got down on his all fours to pacify her, and she took to laughing and singing.

> Ha ha—There was an old man lived on a hill, ha ha
> If he hain't moved away he's a-living there still, ha ha
> Ha ha ha ha ha ha ha ha ha ha, ha ha.

But George, he was awkward at the crawling and meowing, not seeming naturalized to it like Cathey seemed. I named it to Ma when I got to the house. And Ma just said, "Cathey's bounden to a-learnt sech from her Ma." But afterwards I took note that she looked bothered in her mind a little and that she tried to keep George from playing with Cathey so much. But it was like trying to keep a mule from kicking. For George was nigh twelve year old then.

He was nigh twelve and Cathey was going on ten; and they took to the woods. Pa didn't make George work in the field much; so him and Cathey played in the woods nigh all the time, climbing trees and chasing after butterflies and bees and such as

Cathey wanted to chase after. Cathey knowed heart's ease, and sang too, and all the flowers and herbs and where they growed and what every one was used for; and her and George gathered them for Old Lady Hancock. And once I seed her make George cut a limb from off a thorn tree and tote it to Hancocks' house. I told Ma again, and she asked Pa if he reckoned Cathey knowed love weed and might feed it to George when he was older. Pa laughed and poked fun at her and said he didn't believe in any such weed. And she didn't name it to him any more. But just said she wished Old Lady Hancock wouldn't ever talk to George. And was proud when Pa started making George go to the field.

George sometimes jested Cathey about eating the grass and bushes. But she did eat them—sweetgum and sassafras and sheep sours and things I didn't know— bushes and leaves and roots. Just eat them raw. And sometimes George would eat them too, when she begged him. He would chew them up and spit out the spit or swallow it. Whatever she told him to do.

Till George was nigh about fifteen year old. Then he quit playing and took to working all the week without Pa having to make him or to ever tell him to. And on a Sunday evening—every Sunday evening—he would put on his suit of clothes and go to court Cathey. He took her to a poke supper down at Low Land and to the Saturday night singings over at Campbells' and to a cake-walk down at Springvale and had a ruckus with Pal Hawkins over her because Pal asked her to cake-walk with him. And Ike Thompson had to hold George to keep him from getting into a fight with Pal.

At first Ma fussed at George and told him Cathey wasn't his kind and that some folks were dubious of her ma. She named other girls that he could pay his court to. But she soon give up her talking, for George was logger headed as a sow and said he set a heap a store by Cathey and he aimed to marry her for his wife if she would have him. But Cathey, she wouldn't hear his talk about marrying. She would start running. When he named marrying to her she started running. He would start talking to her about it and she would up and flounce out of the room. And if he followed her she would run, skipping along over the rocks like the wind a-blowing, not looking back at him. Or she would shake her head, letting her long thick hair fly through the air and not make him any answer. But he kept on a-asking her. I watched him practice on the bank of the creek, holding his arms first one way then tother and working his mouth up and down and shutting his eyes and groaning it out: "Cathey, will you—I'll make money by the bushels—my wife—why won't you marry me?"

He set around and talked about it to Ma and sometimes to me when we were doing up the work at night or early of a morning. And sometimes he laid the blame on Ma, saying she didn't like Hancocks because they didn't own land of their own. He fell off till he was slim as a rail almost and took to groaning in his sleep and singing love songs about hard-hearted girls and every day he sung that one about

> You should have employment then
> And to her your wages lend
> When you ask a girl to leave
> Her happy home.

He said he believed Cathey wanted to marry a rich man and he was going to make himself rich so she would have him. That's why he took out to Virginia. Him and Cathey had rid the horses two or three times on Saturday evening and gone to Russellville. And George talked with Abe Drennon out there. Abe had a map that he claimed was made by them men—Swift and Munday, their names were—that had found a silver mine up in Virginia. Abe got it, he claimed, from his pa, who had got it from the man that stole it from Old Man Swift at an inn somewhere when the old man was coming out from finding the mine. It was drawed on something that looked like paper but wasn't.

So George, he told Abe he would go help him find it. George said the map was nigh wore out—just ready to split at every place where it was folded. And it begun cracking up into little squares—twelve of them—every time they tetched it. But they could read it clear, and George set his head on finding the silver for Cathey.

He went to see her the evening before he started. Right after dinner he went and didn't come home for supper. He didn't come home till it was time for Ma to get his breakfast for him. She got his breakfast and filled Pa's old saddlebags full of victuals for him; and him and Abe got a soon start.

They walked fast as an ant, George said, and made it to the first hog drover's shelter by midnight or before, maybe, and rested there till daylight, sleeping. Then went on their way again. The next night they slept in a sheep shelter nigh the top of Reds Run Mountain. And there were two other men that come along and spent the night there too, in the shelter, and slept on the floor with them. Claimed they were mule traders from South Carolina. But George said he never named e'er a word about the mine when he talked to them. What little he talked.

Him and Abe parted with the stranger men the next morning and set out on their way again. They come to Four Hills, up in Virginia, before nightfall and seed and talked to a man there that asked them to stay the night with him. They did, and he put them off up in the loft by theirselves and they felt safe up there and like they were nigh to the silver and could almost feel it in their hands. They whispered back and forth to one another and lit the candle and propped the door fast with a chair so they could look at the map to tell which way to go from there. And Abe pulled off his right boot.

He took out the map and started putting the pieces together. But all at once he jumped up so high he nigh hit the ceiling with his head and yelled out to the top of his voice and kept a-yelling: "The balance—the balance—where is the balance of hit?" For there were just six pieces to be found. He took off all his clothes and turned them wrong side outwards and shook them and took the insoles out of his boots and still the map wasn't there—the other six pieces of it. And he set in on George, saying George had told them men; but George said he hadn't. And Abe and George took to argufying back and forth and fussing with one another and got dubious of one another and sullen. But neither one of them was willing to turn back towards home.

So they set out to find their way through the woods without the map. They couldn't tell much with just having half of it. And at nighttime George was afeared to sleep sound for fear Abe would kill him. For Abe took to claiming he believed

George had stole part of the map out of his boot whiles he slept in the night. George stripped off naked as the bare ground to prove he didn't have it, but still Abe was dubious of him and was short in talking to him. Then he took to saying he believed Old Man Swift's ghost come and took the map and he told George such tales till George got so he seed ghostes and empty caving-in mines in his sleep—when he slept. But he kept his heart set on the silver for Cathey.

George stayed with Abe in the woods for a whole year and wandered around in the wind and rain and slept in caves and hollow trees. Till one day he found a lump of something—something he thought might have silver in it. He marked the spot some-how and in a branch that runned there close he found another lump. He put both of them in Pa's saddlebags and fastened them in there tight as skin, telling Abe he would be back, or maybe would, as soon as he married Cathey. That would be enough, he thought, to show her he could be a rich man for the asking. So he left Abe up there and set out to find his own way home. And didn't have any trouble a-getting here.

He set by the fire three days straight hand-going—the first three days—and pid-dled with the lumps before he went to see Cathey. He melted one of the lumps and got the silver—for sure enough they both were silver—from it to make the chain. He melted it and drawed it out into a wire and quiled the wire up in little round rings and made the chain to fasten the other piece onto. It did make a pretty neckpiece, and he set out up the hollow with it, strutting like a turkey gobbler in the springtime, thinking on how proud Cathey would be. "I'll tell her there's more than this that I'll go back for. Hit'll look pretty on Cathey's white throat, won't hit?" And he strutted and strutted—with his long legs. And told me to keep mum about the lost map and not name it to Cathey.

But he come back soon. And yelt out at me, and dared me to talk to him or ask him any questions. And he wasn't ever the same afterwards. Ma named it several times about him being changed and about him not going to see Cathey. Nor making any mention of her. Then one day he told it. Me and Ma was setting a-picking out walnut kernels when he told it. He just kept a-staring at the kernels.

"Do you want some of these?" Ma said. And handed him some picked-out boy's britches.

"No," he said, "I don't want anything—I don't know what I want."

And he set into talking and told it. The silver piece scared Cathey. He handed it to her and she retch out her hand towards it saying, "Hit is pretty, hain't it?" Then the wild look come into her eyes, like in the eyes of a scared deer, he said, and she drew back her hand and never tetched it.

"Hit's yourn," he said. "I will go back for more—some day, when we need it, I will go back."

"George!"

"That's why I went."

She started to open her mouth and didn't. And run out of the house and up through the pine thicket like a streak of lightning, by leaps and bounds—so quick George couldn't think to try and follow after.

He didn't go back to spark her on Sunday any more. And Old Lady Hancock, when she come to help Ma make apple butter, named it about George not finding the mine. "'Did he tell you he didn't?" Ma said. "No," Old Lady Hancock said, "I just thought maybe part of the map got lost or something—I didn't know."

But soon Cathey took to coming here again. Ma made note of the way she feisted around George when she come. And George, he appeared to like it whiles she was here. He would ask her in and set a chair for her and tell her her dress was pretty. She did have pretty clothes, Cathey did, that she made; always with low-cut necks that showed her white chest; and she was proud as a king with her long hair slicked back and shining. George, he would set and look at her and smile, and when she rubbed herself up against him he would feel all over her with his hands. But he never named her after she was gone. And never made offer to walk a piece of the way home with her. Just set and stared at her leaving.

When she was gone, if it was in the wintertime, he would set and look into the fire. Or if it was summer he would set on the front steps staring at the sky or at the bull bats darting down toward the ground. Or at the calves over in the horse lot playing. And not say anything or answer me or Ma when we spoke a word to him. Till Ma took it into her head to tell Old Lady Hancock she didn't think it looked right for Cathey to come down here feisting around George, and Cathey didn't come any more.

Then George took to working and kept hisself busy as a bird all day every day. He took all the feeding and wood-chopping off Pa and stayed in the field from daylight till dark in crop time. During the winter days he was ever busy piddling in the barn or in the tool shed, till Pa was proud of him, saying his trip to the silver mine had done him good—made him know that the only way to get what a body wanted was to dig for it, and to dig in his own ground. Him and Pa cleaned out the fence rows and fixed the porch and Ma, she looked contented in her mind. And peaceful.

Save that Pa kept seeing a deer that come nigh and played around close to the house late in the evening, nigh every evening. The prettiest deer, he said, that he ever seed in his born days, with a white breast. But he had a feeling that it somehow boded bad luck the way it kept a-coming. And he set his mind on killing it. He took to setting out behind the smokehouse a-watching for it. Eight different times it come close up and he shot. But somehow he couldn't ever kill it. He was a good shot, Pa was, and said he knowed he hit it. But every time he shot, it lept into the air and kicked its heels high and went running off so fast Pa just stood with his mouth open a-looking at it.

Till after the eighth time, when he got more dubious of it, I reckon, for he looked in the washstand drawer, where he knowed George's silver piece was at and took the neckpiece from off the chain. He melted it in the ladle and poured it into the bullet moulds like it was lead. And didn't name it to George and I didn't either. Nor Ma.

Pa loaded the rifle with the silver bullet and set out behind the smokehouse every evening watching. Then one evening the deer come—right up to the rail fence, held up its head and looked across. Pa, he took good aim at the white breast, and shot. The deer fell over. He went running up to it. It was heaving its sides up and down a-dying, and he called George to come from the barn and see it. George, he looked and somehow, I don't know how, got the bullet out of its flesh. Not thinking, I reckon. But instead of dying, it jumped up and run away as hard as it could run. And Pa said the blood was dark and thick and not bright like deer's blood was wont to be. And Ma, she took to shaking like a cold dog when she seed the blood on George's hands and made him wash it off quick. And she looked uneasy and troubled in her thinking.

Soon the next morning, Glen—he was Cathey's brother—brought word down here that Cathey was dead. Said she died from a big boil that come on her chest and when the core come out it took to bleeding and wouldn't ever stop bleeding—no matter how much spiderweb and devil's snuff they dusted on it.

Ma went to help lay her out. George, he went over there too. And Ma come home and told about it—told me. Said whiles she was washing Cathey she had to go back through the room where George was setting and that Old Lady Hancock was setting square dab in front of him, eyeing him up and down from toe to head a-staring. And then when she was through with Cathey the old lady said to her: "You thought him not her kind, didn't you?" And Ma said she reckoned it must a-been in her own mind's eye she seed it but said she thought she seed the devil a-working in Old Lady Hancock's eyes. Thought she seed some kind of picture there.

After the burying George just set with his head bent low and his hand in his pocket. He nigh quit working. No matter how much Pa fussed at him or cussed. Then at times he would take something out of his pocket and stare at it full half a day, setting out under the sugar tree or behind the smokehouse, one. Then one day when Pa had gone to the mill, and Ma to Old Man White's burying at Cedar Knob, George made me go to the kitchen and set with the door closed, not giving me any reason for it. I peeped through the slats anyways to watch him. I seed him before the fire melting something in the ladle. But I didn't tell Ma.

Pa, of course, tried to make him work and George took umbrage at it and took to going away from home. At first it was just from meal time to meal time. Then it was from daylight till dark; and Ma said she hoped he wasn't asking victuals from Hancocks; so she left something on the table for him and his plate set, day and night, all the time.

He sometimes talked to Ma in the kitchen when he come in and soon he got to making wild talk, about finding a silver mine on our place and about talking to a deer in the woods and what the deer said to him. And about Cathey. Strange things about how he could still see Cathey. And how she run from him. Once I laughed when he was telling it and Ma shook her head at me and frowned. And when he left again she threatened me to box my ears if I should ever laugh at him again.

Then three days went by when he didn't come in. Me and Ma took victuals and set them around here and there. And everywhere, almost. We took some bread and meat and put it on that old flat rock up there on Slate Hill. The next day I looked and all the victuals was gone. And I took to thinking about the old tree by the spring. And couldn't ever get it off my mind.

George come in and stayed one day and left and didn't come back for a week. Then he come in during the night, early in the night, and come on into the lean-to where I was sleeping. Ma heard the racket. And she run in with a lit candle. "Hit's you," she said to him. And I riz up to speak to him and seed that he was trying to pull off his clothes. But he was awkward as a blind buzzard at it. Seemed like he couldn't straighten himself out or that he was stiff all over and drawing toward the floor. But he kept his fist, his right fist, closed tight as a turtle's mouth.

Ma asked him if he didn't want something to eat before he got in bed; and he went to the kitchen with her. I heard her talking but never did hear him say e'er a thing save "uh-huh" and "huh-uh," grunting the words out to her. When they come back into the lean-to I asked him if he wanted to sleep in front and he just looked at me like maybe he didn't know what I meant; but I moved over and ater a while he crawled in. I took note that it seemed hard for him to stretch out straight; but Ma took the candle on out and I went off to sleep.

And slept till it was nigh daylight and I heard a racket. I riz up quick and got a glimpse of George going out the door. I seed his clothes still on the chair round and I yelt for Ma. She come running; but it was done too late, for he was quick away. And gone out of our sight. Me and her and Pa tried to track him; but it was dry weather and we didn't have any tracks to go by.

Ma took me with her the next day and we went up to Hancocks' to ask them if they had seed him; and the old lady just set and grinned at us and said over and over and didn't say anything else, nor answer Ma what she asked, "You thought he wasn't Cathey's kind." So we kept on a-taking victuals to the woods and looking for him. But we never seed hide nor sole leather of him again. Ma didn't name it to Pa about the clothes on the chair and Pa said George had gone back to Virginia to look for the mine and told everybody that: that George had the wanderlust and had gone back to find more silver. But Ma, she didn't say anything, and I took note of the piece of slat, the piece of ash wood, nailed with three nails and tight across the washstand drawer. Me and her kept on taking victuals to the rock and leaving them there.

Till winter come and the big snow started falling. Early on a Sunday morning it got dark as night; the clouds were down so low, and Pa said we were in for a snowstorm. He made me hold candles for him whiles he laid feed by for the cows and horses, and Ma stuck a pine torch up in a tub of ashes and carried in wood by it, filling the big house full and stacking it on the back porch and in the kitchen.

Then the snow commenced to fall and it lightened up some. I looked at Ma and she looked at me and we set out in search. I yelt and whistled and looked in every fence corner and brushpile. And the snow soon started laying. Then it got dark and we couldn't tell whether the clouds was low again or if it was nighttime.

But it come light again in the morning and we started our searching over—save that the snow was sticking to briars and trees and bushes and nothing looked the same when it was covered—till the first thing we knowed we was going around and round in circles and stepping in our own tracks. The snow kept getting deeper and Ma took to lagging behind and panting. And it was away up into the shank of the evening before Pa come with Old Shep and the horses and found us.

It was two weeks before the snow melted much. Ma and Pa, they both just set and looked at the fire and first one and then tothern went to the window. And once Pa said, "If George finds a cave he will stay in hit—George is good at telling weather."

Ma didn't say anything, and every time Old Shep moved on the porch she run to the door. And at nighttime I dreampt. Seemed like every night I dreampt. About Cathey and George mostly—how they played. And about the tree. They would wake me up from hollering at one another and I could hear her singing down to him:

> Raccoon said to the possum
> Shake them simmons down.

And I could see him jump out of the hollow trunk and start running. I would wake up just as he got out of my sight and not ever get to see him good. But it always seemed that he was somehow different. It bore on my mind so that I told Ma about it one morning. She listened. Then she just said, offhand like, "And you hain't et your breakfast yet." And she didn't say any more save to ask about the tree. "The hollow trunk is big, hain't it?" she said. I told her it was. And she seemed eased in her mind a little. And not so jumpy.

But the snow melted fast when it started. And soon as it was off the trees enough for me to tell my way I set out—without the rifle. And stopped and whistled. The deer jumped out—a buck, it was. And looked at me. I stood awhile. Then went on up to the tree. And there it was in the trunk a-shining. The piece of silver was. And I retch in and got it.

Harriette Simpson Arnow

1908–1986

Born in Wayne County, Kentucky, on the western edge of the Cumberland Plateau, Harriette Simpson attended Berea College and the University of Louisville and taught school in rural Appalachian Pulaski County, Kentucky, until moving to Cincinnati in 1934 to pursue a writing career. There, she worked for the Federal Writers' Project and met Harold Arnow, a journalist from Chicago. After their marriage in 1939, Harriette and Harold moved to a farm in eastern Kentucky, where they remained until 1944. They then moved to Detroit, living briefly in wartime housing before buying a farm near Ann Arbor, Michigan, which became their permanent home.

Arnow is best known for her fiction and nonfiction set in Kentucky's Cumberland Plateau. Her first three novels—*Mountain Path* (1936), *Hunter's Horn* (1949), and *The Dollmaker* (1954)—examine the effect of modernization on rural mountain life in the early to mid-twentieth century. This early fiction met with popular and critical acclaim: *Hunter's Horn* and *The Dollmaker* (a best seller) were nominated for National Book Awards; *Hunter's Horn* was a runner-up for the Pulitzer Prize; and *The Dollmaker* is considered a masterwork in the Appalachian, feminist, and American literary traditions.

In the short story "The Un-American Activities of Miss Prink," Arnow explores themes present in *The Dollmaker,* such as the McCarthy-era witch hunts against supposed Communists. Furthermore, the student who actively supports the story's narrator, a teacher, sounds notably like *The Dollmaker*'s Appalachian-born protagonist, Gertie Nevels. Unpublished until 2005, the story seems to have been written in the 1950s, when Arnow expressed concern about McCarthyism in letters to a number of correspondents.

The Un-American Activities of Miss Prink

Did he mean everybody?

The voice had spoken out of turn, no lifted hand above it.

Still, she nodded, smiling, seeing past it as she always did, the red dust of Virginia stirred by a breath of warm wind, the people crowding by the jail window, looking upward, listening, some frowning in disapproval, as Patrick McSnarty frowned now, others eager, drinking it in, believing, trying hard but not succeeding like those of the sober eyes.

"Yes, for every one— . . . —For some of religious thought—you see, even then in Virginia when Washington was young—preachers of many sects such as we have today—Unitarian and Baptist—were jailed for preaching, but preached from the jail house gratings—Patrick Henry—and just as this pilgrim left England for religious freedom, so did many push west from over the Wilderness Road—and now I wonder."

Several hands waved among the class of forty-seven, and she turned toward the map—eager—thinking a little of all the other times—fifty at least for she had developed this unit in social studies must be twenty-five years ago—and twice a year in social studies with the 8B that until the war—and the children came in shifts—and kept coming in shifts in this factory workers' neighborhood.

And now the Wilderness Road seemed fresher than ever, the children more eager—there were since the war more Southerners—hill children who had known and seen the white water and the smell of azaleas in bloom—and . . .

"Dey hadda go dis way on—dey couldn't get truda mountains no place . . ."

Fingers were snapping behind her and she turned to face the marble-like eyes, the smiling Jerry McSnarty, "Bud teacher, would Patrick Henry—would he ha stood still fuda Reds?"

"Reds."

He smiled at her. "Sure, yu know—du Communists like—yu know . . ." And his pleased glance went with no searching to Benton Skyros, two aisles over, six seats in front.

She looked into the blue eyes, but felt the black eyes on her face—thirsty—drinking from her as men drank from Patrick Henry—from preachers holding services through the jailhouse windows. "Communists," she said at last. "There were no communists then."

"Sure—sure, I know, but Patrick Henry, he u let um tell?"

"He wouldn't have agreed with them," she went on, conscious that even Junie Mae Branchcomb was still, her gum still, everybody still—as if they were grown people who'd read the papers for the past two weeks—had read how [a man, the father of one of their classmates,] had been called along with days and days of others before the unAmerican activities investigating committee. He had been called because an ex-cook had infiltrated and seen him at meetings in 1946—his picture had been [published] yesterday—a tired-looking man with somber eyes and he had said, "I refuse to testify on the grounds of self-incrimination."

Yesterday at lunch when the teachers ate their home-packed lunches in the sewing room, they had discussed it, remembering his children. Some like young Mrs. [Stanhope] had been critical. "Why didn't he tell the truth like a man," she had said, and now feeling the hungry eyes, Miss Prink was glad she had spoken out with a kind of authority that came partly from her years in the school and partly from a wide reading on such matters.

"Had he said he was not a Communist, they might have got him later for perjury—if he had admitted membership he would have had to testify against many others."

"Ugh," Miss Jameson had said. "Do you know in folk games none—not one—of the girls would dance with Jamie—it would have been all right—you know—the girls are often choosy but that horrible Junie May Branchcomb—nobody, of course, had chosen her—she grabbed him. 'It won't rub off,' she said. 'I ain't afeared.'" She sighed. "He looked so sick and pale."

"We must be kind to him in spite of . . ." Miss Prink had said with decision.

That was two days ago—the headlines had widened and blackened when yesterday a teacher from another school had been named by the ex-cook—and fired—nineteen years with no complaints and fired.

"But would Patrick Henry ha stood still an let them Commies tawk?"

"He wouldn't have agreed with them," she said, "but . . ." She drew a long breath—heard it—smiled to show she had not sighed into the silence—"but I don't think he would have been afraid to let them have their say. You see," she said, smiling now, "Patrick Henry had so much faith in our form of government—the government that was to be—that he wouldn't have minded the silly talk of a few Communists."

"Yu mean he would u wanted dem to tawk." The smile was unpleasant now.

"Oh, no—not wanted," she said. "But he wouldn't have been afraid."

The Wilderness Road was waiting and on this, the second day, she must always get Preacher Craig's company to the mountains where they had to leave their wagons for pack horses—and usually it was here she introduced Daniel Boone, the scout who had gone before.

Gradually thus the unit built around transportation would be complete—the Licking River went down from Boone's country close to Cincinnati—early water transportation—the German immigrants—the French—the trip this year promised well.

Once in the last war—a dark face with rotted teeth was waiting by her door. "Yu gotta cut out da 'Germans was good' stuff. I'm gonna git u FBI after you." And the face, lowering, sullen, turning away before she could explain, "always I try to teach here—it is so important here—that America owes her greatness to many nations and races—religions."

She had mentioned the matter to the former principal— . . . old she was to weariness—working past her retirement because of the war. The principal had snapped, "Can't you remember the last war? The music teacher had to be careful—even 'Silent Night, Holy Night' was criticized . . ."

"And then remember it was no more war and leave the Germans—and speak well of the Russians because they were buying American-made machinery—creating jobs, as it were, for Americans in the Depression—just be careful."

Miss Prink had been glad—her special field of social studies was always centered on America—tried to remember troubles with the Germans in the first World War—but could not—and anyway, she'd been teaching straight history and geography then.

She never mentioned the matter of Patrick Henry to the new principal—he was young—so young—not an ex-teacher at all but a school administrator. She did think briefly of bringing it up at lunch—but . . . forgot it until she reached the lunch room, a little late as always.

She couldn't remember her first awareness of their looking at her, silent, not eating, but she knew it was when she was unwrapping the Swiss cheese, domestic, on rye that young Mrs. Stanhope, Section B, third grade asked, "You knew her, didn't you?"

"Who?" she asked, unscrewing her thermos of Postum.

"Mrs. Maki in Wheatley Elementary."

"Quite well," she said. "Wonderful teacher—she's developed a whole unit built around Father Gabriel . . ."

"Oh," said Mrs. Stanhope.

Miss Prink paused, the red cup of hot Postum halfway to her mouth; they— the five of them who brought their lunches—were staring at her so. Miss [Bilky] in English—she'd looked at her that way before; no, it was the McSnarty boy on the Wilderness Road. Miss Duffy was asking, "Haven't you seen anything? *The Morning Bugle* or even last night's *Post*. It said she would be called."

"Called?"

Miss Pumphrey glanced at the door, fished down into her lap, then carefully flattening it, laid the front page of a Detroit paper on the table. "The children shouldn't know we're taking too much interest."

"Why?" Miss Prink asked, and then as Mrs. Shipley spun the paper round for her to see, she was still, the Postum in one hand, the lines in her forehead sharpening for the lines at the top were so big and so black each seemed more an exclamation than a letter spelling out the words, "REDS INFILTRATE PUBLIC SCHOOLS."

Under it, blown up and distorted, smooth, pretty, simpering was Mrs. Maki's picture, and by it were more black letters.

"It can't be true. She's such a good teacher," Miss Prink said, setting the Postum down at last, bending over the paper.

"Was, you mean," Miss Bilky said. "Of course, she'll be fired."

"But," Miss Prink said, "she must have taught at least twenty years—I taught her social studies, history it was then—must . . ."

"I wouldn't try to remember," Miss Payne said, looking at her too sharply.

"The Teachers' Association won't stand for it. I'm sure she's signed her loyalty pledge like—all the rest of us."

"But—well—commies sign pledges quicker than anybody—that is, they say after the pledges are signed," Miss [Bilky] said, and looked hard at her paper napkin tablecloth.

"But that girl can't be a—well, communist," Miss Prink said.

"She's attended proscribed meetings and she won't talk—that's enough to prove she's subversive."

"But they weren't proscribed when she attended. She told me once of marching in a protest parade—she was badly worried but she marched anyway."

"Oh," Miss O'Toole said, looking more interested. "What parade?"

"Something—two or three years ago. A young Negro boy was clubbed to death by police, you know."

"I wouldn't," Miss O'Toole said, reaching for the [paper].

"Mrs. Maki," Miss Prink went on, "took a lot of interest in bettering race relations and . . ."

"She would have done better," Mrs. Thompson said, finding Miss Prink's glance, fastening on it eagerly as if she had been searching a long while, "to have spent her time in going to church learning how to treat her fellow man instead of just treating him. Let's change the subject; it's only one teacher in all the thousands of us. No need to get excited."

"Who's excited?" Miss O'Toole said. "But it isn't just one," she added. "The paper says at least two hundred are suspect."

"There'll be a big murder or some minister will run a red light—you know and they won't be so short on headline stuff. And reds in the schools will be back page stuff."

"They won't fire her without proof," Miss Prink said, picking up her sandwich, laying it down again.

"Oh, but they—we will," Miss O'Toole said, giving the older woman a quick sharp look. "She could at least talk—clear herself, if she can be cleared."

Miss Prink looked toward Mrs. Sheridan, waited a moment for her to repeat what she had already said about rights and principles, but Mrs. Sheridan was busy pouring tomato soup from her red vacuum bottle and did not look up.

The wonder on Mrs. Maki who had taught twenty years, and was now fired on testimony of this ex-cook-waitress lay uneasily in the back of her mind through the afternoon. She kept backing away from the thing, trying to get a better look at it. People were innocent until proven guilty—but guilty of what and where was the proof?

The thought kept coming between her and the 3B's, working on early Detroit—building a city by a lake in the sand box, with two making a church for Father Gabriel.

The last class, then her homeroom in and out again—ordinarily she stayed late on Wednesdays till the janitor was leaving and worked on records and papers—but today she hurried, even rushing the studies a little—even the forever lagging Junie Mae who had come rushing back for forgotten homework in math. She wanted to telephone Mrs. Maki, reassure her, tell her she was certain the teachers' union would stand up for her. It must have been a terrible ordeal—after twenty years of teaching, no complaints on her work—even the paper had said that. She was welcome to the use of the telephone in the principal's office—but well—she would wait until she got home. Her father and Mr. Cramer from The Charleston would be deep in their chess game.

"Yu Miz Prink."

She turned, half startled, and saw the face glowering at her from the doorway.

"I'm Mary McSnarty," the voice went on, its owner a still bulky mass in the door, crisp curls of bright gold hair fringing a green scarf, too bright above a wrinkled red-cheeked face.

"Yes," she said, smiling her teacher's smile, moving toward the doorway.

"Don't grin at me," the woman said. "All I gotta say's yu gotta quit teaching mu kids that this guy—Patrick, Patruck—s' funny last name."

"Henry," Miss Prink said.

"Yu know, kids. Yu gotta quit teachen my kids that he'd u stood up fuda commies. You'se gotta learn u kids won't stand still fudu likes a youse—Communist." The word fell over her, hissing, spattering, somehow like a too wet snowball, and Mary McSnarty was disappearing down the hall.

Miss Prink was for a moment still, then started almost running after the sound of the steps, thumping down the stairs now.

"Aw, leave her be, teacher," Junie Mae said. "Nobody cain't never do nothen with that old son of a—that ole SOB—on account she all lies an tongue like her kids. You'd oughta hear th way they talk to Jimmy; gonna beat him up on account a his pop bean called in front a that American thing."

"UnAmerican," Miss Prink corrected automatically from long habit.

"You said it. That's right."

[Junie Mae] gave the slumped shoulders a reassuring pat as she sped out the door. "I gotta hurry. Them uns is aimen to be ganging up on Jimmy so's me and me brudder an u Shakovitch kids—why, we'll be there."

Miss Prink looked after her a moment, then turned back to her desk and began slowly, deliberately gathering up the papers.

Even though it meant hunting a place to park, she stopped on the way home and bought a Valentine—a pretty lacy thing. It had just occurred to her that Mrs. Maki, if home at all, would be too tired for a telephone conversation—Valentine's Day wasn't too far away—her homeroom was already planning the box—still it might be best to wait a day or so—people never sent Valentines early like Christmas cards.

She thought of the Valentine again the night the Teachers' Union met to vote whether or not to take action in the case of Mrs. Maki, discharged because she would not testify before the committee.

Important questions were usually decided by ballot, and when Mrs. Grinki, the president, called for a standing vote, Miss Prink, already unscrewing the top on her pen for long habit of doing the things she had planned to do, was standing.

There was an instant when she thought, looking about, that it was like in Church—she must go to church more often—when the minister asked the congregation to stand and sing or pray—there was always a moment's fluttering—women clearing their laps of hymnbooks and purses—only now it was very still—too still, like her room when Mrs. McSnarty and Junie Mae were gone—or even the lunchroom [when] they said they had read the paper.

She turned her head at last, looking about her. The next person standing was a young man—and he seemed far way. She straightened a little, conscious of twisting head and searching eyes—Miss O'Toole—past her face flashed a smile—and she realized it was Mrs. Maki. She wished the other had not smiled—it looked, well, as if they were close friends.

Light burst about them. She blinked, realizing at last that the huddle of men in front she had taken for teachers were photographers.

Next morning, as she got her own breakfast, her father's breakfast, her lunch, his lunch, she glanced now and then at the paper, folded in half, but open enough that she could read the double headline, for the Teachers' Union must share with a man who had loved his divorced wife and so had killed.

"Teachers Favor Ouster of Subversive."

"Only fourteen teachers voted in favor of retaining the Communist to teach the overthrow of the government to our young children."

She realized as she poured her Postum into her thermos and watched the coddling of her father's egg that she was whispering. "We didn't vote for that." She, Mrs. Maki, was a good teacher—they said. You can't fire a person just—just for thinking—maybe she was just curious—maybe she really should send the Valentine.

She would explain to the teachers at noon why she had voted as she had—she'd taught freedom of speech—freedom close to forty years—and could she deny freedom of thought?

She never did explain. The teachers never asked. There was, it seemed to her, a peculiar moment of silence, though of late, years when the sections had gone up to thirty-five, forty, forty-five—two shifts, the teachers talked little—mostly they just sat, savoring silence.

Mrs. Clawson asked about her father. They lived in the same section of town and often they had exchanged car rides or even visits with an occasional trip together downtown. "He's fine," she said, "remarkably active for his years."

Miss O'Leary gave her a quick glance. "He must have married awfully young."

Miss Prink nodded, smiling even though Mrs. Dawson gave the other a quick silencing look—youth had gone, slipped away before she knew it to the 3B's down at the old Tomkinds School—she'd never been pretty—it was like she'd looked away and then back and retirement was close—something she could see and plan for.

"He's getting close to eighty," she said. "Funny thing, he's never lost his love of people. He wants to move into the Charlestown—it's more like a hotel than an old man's home—but frightfully expensive."

"What isn't?" Mrs. Dawson said, and they were silent again until Miss O'Toole wanted to know if they'd read about the Craw Chuck Man.

They were silent, none saying they had read, and Miss O'Toole went on to tell of how the union had taken the nervy stand that no man unless he be an official should be fired because he was a Communist.

"But there's no proof he is a Communist," Miss Prink said, knowing after she had spoken that she should keep her silence, but going on, like one of the Wilderness Road people in the middle of a swift river but unable to turn back. "And the last of that woman's testimony was for 1946 and . . ."

"I wouldn't call her 'that woman,'" Miss O'Toole said. "She's a great patriot, giving her time."

"She got paid for her espionage. And now she got paid $25 a day for her work as a witness. That's more than she was ever able to earn as a cook."

"'You know a lot about her," Miss O'Toole said, giving her a sharp look.

"All Federal witnesses get that," Miss Prink said, sipping her Postum.

"Anyway, the men who have to work with that man threw him out yesterday. He bragged he'd come back today. I wonder if he did."

Miss Prink wondered through the afternoon—Jimmy was absent at the brief check-in of the homeroom—maybe he was only tardy.

At dismissal time, when her homeroom came trooping back again, she found herself staring at his empty seat and Mike Shenkey said, giggling, "Teacher's pet ain't here. Dey beat up his old man. He got tough wit um."

"Dey hadda fire his old man. He took a blackjack tu work wit him. S'againsa union rules—taken a weapon into du shop."

"He hadda right," Junie Mae said, her voice trembling as if underneath it there could be a cry.

"Commies ain't got no rights," Mike said.

Miss Prink opened her mouth, closed it firmly. "This is not a discussion period," she said.

"Didja know, Teacher, dey're gonna investigate u schools—clean out u Reds," Mike said, glancing briefly at her, then his pleased glance, going swiftly about the silent watching room. She knew, learning it slowly bit by bit, unconsciously through the years, that the fathers of some children, and the mothers, too, worked in Griggs plant, No. 4, where Jimmy's father worked. And some of these same fathers had no doubt helped throw him out, threatened him—and now they sat too silent and too watchful.

Mike who was often out of hand was repeating, "Didn't chas know dey're gonna investigate du teachers—send men all u way from Washington. T'row out u Reds—not jist u card-carrying communists but all u subversives."

"Row one may pass to the door," she said, realizing as she spoke it was almost a minute early—she heard the tramp of 4B's on the stairs.

She opened the door at last and stood in front of it and watched them down the hall. Mr. Banks, the principal, stood as was his custom watching them down the stairway, first holding them, the long line of them, waiting in the hall until section one of the 3B's had come up from the basement and cleared the main hall below.

The words of apology were there waiting when he stopped by the doorway. "I must have been in a hurry," she said. "It's my afternoon for the downtown library. There's a new book of sources, a lot of Christopher Gist's journal of his travels—it would enrich this unit on the Wilderness Road, for Gist, you know, explored some of the same . . ." She saw he wasn't listening, though he looked at her with the polite smile—that made her think somehow of—well, a department store manager—so young, so well-dressed—she rubbed her forehead. It had gone so quickly—everything seemed old yesterday [when] the men teachers she knew had all been like Mr. Miles—ink-stained and chalky-fingered, their pants shiny—and their ties just something black to cover the shirt buttons. This man's coat was tweed, almost seemed like to his knees, and his tie—she mustn't look at it—he might think . . .

"Still on the Wilderness Road," he said.

She nodded, bright again. "We're studying pioneer life in Kentucky now. Almost ready for George Rogers Clark and his part in the Revolution."

"It must be a job," he said, "tying it altogether like that." He glanced about the room, crowded almost with the sand table, the work table, the posters, the pictures the children made, the bulletin board with clippings, pictures they had brought.

"It seems that Daniel Boone would be less work—and more suited to this age level," he said, and all at once he seemed to her, this neatly dressed young man with no smear of chalk or stain of ink about him, was critical, politely critical, the way teachers had been last night when she stood up.

She wished all at once she'd told him of Mrs. McSnarty—Mrs. McSnarty had been to him—that was it—and with times the way they were—he was trying to tell her—What was he trying to tell her?—to quit teaching Patrick Henry.

He was turning slowly about the room. "You get a wonderful pupil response," he said, studying the bulletin board now. "But with such a heavy teaching load—I'd simplify things—so much research for source materials—do you think children this age can grasp source materials?"

She nodded, trying not to look defiant. "Some of Daniel Boone's writings—well, like the letter in which—when he was old and tired—he asked for the job of improving the Wilderness Road—arouse much interest," she said. "And I remember . . ." But already he was turning away with the look she thought of a man who has not done all of what he planned to do.

She was glad she hadn't told him of how when she was a girl in the old Hancock school under Dr. ——, the Indian, they always called him, she'd cried when the old man had recited Logan's speech—but that was all so long ago. Old Dr. ——could remember the Civil War; old she was and times had changed.

She was half way home before she remembered she should be driving to the library. She hesitated in the right turn lane until the man behind her tooted. She drove straight on; maybe she did work too hard—but she'd never somehow thought of it as work. The afternoon at the library, the evenings over papers, lesson plans, the array of cards of all colors, shapes and sizes. What else was there? her father—the lawn—church. She ought to go to church more often. She'd read the moving speech Supt. Morgan had made on God—good teachers had God in their lives.

She remembered she and the others had discussed his speech, and she had remarked aloud that she had wondered at times what Benjamin Franklin and Thomas Jefferson and Abraham Lincoln had thought of God, even George Washington when he was young.

Miss O'Toole had given her, well, the same look that time she brought *The Nation*—there'd been part of a book review she'd wanted to read, quoting three sentences. . . . She should have clipped it.

The mail had brought Valentines—two she saw were postmarked Korea, and suddenly she cried a little soundlessly sniffling; so many Valentines through so many wars—so many places—seemed only yesterday she'd had her first one from France. She'd been young enough for tears then—but years later she should have kept silent about the one she got from Spain—she'd cried so—but all that war on—his side had lost there—had won in Germany but—he was dead.

She should have sent more Valentines—it was too late now—even for Mrs. Maki. A shame to waste such a pretty Valentine—she took it out of its envelope—stared at it critically a moment—it wasn't too lacy and sweet for a boy—there would be a Valentine box in her homeroom. Jimmy, she thought, wouldn't get any; she'd write just his name, not her own for it would look strange for only one child to get a Valentine from his teacher. No, she'd print his name.

Jimmy, however, got more than one Valentine. She couldn't be certain, but she'd heard his name called six times. Some of the tightness, the coldness that had lain in her was gone. It was snowing past the windows, but inside her room it was brightly red and white with Valentines, red hearts of the children's drawings were bright on the blackboards, and the gay Valentines box, an enormous thing of white crepe, bright with pink hearts and the gold of radio paints, was empty.

The children crunched cinnamon hearts and bigger fatter hearts with greetings of "I love you" and "be my Valentine," her Valentine to all of them, and blushed and giggled over the greetings heaped on their desks. Even Junie Mae seemed softened, surprised, for she, quite new to the group, and among its many cliques and minor groupings, there had never seemed a place for her.

Miss Prink glanced quickly at the good sized pile in front of Jimmy, then down at her own desk, seeming no different from the other years when factory workers' children had money for Valentines—there were big envelopes with fancy things of lace, smaller ones with the hasty scribble of the child who'd just remembered teacher, chocolate hearts in gilded paper, two handkerchiefs decorated with pinch hearts. She, as always, opened them, the children crowding around to see, a few like McSnarty giggling in expectancy for as always there would be the comic ones—a teacher like in the comic strips with buck teeth and skinned back hair, and if they were not obscene, she always held them up for them to see, and shared in the laughter.

She unfolded a handkerchief, murmured "so beautiful," and glanced uneasily at Jimmy. He had opened one Valentine and sat now staring down at it, stiff and still, his face red, his eyes bright with hurt and anger. Junie Mae leant above him frowning and Mike Pavlovitch was calling, "Let's see yer Valentines, Jimmy. Let's see." But Andy McSnarty jeered looking from Jimmy to her, "Let's see Teacher's first."

Miss Prink smiled at him, smiled and resolutely dove into the Valentines, found the neat and even McSnarty writing—for good penmanship was the pride of the McSnartys—and opened it. A homemade Valentine—a single sheet of drawing paper folded—inside a huge crimson heart and underneath, "This heart ain't half so red as yours."

She choked and hastily refolded it, though Jerry and other voices—a few girls now were calling, "Show us. You gotta show us."

Blindly she groped for a chocolate heart and held it up for them to see—there was a motto on it in curls of white frosting—and there was a moment's panic of wondering what the motto said.

It must have been all right for Catherine Schultz was giggling, nudging, "Boy, wait ull she sees mine."

The children were crowding round her now. She felt Michael Angelo's garlic-flavored breath, and Jimmy's, touched still with boiled beans and onions. Someone laughed and shoved another one under her hand. She saw that it was homemade, and reached past it, and smiling, fumbling, opened a lacy heart for them to see, but it seemed like all around her there were jeering cries, "Open this one, Teacher. Yu gotta show us whatcha got."

She glanced hopefully toward the door. Once when Jerry McSnarty threw a book at the young English teacher, the principal had happened by—maybe he would come now—they were making so much noise. The Indians screaming about Crawford with the hot coals pressed into his scalpless head.

She stiffened, and slowly her fingers numb, the paper crackling in the sudden silence, she opened the Valentine, large, the heart a sticky, vivid red, painted with fingerpaint, below it drops and splashes, only the printed words were black and clear. "We're going to shoot that Commie bleeding heart right out of you."

She studied it a moment, spread as it was on her desk, then conscious of the heads crowding to see, she stepped backward, lifted it, and stood an instant still, the red dripping heart held in front of her.

There was silence broken at last by Jerry McSnarty's exultant giggle. A short giggle, cut off by Junie Mae's resounding smack and her flat voiced, "You dirty, dirty bastard."

There had been a little flurry, but fortunately at least for the moment, Jerry had assumed the role of silent martyrdom, and had gone silently home, careful to let the blood stream down his lips and onto his clothing for Junie Mae's hand was large and tough and hard like the rest of her.

She thought of it now, as she turned into the narrow street of small homes close together. She should not let them see the Valentine in the first place and, above all, she should have marched Junie Mae to the principal for quick discipline—but she had done nothing.

Then, that is a moment later, her own Valentines had seemed a small matter. She'd somehow found, not hunting just finding among the other forty-four, Jimmy's face, saw his fist tighten above his thin heap of Valentines, and known that Jimmy's Valentines were like her own. She had folded her Valentines, laid them aside; the bell had rung, and the children gone to their cloak room.

They'd been strangely quiet after Junie Mae's slap—only Jerry's mumbling and groaning through the blood, making a slow seep down his chin, and above the shuffling feet, she'd heard the girlish whispers, hissing, curse like. "How come yu gotta send me a Valentine?—Gonna try tu make u other kids think we're buddies, huh. I ain't want nothen off u th likes a yu. See."

She looked up in time to see a blur of pinky whiteness strike Jimmy in the face and Catherine's yellow head gave a disdainful toss as she marched down the aisle.

She slowed, carefully, to eighteen miles [per hour], shifted, glanced in her rear view mirror, swung out, then turned slowly into her drive. She mustn't think of all that—such little silly stupid things—that Valentine's Day was a year ago—almost.

Nobody remembered it. Mr. [Banks] had probably forgotten the dressing down he gave Junie Mae after Mrs. McSnarty came with Mike the next day—the lip only slightly swollen . . . "Mu kid's heart blood," but the shirt, the jacket, the sweater, ruined, "wit mu kid's heart's blood."

Miss Prink had, when called in, apologized for Junie Mae's outbreak and—she shivered—why think of it—the choking fear that followed her for days—suppose it got into the papers—the papers were forever eager for stories of poor discipline and teaching in the public schools. The story would have gone well with the headlines.

Two Hundred Reds in Public Schools—then smaller, much smaller, the story of how Stella Dodd, ex-communist, had come forward in Washington with testimony about the public schools across the land. Detroit was named along with other cities.

War and national politics, three sex murders, and the defections of a thrice-married minister had claimed the headlines through the fall. School officials had gone ahead with old plans for a bond issue to be put before the voters, of course, for badly needed buildings.

Miss Prink had thrown herself into that—well, not too actively—she attended a few meetings, and it was surprising the popular interest in public education. The press was, of course, unfriendly and one of the council men, who liked to boast that neither he nor any of his children had ever been inside a public school, got several front page stories by his charges of over much luxury in the building of schools, and in all the Letters to the Editors columns there were the usual complaints by business-men that their stenographers couldn't spell, by parents who wanted religion, morals, manners taught in the schools; the number charging socialistic tendencies and red infiltration had been no higher than usual, or so it had seemed to Miss Prink.

And she had for the past few months read the daily papers, more than usual. They kept some of the lonesomeness, not lonesomeness either—a teacher teaching eight groups of forty odd four times a week couldn't be lonesome—more like an emptiness.

She'd left out Patrick Henry and the Craigs—the Regulators—even the speech of Dragging Canoe—frontier thoughts she had called them for the frontier had thoughts as well as guns—the class periods, the days and the months had slid smoothly by—she switched off the ignition, sat a moment staring at the key—too smoothly somehow—of course, she only imagined it but seemed like Mr. [Banks] lingered more often in the hall by her door—she would glance up and through the glass she'd glimpse the shoulder of the well-cut tweed just turning away—the teach-ers talked less as they ate together—and there were fewer. Miss O'Toole and Mrs. Briggs went out for lunch most always now—and Mrs. Brown hadn't visited in a long while or suggested that they go out together to a play or a lecture or the symphony as in other years.

Mrs. Maki had written from another city—she had answered—should have answered.

She glanced once at the folded paper in the car seat, lifted her hand part way, dropped it and sat, staring straight in front of her.

She stared and tried to find pleasure in the rows of shelves, filled with labeled boxes and books and old lesson plans, as she had used to. Sometimes on rainy Sat-urdays she had used to come and file and sort her things, for in the boxes were all the Christmas cards, the Valentines, the foolish gifts, loud handkerchiefs, cheap per-fumes, cheap glass and dinnerware—all cherished because they were the gifts of the children—so many small things and she could not use them all.

She glanced toward a box marked Valentines and looked away. Last year's Val-entines were there—all of them—even the big red hearts. Tomorrow was Valentine's Day and what would she get—after this. She reached again for the paper. She was so tired—too tired to unfold it and read—she knew the headlines. Mrs. Dawson had wept suddenly in a great soundless outburst over them at noon, whispering, "Why? WHY?—Some—my own children might even think it could be me."

"Don't be silly," Miss O'Toole had said fiercely, and all day long the principal had tramped the halls, pausing at times to scrutinize some teacher's door as if asking, "Could it be she?"

She remembered the garage doors, not closed, and pulled the rope by which one could close the door without getting out of the car.

Then she looked down at the unfolded paper, the great headlines were like a black mist before her eyes, but she knew what they said. "Name twenty-eight schools harboring Reds."

She did not read the column, the upper part, but only the last part of the big print—"particularly was the Dewey School."

All afternoon she'd felt the children watching her, knowing she was the red. She was what the superintendent meant when, in a news release, he had complained that he as yet had been handed no list of subversives by any one of the four separate agencies he presumed was investigating Detroit's public schools—the state anti-subversive commission, the City Loyalty Commission, the unAmerican activities, the FBI, the American Legion, the Loyalty Review Board of the Teachers' Union, and the city police Red squad. None of these had as yet handed him a list. Oh, of course, the Board of Education checked on all possible subversives, reports of parents concerning the attitude and acts of some teachers—reports of other teachers.

That was it—she listed in her head the things she had done to arouse suspicion— the list seemed almost endless. Tomorrow there would be Valentines—maybe vandalism with COMMUNIST written on the wall.

Jonathan Williams

1929–2008

Poet and publisher Jonathan Williams was born in Asheville, North Carolina. He studied at the experimental Black Mountain College, located near Asheville, as well as at Princeton University and the Chicago School of Design. As an adult, Williams and his partner, Thomas Meyer, divided their time between North Carolina's Blue Ridge Mountains and England. In addition to writing poetry, Williams founded the Jargon Society in 1951. Jargon published avant-garde poetry and fiction, photography, and folk art.

Williams was associated with the avant-garde Black Mountain Poets, who include Charles Olson, Robert Creeley, and Robert Duncan, and who take their name from their association with Black Mountain College and the *Black Mountain Review*. Black Mountain College was founded in 1933 as a holistic, alternative approach to higher education. Although the college closed in 1957, it made a lasting impact on the arts in the United States; many innovative artists, dancers, musicians, and poets of the mid- to late twentieth century were faculty or students.

Presented here are two of Williams's early poems and four found poems gleaned from his Blue Ridge neighbors' speech and from various signs he saw as he drove through the mountains.

The Chameleon

at 14 I decided it was avant-garde to dig
women

but, man if I were just the least
bit queer, boy, you know, man, wow,

and then some; but, like
I'm not, but

when I write *Dearest* to you in a letter, then
that's different,

isn't it?

To Charles Oscar

may there be stiff reeds
for your hands
among the asphodels,
Charles

and wind
to move them
over the bronze water
onto paper

and Lethe for us,
left
with your shattered
inkstone

The Epitaph on Uncle Nick Grindstaff's Grave
on the Iron Mountain above Shady Valley, Tennessee:

LIVED ALONE   SUFFERED ALONE   DIED ALONE

Paint Sign on a Rough Rock
Yonside of Boone Side of Shady Valley:

BEPREPA
REDTO
MEETGO
D

Jeff Brooks, Wagon-Master of Andrews,
en Route to Franklin through the Nantahalas

no
other
sound

except

the creak
of leather

Aubade

you could hear an ant
fart
it was that
quiet

James Wright

1927–1980

Poet James Wright was born in Martins Ferry, Ohio, across the Ohio River from Wheeling, West Virginia. His father worked at a glass factory and his mother at a laundry. The poverty of Martins Ferry, his parents' working-class existence, and the Great Depression affected Wright, and at age sixteen he suffered a nervous breakdown. He later enlisted in the army, serving in Japan. Upon his return, he attended Kenyon College on the GI bill. There Wright studied under John Crowe Ransom and received a foundation in New Criticism, a critical approach that heavily influenced Wright's early poetry.

Wright wrote numerous collections of poetry, the last three published posthumously. By the time Wright won the Pulitzer Prize (1972), his style was conversational and he was recognized by a generation of poets and critics as the foremost practitioner of a "pastoral surrealism."

Although Wright could express affection for his home, many of his poems paint an Appalachian landscape that is far from idyllic. "Lament for my Brother on a Hayrake," an example of his early formal work, depicts the sacrifice of a farmer's life during the October harvest. "Autumn Begins in Martins Ferry, Ohio" portrays the defeated spectators of his hometown as they watch "their sons grow suicidally beautiful" on the football field.

Lament for My Brother on a Hayrake

Cool with the touch of autumn, waters break
Out of the pump at dawn to clear my eyes;
I leave the house, to face the sacrifice
Of hay, the drag and death. By day, by moon,
I have seen my younger brother wipe his face
And heave his arm on steel. He need not pass
Under the blade to waste his life and break;

The hunching of the body is enough
To violate his bones. That bright machine
Strips the revolving earth of more than grass;
Powered by the fire of summer, bundles fall
Folded to die beside a burlap shroud;
And so my broken brother may lie mown

Out of the wasted fallows, winds return,
Corn-yellow tassels of his hair blow down,
The summer bear him sideways in a bale
Of darkness to October's mow of cloud.

Autumn Begins in Martins Ferry, Ohio

In the Shreve High football stadium,
I think of Polacks nursing long beers in Tiltonsville,
And gray faces of Negroes in the blast furnace at Benwood,
And the ruptured night watchman of Wheeling Steel,
Dreaming of heroes.

All the proud fathers are ashamed to go home.
Their women cluck like starved pullets,
Dying for love.

Therefore,
Their sons grow suicidally beautiful
At the beginning of October,
And gallop terribly against each other's bodies.

In Response to a Rumor That
the Oldest Whorehouse in Wheeling,
West Virginia, Has Been Condemned

I will grieve alone,
As I strolled alone, years ago, down along
The Ohio shore.
I hid in the hobo jungle weeds
Upstream from the sewer main,
Pondering, gazing.

I saw, down river,
At Twenty-third and Water Streets
By the vinegar works,
The doors open in early evening.
Swinging their purses, the women
Poured down the long street to the river
And into the river.

I do not know how it was

They could drown every evening.
What time near dawn did they climb up the other shore,
Drying their wings?

For the river at Wheeling, West Virginia,
Has only two shores:
The one in hell, the other
In Bridgeport, Ohio.

And nobody would commit suicide, only
To find beyond death
Bridgeport, Ohio.

Wilma Dykeman

1920–2006

As a journalist, historian, essayist, novelist, and short story writer in the mid-twentieth century, Wilma Dykeman was in the vanguard of the new Appalachian studies movement. Dykeman was born in Asheville, North Carolina, where her mother's family had lived for generations. After graduating from Northwestern University in 1940, she married James Stokely Jr., a poet and son of an East Tennessee canning company magnate, with whom she reported on the civil rights movement in the 1950s.

Dykeman's literary career began in 1955 with her first and perhaps most widely known book, *The French Broad,* an account of the environmental, cultural, and historical impact of western North Carolina's French Broad River. Dykeman's attention to pollution in the river foreshadowed environmental concerns that would emerge nationally in the 1960s.

Dykeman's fiction explores themes of family and community, connection to the land, and women's roles in public and private life in the mountains. Two of her novels, *The Tall Woman* (1962) and *The Far Family* (1966), trace, through strong female characters, the Civil War's legacy for generations of mountain people in western North Carolina. Dykeman's third novel, *Return the Innocent Earth* (1973), a fictionalized account of a rising East Tennessee canning company, loosely based on her husband's family's experiences, examines the benefits and costs of exploitation, and the influence economic success has on individuals, families, and communities.

FROM **Return the Innocent Earth**

FROM CHAPTER I

Friday afternoon in Clayburn-Durant's computer department I was ambushed by the smell of ketchup. Tomorrow's mechanized memory and brain was wrapped in the rich cocoon of that earthy aroma, old and warm, familiar and wrenching. Nothing since then has been the same.

The day had started with a phone call from Stull.

"Jon." Not a question, not a greeting, a flat statement and assumption. He did not wait for me to answer. "Wanted you to fly down with Nat and me for the Jackson U. game tomorrow."

I resented that voice—especially at a quarter till seven on Friday morning—arranging my weekend. I did not want to traipse down south to watch the Jackson U. football squad grunt and crunch. I wanted to go to New York and be with Deborah Einemann.

Stull caught my hesitancy. He wasn't stupid. No one had ever accused Stull Clayburn of stupidity, not even when he was a plump, quiet boy standing around awkwardly watching with milky blue eyes which looked and probed and never betrayed the barest hint of emotion or reaction going on in the restless mind behind those eyes.

"First game of the season. And Tech's rated the number two team in the country this year."

"Number one in the Southeast," I said, programmed to a right response.

"Screw the Southeast. It's national that counts. That ought to give the Jackson boys something to fight for."

That's right, Stull: think big. Out loud I said, "It ought to be a good game."

"We'll pick you up at eight-thirty," he said.

"Hold on, Stull." I was sitting on the edge of my twin mahogany bed looking at the empty, neatly made twin bed next to me, and suddenly my feet were chilly and the phone was hard against my shoulder and ear as I tried to light a cigarette and I was chilly all over. "I had other plans for tomorrow."

There was the briefest pause at the other end of the line. From the thickness of Stull's voice I could tell he was having a bad morning, but my sympathy for those bad mornings had run short a long time ago. "There's something else, Jon—"

With Stull there was always something else. Most of us had learned that a long time ago—the hard way. Had I thought for one crazy minute that he only wanted to take me to a ball game to bask forty years later in his glory at Jackson U.? Only?

"What else, Stull?"

"A little problem at the Churchill plant."

"But tomorrow's Saturday. It'll be two-thirds shut down—"

"It's not that kind of a problem." I didn't answer and he went on. "You remember somebody named Burl Smelcer?"

Stull made him sound like an interchangeable part of one of the cabbage cutters. "Of course I remember Burl Smelcer," I said. "Foreman at the Riverbend Farm for twenty or thirty years. I used to pull beets and pick tomatoes on his crew. Two teeth, eleven children, fourteen dogs."

"His wife's sick."

"Perlina." I could see Perlina Smelcer's great freckled arms bulging from the sleeves of her sweat-stained gingham dress whenever she drank from the dipper at the water bucket where a motley crew of pickers would be stripping green bean vines when I was a boy. In her greed for the water, rivulets ran from the sides of her mouth faster than she could swallow and fell on the red, heaving flesh of her neck, then disappeared in the depths of her bosom like a stream soaked up by desert sand dunes. She would see me watching her and she would grin with friendliness and satisfaction, fanning the neck of her dress back and forth to enjoy the full benefit of the cool water trickling down her front.

"Perlina her name?" Stull asked, making it the most inconsequential knowledge since the date of the invention of the yo-yo.

"All right, Stull. Tell me why you've got me sitting here on the side of the bed at this time of the—"

"I thought you might like to see Jackson U. beat Tech—"

"And?"

"And afterward I thought you might run on up to Churchill and check on a few things."

"Such as?"

"The Smelcer woman."

"I'm no damn doctor, Stull. Besides—"

"You haven't waked up yet have you, Jon? The Riverbend is the farm where we've been trying that Morrison fellow's new spray."

"Oh my God!" The chill reached up my back. "How sick is she, Stull?"

"Sick enough. Price Sims called last night, told Nat Lusk about it. She's running a fever, vomiting, on the verge of convulsions."

My mental picture of Perlina Smelcer in a convulsion seemed totally absurd. All her life she had cared for a lazy husband and sickly children who bought third-hand Chevvies and Fords and pulled out for Cleveland or Detroit or New Jersey as soon as they were beyond school truancy age. Perhaps she had earned her own respite from the rigors and duties of health. "And why did Price Sims think all that had anything to do with our spray?"

"Because Perlina had eaten herself a bait of greens the picking machine left behind."

"What about Burl and the children?"

"Price went into that, too. Burl was ailing and didn't eat. As for the others, none of them were home this week—the last two youngsters were in Churchill staying with a cousin to go to the fair."

It all came back to me in a flood of smells and sounds—the September dust and rotten canvas, bawling calves, tattooed sideshow hustlers, glittering prizes, and the music of the ferris wheel as its rickety seats floated up and over and around between the sawdust underfoot and the velvety night sky above. "So it's Perlina."

"We don't know that there's any connection at all between the new spray and her troubles," Stull said. His tongue had lost most of its furred thickness now. "We don't know anything at all. That's why you might do some good down there just looking, listening for a couple of days."

Why me? But I did not ask it. Who else was there? Only Stull and Nat Lusk and I, of all the people who made up the midwestern home office of Clayburn-Durant, knew Churchill, had been born there, lived there, knew the way winter slipped in late or apple blooms broke through early or that a man would shoot his brother's son through the heart because of a rawboned black-and-tan foxhound.

"Jon?"

"Yes, Stull?"

"We can't mess this one up. This spray could mean the biggest break C-D has had in a long time. We can't let some loud-mouthed old mountain woman who doesn't know a snuff stick from a chopstick ruin the whole ball game for us."

I didn't answer.

"You hear, Jon?"

"Sure, Stull. I hear."

"Then I can count on you? I've got Morrison coming in this morning to tell us what the hell may be going on. If he's such a big plant expert and chemist, he ought to know what our risks are."

"I hope so."

"You come by. At ten."

As he hung up I added what he failed to order: "And pack your two-suiter for Churchill." Before I left the phone or even turned on a hot shower to thaw out my chill, I called New York.

Deborah's voice was all that Stull's was not: soft and clear, resonant with her warmth, her inescapable memories, her caring. When I told her I would not be arriving at La Guardia that night, she asked no questions. It was one of her special virtues—this restraint, this lack of prying or probing. "If I listen you'll tell me all I need to know, all I want to know—now or sometime," she said once, soon after we met. Then, with that half-sad smile, "And I shall listen."

(In the beginning was the number, and the number was of Deborah and the number was with Deborah and the number was Deborah.)

When I told her I would be in Churchill and that I might be there all week, she paused a moment and then said, "Don't be homesick, Jon."

How odd—when I would be at home, or where my home once was. "I'm not worried about homesickness," I said. "It's just this damn food business that gets to you after a while."

"I'll be here, Jon, whenever you can come."

I could see the thin scarred wrist and hand laying the phone back in its cradle, her wretched fingers a contrast to the richness of her voice and dark eyes.

When I walked into Stull's office at ten o'clock, Lex Morrison from National Laboratories was already sitting stiffly in one of Stull's Spanish chairs. There was no other way to sit against those hard high backs. The fellow had been to Clayburn-Durant before. The first time, he had done most of the talking, not because he was a talkative fellow but because he had the information we needed. This time Stull was talking. I tried to size up Stull's condition. He was all right, at least for the moment.

"You two met before—" Stull's cryptic introduction left both of us dangling until I crossed the room and shook hands again.

"Jon Clayburn," I said. "You're Morrison—"

The man was pleased. "Lex Morrison, from National Commercial and Botanical Research Lab." He had a good firm grip and his gray-green eyes met a stranger's gaze openly and directly. He was tall and lean and slightly awkward. The sleeves of his coat were a couple of inches too short. His cheekbones were high and stood like small plateaus on his face.

"Your arrested-growth discovery. You've made more tests?"

Lex Morrison looked at Stull. "I guess we're all up against the same shortage: time." He and I sat down on the black leather upholstery of the carved chairs.

Stull pushed himself back from his wide cluttered desk so that the smoggy morning mist rising from the concrete and steel outside created a pale aura behind his large round head. Before him an ornate inkwell and pen, an electric clock with calendar attached, and a tarnished sterling silver cigar and cigarette box were small islands in a sea of letters, envelopes, clippings, reports, and memoranda. To a stranger, Stull's desk must seem incredible, but I know that what he needs to remember is not on file there.

Stull gazed down attentively at his hands. He seemed to be studying the wide flat fingernails, cuticle, pale skin, hair follicles with minute concentration. To Morrison he might have seemed inattentive and indifferent. He wasn't.

"The crunch is on," he had said to me last week when we went down to the company kitchen together to see if the cooking tests had been run on any of the newly sprayed vegetables. "This arrested growth could give us the edge we want in next year's market." I had been surprised but Stull was usually miles ahead of the rest of us in foreseeing what might happen in the canning business.

"Cut the waste at our growers' level," he went on, "ensure peak ripeness in taste and color quality at production level. And if those fellows bitching around down in sales can't sell that, then they ought to be out on their butts."

Stull's vehemence had caught me by surprise. Then I realized there were no positions, not even the president's, secure in this game.

"I was just telling Morrison," Stull said to me now, "that we've tried his chemicals on some of our turnip greens down around Churchill—and a few late tomato vines."

"How did it work?" The scientist was eager as a boy. Perhaps it was asking questions that kept him young.

I grinned at him. "Price Sims, he's our Churchill manager, says the foreman down there claims it's magic. Tomatoes on the vine stayed exactly like they were for ten days. No over-ripening, no spoiling, no rotting."

He was leaning forward in his chair. "And the turnip greens?"

I glanced at Stull. "After a week of sun and rain, less than an inch more growth. Not a tough stalk among the lot. Tender as a baby's bottom."

He nodded. "That's the way it worked on our best farms," he said. "Complete stabilization of the crop. Total interruption of the growth process."

"There are all kinds of possibilities for something like this. That is, if it really works—"

There was a moment's pause.

"You develop this spray on your own time?" Stull hurled the question like a javelin, hard and fast. "University time? Government time?"

Lex Morrison looked straight at us. Obviously he had not expected this interrogation but it did not put him off balance. "It's a sticky question. I teach botany and do research at the state university. Our laboratory has received several grants from the federal government. But none of my college or government time has gone into this. It was my own pet project."

"Why?"

"Plants are what I know. Ever since I was a boy I've studied plants. I care about them. My grandmother taught me that almost before I could walk." He hesitated.

"You know she was from your part of the country." He paused but Stull did not pursue the geography. "Down there in the mountains. It's a botanist's paradise."

Haze of smoke, autumn, and exhaust fumes shimmered just beyond the dimness of the room. Then the stranger said, with some embarrassment, "I have a hang-up about time. Since I was a kid, the clock's been my enemy. The changes it brings, the deterioration, the withering—"

"You want to play God?" Stull's voice carried a hint of a dry chuckle.

He flushed. "Don't most of us?" His jaw was hard and set as he answered.

There was a pause before Stull asked if the scientist could give any analysis or reassurance about residual effects.

"No. That's where the time factor enters. It's only been in usable form since last spring. Tested it during my vacation down in Florida and then this summer in my own garden. Arrested plant growth completely—and I ate the fruits and vegetables myself. No harmful effects."

"It arrest your growth?" Stull asked.

"A little late for that, I'm afraid." He half-smiled. "No, it didn't seem to do that, either."

"You find something to keep people from aging," I was trying to relieve the inquisitional air Stull created, "find something to stop this old human machine from what you so nicely call withering—and you can match pennies with J. Paul Getty."

Of course. That was what was in all our minds—from Lex Morrison's and Stull Clayburn's to the Hollywood starlet's and the toothless old farmer's down in Churchill: no change. The great American Dream: Ever Young. Everlasting Eighteen. And if this chemical concoction could achieve that ultimate goal for a plant why not the possibility that it could do as much eventually for a man?

"What do you think about it? Any danger?" Stull laid his hands on the arms of his chair and his eyes narrowed. His hands hardly shook at all when they had something to grasp. "You made the stuff, by God, you ought to have some idea of whether or not we can use it without having our tail shot off."

Morrison answered in the same tone Stull had used. "I know it's all right by itself. I can guarantee that."

"But?"

"But nothing is by itself any more. What I can't guarantee is the effect of any powerful chemical compound in relation to other sprays and fertilizers and additives and even water purifiers."

There was a silence. He went on. "I think it will be okay. But I'm a scientist and I like to be sure."

"And I'm a businessman and I like to be first," Stull Clayburn said.

In the pause I considered why Stull was on the attack, setting up the situation of offense-defense rather than of cooperation in a mutual enterprise. I had personally encountered this arrangement too many times before. When I first joined the company. When Teena and I were married. Stull wanted something. And whatever it was, he wanted it exclusively and totally and at the cheapest price possible. Whoever sat opposite him was automatically an adversary. Winning was all.

Sounds of traffic in the streets below came up in blurred noisy waves—crunching gears and the roaring labor of trucks and screaming brakes. The silence of the room was enclosed in dark paneling and heavy carpet but it was an artificial silence surrounded by the city's clamor.

I broke the pause. "Isn't there a way to be both? Be sure and be first? Take another year for tests but let us have the option until the safety factor is proved and we can begin to use the spray. Then you can be sure and we'll still be first to reap the advantage."

Morrison was nodding. "That might work."

"And it might not." Stull dismissed me in disgust. "You think you're the only fellow working on such a discovery, Morrison? If you've done it, that means there are a dozen bright boys just like you swarming all over the lot, right on the edge of a breakthrough. And a dozen companies right there waiting to grab first. Read your history. That's the story of progress. The names are all there. And they're Fulton and Edison and Bell and Ford and the Wright boys, not the ones who were backing and filling and testing till everything was sure as sunrise. Who the hell remembers the name of the second man to fly an airplane? Or the second man who worked on Salk's vaccine?"

I looked at the photographs on the wall to his left. One family picture of the Clayburn brothers, all the rest glossy photographs of Stull with various groups and individuals, many of the familiar faces around the world. The largest, most prominent, however, was a blown-up news shot of Stull surrounded by the Jackson U. football team. I knew what that picture meant to Stull.

"And what about the Feds?" I intercepted. I knew the question would block Stull for at least one play. I wondered when he was going to bring up the problem of Perlina Smelcer.

He frowned. I saw his old suspicion of me revive. "Agriculture won't have to know anything for a while. We'll go through channels, and channels are slow." He tapped his hands lightly on the desk. "As for Food and Drug, some of these young do-gooders that never had a day's practical experience in their lives are putting the bite on the FDA inspectors, keeping everything unsettled. We'll register our new spray, report in Morrison's own successful tests, ask to be allowed to proceed while we wait for a ruling. Emergency use."

"Sounds all right if it works."

"Sure it'll work—till they can prove something is wrong," Stull said. "Then maybe we can put one of our great senators into the game. Take your choice: an old-guard Republican who understands your problems but won't work on them, or a bright young Democrat who doesn't understand but goes right to work."

Lex Morrison was frowning. "This is something people eat. I wouldn't want—"

The light on Stull's private telephone winked on and off. Without seeming to notice that anyone was talking, Stull pressed a button. We heard his secretary's voice. "I'm sorry to interrupt, Mr. Clayburn, but it's Mr. Lusk here. He says you'll want to see him right now."

"All right." Stull's face held no expression. "Let me see him right now."

The big door swung open immediately. As Nat Lusk entered he nodded to Stull and me but directed his greeting to Lex Morrison. "Just the man I wanted to reach. Met you first time you came here with your snake oil."

"I remember."

"Just had a call from Churchill—"

"Sit down, Nat," Stull said.

Nat Lusk hesitated. His opening run had been thrown off-balance. The deep lines crevassing the leathery skin of his heavy suntanned face were even more prominent than usual.

"How's it going?" Stull asked.

And Nat knew that this was a warm-up play. He went along. "Okay," he said, "considering that everything I like nowadays either makes you fat, pollutes the air, or adds to the population explosion."

I managed a smile, but Lex Morrison did not laugh. He was looking at his large bony hands—and thinking.

Nat's Italian tailored suit could not camouflage the rolls of fat which spilled out over his black alligator belt, as the heavy lids could not hide the worry behind his dark eyes. (I recalled the night several years before when Teena had said to me, "There are women, you know, Jon, who like the hint of brutality in a man. Brutality cushioned with luxury. Maybe that's Nat Lusk's appeal." "In that case woman—" I had whacked her lightly on the backside. "It's an appeal I find utterly resistable," she added hastily, laughing. It was one of the last times we laughed together easily, without forcing the gaiety. The next day she went to the doctor and he advised surgery.)

As Nat Lusk sat down he lit a cigarette and took a deep drag on it, then leaned forward, an elbow on each knee, hands dangling loosely between. He looked around like an uneasy old sea lion I had watched once on the water-slick rocks along the California coast, swinging his head from side to side in alert and rhythmic unease.

"Well, Nat?" Stull said.

"I just talked with Price Sims down in Churchill. The Smelcer woman died."

"Damn." As Stull breathed it, it was more a sigh than a word.

I could visualize the scene at the Churchill clinic first and now at the funeral home, although I've been away for many years—can it be more than twenty? Smelcers (the mountains are full of sawbriars and Smelcers, Uncle Whit Ransom used to say) of every size and age, in overalls or housedresses or uniforms, crowding into the poor woman's sick room, certain that this succumbing to a hospital was only a prelude to the final surrender to the grave. And while they watched and waited they would talk and socialize, spying out places to secretly unload streams of tobacco juice. Using up the oxygen in her tight little room, perching on the foot of her bed, they would nevertheless provide Perlina with an indispensable ingredient: the certainty that she belonged, had a place, an identity, relationships.

Nat was explaining the circumstances of Perlina Smelcer's sickness and death to the scientist.

"That was the farm where the spray was used?" Lex Morrison asked.

"It sure as hell was—is," Nat said.

For a moment there was no sound or movement in the office except for the faint wheezing rasp of the electric clock on Stull's desk.

"And there goes the ball game," Nat said.

"Had she eaten the turnip greens more than once?" Morrison asked.

Stull looked at him. "There's the scientist," he nodded, and for the first time there was genuine admiration in his voice. "No hasty conclusions. No pressing the panic button. Questions. Facts."

"How the hell do we know how much the Smelcers have been eating?" Nat Lusk was stung by the implicit reprimand. "Most of those farm tenants just go out and help themselves to the crops whenever they want to. And they glean the fields—get whatever the machines leave behind."

"She probably ingested some of the spray," Morrison said slowly.

"We don't know," Stull repeated. His voice and face were troubled. "But we'll find out—in an orderly fashion." He glanced at me, then looked away. I took the signal, said nothing about my plans for Churchill.

"Those mountain folks are superstitious." Nat lit another cigarette.

Stull spoke on, half to himself. "She might have eaten some other questionable food that same day. Or she may have had some disease for years—all those mountain women are sick half the time. Neither Morrison nor any of his assistants had any side-effects when they ate fruits and vegetables that had the spray."

"Of course, those were controlled situations—"

"Well, I didn't tell Mama Smelcer to go out in our fields and help herself to our crops. If that's what she did. Hell, I don't want to put anything dangerous out on the market. On the other hand, I don't want to pass up a good thing, work with one hand tied behind me in a competitive situation just because of a scare story."

"Why don't we just by-pass the whole stinking bit, forget about putting ever-fresh fruits and vegetables in our cans?" Nat Lusk stood up and paced across the room, introducing once again his pet idea. "I say switch to some of the cheap and easy, look-alike artificial foods. Most of the half-assed people in the grocery stores and restaurants today don't know what they're getting anyway. Sugar that never came from any plant, cream that was never yanked from any cow's tits, meat that was never on any hoof or wing. If that's what they'll pay for, I say give it to them."

Stull had turned his back on Nat Lusk and sat looking out the window. There was a real splash of gray even in the hair on the back of his head. "No, Nat. We don't want to hurt anybody. We're here to feed people. That's what my father used to say." (*Your* father! I thought. You mean your Uncle Jonathan. Isn't that who you mean, Stull, deep down in your memory?) "We'll set up some more tests in our laboratories. Meanwhile—" he swung back to his desk. His face had tightened, lost much of its flabbiness. In a crisis, his flesh and voice pulled together to become almost firm. "—What's Price Sims doing?"

"Sitting tight," Nat said.

The thought occurred to me that this was no news. By this time of day Price was usually walking tight, too.

"No one down there saying anything about the spray?" Stull went on.

"We didn't exactly advertise," Nat said. "It was all a pretty secret trial run."

"Then they, or we, don't really have any idea what caused Smelcer's wife to be sick, do we?" No one answered Stull. "Maybe it was a new brand of snuff she was dipping."

Nat Lusk was pulling hard on his cigarette. Lex Morrison looked at the three of us Clayburn-Durant men. "I'm not sure I know what you're saying."

"All right. Let's put it right up front where it belongs and look at it. As you yourself asked, what do we know—for sure?" Stull's pale blue gaze, like the level tone of his voice, demanded attention. "Morrison, let's find out why you came to Clayburn in the first place."

The young scientist was surprised. "I told you at our first meeting. There may have been several reasons. I suppose one was the memory of my grandmother talking about the Clayburn cannery, the Clayburn family—"

"Your grandmother?" I asked. I tried to ignore the grim impatience on Stull's face. "Who was your grandmother?"

"Laura Morrison."

I had heard the name before. But this time there seemed to be an echo in my mind. "Before she married, what was her name? Could she have been Laura Rathbone?"

Lex Morrison nodded.

"Well, I'll be damned." I looked up at the picture of five brothers which hung on Stull's wall—five tall, serious young men wearing high, stiff Sunday collars and proper parlor expressions, and I looked at the second one particularly. Jonathan, my father. "Your grandmother and my father—" I began, not really knowing what to say, but Stull interrupted.

"Didn't you actually come to us," he drove the conversation back into line, "because you thought we had the know-how to put your little discovery to good use?"

"The know-how *and* the need," Morrison agreed mildly. "Yes, that was part of it."

"Right now we've got a great big need," Stull spoke softly. "Let's call the game like it is: harvesting crops at their split-second peak of ripeness isn't the biggest hurdle we have to overcome in the canning business. It's just one part of the whole damned obstacle course. But every problem we can lick, or minimize, puts us just that much ahead of the others."

"Of course," Lex Morrison said.

"The way any single plant in a canning company can make us money, Morrison, is to run as near capacity for as many days and nights over as long a season as possible. It costs us almost as much to get everything in motion, cleaned up afterward, for a three-hour day as for a sixteen-hour day. And when we lose time because of lousy harvesting conditions, it costs. And when it costs, we hurt."

Nat Lusk sat down heavily, bored by Stull's elementary education of Morrison. Stull quieted him. "Nat, I want our scientist to understand the basics of the situation."

"Hell yes," Nat agreed. "Let's all understand."

"Well, then," Stull folded his hands together. "We try to regulate our crops by planting at intervals, a week or two apart, and by irrigation. But that fickle lady weather is still hard to manipulate. Too cool, too hot, too rainy—"

"Like most women," Nat muttered.

"But if we could get our pack in the cans, on the shelves, into the kitchens, fresher and quicker and cheaper than the competition"—Stull's milky blue gaze had frozen and fixed on each of us—"we'd show a profit. That spray of yours, Morrison, might make the difference."

It was as long a speech as I had ever heard Stull deliver, except at a board meeting.

"A helluva advertising gimmick, too," Nat broke the silence. "Every bite captured at the tender moment of summer-fresh maturity." His voice assumed the oracular tones of a radio or television announcer.

"I'm not talking about gimmicks, dammit, Nat," Stull said. "This isn't some expensive plan to pour more money into the tube for a return nobody can measure. It isn't some come-on for contests or packaging or promoting. It's good sound production."

"Okay, okay," Nat was waving his hand. His survival instinct told him better than to reopen a basic conflict with Stull now. "But whatever we produce we have to sell—and I kid you not."

Stull was looking at Morrison. "Earlier this summer your spray might have saved us nearly a million dollars."

"That bastard strike," Nat growled.

"Right," Stull said. "This summer, Morrison, three places where our careful planning and growing program brought in bumper tomato crops right on the nose—California, Indiana, and New Jersey—went out on strike. Those tomatoes mildewed, scalded, rotted in the fields. We plowed some under. And we lost a million-two on the whole stinking deal."

All of us winced at the memory.

"Your spray could have saved our damn ass," Stull said to Morrison. "Now we're talking about next season. Not two seasons from now, not a year from now. Next season. Spray in full production ready for our earliest pack, if necessary."

Morrison nodded very slowly. "I understand."

"I doubt that you understand, Mr. Morrison. You've never met a payroll. You've never faced a room full of stockholders who've gone without a dividend twice in a row." Stull leaned back in his chair, but he was tense as a wire stretched for tightrope walkers. "You've never watched a hundred acres of sugar peas rot because they grew too full before the machines could get into the wet fields. But there's no law says you have to understand, as long as you know that we want a reasonably safe spray. We don't ask for the moon. But we want it now or not at all. We'll pay you a fair price. You might even get rich from it."

There was another pause. Morrison shifted in his chair. Nat Lusk took two final draws on his cigarette and smashed the stub in an ash tray on the windowsill.

"And what about Perlina Smelcer?" I asked.

"We hope," said Stull evenly, turning a silver pen around and around in his fingers, not looking at me, "that Mrs. Smelcer wasn't ailing from our spray. And that no one else will be. We wish Mr. Smelcer a long and healthy life."

You could hear the four of us breathing in the room. Morrison was glimpsing the sudden possibility of riches. Stull was grasping at the possibility of stability in an unstable production situation. And Nat and I were groping along in their wake with our own possibilities to push: his for Clayburn-Durant Food Company to go essentially non-food, and mine for us to find a new direction which I couldn't even clearly define.

I looked at Stull's immobile face and the eyes as impenetrable as a pool glazed with ice. Only the hands, locked into a double fist on the pile of papers before him, betrayed any reaction. I was aware of Nat Lusk's disintegrated features and of the eager, troubled openness of Laura Rathbone's grandson. But the other two were only at the periphery. It was Stull Clayburn I saw.

"And do we intend in any way to investigate Perlina Smelcer's illness and death?" I asked.

"We don't intend to throw the goddamned alarm switch," Stull said.

I could feel the hostility fermenting in the room, oppressive as the smog which thickened the air just beyond the windows. But I would not stop. Suddenly I felt quite removed from the executive team of Clayburn-Durant Foods. I was back in Churchill listening to the tales about my great-uncle Whitley Ransom or my uncle Jack Montgomery, who tried to match life's absurdities with their own. Now I was not sure whether I really cared about Perlina Smelcer or whether I wanted to bait Stull.

"Don't we have any responsibility toward her? Not even any curiosity?"

"We have a responsibility to nineteen thousand and twenty-two stockholders." Stull's face was flushing. The change from his normal indoor pallor to this unnatural ruddiness reminded me of watching a summer storm distress the sky with feverish clouds while everything underneath grew motionless.

"And our duty to them begins with Perlina Smelcer," I suggested. Stull and I stared at each other across the desk.

"My duty to them is to keep this company alive."

"And profitable."

"You'd better believe it!" Stull's fist came down on the desk like a thunderclap. The cigarette box rattled. "What's the matter, Jon? No guts to take a risk?"

I smiled. It cost an effort, but I knew that smile would infuriate Stull more than anything else I could say. "I'll tell you what I don't have the guts for. Perlina Smelcer taking my risk for me. Especially when she's not even been told—or asked."

"And now," Stull's voice showered sarcasm, "our executive vice-president massages his bleeding heart. Sweetness and light—and bullshit!" he finished savagely.

I had known for a long time that this moment would arrive. Stull and me. I had not expected it today.

He leaned toward me, his eyes narrow and mean. "We've got a company to run. Whose side are you on, anyway?"

Maybe this was as good a time and outward reason as any. I stood up, shoved away the chair. "I'll have to let you know, Stull," I said.

I turned my back and walked out of the room. Behind me Nat Lusk was making some move and Lex Morrison was saying something, but clearer than their actions and louder than their words was Stull's anger which rode on my back as I left his office.

PART VII
The Appalachian Renaissance
Jessie Graves, Katherine Ledford, and Theresa Lloyd

In Appalachian literature, the 1960s through the 1990s saw a creative explosion that is sometimes referred to as the Appalachian Renaissance. Several factors were behind this great flowering. In the 1960s, national attention focused on Appalachia with an intensity not seen since extractive industries and social reform movements entered the region in the late nineteenth and early twentieth centuries. As the War on Poverty, a federal initiative inspired by the late president John F. Kennedy and created under the leadership of President Lyndon Johnson, sought to end economic privation in the United States, the media often used Appalachia as a symbol for the worst conditions in the nation. In response, Appalachian writers—inspired by women's studies, Native American studies, African American studies, Chicana/o studies, and other movements rooted in the nascent identity politics of a nation undergoing significant social and cultural change—countered media stereotypes with literary texts that explored pride, resilience, and positive values in the region.

Much of the poetry published during this era shows the physical, psychological, and spiritual displacement that resulted when industrialism finally supplanted the region's predominantly rural agricultural economy. Jim Wayne Miller's Brier poems are emblematic of this theme. The poetry of Jeff Daniel Marion, Don Johnson, and Irene McKinney also deals with these issues.

Formally, poetry written during the Appalachian Renaissance may be the most experimental of all writing from the region. Language is as much the subject of Charles Wright's poetry as is the landscape or the spirit-world with which the poems also engage. Conversely, Robert Morgan writes of landscape as text or language, viewing nature as a written text to be read and interpreted by those who pay careful attention. Great erudition, coupled with humor from the oral storytelling tradition, is the signal quality of Fred Chappell's poetry.

Like their counterparts in poetry, Appalachian fiction writers from the 1960s through the 1990s grapple with identity, with love *and* hate of people and place, with the hard realities of both leaving home and returning home, and with the even harder choice, sometimes, of staying put. Gurney Norman's counterculturalist Divine Right contemplates reintegration into his Eastern Kentucky family and community after a frenetic sojourn in the American West. In contrast, Breece D'J Pancake's Hollis fumes at the restrictions of farm life and the responsibility for aging parents forced upon him by his absent brother.

Late twentieth-century Appalachian nonfiction saw the same exciting developments that characterized American nonfiction more broadly, particularly the combination of fact, story, and emotion into what is called literary or creative nonfiction. The genre was especially effective in exposing systemic exploitation of the region and engendering a sympathetic or even an activist response in readers. The concept of literary nonfiction provides a useful lens for viewing Harry Caudill's writings about Appalachia, controversial among readers today yet highly influential when published.

Creative nonfiction has also been important in the region's environmental literature. In addition to Caudill, environmental authors represented in this section include Harry Middleton and Harvey Broome, whose reflective, philosophical writings explore the line between nature and culture, fully accepting the idea that unpeopled wilderness never existed and that even the remotest Appalachian landscapes are inevitably altered by modern humans.

If the term "Appalachian Renaissance" describes a huge outpouring of literature from the region in the last third of the twentieth century, using the phrase to refer to drama of the period may seem contradictory. By this time, few playwrights *from* the region were working *in* the region, and most of the playhouses were closed. However, many dramatists writing from an Appalachian sensibility produced highly compelling work. Although some late twentieth-century Appalachian dramatists received national attention by presenting predictable notions of the region's history and culture, the playwrights represented in this anthology indicate that dramatic explorations of Appalachian life need not be limited to stereotypes. Jason Miller's *Nobody Hears a Broken Drum* (1970) is a historical drama about coal miners' lives in the southern anthracite region of Pennsylvania. *The Janitor* (1985) is a short piece by distinguished Pittsburgh playwright August Wilson. Jo Carson's *Daytrips* (1990) is a powerful experimental play about Alzheimer's disease and family responsibility.

During the 1970s, community-based theater (an offshoot of street theater) became an exciting aspect of the theatrical landscape. Some of these grassroots theatrical companies, such as the Roadside Theater of Whitesburg, Kentucky, and the Bloomsburg Theatre Ensemble of Pennsylvania, are professional and pay their performers. Others, such as EcoTheater of Lewisburg, West Virginia, are more closely aligned with the participatory street theater of the 1960s and believe that nonprofessional local people are best suited to tell their own stories.

Finally, one should note that Appalachian Renaissance authors in all genres display a greater diversity than previously represented in the region's literature. The poems of Marilou Awiakta consider the many facets of the identity of a modern Cherokee. John Edgar Wideman, August Wilson, and Nikki Giovanni give strong voice to the African American experience in Northern and Southern Appalachia. Many women fiction writers came to the forefront during the Appalachian Renaissance. Denise Giardina, Lee Smith, George Ella Lyon, Lisa Alther, and Jayne Anne Phillips explored female characters and their places in families and communities, and, ultimately, shaped them as individuals with agency of their own.

Sources: Danny Miller, Sharon Hatfield, and Gurney Norman, eds., *An American Vein: Critical Readings in Appalachian Literature* (2005); John Lang, *Appalachia and Beyond: Conversations with Writers from the Mountain South* (2006); John Lang, *Six Poets from the Mountain South* (2010).

Marilou Awiakta

1936–

Poet, storyteller, and essayist Marilou Awiakta explores the intersection of traditional and modern Appalachian life by blending her Appalachian and Cherokee heritages with the legacy of post–World War II nuclear energy research in her hometown of Oak Ridge, Tennessee. Born Marilou Bonham in Knoxville to a family with Scots-Irish and Native American roots reaching back to the 1730s, Awiakta (her middle name) was raised with an awareness of social and environmental responsibility. When Awiakta was nine, her family moved to Oak Ridge, where her father agreed to work for two years in the nuclear facility, known locally as "the secret city." After graduating from the University of Tennessee in 1958, Awiakta moved to France with her husband, a physician with the US Air Force. While there, she worked as a liaison and translator for the base.

In *Abiding Appalachia: Where Mountain and Atom Meet* (1978), from which the following poems are taken, Awiakta weaves together her diverse heritages with the language of atoms, inviting readers to explore unexpected interconnections in their own fractured identities. The four sections of the book span generations, beginning with the Cherokee removal and ending with the construction of the deep fusion reactor in Oak Ridge. In the first section, Awiakta examines her Cherokee identity; in the second, her Appalachian pioneer heritage; in the third, the disconnection caused by the scientific frontier at Oak Ridge; and in the fourth, the space where these multiple strands are united.

An Indian Walks in Me

An Indian walks in me.
She steps so firmly in my mind
that when I stand against the pine
I know we share the inner light
of the star that shines on me.
She taught me this, my Cherokee,
when I was a spindly child.
And rustling in dry forest leaves
I heard her say, "These speak."
She said the same of sighing wind,
of hawk descending on the hare
and Mother's care to draw
the cover snug around me,
of copperhead coiled on the stone

and blackberries warming in the sun—
"These speak."   I listened . . .
Long before I learned the
universal turn of atoms, I heard
the Spirit's song that binds us
all as one. And no more
will I follow any rule
that splits my soul.
My Cherokee left me no sign
except in hair and cheek
and this firm step of mind
that seeks the whole
in strength and peace.

Smoky Mountain–Woman

I rise in silence, steadfast in the elements
with thought a smoke-blue veil drawn round me.
Seasons clothe me in laurel and bittersweet, in ice
but my heart is constant . . . Fires scar and torrents
erode my shape . . . but strength wells within me
to bear new life and sustain what lives already . . .
For streams of wit relieve my heavy mind
smoothing boulders cast up raw-edged . . . And the
raven's lonesome cry reminds me that the soul is
as it has ever been . . .
Time cannot thwart my stubborn thrust toward Heaven.

Marriage

Two peaks
Alone . . . apart . . .
yet join at the heart
where trees rise green
from rain-soaked loam
and laurel's tangled skeins
bear fragile blooms
and wind, a honing, ceaseless
sigh, blends with mirth
of streams defying heights
to wend their way unquenched.
Two peaks
they stand against the sky
spanned by a jagged arm of rock
locked in an embrace

elements cannot destroy
or time erase.

Genesis

Settlers sowed their seed.
Then their sons took the plow and in their turn grew old.
And the mountains abided, steeped in mist.
But in the deep was a quickening of light, a freshening of wind . . .
And in 1942, as fall leaves embered down toward winter,
   new ground was turned near Black Oak Ridge.
   The natives pricked their ears.
   These descendants of old pioneers
    lifted their heads to scent the wind—
   A frontier was a-borning.
Many had to pack up hearth and home and go.
But others joined the energy that flowed toward Black Oak Ridge
as to a great magnetic power:
   Thousands of people streamed in.
   Bulldozers scraped and moved the earth.
   Factories rose in valleys like Bear Creek
   and houses in droves sprang up among the trees
   and strung out in the lees of ridges.
A great city soon lay concealed among the hills.
   Why it had come no one knew.
   But its energy was a strong and constant hum,
   a new vibration, changing rhythms everywhere . . .

It charged the air in Knoxville, where we lived
and when I saw my parents lift their heads,
I lifted my head too, for even at seven
I knew something was stirring in our blood,
something that for years had drawn the family along frontiers
from Virginia to West Virginia, on to Kentucky and Tennessee.
And now, a few miles away, we had a new frontier.

Daddy went first, in '43—leaving at dawn, coming home at dark
and saying nothing of his work except,
"It's at Y-12, in Bear Creek Valley."
The mystery deepened.
The hum grew stronger.
And I longed to go.
Oak Ridge had a magic sound—
They said bulldozers could take down a hill before your eyes
and houses sized by alphabet came pre-cut and boxed, like blocks,

so builders could put up hundreds at a time.
And they made walks of boards and streets of dirt (mud, if it rained)
and a chain-link fence around it all to keep the secret.

But the woods sounded best to me.
My mind went to them right away . . .
      to wade in creeks and rest in cool deep shadows,
      watching light sift through the trees
      and hoping Little Deer might come.
      In the Smokies I'd often felt him near
      and I knew he'd roam the foothills too.
Woods were best. And if the frontier grew too strange
      my mountains would abide unchanged,
      old and wise and comforting.

So I kept listening to the hum, and longing . . .
Mother said we'd go someday, in the fullness of time.
And when I was nine the fullness came,
exploding in a mushroom cloud that shook the earth.

Where Mountain and Atom Meet

Ancient haze lies on the mountain
smoke-blue, strange and still
a presence that eludes the mind and
moves through a deeper kind of knowing.
It is nature's breath and more—
an aura from the great I AM
that gathers to its own
spirits that have gone before.

Deep below the valley waters
eerie and hid from view
the atom splits without a sound
its only trace a fine blue glow
rising from the fissioned whole
and at its core
power that commands the will
quiet that strikes the soul,
"Be still and know . . . I AM."

Nikki Giovanni

1943–

The influential African American writer, activist, and editor Yolande Cornelia "Nikki" Giovanni Jr. pushes people to ask difficult questions about racism and the African American experience, especially the experiences of black women. Her activism and poetry have been recognized since the early 1970s through numerous local, state, regional, and national awards.

Giovanni's connections to Appalachia emerge from her family life and are woven into her poetry. Born in Knoxville, Tennessee, Giovanni was reared in Cincinnati, Ohio, by her parents, who were teachers and a part of the black diaspora seeking expanded opportunities outside the segregated South. With her sister and cousins, Giovanni returned to Knoxville in the summers for extended visits with her maternal grandparents and moved back to Knoxville to live with her grandparents during her high school years before enrolling at Fisk University. Giovanni's faculty position at Virginia Tech, which she accepted in 1989, has offered her the opportunity to live in Appalachia again. Giovanni has expressed discomfort with the label "Appalachian writer," preferring to call herself an "urban writer," but she attributes her own independent nature to her Appalachian roots.

"Knoxville, Tennessee" is a reflection on a childhood summer.

Knoxville, Tennessee

I always like summer
best
you can eat fresh corn
from daddy's garden
and okra
and greens
and cabbage
and lots of
barbecue
and buttermilk
and homemade ice-cream
at the church picnic
and listen to
gospel music
outside
at the church
homecoming

and go to the mountains with
your grandmother
and go barefooted
and be warm
all the time
not only when you go to bed
and sleep

Fred Chappell

1936–

Poet, fiction writer, essayist, and educator Fred Chappell was reared on his grand-parents' farm in Canton, North Carolina. He began writing poems when he was fifteen. While attending Duke University (receiving his AB in 1961 and his MA in 1964), he became friends with southern writers Reynolds Price, Anne Tyler, and James Applewhite. Chappell taught creative writing at the University of North Carolina at Greensboro from 1964 until 2004 and was poet laureate of North Carolina from 1997 until 2002. Although claimed by the southern literary canon, Chappell considers himself an Appalachian author, believing that Appalachian literature is distinct from its southern cousin.

Chappell's major poetic work is *Midquest,* from which the following poem comes. Each of the four separately published volumes of *Midquest—River* (1975), *Bloodfire* (1979), *Wind Mountain* (1979), and *Earthsleep* (1980)—centers on a different element: water, fire, air, and earth. The collection weaves Dante, the Bible, Wittgenstein, Schopenhauer, and a host of allusions to contemporary and ancient works with Appalachian traditions such as the tall tale. Ultimately, *Midquest* attempts to bridge the gap between the unlettered and the scholarly, the personal and the universal, Appalachia and the world.

My Grandmother Washes Her Vessels

In the white-washed medical-smelling milkhouse
She wrestled clanging steel; grumbled and trembled,
Hoisting the twenty-gallon cans to the ledge
Of the spring-run (six by three, a concrete grave
Of slow water). Before she toppled them in—
Dented armored soldiers booming in pain—
She stopped to rest, brushing a streak of damp
Hair back, white as underbark. She sighed.

"I ain't strong enough no more to heft these things.
I could now and then wish for a man
Or two . . . Or maybe not. More trouble, likely,
Than what their rations will get them to do."

The August six-o'clock sunlight struck a wry
Oblong on the north wall. Yellow light entering
This bone-white milkhouse recharged itself white.

Seeped pristine into the dozen strainer cloths
Drying overhead.

        "Don't you like men?"

Her hand hid the corner of her childlike grin
Where she'd dropped her upper plate and left a gap.
"Depends on the use you want them for," she said.
"Some things they're good at, some they oughtn't touch."

"Wasn't Grandaddy a good carpenter?"

She nodded absentminded. "He was fine.
Built churches, houses, barns in seven counties.
Built the old trout hatchery on Balsam . . .
Here. Give me a hand."

        We lifted down
Gently a can and held it till it drowned.
Gushed out of its headless neck a musky clabber
Whitening water like a bedsheet ghost.
I thought, Here spills the soldier's spirit out;
If I could drink a sip I'd know excitements
He has known; travails, battles, tourneys,
A short life fluttering with pennants.

        She grabbed
A frazzly long-handled brush and scrubbed his innards
Out. Dun flakes of dried milk floated up,
Streamed drainward. In his trachea water sucked
Obscenely, graying like a storm-sky.

"You never told me how you met."

        She straightened,
Rubbed the base of her spine with a dripping hand.
"Can't recollect. Some things, you know, just seem
To go clear from your mind. Probably
He spotted me at prayer meeting, or it could
Have been a barn-raising. That was the way
We did things then. Not like now, with the men
All hours cavorting up and down in cars."

Again she smiled. I might have sworn she winked.

"But what do you remember?"

                              "Oh, lots of things.
About all an old woman is good for
Is remembering. . . . But getting married to Frank
Wasn't the beginning of my life.
I'd taught school up Greasy Branch since I
Was seventeen. And I took the first census
Ever in Madison County. You can't see
It now, but there was a flock of young men come
Knocking on my door. If I'd a mind
I could have danced six nights of the week."

We tugged the cleaned can out, upended it
To dry on the worn oak ledge, and pushed the other
Belching in. Slowly it filled and sank.

"Of course, it wasn't hard to pick Frank out.
The straightest-standing man I ever saw.
Had a waxed moustache and a chestnut mare.
Before I'd give my say I made him cut
That moustache off. I didn't relish kissing
A briar patch. He laughed when I said that,
Went home and shaved. . . . It wasn't the picking and saying
That caused me ponder, though. Getting married—
In church—in front of people—for good and all:
It makes you pause. Here I was twenty-eight,
Strong and healthy, not one day sick since I
Was born. What cause would I have to be waiting
On a man?"

                    Suddenly she sat on the spring-run edge
And stared bewildered at empty air, murmuring.

"I never said this to a soul, I don't
Know why . . . I told my papa, 'Please hitch me
The buggy Sunday noon. I can drive
Myself to my own wedding.' That's what I did,
I drove myself. A clear June day as cool
As April, and I came to where we used to ford
Laurel River a little above Coleman's mill,
And I stopped the horse and I thought and thought.
If I cross this river I won't turn back. I'll join
To that blue-eyed man as long as I've got breath.

There won't be nothing I can feel alone
About again. My heart came to my throat.
I suppose I must have wept. And then I heard
A yellowhammer in a willow tree
Just singing out, ringing like a dance-fiddle
Over the gurgly river-sound, just singing
To make the whole world hush to listen to him.
And then my tears stopped dropping down, and I touched
Nellie with the whip, and we crossed over."

Irene McKinney
1939–2012

Poet Irene McKinney was born in Belington, West Virginia, and grew up on her family's farm. Rural life and connection to place—the mountains of West Virginia specifically—proved to be a source of poetic inspiration throughout her life. She earned a BA in English literature at West Virginia Wesleyan College, an MA at West Virginia University, and a PhD at the University of Utah.

McKinney taught at West Virginia Wesleyan College, where she founded and directed an MFA program. She received a National Endowment for the Arts award for poetry and a residency at the Bread Loaf Writers' Conference, among other honors. In 1994, McKinney was appointed poet laureate of West Virginia, a post she retained until her death.

McKinney's lyrical poetry takes a hard look at the mountainous landscape with its reality of austerity, isolation, and economic stagnation. Her speakers search not for a way out of difficult terrain, both physical and social, but for a way into spiritual lessons of compassion and joy. In "Twilight in West Virginia: Six O'Clock Mine Report," McKinney turns a matter-of-fact bulletin on mine activity, a staple of West Virginia news, into a report on the problematic effects of mining.

Twilight in West Virginia: Six O'Clock Mine Report

Bergoo Mine No. 3 will work: Bergoo Mine
No. 3 will work tomorrow. Consol. No. 2
will not work: Consol. No. 2 will not
work tomorrow.

Green soaks into the dark trees.
The hills go clumped and heavy
over the foxfire veins
at Clinchfield, One-Go, Greenbrier.

At Hardtack and Amity the grit
abrades the skin. The air is thick
above the black leaves, the open mouth
of the shaft. A man with a burning

carbide lamp on his forehead
swings a pick in a narrow corridor

beneath the earth. His eyes flare
white like a horse's, his teeth glint.

From his sleeves of coal, fingers
with black half-moons: he leans
into the tipple, over the coke oven
staining the air red, over the glow

from the rows of fiery eyes at Swago.
Above Slipjohn a six-ton lumbers down
the grade, its windows curtained with soot.
No one is driving.

The roads get lost in the clotted hills,
in the Blue Spruce maze, the red cough,
the Allegheny marl, the sulphur ooze.

The hill-cuts drain; the roads get lost
and drop at the edge of the strip job.
The fires in the mines do not stop burning.

Don Johnson

1942–

Poet Don Johnson was born and reared in Poca, West Virginia, a small town near a coal-fired energy plant. He earned a BA (1964) and MA (1966) from the University of Hawaii, where he played football, and a PhD (1972) from the University of Wisconsin–Madison. Johnson served as editor of *Aethlon,* a scholarly journal of sports literature published at East Tennessee State University, where he was a professor of English and the university's poet in residence.

Johnson's biography informs his poems, many of which deal with the Appalachian landscape and culture, with Hawaii, or with sports. Although his poetry is at times personal and meditative, Johnson often allows other speakers to narrate the poems.

Watauga Drawdown (1990), from which the following selections were chosen, recounts the history of the Watauga Valley, focusing on the town of Butler, Tennessee, which was flooded by the Tennessee Valley Authority in 1948 as part of post–World War II efforts to control flooding in the region and to generate hydroelectric power. When Watauga Lake was drained for dam repairs in 1983, former residents and others visited the site. The poems included here feature the voices of those who used to live in the area who struggle to make sense of relocation. In "1946," for example, a recently returned World War II veteran sees the destruction he witnessed during the war mirrored in the flooding of his hometown. Ultimately, then, Johnson's depiction of Butler takes on mythic dimensions.

1946

After Europe
he returned to a valley like the war,
a town of cellar holes and stumps
where yard trees, homeplace oaks and walnuts,
had been lumbered.
                    Farmhouses, jacked loose
from foundations, waited like dazed refugees
for trucks.
                He couldn't separate the tanks
and half-tracks that clanked and back-fired
in his dreams
                  from the rumble and scrape
of bulldozers under arc lights at the dam site.

Roads were dust or mud.

Twice he dived in the ditch
when unscheduled charges went off on the bluff.

No one cleaned or planted.

The day his family moved, he sat on the front porch
chain-smoking Luckies, as he had the evening
he paced the Marktplatz in Hanau.

The only things left standing in the square
were one Grimm brother's statue
and a figure that hunched from the rubble
when his back was turned

to glean his discarded butts
that the moonlight made shine
like white pebbles on the dark cobblestones.

And the River Gathered Around Us

After they wheeled away the town,
when the floodgates closed
and the river turned on itself,
we came back day after day
to watch the coves slowly fill up.

At the end of a week one road in
lay open. We drove it in three
Ford cars and a pick up towing
Wash Holt's rubber-tired wagon
that the boys from Mountain City rode.

It was not a Sunday. Most of us
had jobs, but we agreed to one more
game of ball before the smoothest
diamond in three counties
turned to lake bottom.

Water already lapped at the right field
fence where I killed a snake
before the first pitch, a fast ball
the batter himself called
a strike since we had no umpire.

Right went under with two out
in their half of the third
and we declared a ground ball
to that field an out. I played
barefoot and cheated toward

the infield, but it didn't matter.
Before the fifth was over,
water covered all but the mound
and the raked dirt at the plate.
By then, anything not a bunt

or fly ball was an out
and we were losing 6-2
when their pitcher called time
and said all three balls we had
were water-logged and that

he wouldn't ruin his arm
for no damn game in a lake,
so we brought him in half-way
where it was wet but close enough
to lob those melons in

with no pain. Then we lost
the bases, but ruled that running
in the right direction counted
if the runner didn't stop
until he made it home

or got out. We tied the score
on four straight hits to left
when a jon boat floated through
and blocked the fielder's way.
We called anything that hit

the boat a homer and it rained
that inning, the score tied
and water finally touching
the plate where both teams
congregated, soaked and up

to our knees in a field
without bounds, where everything

slowed and floated and nothing
sliding beneath the flood
would ever be forgotten.

Raymond Pierce's Vietnamese Wife

couldn't understand milk gravy,
how her mother-in-law could brown
biscuits, keeping their insides white
and flaky, and her family transform
them into sodden lumps of dough
and warm liquid. She could not
fathom the distance and space
in her new life: vacant acres
of land between towns,
the squat brick ranches
shadowed by empty-windowed farmhouses
abandoned and allowed to fall.

Afternoons, she would cry
on the floor of the walk-in closet,
her husband's shirts crowded
along the wall like ghostly applicants
for visas. When he found her there
he couldn't understand her tears.
She had so much, now. In 'Nam
her people slept and ate in a room
no bigger than that closet.

When he drove her out to the lake,
he pointed at blank water, saying,
"I was born there, a hundred feet
down," thinking she would not
understand a valley flooded
so there would be no more floods.
But she did understand, as she
stared at the water's sheen
baring no hint of village, only sky
and the deep mountain of green.

Robert Morgan

1944–

Born in Hendersonville, North Carolina, Robert Morgan grew up on his family's farm and wrote his first short story in the sixth grade at the prompting of a teacher. During college, after a professor said reading one of Morgan's stories moved him to tears, Morgan transferred from North Carolina State University, where he was studying mathematics and engineering, to the University of North Carolina at Chapel Hill, majoring in English. He began encouraging young writers himself when he accepted a teaching position at Cornell University in 1971. Since then, Morgan has made his academic home at Cornell in Ithaca, New York, on the northern edge of Appalachia, but his creative home is the southern mountains of his boyhood and young adult years.

In college, Morgan began writing short stories seriously but shifted to poetry in graduate school while studying with Fred Chappell at the University of North Carolina at Greensboro, earning an MFA degree in 1968. Morgan's first book, *Zirconia Poems* (1969), illuminated his home community in Henderson County. His first collection of short stories, *The Blue Valleys,* appeared in 1989. A prolific and critically acclaimed writer, Morgan gained popular attention nationwide via an endorsement from Oprah's Book Club for the novel *Gap Creek* (1999). Morgan's careful attention to poetic structure is informed by his broad reading in Chinese, Japanese, French, American, and British poetry. His concern with place, land, and people in western North Carolina has captured the interest of a large number of readers and critics, especially as his poetry has moved from a formal to a more speaker-focused and narrative expression.

High Wallow

North end of the mountain's summit
the ground's all bare and hollowed out
like some bull has been wallowing,
no trees, not even grass gathering
on the brow, and pebbles collect
in the holes of kicked-up sods plucked
naked of leaves and weeds. For high
wind, the hard wind, hits here all night
and day, all year, knocking the peak
and scrubbing away all grit like
chalk. The prevailing voice stunts
and bullies vegetation, grunts

up the slope until nothing grows
at the crest, and weeds uprooted blow
past, leaves caught in the updraft swirl.
And the soil is pitted where shrill
wind has dug for centuries loosening
clay and mica, tearing, tossing
any thaw crumbs, dashing water
from catchment pools, rubbing over
any sign or track left there, as
the fury of the air erases
and abrades whatever history
the mountain offers to the sky.

Double Springs

I used to wonder how
two springs could issue from the hill
a yard apart. Why not dig deeper
and unite their flow?

And later realized they
surfaced close from opposite
directions. The southern
sweeter, though the northern's steady

effluence came cold, even in the dry
months when its neighbor
slacked and almost stood, with
algae thickening the edges.

In the church nearby I've heard
sermons on the trinity describe
their separate currents merging to
one branch. The sweet uneven

head rose from the hillside leaning toward
Dark Corner, while the constant
icy thread emerged
from the farm country. In summer

they condemned the slow one and
when I came down to drink before
or after preaching its partner sure
enough ran clear, with ebullition

dimpling the surface above the pores,
and purifying lizards gripped
the sandy floor. But after swilling
there I'd dip the gourd

into the slightly silty left
embellished now with leaves and spiders
and aquatic mosses for a richer sip.
That ungodly taste I'd carry home.

Paradise's Fool

In the appletree abloom at the field's
edge and the hummingbird's
nest of moss and plantdown,

in the canticles of the star maiden
and subtle
aesthetics of failure,

the severalty of tidelands, duff
of fencerows, word amulets, stench of traffic
in the electron, I

am paradise's fool.
See the grapery and mariculture, whole
alloys of people, singing plants,

nut groves and
the clitoris sharp as a phonograph needle
scoring circles of music.

Lo, worlds without beginning in
the spring's contact lens,
the haunted well and camphorwood.

Neither in surview nor sweet veld
do I escape the terror,
the presence of the comforter.

Mountain Bride

They say Revis found a flatrock
on the ridge just

perfect for a natural hearth,
and built his cabin with a stick

and clay chimney right over it.
On their wedding night he lit
the fireplace to dry away the mountain
chill of late spring and flung on

applewood to dye
the room with molten color while
he and Martha that was a Parrish
warmed the sheets between the tick

stuffed with leaves and its feather
cover. Under that wide hearth
a nest of rattlers,
they'll knot a hundred together,

had wintered and were coming awake.
The warming rock
flushed them out early.
It was she

who wakened to their singing near
the embers and roused him to go look.
Before he reached the fire
more than a dozen struck

and he died yelling her to stay
on the big four-poster.
Her uncle coming up the hollow
with a gift bearham two days later

found her shivering there
marooned above a pool
of hungry snakes,
and the body beginning to swell.

Audubon's Flute

Audubon in the summer woods
by the afternoon river sips
his flute, his fingers swimming on
the silver as silver notes pour

by the afternoon river, sips
and fills the mosquito-note air
with silver as silver notes pour
two hundred miles from any wall.

And fills the mosquito-note air
as deer and herons pause, listen,
two hundred miles from any wall,
and sunset plays the stops of river.

As deer and herons pause, listen,
the silver pipe sings on his tongue
and sunset plays the stops of river,
his breath modeling a melody

the silver pipe sings on his tongue,
coloring the trees and canebrakes,
his breath modeling a melody
over calamus and brush country,

coloring the trees and canebrakes
to the horizon and beyond,
over calamus and brush country
where the whitest moon is rising

to the horizon and beyond
his flute, his fingers swimming on
where the whitest moon is rising.
Audubon in the summer woods.

Jeff Daniel Marion
1940–

Poet, educator, editor, and publisher Jeff Daniel Marion was reared in the small northeastern Tennessee town of Rogersville. The time he spent on his grandmother's and uncle's nearby farms contributed to the pastoral sensibility underlying his poetry.

Marion received his BS and MA from the University of Tennessee and began writing poetry in 1968, shortly before beginning to teach creative writing at Carson-Newman College in Jefferson, Tennessee. To date, nine volumes of Marion's poetry have been published; his poems have also appeared in dozens of journals. After Marion's retirement from Carson-Newman, he relocated to Knoxville, where he served as poet in residence at the University of Tennessee Library.

Marion was the founding editor of two literary journals, the *Small Farm* (1975–1980) and the *Mossy Creek Reader* (1990–2001). He also established the Mill Springs Press, which he operated from a cabin near the Holston River in East Tennessee and which produced chapbooks and broadsides on a hand-set printing press.

Marion's poetry evinces a personal connection to the natural world and a wistful connection to the past, both of which, the poems indicate, have bracing, restorative powers. Tender and clear, his verse mourns a way of life that is disappearing as he writes. Marion's interweaving of memories, natural imagery, and spirituality invites comparison with poetry as diverse as that of Robert Frost and the classic Chinese mountains and rivers poets.

Ebbing & Flowing Spring

Coming back you almost
expect to find the dipper
gourd hung there by the latch.
Matilda always kept it hidden
inside the white-washed shed,
now a springhouse of the cool
darkness & two rusting milk cans.
"Dip and drink," she'd say.
"It's best when the water is rising."
A coldness slowly cradled
in the mottled gourd.
Hourly some secret clock
spilled its time in water,
rising momentarily only
to ebb back into trickle.

You waited while
Matilda's stories flowed back,
seeds & seasons, names & signs,
almanac of all her days.
How her great-great grandfather
claimed this land, gift
of a Cherokee chief
who called it Spring of Many Risings.
Moons & years & generations
& now Matilda alone.
You listen.
It's a quiet beginning
but before you know it
the water's up & around you
flowing by.
You reach for the dipper
that's gone, then
remember to use your hands
as a cup for the cold
that aches & lingers.
This is what you have come for.
Drink.

The Man Who Loved Hummingbirds

Once I saw my father
    lift from last fall's leaves
        below our wide picture window

a hummingbird, victim
    of reflected surfaces, the one clue
        a single feather clinging above the sill.

He cradled its body in his cupped
    hands and breathed across the fine
        iridescent chest and ruby throat.

I remembered all the times
    his hands became birdcalls, whistles,
        crow's caw from a blade of grass.

Then the bird stirred and rose
    to perch on his thumb.
        As he slowly raised his hand

the wings began to hum
and my father's breath lifted
and flew out across the world.

Lynn Powell
1955–

Born and reared in Chattanooga, Tennessee, Lynn Powell often focuses her poetry on spirituality and its infusion into daily life. She attended Carson-Newman College, where she received her BA (1977), and she earned her MFA at Cornell University (1980). Powell has focused on bringing poetry into public schools, both during her work as a writer in the schools for the Tennessee Arts Commission and in her later role as the director of the Writers in the Schools program at Oberlin College.

Powell's poetry has been published in several venues, and she has won multiple awards for her writing. In addition to her poetry, Powell has written two works of nonfiction; the first, *Framing Innocence: A Mother's Photographs, a Prosecutor's Zeal, and a Small Town's Response* (2010), dealt with the way a small town rallied around a well-liked but unconventional mother whose innocent pictures of her young child bathing resulted in her arrest and a lengthy trial.

Old and New Testaments (1995), from which the following poems are taken, is divided into four sections, each prefaced with a Bible verse that introduces that part's theme. While the narrative voices are diverse, each poem serves as a testament to a stage of life and offers insight into the wisdom gained from a community of believers. Even the most ordinary of moments, rendered both intimate and relatable, become revelations in these poems.

Raising Jesus

How in the world did Mary do it?
After the remarkable birth in the company of beasts,
the gospels edit out her ordinary work—kneading loaves
and frying fishes, healing the daily hurts, giving the ten times
ten thousand reprimands and kisses that make
a learned boy in the temple from a squalling newborn.

My own son growls, *When I grow up I want to be a Bad Guy,*
then swaggers from the kitchen, his tinkertoy sword raised.
When he was born, his sister converted to a Crocodile
and warned, *I'll swallow up that little Captain Hook!*
Now she's Wendy, walking the plank, her arms
outstretched so Peter Pan can save her.

The Bad Guy stops, observes her cool mutiny
of the couch, and is shaken by an insight:

Hey! There is *no Peter Pan!*
At three, he doesn't pause to ponder
the evolution of good, the availability of God,
the reptilian brain and its housemate, the soul—

he just tosses his sword in the sea of blue carpet,
and raises his sister from the waves.
The story is solved by a kiss—not
the perfunctory kind I coax from one to the other
after insult or injury, but a real smooch the rapt
Wendy bestows on the born-again Pan.

I'm grinding mustard seeds for the curry
and suddenly everybody wants to help, jostling
for the mortar and pestle till there's sobbing and stomping
off to other rooms. How did Mary judge,
when little Jesus wept, if tears were real, or crocodile?
How did she perform that first miracle, teaching him to love?

Outside, our yard is full of the prerequisites
of parable: bulbs buried like talents,
a garden sown on rocky ground,
the dessicated grapevine stubbled with bud.
But the moment for instruction passes.
The household enemies make up on their own.

Just as I leave the kitchen and wade
into the day's first pool of quiet,
my daughter appears, draped in shawls and towels,
and leading her brother, naked except for the scarf
wrapped twice round his waist and knotted in front.
Guess who he is, Mama! Jesus—grown-up!

That's fine, I say, as they tramp away
across the warm afternoon rugs of windowlight. . . .
Oh God, keep me a mediocre Mary!
Dilute my children's love with selfishness,
let them refuse the treacherous kiss, never know
the miserable cup. Make their lives long, happy, ordinary—

and forgive the mother, reaching for Your hem, craving that miracle.

At Ninety-Eight

> I sure as hell hope the Lord's got beans
> to break and string in heaven.
> —Aunt Roxy

Her mind goes blank
imagining what pearly gates
and boulevards of gold—what
contraption of an afterlife—
could matter more than sweet
potatoes garden dug, still damp,
a green bonfire of mustards,
the pumpkin fattening like a golden calf.
She's lost patience
with that infernal flirt, the future,
outlived the widowed longings of the past.

And though I needle her to tell me
who 80 years ago she loved,
who 60 years ago she nursed,
her loss has turned as silver
and familiar as the moon.
She'd rather go buy nylons at the 5 & 10,
then, holding to me like a lover,
try on her bright new lipstick, red as fruit.

Jim Wayne Miller

1936–1996

Reared in western North Carolina on a farm in Buncombe County near his maternal and paternal grandparents, Jim Wayne Miller completed his undergraduate work at Berea College in 1958 and earned his doctorate in German literature at Vanderbilt University in 1965. Throughout his professional life, he taught German at Western Kentucky University.

In *The Mountains Have Come Closer* (1980), Miller first presents the persona for whom he would become best known—the Brier, whose name Miller co-opted from a midwestern epithet for outmigrant Appalachians. The Brier—who is simultaneously a spokesperson for Miller; a representative Appalachian person living in the post–World War II era; and anyone dislocated by rapid cultural change—is aware that he and other southern mountain people live in two worlds: no longer isolated subsistence farmers, they have modern lives like other Americans, yet they are rooted in older traditions as well.

In the "Brier Sermon," the shape-shifting Brier assumes the persona of a street preacher. Although religion suffuses the poem, Miller uses it metaphorically rather than doctrinally. Not affiliated with a denomination, Miller said that the poem's numerous diverse sources include Zen Buddhism and Friedrich Nietzsche's *Thus Spake Zarathustra*.

Along with poetry, Miller wrote fiction and nonfiction and worked with other influential figures of Appalachian studies and literature such as Robert Higgs and Ambrose Manning to edit important Appalachian literary collections. Additionally, Miller taught writing workshops, including at Hindman Settlement School.

Brier Sermon—*"You Must Be Born Again"*

One Friday night the Brier felt called to preach. So Saturday morning, early, he appeared on a street corner in town and started preaching, walking up and down the sidewalk in front of a hardware and sporting goods store, back and forth in front of the shotguns and spin casting rods and Coleman camp stoves in the window, and looking across the street to the Greenstamp Redemption Store, where all the women brought their trading stamps. Cars and trucks were passing on the street, women were going in and out of the Redemption Store; and a few men and boys were standing around, in groups of three or four. The Brier knew they were listening even though they were not looking at him. He took as his text, "You Must Be Born Again," and started drawing the people closer, saying:

You may say, Preacher, where is your black Bible?

Why ain't you preaching down sin?
You may say, Preacher, why ain't you talking about hell?
What about lipstick and short dresses?
What about cigarettes and whiskey?
What about dope and long hair?

Well, I didn't bring my Bible for a purpose.
Because this morning I wanted to say to you
I've been through all the books and come out yonside.
I'm educated, but not like the Brown boys.
Let me tell you about the Brown boys.

Feller over close to where I live
wanted some little cedar trees dug up
and planted in a row beside his house.
Tried to hire the Johnson boys, his neighbors,
but they were too scared to do it, didn't believe
in digging up cedar trees; they'd always heard
you'd die whenever the trees got tall enough
for their shadow to cover your grave. Get somebody else,
they said. Get old Jim Brown and Tom Brown.
They're educated, don't believe in nothing.
Well, I'm educated, but not like the Brown boys.
There's something I believe in:
You must be born again.

When he told about the Brown boys, the Brier heard some of the men laugh and say
things to one another. Across the street at the Redemption Store a woman had come out
and stopped, holding a little boy by the hand. The Brier figured the woman and the little
boy would like a story, too.

You hear preachers talk about being lost.
What does it mean? What's it got to do
with being born again?—Feller I know,
he didn't go to church, but a church bus
always ran right by his house, and his boy,
about five or six years old, wanted to ride it.
So he let him go. Little boy got over there
in church and they were having a revival. Preacher
knelt down by the little boy, said, Son, are you lost?
Little boy said, Yes, for the bus had gone up several
creeks and hollers, picking up other people,
and carried the little boy so far from home
he didn't know where he was.

We're not so different from that little boy.
We can be lost, sitting right in the church house.
Because we've been carried a long way around,
we've got so far away from home, we don't know where
we are, how we got where we are, how to get home again.
I know I wasn't so different from that little boy.

In my father's house, Jesus said.

Our foreparents left us a home here in the mountains.
But we try to live in somebody else's house.
We're ashamed to live in our father's house.
We think it too old-fashioned.
Our foreparents left us a very fine inheritance,
but we don't believe it.
I just want to set you down, gather you together,
and read you the will!

You've wanted to run off and leave it, this inheritance.
You didn't want to see it,
ashamed to hear about it,
thought it wasn't pretty because it wasn't factory-made.
You put it back in the attic,
you've thrown it off in a corner of the barn,
thrown it down into a ditch.

In my father's house.

The house our foreparents left had a song, had a story.
We didn't care.
We said:
them old love songs
them old ballets
them old stories and like foolishness.

We were too busy anyway
giving our timber away
giving our coal away
to worry about love songs
to worry about ballets
to worry about old stories
and like foolishness.

But I know a man

he had a song from his foreparents.
It got carried off to New York City
and when he heard it played on tv one night
by three fellers who clowned and hip-swinged
he said he began to feel sick,
like he'd lost a loved one.
Tears came in his eyes
and he went out on the ridge and bawled
and said, "Lord, couldn't they leave me the good memories?"
Now that man wasn't lost
but he knew what he had lost.

You've done your best to disremember
what all you've lost.
You've spoiled the life that's yours
by right of inheritance.
You have to go around to the back door
of the life that belongs to somebody else.
You're neither here nor there.
You're out in the cold, buddy.

But you don't have to live in the past.
You can't, even if you try.
You don't have to talk old-fashioned,
dress old-fashioned.
You don't have to live the way your foreparents lived.
But if you don't know about them
if you don't love them
if you don't respect them
you're not going anywhere.
You don't have to think ridge-to-ridge,
the way they did.
You can think ocean-to-ocean.

You say, I'm not going to live in the past.
And all the time the past is living in you.
If you're lost, I say it's because
you're not living in your father's house.
It's the only house you've got
the only shelter you've got.
It may be just a mountain cabin,
but it's shelter and it's yours.

I left my father's house. Oh, I was moving.

But I noticed I wasn't getting anywhere.
I was living in somebody else's house.
I kept stepping out somebody else's door
and the roads I traveled kept winding, twisting,
had no beginning, had no end.

My own house, heired to me by my foreparents,
was right there all the time
yours is too
but I wasn't living in it. Well, I went home.
And when I stepped out of my own front door
when I knew where I was starting from
I knew then where I was going.
The only road I could go was the road
that started from my own front door.
—In my father's house, that's what the Bible says.

And it speaks of the sins of the fathers
sins of the fathers visited on the children
unto the fourth generation
says the sins of the fathers
will set the children's teeth on edge.
You were probably wondering why
I wasn't talking about sin. Well, I am.
But I say, Forget the sins of the fathers.
What about the sins of the sons and daughters?
We've got enough sins of our own to think about.
We're able to set our own teeth on edge.
Ours is the sin of forgetfulness
forgetfulness of the fathers
forgetfulness of a part of ourselves
makes us less than we ought to be
less than we could be.
Forgetfulness of the fathers makes us a people
who hardly cast a shadow against the ground.

You've heard it said you can't put new wine in old bottles.
Well, I don't know.
But don't be too sure you're new wine.
Maybe we're all old wine in new bottles.

*The Brier was walking up and down the sidewalk, in front of the hardware and sporting
goods store, passing back and forth in front of the guns and fishing rods and catalytic
heaters, and a good crowd was gathering across the street in front of the Redemption*

Store. He was pacing to the corner and back, stopping to lay a hand on a parking meter. Traffic was increasing in the street. Some of the people passing nodded or waved a hand, for they knew the Brier. He nodded, and waved back. When the light stopped traffic in the street, he stood on the balls of his feet and talked across the tops of cars to the crowd in front of the Redemption Store. The light would turn and the traffic would move on— cars and pickup trucks, motorcycles, RV's pulling boats. A boy parked his wide-tired jacked-up car at the first parking meter in front of the Brier, got out and went into the hardware store. The Brier moved down and talked across the car's hood.

> I see these boys with their old cars jerked up
> on a pulley out under a tree somewhere.
> I see the cars looking like monster-beasts
> that have these boys' heads bit off
> and half of their bodies already eaten up.
> I see them lying flat on their backs
> with their heads up under cars,
> nothing but their feet a-sticking out,
> their hands mucking around in grease and gears.
> And I think, buddy, that's how America's got you,
> that's just the view you have of this country.
> You've had your head eat off,
> or else you're flat of your back
> looking up into the guts and gears of America,
> up to your elbows in her moving parts,
> flat of your back, always looking up.
>
> And I think to myself
> I'd like to open up your heads
> just like you raise the hood or go into a gearbox.
> I'd like to rewire your heads
> and gap your spark plugs and reset your timing.
>
> Because you can get off your back
> you can have a new view
> you can get behind the wheel of America.
> You can sit in the smooth upholstered seats of power
> and listen to the music playing.
>
> But first you've got to come home
> and live in your father's house
> and step out your own front door.
> There's a road back, buddy.
>
> Let me go back a little, let me tell you

how we got in this fix in the first place.
Our people settled in these mountains
and lived pretty much left to themselves.
When we got back in touch we started seeing
we had to catch up with the others.
And people came in telling us,
You've got to run, you've got to catch up.

Buddy, we've run so fast
we've run off and left ourselves.
We've run off and left the best part of ourselves.

And here's something peculiar:
running we met people on the road
coming from where we were headed,
wild-eyed people, running away from something.
We said, What'll you have? and it turned out
they were running away from what we were running after.
They were on their way to sit a spell with us.
We had something they wanted.
When they got here, a lot of us weren't to home.
We'd already run off and left ourselves.
So they set to picking up
all the things we'd already cast off—
our songs and stories, our whole way of life.
We couldn't see the treasures in our own house,
but they could, and they picked up what we'd abandoned.

You say, Preacher, you must be touched, that's foolishness.
How can anybody run off and leave himself?
I say, Don't ask me. You're the one who's done it.
You've kept the worst
and thrown away the best.
You've stayed the same where you ought to have changed,
changed where you ought to have stayed the same.
Wouldn't you like to know what to throw away
what to keep
what to be ashamed of
what to be proud of?
Wouldn't you like to know
how to change and stay the same?

You must be born again.

Say you were going on a trip
knowing you wouldn't ever be coming back
and all you'd ever have of that place you knew,
that place where you'd always lived
was what you could take with you.
You'd want to think what to take along
what would travel well
what you'd really need and wouldn't need.
I'm telling you, every day you're leaving
a place you won't be coming back to ever.
What are you going to leave behind?
What are you taking with you?
Don't run off and leave the best part of yourself.

And what is that best part? It's spirit.
I tell you, I know places in these mountains,
back off the big roads,
up the coves and hollers
old homeplaces
with barns and apple orchards, cattle gaps,
haunted by spirits
spirits of people who left there
taking everything with them but their spirits
for their spirits wouldn't leave that place
and their spirits are there yet
like half-wild dogs or cats that will live on
around a place after the people are gone.

And I know other places
in our towns and cities
where the people have moved to without their spirits.
Do you believe in signs? I do.
I believe in signs.
And when I see people living in dirt
living in filth and trash
I believe it's a sign.
It believe it's a sign the spirits of those people
are living somewhere else.
For a spirit won't live in filth and nastiness.
A spirit keeps its own place clean
like around a fox's den
when the little foxes come out and play in the evening
and it's clean around the den.

Yes, foxes have their dens
but what do we have?

We've lost the ground from underneath our feet,
lost the spiritual ground.
We've run off and left the best part of ourselves.
We've moved to the cities
moved to town
and left our spirits in the mountains
to live like half-wild dogs around the homeplace.

You say, Preacher, we have to change.
That's right.
But we're forgetful.

It's our forgetfulness that's a sin against ourselves.
We don't know any more about our history
than a dog knows about his daddy.
We're ignorant of ourselves
confused in what little we do know.
All we know is what other folks have told us.
They've said, You're fine Anglo-Saxons,
pioneer stock.
Then we went to the cities.
They said we were trash, said we were Briers.
They said, You're proud and independent.
They said, You're narrow-minded.
They said, You're right from the heart of America.
They said, You're the worst part of America.
They said, We ought to be more like you.
They said, You ought to be more like us.

You've heard that prayer that goes:
Help us to see ourselves as others see us.
Buddy, that's not a prayer we want to pray.
I believe we ought to pray:
Lord, help us to see ourselves—and no more.

Or maybe: Help us to see ourselves,
help us to be ourselves,
help us to free ourselves
from seeing ourselves
as others see us.

I know it's hard
to turn loose of that old self,
that confused self.

You think, That's the only thing I am,
what someone else has told me I am.
I've hung there, I know.
I've twisted in that wind.
But you can turn loose, you can do it.

One dark night in the fall of the year
a man went out to coonhunt—went by himself.
His dogs they struck a trail and he followed
up the ridge, stopping to listen, moving on,
moving through the dark.
And when his dogs barked treed, way over yonder,
he hurried on through the brush, moving faster,
and walked, yes, walked right over a cliff.
You'll do that in these mountains if you're not careful.
Well, he managed to grab a hold as he went over.
A little twisty, runty tree was growing out,
out from a crack in the cliff, and he hung by it,
held on in the dark.

But he couldn't do anything but just hang there.
He couldn't get back up, there was no footing.
And nothing but death and darkness there below him.
But he couldn't hold on much longer, either.
Finally all the strength in his hands was gone.
He couldn't hold on any longer, and he fell—
about a foot. Yes, fell about a foot.
He'd hung as long as he could. He'd held to dear life,
just as anybody will.
Having no choice, he turned loose of his life.
But he didn't lose it.
He didn't lose himself, he found himself,
found himself on firm ground. And he went home.
But he went home a changed man.

You're hanging like that man.
You're struggling for a toehold in the dark.
You're holding on to that old self
but your grip is growing weaker all the time.
Turn loose.

All you'll do is fall about a foot.
You'll fall about a foot to spiritual ground.
You'll fall home.
You'll walk away a different man or woman.

Oh, you'll think, I'm going to die.
But you won't die.
I'm not talking about physical death.
When you die a physical death
you're put into the ground.
And the Bible teaches you'll be raised up,
resurrected from that physical death.

But I'm not talking about physical death.
I'm talking about spiritual death.
I'm not talking about life after death.
I'm talking about life before death.
I'm saying if you're dead in life,
spiritually dead in life,
you must be born again,
you must be born again and again and again.

You say, Preacher, what's it like? I'm here to tell you:
It's like becoming a little child again
but being grown up too.
It's the best of both.
It's being at home everywhere.
It's living in your own house.
It's stepping out your own front door every morning.
It's being old wine in a new bottle.

It's getting to know another side of yourself.
You know how sometimes when you squirrel hunt
a squirrel will get on the back side of a tree
and if you step around there, he just goes
around to the side of the tree where you were standing,
and if you step back around to that side again,
he goes to the side where he was in the first place
and on and on and you never get him that way.
You've got a side of yourself that's like that squirrel,
always out of sight.

What's it like—being born again?

It's going back to what you were before
without losing what you've since become.

They say people can go blind gradually.
They say people can go deaf gradually.
Lose the sense of taste little by little.
They forget the shapes of leaves on trees,
forget the sound of the creek running,
the world just blurs, grows silent.
They forget the taste of coffee and all their food.
Now what would it be like if that sight were given back?
If they heard the creek running again, or a crow call?
If suddenly they could taste their food again?
Something is restored to them, a richness.
They've found something they didn't even know they'd lost.
They're born again to sights and sounds and tastes.

Oh, you must be born again.

Do you remember, back when you were little,
and wore brogans or heavy shoes all winter?
And do you remember that first day in spring
when you took them off and started going barefoot?
The air was warm but the ground was still so cool,
your feet were white and tender
but you felt light-footed
you had good wind
and you felt like you could fly right off the earth.

You must be born again!

The crowd had scattered now. The street was almost empty when he finished. He stood a moment like a blind man smiling and gazing past people he spoke to. Then he reached out, as if to gather something in and, raising his hand higher still, he blessed an invisible crowd on the sidewalk. Traffic stopped at the light, and the Brier on the corner disappeared behind a motor home. When it pulled away, he had gone.

Kathryn Stripling Byer

1944–2017

Kathryn Stripling Byer grew up in southwest Georgia, but her professional life was spent in southern Appalachia. Byer earned an MA from the University of North Carolina at Greensboro, studying with Alan Tate, Fred Chappell, and Robert Watson. Her first collection of poetry, *The Girl in the Midst of the Harvest,* was published in 1986. Nine more collections followed, culminating in a 2015 work titled *Intimacy.* During the 1990s, Byer served as poet in residence at Western Carolina University, the University of North Carolina at Greensboro, and Lenoir-Rhyne University and as North Carolina's first woman poet laureate from 2005 to 2009.

Adopting North Carolina as her literary home, Byer set almost all of her poems in the southern mountains; many focus on the lives of rural or small-town Appalachian women. A prominent theme in Byer's poetry is the presence of the past in the modern world, often represented by mountain women who may be ghosts. Drawing upon cultural traditions, community, and individual strengths, Byer creates female characters who serve as bridges between the agrarian past and contemporary mountain communities and families coping with change, as exemplified in "The Still Here and Now." Reliance on local knowledge, sometimes to the exclusion of outside opinions and influences, characterizes her poems. Byer's poetry also addresses the aging process, especially as experienced by women, both individually and as part of a larger community.

Full Moon

Full moon says look I am
over the pinebreak, says give me
your empty glass, pour
all you want, drink, look
out through your windows of ice,
through the eyes of your needles
observe how I climb, lay aside
what you weave on your looms

and see clouds fall away
like cold silk from your shoulders,
be quiet, hear the owl coming back
to the hayloft, shake loose
your long braids and rise up
from your beds, open

windows and curtains, let light
pour like water upon your heads,

all of you women who wait, raise
the shades, throw the shutters
wide, lean from your window ledge
into the great night that beckons
you, smile back at me
and so quietly nobody can hear you
but you, whisper, "Here am I."

The Still Here and Now

This fragrance I've never been able to name,
floating past on the skin of an eighteen year old,
still invites me to stand on the loggia again,
afternoon ticking down into dark,
asking *What am I doing here?*
lost among strangers with hair more
bouffant than mine, clothing more stylish.

Soon I'd learn the words for what I couldn't find
in my closet: Bass weejuns, madras, and Villager.
As for the name of that scent mingling
now with aroma of barbecue served on the porch,
it would have to be French, I imagined,
Ma Griffe, L'air du Temps, Insouciance,
not my mother's stale *Emeraude* clinging to me
from our goodbye embraces. Now dusk would be
shrouding my father's farm, doves mourning
out in the empty fields. I knew my way back
to all that. Don't think for a moment I didn't

wish I had the courage to set out for home.
But just then the sun set. The lamps bloomed
like storybook tulips. The campus unfolded
around me its labyrinth that like a medieval pilgrim
I'd walk until I reached the center where I'd find
no Rose Window as I saw later at Chartres
sifting light down upon us, but tall classroom windows
that shook when the Rivoli train passed. I still walk
those pathways at night, dreaming arias spiraling
forth from the practice rooms, each dorm a beehive
of desk lamps and phones ringing endlessly.

Time, say some physicists, does not exist.
Sheer Illusion. Each moment a still frame,
as though in a movie reel unspooling out to the edge
of the universe. Each now forever.
So let my first afternoon darken to first night.
Inside a small room overlooking a golf course
and woodland, a small bed waits,
heaped with my unpacked belongings.
I slowly walk toward it, my nostrils still seeking
a fragrance I now name *Siempre* because
the next day I sit down to learn Spanish,
not French. In my best cursive
I write my name on each blank sheet I'm given.
The ginkgo trees flutter their luminous handkerchiefs:
Buenos Dias, Bonjour, Wilkommen.

Again and again I come back
to the start of this journey. I stand looking down
at the fountain, as if to say *Here I am.*
There you are, water sings to our gathering voices.
The loggia is filling with girls wanting supper,
and now she whose fragrance awakened my senses
so many years back brushes by and the wake
of her passage still trembles around me.

Charles Wright

1935–

Charles Wright was born in West Tennessee. During his youth, his father's work as a civil engineer for the Tennessee Valley Authority required that the family move frequently, first to Corinth, Mississippi, and eventually to three Appalachian locations—Kingsport, Tennessee; Hiwassee Dam, North Carolina; and Oak Ridge, Tennessee. After graduating from Davidson College in 1957, Wright enlisted in the army; while stationed in Italy, he discovered Ezra Pound's *Cantos* and began reading and writing poetry. In 1963, he earned an MFA from the University of Iowa, studying under the poet Donald Justice. Wright taught for nearly two decades at the University of California, Irvine, and then at the University of Virginia in the foothills of the Blue Ridge Mountains.

Wright's poetry defies regional categorization. He grounds his poems not only in Appalachia but also in diverse geographic locations and intellectual traditions. In a wary search for spirituality, the poems explore the landscape and the flicker of the transcendent in the everyday. Wright has grouped nine of his collections into a single "trilogy of trilogies." Loosely modeled on Dante's *Divine Comedy,* the three trilogies' individual volumes thematically represent *inferno, purgatorio,* and *paradiso.* Wright connects his Blue Ridge backyard with ancient Chinese poetry, Egyptology, modern Italian painting, and the blues.

Wright has earned numerous awards for his work, including the Pulitzer Prize and the National Book Award. He was named poet laureate of the United States in 2014.

Appalachian Farewell

Sunset in Appalachia, bituminous bulwark
Against the western skydrop.
An Advent of gold and green, an Easter of ashes.

If night is our last address,
This is the place we moved from,
Backs on fire, our futures hard-edged and sure to arrive.

These are the towns our lives abandoned,
Wind in our faces,
The idea of incident like a box beside us on the Trailways' seat.

And where were we headed for?

The country of Narrative, that dark territory
Which spells out our stories in sentences, which gives them an end and
    beginning . . .

Goddess of Bad Roads and Inclement Weather, take down
Our names, remember us in the drip
And thaw of wintery mix, remember us when the light cools.

Help us never to get above our raising, help us
To hold hard to what was there,
Orebank and Reedy Creek, Surgoinsville down the line.

Morning Occurrence at Xanadu

Swallows are flying grief-circles over their featherless young,
Night-dropped and dead on the wooden steps.
The aspen leaves have turned gray,
                slapped by the hard, west wind.

Someone who knows how little he knows
Is like the man who comes to a clearing in the forest,
                      and sees the light spikes,
And suddenly senses how happy his life has been.

Gurney Norman

1937–

Gurney Norman was born in the coalfields of Virginia in 1937 and spent his childhood under the care of his grandparents in that state and Kentucky. As an undergraduate student at the University of Kentucky, Norman met future writers Wendell Berry, James Baker Hall, and Bobbie Ann Mason. Norman continued his study of writing at Stanford University. From 1963 to 1965 Norman worked as a reporter at the *Hazard Herald,* witnessing coal-mining strikes, strip mining, and grassroots activism.

While living on the West Coast, Norman published *Divine Right's Trip: A Novel of the Counterculture* in *The Last Whole Earth Catalog,* which was a source book for the back-to-the-land and counterculture movements. Revised slightly and republished in 1972 as *Divine Right's Trip: A Folk Tale,* the novel recounts the road trip of its stoned protagonist, David Ray, or Divine Right, from California across the United States to reconnect with his Kentucky mountain community and family.

Norman's oeuvre has spanned genres and media. In 1976 he released a spoken-word album, *Ancient Creek,* an original folktale examining environmental degradation in the coalfields. The tale was issued as a book in 2012. A collection of short stories, *Kinfolks,* also set in eastern Kentucky, appeared in 1976. Three stories from *Kinfolks* have been made into films. In 1990 Norman published *Book One from Crazy Quilt: A Novel-in-Progress,* and in 2020 *Allegiance: Stories* appeared.

Norman has mentored young writers and community members and supported the formation of the Affrilachian Poets. In 2009 and 2010 he served as the poet laureate of Kentucky.

FROM Divine Right's Trip: Novel of the Counterculture

Sunday: The Mine

Walking, body jolting, downhill. It's Sunday morning now and D.R. is on his way to explore the old abandoned coal mine he'd freaked out in his first day back at Trace Fork. Every time he has gone in or out of the hollow he has passed the ruins of the tipple, and it's been on his mind to crawl back in with a light of some kind and get a real look at the place. But 'til this morning he has always been on one specific errand or another, and there has been no chance to stop and look around.

But it's Sunday now, his day of rest and leisure. D.R. slept 'til almost ten, fixed himself some eggs and fried a slice of green tomato for breakfast, and now at about the hour the other people of the community are gathering for Sunday worship at the church, D.R. has set out from the house with this very special destination in mind.

It was an easy entrance this time. The little furrow he had made before was still there, a little tunnel through the rotting wood and dusty earth that led him to the center of the pile of beams and timbers across the drift mouth. Lying in the drift mouth, D.R. felt the cool air from the mine blow across his neck and face and arms. He smelled the coal-ness of the mine, the slate-taste-color flowing from the earth into his nostrils like some subtle gas that soothed and calmed his mind. Cool. Dark. Quiet, except for the sound of his own body crawling now, easing into the hole.

Then, when he was still again, it was utterly quiet, except for the sound of water slowly dripping, and except for the way the very silence was a kind of noise.

He was actually *there,* beneath the mountain, quiet in the bosom of the world. And conscious of it this time, there freely, there simply, without all the smoke and swirl. On his way down the hill to the mine his thought had been that he would go inside, maybe deep inside, and explore by the light of his candle. That impulse was gone now. Within thirty feet of the entrance D.R. found what he had come for. He hadn't known, really, just what he was going there for. But now he knew. It was just to sit a while, at rest in a cool, quiet place. That was all.

D.R. sat holding the candle in his hand, looking around him in the circle of light at the ragged posts on either side that held the roof in place.

The roof was slate, and the color of slate.

The walls were solid coal.

The floor was dusty near the walls, but in the center it was moist, with here and there a pool of water gathered from the dripping above.

He sat a long time without moving. There was the roof above, the floor beneath him, and the walls on either side. And the candle, in the center of the circle of the light.

After a while, without deciding to, D.R. leaned forward and set his candle in the mud beside a little pool near his feet. The reflection in the water was a perfect reproduction of the real, and D.R. marveled at it. One above, one below, the two candles shone together in the vastness of the cavern, and D.R. sat crosslegged on the floor in total fascination.

Behind him in the dark was the entrance to the mine, and the world of day beyond. Behind the candles was the deeper vastness of the mine.

Neither attracted him.

D.R. didn't want to go in motion either way.

He was where he was.

This was his place to be.

And that stayed true even after he blew the candle out.

Without deciding to, D.R. crawled forward and blew the candle out. And then, for longer than he knew, he sat there where he was, within and of the dark.

Monday: The Scheme

On Monday morning, D.R. went to work expanding Emmit's scheme.

He had tinkered with it and nursed it along, doing chores, in the time he had lived alone as Emmit's successor at the homeplace. But it wasn't until this particular

Monday morning that D.R. took up tools to enlarge and make his own mark on the work that Emmit had begun the last year of his life.

It was a scheme to reclaim the soil of the homeplace that had been killed by the mining on the slopes above the farm. Until Emmit started rebuilding the garden soil with rabbit shit behind the barn. The only living spot on the homeplace was the little triangle of green in front of the house, where some grass still grew and the poplar trees and the silver-leaf maple tree had leaves. It was only a matter of time before that little patch would be destroyed too, however, and the old family house along with it. For behind the house was a wall of dried mud and shale and blasted rock high as the roof in places. It had rolled down from the bench above, and then in two wet winters continued to slip until now it looked like a frozen ocean wave, waiting for another winter to melt it and send it flowing through the house and on across the yard toward the road and Trace Fork creek below.

But out near the barn, which stood a little uphill from the house and on a kind of roll in the slope, the overburden had stabilized. It had slipped as far as it was going to, and it was there that Emmit had chosen to make his effort and invest his work the last few months of his life.

The barn had been pushed off its foundation by the wash of overburden, flowing down. A rock big as a car, set rolling by a bulldozer up above, had smashed into the upper end of the barn and ripped a big hole in the wall. But in spite of the damage the barn was still a fairly solid structure, and when the mud had dried and settled Emmit had gone to work behind the barn, spreading all the manure and organic matter he could get, in an effort to create enough new topsoil to make a garden.

There'd been some old rotted manure in the stalls in the barn, left from the days when the Colliers kept cows and a workhorse. Emmit had shoveled it out and scattered some spoiled hay over it, and then worked that into the spot he intended to garden. Emmit's health was starting to fail him even then. That shoveling was among the last heavy work he tried. It was then he got his idea to raise rabbits in hutches as a source of manure for the garden he intended to create below the barn.

A friend of Emmit's on Upper Rockhouse Creek who raised rabbits for meat sold him the buck and the first two does. Emmit built hutches for them out of weather boarding he ripped off the back of the old doomed house he lived in. In a year's time he built eleven hutches from lumber off the house, and his herd grew to nearly fifty rabbits. He fed them commercial rabbit feed that Leonard hauled up the creek in the sled by the hundred-pound bag. It cost him, but the project was important to Emmit and he was willing to pay. Emmit received a disability pension from the government for his war wound, a hundred and forty some dollars every month. His personal expenses were rarely more than half of that, so he could afford his herd of rabbits. Leonard said that Emmit would eat a rabbit now and then, but what he kept them for was the first-class shit they produced. As it accumulated beneath the hutches he spread it on the sterile soil, and in a year's time he had redeemed a patch twenty feet by ten, and it was now growing short, single rows of lettuce, carrots, turnips, cucumbers, potatoes, beans, tomatoes and comfrey, and two longer rows of beans.

The rabbits were the central project in Emmit's scheme, but he had other things going too that he had worked at as he had the time, and strength. He had a worm pit going by one of the walls inside the barn. He'd built it when he first got his rabbits, filled it with manure and stocked it with five thousand red worms he'd ordered through the mail. A year later there were so many worms in it he was scooping them out by the pitchfork full and planting them in the garden rows to go to work on the mulch of shit and hay. But as the garden expanded and the rabbit population increased, Emmit wanted still more worms, and the extension of the pit was one of the projects he left unfinished when he died.

D.R. intended to finish that pit, and perhaps build another one along the facing wall.

It would not be possible to breed too many worms for the work he had in mind.

He also intended to go on dismantling the old house, to tear as much of it down for salvage as he possibly could before the coming winter's rains. Emmit had only taken boards off as high as he could comfortably reach. He had stripped the weather boarding from the lower portions of the house on three sides. With a ladder D.R. would be able to get three times as much lumber as Emmit had before he even touched the insides of the house. Emmit had worked the lumber with a hammer and a wrecking bar, pulling out the nails and trimming up their edges with a saw. As he cleaned the boards he had stacked them neatly in a corner of the barn. He had scavenged more lumber than he needed for his hutches. It wasn't clear what he had intended to do with the extra, but D.R. knew exactly what his own intentions were: he was going to remodel two of the stalls into a weather-tight room, and live in it that winter.

Two rooms, if he could get them done.

And three rooms, if Estelle would come to live there with him, and help him with the work.

If Estelle would come, they would convert one whole end of the barn into a house, and live there together by the rabbits and the worms and near the garden. They would get up early every morning and work to improve their place. If they wanted to, they could have a hundred hutches full of rabbits, and a million worms a year. They could have five hundred hutches full, and ten million worms at work in their manure, if they wanted to. If they wanted to, they could have a thousand hutches, one standing on every five square yards of that old ruined mountain, shitting pure worm food onto the ground, creating perfect lettuce beds and comfrey stands, and alfalfa fields galore.

They could do that if Estelle would come to live there with him.

They'd do all of that, and more.

If Estelle came.

Tuesday: The Magic Rabbit

Until the work was done, Tuesday was very much like Monday.

D.R. spent the morning turning under the manure he had spread the day before. He planted the little new ground with worms and humus from the pit, then worked a while tearing boards off the side of the house, dressing them and stacking them in the barn. Already the stack was waist-high and five boards across, enough to begin the work of converting the stalls to rooms. D.R. had an impulse to commence it then and there, but he knew he ought to talk to Leonard first. He could probably bang a room of some sort together by himself; but this was no crude project he had in mind. There are ways to go about certain kinds of work; there are rules in building and D.R. wanted to learn them. He wanted to do a good job, and know something truly useful when he was done. So he left the room alone 'til Leonard could come up to advise him on it, and worked some more in the afternoon on the new worm pit instead.

D.R. worked the whole day through, going from job to job. It tired his body in that satisfying way he'd come to relish the last few days, and after supper he was glad to sit in Emmit's rocking chair on the front porch and rest himself a while. His body sank into the chair and without reluctance let go of the day in anticipation of the night.

But D.R.'s mind wasn't ready for that yet. His mind was still excited, eager for some action, some outlet for the words that had built up through the day and gone unsaid. And so he went in the house and got his tablet and his pen, came back to his chair and wrote another letter to the Flash.

Dear Flash,

Here's what's going on:

Saturday I helped Leonard build a new pen for his hogs.

Sunday I crawled back in an old coal mine and watched a candle burn. Then I sat a long time in the dark, just being quiet.

Yesterday I spread rabbit shit on some old dead ground, and today spaded it in and sprinkled two gallons of red worms on it.

I also ripped a lot of boards off this old house I'm living in, and cleaned them up to use building myself a pad in a corner of the barn.

This house I'm living in is dead.

There are people living who have memories of it, and things that happened here. I remember things, and my sister, and there are a few others scattered around with old home movies in their brains they filmed in years gone by.

But the house itself is dead, and within the year it will be buried by about a million tons of mud and crap piled up behind it.

The barn is where the life is now. The garden is behind it. The worms live inside it in a pit. There's a chicken lot on one side, and on two sides all the rabbits in their hutches that I told you about. They're in those hutches right this minute, Flash, wondering when I'm going to come and live there as their neighbor.

This afternoon I stuck my head in one of the hutches and breathed awhile with the old momma and her litter. She's brown and white and solemn. The babies are about three weeks old, just starting to hop in and out of the nest box on their own, and sniff their mother's solid food. They're getting curious about the larger world. The old momma already knows. She's wise and proud and I think satisfied. We looked deeply into one another's eyes a time or two. I'm her bringer of food. That's my whole function in the world as far as she's concerned. As a matter of fact, it's my function in the world as far as I'm concerned too, except that what I know that she doesn't is that there's this whole larger scheme going on. What I know that she doesn't is that her produce—the manure; those thousands of little pellets that gather beneath her hutch—is food too, in this amazing scheme that my uncle started before he died, and that I'm now in the process of expanding.

It's a business, actually. I mean, just this very second I flashed that this enterprise of mine is actually a business. It's called the Magic Rabbit. The rabbits are my employees. They shit all week, around the clock, and I pay them with food. Our purpose is soil redemption. Salvation! Healing, by miracles, signs and wonders. The theme song of our commercials is "The Old Rugged Barn."

> On a hill far away,
> Stood an old rugged barn,
> The emblem of effort and pride.

Far out!

Come be my partner, Flash. Go find Estelle and bring her with you, and join the Magic Rabbit, Incorporated, and we'll get into soil salvation. First we'll save our own; we'll breed ten thousand rabbits and twenty million worms, and make this dead old hillside bloom. Then if other people feel like they've got a troubled soil, why let them call upon us, and we'll respond, with miracles, signs and wonders.

Faith, brother! Faith and rabbit shit, that's the theme!

> On a hill far away,
> Stood an old rugged barn,
> The emblem of effort and pride.
> How I love that old barn,
> So despised by the world,
> For the weirdness that happens inside.

You've got forty-eight hours to reply to this business proposal, Flash. Refuse it at the peril of your soil.

Your associate,
D.R.

Wednesday: Urge's Bath

When D.R. went off the hill late Wednesday to mail his letter to the Flash he was almost certain there'd be a letter waiting for him at the store. From the Flash, from Marcella, maybe even, by sudden cosmic arrangement, some word from Estelle. A post card, a note, *some*thing, from *some*body.

But there wasn't, and D.R. had to fight his disappointment down.

He bought a Coke from Mrs. Godsey, and after he had drunk it he bought a few more groceries to see him through the remainder of the week. Mrs. Godsey asked D.R. how he was and he said fine, but it was clear to her that he wasn't fine, and Mrs.

Godsey found herself worrying about D.R. a little. She tried to think of something to say that might make him feel better, but she didn't have any confidence in any of the words that occurred to her. She wrote his groceries up in the account book, and wished him a good day as he carried them out the door. But that wasn't enough, it wasn't enough at all and she felt bad about D.R. as the screen door slammed behind him.

Before he started back up the hill, D.R. went around in back of Godsey's store to look in Urge a minute. Urge had still not been given a thorough cleaning since he had been in Kentucky. A little at a time, D.R. had been taking stuff out of the bus and either throwing it away or carrying it with him up the hill. But the great bulk of their stuff still had not been touched, and in looking at it now D.R. felt suddenly inspired to pitch in then and there and clean it out once and for all.

As soon as he decided that's what he'd do, he felt instantly better, and better still when he started dumping junk out of the bus left and right. He spread their old stale sleeping bags on top of the bus to air. He dragged the mattress out and laid it on the grass in Leonard's yard. He collected the worst of the actual trash, the empty bottles, old apple cores, old smashed Kentucky Fried Chicken buckets, paper cups, old magazines, and grubby old paper napkins, and threw it all outside in a pile. Beside it he piled an old quilt that had had a chocolate milkshake spilled on it, and a towel too far gone to preserve. A pair of his own worn-out jeans wound up on the pile.

When he started coming to things he wasn't sure what he should do with, he began a separate pile. He found one of Estelle's blue sneakers, worn through at the little toe, laced with binder twine. He found a pair of her cut-off Levis, and three dirty socks. In a pillow case he found two of her special outfits, the gingham frontier dress, and the tie-dyed jumpsuit she'd made out of a mechanic's coveralls. He found their kitchen stuff in a box lined with the green sports section of the *San Francisco Chronicle*. The pots and pans and skillet and plastic plates and bowls were piled in with the Mazola Corn Oil, a box of salt, some spices in little cans, brown sugar in a jar, some old rice. He found their mangled copy of *The Whole Earth Catalog*, the paperback of *Stranger in a Strange Land* that Estelle had made so many notes in. And then, way back under the bed, face down on the floor, opened at the hexagram called Youthful Folly, D.R. found their *I Ching*.

Far out.

The *Ching*.

It was like running into an old friend. D.R. picked it up and dusted it off, and sat for a while holding it in his hand. He had been wishing for the *Ching*. It was time for him to start consulting it again. And maybe he could find some shit to order from the *Catalog*, too. The found books pleased D.R. enormously, and lifted him past the little desire that had begun to build in him to stop working on the bus and go flake out somewhere. D.R. was suddenly filled with tenderness and affection for Urge, and he went the whole way with his cleaning job.

When he had emptied the bus completely, he went to Roxie's house and borrowed a broom, and swept everywhere in the bus the broom could touch. Roxie showed him where the outdoor faucet was, and Leonard's hose. D.R. took the sleeping bags off the top, spread them out beside the mattress, and moved Urge until the hose could reach. And then he washed him good, all over, inside and out, with soap and warm water from Roxie's kitchen, and then a cold rinse with the hose. It was the first bath Urge had had since the west coast, and you could tell by the sound of the motor how much the old bus dug it. When he went back in the store to get some cardboard boxes, Mrs. Godsey told him he could store anything he wanted to in her basement. D.R. spent the rest of the afternoon sorting through the stuff that he would keep, getting it into boxes, four of them, and then stacking the boxes on the floor of Mrs. Godsey's basement.

Leonard came home from another day with the Grand Jury in town as D.R. was finishing up and asked if he would like to stick around for supper. D.R. said no thanks. He had a whole new fund of energy now, and he wanted to get back up on the hill with it, and use it well. He gathered up his books and his groceries and set out whistling, back up Trace Fork again.

Lisa Alther

1944–

Novelist and nonfiction writer Lisa Alther was reared in Kingsport, Tennessee. For college, she moved north to attend Wellesley College, where she received a BA in English in 1966. After college, she lived in Vermont, New York City, London, and Paris. In the 1990s, Alther returned to live part-time in Tennessee (Vermont remained her other home), and southern Appalachia became an increasingly central topic in her writing.

Alther's geographic transitions inform her work, as her characters frequently move from southern Appalachia to the North. The settings of *Kinflicks* (1976) include "Hullsport" (a fictionalized Kingsport), Massachusetts, and Vermont. *Original Sins* (1981) and *Five Minutes in Heaven* (1995) also have dual southern and northern settings.

One of the primary topics of Alther's often comic fiction is women's lives, especially women's sexuality. Alther was a pioneer in this regard; when the openly sexual *Kinflicks* was published in 1976, it caused a sensation. Alther was also ahead of her time in writing candidly about lesbianism.

In the following excerpt from *Kinflicks,* Alther examines adolescent courting rituals and satirizes hypocrisy in religion as she utilizes a rhetorical genre that has fascinated other southern Appalachian authors such as George Washington Harris—the revival preacher's sermon.

FROM Kinflicks

On Friday night we cruised Hull Street in Sparkplug with its top down, along with all the other students worthy of note from Hullsport High. We started at the church circle and drove slowly up Hull Street through three intersections to the train station, Sparkplug's engine idling with noisy impatience. At the train station we circled around and headed back down Hull Street to the church circle, with Joe Bob playfully revving the engine in competition with whoever was stopped next to us at the lights. Then we repeated the circuit.

The other cars accompanying us in this rite contained either established couples from school, or a bunch of unclaimed boys on the prowl, or a bunch of unclaimed girls trying to feign lack of interest. Occasionally, at a stop light, as though compelled by cosmic signals, half the unclaimed girls in one car would leap out and exchange places with half the unclaimed boys in another car in an adolescent version of fruit-basket-upside-down; it was as though each car were an atom exchanging electrons with another atom so as to neutralize their charges. From the air it would have looked like an intricate square-dance figure. It was the modern American adaptation of the old Spanish custom in which the single young people stroll around the town plaza eyeing each other with scarcely concealed desperation and desire, in full view of placid but watchful adults. In this case the chaperones were the highway patrolmen, not long ago students at Hullsport High themselves, but gone over now to the enemy. Taking their revenge on us for their no longer being young and unfettered by families, they liked nothing better than to ticket someone for driving in the wrong direction around the church circle. Their formerly athletic bodies gone to flab under their khaki shirts, they now cruised for a living and delighted in breaking up backseat tussles on dark dirt roads. As I soon learned—which was why I finally "went all the way," as the teen jargon discreetly put it, only when locked securely in the bomb shelter in my basement. But I'm getting ahead of myself again.

After half a dozen trips up and down Hull Street, Joe Bob pulled into a parking spot. We got out and sauntered along the sidewalk and looked in the shop windows at the latest in teen fashions, each subtly instructing the other on what outfits to buy next. We lingered long in front of the display windows of Sparks Shoe Store, owned by Joe Bob's father. We both agreed that it had the nicest selection of shoes in town. I noted with approval that, each time we came to a Dixie cup or a candy wrapper wantonly discarded, Joe Bob would pick it up, wrist weights clanking on the sidewalk, and deposit it in a trash can saying "Keep Hullsport Beautiful."

"You can hardly walk down the street anymore without tripping over somebody's garbage," I said appreciatively.

"Do whut?" he asked with a grin, chomping on his Juicy Fruit with his front teeth.

"Garbage. People throw it all over the place."

He nodded serenely, munching.

We got back into Sparkplug and did another half dozen circuits of Hull Street. After which we pulled into the parking lot of the most popular drive-in restaurant, the Dew Drop Inn. The Dew Drop had asphalt ridges in its parking lot to discourage its inclusion in our cruising route. Joe Bob went over the bumps reverently, careful not to scrape his chrome tail pipes. But the following year Clem and I raced over them on his cycle, leaning from side to side, like Eddie Holzer negotiating moguls on cross-country skis on the slopes of Vermont.

Through the microphone next to the car, Joe Bob ordered six half-pints of milk in waxed cardboard containers for himself and a small Seven-Up laced with cherry syrup for me. When the car hop brought them, Joe Bob said, "Thank you, ma'am," in his soft babyish voice with his mad contorted smile, all the time eyeing her ample chest out the window. Then he removed his wad of Juicy Fruit and stuck it on the dashboard. One after another, he opened the cartons and tossed down the milk, scarcely pausing for breath. He winked at me and smiled dementedly and said, "Trainin."

I had just begun to sip my cherry Seven-Up by the time he had drained all six of his milk containers. He stuck his Juicy Fruit back in his mouth and turned to watch me drink. The be-bosomed carhop whipped by, and Joe Bob's eyes followed her chest. Finally he said, "One time I was here with this cousin of mine. Jim, he's got him this Fairlane 500 with push-button windows. Well, that girl over yonder—I *think* it was that ole girl—anyhow, she brung him this pack of Pall Malls. The window was partway down, and ole Jim, he reached over to roll the window the rest of the way down. Well, he wasn't watchin what he was doin. He was lookin at his change to see if he'd have to break a bill to pay her." I nodded frantic encouragement. I'd never before heard him say so many words at one time. He took a deep breath and continued in his scarcely audible voice. "Well—it turns out he's not rollin the window *down*, he's rollin it *up!*" His grin was pushing his crew cut up. I hadn't caught the joke yet. I smiled uncertainly, hoping for a punch line.

After waiting for an appropriate amount of time, I said hesitantly, "I'm not sure I get it."

He blushed. "Well, she was standin right up against the window of the Fairlane, see? The window rolled up without him knowin it, and he like to chopped off her— you know." I flinched reflexlike, imagining the pain of having a push-button window close on my breasts; then I too blushed at this open reference to crucial female anatomy, even though it was obviously the cornerstone of our impending relationship; then I grinned idiotically as the tale began to appeal to me; then I smiled sweetly at Joe Bob for his delicacy in referring to tits as "you know."

Joe Bob pushed back his left wrist weight and glanced at his watch. He sat up straight, hurriedly flashed his headlights, and started up the motor with a roar. The carhop, blessed with chest, sauntered out to retrieve the tray. As Joe Bob threw the car into gear and backed out, he said anxiously, "I like to forgot trainin. Lord, Coach'll kill me!" We roared down Hull Street in the direction of my house.

"What do you mean?" I demanded, injured.

"Got to be in bed by ten," he notified me grimly, weaving Sparkplug in and out of the frivolous cruising traffic.

"You're *kidding!*" My heart sank. A ten o'clock curfew definitely dampened the possibilities for lingering exchanges of sweet nothings. He dumped me at the foot of our driveway and left me to find my own way through the magnolia thicket to the house.

Our courtship was like a silent movie. In those days before the raising of the public's seat-belt consciousness, the progress of a couple's relationship could be gauged by the distance between them as they drove down the street. Who knows how many budding romances have been nipped by the surge in popularity of bucket seats? I started out that first night of cruising crammed next to the door with my hand on the handle so that I could leap out if Joe Bob were transformed into a rape-strangler. But he didn't so much as shake my hand for weeks, first to my relief, and eventually to my distress. Gradually, I began scooting over slightly on the seat after he let me in and before he got back around to his side. In a month's time I had worked my way over almost to his side, under the guise of constantly tuning the radio.

And then it happened! We were at the city-wide Preaching Mission, being held in the cavernous gymnasium of the Civic Auditorium, which, on less sacred occasions, hosted roller derbies and wrestling matches. Joe Bob and I sat on bleachers along one wall with the rest of the student population. The adults sat in rows of folding chairs set up across the floor. It was a Friday night, the climax of the week-long mission.

The speaker tonight was Brother Buck Basket from Birmingham, Alabama, come all the way to Hullsport just to spread the good news to his Tennessee brothers and sisters that Death had lost its sting. Joe Bob was all ears. Brother Buck was his idol. He had been a famous All-American guard from the University of Alabama a decade earlier. And then a Baltimore Colt, until he had run into a goal post and suffered a head injury which had left him unconscious for days and then bound up in gauze for a month or more, with every football fan in the country in a frenzy of anxiety. Upon returning to the land of the living, however, Brother Buck had renounced his gridiron glory and dedicated his life to Christ.

His massive, dedicated frame dwarfed the podium. He wore a tan western-cut suit and a string tie and cowboy boots. I knew that soon Joe Bob would own a tan western suit and a string tie.

"*Death! Where is your sting? Grave, where is your victory?*" Brother Buck thundered. The steel I beams that held up the roof seemed to tremble. He was holding up one fist in a gesture of defiance and was gazing intently at a spot near the rear ceiling. All of us automatically turned in that direction, expecting to see at least the Four Horsemen of the Apocalypse, if not the Four Horsemen of Notre Dame.

"Ah know what you think," he assured us quietly, returning his fist to the podium and his fervid blue gaze to the audience. "You think: It don't matter none *what* kind of life ah live. Ah can read these here pornographic books, and look at nasty pictures, and defile my body with all manner of vile corruption. Ah can stay up all night drinkin, and ah can run round with fallen women and sleep through church on Sundays. It don't matter none. That's what you think, don't you, now? Admit it right here tonight to ole Brother Buck. You think, ah'd better just live it up today cause tomorrow ah may lie dyin in a pool of black gore, with mah bones smashed and pokin up through mah flesh; with mah guts trailin out and tangled round mah twisted car; with mah brains dribbled acrost the highway like cornmeal mush . . ."

I glanced wearily at Joe Bob. I'd had enough of this from my Cassandran parents to last me a lifetime, which lifetime was apparently predestined to brevity and a bloody ending. But Joe Bob was grinning insanely and was mincing his Juicy Fruit, thrilled at this proximity to his hero.

". . . and tomorrow that there bomb ah'm always hearin about will go off and blow us all sky high in little red pieces, like chaff before the whirlwind. Tomorrow mah plane flight will smash into the side of some mountain, and there'll be jagged bloody chunks of mah body strewn all acrost the forest floor for the wild animals to feast on. Tomorrow some madman with a telescopic sight will use mah eyes for target practice. So ah'd better live it up now while ah can. Ah'd best titillate mah flesh ever which way, cause this breath ah'm takin"—he paused to take a deep illustrative breath—"may be mah last.

"Oh, Brother Buck *knows* how most of you folks live, friends." The suspicion that this might be true, that Brother Buck really *did* know all about my feminine napkins and my padded bra, filled me with the same outraged sense of exposure I used to feel as a child at the line in "Santa Claus Is Coming to Town" that goes, "He sees you when you are sleeping. / He knows if you're awake."

"*How* does Brother Buck know? He knows because he's been there hissef. He knows because he's thought corrupt thoughts. Because he's broken heavenly trainin and lived a pre-verse life hissef, friends, usin ever chanct he got to provoke tinglin sensations in his mortal flesh. Yes, Brother Buck has lived a lustful life full of sin!

"When he played pro ball, he went to all the fancy places where wicked women sold theirselves up to vile corruption The temptations were many and wondrous to behold for a country boy from Alabama, and Brother Buck failed the test, friends. Yes, he did. He tried em all." I looked over at Joe Bob and discovered that a thin line of saliva was drooling out the corner of his mouth as he munched his Juicy Fruit. His eyes were gleaming.

"But do you *know* what happened to Brother Buck with his wretched ways, friends? He ran into the goal post one night on a football field in Baltimore, Maryland. Yes, he did. And he landed up in a Baltimore hospital. Yes, friends, ah lay with mah entire head wrapped up in bandages for one solid month, alone there in mah private darkness, unable to speak, unable to see. And that solitude, brothers and sisters, that lonely month there in the dark on mah back in bed all alone, was the turning point in mah preverse and sinful life!

"Ah want to tell you what happened to me as ah lay there, not knowin if ah'd ever see again, much less play ball." We were all hanging on the edges of our bleachers waiting for the punch line. "*Jesus* came to me! Yes, he did! He come to me and He says, 'Brother Buck, don't you fret none, son. We're gonna clean out the temple of your soul, buddy, that body of yours whose pleasures you set so much store by. The *devil* has been lyin in wait for you, brother, behind them rhinestone pasties. But ah got plans for you on *mah* team, fella!'

"And that's why ah'm here tonight, friends, Brother Buck right here in—ah—here with all you fine people tonight in—uh—this lovely town of—uh—." He turned around quickly to the clerical-collared men on the stage behind him. Then he turned back around and said casually, "Here in Hullsport, Tennessee. Yes, ah'm here to let you all in on a li'l ole secret."

Joe Bob and I strained forward in our seats, since all the world loves a secret. As we did so, our thighs rubbed together. I hastily moved my legs to one side—and bumped into the thighs of the strange boy next to me. I appeared to have no choice but to allow my left thigh to nestle up against Joe Bob's muscled right one. We sat rigid, pretending not to notice, as Brother Buck told us his secret in a voice that boomed to the rafters: "*You don't have to die, friends!*"

He paused until the echo faded, then continued in a shout: "That body you're abusin, buddy, with your liquor and your lusts, that *body,*" he roared, then instantly dropped his voice almost to a whisper so that the audience strained forward as one to hear him, "is the sanctuary of your soul." He stopped, sweat glistening on his forehead beneath his light brown crew cut. "*Your soul!*" he shouted again, so that everyone sat back startled. "The Bible says, 'Know ye not that your body is the temple of the Holy Ghost which is in you, which ye have of God? Ye are not your own.'"

By now Joe Bob's and my thighs were pressed together tightly and were generating hot secrets within our respective soul sanctuaries.

Suddenly Brother Buck burst into the feverish pitch of revival preaching. It was like a thunderstorm finally breaking after hours of black clouds amassing. "Ah came here to save *souls!* Ah came here to share with you mah joy in the *Lord!* Yes, Jesus!" Brother Buck could have been quoting stock prices now and none of us would have noticed.

"'The Lord is mah *Shepherd!* Ah shall not want!' Yes! The Lord says, He says in that last awful day of reckonin, brothers, on that day when your lungs fill up with blood, yes, and you can't call out to no one to come hep you! Yes! On that day, friends, when the film of death draws acrost your eyes and you can't *see* the loved ones around you! Yes! On that *day,* friends, when your ears are roarin with the sound of your own organs collapsin inside you! Yes! On that *day,* oh dear God that *day,* when your teeth won't stop chatterin from fear, and your bones turn to jelly and your legs collapse underneath you! Oh, *friends!* That day when your precious body is crumblin into dust and swirlin away! Yes! 'Behold!' Isaiah says. 'Behold the Lord maketh the earth empty.' Yes! 'And wastes it, and turns it upside down, and scatters abroad the inhabitants thereof!' Oh *yes,* sweet Jesus! 'The land shall be utterly *spoiled,*' Isaiah says, 'for the earth is *defiled* under the inhabitants thereof!' Yes, praise God!"

The emotional climate in the auditorium was rising now, particularly in the immediate vicinity of Joe Bob and me. Our thighs were positively aglow. People in the audience were starting to shout back at Brother Buck: "Yes, Jesus!" "Praise God!"

"Think about it," he invited us, suddenly quiet. He was playing us as though we were hooked fish, giving us emotional slack now in order to reel us in more quickly later. "You've broken trainin all your life. Your body's a stinkin sewer of ever vile corruption you can name. Your team has lost the game because you're all just reekin with sin. You're slouchin toward the dressin room thinkin bout the hot shower that's gonna feel so great on your bruised body. But as you walk into the locker room, friends, you hear your teammates weepin and howlin with anguish.

"What's waitin for you there in your dressin room, friends! Do you know? Let's listen to the Bible and see," he suggested, holding up a black book as though fading back to pass it into the audience. Flipping through it nonchalantly, he stopped and read slowly, 'Behold,' Isaiah says, 'the Lord will come with fire, and his chariots like a whirlwind, to render his anger with fury, and his rebuke with flames of fire.'"

His tempo and pitch were picking up again. "'The people shall be as the burnins of lime, as thorns cut up shall they be burnt in the fire,' says Isaiah. Oh dear God! 'Ah will tread them in mine anger!' Yes! 'Ah will trample them in mah fury!' Yes! 'Their blood shall be sprinkled upon mah garments, and ah will stain all my raiment!' Oh sweet Jesus! 'They shall go forth, friends, yes, and they shall look upon the carcasses of the men that have transgressed against me,' says the Lord. 'Their *worm* shall not die, neither shall their *fire* be quenched!' No! 'And they shall be an *abhorrin* unto all flesh!' Oh woe! *Woe!* Listen to this from Corinthians, brothers and sisters, ah beg of you! 'Be not deceived: neither fornicators, no, nor idolaters, nor adulterers, nor effeminate, nor abusers of themselves, shall inherit the kingdom of God! *The body is not for fornication but for the Lord!* Yes, praise Jesus! '*Know ye not* that your bodies are the members of Christ?' *Know ye* not? 'Shall I then take the members of Christ and make them the members of an harlot? *God forbid,'* says Corinthians! Rather, 'Flee fornication!'"

Joe Bob and I were unable to sit still. Blood was throbbing in my thigh along the area where it contacted Joe Bob's. The entire audience was squirming. If Brother Buck had told us all to go burn down the Major's munitions factory, we probably would have.

Sweat was dripping from Brother Buck's face as though he had been standing under a shower. "On that horrible last day, friends, when the losin team is howlin in the locker room, what about the winnin team? What happens to them, do you think? 'We need not fear,' says the Psalm, 'though the earth be moved, and though the hills be carried into the midst of the sea; though the waters thereof rage and swell,' friends; 'though the mountains shake at the tempest. We need not fear.' *We need not fear!"* he announced, his face expressing delighted astonishment through its layer of sweat. "'Be not afraid of them that kill the body and after that have no more that they can do!'

"And so Brother Buck pleads with you tonight, folks: Turn your back on the corruption of this vile and hateful world, and purify yourself to be worthy of the next. Yes! It's not too late to swap teams if you start followin trainin tonight. 'Flesh and blood cannot inherit the Kingdom, neither doth corruption inherit incorruption. But when the corruptible shall have put on incorruption, the mortal shall have put on immortality.'

"Do it tonight, friends. Brother Buck begs you. He pleads with you from the depths of his heart. Put on incorruption. Put it on tonight. 'Cause then only shall be brought to pass the sayin that is written, 'Death is swallowed up in victory. *O death, where is thy sting? O grave, where is thy victory?'"*

In an exhausted voice, Brother Buck invited everyone who intended to lead a new life as a teammate of Christ to come forward. "Do it tonight, brothers and sisters," he intoned as Joe Bob and I walked automatonlike toward the stage. "Give up your wicked ways and inherit eternity. Shed dishonor and put on glow-ry." If he had invited us to come sip his bathwater, as medieval messianic figures did, Joe Bob and I would have gone forward as obediently. We joined about two hundred people at the foot of the stage.

"Take the hand of the person on either side of you, brothers and sisters," he panted, loosening his string tie as though it were a noose. Joe Bob and I obediently clutched hands, and at that point the dove descended. We stood there, Joe Bob and I, our clasped hands sweating and trembling.

"Let us pray," Brother Buck instructed. "Father, our Coach, hep us, Father, to run Thy plays as Thou wouldst have them run. Knowing, Lord, that Christ Jesus Thy quarterback is there beside us with ever yard we gain, callin those plays and runnin that interference. Hep us, Lord, to understand that winnin ball games depends on followin trainin. Hep us not to abuse our minds and bodies with those worldly temptations that are off-limits to the teammates of Christ . . . " Joe Bob was stroking my palm with his finger tips. Shivering sensations were running up my arm like an electric current and were grounding out somewhere below the navy stretch straw belt of my Villager shirtwaist.

" . . . and hep us, Celestial Coach, to understand that the water boys of life are ever bit as precious in Thy sight as the All-American guards. And when that final gun goes off, Lord, mayst Thou welcome us to the locker room of the home team with a slap on the back and a hearty, 'Well done, my good and faithful tailback.'

"A-man," Brother Buck added as an afterthought.

"A-man," echoed the rest of us.

"All right, you can drop hands now," Brother Buck said sotto voce to the group up front. Regretfully, Joe Bob and I peeled apart our sticky palms. "Now what ah hope," Brother Buck said into the microphone, "is that some of the young people in this group down front here—and any of the rest of you kids in the audience who didn't bother to come down because you've already received the Lord as your Savior—these fine kids, ah hope, will form the nucleus of a Brother Buck Teen Team for Jesus, right here in—ah—Hullsport, Tennessee. There are groups all *over* the South, and ah think you'll find that they're the comin thing in our high schools. Soo . . . that's all for tonight, friends. And God love you!" He waved to the audience, who stood up with much rumbling of folding chairs.

Several dozen of us remained down front—Hullsport's saving remnant. Most were Joe Bob's fellow football players and their girl friends. Joe Bob squared his massive shoulders and walked boldly over to Brother Buck, who was squatting on the edge of the stage talking to prospective Teen Team members.

Joe Bob introduced himself and pointed to me saying, "And this here's my friend Virginia. I'm—uh—the captain of the Hullsport Pirates." He looked at the floor with modesty and minced his Juicy Fruit with his front teeth.

Brother Buck said thoughtfully, "Just a minute now. Joe Bob Sparks, you said? Why, yes, ah do believe ah've heard of you, son." Joe Bob glowed. "You've had a good season so far, as I recall."

"Six and O," Joe Bob confirmed.

By the time I dragged him away, he had signed us both up for the Teen Team for Jesus, Hullsport branch.

The next night at the Family Drive-In Joe Bob and I were watching a movie called *Girls in Chains,* to which no one under eighteen was supposed to have been admitted. It involved a gang of female motorcyclists who roared around cutting the safety chains off the cycles of their male counterparts and then hiding the cycles in clever places, like in the trunk of a police cruiser.

Joe Bob took his right hand off the steering wheel, which he'd been gripping tightly. Without taking his eyes off the screen, he reached down and groped for my hand, which lay panting, palm up, on the seat next to him. After all, Brother Buck himself had told us to join hands. We knitted our fingers together, both studying the screen intently and trying to pretend that nothing out of the ordinary was happening. His huge hand with its stove-in knuckles enfolded my small skilled flag-twirling hand like a pod around a pea.

This was my first experience with the concept that I have now, after extensive experimentation, formulated into a postulate: It is possible to generate an orgasm at any spot on the human body. Our hands, thus interlocked, took on lives of their own.

They trembled and shuddered for the rest of the movie, as Joe Bob and I, though pretending to watch the antics of the girls and their safety chains, made our captive hands the focus of our entire existence.

The movie over, neither of us knew how to disengage ourselves in a nonrejecting fashion, although by now both palms were slimy with stale sweat. Joe Bob shifted into reverse, using our clasped hands as a unit. On the way home I asked, "Do you ever think about stuff like what Brother Buck was saying last night?"

"Naw, never do," Joe Bob replied proudly, mincing his Juicy Fruit daintily.

Jayne Anne Phillips

1952–

Novelist and short story writer Jayne Anne Phillips was born in Buckhannon, West Virginia. She began writing at the age of nine, inventing wild adventure stories about herself and her friends, before turning to poetry in her teens at the encouragement of her teachers. She earned a BA in 1974 from West Virginia University and an MA in 1978 from the University of Iowa, where she studied at the Iowa Writers' Workshop, publishing two collections of short stories while still a graduate student. With the publication of her critically acclaimed short story collection *Black Tickets* (1979), Phillips established herself as an important voice on the American literary scene.

Although Phillips has lived most of her life outside Appalachia, teaching creative writing at universities, including Harvard and Brandeis, and founding an MFA program at Rutgers University–Newark, the Appalachian region informs the subject matter of much of her fiction. Phillips is sometimes considered a member of the school of dirty realism, a subset of minimalism, along with non-Appalachian writers such as Raymond Carver and Tobias Wolff. Disintegration of the family unit, personal isolation, the abandonment of traditional gender roles, raw sensuality, and changes in American society in the wake of the Vietnam War are among Phillips's concerns. Her working-class characters seek escape and transcendence while grappling with everyday tragedy in a world coming unhinged.

In "Souvenir," which comes from the collection *Black Tickets,* Phillips examines the distances family members must bridge in order to rejoin one another and come to terms with sickness and death.

Souvenir

Kate always sent her mother a card on Valentine's Day. She timed the mails from wherever she was so that the cards arrived on February 14th. Her parents had celebrated the day in some small fashion, and since her father's death six years before, Kate made a gesture of compensatory remembrance. At first, she made the cards herself: collage and pressed grasses on construction paper sewn in fabric. Now she settled for art reproductions, glossy cards with blank insides. Kate wrote in them with colored inks, "You have always been my Valentine," or simply "Hey, take care of yourself." She might enclose a present as well, something small enough to fit into an envelope; a sachet, a perfumed soap, a funny tintype of a prune-faced man in a bowler hat.

This time, she forgot. Despite the garish displays of paper cupids and heart-shaped boxes in drugstore windows, she let the day nearly approach before remembering. It was too late to send anything in the mail. She called her mother long-distance at night when the rates were low.

"Mom? How are you?"

"It's you! How are *you?*" Her mother's voice grew suddenly brighter; Kate recognized a tone reserved for welcome company. Sometimes it took a while to warm up.

"I'm fine," answered Kate. "What have you been doing?"

"Well, actually I was trying to sleep."

"Sleep? You should be out setting the old hometown on fire."

"The old hometown can burn up without me tonight."

"Really? What's going on?"

"I'm running in-service training sessions for the primary teachers." Kate's mother was a school superintendent. "They're driving me batty. You'd think their brains were rubber."

"They are," Kate said. "Or you wouldn't have to train them. Think of them as a salvation, they create a need for your job."

"Some salvation. Besides, your logic is ridiculous. Just because someone needs training doesn't mean they're stupid."

"I'm just kidding. But *I'm* stupid. I forgot to send you a Valentine's card."

"You did? That's bad. I'm trained to receive one. They bring me luck."

"You're receiving a phone call instead," Kate said. "Won't that do?"

"Of course," said her mother, "but this is costing you money. Tell me quick, how are you?"

"Oh, you know. Doctoral pursuits. Doing my student trip, grooving with the professors."

"The professors? You'd better watch yourself."

"It's a joke, Mom, a joke. But what about you? Any men on the horizon?"

"No, not really, A married salesman or two asking me to dinner when they come through the office. Thank heavens I never let those things get started."

"You should do what you want to," Kate said.

"Sure," said her mother. "And where would I be then?"

"I don't know. Maybe Venezuela."

"They don't even have plumbing in Venezuela."

"Yes, but their sunsets are perfect, and the villages are full of dark passionate men in blousy shirts."

"That's your department, not mine."

"Ha," Kate said, "I wish it were my department. Sounds a lot more exciting than teaching undergraduates."

Her mother laughed. "Be careful," she said. "You'll get what you want. End up sweeping a dirt floor with a squawling baby around your neck."

"A dark baby," Kate said, "to stir up the family blood."

"Nothing would surprise me," her mother said as the line went fuzzy. Her voice was submerged in static, then surfaced. "Listen," she was saying, "Write to me. You seem so far away."

They hung up and Kate sat watching the windows of the neighboring house. The curtains were transparent and flowered and none of them matched. Silhouettes of the window frames spread across them like single dark bars. Her mother's curtains were all the same, white cotton hemmed with a ruffle, tiebacks blousing the cloth into identical shapes. From the street it looked as if the house was always in order.

Kate made a cup of strong Chinese tea, turned the lights off, and sat holding the warm cup in the dark. Her mother kept no real tea in the house, just packets of instant diabetic mixture which tasted of chemical sweetener and had a bitter aftertaste. The packets sat on the shelf next to her mother's miniature scales. The scales were white. Kate saw clearly the face of the metal dial on the front, its markings and trembling needle. Her mother weighed portions of food for meals: frozen broccoli, slices of plastic-wrapped Kraft cheese, careful chunks of roast beef. A dog-eared copy of *The Diabetic Diet* had remained propped against the salt shaker for the last two years.

Kate rubbed her forehead. Often at night she had headaches. Sometimes she wondered if there were an agent in her body, a secret in her blood making ready to work against her.

The phone blared repeatedly, careening into her sleep. Kate scrambled out of bed, naked and cold, stumbling, before she recognized the striped wallpaper of her bedroom and realized the phone was right there on the bedside table, as always. She picked up the receiver.

"Kate?" said her brother's voice. "It's Robert. Mom is in the hospital. They don't know what's wrong but she's in for tests."

"Tests? What's happened? I just talked to her last night."

"I'm not sure. She called the neighbors and they took her to the emergency room around dawn." Robert's voice still had that slight twang Kate knew was disappearing from her own. He would be calling from his insurance office, nine o'clock their time, in his thick glasses and wide, perfectly knotted tie. He was a member of the million-dollar club and his picture, tiny, the size of a postage stamp, appeared in the Mutual of Omaha magazine. His voice seemed small too over the distance. Kate felt heavy and dulled. She would never make much money, and recently she had begun wearing make-up again, waking in smeared mascara as she had in high school.

"Is Mom all right?" she managed now. "How serious is it?"

"They're not sure," Robert said. "Her doctor thinks it could have been any of several things, but they're doing X rays."

"Her doctor *thinks*? Doesn't he know? Get her to someone else. There aren't any doctors in that one-horse town."

"I don't know about that," Robert said defensively. "Anyway, I can't force her. You know how she is about money."

"Money? She could have a stroke and drop dead while her doctor wonders what's wrong."

"Doesn't matter. You know you can't tell her what to do."

"Could I call her somehow?"

"No, not yet. And don't get her all worried. She's been scared enough as it is. I'll tell her what you said about getting another opinion, and I'll call you back in a few hours when I have some news. Meanwhile, she's all right, do you hear?"

The line went dead with a click and Kate walked to the bathroom to wash her face. She splashed her eyes and felt guilty about the Valentine's card. Slogans danced in her head like reprimands. *For A Special One. Dearest Mother. My Best Friend.* Despite Robert, after breakfast she would call the hospital.

She sat a long time with her coffee, waiting for minutes to pass, considering how many meals she and her mother ate alone, similar times of day, hundreds of miles apart. Women by themselves. The last person Kate had eaten breakfast with had been someone she'd met in a bar. He was passing through town. He liked his fried eggs gelatinized in the center, only slightly runny, and Kate had studiously looked away as he ate. The night before he'd looked down from above her as he finished and she still moved under him. "You're still wanting," he'd said. "That's nice." Mornings now, Kate saw her own face in the mirror and was glad she'd forgotten his name. When she looked at her reflection from the side, she saw a faint etching of lines beside her mouth. She hadn't slept with anyone for five weeks, and the skin beneath her eyes had taken on a creamy darkness.

She reached for the phone but drew back. It seemed bad luck to ask for news, to push toward whatever was coming as though she had no respect for it.

Standing in the kitchen last summer, her mother had stirred gravy and argued with her.

"I'm thinking of your own good, not mine," she'd said. "Think of what you put yourself through. And how can you feel right about it? You were born here, I don't care what you say." Her voice broke and she looked, perplexed, at the broth in the pan.

"But, hypothetically," Kate continued, her own voice unaccountably shaking, "if I'm willing to endure whatever I have to, do you have a right to object? You're my mother. You're supposed to defend my choices."

"You'll have enough trouble without choosing more for yourself. Using birth control that'll ruin your insides, moving from one place to another. I can't defend your choices, I can't even defend myself against you." She wiped her eyes on a napkin.

"Why do you have to make me feel so guilty?" Kate said, fighting tears of frustration. "I'm not attacking you."

"You're not? Then who are you talking to?"

"Oh Mom, give me a break."

"I've tried to give you more than that," her mother said. "I know what your choices are saying to me." She set the steaming gravy off the stove. "You may feel very differently later on. It's just a shame I won't be around to see it."

"Oh? Where will you be?"

"Floating around on a fleecy cloud."

Kate got up to set the table before she realized her mother had already done it.

The days went by. They'd gone shopping before Kate left. Standing at the cash register in an antique shop on Main Street, they bought each other pewter candle holders. "A souvenir," her mother said. "A reminder to always be nice to yourself. If you live alone you should eat by candlelight."

"Listen," Kate said, "I eat in a heart-shaped tub with bubbles to my chin. I sleep on satin sheets and my mattress has a built-in massage engine. My overnight guests are impressed. You don't have to tell me about the solitary pleasures."

They laughed and touched hands.

"Well," her mother said. "If you like yourself, I must have done something right."

Robert didn't phone until evening. His voice was fatigued and thin. "I've moved her to the university hospital," he said. "They can't deal with it at home."

Kate waited, saying nothing. She concentrated on the toes of her shoes. They needed shining. *You never take care of anything*, her mother would say.

"She has a tumor in her head." He said it firmly, as though Kate might challenge him.

"I'll take a plane tomorrow morning," Kate answered, "I'll be there by noon."

Robert exhaled. "Look," he said, "don't even come back here unless you can keep your mouth shut and do it my way."

"Get to the point."

"The point is they believe she has a malignancy and we're not going to tell her. I almost didn't tell you." His voice faltered. "They're going to operate but if they find what they're expecting, they don't think they can stop it."

For a moment there was no sound except an oceanic vibration of distance on the wire. Even that sound grew still. Robert breathed. Kate could almost see him, in a booth at the hospital, staring straight ahead at the plastic instructions screwed to the narrow rectangular body of the telephone. It seemed to her that she was hurtling toward him.

"I'll do it your way," she said.

The hospital cafeteria was a large room full of orange Formica tables. Its southern wall was glass. Across the highway, Kate saw a small park modestly dotted with amusement rides and bordered by a narrow band of river. How odd, to build a children's park across from a medical center. The sight was pleasant in a cruel way. The rolling lawn of the little park was perfectly, relentlessly green.

Robert sat down. Their mother was to have surgery in two days.

"After it's over," he said, "they're not certain what will happen. The tumor is in a bad place. There may be some paralysis."

"What kind of paralysis?" Kate said. She watched him twist the green-edged coffee cup around and around on its saucer.

"Facial. And maybe worse."

"You've told her this?"

He didn't answer.

"Robert, what is she going to think if she wakes up and—"

He leaned forward, grasping the cup and speaking through clenched teeth. "Don't you think I thought of that?" He gripped the sides of the table and the cup rolled onto the carpeted floor with a dull thud. He seemed ready to throw the table after it, then grabbed Kate's wrists and squeezed them hard.

"You didn't drive her here," he said. "She was so scared she couldn't talk. How much do you want to hand her at once?"

Kate watched the cup sitting solidly on the nubby carpet.

"We've told her it's benign," Robert said, "that the surgery will cause complications, but she can learn back whatever is lost."

Kate looked at him. "Is that true?"

"They hope so."

"We're lying to her, all of us, more and more." Kate pulled her hands away and Robert touched her shoulder.

"What do *you* want to tell her, Kate? 'You're fifty-five and you're done for'?"

She stiffened. "Why put her through the operation at all?"

He sat back and dropped his arms, lowering his head. "Because without it she'd be in bad pain. Soon." They were silent, then he looked up. "And anyway," he said softly, "we don't *know*, do we? She may have a better chance than they think."

Kate put her hands on her face. Behind her closed eyes she saw a succession of blocks tumbling over.

They took the elevator up to the hospital room. They were alone and they stood close together. Above the door red numerals lit up, flashing. Behind the illuminated shapes droned an impersonal hum of machinery.

Then the doors opened with a sucking sound. Three nurses stood waiting with a lunch cart, identical covered trays stacked in tiers. There was a hot bland smell, like warm cardboard. One of the women caught the thick steel door with her arm and smiled. Kate looked quickly at their rubber-soled shoes. White polish, the kind that rubs off. And their legs seemed only white shapes, boneless and two-dimensional, stepping silently into the metal cage.

She looked smaller in the white bed. The chrome side rails were pulled up and she seemed powerless behind them, her dark hair pushed back from her face and her forearms delicate in the baggy hospital gown. Her eyes were different in some nearly imperceptible way; she held them wider, they were shiny with a veiled wetness. For a moment the room seemed empty of all else; there were only her eyes and the dark blossoms of the flowers on the table beside her. Red roses with pine. Everyone had sent the same thing.

Robert walked close to the bed with his hands clasped behind his back, as though afraid to touch. "Where did all the flowers come from?" he asked.

"From school, and the neighbors. And Katie." She smiled.

"FTD," Kate said. "Before I left home. I felt so bad for not being here all along."

"That's silly," said their mother. "You can hardly sit at home and wait for some problem to arise."

"Speaking of problems," Robert said, "the doctor tells me you're not eating. Do I have to urge you a little?" He sat down on the edge of the bed and shook the silverware from its paper sleeve.

Kate touched the plastic tray. "Jell-O and canned cream of chicken soup. Looks great. We should have brought you something."

"They don't *want* us to bring her anything," Robert said. "This is a hospital. And I'm sure your comments make her lunch seem even more appetizing."

"I'll eat it!" said their mother in mock dismay. "Admit they sent you in here to stage a battle until I gave in."

"I'm sorry," Kate said. "He's right."

Robert grinned. "Did you hear that? She says I'm right. I don't believe it." He pushed the tray closer to his mother's chest and made a show of tucking a napkin under her chin.

"Of course you're right, dear." She smiled and gave Kate an obvious wink.

"Yeah," Robert said, "I know you two. But seriously, you eat this. I have to go make some business calls from the motel room."

Their mother frowned. "That motel must be costing you a fortune."

"No, it's reasonable," he said. "Kate can stay for a week or two and I'll drive back and forth from home. If you think this food is bad, you should see the meals in that motel restaurant." He got up to go, flashing Kate a glance of collusion. "I'll be back after supper."

His footsteps echoed down the hallway. Kate and her mother looked wordlessly at each other, relieved. Kate looked away guiltily. Then her mother spoke, apologetic. "He's so tired," she said. "He's been with me since yesterday."

She looked at Kate, then into the air of the room. "I'm in a fix," she said. "Except for when the pain comes, it's all a show that goes on without me. I'm like an invalid, or a lunatic."

Kate moved close and touched her mother's arms. "That's all right, we're going to get you through it. Someone's covering for you at work?"

"I had to take a leave of absence. It's going to take a while afterward—"

"I know. But it's the last thing to worry about, it can't be helped."

"Like spilt milk. Isn't that what they say?"

"I don't know what they say. But why didn't you tell me? Didn't you know something was wrong?"

"Yes . . . bad headaches. Migraines, I thought, or the diabetes getting worse. I was afraid they'd start me on insulin." She tightened the corner of her mouth. "Little did I know . . ."

They heard the shuffle of slippers. An old woman stood at the open door of the room, looking in confusedly. She seemed about to speak, then moved on.

"Oh," said Kate's mother in exasperation, "shut that door, please? They let these old women wander around like refugees." She sat up, reaching for a robe. "And let's get me out of this bed."

They sat near the window while she finished eating. Bars of moted yellow banded the floor of the room. The light held a tinge of spring which seemed painful because it might vanish. They heard the rattle of the meal cart outside the closed door, and the clunk-slide of patients with aluminum walkers. Kate's mother sighed and pushed away the half-empty soup bowl.

"They'll be here after me any minute. More tests. I just want to stay with you." Her face was warm and smooth in the slanted light, lines in her skin delicate, unreal; as though a face behind her face was now apparent after many years. She sat looking at Kate and smiled.

"One day when you were about four you were dragging a broom around the kitchen. I asked what you were doing and you told me that when you got old you were going to be an angel and sweep the rotten rain off the clouds."

"What did you say to that?"

"I said that when you were old I was sure God would see to it." Her mother laughed. "I'm glad you weren't such a smart aleck then," she said. "You would have told me my view of God was paternalistic."

"Ah yes," sighed Kate. "God, that famous dude. Here I am, getting old, facing unemployment, alone, and where is He?"

"You're not alone," her mother said, "I'm right here."

Kate didn't answer. She sat motionless and felt her heart begin to open like a box with a hinged lid. The fullness had no edges.

Her mother stood. She rubbed her hands slowly, twisting her wedding rings. "My hands are so dry in the winter," she said softly, "I brought some hand cream with me but I can't find it anywhere, my suitcase is so jumbled. Thank heavens spring is early this year. . . . They told me that little park over there doesn't usually open till the end of March . . ."

She's helping me, thought Kate, I'm not supposed to let her down.

" . . . but they're already running it on weekends. Even past dusk. We'll see the lights tonight. You can't see the shapes this far away, just the motion . . ."

A nurse came in with a wheelchair. Kate's mother pulled a wry face. "This wheelchair is a bit much," she said.

"We don't want to tire you out," said the nurse.

The chair took her weight quietly. At the door she put out her hand to stop, turned, and said anxiously, "Kate, see if you can find that hand cream?"

It was the blue suitcase from years ago, still almost new. She'd brought things she never used for everyday; a cashmere sweater, lace slips, silk underpants wrapped in tissue. Folded beneath was a stack of postmarked envelopes, slightly ragged, tied with twine. Kate opened one and realized that all the cards were there, beginning with the first of the marriage. There were a few photographs of her and Robert, baby pictures almost indistinguishable from each other, and then Kate's homemade Valentines, fastened together with rubber bands. Kate stared. *What will I do with these things?* She wanted air; she needed to breathe. She walked to the window and put the bundled papers on the sill. She'd raised the glass and pushed back the screen when suddenly, her mother's clock radio went off with a flat buzz. Kate moved to switch it off and brushed the cards with her arm. Envelopes shifted and slid, scattering on the floor of the room. A few snapshots wafted silently out the window. They dipped and turned, twirling. Kate didn't try to reach them. They seemed only scraps, buoyant and yellowed, blown away, the faces small as pennies. Somewhere far-off there were sirens, almost musical, drawn out and carefully approaching.

The nurse came in with evening medication. Kate's mother lay in bed. "I hope this is strong enough," she said. "Last night I couldn't sleep at all. So many sounds in a hospital . . ."

"You'll sleep tonight," the nurse assured her.

Kate winked at her mother. "That's right," she said, "I'll help you out if I have to."

They stayed up for an hour, watching the moving lights outside and the stationary glows of houses across the distant river. The halls grew darker, were lit with night lights, and the hospital dimmed. Kate waited. Her mother's eyes fluttered and finally she slept. Her breathing was low and regular.

Kate didn't move. Robert had said he'd be back; where was he? She felt a sunken anger and shook her head. She'd been on the point of telling her mother everything, the secrets were a travesty. What if there were things her mother wanted done, people she needed to see? Kate wanted to wake her before these hours passed in the dark and confess that she had lied. Between them, through the tension, there had always been a trusted clarity. Now it was twisted. Kate sat leaning forward, nearly touching the hospital bed.

Suddenly her mother sat bolt upright, her eyes open and her face transfixed. She looked blindly toward Kate but seemed to see nothing. "Who are you?" she whispered. Kate stood, at first unable to move. The woman in the bed opened and closed her mouth several times, as though she were gasping. Then she said loudly, "Stop moving the table. Stop it this instant!" Her eyes were wide with fright and her body was vibrating.

Kate reached her. "Mama, wake up, you're dreaming." Her mother jerked, flinging her arms out. Kate held her tightly.

"I can hear the wheels," she moaned.

"No, no," Kate said. "You're here with me."

"It's not so?"

"No," Kate said. "It's not so."

She went limp. Kate felt for her pulse and found it rapid, then regular. She sat rocking her mother. In a few minutes she lay her back on the pillows and smoothed the damp hair at her temples, smoothed the sheets of the bed. Later she slept fitfully in a chair, waking repeatedly to assure herself that her mother was breathing,

Near dawn she got up, exhausted, and left the room to walk in the corridor. In front of the window at the end of the hallway she saw a man slumped on a couch; the man slowly stood and wavered before her like a specter. It was Robert.

"Kate?" he said.

Years ago he had flunked out of a small junior college and their mother sat in her bedroom rocker, crying hard for over an hour while Kate tried in vain to comfort her. Kate went to the university the next fall, so anxious that she studied frantically, outlining whole textbooks in yellow ink. She sat in the front rows of large classrooms to take voluminous notes, writing quickly in her thick notebook. Robert had gone home, held a job in a plant that manufactured business forms and worked his way through the hometown college. By that time their father was dead, and Robert became, always and forever, the man of the house.

"Robert," Kate said, "I'll stay. Go home."

After breakfast they sat waiting for Robert, who had called and said he'd arrive soon. Kate's fatigue had given way to an intense awareness of every sound, every gesture. How would they get through the day? Her mother had awakened from the drugged sleep still groggy, unable to eat. The meal was sent away untouched and she watched the window as though she feared the walls of the room.

"I'm glad your father isn't here to see this," she said. There was a silence and Kate opened her mouth to speak. "I mean," said her mother quickly, "I'm going to look horrible for a few weeks, with my head all shaved." She pulled an afghan up around her lap and straightened the magazines on the table beside her chair.

"Mom," Kate said, "your hair will grow back."

Her mother pulled the afghan closer. "I've been thinking of your father," she said. "It's not that I'd have wanted him to suffer. But if he had to die, sometimes I wish he'd done it more gently. That heart attack, so finished; never a warning. I wish I'd had some time to nurse him. In a way, it's a chance to settle things."

"Did things need settling?"

"They always do, don't they?" She sat looking out the window, then said softly, "I wonder where I'm headed."

"You're not headed anywhere," Kate said. "I want you right here to see me settle down into normal American womanhood."

Her mother smiled reassuringly. "Where are my grandchildren?" she said. "That's what I'd like to know."

"You stick around," said Kate, "and I promise to start working on it." She moved her chair closer, so that their knees were touching and they could both see out the window. Below them cars moved on the highway and the Ferris wheel in the little park was turning.

"I remember when you were one of the little girls in the parade at the county fair. You weren't even in school yet; you were beautiful in that white organdy dress and pinafore. You wore those shiny black patent shoes and a crown of real apple blossoms. Do you remember?"

"Yes," Kate said. "That long parade. They told me not to move and I sat so still my legs went to sleep. When they lifted me off the float I couldn't stand up. They put me under a tree to wait for you, and you came, in a full white skirt and white sandals, your hair tied back in a red scarf. I can see you yet."

Her mother laughed. "Sounds like a pretty exaggerated picture."

Kate nodded. "I was little. You were big."

"You loved the county fair. You were wild about the carnivals." They looked down at the little park. "Magic, isn't it?" her mother said.

"Maybe we could go see it," said Kate. "I'll ask the doctor."

They walked across a pedestrian footbridge spanning the highway. Kate had bundled her mother into a winter coat and gloves despite the sunny weather. The day was sharp, nearly still, holding its bright air like illusion. Kate tasted the brittle water of her breath, felt for the cool handrail and thin steel of the webbed fencing. Cars moved steadily under the bridge. Beyond a muted roar of motors the park spread green and wooded, its limits clearly visible.

Kate's mother had combed her hair and put on lipstick. Her mouth was defined and brilliant; she linked arms with Kate like an escort. "I was afraid they'd tell us no," she said. "I was ready to run away!"

"I promised I wouldn't let you. And we only have ten minutes, long enough for the Ferris wheel." Kate grinned.

"I haven't ridden one in years. I wonder if I still know how."

"Of course you do. Ferris wheels are genetic knowledge."

"All right, whatever you say." She smiled. "We'll just hold on."

They drew closer and walked quickly through the sounds of the highway. When they reached the grass it was ankle-high and thick, longer and more ragged than it appeared from a distance. The Ferris wheel sat squarely near a grove of swaying elms, squat and laboring, taller than trees. Its neon lights still burned, pale in the sun, spiraling from inside like an imagined bloom. The naked elms surrounded it, their topmost branches tapping. Steel ribs of the machine were graceful and slightly rusted, squeaking faintly above a tinkling music. Only a few people were riding.

"Looks a little rickety," Kate said.

"Oh, don't worry," said her mother.

Kate tried to buy tickets but the ride was free. The old man running the motor wore an engineer's cap and patched overalls. He stopped the wheel and led them on a short ramp to an open car. It dipped gently, padded with black cushions. An orderly and his children rode in the car above. Kate saw their dangling feet, the girls' dusty sandals and gray socks beside their father's shoes and the hem of his white pants. The youngest one swung her feet absently, so it seemed the breeze blew her legs like fabric hung on a line.

Kate looked at her mother. "Are you ready for the big sky?" They laughed. Beyond them the river moved lazily. Houses on the opposite bank seemed empty, but a few rowboats bobbed at the docks. The surface of the water lapped and reflected clouds, and as Kate watched, searching for a definition of line, the Ferris wheel jerked into motion. The car rocked. They looked into the distance and Kate caught her mother's hand as they ascended.

Far away the hospital rose up white and glistening, its windows catching the glint of the sun. Directly below, the park was nearly deserted. There were a few cars in the parking lot and several dogs chasing each other across the grass. Two or three lone women held children on the teeter-totters and a wind was coming up. The forlorn swings moved on their chains. Kate had a vision of the park at night, totally empty, wind weaving heavily through the trees and children's playthings like a great black fish about to surface. She felt a chill on her arms. The light had gone darker, quietly, like a minor chord.

"Mom," Kate said, "it's going to storm." Her own voice seemed distant, the sound strained through layers of screen or gauze.

"No," said her mother, "it's going to pass over." She moved her hand to Kate's knee and touched the cloth of her daughter's skirt.

Kate gripped the metal bar at their waists and looked straight ahead. They were rising again and she felt she would scream. She tried to breathe rhythmically, steadily. She felt the immense weight of the air as they moved through it.

They came almost to the top and stopped. The little car swayed back and forth.

"You're sick, aren't you," her mother said.

Kate shook her head. Below them the grass seemed to glitter coldly, like a sea. Kate sat wordless, feeling the touch of her mother's hand. The hand moved away and Kate felt the absence of the warmth.

They looked at each other levelly.

"I know all about it," her mother said, "I know what you haven't told me."

The sky circled around them, a sure gray movement. Kate swallowed calmly and let their gaze grow endless. She saw herself in her mother's wide brown eyes and felt she was falling slowly into them.

Lee Smith

1944–

Born in Grundy, Virginia, in the coalfields of the southwestern section of the state, Lee Smith depicts an Appalachia steeped in family and community relationships, in supernatural and religious powers, and in musical and cultural traditions through which characters navigate a changing and modernizing world. Smith attended Hollins College, then a women's college. While there, she studied with Louis Rubin, a leading scholar of southern literature; her classmates included a remarkable number of women who, like Smith, went on to pursue literary careers—for example, author Annie Dillard and literary scholars Lucinda MacKethon and Anne Goodwin Jones.

Smith has written more than a dozen novels, four collections of short stories, and a novella. Although she has spent much of her adult life in the North Carolina Piedmont teaching at North Carolina State University, she remains active in Appalachia. She frequently teaches at the Hindman Settlement School's Appalachian Writers' Workshop in Hindman, Kentucky. In 1988 she was recognized for her contribution to Appalachian writing with the Weatherford Award for Appalachian fiction.

Smith's Appalachian novels, which are often multigenerational, explore how historical events have affected mountain life and culture in the twentieth century. Smith is especially concerned with women's experiences in a patriarchal society. The sassiness of many of her female narrators—evident in "Folk Art," the story presented below—is often in tension with the pathos of her fiction, which chronicles the difficult choices and missed opportunities that women (and men) face.

Folk Art

Lord have mercy! You liked to scared me to death! Come on out of there this minute. You're tramping on my daylilies. There now. That's better. Let me get a good look at you. You don't say! Why you don't look hardly old enough to be a art professor, I'll tell you that. I would of took you for a boy. Just a little old art boy, how's that? Me, I'm Lily Lockhart. I reckon you know that already. How'd you get in here anyway? Well, it don't matter. Honey, you have come to the right place! Art is my life, if I do say so myself.

Why sure, I'll be glad to show you around my backyard, now that you've got in here. It'd be my pleasure. It's not much to see, though. Not much to show somebody like you. Why thank you. I appreciate that. Mama planted a lot of them herself. She used say, "Lily, I want our backyard to look just like the Garden of Eden." That's bee balm. Mama planted it years and years ago. Them wild spiky flowers, them's cleomes. And these here is hollyhocks, of course, they're my favorite. Me and Daisy used to take a blossom and hold it just so, and pretend it was a dolly, going to a dance. See here? This is her party dress. Why no, they're easy, once they get a good start, just like anything else. Once you get something going, it takes on a life of its own, seems like. Looky here how tall they get! Taller than Billy, and Billy's tall. He's in the house, he don't get out much anymore. You're the first visitor I've had in—Lord, I don't know how long! Of course I've got lots of company out here in the yard. You want to meet my people? Come on then. I'll be glad to introduce you.

Now this here is Mama, who loved flowers and songs and every pretty thing. Oh, I wish you could have seen her in life! She was the sweetest thing, she reminded me of a butterfly somehow. Yellow hair hanging down to her waist, and the littlest, whitest feet! She used to paint her toenails fire-engine red, and then she'd paint our little toenails red, too. She'd put cotton between our toes, to let our toenails dry, and then we'd dance and dance in the garden, Daisy and me and Iris Jean, and Mama would sing.

Oh, I don't know. Songs she made up out of her head, I reckon. Daddy didn't like it. He thought all music ought to be church music, but he didn't say a thing. He never spoke a word when it came to Mama, she meant the whole world to him, which was true from the minute he first laid eyes on her at that little church up in the Blackey coal camp where she was born. She was one of nine children, and the oldest, though she was not but fourteen years old when Daddy came riding up the holler to preach that first time. She stood up in front of the altar all by herself and threw back her head and closed her eyes and sang "Beulah Land" in her pure gold voice that never faltered, sang so beautiful Daddy said you could see the notes floating out perfect and visible in the air. Daddy was thirty years old at the time. He had already been out west, gone to jail, married a Mexican, got shot in the leg, you name it! All of these things before he got religion, after which he had took to the road for the Lord. Oh, he'd been places, and seen things. But he had never seen nothing like Mama the day he came to the church at Blackey when she was singing "Beulah Land." Mama noticed him too, of course, the handsome stranger with the snapping black eyes and the big black hat standing thunderstruck in the open door at the back of the church.

And then he *did* preach, though he hardly knew what he said, and after it was all over, Daddy exchanged a few words with Mama and then went right up to her father, old Joe Burns, and said, "Sir, I want to marry your daughter Evalina."

Old Joe Burns looked Daddy in the eye. "I appreciate the offer," he said, "for times is hard, but Evalina is too young, sir. Come back next year and you can have her." And so he did, and brought her over here to Rockhouse Branch, and built this house for her, meantime farming and preaching down at the Mount Gilead church which you must of passed on your way up here.

Why, I don't know as she thought *anything* about it! Girls in those days did as they were told, not like they do now, not like Daisy and Iris Jean have done! Anyway, it was plain to see that Daddy doted on her and got her anything she could think of, though he did not like for her to go off the place except to church. He was always worried that something bad might happen to her. He brought pearl buttons and ribbons and pretty cloth from town, and was real proud of how nice she could sew, and she did make beautiful dresses for us girls and for herself, though there were always those at church that talked about it, and about the sin of vanity.

"My little flowers," Mama called us, and in fact we truly were her garden as she said, Iris Jean the oldest, born when Mama was sixteen, and then me and Daisy my sweet twin, and then Billy, three years later. I know it was a lot of children for a slip of a girl to bear, and sometimes I have felt that what happened was *our fault*, somehow, for coming on her so fast.

I remember so clearly one thing I heard her say to Daddy when we were all just little and Billy was newborn. She was lying in the big old bed with Billy nestled up close by her, and Daddy though fully clothed lay by her side and stroked her long bright hair. I stole in the room and stood at the other side of the bed, where they did not see me. "Gabriel Lockhart," Mama said, as if in a dream, "where did all of them come from? Don't you remember back when it was just me and you? But now there is so many. I keep thinking, oh who are they all? and where have they come from?"

"Now Evalina," Daddy said, "you know they have come from God." And she smiled at him, and then she started humming a little faraway tune while Billy nursed. Everybody was worried about Billy, who came out backward with the cord wrapped around his neck and had terrible seizures as a little child.

I was more worried about Mama, who started talking to Billy in his illness the way you do talk to a baby but then kept on talking to herself, and pacing the house all night. I was not surprised when she left us, as she had been mostly gone in her mind for a while, though Daddy would never admit it. It was true that she might never have left had it not been for John Astor Sneed who came out here from town selling dry goods and notions. He came once, twice, and the third time Mama went with him in that wire-wheeled buggy he had hitched to the cherry tree. John Astor Sneed wore red suspenders, I will never forget it. Had a fat gray horse. Billy stood in the yard and waved good-bye when they left, Billy loves to wave, but I was crying. She said she was coming back, but I knew somehow she never would, not unless I made her, which I have now done. She is the first one I made when I started doing my art.

Shoot, no! Take all the pictures you want. It's real pretty back here, ain't it? Every one of my people has got their own little garden, you might say. Of course it just about kills me, trying to keep it all up. Poor Billy now, he never was a bit of help. Just as soon pull up a rose as a weed. He don't know no better. But he sure has brought me a lot of nice art supplies.

Well, I don't know. I can't exactly tell you. All of a sudden I thought, *Lord, how much I miss Mama!* It had come a real bad thunderstorm that night, and I came out here in the yard to find a big branch snapped right off this little dogwood tree, and something about the way it was standing there, that little jaunty angle of it—see how it looks like it is fixing to dance?—put me in mind of Mama, and how graceful she was, and how light of foot.

The first thing I done was wrap chicken wire all around it, and then I started hauling some clay mud up here from the branch to pack in around it—Daisy and me had always made little people out of that old red clay—but then all of a sudden I thought, *Well, shoot! Why not get some of that instant concrete from the hardware store, might as well be modern.* And so I did, and so I made her. All the quartz? It's down at the branch. That's where the name comes from, Rockhouse Branch. Sure it took a long time. Months. Every day or so I'd put me a little dab of concrete and a little piece of quartz. Gave me something to do. Then Billy got the idea and he started bringing me this mica, see here? Isn't that pretty? Lord knows where he got it, he just walks and walks everplace. That's salvia, blooming at her feet. Fire-engine red! She loves it.

Now what did you say your name was? I was wondering if you might be kin to any Goodys. You look just like a boy I used to know, name of Ray Goody, a long time back. You kindly favor him.

No? Well, anyway, Daddy was a handsome man as I said, but oh how he declined after Mama left! For he used to call her his little sunshine, and now his sunshine was gone. A blackness fell upon him like a cloak. He turned dark and sad and could not see the good of anything. It seemed like even God had turned His back on Daddy, and on us.

We just did the best we could, naturally. That's all you *can* do! Daddy was so sweet and broken that I had to take care of Billy the best I could, and keep house. Oh, Iris Jean didn't care a fig for all that. It was all school, school, school for Iris Jean, who *was* smart—I'll admit it—but would not stay home from school for one single day, not even when Billy had double pneumonia. Furthermore Iris Jean would not go to church or mention Mama's name, either one. Kept her nose stuck in a book all the time. Poor Daddy! First he lost Mama to John Astor Sneed, then Iris Jean to education. Now I'll tell you frankly, I might of liked some of that education myself—I've always been real smart—but *somebody* had to stay here and cook for Daddy and take care of Billy! Everybody can't just run off and do whatever they please!

Of course Iris Jean came back into the picture from time to time with her fancy degrees and big ideas, such as getting papers on Billy and sending him off to the special school, which liked to kill Daddy and me, though it did not last long, I will tell you. Lord, I won't forget how happy I was the day I was sitting right out here in a lawn chair snapping beans and I heard that little whistle I knew so well, and it was Billy! Grinning like the sun, arms full of old stuff he'd picked up along the way. "Here, Sissy," he said—that's what he calls me, Sissy. "All for you, Sissy," he said.

I used bottle pieces on Iris Jean—look how they catch the sun! Those blue ones come from Milk of Magnesia bottles, they're my favorite.

And mirror pieces of course for Daisy, who looked like me but did not have any character to speak of, unlike myself. I am afraid Daisy took after our sweet Mama in the worst possible way. It all happened in the blink of an eye. One minute Daisy was playing hollyhock dolls with me, and the next minute she was jumping into pickup trucks with complete strangers. I am not even sure how she met those boys in the first place, as Daddy had started keeping us home from school for our own protection right after we lost Iris Jean. Poor Daddy! He begged and pleaded and cried and prayed over Daisy to no avail. He locked her in her room and switched her with a locust branch until her skinny white legs had long red welts and even I had to feel sorry for her.

I will not forget the time I woke up in the middle of the night to feel a boy's long hard body pressing mine, his warm lips on my face. "Ssshh," he said. In a flash I knew it was Lewjack Jones, sneaking in the wrong window. But I confess I didn't say a word. I lay there and let him kiss me for the longest time before I jumped up and hollered "Daddy!" real loud and scared them all to death. It was funny, really. But then after Daddy ran him and Daisy off, I laid back down on my bed and cried and cried as if my heart would break, as if I even *cared* what that boy and my sister did in the dead of night! So—that's Daisy! Right over there, surrounded by zinnias.

This left Daddy and Billy and me. I got Billy to help me switch the mattresses around until I got the best one, which had been Iris Jean's, and the prettiest quilt, which used to be on Mama and Daddy's bed. Fan pattern, Mama made it herself. Daddy never missed it. He was not into details by that time, all he did was lie in the bed and cry until finally he lost his church and all of them started coming around here with casseroles, and then they stopped. I love that kind of casserole you make with French-style green beans and mushroom soup and onion rings on top, you know which one I mean? Church women all know how to make that casserole, it must be the law! Well, I miss that. I have never been one to cook, I've got too much to take care of out here in the yard.

Yes, I *did* think about it, just once. It was about then, in fact. Now I was accustomed to walking into town to buy groceries and what all else we needed, such as aspirin from the drug store, or whatever. It *is* a long way. Three miles, I reckon. At least. Well, Daddy used to drive me, but then he got so poorly, and of course I didn't have a driver's license, he never held with us girls driving a car—anyway, I was walking out of the hardware store one day when I heard this high-pitched voice yelling my name. "Lily Lockhart! Lily Lockhart! Wait a minute!" and so I did, and it turned out to be Ray Goody, who worked for Mr. Gray and rented a room right upstairs. Ray Goody was slight-built and sandy-haired, like you are, and had him some of those little gold-frame glasses too. He was real shy. His face turned the brightest red when he talked to you. "Lily Lockhart!" he said again. "I'm going to drive you home." And so he did. And came in the backyard carrying a bag of concrete, and put it down, and admired my people, and said hello to Billy and Daddy who had come out there to gawk at him. Ray Goody acted just like we were anybody. So I did too. "Sit down here and let me get you a cold drink," I said, and he did. He sat on that little stone bench you're sitting on now, and I came back with two glasses of ice water. It was summertime, real hot, and the glasses were all beaded up with sweat by the time I got back with them.

"This is the best water I have ever tasted," Ray Goody said, and proceeded to drink every drop without taking his eyes off me. His eyes looked like china plates behind his glasses. "It's nice here," he said, putting the glass down when he had finally drunk his fill.

"Come back anytime," I said. I don't know what got into me! But the fact is, he did. He came back and sat under the cedar tree and told me how he had been sick in the hospital but was now better and had come to work at Gray's Hardware because Mrs. Gray was his mother's cousin. He was really a writer, he said. "I have been watching you come in the store," he said. "In fact I couldn't take my eyes off of you," he said. This embarrassed us both so much it seemed we might die on the spot, but we did not, and as Ray Goody's visits continued, he started bringing us all manner of gifts from the hardware store, bird feeders and wind chimes and grapefruit spoons with little ridges on them and a new hose and an ashtray shaped like North Carolina. Chewing tobacco for Daddy and butter-rum Life Savers for Billy. Ray Goody spoke of this as his courtship. "How am I doing with my courtship?" he used to ask me, bright red but determined, and soon he took to sneaking up behind me and putting his arms around my waist and rubbing his face in my hair.

As for me, I went around in a dream, and my heart beat too fast all the time. I could see right where we were headed, like leaves floating down Rockhouse Branch to that little waterfall. Then one October day he popped the question. He wanted to marry me, and we would live together in his room in town over the hardware store where I would have a job too, in the arts and crafts. Ray had already asked Mr. Gray about it, and Mr. Gray said it was fine, that he and Mrs. Gray had been thinking about buying an RV vehicle and seeing something of the world themselves.

"What do you say?" Ray Goody asked me, but I was flabbergasted. "Well, think about it," he said, and then he kissed me and drove back into town, saying he'd be back that evening. Well! I had to sit down. I thought about it while scarlet leaves from the maple tree fell on the grass and the wind blew my hair around. My face felt hot, like I had a fever. *Why not?* I thought. *Why not?* I could scarcely breathe. Then I started thinking about making a concrete birdbath shaped like a leaf, and some stepping stones. Those things would be easy to mass produce. My heart on fire, I went in to tell Daddy.

He was standing by the window looking out, and did not turn around when I told him. "Why, that is wonderful," he said. Then he bent over double with the pain that would take several years to kill him. "You go on," he said. "It's not anything. I just want you to be happy," Daddy said. He was so sweet, wanting nothing more than to lie down by himself until it passed. Oh, he was so brave! But of course I did not go with Ray Goody when he came back that evening, I did not go with him then or anytime, and sometime during Daddy's long illness, Ray just slipped away. Left town. I don't know if he told the Grays where he was going or not—he sure didn't tell me! One week he was in there selling nails and saying, "How is your Daddy today, Lil?" and the next week he was gone, that lace curtain fluttering out of his open upstairs window like a sign. Oh, I was a pure-tee fool to think I could have done it anyway! I had to wait on Daddy hand and foot from then on. And he wrestled with the angel of death as hard as he'd wrestled with God, I swear it. You'd think he would have been glad to go, after everything that had happened to him, but he was not. Lord, no! He fought it tooth and nail, I'll tell you. He was all wore out by the end, and light as a feather, and we put him right over there, me and Billy. Sure thing! That's him all right, all them dark rocks in the shape of the cross. Then I built the arbor and planted the grapevine in memory of how hard he hung on, you have to admire that in a man. You have to.

You mean this here pile? Well, I don't know, it gives me something to do while I'm taking care of Billy, he sleeps so much now. Poor thing. He couldn't do without me. And it will not be long, I can tell you. You know how I know? It's when their fingers start curling up like ferns. In fact I may bring me some ferns up here from the creek, now that's a thought. But I'll swear it don't seem like no time at all to me since Billy was just a little boy, making mudpies down there with me and Daisy.

Well, I wish you didn't have to rush off. But you come on back *anytime!* You can sit right there on that bench and write in your notebook, just like you used to. I bet you could get a lot of work done. It's nice, in a garden. Why there's something happening all the time out here, first daffodils and forsythia in the spring, then roses and daylilies and I don't know what all in the summertime, then chrysanthemums and asters and nandina in the fall, everything comes and goes and comes again in its season. You're going to like it out here. It's real peaceful, and there is always a little wind up in them cedar trees, it's like they catch the wind somehow, and trap it up in there, and it sounds so pretty, like wind chimes. Why, you can hear it right now. Just listen.

John Edgar Wideman
1941–

John Edgar Wideman was born in Washington, DC, and reared in Pittsburgh's Homewood community, which was predominately African American. At both top-ranked Peabody High School and the University of Pennsylvania, where he received his BA in 1963, he excelled academically and athletically. He was only the second African American to receive a Rhodes Scholarship (1966) to study at Oxford University. He taught at the University of Iowa's Writers' Workshop, the University of Massachusetts at Amherst, Brown University, and other institutions.

Wideman's award-winning work provides an important examination of the African American experience in urban northern Appalachia. His Homewood trilogy of novels—*Damballah* (1981), *Hiding Place* (1981), and *Sent for You Yesterday* (1983)— are reflections on the Pittsburgh neighborhood in which he grew up.

Like the influential African American sociologist W. E. B. DuBois, Wideman believes that "twoness" is central to the African American experience, and Wideman's writings frequently use doubling to explain African American biculturalism. In his memoir *Brothers and Keepers* (1984), for example, Wideman uses his brother, sentenced to life in prison for murder, as a double to examine issues of racism, the injustice of the prison system, and the influence of family history and geography on identity formation. Wideman's work exposes the fallacy of racial binaries and searches for points of interconnection between races and cultures.

Lizabeth: The Caterpillar Story

Did you know I tried to save him once myself. When somebody was dumping ashes on the lot beside the house on Cassina Way. Remember how mad Daddy got. He sat downstairs in the dark with his shotgun and swore he was going to shoot whoever it was dumping ashes on his lot. I tried to save Daddy from that.

It's funny sitting here listening at you talk about your father that way because I never thought about nobody else needing to save him but me. Then I hear you talking and think about John French and know there ain't no way he could have lived long as he did unless a whole lotta people working real hard at saving that crazy man. He needed at least as many trying to save him as were trying to kill him.

Knew all my life about what you did, Mama. Knew you punched through a window with your bare hand to save him. You showed me the scar and showed me the window. In the house we used to live in over on Cassina Way. So I always knew you had saved him. Maybe that's why I thought I could save him too.

I remember telling you the story.

And showing me the scar.

Got the scar, that's for sure. And you got the story.

Thought I was saving Daddy, too, but if you hadn't put your fist through that window I wouldn't have had a Daddy to try and save.

Had you in my lap and we were sitting at the window in the house on Cassina Way. You must have been five or six at the time. Old enough to be telling stories to. Course when I had one of you children on my lap, there was some times I talked just to hear myself talking. Some things couldn't wait even though you all didn't understand word the first. But you was five or six and I was telling you about the time your Daddy ate a caterpillar.

The one I ate first.

The very one you nibbled a little corner off.

Then he ate the rest.

The whole hairy-legged, fuzzy, orange and yellow striped, nasty rest.

Because he thought I might die.

As if my babygirl dead wouldn't be enough. Huh uh. He swallowed all the rest of that nasty bug so if you died, he'd die too and then there I'd be with both you gone.

So he was into the saving business, too.

Had a funny way of showing it but I guess you could say he was. Guess he was, alright. Had to be when I look round and see all you children grown up and me getting old as sin.

Nineteen years older than me is all.

That's enough.

I remember you telling me the caterpillar story and then I remember that man trying to shoot Daddy and then I remember Albert Wilkes's pistol you pulled out from under the icebox.

That's a whole lot of remembering. You was a little thing, a lap baby when that mess in Cassina happened.

Five or six.

Yes, you were. That's what you was. Had to be because we'd been on Cassina two, three years. Like a kennel back there on Cassina Way in those days. Every one of them shacks full of niggers. And they let their children run the street half-naked and those burr heads ain't never seen a comb. Let them children out in the morning and called em in at night like they was goats or something. You was five or six but I kept you on my lap plenty. Didn't want you growing up too fast. Never did want it. With all you children I tried to keep that growing up business going slow as I could. What you need to hurry for? Where you going? Wasn't in no hurry to get you out my lap and set you down in those streets.

I remember. I'm sure I remember. The man, a skinny man, came running down the alley after Daddy. He had a big pistol just like Albert Wilkes. And you smashed your fist through the glass to warn Daddy. If I shut my eyes I can hear glass falling and hear the shots.

Never knew John French could run so fast. Thought for a moment one of them bullets knocked him down but he outran em all. Had to or I'd be telling a different story.

It's mixed up with other things in my mind but I do remember. You told me the story and showed me the scar later but I was there and I remember too.

You was there, alright. The two of us sitting at the front window staring at nothing. Staring at the quiet cause it was never quiet in Cassina Way except early in the morning and then again that time of day people in they houses fixing to eat supper. Time of day when the men come home and the children come in off the streets and it's quiet for the first time since dawn. You can hear nothing for the first time and hear yourself think for the first time all day so there we was in that front window and I was half sleep and daydreaming and just about forgot I had you on my lap. Even though you were getting to be a big thing. A five- or six-year-old thing but I wasn't in no hurry to set you down so there we was. You was there alright but I wasn't paying you no mind. I was just studying them houses across the way and staring at my ownself in the glass and wondering where John French was and wondering how long it would stay quiet before your sister Geraldine woke up and started to fuss and wondering who that woman was with a baby in her lap staring back at me.

And you told the caterpillar story.

Yes, I probably did. If that's what you remember, I probably did. I liked to tell it when things was quiet. Ain't much of a story if there's lots of noise around. Ain't the kind you tell to no bunch of folks been drinking and telling lies all night. Sitting at the window with you at the quiet end of the afternoon was the right time for that story and I probably told it to wake myself up.

John French is cradling Lizabeth in one arm pressed against his chest. She is muttering or cooing or getting ready to throw up.

"*What did she eat? What you saying she ate? You supposed to be watching this child, woman.*"

"*Don't raise your voice at me. Bad enough without you frightening her.*"

"*Give it here, woman.*"

His wife opens her fist and drops the fuzzy curled remnant of caterpillar in his hand. It lies there striped orange and yellow, dead or alive, and he stares like it is a sudden eruption of the skin of the palm of his hand, stares like he will stare at the sloppy pyramids of ash desecrating his garden-to-be. He spreads the fingers of the hand of the arm supporting the baby's back; still one minute, Lizabeth will pitch and buck the next. He measures the spiraled length of caterpillar in his free hand, sniffs it, strokes its fur with his middle finger, seems to be listening or speaking to it as he passes it close to his face. His jaws work the plug of tobacco; he spits and the juice sizzles against the pavement.

"*You sure this the most of it? You sure she only ate a little piece?*"

Freeda French is still shaking her head yes, not because she knows the answer but because anything else would be unthinkable. How could she let this man's daughter chew up more than a little piece of caterpillar. Freeda is crying inside. Tears glaze her eyes, shiny and thick as the sugar frosting on her Aunt Aida's cakes and there is too much to hold back, the weight of the tears will crack the glaze and big drops will steal down her cheeks. While she is still nodding yes, nodding gingerly so the tears won't leak, but knowing they are coming anyway, he spits again and pops the gaudy ringlet of bug into his mouth.

"I got the most of it then. And if I don't die, she ain't gonna die neither, so stop that sniffling." He chews two or three times and his eyes are expressionless, vacant as he runs his tongue around his teeth getting it all out and down. . . .

Someone had been dumping ashes on the vacant lot at the end of Cassina Way. The empty lot had been part of the neighborhood for as long as anybody could remember and no one had ever claimed it until John French moved his family into the rear end of the narrow row house adjoining the lot and then his claim went no farther than a patch beside the end wall of the row houses, a patch he intended to plant with tomatoes, peppers and beans but never got around to except to say he'd be damned if he couldn't make something grow there even though the ground was more rock and roots than it was soil because back home in Culpeper, Virginia, where the soil so good you could almost eat it in handfuls scooped raw from the earth, down there he learned about growing and he was going to make a garden on that lot when he got around to it and fix it to look nearly as good as the one he had loved to listen to when he was a boy sitting on his back porch with his feet up on a chair and nobody he had to bother with from his toes to the Blue Ridge Mountains floating on the horizon.

Ashes would appear in gray, sloppy heaps one or two mornings a week. The shape of the mounds told John French they had been spilled from a wheelbarrow, that somebody was sneaking a wheelbarrow down the dark, cobbled length of Cassina Way while other people slept, smothering his dream of a garden under loads of scraggly ash. One afternoon when Lizabeth came home crying with ash in her hair, hair her mother had just oiled and braided that morning, John French decided to put a stop to the ash dumping. He said so to his wife, Freeda, while Lizabeth wept, raising his voice as Lizabeth bawled louder. Finally goddamned somebody's soul and somebody's ancestors and threatened to lay somebody's sorry soul to rest, till Freeda hollering to be heard over Lizabeth's crying and John French's cussing told him such language wasn't fit for a child's ears, wasn't fit for no place or nobody but the Bucket of Blood and his beer drinking, wine drinking, nasty talking cronies always hanging round there.

So for weeks Lizabeth did not sleep. She lay in her bed on the edge of sleep in the tiny room with her snoring sister, afraid like a child is afraid to poke a foot in bath water of an uncertain temperature, but she was frozen in that hesitation not for an instant but for weeks as she learned everything she could from the night sounds of Cassina Way, and then lay awake learning there was nothing else to learn, that having the nightmare happen would be the only way of learning, that after predictable grunts and alley clamors, the cobblestones went to sleep for the night and she still hadn't picked up a clue about what she needed to know, how she would recognize the sound of a wheelbarrow and find some unfrightened, traitorous breath in herself with which to cry out and warn the man who pushed the barrow of ashes that her father, John French, with his double-barreled shotgun taller than she was, sat in ambush in the downstairs front room.

Even before she heard him promise to shoot whoever was dumping ashes she had listened for her Daddy to come home at night. He'd rummage a few minutes in the kitchen then she'd listen for the scrape of a match and count his heavy steps as he climbed to the landing; at *twelve* he would be just a few feet away and the candlelight would lurch on the wall and her father would step first to the girls' room, and though her eyes were squeezed as tightly shut as walnuts, she could feel him peering in as the heat of the candle leaned closer, feel him counting his daughters the way she counted the stairs, checking on his girls before he ventured the long stride across the deep well of the landing to the other side of the steps, the left turning to the room where her mother would be sleeping. Once in a while partying all by himself downstairs, he would sing. Rocking back and forth on a rickety kitchen chair his foot tapping a bass line on the linoleum floor, he'd sing, *Froggy went a courtin and he did ride, uh huh, uh huh.* Or the songs she knew came from the Bucket of Blood. His husky voice cracking at the tenor notes and half laughing, half swallowing the words in those songs not fit for any place but the Bucket of Blood.

Most times he was happy but even if she heard the icebox door slammed hard enough to pop the lock, heard his chair topple over and crash to the floor, heard the steps groan like he was trying to put his heel through the boards, like he was trying to crush the humpback of some steel-shelled roach with each stride, hearing even this she knew his feet would get quieter as she neared the end of her count, that no matter how long it took between steps when she could hear him snoring or shuffling back and forth along the length of a step like he had forgotten *up* and decided to try *sideways,* finally he would reach the landing and the staggering light from the candle her mother always set out for him on its dish beside the front door would lean in once then die with the bump of her parents' door closing across the landing.

Lizabeth could breathe easier then, after she had counted him safely to his bed, after the rasp of door across the landing and the final bump which locked him safely away. But for weeks she'd lain awake long after the house was silent, waiting for the unknown sound of the wheelbarrow against the cobblestones, the sound she must learn, the sound she must save him from.

"It got to be that bowlegged Walter Johnson cause who else be cleaning people's fireplaces round here. But I'll give him the benefit of the doubt. Every man deserves the benefit of the doubt so I ain't going to accuse Walter Johnson to his face. What I'm gon do is fill the next nigger's butt with buckshot I catch coming down Cassina Way dumping ash."

She knew her father would shoot. She had heard about Albert Wilkes so she knew that shooting meant men dead and men running away and never coming back. She could not let it happen. She imagined the terrible sound of the gun a hundred times each night. If she slept at all, she did not remember or could not admit a lapse because then the hours awake would mean nothing. Her vigilance must be total. If she would save her father from himself, from the tumbling cart and the gray, ashy faced intruder who would die and carry her father away with him in the night, she must be constant, must listen and learn the darkness better than it knew itself.

"Daddy." She is sitting on his knee. Her eyes scale her father's chest, one by one she climbs the black buttons of his flannel shirt until she counts them all and reaches the grayish neck of his long johns. Their one cracked pearl button showing below his stubbled chin.

"Daddy. I want to stay in your hat."

"What you talking about, little sugar?"

"I want to live in your hat. Your big brown hat. I want to live in there always."

"Sure you can. Yes indeed. Make you a table and some chairs and catch a little squirrel too, let him live in there with you. Now that sounds like a fine idea, don't it? Stay under there till you get too big for your Daddy's hat. Till you get to be a fine big gal."

Lizabeth lowers her eyes from his long jaw, from the spot he plumped out with his tongue. He shifted the Five Brothers tobacco from one cheek to the other, getting it good and juicy and the last she saw of his face before her eyes fell to the brass pot beside his chair was how his jaws worked the tobacco, grinding the wad so it came out bloody and sizzling when he spit.

She was already big enough for chores and hours beside her mother in the kitchen where there was always something to be done. But hours too on the three steps her Daddy had built from the crooked door to the cobbled edge of Cassina Way. Best in the summer when she could sit and get stupid as a fly in the hot sun after it rose high enough to crest the row houses across the alley. If you got up before everybody else summer mornings were quiet in Cassina, nothing moving until the quiet was broken by the cry of the scissors-and-knife man, a jingling ring of keys at his waist, and strapped across his back the flintstone wheel which he would set down on its three legs and crank so the sparks flew up if you had a dull blade for him to sharpen, or by the iceman who would always come first, behind the tired clomp of his horse's hooves striking Cassina's stones. The iceman's wagon was covered with gray canvas that got darker like a bandage on a wound as the ice bled through. *Ice. Ice. Any ice today, lady?* The iceman sang the words darkly so Lizabeth never understood exactly what he cried till she asked her mother.

"He's saying *Any ice today, lady,* least that's what he thinks he's saying. Least that's what I think he thinks he's saying," her mother said as she listened stock-still by the sink to make sure. For years the iceman was Fred Willis and Fred Willis still owned the horse which slept some people said in the same room with him, but now a scowling somebody whose name Lizabeth didn't know, who wore a long rubber apron the color of soaked canvas was the one talking the old gray horse down the alley, moaning *Ice, ice, any ice today, lady* or whatever it was she heard first thing behind the hollow clomp of the hooves.

Stupid as a fly. She had heard her Daddy say that and it fit just how she felt, sundazed, forgetting even the itchy places on her neck, the cries of the vendors which after a while like everything blended with the silence.

Stupid as a fly during her nightlong vigils when she couldn't learn what she needed to know but she did begin to understand how she could separate into two pieces and one would listen for the wheelbarrow and the other part would watch her listening. One part had a Daddy and loved him more than anything but the other part could see him dead or dying or run away forever and see Lizabeth alone and heartbroken or see Lizabeth lying awake all night foolish enough to think she might save her Daddy. The watching part older and wiser and more evil than she knew Lizabeth could ever be. A worrisome part which strangely at times produced in her the most profound peace because she was that part and nothing else when she sat sun-drugged, stupid as a fly on the steps over Cassina Way.

Bracelets of gray soapsuds circled her mother's wrists as she lifted a china cup from the sink, rinsed it with a spurt of cold water and set it gleaming on the drainboard to dry. The same froth clinging to her mother's arms floated above the rim of the sink, screening the dishes that filled the bowl. Each time the slim hands disappeared into the water there was an ominous clatter and rattle, but her mother's fingers had eyes, sorted out the delicate pieces first, retrieved exactly what they wanted from the load of dishes. If Lizabeth plunged her own hands into the soapy water, everything would begin to totter and slide, broken glass and chipped plates would gnaw her clumsy fingers. Some larger pieces were handed to her to dry and put away which she did automatically, never taking her eyes from her mother's swift, efficient movements at the sink.

"Lizabeth, you go catch the iceman. Tell him five pounds."

Lizabeth shouted, *Five pound, we want five pound.* She knew better, her mother had told her a hundred times: pounds and miles, *s* when you talking bout more than one, but her Daddy said *two pound a salt pork and a thousand mile tween here and home* so when the wagon was abreast of the last row houses and the echo of the hooves and the echo of the blues line the iceman made of his call faded down the narrow funnel of Cassina Way she shouted loud as she could, *Five pound, five pound, Mister.*

The horse snorted. She thought it would be happy to stop but it sounded mad. The driver's eyes went from the little girl on the steps to the empty place in the window where there should be a sign if anybody in the house wanted ice. When his eyes stared at her again, they said you better not be fooling with me, girl, and with a grunt much like the horse's snort he swung himself down off the wagon seat, jerked up an edge of the canvas from the ice and snapped away a five pound chunk in rusty pincers. The block of ice quivered as the iron hooks pierced its sides. Lizabeth could see splintered crystal planes, the cloudy heart of the ice when the man passed her on the steps. Under the high-bibbed rubber apron, the man's skin was black and glistening. He hollered once *Iceman* and pushed through the door.

If she had a horse, she would keep it in the vacant lot next door. It would never look nappy and sick like this one. The iceman's horse had bare patches in his coat, sore, raw-looking spots like the heads of kids who had ringworm. Their mothers would tie a stocking cap over the shaved heads of the boys so they could come to school and you weren't supposed to touch them because you could get it that way but Lizabeth didn't even like to be in the same room. Thinking about the shadowy nastiness veiled under the stockings was enough to make her start scratching even though her mother washed and oiled and braided her thick hair five times a week.

She waited till the wagon had creaked past the vacant lot before she went back inside. If her pinto pony were there in the lot, nibbling at the green grass her Daddy would plant, it would whinny at the sad ice wagon horse. She wondered how old the gray horse might be, why it always slunk by with its head bowed and its great backside swaying slowly as the dark heads of the saints in Homewood A.M.E. Zion when they hummed the verses of a hymn.

"That man dripping water in here like he don't have good sense. Some people just never had nothing and never will." Her mother was on her hands and knees mopping the faded linoleum with a rag.

"Here girl, take this till I get the pan." She extended her arm backward without turning her head. "Pan overflowed again and him slopping water, too." She was on her knees and the cotton housedress climbed up the backs of her bare thighs. Her mama's backside poked up in the air and its roundness, its splitness made her think of the horse's huge buttocks, then of her own narrow hips. Her mama drew the brimful drain pan from under the icebox, sliding it aside without spilling a drop. "Here," her arm extended again behind her, her fingers making the shape of the balled rag. She had to say *Here girl* again before Lizabeth raised her eyes from the black scarifications in the linoleum and pushed the rag she had wrung into her mother's fingers.

"I don't know why I'm down here punishing these bones of mine and you just standing there looking. Next time . . ."

Her mother stopped abruptly. She had been leaning on one elbow, the other arm stretched under the icebox to sop up the inevitable drips missed by the drain pan. Now she bowed her head even lower, one cheek almost touching the floor so she could see under the icebox. When her hand jerked from the darkness it was full of something blue-black and metal.

"Oh, God. Oh, my God."

She held it the way she held a trap that had snared a rat, and for a moment Lizabeth believed that must be what it was, some new rat-killing steel trap. Her mama set the wooden kind in dark corners all over the house but when one caught something her mother hated to touch it, she would try to sweep the trap and the squeezed rat body out the door together, leave it for John French to open the spring and shake the dead rodent into the garbage can so the trap could be used again. Her mama held a trap delicately if she had to touch it at all, in two fingers, as far from her body as she could reach, looking away from it till she dropped it in a place from which it could be broomed easily out the door. This time the object was heavier than a trap and her mama's eyes were not half-closed and her mouth was not twisted like somebody swallowing cod liver oil. She was staring, wide-eyed, frightened.

"Watch out . . . stand back."

On the drainboard the gun gleamed with a dull, blue-black light which came from inside, a dead glistening Lizabeth knew would be cold and quick to the touch, like the bloody, glass-eyed fish the gun lay next to.

"You've seen nothing. Do you understand, child? You've seen nothing and don't you ever breathe a word of this to a soul. Do you understand me?"

Lizabeth nodded. But she was remembering the man in the alley. Must remember. But that afternoon in the kitchen it was like seeing it all for the first time. Like she had paid her dime to the man at the Bellmawr Show and sat huddled in the darkness, squirming, waiting for pictures to start flashing across the screen. It had to begin with the caterpillar story.

"I got the most of it then. And if I don't die, she ain't gonna die neither, so stop that sniffling."

Lizabeth has heard the story so many times she can tell it almost as well as her mother. Not with words yet, not out loud yet, but she can set the people—her father, her mother, herself as a baby—on the stage and see them moving and understand when they are saying the right words and she would know if somebody told it wrong. She is nearly six years old and sitting on her mother's lap as she hears the caterpillar story this time. Sitting so they both can look out the downstairs window into Cassina Way.

Both look at the gray covering everything, a late afternoon gray gathered through a fall day that has not once been graced by the sun. Palpable as soot the gray is in the seams between the cobblestones, seals the doors and windows of the row houses across the alley. Lights will yellow the windows soon but at this in-between hour nothing lives behind the gray boards of the shanties across the way. Lizabeth has learned the number *Seventy-Four-Fifteen* Cassina Way and knows to tell it to a policeman if she is lost. But if she is Lizabeth French, she cannot be lost because she will be here, in this house certain beyond a number, absolutely itself among the look-alikes crowding Cassina Way. She will not be lost because there is a lot next door where her Daddy will grow vegetables, and her mother will put them in jars and they will eat all winter the sunshine and growing stored in those jars and there are three wooden steps her Daddy made for sitting and doing nothing till she gets stupid as a fly in that same sun, and sleeping rooms upstairs, her sister snoring and the candle poked in before her Daddy closes the door across the deep well.

The end house coming just before the empty corner lot is Lizabeth and Lizabeth nothing more nor less than the thinnest cobweb stretched in a dusty corner where the sounds, smells and sights of the house come together.

Lizabeth watches her mother's eyes lose their green. She sits as still as she can. She is not the worm now like her mama always calls her because she's so squirmy, she is nothing now because if she sits still enough her mother forgets her and Lizabeth who is nothing at all, who is not a worm and not getting too big to be sitting on people's laps all day, can watch the shadows deepen and her mama's green eyes turn gray like the houses across Cassina Way.

"There was a time Cassina Way nothing but dirt. Crab apple trees and pear trees grew where you see all them shacks. Then the war came and they had a parade on

Homewood Avenue and you should have seen them boys strut. They been cross the ocean and they knew they looked good in their uniforms and they sure was gon let everybody know it. People lined up on both sides the street to see those colored troops marching home from the war. The 505 Engineers. Everybody proud of them and them strutting to beat the band. Mize well been dancing down Homewood Avenue. In a manner of speaking they were dancing and you couldn't keep your feet still when they go high stepping past. That big drum get up inside your chest and when Elmer Hollinger hits it your skin feels about to bust. All of Homewood out that day. People I ain't never seen before. All the ones they built these shacks for back here on Cassina Way. Ones ain't never been nowhere but the country and put they children out in the morning, don't call them in till feeding time. Let them run wild. Let them make dirt and talk nasty and hair ain't never seen a comb.

"That's why I'ma hold on to you, girl. That's why your mama got to be mean sometimes and keep you in sometime you want to be running round outdoors."

Lizabeth loves the quiet time of day when she can just sit, when she has her mama all to herself and her mama talks to her and at her and talks to herself but loud enough so Lizabeth can hear it all. Lizabeth needs her mother's voice to make things real. (Years later when she will have grandchildren of her own and her mother and father both long dead Lizabeth will still be trying to understand why sometimes it takes someone's voice to make things real. She will be sitting in a room and the room full of her children and grandchildren and everybody eating and talking and laughing but she will be staring down a dark tunnel and that dark, empty tunnel is her life, a life in which nothing has happened, and she'll feel like screaming at the darkness and emptiness and wringing her hands because nothing will seem real, and she will be alone in a roomful of strangers. She will need to tell someone how it had happened. But anybody who'd care would be long dead. Anybody who'd know what she was talking about would be long gone but she needs to tell someone so she will begin telling herself. Patting her foot on the floor to keep time. Then she will be speaking out loud. The others will listen and pay attention. She'll see down the tunnel and it won't be a tunnel at all, but a door opening on something clear and bright. Something simple which makes so much sense it will flash sudden and bright as the sky in a summer storm. Telling the story right will make it real.)

"Look at that man. You know where he been at. You know what he's been doing. Look at him with his big hat self. You know he been down on his knees at Rosemary's shooting crap with them trifling niggers. Don't you pay me no mind, child. He's your Daddy and a good man so don't pay me no mind if I say I wish I could sneak out there and get behind him and boot his butt all the way home. Should have been home an hour ago. Should have been here so he could keep an eye on you while I start fixing dinner. Look at him just sauntering down Cassina Way like he owns it and got all the time in the world. Your sister be up in a minute and yelling soon as her eyes open and him just taking his own sweet time.

"He won too. Got a little change in his pocket. Tell by the way he walks. Walking like he got a load in his pants, like other people's nickels and dimes weigh him down. If he lost he'd be smiling and busting in here talking fast and playing with youall and keep me up half the night with his foolishness. Never saw a man get happy when he gambles away his family's dinner. Never saw a man get sour-faced and down in the mouth when he wins."

Lizabeth doesn't need to look anymore. Her Daddy will get closer and closer and then he'll come through the door. Their life together will begin again. He is coming home from Rosemary's, down Cassina Way. He is there if you look and there if you don't look. He is like the reflection, the image of mother and daughter floating in the grayness of Cassina Way. There if she looks, there if she doesn't.

She stares at the pane of glass and realizes how far away she has been, how long she has been daydreaming but he is only a few steps closer, taking his own good time, the weight of somebody else's money in his pockets, the crown of his hat taller than the shadowed roofs of Cassina Way.

Her mama's arms are a second skin, a warm snuggling fur that keeps out the grayness, the slight, late-afternoon chill of an October day. She hums to herself, a song about the caterpillar story her mama has just told. Her baby sister is sleeping so Lizabeth has her mother to herself. Whenever they are alone, together, is the best time of the day, even if it comes now when the day is nearly over, sitting at the window in her mama's lap and her mama, after one telling of the caterpillar story, quiet and gray as Cassina Way. Because Lizabeth has a baby sister Geraldine she must love even though the baby makes the house smaller and shrinks the taken-for-granted time Lizabeth was used to spending with her mama. Lizabeth not quite six that early evening, late afternoon she is recalling, that she has not remembered or relived for five years till it flashes back like a movie on a screen that afternoon her mother pulls the revolver from under the icebox.

Her mother screams and smashes her fist through the windowpane. A gunshot pops in the alley. Her Daddy dashes past the jagged space where the windowpane had been, glass falling around his head as he bounds past faster than she has ever seen him move, past the empty, collapsing frame toward the vacant lot. A gun clatters against the cobbles and a man runs off down the corridor of Cassina Way.

My God. Oh, my God.

Her mama's fist looks like someone has tied bright red strings across her knuckles. The chair tumbles backward as her mother snatches her away from the jagged hole. Baby Geraldine is yelping upstairs like a wounded animal. Lizabeth had been daydreaming, and the window had been there between her daydream and her Daddy, there had been separation, a safe space between, but the glass was shattered now and the outside air in her face and her mama's hand bleeding and her mama's arms squeezing her too tightly, crushing her as if her small body could stop the trembling of the big one wrapped around it.

"Lizabeth . . . Lizabeth."

When her mama had screamed her warning, the man's eyes leaped from her Daddy's back to the window. Lizabeth saw the gun but didn't believe the gun until her mama screamed again and flung her fist through the glass. That made it real and made her hear her own screams and made her Daddy a man about to be shot dead in the alley.

If a fist hadn't smashed through the window perhaps she would not have remembered the screaming, the broken glass, the shots when she watched her mama drag a pistol from under the icebox and set it on the bloody drainboard.

But Lizabeth did remember and see and she knew that Albert Wilkes had shot a policeman and run away and knew Albert Wilkes had come to the house in the dead of night and given her father his pistol to hide, and knew that Albert Wilkes would never come back, that if he did return to Homewood he would be a dead man.

"You're a fool, John French, and no better than the rest of those wine-drinking rowdies down at the Bucket of Blood and God knows you must not have a brain in your head to have a gun in a house with children and who in the name of sense would do such a thing whether it's loaded or not and take it out of here, man, I don't care where you take it, but take it out of here." Her mother shouting as loud as she ever shouts like the time he teased her with the bloody rat hanging off the end of the trap, her Daddy waving it at her mama and her mama talking tough first, then shouting and in tears and finally her Daddy knew he had gone too far and carried it out the house. . . .

Lizabeth remembered when the gun was dragged from under the icebox so there was nothing to do but lie awake all night and save her Daddy from himself, save him from the trespassing cart and smoking ashes and the blast of a shotgun and dead men and men running away forever. She'd save him like her mama had saved him. At least till he got that garden planted and things started growing and he put up a little fence and then nobody fool enough to dump ashes on something belonged to John French.

You ought to paint some yellow stripes and orange stripes on that scar, Mama.

Don't be making fun of my scar. This scar saved your father's life.

I know it did. I'm just jealous, that's all. Because I'll never know if I saved him. I'd sure like to know. Anyway an orange and yellow caterpillar running across the back of your hand would be pretty, Mama. Like a tattoo. I'd wear it like a badge, if I knew.

Don't know what you're talking about now. You're just talking now. But I do know if you hadn't been sitting in my lap, I'da put my whole body through that window and bled to death on those cobblestones in Cassina Way so just by being there you saved me and that's enough saving for one day and enough talk too, cause I can see John French coming down that alley from Rosemary's now and I'm getting sad now and I'm too old to be sitting here crying when ain't nothing wrong with me.

Breece D'J Pancake

1952–1979

Although Breece D'J Pancake published only a handful of short stories during his brief life, their mastery has secured him a high ranking in Appalachian literature. Born and reared in Milton, West Virginia, Pancake completed his BA degree in English education at Marshall University in 1974. He taught at two military high schools, Fort Union and Staunton, before studying creative writing at the University of Virginia. Pancake felt culturally at odds with the university's traditionally elite student body, and while there, he cultivated a "mountain man" persona. (In truth, Pancake did enjoy hunting and fishing throughout his life.) Pancake's unusual middle name was the result of a printer's error at the *Atlantic Monthly*. Pancake was charmed by the error and retained it for his nom de plume. Shortly before his death, Pancake converted to Catholicism. His depression, revealed in his writing and his correspondence with friends and family, led to his early death in 1979, when he was found dead from a self-inflicted gunshot wound at the age of twenty-six.

Pancake published six short stories, most in the *Atlantic Monthly*. These and six more unpublished stories were collected with the help of James Alan McPherson and John Casey, Pancake's professors at the University of Virginia, in a posthumous volume, *The Stories of Breece D'J Pancake* (1983). Pancake's biggest writing influence was Hemingway, whose economical writing style Pancake utilized.

Though he grew up in a conventional middle-class household, Pancake demonstrated an intimate understanding of poverty. His stories are chilling narratives of greed, lust, and lost hope. "First Day of Winter" depicts the relationship between aging parents and their sons cast against the landscape of the family's failing farm. Pancake's work is memorable for its ability to weave theme with setting in a narrative of bitterness and frustration that captures what many authors of his period saw as a crisis of identity in an evolving Appalachia.

First Day of Winter

Hollis sat by his window all night, staring at his ghost in glass, looking for some way out of the tomb Jake had built for him. Now he could see the first blue blur of morning growing behind bare tree branches, and beyond them the shadows of the farm. The work was done: silos stood full of corn, hay bales rose to the barn's roof, and the slaughter stock had gone to market; it was work done for figures in a bank, for debts, and now corn stubble leaned in the fields among stacks of fodder laced with frost. He could hear his parents shuffling about downstairs for their breakfast; his old mother giggling, her mind half gone from blood too thick in her veins; his father, now blind and coughing. He had told Jake on the phone, they'll live a long time. Jake would not have his parents put away like furniture. Hollis asked Jake to take them into his parsonage at Harpers Ferry; the farm was failing. Jake would not have room: the parsonage was too modest, his family too large.

He went downstairs for coffee. His mother would not bathe, and the warm kitchen smelled of her as she sat eating oatmeal with his father. The lids of the blind man's eyes hung half closed and he had not combed his hair; it stuck out in tufts where he had slept on it.

"Cer'al's hot." His mother giggled, and the crescent of her mouth made a weak grin. "Your daddy's burnt his mouth."

"I ain't hungry." Hollis poured his coffee, leaned against the sink.

The old man turned his head a little toward Hollis, bits of meal stuck to his lips. "You going hunting like I asked?"

Hollis sat his cup in the sink. "Thought I'd work on the car. We can't be with no way to town all winter because you like squirrel meat."

The old man ate his cereal, staring ahead. "Won't be Thanksgiving without wild game."

"Won't be Thanksgiving till Jake and Milly gets here," she said.

"They said last night they ain't coming down," his father said, and the old woman looked at Hollis dumbly.

"I got to work on the car," Hollis said, and went toward the door.

"Car's been setting too long," the old woman yelled. "You be careful of snakes."

Outside, the air was sharp, and when the wind whipped against his face, he gasped. The sky was low, gray, and the few Angus he had kept from market huddled near the feeder beside the barn. He threw them some hay, brought his tool chest from the barn, began to work on the car. He got in to see if it would start, ground it. As he sat behind the wheel, door open, he watched his father come down from the porch with his cane. The engine's grinding echoed through the hollows, across the hills.

Hollis's knuckles were bloody, scraped under the raised hood, and they stung as he turned the key harder, gripped the wheel. His father's cane tapped through the frosty yard, the still of December, and came closer to Hollis. The blind man's mouth was shut against the cold, the dark air so close to his face, and Hollis stopped trying the engine, got out.

"You can tell she's locking up." The blind man faced him.

"This ain't a tractor." Hollis walked around, looked under the hood, saw the hairline crack along one side of the engine block. His father's cane struck the fender, and he stood still and straight beside his son. Hollis saw his father's fingers creeping along the grille, holding him steady. "She sounded locked up," he said again.

"Yeah." Hollis edged the man aside, shut the hood. He didn't have the tools to pull the engine, and had no engine to replace it. "Maybe Jake'll loan you the money for a new car."

"No," the old man said. "We'll get by without bothering Jake."

"Put it on the cuff? Do you think the bank would give us another nickel?"

"Jake has too much to worry with as it is."

"I asked him to take you-all last night."

"Why?"

"I asked him and Molly to take you in and he said no. I'm stuck here. I can't make my own way for fighting a losing battle with this damn farm."

"Farming's making your way."

"Hell."

"Everybody's trying for something better anymore. When everybody's going one way, it's time to turn back." He rationalized in five directions.

In the faded morning the land looked scarred. The first snows had already come, melted, and sealed the hills with a heavy frost the sun could not soften. Cold winds had peeled away the last clinging oak leaves, left the hills a quiet gray-brown that sloped into the valley on either side.

He saw the old man's hair bending in the wind.

"Come on inside, you'll catch cold."

"You going hunting like I asked?"

"I'll go hunting."

As he crossed the last pasture heading up toward the ridges, Hollis felt a sinking in his gut, a cold hunger. In the dry grass he shuffled toward the fence line to the rising ridges and high stand of oaks. He stopped at the fence, looked down on the valley and the farm. A little at a time Jake had sloughed everything to him, and now that his brother was away, just for this small moment, Hollis was happier.

He laid down his rifle, crossed the fence, and took it up again. He headed deeper into the oaks, until they began to mingle with the yellow pine along the ridge. He saw no squirrels, but sat on a stump with oaks on all sides, their roots and bottom trunk brushed clean by squirrel tails. He grew numb with waiting, with cold; taking a nickel from his pocket, he raked it against the notched stock, made the sound of a squirrel cutting nuts. Soon enough he saw a flick of tail, the squirrel's body hidden by the tree trunk. He tossed a small rock beyond the tree, sent it stirring and rattling the leaves, watched as the squirrel darted to the broadside trunk. Slowly, he raised his rifle, and when the echoes cleared from the far hills across the valley, the squirrel fell. He field-dressed it, and the blood dried cold on his hands; then he moved up the ridge toward the pine thicket, stopping every five minutes to kill until the killing drained him and his game bag weighed heavily at his side.

He rested against a tree near the thicket, stared into its dark wavings of needles and branches; there, almost blended with the red needles, lay a fox. He watched it without moving, and thought of Jake, hidden, waiting for him to break, to move. In a fit of meanness, he snapped his rifle to his shoulder and fired. When he looked again the fox was gone, and he caught a glimpse of its white-tipped tail drifting through the piny darkness.

Hollis dropped the gun, sat against the tree, and, when the wind snatched at his throat, fumbled to button his collar. He felt old and tired, worn and beaten, and he thought of what Jake had said about the state home he wanted the folks in. They starve them, he said, and they mistreat them, and in the end they smother them. For a moment, Hollis wondered what it would be like to smother them, and in the same moment caught himself, laughing; but a darkness had covered him, and he pulled his gloves on to hide the blood on his hands. He stumbled up, and, grabbing his gun, ran between trees to the clearing nearest the fence, and when he crossed into the pasture felt again a light mist of sweat on his face, a calming.

He crossed the fields and fences, slogged across the bottoms and up to the house. Inside, his mother sat in the tiny back room, listening, with the husband, to quiet music on the radio. She came to Hollis, and he saw in her wide-set eyes a fear and knowledge—and he knew she could see what insanity had driven him to.

He handed her the squirrels, dressed and skinned, from his game bag, and went to wash his hands. From the corner of his eye, he saw her, saw as she dropped the squirrels into soaking brine, saw her hand go up to her mouth, saw her lick a trace of blood and smile.

Sitting at the table, he looked down at his empty plate, waited for the grace, and when it was said, passed the plate of squirrel. He had taken for himself only the fore-quarters and liver, leaving the meaty hinds and saddles.

"Letter come from Jake." The ol man held a hindquarter, gnawed at it.

"And pitchers of them." His mother got up, came back with a handful of snapshots.

"He done fine for himself. Lookee at the pretty church and the children," she said.

The church was yellow brick and low, stained windows. In the picture Jake stood holding a baby, his baby girl, named after their mother. His face was squinted with a smile. The old woman poked a withered finger into the picture. "That's my Mae Ellen," she said. "That's my favorite."

"Shouldn't have favorites." His father laid down the bones.

"Well, you got to face that he done fine for himself."

Hollis looked out the window; the taste of liver, a taste like acorns, coated his mouth with cold grease. "Coming snow," he said.

His father laughed. "Can't feel it."

"Jake says they're putting a little away now. Says the church is right nice people."

"They ain't putting away enough to hear him tell it."

"Now," she said, "he's done fine, just let it be."

When the meal was finished, Hollis pushed back his chair. "I asked Jake to help by taking you-all in; he said no."

The old man turned away; Hollis saw tears in his blind eyes, and that his body shook from crying. He wagged his head again and again. The old woman scowled, and she took up the plates, carried them to the sink. When she came back, she bent over Hollis.

"What'd you figure he'd say? He's worked like an ox and done good, but he can't put us all up."

The old man was still crying, and she went to him, helped him from the chair. He was bent with age, with crying, and he raised himself slowly, strung his flabby arm around the woman's waist. He turned to Hollis. "How could you do such a god-damned thing as that?"

"We'll take our nap," she said. "We need our rest."

Hollis went to the yard, to where his car stood, looked again at the cracked block.

He ran his hand along the grille where the old man's hands had cleared away dust. The wind took his breath, beat on him, and the first light flecks of ice bounced from the fenders. The land lay brittle, open, and dead.

He went back to the house, and in the living room stretched out on the couch. Pulling the folded quilt to his chest, he held it there like a pillow against himself. He heard the cattle lowing to be fed, heard the soft rasp of his father's crying breath, heard his mother's broken humming of a hymn. He lay that way in the graying light and slept.

The sun was blackened with snow, and the valley closed in quietly with humming, quietly as an hour of prayer.

Fred Chappell

1936–

For biographical information about Fred Chappell, see the headnote provided above for his poem "My Grandmother Washes Her Vessels." The following story comes from Chappell's *I Am One of You Forever* (1985), the first novel in his Kirkman tetralogy. These novels share characters and structure with Chappell's long poem *Midquest*. Ole Fred of the poems becomes the novels' narrator, Jess Kirkman.

FROM I Am One of You Forever

CHAPTER THREE: THE BEARD

Uncle Gurton's beard had a long and complex history, but I will try not to bore us with much of that. Enough to say that it was a fabled beard and that when my father and I heard that Uncle Gurton was coming to visit we were thrilled at the prospect of viewing the legendary fleece.

"How long is that beard of his now?" my father asked my grandmother.

She smiled a secret smile. "Oh, I wouldn't have no idea," she said. "But he's been growing it for forty years or more and ain't once yet trimmed it. That's what I hear tell."

"And he's coming here to our house to visit?" I asked.

"That's what Aunt Sary says in her letter." She held up the scrawled bit of paper, but not close enough for us to read the writing.

"And when is he going to get here?"

"She wouldn't know about that. You'll just have to wait."

"Hot damn," my father said. "If this ain't the biggest thing since Christmas. We're going to make that old man plenty welcome."

"Now, Joe Robert, don't you be deviling Uncle Gurton," she said. "Leave him in peace."

"Oh, I wouldn't harm a hair of his face," he said. "When you say he's coming?"

She smiled again. "You'll just have to wait till he shows up."

Show up is exactly what Uncle Gurton did. We heard no car or truck arrive, and he didn't walk into the house or knock at the door. One Tuesday noon he was just there, standing under the walnut tree in the side yard and staring at our chopblock and pile of kindling as if he'd never seen such objects upon the face of the earth. An apparition, he simply became present.

The three of us raised our heads from our dinner plates at the same time and saw him, and a spooky feeling came over us.

"What in the world is *that?*" my father asked.

"Uncle Gurton," said my grandmother in her serenest voice.

His back was toward us, so that all we could tell was that he was a very tall man, his white head bare, and dressed in faded overalls and a green plaid shirt, as lean and narrow as a fence rail, and warped with age and weather. Then, as if presenting himself formally to our gaze, he turned around.

I was profoundly disappointed. The famous beard that he had been working on for forty years and more, the beard that was the pivot of so many stories, was tucked down inside his overalls bib.

My father and I had made bets whether it would hang down to his belly button or all the way down to his knees, and now we couldn't say.

But even apart from his beard he was an extraordinary-appearing person. His arms were too long for his shirt sleeves and his hands dangled out like big price tags. His overalls legs were too short and his skinny legs went naked into his high-topped brogans. His long hair was white and hung down both sides of his ruddy sharp-featured face. The beard, as purely white as a morning cloud, went down behind his overalls bib, and what happened to it after that, what it truly looked like, only Uncle Gurton and the almighty and omniscient God could say.

"Jess," my grandmother said, "go out and welcome Uncle Gurton to the house."

"Please, ma'am, no," I said. Uncle Gurton was too famous in my mind. It would have been easier to shake hands with Lou Gehrig.

"He does look kind of fearsome," my father said. "I'll go gather him in."

He went out and talked and Uncle Gurton gave him one short nod and then they came into the house. When the old man entered our small alcove dining space he looked even taller and odder than he had outdoors. His head nearly scraped the low ceiling.

My grandmother told him how glad we were to see him and how we hoped he would stay a long time, and asked him to sit and eat with us. Which he did with right good will. She brought flatware and a glass of buttermilk and a plate piled full of green beans, cornbread, and fried rabbit. Then she sat down at the end of the table and began to question him.

"How is Aunt Jewel getting along?" she asked.

Uncle Gurton smiled and was silent.

She waited a space of time and asked, "How is Cousin Harold doing?"

He gave her a smile as warm and friendly as the first, and as informative as a spoon.

In a while she lit on the correct form. "Has Hiram Williams got him a good tobacco crop set out?" He smiled and gave a vigorous affirmative shake of his head. After this, she asked questions that could be answered yes or no, and Uncle Gurton would nod a cheerful Yes or wag a downcast No.

And all during this exchange he was feeding voraciously. Great heaping forkfuls went into his hirsute mouth with mechanical accuracy and rapidity. A sight awesome to behold. My father kept filling his plate and Uncle Gurton kept emptying it. My father described it later: "The way he was forking at it, and with all that hair around his mouth, I kept thinking it was a man throwing a wagonload of alfalfa into a hayloft."

He finished by downing a whole glass of buttermilk. We came to find out that buttermilk was his sole beverage, breakfast, dinner, supper. He never touched anything else, not even water.

He edged his chair back from the table.

"Uncle Gurton, won't you have a little something else?" my grandmother asked.

"No thank you," he said. "I've had an elegant sufficiency; any more would be a superfluity."

That was his one saying, the only one we ever heard him utter, and he was as proud of it as another man might be of a prize beagle. He said this sentence at the end of every meal, and we came to realize that he got mighty upset, his whole day was lusterless, if you didn't ask him to have a little more something, and give him occasion to say his sentence.

My father's mouth flew open like a phoebe's after a fly. His eyes lit up with surprise. "Would you mind saying that again, Uncle Gurton?" he asked. "What you just said?"

Uncle Gurton gave him a sweet warm smile and disappeared.

I don't mean that he dissolved into nothingness before our watching eyes like a trick ghost in a horror movie. But he evaded my father's request with one of those silent smiles, and when we had got up and scraped our dishes into the slop bucket and stacked them on the drainboard of the sink and turned around, Uncle Gurton was gone. His chair was angled back from the table, his red and white checked napkin folded neatly and laid in the seat, and he was nowhere to be seen. If it weren't for the soiled plate with the knife and fork primly crossed and the empty streaked glass, we might not have believed that he had been there. No footsteps of departure, no sound of the side door, nothing.

"Our Uncle Gurton has got some interesting ways about him," my father said.

"Poor old soul," my grandmother murmured.

This habit of absenting and distancing himself we learned to know as an integral part of Uncle Gurton's character, as one with the man as his silence. You would sight him on the ridge of the pasture above the farther barn, his stark figure scarecrowlike against the sky and leaning into the wind, and then if you glanced off into the pear tree to see a bluejay, he was no longer on the ridge when you looked again. Snuffed out of the present world like a match flame. Translated into another and inevitable dimension of space. What? Where? When was he? He was an enigma of many variations, and his one answer, silence, satisfied them all as far as he was concerned.

"There's one thing, though, you can be certain of," my father said. "He won't miss a mealtime."

And this was true. As soon as the first steaming dish of corn or squash or squirrel burgoo was set out, Uncle Gurton *arrived* from whatever mystery world otherwise absorbed him.

My father kept testing him. "Uncle Gurton," he said, "this afternoon Jess and me have got a little fence mending to do along the back side of the far oatfield. Restring some barbwire, reset a few posts. How'd you like to go along and keep us company?"

There was the smile, sweet and friendly and utterly inscrutable.

My father rephrased the question. "I mean," he said, "would you be willing to go along with us, maybe lend a hand?"

Uncle Gurton nodded.

My father leaned back in his chair. "That's fine," he said. "We'll go catch us a smoke out on the porch here after lunch and then we'll go on over to the oatfield."

What distracted us? When we finished eating and tidied up a bit, Uncle Gurton was gone again. The folded napkin, the crossed knife and fork; and no Uncle Gurton.

"I'm going to get me a moving picture camera," my father said. "Because I want to find out how he does that. I believe that it's a truly rare gift that he has."

He pondered the matter all the way out to the fence line, the roll of barbwire hoisted on his shoulder and bouncing on the burlap-sack pad with every stride. I walked at his side, toting the awkward posthole diggers and the wire stretcher. "I put the question to him wrong," he said at last. "I didn't ask him was he actually going to go with us, but was he *willing* to go."

"What's the difference?" I said.

"He was willing to go, all right, but he was even more willing not to."

At the top of the high second hill of the pasture we turned to look back. There in the dusty road between the house and the first barn, as steady as a mailbox post, stood Uncle Gurton.

I dropped the posthole diggers with a loud clatter. When we looked again, the road was empty.

"No, a movie camera wouldn't capture it," my father said. "It would take some kind of invention that is beyond the capacity of present-day science."

We were resting from the fence work. We sat in the shade of a big red oak and watched the wind write long cursive sentences in the field of whitening oats.

"One question we don't need to ask," my father said. "Whether he sleeps with his beard inside or outside the covers. Stands to reason that a man who would tuck his beard down in his overalls will sleep with it under the covers."

"How long do you reckon it is?" It was the thousandth time I had asked that question.

"Before he got here, I would've guessed it was a foot and a half," he said. "And then when I saw him first, I'd've said two feet. But now the more I don't see it the longer it gets. I've been imagining it four or five feet easy."

"You really think it's all that long?"

"I've got to where I'll think anything when it comes to that beard."

"If it's that long he has to let it run down his britches leg," I said. "Which one you think, left or right?"

"Kind of a ticklish decision," he said. "Maybe he divides it up, half down one leg, half down the other."

"You reckon it's the same color all over?"

He gave me a level look. "Jess, for anything I know, it's green and purple polka-dotted under them overalls and he's got it braided into hangnooses. But I'll tell you what. I'm bound and determined to see that beard, every inch of it. I'll never sleep easy again till I do."

"How are you going to do that?"

"I'll let you know."

It was three days later, the hour before suppertime, when he revealed his grand and cunning design. He took a thumb-sized blue bottle out of his pocket. "You see this? This is our beard-catcher; this is going to turn the trick."

"What is it?"

"It's a sleeping draught I got from Doc McGreavy."

Doc McGreavy was our veterinarian, an old man who lived with his wife in a dark little house three miles from us, at the very end of the road where the mountainside pines took possession and human habitation left off.

"What are you going to do?"

"Slip it in his buttermilk. When he goes to bed he'll sleep as sound as a bear wintering in. Then we'll have us a look at that beard."

"You think it'll work?"

"Doc says it'll lay a horse down, he's put many a horse to sleep with it. I'll give Uncle Gurton just a little bit. We won't be hurting him any."

"You sure?"

He was impatient. "Sure I'm sure."

And so at supper my father kept close watch on Uncle Gurton's buttermilk. When he had drunk off the first glass, my father picked it up. "Here," he said, "let me get you some more, Uncle Gurton." He tipped me an evil wink and I knew he was going to drop the powders.

Uncle Gurton nodded and flashed the friendliest smile in his smile box, and when the buttermilk came he drained it in two swallows. My father looked so gleeful I was afraid he'd bust out laughing and spoil it all.

Then I was afraid he'd got hold of the wrong powders because nothing seemed to be happening. Uncle Gurton was as bright eyed silent as ever and was forking into the stewed tomatoes with devastating effect. But in a few minutes I saw that his eyes were growing faraway cloudy and the lids were drooping.

"Have another piece of cornbread," my father suggested.

"No thank you," he said. "I've had an elegant sufficiency—"

But he didn't say on to *the superfluity* and we knew we had him. He rose from the table and stumbled through the kitchen and out the door, headed down the hall for the stairway. He didn't cross his knife and fork on the plate, and the checked napkin lay on the floor where he'd dropped it. My father retrieved it and laid it by his plate.

My grandmother followed his progress with curious eyes. "Uncle Gurton is right strange-acting. I wonder is he feeling poorly."

"Aw, he's okay," my father said. "He's just plumb tuckered from appearing and disappearing out of thin air all day."

We cleaned and stacked our dishes and then retired to the side porch where my father smoked his cigarette after meals.

"We going to see the beard now?" I asked.

"Better give him a little while, make sure he's sound asleep. Let's go out to the shed a minute."

In the woodshed he took a dusty kerosene lantern off a hook and shook it to hear if there was oil in the reservoir. He reached an old motheaten blue sweater off a nail and wiped the cobweb off the lamp. "We'll need this if we're going to be good and sneaky," he said. He brought the lamp and the sweater and we returned to the porch and he smoked two slow cigarettes and we watched the first stars pierce the western sky. The far hills went hazy blue and then purple-black.

"Let's go," he said, and we opened the forbidden door and tiptoed through the dark sun parlor. The souvenir teacups rattled on the glassed-in shelves. It was stale in here and dusty. I was afraid I'd sneeze and trumpet our crime to the world at large.

We entered into the dark stairway hall and stood for a moment to listen. My father struck a kitchen match with his thumbnail and lit the wick and let the shell down. The pale orange light made our shadows giant on the walls, and everything was strange in here in the hallway, all silent, and in the stairwell above in the hovering darkness. I felt a way I'd never felt before, like a thief or a detective. My breath was quick, the pulse tight in my temples.

We climbed the stairs one careful step at a time. Our shadows fell behind us and washed up on the far wall and the shadows of the banister posts spun like ghostly wheel spokes. My father held the lantern by his side in his left hand and I hid in his righthand shadow, moving when he did.

We paused at the top of the stairs and he raised the lantern. The door to Uncle Gurton's room was at the end of the hall and we edged toward it. Every snap and squeak of the floor made me fearful; I was certain we'd be discovered. What could we say to Uncle Gurton or my grandmother when they found us? I realized, maybe for the first time, that my father wasn't always the safest protection in the world.

At that fateful door we stopped and held our breaths to listen. My father began to ease the door open, turning the knob slowly, slowly, until it ceased and the door swung open upon blackness. We heard the sound of heavy breathing and I felt relieved to know we hadn't poisoned the old man to death. My father had wrapped the wool sweater around the lantern and now he rolled it up from the bottom, showing a little light at a time.

We needn't have been so precisely stealthy. Uncle Gurton's mouth was open and, lying flat on his back, he uttered a gurgling half-snore. We could have dropped a wagonload of tin kettles on the floor and he wouldn't have stirred an ounce.

I was impressed by how Uncle Gurton lived. There were a few shirts on hangers in the open closets and one shirt hung on the back of a chair by the foot of the bed. In front of this chair his battered brogans sat, a sock dangling out of the top of each. And that was all I saw there. He led a simple existence.

My father handed me the lantern and we advanced to the edge of the bed. After giving me one significant and thrilling glance, he began to turn the sheet down from under the old man's chin. We were dismayed to discover that Uncle Gurton slept in his overalls. He wore no shirt; his naked freckled arms lay flat beside him, but the blue denim bib still hid what we had schemed so anxiously to disclose. My father rolled the sheet down to Uncle Gurton's waist, then leaned back from the bedside.

He gave me another look, this one of bewilderment and frustration. Little beads of sweat stood on his forehead. I shrugged. I was ready to leave, figuring Uncle Gurton was just one too many for us. He was a coon we couldn't tree.

But we'd come too far for my father to let it go. He reached and unhooked the gallus on the far side; then loosed the one nearer. Then he inched the bib down.

We were not disappointed; it was everything we had come to see. A creeklet of shining white lay over Uncle Gurton's skinny chest and gleamed in the lantern light like a drawer of silver spoons. It was light and dry and immaculately clean—a wonder because we'd never known Uncle Gurton to bathe. We'd never seen him do much but eat.

I thought the beard was marvelous, and I couldn't regret all our trouble and terror. It was like visiting a famous monument—Natural Bridge, Virginia, say; and I felt a different person now I'd seen it.

But the great question went begging. How long was it? We couldn't tell, and there didn't seem to be any way to find out unless we stripped him naked or tugged the beard to light by handfuls.

We stood gazing dejected until the beard began to move. It was a movement hard to distinguish. At first I thought it was flowing away to the foot of the bed like a brook, and then I thought it was rising like early mist over a pond. My father clutched my shoulder and I knew he saw this motion too.

Then suddenly it was out upon us, billow on billow of gleaming dry wavy silver beard, spilling out over the sheet and spreading over the bed like an overturned bucket of milk. It flowed over the foot of the bed and then down the sides, noiseless, hypnotic. There was no end to it.

I felt it stream over my shoe tops and round my ankles and it was all I could do to stifle a shriek. I dropped the lantern and my father bent and picked it up before it could set fire to the beard, to the house. We retreated, stepping backward quickly, but always facing the bed. We were afraid to turn our backs on that freed beard.

Now over Uncle Gurton's torso it began to rise into the air, mounding up dry and white and airy. It was like seeing a frosty stack of hay rising of its own volition out of the ground. Little streamers of beard detached from the mass and began to wave in the air like the antennae of butterflies. They searched around the tall flat headboard of the bed and went corkscrewing up the curtain drawstrings. In just a moment the beard had curled in and out, around and over, the chair in the middle of the floor like wisteria overtaking a trellis.

At last my father said something; speaking out loud. *My God,* was what he said.

"Let's please leave," I said. The flow of beard was up to my calves now and I was afraid it would start wrapping around my legs the way it had gone over the chair. Then what would happen?

"Go on," my father said. "I'm right behind you." Then he pointed and said *My God* again.

Over the bed the beard had climbed until it was like a fogbank, only more solid, and threatened to topple forward. But it was still sliding underneath in sheets off the bed like a small waterfall, and now out of that misty mass and down over the edge of the bed came a birchbark canoe with two painted Cherokee Indians paddling with smooth alacrity. Above them, out of the mist-bank of beard, flew a hawk pursued by a scattering of blackbirds. We heard a silvery distant singing and saw a provocative flashing and then a mermaid climbed out of the beard and positioned herself in the streaming-over straight chair. She did not seem to see my father and me, but gazed into some private distance and sang her bell-like song; the hair that fell over her shoulders, hiding her breasts, was the same color as Uncle Gurton's beard.

Behind the mermaid's singing all sorts of other sounds emerged, squeaks and squawks, chatterings, chitterings, muffled roars, howls, and thunderings: the background noises in a Tarzan movie. In the corner of the room was a sudden and terrific upheaval and a great mass of beard lifted to the height of the ceiling, then subsided to ominous silence. We glimpsed the movement of a huge indistinct bulk beneath the surface, moving stately-swift toward the far wall.

"What's that?" I whispered.

My father said *My God* once more and then murmured, "I believe to my soul it's a damn big white whale."

"I really think it's time to get out of here."

"I do believe you're absolutely right, Jess," he said. He pointed at three dark sharp triangles cutting through the surface. "Sharks in here too. Well, that settles that. We'd better go, I reckon."

He slipped the lantern bail up over his shoulder and dropped the old wool sweater. It floated for a moment on the surface of the silver hair and suddenly submerged. Something had snatched it under, I didn't want to know what.

We made our way to the door, lifting our feet high, and after a minute of straining together, managed to push the slowly closing door against the wall. The river of beard was already out into the upper hall, spreading both ways along the corridor. We stopped at the top of the stairs and my father unslung the lantern from his shoulder and held it up. The beard was flowing steadily down the steps, and the footing on the stairway looked plenty treacherous.

"What do you think?" I asked.

"I don't know. I don't trust it."

"I know what," I said. "Let's slide down the banister."

"Yeah, that's the ticket," he said. "I'll go first and hold the lantern for you. You can see your way down better."

"I'll go first."

"Stay right here and watch if I get down okay." He clenched the tin wire bail in his teeth. Then he straddled and lifted his feet and slid to the bottom pretty nifty. But he hit the newel post there hard and I knew if he hadn't had a mouthful of lantern bail I'd have heard some hair-singeing curses. He got off and stepped back, holding the lantern with one hand and rubbing his ass with the other. "Come on," he said, "you can make it just fine."

But as I was getting set to mount the banister, my left foot tangled in a wavelet of beard and I pitched forward. I was sure I was drowned or strangled, but my right hand on the banister held me up and I twisted over and got hold with my left hand and pulled myself up. Then I got on and slid down.

"I was worried about you for a second there," he said. "Come on, let's go."

"I was a little worried myself."

The beard was only shoe top deep down here and we went padding through it into the little sitting room, then through the kitchen hallway and out the back door.

In the yard stood a startling black apparition, but when my father held the lantern toward it, it was only my grandmother standing straight and narrow and angry in a wine-colored bathrobe. "What have you boys been doing?" she asked.

We said nothing and turned to look at the house. The upstairs windows were packed solid white with beard, and there were trailers coming out of the downstairs kitchen windows, and from the chimney a long flamelike banner of it reached toward the stars and swayed in the cold breeze.

"We just wanted to see Uncle Gurton's beard," I told her.

She clucked her tongue. "Well, do you think you've seen enough of it?"

My father looked at her and gave a deep and mournful sigh. "Yes ma'am," he said. "I've seen an elegant sufficiency. Any more—" He choked on a giggle like a bone in his throat. "Any more would be a superfluity."

George Ella Lyon

1949–

Born in Harlan, Kentucky, George Ella Lyon began writing in the third grade and playing guitar in the eighth grade. As an adult, after establishing herself as a poet, Lyon was recruited to her well-known role as children's author by influential children's book editor Richard Jackson. In addition, Lyon is a novelist, playwright, essayist, and musician. Using word and song, she advocates for social and environmental justice. After teaching and serving as a writer in residence for many years, Lyon conducts writing workshops for children and adults throughout Appalachia.

Lyon uses the rich musical and labor history of her home to inform her work, including children's books such as *Mama Is a Miner* (1994) and an account of Florence Reece's composition of the union standard "Which Side Are You On?" While Lyon writes about diverse subjects—from childhood disability to teenage pregnancy to the woman who founded the Bronx Zoo's animal nursery—the mountains of eastern Kentucky and the people who live among them remain her most consistent inspiration.

In this excerpt from the young adult novel *With a Hammer for My Heart* (1997), fifteen-year-old Lawanda Ingle sells magazines to help finance her college education, her path out of her close-knit coal town. On her rounds, she befriends Amos Garland, a mentally scarred World War II veteran and alcoholic living in a school bus at the edge of town. Parts of the novel are narrated by Nancy Catherine, Garland's estranged adult daughter, who remembers her father only as an abusive alcoholic. Garland is jailed for writing about Lawanda in his private journal, observations that some in the town, including Lawanda's parents, regard as sexually inappropriate. Lawanda, who insists nothing inappropriate happened, seeks assistance for her friend from Nancy Catherine and from her own grandmother, Mamaw, who was kicked out of church for claiming she has visions of a female God who grants her healing powers.

FROM With a Hammer for My Heart

NANCY CATHERINE: So she comes blazing into my life with a wild tale about my daddy and a mane of hair like the youth of steel wool: Lawanda Ingle—is that a name? Gets me off center, all wobbled into memory, promising to go back with her to Cardin, and then gives me a feather. You know, like from a bird. I don't know what kind. I have enough trouble with flowers. And she says her mamaw uses it in some primitive ritual. You have to admit this is interesting. My daddy's a *nut,* but her grandmother is a *witch.*

She tells about the old woman while I finish out the afternoon. Also she eats her lunch. You would not believe it. A sandwich of something she calls dog meat—they make it from ground-up bologna seasoned with peanut butter and vinegar. She has a hod of this stuff between two pieces of balloon bread. Also she has an RC. I think of my yogurt, rice cakes, miso spread, and sprouts. Of herb tea. Then I think how Lawanda looks new and healthy as all get-out, while I look like what the garbagemen won't take. Well, it's because I ate the equivalent of dog meat when I was her age, that's all. Moon Pies and fatback and soup beans, slabs of commodity cheese. Mother probably put Kool-Aid in my bottle. I know she did in Eddie's. It's what she could afford and it kept him quiet.

I am stunned by this whole thing. I take the feather and blow on it. The sensation I get is like glitter spilled down my back. I shake my head. Lawanda watches.

"What's your mamaw's name?"

"Ada Smith. She was a Holcomb."

I laugh. "Holcombs don't mean a thing to me."

There's a frown between her eyebrows, but otherwise she just gazes. This girl is too calm.

"Does Ms. Smith have visions all the time?"

"No," Lawanda says. "Just that one."

"And it was enough?"

"I guess so. Enough to make her a healer, anyway. That keeps her busy."

"A lot of sickness in this world."

Lawanda nods. I think how to her that means cancer and black lung, while to me it means old Amos. AG, his initials say. *Ag. Gag.* Some dictionaries say Amos means "burden." Why look it up? I say. Why drive five hours to meet it?

But that's what I'm doing, caught in his ego undertow. Viola says she can keep store. I close at four and Lawanda helps me deliver orders on the way home.

"I've done this sometimes with Dad," she offers.

"Yours or mine?"

She takes a deep breath. Maybe she's not all that calm.

"Sorry," I say. "Done what?"

"Delivered stuff. He's the route man for the We-Suit-U cleaners."

"At least when you get the dry cleaning to the door, they don't say it's all wilted."

"Sometimes they do," she says. There's a break while she takes the Pine Cone Supreme to the Haddixes'. "One woman won't allow her curtains to be put on hangers. I have to stand in the back of the truck and hold them over my arms."

I hoot and her gray eyes widen as if she never thought that could be funny. I practice deep breathing till we get home. Beechwood Estates, and not a tree in sight. Upstairs, end apartment, 43A—small but full of light. And the living room corner is a bay window, faceted out like a lute back. That's where I have my cacti and crystals. Lawanda goes right over to it.

"What a great lookout!"

"Yeah. It's a powerful place for me."

"I have a place like that," she says. "The laurel rock up the hill behind our house. I go there to think."

"You're young," I tell her. "In twenty years, you won't try to think."

"Excuse me?" She turns around, the last winter daylight her aura.

"You'll just be trying to get congruent."

She shakes her head.

"Well, never mind. You want some juice or something before we go?"

"No, but I need to call Mamaw."

"Sure. The phone is on the wall by the microwave." I point her toward the kitchen. I really want to hear what she says to this woman, but nothing carries.

When I come out with my stuff, she doesn't look so good. She's sitting in the corner of the couch.

"You get her?"

She just nods.

"What did she say?"

"Said my mom pitched a fit even Dad couldn't catch."

"So?"

"The two of them drove all the way to Sexton before Dad persuaded her I'd beat them home."

"Sounds like you're in hot water."

"Boiling."

She smiles a little.

"Let's go then. I expect the longer you're gone, the hotter it will get."

"Can it get any hotter than boiling?"

"It could boil dry," I say, "and ruin the pan."

"Okay."

We head out.

It's not a bad trip once we make it through the traffic. I like getting out of Louisville, so something besides the river can shape my mind. I just wish it wasn't Amos. I suggest Lawanda look through my tapes.

"Ocean," she says, holding one up. "What does it mean?"

"Just that. Waves, surf, wind, birds. What you'd hear if you were on the beach."

"Wow! Can we listen to it?"

"That's the idea." I snap it into the cassette player and soon we're driving through foothills, earth swell, and the ocean roars in the car.

She's leaning back, her eyes closed.

"You can recline the seat if you want to. There's a handle on the side by the door."

"You don't mind?" she asks. I shake my head. "Wake me up when you need directions."

"Yes ma'am. I wouldn't want to miss the jail."

That's a lie. Anyway, I take Lawanda home first. Her house sits right on the narrow road. Green foundation, white picket porch on a little white box. "Dwelling house," my mother would say, to distinguish it from smokehouse, outhouse, and so on. There's barely room to pull off, so I start to follow Lawanda out the passenger's side, but she is up the steps with two sets of arms around her before I even get my feet on the frozen mud. I'm sliding back toward the driver's seat when I see a big figure come down the steps. Could this be the wild mamaw, bird woman whose feather is in my bag? I get out.

She comes toward me, her left hand hitching stray hair into a bun, her right hand offered.

"You're a good girl, Nancy Catherine," she says. "You've done right to come."

"You must be Lawanda's grandmother."

"Yes, her ma's ma. Ada Smith."

"You knew my aunt?"

"Law, yes."

"And you know my father."

"I'm proud to say I do."

"You're about the only one!" I laugh.

She just pats her dress front. I wonder if she's got feathers in there nesting with those soft eggs.

"He's a man out on a limb," she says, "but I see the tree's yet living." Her nod indicates me.

"Knock on wood?" I ask.

A smile pulls her cheeks into furrows.

"Depends if you're ready to answer the door."

LAWANDA: I listened to Nancy Catherine pull out, Mamaw labor up the porch steps, Mom rant. Then we went, all knotted up, into the house. Mom and Dad sat on the couch, I sat in the dump chair, and Mamaw took the rocker in the corner. Taking a deep breath, I reached back and flipped the elastic loop to let my hair loose. I was home.

"I apologize for worrying you," I said, "and for going where you told me not to. But I don't think it's wrong. Being friends with Garland, I mean."

"Friends!" Mom said this like a dirty word.

"I don't know what he wrote, but I know he didn't *do* a thing except talk to me. And listen. He took me seriously!"

Dad sucked in his breath. "God Almighty, Lawanda! Serious is just what this is."

"I know that!"

"Then why didn't you come to me? Why did you head off into more danger?"

"Everything is dangerous," I told him.

"Oh, honey," Dad said. "You don't know the half of it."

"I know *my* half, which is more than you know!" I stood up. Anger hit me full force. "You don't know Garland! You don't know what he wrote! Galt could be the sick old man. Did you think of that? How do you know it's not that fat jailer with a dirty mind?"

"Lawanda!" Mom stood up too, her face patchy red. "Watch your tongue! Ray will be back with the rest of the kids any minute. Besides, this is your daddy you're talking to, not somebody on TV. This is the man who keeps a roof and clothes over you and food in your ungrateful mouth."

"Yeah, well, he won't be much longer. I'm not a baby!"

Mom's face drew up. It shut on me like a door. "I'd be ashamed!" she hissed.

"Junie . . ." Dad got to his feet and put his arm around her shoulder. Her hands slashed out.

"No!" she shouted. Dad jumped back. "We'll deal with this. We'll not smooth it over. Lawanda thinks she can go off and do whatever she takes a notion to. Thinks she knows better than us. And it's partly your fault, Mommy. Because you make your own rules . . ."

We all looked at her. I'd about forgot she was there.

"Sit down," she told us.

We sat.

"We don't know about right nor wrong here yet. I prayed and I steered Lawanda, it's true. If that was wrong, I'll repent as soon as we get to it. But right now, what we need is to sit still and see what's going on."

"Okay," I said. "But don't tell us to pray about it."

"Lawanda Ingle!" That was Mom.

"Your heart has to tell you that, Lawanda. And you can't hear your heart for your tongue."

I felt like she'd slapped me.

"Garland's got to pay," Dad said. "And *you*, Lawanda, you who are so all-fired grown-up that you can leave town without a word, you've got to tell us what he's paying for."

"I already *told* you—"

Mamaw cut in. "You won't find the truth by knocking people's teeth out of their heads," she said.

We breathed that in.

"And hate don't heal a thing."

She's got her text, I thought. Here comes the sermon.

But the phone rang.

"You get it, Howard," Mom said. "I'll put on some coffee. My head feels like a dishrag."

"Ngya-hello," Dad said. He answers the phone like a cat. "Who? Oh. Can you hold on a minute?" He snagged the phone cord with his free hand and slipped around the corner to the hall.

Mamaw's eyes caught mine. "Bird on a wire," she said.

"What?"

"Nancy Catherine."

"What about her?"

"That's her on the phone."

Mom came in. She had Hi Ho crackers and Cheez Whiz all laid out on a plate.

"Coffee'll be done in a minute," she said, setting the snacks on the couch. "Eat something, Mommy. You look peaked."

Mamaw took a kniful of cheese and made a cracker sandwich. "Here, Lawanda," she said, holding it out.

To carry this on, I should have passed the cracker to Mom, but I ate it in two bites. "Thanks," I told Mamaw.

We sat silent except for the crunch of crackers and the drone of Dad's voice. Then the coffeepot made its last gasp. Mom went back to the kitchen.

"Your trip okay?" Mamaw asked.

"I guess so. I found Nancy Catherine, and some man asked me to marry him."

"I forget how far Louisville is," she said, taking off her glasses.

Mom and Dad almost collided, her coming from the kitchen, him through the hall door. When that happens Dad usually says, "Going to have to put a stoplight at this corner." Not tonight.

Mom brought two mugs of coffee. Dad got the rest. We all drink it black.

When everybody was settled Dad announced, "That was Nancy Catherine."

"Don't bring her into this," Mom said.

"I already did," I reminded them.

"You already did a lot of things," Mom snapped.

"What did she want?" I asked.

"*I* want her daddy to stay locked up," Dad put in.

"Children," Mamaw said. "Stop agitating and listen."

But Dad wouldn't. "I've got my rights—"

"And Amos Garland has his," she insisted.

"I've got some too," I told them. "As much as anybody in this. And the first thing I want is to read that notebook."

"Oh no!" Mom said. "I'd not allow that."

"You let me go to school and read the bathroom walls!"

"That's the law, Lawanda. I have to let you go to school."

"Well, it's a law that being accused doesn't mean you did it either."

"Innocent until proved guilty," Mamaw said.

"That's right. We all have to read the notebook and decide what we think."

"And then whatever we want to charge him with . . ." Dad paused.

"It's your word against mine," I told him.

"And I'll tell them not to trust you," he fired back. "*I* can't."

There was silence for a second, as if even the furniture was letting that sink in.

Then Mamaw asked, "Would you *do* that, Howard Ingle?"

"Old woman," he said, "I don't know what I might do."

NANCY CATHERINE: It's well past dark and into high stars when I get to the jail. There's a trio of wise men in lights on the courthouse lawn. All they are is lights, like low constellations. My horoscope. What am I doing here, old man, boozer and beater? Have I come back for more? What could you do to me in jail?

That's what I'm asking myself when I tell Mr. Galt who I am.

"I reckon you got your rights," he says, "but don't look for no reunion."

Amos Garland lies on his side under a blanket. His silhouette is like mountains, folded and faulted. Mr. Galt flips on the light.

"Company!" he hollers. "Are you decent?" Then he adds, "She's come a far piece."

The mountain rolls. "They can't whip you in here," it says. "They just shoot you with light."

I want to announce myself, but there's no name I can call him. The cold boot of my stomach kicks and kicks. He sits up.

"Well, speak, woman! Or are you a ghost?"

"It's Nancy Catherine," I say.

"Nancy . . ."

"Your daughter. You may have forgotten."

"You had a big mouth when you was born," he says. Anger strikes like lightning and lifts my arms.

"Beat up on me real good," he says. "It might make them bastards take pity. At least make them laugh. You know I'm going to court, I reckon. You know I'm to be tried for spoilation of the purest of the pure?"

"Lawanda Ingle came to get me," I tell him.

"Aw God," he moans, doubling over on the bunk.

"She slipped off and came on the bus."

"No, no, honey," he croons, rocking back and forth, like he could put his pain to sleep.

"Are you talking to Lawanda or me?"

He lifts his head. I see what could happen to my face. "Yeah," he says. "What'd you cut off your hair for?"

"I'm not Lawanda!"

"I mean all that hair you had when you was little."

"Oh."

"It was black, too. What'd you spatter it with paint like that for?"

His words scrape my throat. "I'm thirty-eight years old," I tell him.

"It was so black I used to say coal dust came off on the brush."

"You do remember me."

He strikes a pose, stroking and fluffing his beard.

"Does the Lord remember Moses? Does Moses recall the Promised Land?"

"I don't guess you could quote the Bible without making yourself the Lord."

"Set down, N.C. Pull up that rusty, urinous chair."

I do.

"What's on your mind now? Something your old daddy could help you with?"

I cover my eyes, not because I'm crying, but because I don't want to look at his face.

"I guess I'm here to save your hide," I say, "although I don't know why."

He spits. "Save it, tan it, make you a pocketbook. Or cut it up and braid it for a bullwhip. 'O death, where is thy sting?'"

"Has Ada Smith been preaching to you?"

He looks around. "These walls preach. Even that drain has exhortations, but no matter. I've got Scripture written in my groin."

"That'd be okay if you just wouldn't make other people read it."

He's up so fast, the breath goes out of me, his hands hard on my throat, pulling me to my feet, pushing, twisting the root of my voice.

"Daddy!" I make this pitiful sound.

Then his head butts my shoulder and his hands drop.

"I wouldn't hurt you for the world," he says, stepping back.

"Could have fooled me," I tell him, and then holler for Galt to set me free.

When I get out, I call the Ingles from a pay phone across from the jail. It doesn't surprise me that I can't talk to Lawanda—they've got to have their scene, too—I just need to make sure I can see her tomorrow. Make sure that she, who got me here, is real. It's bad when your reality check is somebody you never saw till lunch. But there you have it.

Howard says okay, to come by at four. Talks like I'm not worth wasting words on. He's worried about his precious daughter. Imagine a daddy who does *that*.

Harvey Broome
1902–1968

Harvey Broome was born in Knoxville, Tennessee, within sight of the Great Smoky Mountains. Although his parents lived in town, his grandparents farmed, and as a boy, Harvey was a frequent visitor to their land. Broome graduated from the University of Tennessee in 1923 and Harvard Law School in 1926. Returning to East Tennessee, he worked as a law clerk and attorney for his entire professional career.

Broome was a prolific outdoors writer and an ardent conservationist who can be ranked among environmentalists such as Justice William O. Douglas, with whom he hiked, and Aldo Leopold and Benton McKaye, with whom he and others founded the Wilderness Society in 1935. He was a prime mover behind the creation of the National Wilderness Preservation System and was present when President Lyndon B. Johnson signed the bill mandating the Wilderness Act in 1964.

It was to the Great Smoky Mountains that Broome devoted his primary attention. He helped establish the national park in the Smokies, was active in subsequent preservation fights, hiked there frequently, served as president of the Smoky Mountains Hiking Club, and eventually built a mountain cabin.

After Broome's death, his wife edited three books of his writings. The excerpt in this anthology comes from *Out under the Sky of the Great Smokies: A Personal Journey,* published in 1975. The book is composed of selections from Broome's journals written during or after his visits to the Smokies. The excerpt below details Broome's earliest encounters with his beloved mountains.

FROM Out under the Sky of the Great Smokies: A Personal Journey

FORMATIVE YEARS

From my birthplace on a hill in east Knoxville the Great Smoky Mountains were a pale blue band on the southern horizon. It is significant that my birthplace was also my home. The town had one hospital, seldom used for such natural events as births.

The majority of the streets were rutted surfaces of bare earth over which a layer of stone had been scattered. There were then few automobiles. People walked to their work, to school, to church, or rode the few electric trolleys. There were some private stables among the well-to-do. Bicycles were common, threading the treacheries of gravel and ruts. Sidewalks and a few downtown streets were of brick. But interurban roadways were unknown.

Most people read by the light of coal oil (kerosene) lamps or gas. Some streets were lit by gas—a few by the novel electric arcs. The daily newspapers and a few magazines—*Literary Digest, Review of Reviews, Youth's Companion,* and *World's Work*—

kept the people aware of an outside world. They read the Bible and the newspapers; went to church; went to bed early and arose early for long ten- and twelve-hour work days.

People took an interest in the churches and the new minister, in their children, in politics and elections, in shootings and murder trials, in fires which were frequent and destructive, in deaths and weddings. There were modest excursions on the river, and boating was popular on the tiny lakes of the town park.

Walking was popular on Sunday afternoon after a soporific noon time dinner. With cousins I often went to a bluff which hung above the river. Sometimes we went to the plant down on the river where throbbing steam-powered pumps hoisted water 300 vertical feet to settling basins and the great standpipe which served most of the town from the crest of the hill above our home. Sometimes we went to the "water works" and looked at the raw water, rust-colored and turbid as it came up from the river, and then at the same water, cleansed and sparkling, as it poured into the final tank to be raised thence to the standpipe.

On rarer times we crossed the river and climbed through wooded foothills to the Cherokee Bluffs, where we could see gun emplacements from the Civil War. There we could pick up Minie balls of lead, relics of the war.

About once a month my parents, brother, sister, and I took the steam "dummy" line—a miniature train—five miles toward Fountain City to Grandpa Smith's farm, where there were a two-storied brick house, two barns, several horses, cattle, pigs, chickens, fields, rabbits, an orchard, a springhouse, a smokehouse, woodhouse, and outhouse, each carrying its own odor, delectable or pungent. There were free-flowing springs from which clear pure water was dipped.

Grandpa was someone special. He had been a cavalryman in the Civil War. But he was always a farmer. He could shoe a horse, cradle a field of wheat, make a pair of shoes, slaughter a pig, milk a cow, chop wood, grind a blade, grease a wagon, and handle a horse with certitude. Grandma could weave, knit and quilt, make lard and butter, blackberry jam and apple butter, and soap. Her brown-sugar cookies were incomparable.

On Sundays Grandpa hitched up the surrey and spring wagon and we drove three gritty miles to church. After Sunday School, the catechism, the sermon, hymns, and the socializing, we returned to the Old House where we feasted from Grandma's bountiful table. Then we propped ourselves in chairs on the front porch and watched the people drive by.

In the later afternoon, before the pigs had to be fed and the milking done, if we were lucky we could persuade Father and Grandpa to climb the wooded ridge to the east, whence five long miles away we could just make out the red standpipe on the hill above our house in town. I was astounded that one could see five whole miles.

In this pleasant, peaceful, isolated, and self-contained world I don't recall when I first became aware that there were mountains to the south. But I could not have been very old.

As I have implied, the church was the center of much of the social life. The more sophisticated town churches sometimes chartered a train for their summer pic-

nics. Cinders and black smoke poured in the open doors and windows of the swaying coaches, and the screech of the steam whistle raised the hair on our heads and
allowed the cinders to settle closer to our scalps.

I loved the train rides. I loved the expectancy and the first lurch of the coach. One
time we went beyond Maryville and rolled and jolted to the way-station of Walland.
There our locomotive was detached, rolled onto a turntable, and was rotated by two
straining trainmen. A curious engine with a battery of vertical pistons on the side
was coupled on and we were jerked and towed for miles along a small clear river to
Townsend.

This was a sawmill town with great piles of logs, a log pool at the foot of an
inclined elevator, the high whine of the handmill, and smoking cages of sawdust
burners. Everywhere were bark and lumber piles, and the sour tang of fresh-sawed
boards. I didn't question where the logs came from.

Beyond Townsend we entered a wooded gorge and were snaked up the stream.
The wheels screamed on the curves. Such thrills! We looked down on raw boulders
in water, foaming and clear. The cars crossed the stream on a bridge and everybody
moved, as one, to the windows on the opposite side to continue a love affair with the
river.

It was alive and moving and beautiful.

Something was said about Elkmont. I know now that it was a logging camp,
where there were some rough houses, a small railroad shop, and a commissary
whose steps and floors were chewed and pitted by the needle calks in the Cutter
boots of the lumberjacks. But we rolled on through Elkmont and were pulled a short
distance beyond. We hardly had time for lunch and a furtive retreat to a screen of
bushes to change our clothes for a quick, sharp dip into the clear biting water. I didn't
ask where the water came from.

I do not recall any particular impression made upon me by the rugged surroundings. I do recall that I was reluctant to leave when the long blast of the locomotive
whistle signaled the end of the day.

As the train swept out through a deep water gap into the valley, the glorious
façade of the mountains was broadside to the train. I leaned on the windowsill of the
coach and watched that soft blue wall until it vanished in the twilight.

I had become aware that there were mountains. And after two or three such picnics at Elkmont, I became aware also that the pale blue band which could be seen
from the upstairs front window of my birthplace was mountains. Two new measures
had become a part of my world, a longer horizontal (much farther than the five-mile
view from grandpa's ridge) and a vertical dimension—mountains.

Such was the first phase in the linkage of my life with mountains and the wilds. The
second phase also had an early origin. Illness had touched the first decade and a half
of my life. My body was frail, or so everyone thought; and I was shielded from contact sports. Though I performed my share of the chores—splitting kindling, carrying coal, cutting grass—and though at the age of eleven I got my first bicycle, I was
undersized and weakly and a concern to members of my family.

In 1917, when I was fifteen, an uncle thought a camping trip in the mountains might boost my health. He approached my parents. Father agreed with alacrity; mother, who was always a cautious person, finally yielded to my enthusiasm for the trip. Father and I went to a harness maker with specifications for a knapsack in which to carry my personal belongings. It was made of canvas and leather; and though it cost but $2.00, I was to carry it for a decade.

The great day of departure started with a train ride to the Elkmont of earlier years. We were met by three grizzled mountaineers, whose clothes carried the odor of sweat and of the earth. The scent was not unpleasant but I was aware of it whenever I came near them, and the very experience was a part of this great new adventure.

Our mountain friends had three horses tied in the shade nearby. After an interminable period of weighing and balancing and roping the nondescript bundles of duffle to the pack frames, we got under way. Our destination—twelve miles away and 3500 feet higher—was Silers Bald, near the heart of the Smokies.

Only the camping equipment was to be carried by the horses. The three mountain men, my three uncles, and a cousin and I were to walk. I was uneasy about the hike. I had no inkling of what was involved in walking twelve miles, and of climbing 3500 feet.

It was a hot August afternoon. Ridges towered to unbelievable heights. After climbing a few miles we digressed from the Jakes Gap trail to take the more direct, slippery and inhumanly steep Dripping Springs route to the summit of Miry Ridge. Each of us was carrying an item or two which could not be packed handily on the horses. I had the rifle. Burdened with it and my own inexperience, my struggles in brief slippery spurts up the Dripping Springs mountain added nothing to my self-assurance. My legs were weak; my lungs were shallow. Every lunge upward seemed to bring me close to exhaustion. But the ascent finally dwindled away. The slope leveled off and we moved out on top of Miry Ridge.

That night we slept in a rude enclosure constructed around the "claim cabin" of a lumber company. We lay on the ground with only the folded canvas of a tent underneath us. A round moon arched across the sky. Stimulated by the openness above and by the hard earth beneath, as well as by the day's excitement, I slept little on this my first night, ever, out under the sky.

The next morning we started early. A mist hung close and in its dimness we and the horses wallowed the length of Miry Ridge. Pans clanged as packs collided with trees, and my cherished knapsack was torn on a snag. We avoided the quagmire of the trail and sought out a narrow and incredibly greasy bench of humus alongside. The morning was cool. The mist mingled with the forest in a muted world of rhododendrons and hemlocks, of birch and maples. By mid morning it had vanished, and we emerged into sunshine at a rocky look-off near the junction of Miry Ridge and the Great Smoky divide.

The magnitude of the view was lost upon me. Every sight, every sound and sensation since leaving Elkmont, except the punishing climb up Dripping Springs mountain, had been strange and exciting. The whole trip had been akin to a first breathless glimpse of the Grand Canyon. I had been plunged into wildness. When Uncle Charlie pointed out the one thing in that vastness of which I had previously heard—Silers Bald—I centered my attention upon it.

About noon we pitched our wall tent on a little flat. Slender beech trees, cut from the forest, furnished poles for the tent and frames for our canvas cots. Sam Cook, our guide, found a small overhanging cliff and laid his bedding under it. Sam split bark from a buckeye and flattening it out made a table. A pole squared on one side and braced between two trees provided a seat. We assembled rocks for a fireplace. Our water was obtained from a scooped-out place down the side of the mountain. It was a long walk down, and it was a longer carry back with 40 to 50 pounds of water sloshing in lard cans between us.

A single layer of canvas discouraged the elements. We cut, chopped, and split trees for firewood. Candles supplied light. The day's activities began with the dawn and ended with the dark. There was no outhouse. One quickly found the pattern for more primitive ways. We experienced 48 consecutive hours of rain and fog, and lived with mud and dampness. The rain falling on our tin plates splashed food into our faces. Smoke saturated our clothes as we rotated before the fire on a corduroy of logs laid to raise us above the mud.

On the east horizon four miles away was the rounded bulk of Clingmans Dome— what seemed to me a very high mountain. It was covered with an evergreen forest— denser, darker, and more mysterious than our grove of beeches.

One fine day we followed the divide from Silers to Clingmans. At one spot we looked far down into Tennessee and saw logging trains which resembled toys. At another spot we could both see and hear lumberjacks working in North Carolina.

At the summit of Clingmans we entered a dim, thickset stand of evergreens smaller than telephone poles. I did not inquire why the growth was different from the majestic forest, brilliant with wild flowers, through which we had ascended. But the memory of that dark and closely growing timber has remained with me all my life. Later I was to learn that it constituted a few acres of second growth and that there are differences between a primeval and a regenerating forest.

After two weeks we returned home. I had survived in the outdoors despite rain and bad weather. From Sam Cook I had discovered that one did not need a tent for a snug shelter but could use a cliff. I was sturdier and had gained a few pounds in weight. Under the sharp surveillance of three grown men I had been permitted to use an ax. But I could not have built a fire in the rain or have found my way without a guide. I had not learned what it meant to climb with a pack on my back.

On Silers we had been surrounded by a vast expanse of mountains, blue and inviting when the sky was clear. On the east rim was Clingmans Dome. Far to the west was Thunderhead. And on the north rim were the bold outlines of another great peak, Mt. Le Conte. The huge triangle defined by those summits was a complete unknown to me. My eyes were on Mt. Le Conte, which had come to hold for me an irresistible appeal.

Three years were to pass before I was to climb it. The first World War intervened, curtailing much civilian activity but bringing one boon. Teenagers became a useful commodity upon the labor market and twice I worked for a short period at an apple orchard a few miles from the base of Mt. Le Conte. This spot lay in rough foothill country, and a whole day by truck, wagon, and foot was consumed in covering the 40 miles between Knoxville and the orchard.

The mountains were close and twice we took quick trips around the end and back of Le Conte to a stream of surpassing beauty. We hiked far past the last rough homestead where visitors were so rare that it was the prudent custom to pause outside the fence and call before approaching for fear of being shot.

Here we purchased eggs and obtained permission to use a cabin belonging to a lumber company. Beyond the cabin we entered upon an old trail which had served as access to saltpeter deposits in the Civil War. Since that date it had had limited use for passage between North Carolina and Tennessee. Overgrown and narrow, the trail crossed and recrossed a stream of absolute clarity.

The crossings I approached with real fear. We were backpacking and I reached the stream with rubbery legs and scorched lungs. There were no footlogs, and we waded or leaped from boulder to boulder. If a person slipped, or his knapsack pulled him off balance, he would bang a shin or fall into the water. On the Silers trip my introduction to mountains had been along their ridge tops, but now I received my baptism in their streams.

Our destination was a tiny log cabin which had been erected in a rough clearing above the stream. The gaps between its logs were closed by clean, hand-split shingles which had been nailed horizontally on the inside. The work was crude and the air circulation remained excellent. The cabin had a puncheon floor and a roof of split shingles.

A small iron stove with a flat cooking surface was propped on billets in one corner of the cabin. Pole bedsteads with corn husk mattresses occupied two corners, and a pile of firewood, mostly waste from the cabin construction, was stacked handy to the stove. This was our shelter.

We fished the stream for brook trout. One of my companions was an expert who caught all that we could eat. Our fire of hemlock and spruce chunks popped and crackled as it flickered through the cracks in the stove. The smoke of these woods also has an extreme pungency, and the night breezes swirled it like incense both outside and inside the cabin with separate but equal abandon. At nightfall the vastness and darkness of the uncut forest settled about us, and our whole world centered around the liveliness in that rickety stove. The high beech woods and meadows of Silers Bald had never been like the overwhelming, inky-black forested wilderness at the bottom of that narrow, chill, north-facing valley.

After the camping trip I worked again at the orchard. In good weather the summit of Le Conte was visible eight tantalizing miles distant and 5000 intriguing feet higher. On the weekend before I was to return to Knoxville to the university, I planned to make the climb with some mountain friends. Quite unexpectedly my father appeared on the day before, and quite characteristically joined the party. He knew that his way of life had not conditioned him for such a trip. But he lived his life with a certain quiet élan, often counting the cost of an adventure afterward rather than before. I have always been grateful that he turned up to share this climb with me.

There was a trail less than half the way. When it played out we took the first hollow to the right. And when it became impassable from vertical cliffs made slippery by moss and water, we bore to the left to the ridge on that side of the gulch.

We were now on the side of Le Conte itself and again encountered cliffs and maddening thickets of laurel and rhododendron. We scrambled and we slipped; we clawed and we pulled. This lofty mountain seemed to have no summit, and I was becoming weak from hunger and fatigue. When it seemed I could go no farther I dragged myself over a low ledge and found we had reached the top.

The view from the immediate summit was disappointing because of a screen of balsams. But after lunch we fought our way to a look-off point, and a truly magnificent and tremendous view burst upon us. We were on one of the points of the great triangle of which Silers was the center. But the superior elevation and location of Le Conte produced stupendous views not only of mountains but of the fields and hamlets in the Great Valley. Though the day was brilliant, to the north over Knoxville was a long sooty band touching the horizon. I had not then heard of smoke pollution.

The middle peak, or Cliff Top, to which we proceeded after lunch, was covered with dense stands of windswept balsams, a low-growing rhododendron, and masses of a gorgeous, hedge-like shrub with tiny glistening leaves suggesting a boxwood—Huger's sand myrtle. The leaves of this resplendent plant had a waxy content and were highly inflammable. This fact was discovered by the youngest member of the party, who set fire to an isolated clump. He was scolded by his father who quickly stamped out the blaze.

But when we left the cliffs for the descent this youngster lingered. Later when we looked up from the open summit of the Rocky Spur far below, we saw a column of white smoke hovering over Cliff Top. The sand myrtle was afire and I felt a youthful outrage. For the first time in my life I had wanted to protect a bit of nature from destruction.

We followed no trail down the mountain, as we had followed one but little on the ascent. This trip had been an introduction to bush whacking by my mountain friends who were masters of the art. My fears of the unknown and of getting off a trail had been blunted. The experience led to an awareness that every foot of the mountains was open to me, and that trails, though a convenience, were not a necessity. And on the same trip a lifelong concern for the vegetative cover of the land was kindled by that senseless blaze in the sand myrtle on Cliff Top.

The next years had their frustrations. I was busy at the university and plagued by lack of time and money. Once or twice I managed a prodigious excursion, prompted equally by my love of the mountains and by my desire to measure myself against them.

At Easter we skipped classes and took a trip to Thunderhead—the massive grassy bald which had formed the western tip of the great triangle revealed from Silers.

This was a 40-mile jaunt crowded into three days. We were elated by seeing acres of bird's-foot violets in the foothills and by the sight of a yellow lady's-slipper—my first orchis. Soft from unwonted exercise, we had crammed six months of yearning into one relentless excursion.

Another summer I worked at the very base of Mt. Le Conte. My employer was versed in botany. From him I learned the identity of many trees in this land of many trees. On the weekends his home became an overnight stop for visitors from the "outside" who coveted a look at these great, verdant, little-known mountains. On one weekend two research professors, a botanist and an entomologist, were there. From them I learned the name of the fresh and beautiful pink turtlehead, a flower which grew near the summit of Le Conte.

On another weekend a taxonomist of some note came from a midwestern college. His excitement, as he discovered plant after plant which he had not even seen before, was contagious. In the party that day were several mountaineers. During a rest our visitor reached down and picked a leaf of the dog hobble which covered a whole slope. Musingly, half to himself, he spoke its scientific name, *Leu-cothoë.*

One of the mountain men replied, "'Leucothy,' that's what we calls it." Who was the ancestor who had known and handed down the scientific name of this shrub, and why had he come to these mountains?

In a moist cleft on top we found an exquisite ivory-toned flower, its petals strongly veined with green—Grass-of-Parnassus. I have since seen its long-stemmed cousins in the area of the great limestone springs in Florida and a dwarfed version at timberline in the North Cascades of Washington. The memory in later years of that enchanting plant on Le Conte contributed to my first dim perception of plant ecology on the North American continent.

One autumn I departed East Tennessee for three years at an eastern law school. I came home each summer and worked in a law office, but managed a trip or two to the mountains.

On one of these we hiked from Thunderhead to Clingmans Dome, camping along the way. Sam Cook was again our guide. At Spence Field we found many domestic animals grazing on its expansive summit meadows, the practice of valley farmers being to summer their stock in the mountains.

At our campsites I learned from Sam how to start a fire, how to set up a crane from which to hang a bucket over the fire. At Buckeye Gap we heard a call in the night. The eyes of young John Tittsworth widened with fear.

"What's that?"

Sam chuckled, "That's an owl; he's your friend."

The "whoo whoo" of this bird is one of the startling sounds of the great woods. Its call is yet heard in many areas of our country. Where there are woods enough for it, there is hope for wilderness.

From Buckeye Gap we walked to Silers Bald; John and I went on to Clingmans. The next day we all hiked to Elkmont via Miry Ridge. As we descended through the rain there was smoke in the air and we began to see blackened stumps and snags. The area had been logged, had burned, and was still smoldering. I could not perceive in this open rocky charcoal-black area, the lush and magnificent forest I had traversed in mist eight years earlier. Down in the hollow we ran into the logging operation itself in a land I had known under different conditions on my first trip into the high mountains. I had found the origin of the logs which fed the sawmill at Townsend. The following summer, at Charlies Bunion, I was again to see first-hand the consequences of careless logging.

Whereas Mt. Le Conte had once been my great goal, I now wanted to try Mt. Guyot, a peak second in height only to Clingmans Dome and located in a remote complex of mountains far to the east of Le Conte. I had interested Wiley Oakley in going with me. He was a mountaineer who looked upon the mountains as a source of beauty and inspiration, rather than a resource to be exploited.

We were to hike from Gatlinburg to Le Conte and out the meanders of the ridge, now known as the "Boulevard," to the state line, and thence along the untrailed state line to Guyot.

The Boulevard ridge was trailless. We were slowed by frightful undergrowth and by the battering of a summer storm. By late afternoon we had barely reached the edge of the burn near Charlies Bunion, on which were now stands of blackberry briers eight feet high. We plunged into them hoping to reach Dry Sluice Gap by dark, but were held back by the briers and by partially burned trees which had fallen across our course. The briers had completely engulfed the windfalls so that we were unaware of them until we walked into protruding limbs. Progress was slowed to a quarter of a mile an hour.

Near the gap the briers thinned a bit. The fire had burned the humus down to the mineral soil, and water from the storm was running over the area. We attacked blackened logs with an ax and chopped out dry wood for our camp fire.

A second storm struck and we thatched the fire with bark. Under this cover it outlasted the storm. But there was no dry spot for sleeping. Finally we collected large stones and heated them in the fire. Some of these we placed at our feet and others on the slope as seats. I shall never forget Wiley's tentative test, and how he quickly sprang upright when he found it too hot. Whimsically he said, "My seat is hard as a rock." Over this spot we stretched a poncho and sat out the night.

Dawn came eventually. Our eyes were red from smoke and sleeplessness; our hands and faces were scratched and besmudged. We decided to return to Gatlinburg by the shortest route. This was down the trail from Dry Sluice Gap, and through the Porters Flat of the Greenbrier.

On the descent we followed a deep ravine just east of the Charlies Bunion peaks and ridges. Looking up at them, we were appalled. They had been incinerated down to the bare rock leaving only the blackened trunks of a once virgin forest. Since there had been no logging on the Tennessee side, the fire must have started in the loggings in North Carolina. It had swept across the divide into several hundred acres of virgin woods in Tennessee.

Two miles farther, the valley leveled out into the Porters Flat where grows one of the surpassing deciduous forests on earth. It was as unspeakably beautiful as the area of holocaust had been unutterably blighted.

In the decades following the first Silers trip I grew in assurance and strength. My love for mountains and wild country became a major motivation. My trips there numbered into the hundreds in every season—from the cold dormance of winter, through the perfections of spring and the heavy humidity of summer, to the sharp scintillating delights of the fall. They involved short one-day excursions and week-long back packs. Camp fires were built from wood so damp that moisture pockets, exploding in the wood, blew out the flames. Camps were established in storms so violent that they dumped four inches of rain in a night. I waded streams so cold that my feet became numb, pushed through snow up to my middle, and camped in the deep forest at −15°.

My knowledge grew not only of the terrain of the mountains but of their plant and animal life. Recognition of first- and second-growth forest developed, and likewise perception of the succession of plants involved in the long journey back from disturbance to climax forest. The differences between north-slope and south-slope vegetation became clear.

The movement for a National Park in the Great Smokies got underway during an absence of mine. But upon my return to Knoxville I supported Colonel David C. Chapman and other leaders of this complex and successful undertaking.

In 1930 I learned of the Appalachian Trail and participated in the location of remote stretches of the trail through the mazes of little-known ridges in the Smokies.

I became acquainted with Benton MacKaye, father of the Appalachian Trail; with Stanley Cain, a great and articulate ecologist; with Robert Marshall, a professional forester and a towering figure in the field of wilderness preservation; and with Bernard Frank, a specialist in forest influences, from whose searching eyes little escaped.

On trips into the mountains with these and many others, there came a disturbing awareness of the rift between the untrammeled wilds and the rifled countryside where man had established his civilization. It was not enough to enjoy wild country; one felt compelled to try to conserve and defend the land against further spoliation. With MacKaye, Marshall, Frank, and four other dedicated conservationists [Harold C. Anderson, Aldo Leopold, Ernest Oberholtzer, Robert Sterling Yard], I was associated in the founding of the Wilderness Society.

Some persons hunt for the origins of the wilderness movement in the consciences of big city dwellers, who, seeing about them the shambles of the natural world, seek to protect and restore it elsewhere. But my own beginnings in a provincial valley town, and my youth among a gentle and unassuming people, rebut such a sweeping assumption. The very first time I journeyed the few miles from my home village to the foothills of the Smokies, I found something beautiful, different, and intensely desirable. I had not been conditioned by the fevers of a metropolis. The great bent of my life had been fixed before I set foot beyond the boundaries of Tennessee.

Harry Caudill
1922–1990

Harry Caudill's *Night Comes to the Cumberlands: A Biography of a Depressed Area* (1963) is arguably the most famous book ever written about Appalachia. Caudill was born in a hollow near Whitesburg, Kentucky; his father, active in local politics, was a farmer and a coal miner. Although his family did not suffer from Depression-era poverty, young Caudill was deeply affected by the hardship that he witnessed in coal towns and by the environmental toll that clear-cutting and coal mining took on the landscape. Caudill served in the military during World War II, earned a law degree from the University of Kentucky, and opened a law practice in Whitesburg, Kentucky.

In response to the problems facing the people and the land of the Cumberland Plateau, Caudill wrote *Night Comes to the Cumberlands*. The book contributed to the national attention focused on extreme Appalachian poverty in the early 1960s. An eloquent, angry book, *Night Comes to the Cumberlands* galvanized readers to take action and made Caudill an important spokesperson for Appalachia. However, by the 1980s, problems with Caudill's scholarship and his sometimes stereotypical assessments of mountain culture undermined the book's credibility with some Appalachian studies scholars. Nonetheless, the book remains a powerful indictment of the greed that has assaulted Appalachia's people and land.

The following essay, "O, Appalachia!" (1973), summarizes the main points that Caudill developed in his longer works.

O, Appalachia!

The Appalachian mountain range is the least understood and the most maligned part of America. In the last decade alone it has been the subject of scores of economic and sociological studies. Lyndon Johnson's Great Society made it a principal battlefield in the War on Poverty. And, yet, despite this there persists a monumental unwillingness to recognize the harsh realities of the Appalachian paradox.

"Paradoxical" is the adjective most applicable to that vast region embracing western Pennsylvania, western Virginia, eastern Kentucky, northeastern Tennessee, nearly all of West Virginia, northern Alabama, and bits of Maryland, North Carolina and Georgia. The very name of the region has become synonymous with poverty and backwardness. Arnold Toynbee sees its people and culture as serious internal threats to Western civilization. "The Appalachians," he wrote, "present the melancholy spectacle of a people who have acquired civilization and then lost it." As he sees them, our southern highlanders have reverted to barbarism and are the "Riffs, Albanians, Kurds, Pathans and hairy Ainu" of the New World.

But the land itself is rich in every respect that an ambitious people would find necessary for greatness. To assert that the Appalachian land is poor is to display the same ignorance so often imputed to the mountaineers themselves.

Appalachia is rich. Its heartland is a mere 480 miles from Washington, D. C., and is within easy reach of the populous eastern third of the nation. This huge, sparsely populated region thus lies close to the heart of the most highly industrialized continent in the world.

Its forest—the finest expression of the eastern deciduous—is the most varied and splendid of the globe's temperate zones. Fifty million years old, it contains almost every plant the glaciers shoved down from the north and many that later seeded up from the south. More than 2,000 seed-bearing plants are native to West Virginia alone. Although this forest still covers Appalachia like the folds of a mighty carpet, human greed has reduced it in many places to thickets and stands of new growth.

The bottomlands produce excellent potatoes, grains, berries, grapes and fruit, and a survey by the President's Appalachian National Commission disclosed that there are 9.5 million acres suitable for pasturage.

After a century of mining, Appalachia's coal veins still contain 250 billion tons of the world's best coal. Economists have declared one of its coal beds to be the most valuable mineral deposit on the globe. The first petroleum wells gushed there; its oil and gas resources still boom. And in addition the region ships out limestone, talc, cement rock, iron ore, clays, gneiss, gibbsite and grahamite.

Appalachia has beauty. The ancient crags, timber-cloaked slopes, rhododendron and laurel thickets, beds of ferns and flowers, and creeks and rushing rivers make it a land of stunning loveliness. The Great Smokies is the most visited of U.S. parks, and it is not mere coincidence that two of the nation's greatest aggregations of scientific minds have been brought together within the shadows of the Appalachian hills at Huntsville and Oak Ridge.

Little credence is due the notion that the troubles of the mountaineers stem from the mountainous character of their habitat. Mountains and poverty do not automatically go together, as the little Republic of Switzerland so dramatically proves.

Nor does the mountaineers' failure stem from any genetic deficiency or some ill fortune at the beginning. The settlers—whose descendants are a majority today—were English, Scotch, German and Scotch-Irish, with a virility and toughness legendary on the frontier. In 1780 at Kings Mountain, South Carolina, an army of 30-day volunteers administered a larger British force the most unequivocal defeat in the history of the empire. Of 907 British and Tory soldiers engaged, all were killed, wounded or captured. These backwoodsmen proclaimed American independence and liberty at Mecklenburg Courthouse a year before July 4, 1776. Tough, sturdy stock had a promising beginning in a labyrinth stuffed with riches and bright with promise.

How, then, did it happen that more than a century ago the descendants of Kings Mountain were already so poor and ignorant they had become a matter of grave concern to President Abraham Lincoln and his friend, O. O. Howard, head of the Freedmen and the Refugees Bureau? The essential trouble lay in this reality: from the beginning Appalachian people nurtured a profound distrust of government, sought to elude its influence and consistently refused to use it as a tool for social and economic enhancement.

Appalachia's population was drawn almost entirely from the frontier of the revolutionary war era. The same qualities that made the frontiersmen effective Indian fighters and revolutionaries doomed them and their descendants as social builders. What Toynbee has described as a retreat to barbarism is actually a persistence of the backwoods culture and mores into an age of cybernetics and rockets—nearly two centuries after the frontier itself rolled westward and passed into history.

The Europeans whose descendants filtered into Appalachia were poor. They were landless younger sons, people swept from the farms by landlords, indigents who swarmed into cities in search of work, disbanded soldiers and Ulstermen pauperized by parliamentary acts designed to protect the English wool trade. Many came as indentured servants too poor to pay a shipmaster for their passage. The quest for land took them to the backwoods. They shared a tenacious hatred of the English rulers whose policies had brought them only toil and bitterness. They soon shared another sentiment—disdain for the copper-skinned aborigines who presumptuously claimed to own the virgin lands the newcomers coveted. In their struggles to preserve their ancient domain, Indians fought skillfully against the interlopers and through much of the struggle were supported by the crown. In 1763 His Majesty's government proclaimed the Appalachian crest as the settlement line beyond which no British subject could lawfully build a cabin. Thus, reasoned the King's counselors, peace with the natives would be preserved until they could be civilized and turned into good servants of the crown, the fur trade would be stabilized, and the whites would turn the land east of the line into a vast expanse of orderly, English-style farms. The Proclamation caused the fast-breeding backwoodsmen to pile up on the border and provided the stock for a massive wave of settlers when the revolution shattered English power.

The Indian wars lasted more than 40 fiery years until Anthony Wayne's victory at Fallen Timbers in 1794. Raid and counter-raid, scalped corpses, burned crops, slaughtered livestock, stratagems, counter-stratagems and a perpetual all-pervading unease—these were the elements that etched into the backwoods culture an acceptance of bloodshed as a normal part of life. With no effective government to protect them, the settlers became supremely self-reliant, loyal only to the helpful clans who moved westward as they did. They learned, though, from the enemy; and Cherokee corn bread, parched corn and fondness for the hunt mixed with lively Old World fiddle tunes as part of the burgeoning culture.

Many settlers stayed abreast of the frontier, forming the keen cutting edge of the scythe that reached Oregon a mere 80 years after the Mecklenburg Resolves. But most were absorbed by the Appalachian maze. They stayed, steeping in the backwoods behavioral patterns with their quick violence, subsistence farming, hunting, antipathy to government and, after the revivalist movement of 1800, old-time Baptist religion. All the later migrants—Germans, Poles, Jews, Italians, Scandinavians—went westward without touching the hill people. Until the railroads began to reach out for the coal and timber, they simmered undisturbed, acquiring the characteristics that have led to the present plight.

Having no one else to learn from, they learned from their forebears, repeating the techniques and perpetuating the aspirations of their frontier past. They evolved a traditionalism that ruled out everything unsanctioned by time. The patriarchs cautioned against the untried, and the mountaineer became a conspicuous anachronism.

Like someone of a Swiss Family Robinson within his fold of the mountains and surrounded by foes real or imagined, the mountaineer was crankily individualistic. He tenaciously defended the ideals and freedoms that made his bizarre individualism possible. He became a loner to whom cooperative efforts were distasteful and strange.

The sun began setting long ago for the highlander. His fields eroded and he had to clear new ground, which became barren for the same reasons. The labor of clearing exhausted him, and his unremunerative cropping bound him to subsistence levels except in a few broad and fertile valleys. New waves of out-migration drained off the strong and energetic. The primitive economy generated little money for schools and the traditionalism did not encourage them. E. O. Guerrant, a Presbyterian evangelist, wrote that during the Civil War he crossed the mountains many times without seeing a schoolhouse or a church. The roads remained little better than the ancient buffalo traces. The simplest manifestations of government advanced with glacial slowness. For example, in 1799 all of eastern Kentucky was organized into a new county called Floyd. Sixteen years elapsed before the fathers could complete a log courthouse 22 feet square. And promptly after it was finished someone burned it to the ground.

Ignorant, disorganized, old-fashioned and poor, the people were perfect victims for the mineral and land buyers who came after the Civil War. The buyers knew from their geologists what was in the land. The mountaineers knew nothing and sold everything at prices ranging from a dime to a few dollars per acre. The already precarious plight of the highlanders then became desperate, because the deeds gave to industrialists in New York, Philadelphia and London the legal title to "all mineral and metallic substances." And with the ownership of the mineral reserves passed, also, the political mastery of the region.

Thus, as the West Virginia Tax Commission warned in its 1884 report, "the history of West Virginia will be as sad as that of Poland and Ireland." And indeed all the elements of the Irish famine were present: inadequate agriculture, absentee ownership of the landed wealth, incapacity to generate and follow wise leaders. With the Great Depression and postwar mechanization of the mines, the Appalachian social order collapsed, and large-scale death by famine was prevented only by the largesse of the federal government and the most massive out-migration in U.S. history. If contemporary Appalachia has viable symbols, they are the public assistance check, the food stamp and the ancient sedan wheezing its uncertain way toward Detroit.

Thus two Appalachias grew up in the same domain, side by side and yet strangers to each other. One, the Appalachia of Power and Wealth, consists of huge land, coal, oil, gas, timber and quarry companies that "recover" the minerals from the earth; rail, barge and pipeline companies that convey the minerals to markets; and steel, refining, chemical and utility firms that convert the minerals to marketable products. This Appalachia, headquartered in New York and Philadelphia, is allied to mighty banks and insurance companies. It is exemplified by Edward B. Leisenring, Jr., now president of Penn Virginia Corporation, who boasted (*Dun's Review and Modern Industry*, April 1965), that his company netted 61 percent of gross income.

The second Appalachia is a land devastated by decades of quarrying, drilling, tunneling and strip-mining. Five thousand miles of its streams are silted and poisoned beyond any present capacity to restore them, and as many more are being reduced to the same dismal state. Its people are the old, the young who are planning to leave and the legions of crippled and sick. Its lawyers thrive on lawsuits engendered by an ultrahazardous environment.

Government has never pretended to serve both Appalachias impartially. Appalachia One routinely raises money to persuade and bribe Appalachia Two to elect candidates acceptable to wealth and power. Until recent stirrings of revolt, Appalachia Two invariably elected "bighearted country boys" beholden only to the corporate overlords who financed their campaigns. Invariably, they gave a bit more welfare to the poor and enlarged the privileges and exemptions of the rich. The poor sank into apathy and the rich, all curbs removed from their arrogance, wantonly triggered such calamities as the destruction of towns on Buffalo Creek, West Virginia. On February 26, 1972, a total of 124 people perished after a mountain of mining wastes collapsed.

In 1862, Abraham Lincoln became the first president to pledge aid to the impoverished Appalachians. The war and John Wilkes Booth kept him from acting on his promise. Seventy years later Franklin D. Roosevelt rediscovered them in an even worse situation.

The New Deal spent hundreds of millions of dollars on relief projects. Some of the ugliest schools and courthouses the human mind has ever contrived sprang up as destitute men chipped, hammered and sawed on relief works. The Civilian Conservation Corps and an expanding army and navy lifted thousands of benumbed youths out of idleness and away from moonshine stills. National Youth Administration jobs kept threadbare students in school so that they could graduate into World War II. On the eve of that conflict the New Deal formulated plans to resettle a million highlanders, a goal the postwar coal depression accomplished with dispatch.

It is doubtful that FDR could have done more even if he had wanted to. There were ranks of senators dutifully determined to protect Appalachia One even if Appalachia Two starved to death, and a Supreme Court determined to hold unconstitutional anything that tampered with the vested rights of the Mellons, Rockefellers, Pews and Insulls. A firm commitment to Appalachia Two might have aimed at a TVA-like program designed to use Appalachia's bountiful resources in a job-generating cycle within the region. The Tennessee Valley Authority pioneered in an area with few rich vested interests to offend while the equally destitute hill people were never considered for a federally mandated Appalachian Mountain Authority.

When John Kennedy ran for the White House in 1960 he overruled the advice of his aides and challenged Hubert Humphrey in West Virginia's primary. To the amazement of the nation, he won and went on to the White House. In the mountain state, the young president had seen two million people within the ruinous grip of the

Appalachian culture. To do something, Kennedy appointed PARC—the President's Appalachian Regional Commission—to study the paradox of Appalachian poverty in what John Kenneth Galbraith was pleased to call the "affluent society." PARC was chaired by another Roosevelt, FDR, Jr., who, whatever his father's feelings may have been, displayed little comprehension of his task and learned little at his carefully staged "hearings."

In the bleak autumn of 1963 Homer Bigart of the *New York Times* came to eastern Kentucky and wrote about children so hungry they were eating mud from between chimney rocks, of people living in collapsing shacks, of a society that offered no alternative to the dole. The story roused the lethargic PARC to action. John Kennedy was in his grave when the pallid report went to the president's desk and the recommendations entered the U.S. Code in 1965. Lyndon Johnson signed it in a little ceremony in the White House Rose Garden, made it a part of his Great Society, and in a typical example of rhetorical overkill, declared that in Appalachia "the dole is dead."

The dole remains very much alive, and there is nothing in the much touted Appalachian Regional Development Act that can ever bring it to an end. ARDA was written to please—or at least avoid conflict with—Appalachia One. One of Kennedy's requirements was that it be tailored to gain the support of governors whose states had counties in the region. These ranged from George Wallace to Nelson Rockefeller, and a more safely square, establishmentarian bunch of non-reformers can scarcely be imagined. They tucked in a clincher that allowed a governor to veto for his state any proposal he found offensive. Thus the Appalachia of Wealth was formally secured in its capacity to strike down federal efforts to lift the Appalachia of Poverty.

The initial authorization for LBJ's project to eradicate poverty in a diverse territory as big as Great Britain was by no means so bloated as to alarm fiscal conservatives—$1,092,400,000. And if the financing was modest, the plans, too, were calculated to stir few objections in the most cautious soul.

In America roads are beloved of all men from Paul Mellon's globe-girdling corporations to the humblest welfare recipient in a floorless cabin at the head of Powderhorn Creek. And, since roads are so favored, the governors, FDR, Jr., and Congress agreed that more than 75 percent of the money—$840 million—should be spent to build new highways. But these were not highways of the first quality like the Interstates then beginning to lace the country together. The governors and their highway commissioners decreed 1950-style two-lane affairs, with a third or "passing" lane at intervals. The roads that emerged as a result of this saddle Appalachia with an archaic transportation system of continuing obsolescence.

And though the new highways would be rammed through the endless string of towns that shelter Appalachia Two, the bill provided no homes for the dispossessed. Hundreds of men and women—most of them old and sick, and some helpless from senility—were handed small sums and told to clear out. They did, generally into house trailers strewn about the landscape like huge, oblong dice. And the roads were scarcely completed when immense and immensely overloaded coal trucks began pounding them to pieces. In some instances the last guardrails were not even in place when highway departments started calculating the cost of resurfacing.

Then the lawmakers prepared a small Band-Aid for the staggering devastation inflicted by the strip-mining of coal. They appropriated $36.5 million to patch up some of the worst eyesores. Next they acknowledged that long exploitation had ravaged the hardwood forests and that the owners of small tracts could be helped if their timber stands were improved. Five million dollars went into this task!

The mammoth erosion that was shaving mountains to the bedrock and choking streams in hundreds of counties was combated with $17 million. A study of water resources was financed with another $5 million. Sewage treatment facilities and vocational schools drew $6 million. Demonstration health facilities were financed with $69 million. Vocational schools received $16 million.

Finally, the Act provided for support to local development districts—but only after their "genuineness" had been certified by the governors.

In due time the rest of the Great Society programs were impaled on the horns of the same dilemma: How to aid the region's poor without distressing its rich? It could not be done and the efforts broke down in frustration and failure.

Transferred from the Peace Corps to head the Office of Economic Opportunity, Sargent Shriver sent platoons of young, idealistic VISTA (Volunteers in Service to America) workers into Appalachia. They started "community action" enterprises, summoning the poor to countless meetings and exhorting them to organize. For what? No one had told the volunteers the answer to that or even informed them about the existence of Appalachia One. They promptly perceived the outlines of the truth, however, and began telling audiences about them, whereupon a lively time in the hills ensued. Boards of education were beset by people demanding better schools.

It was all entertaining and encouraging while it lasted. But sleeping dogs were aroused at last and telephones began ringing in the offices of congressmen and senators. VISTA was decried as Communist and un-American. A few of the volunteers were jailed on charges ranging from reckless driving to criminal syndicalism. The Great Society withdrew its soldiers from the War on Poverty, and Appalachia One settled back to digest the region undisturbed.

Henceforth federal funds came down through safe, orthodox channels where the control was well established and the people involved knew how to play the game without causing discontent in powerful quarters. With Richard Nixon came even further routinization of procedures and approaches. All told, billions have been spent on Appalachian renewal in the last 12 years and only a gimlet eye can tell any difference in the homes and lives of that numerous citizenry I have referred to as Appalachia Two.

Except in Kentucky, where a severance tax was imposed in 1972, the endless outflow of natural resources goes almost untaxed to the markets of the world. The flow is so great that as many as 25,000 railroad cars of coal have piled up at Hampton Roads, Virginia, awaiting ships for Europe and Japan. Strip-mining shatters the ancient ecology, and "reclamation" is a sorry joke. The out-migration continues, and new vocational schools supply plumbers and typists to many cities in other states. Silt from mine spoils is ruining lakes the Corps of Engineers has built at enormous costs. After a decade of much publicized "anti-poverty" efforts in the Appalachians, relief rolls have swollen ominously—in some counties to support 65 percent of the population. A whole new generation has come to maturity as public assistance recipients struggle to qualify for a continuance of the grants for the rest of their lives. In growing numbers of families no one has held a job in three generations.

In September 1972, ARDA issued its annual economic report. Within the tenacious hold of the old culture of poverty and of the great corporations that own its wealth and shape its destiny, Appalachia Two reflected the following interesting facts:

(a) Eleven percent of the residents of Central Appalachia had departed in the 1960s.

(b) Thirty-four percent of the homes lacked essential indoor plumbing.

(c) A third of the work force may be jobless.

On August 28, 1972, *Barron's National Business and Financial Weekly* characterized the entire Appalachian Poverty Program as a "costly failure."

The modern Appalachian welfare reservation makes few demands on its inhabitants. They are left alone in their crumbling coal camps and along their littered creeks to follow lives almost as individualistic, as backward looking and tradition ridden, as fatalistic and resigned as in those days three or four wars ago before the welfare check replaced the grubbing hoe and shovel as pot fillers. Then a man needed to know the seasons and the vagaries of the bossman if he were to eat. But new skills are required in an age when government is gigantic, when a few men with giant machines can drag from the ground all the fuel a nation can consume, and when the poor are of little use to the well-to-do. It pays to sense winners and vote for them—and to let them know of one's intention in advance. And one must recognize that there are powers that cannot be overturned or defied, and so one does not resist. Once these concessions are made it is generally possible to enjoy many of the freedoms and prerogatives of the nineteenth century without its toils and dangers. Perhaps Toynbee's "barbarism" is actually a preview of the twenty-first century, when the rich will be truly secure and the poor will not work, aspire or starve. Appalachia was the nation's first frontier. Now it may be foretelling America's final form.

Verna Mae Slone

1914–2009

Author of memoirs and other books about Appalachia, Verna Mae Slone was born in Knott County in eastern Kentucky. Reared from infancy by her father, Isom "Kitten Eye" Slone, after her mother died, Slone attended Hindman Settlement School until the eighth grade, when she left to help support her family. Slone married Willie Slone (to whom she was not related), a bulldozer operator; they had five sons, whose care frequently fell solely to Verna, as her husband's work often took him away from home.

A tenth-generation Kentuckian and a prodigious reader, Slone was acutely aware of the negative stereotypes about Appalachia. When she was in her sixties, she wrote what became her first published book, *What My Heart Wants to Tell* (1979), to record her father's and her own biography and the traditional Appalachian life of the early twentieth century in a way that she felt would be more accurate than popular depictions of mountain life. Although the manuscript was meant only for her immediate circle, an editor at New Republic Books in Washington, DC, heard portions of it being read on National Public Radio and contacted Slone about publishing the book. Slone went on to write five more books and a column for her local newspaper. She also received visitors interested in learning more about Appalachian traditions.

In addition to writing, Slone's creativity found many outlets; for example, she made over fifteen hundred quilts and dolls.

FROM What My Heart Wants to Tell

Of all the things my father taught me, I am thankful that I learned from him the enjoyment one could obtain from work. I did not know until I was grown that there were people who did not like to work, and not until my children were grown did I realize that some folks thought it was shameful to do manual labor. (I must admit, though, I do not like to do housework. I like for a house to be a home, a comfortable place to live, not a "show room.")

I wish I could pass on to my grandchildren how I feel about growing our own food. All good things come from God. But you seem so close to Him, one with nature, when you plant the tiny seeds, in faith that they will grow. Later there is the joy of gathering and storing away these results of your partnership with nature. The food you grow yourself tastes much better and seems a lot cleaner to me. It may not be "untouched by human hands," but at least you know whose hands they were.

Mike was once helping me to dig a mess of potatoes for supper and asked, "Granny, why do you put your potatoes in the ground? Is it so your chickens can't get at them? Mother gets hers at the market."

I've always been thankful we owned a farm of our own, to grow corn, for example. A "new ground" (pronounced as one word) was best. This meant the ground had been cleared of all the trees and underbrush, and was now ready to be planted.

If you were lucky enough to have a new ground you would be assured of a good crop but a lot more work. It had to be all done by hand, using only hoes. Although most of the larger roots and stumps were removed—either by burning or dynamite, or sometimes pulled out by oxen—there were still too many small roots and sprouts to make plowing possible.

So, early in the spring, sometimes as early as January or February, we would begin "grubbin'," digging the young sprouts that were beginning to grow around where the trees had grown. After these were all dug, they were raked into piles and burned. Then we took hoes and shaved off the weeds. Each one working would take a "swith" and distance themselves as long as they could reach with a hoe, one above the other, each one just a little ahead of the one above. Around the hill they would go, raking a very small layer of the topsoil along with the weeds onto the row below. After this was finished, they would "dig in" the corn, about every three feet, in rows about four feet apart. A small loose hole was dug, with three to five grains of corn dropped inside, and the dirt spread over it. My father always said to plant five,

> One for the ground squirrel,
> One for the crow,
> One to rot,
> And two to grow.

When the corn was about a foot high, you began to hoe it, cutting all the weeds, and thinning it to two stalks to a hill. Someone would always joke and say, "Pull up the large ones and give the little ones room to grow." We replanted any missing hills and a few weeks later we hoed it again. This second hoeing was called "laying it by," because this finished all the work with the corn until time to save the fodder and gather the corn. The fodder was gathered in September and the corn brought to the barns in November. When we "layed by our corn" it called for a wild celebration. Folks on adjoining farms were always in friendly competition. Each would rush to beat the others. Our hills are so close, many different family groups could see and hear each other. When the last "hill of corn" was hoed they would begin to yell, beating their hoes together or against rocks, thumping on the dinner bucket, anything to make a noise. Someone at the house would ring the dinner bell, telling all their friends that they were through with their corn. An extra good dinner or supper, as the case might be, would be cooked, and everyone had at least one whole day's rest. Even the mules got this one day without working.

Another little saying of my father's helped us remember what happened when you waited too long to plant your corn:

> In July, corn knee-high,
> In August, he layed it by,
> In September there came a big frost.
> Now you see what corn this young man lost.

Fodder also had to be saved. All the blades from where the ear of corn grew down were stripped from the stalk, leaving the one on which the corn grew. Every few handfuls were placed between two stalks close to the ground; here they would cure out. After a few days, these would be tied into bundles, and stacked in a shock, or hauled to the barn. The remaining stalk was cut off just above the ear of corn, and tied into bundles and placed together in smaller shocks. These were called "tops" and were not as valuable as the blade fodder. The tops were usually fed to the cows, and the rest kept for the horses. Taking care of fodder was one work I could never do. I know now I was allergic to the smell, though I did not know what was wrong then. I just knew I always got sick when I pulled fodder or cut tops, but it never seemed to bother me once it was cured out, and I could help put it away.

My father's generation had no glass jars, so they did not can fruits or vegetables. They filled large crocks or churns with applebutter. When boiled down very stiff and sweetened with molasses, it would keep fresh for many weeks. Big barrels were filled with smoked apples; a few holes were made in the bottom of the barrel so the juice would run out, then filled up a few inches with apples that had been pared and sliced, with the core removed. On top of these a dish was placed in which a small amount of sulfur was slowly burned by placing a heated piece of iron inside the dish. A quilt over the top kept the smoke from escaping. Next day, another layer of apples and more sulfur was burned and so on, until the barrel was full. The sulfur gave the apples an "off" flavor that took a little getting used to, but was supposed to be good for you. I loved the taste myself, and always served them topped with blackberry jelly.

The late apples could be "holed away" in the ground. Often the floor of the house was removed and the hole dug there. It was lined with straw, the apples were poured in, and more straw and dirt were mounded over the top. You had to be very careful that none of these apples were bruised or rotten. Some were kept in barrels, each wrapped separately in a piece of paper. Sweet potatoes were also kept this way. Many times these barrels were left all winter in a corner of the bedroom, hid from view by a curtain or quilt. Apples were fried, or made into pies and dumplings.

Peaches were canned in syrup. We had a "cling stone" peach, so small that the stone could not be removed as in other peaches. Often we would peel these and can them whole—the stone gave them a very nice flavor—sometimes using sugar, and some in sugar, vinegar, and spice. We had a few pears, and I remember my sister, Frances, had a quince tree. Some folks, not many, had cherries and plums, but almost everyone had a gooseberry patch, and strawberries grew wild in many places. We picked and canned huckleberries and raspberries, but we used blackberries the most; from these we made jelly and jam. Dumplings were made by bringing the sweetened, cooked berries to a boil and dropping in fist-sized balls of biscuit dough.

Berry "sass" was a breakfast dish. The boiling berries were thickened with a little flour and water—not quite as heavy as the sauce used for a pie filling—sweetened and served like a pudding. I always loved to pick berries. No one ever went alone, because of snakes. The huckleberries grew on the tops of ridges. Every year, when they began to ripen, someone would start a rumor that a bear or wildcat had been seen on such and such a hollow, or maybe the story would be that some crazy man or desperate criminal was loose. Moonshiners started these tales so as to scare the women. They were afraid the women would find the moonshine stills while hunting huckleberries.

No one picks berries anymore; almost all the old orchards are gone. Of the fourteen apple trees that grew in my yard when I moved here, only four remain, too old for fruit, giving little shade, and almost dangerous to let stand. In fact, during the severe cold weather this past winter we reopened our fireplace, and chopped one of our apple trees into firewood. I almost felt like I was forsaking an old friend.

All fruits and berries were eaten raw, or cooked in syrup, and made into jelly and jam, but most were used for dumplings or pies. For peach cobbler the slices were baked with layers of biscuit dough. Apples were used in fried pies, apples or apple-butter, folded into small thin sheets of dough and fried in deep fat. I have also heard these called half-moon pies or moccasin pies. We also used vinegar as a substitute for fruit, making pies or dumplings flavored with vinegar, sugar and spice. A "barefoot dumpling" was when the balls of dough were cooked in boiling water, containing only salt and lard. Of course, they were better in chicken broth or fresh meat "sop."

We grew corn for feed and bread, but we also used it as a vegetable, canning it and pickling it in brine salt water for winter use, while the kernels were still young enough to be soft. Pickled corn is good fried in a little sugar, but it's best to eat as a snack, sitting around the fire at night and biting it directly off the cob. "Gritted bread" (probably from the word grater) was made from young corn; a gritter was made by driving holes in a piece of tin, maybe an empty peach can, with a nail, then fastening the tin to a board. The ears of corn were rubbed over the sharp edges made by the nail holes, to make meal. If the corn was young enough, no water needed to be added, just a little salt and baking soda, baked in a greased pan. Eaten with sweet milk, it was a meal in itself. You can use corn to grit until it gets old enough to shell from the cob. After the juice or "milk" on the inside of the grains begins to dry, the water must be added, to make soft dough before baking.

I guess of all vegetables, beans were used the most. There were many kinds of seeds, from the "bunch" beans grown in the garden, to field beans planted along with the corn. The stalks of corn make a place for the bean vines to grow. Beans were pickled in brine salt water in large wooden barrels. We also canned them. Many times we placed the closed glass jars full of beans in a washtub filled with water allowing them to cook for several hours on a fire outside.

Then there was a "tough" bean. The hull was too hard to eat. These were used for soup beans, cooked by themselves or mixed with the dried beans. Salt pork or hog's jowl was added to the beans while they cooked. A friend once told me how every night, before being allowed to go to bed, he and his brothers and sisters each had to shell enough beans to fill a large cup.

We always raised two crops of cabbage. The later one was planted in early July in the hill and not transplanted. These were "holed away" for winter use. A long trench, or "fur," was made with the plow. The fully grown cabbages were pulled up "by the roots," with a few of the bottom leaves broken off. The remaining excess leaves were wrapped around the "head" and placed side by side with the roots turned up in the hole made by the plow; then dirt was thrown up around the cabbages, leaving part of the stalk and the roots exposed. This way they were easily found and removed. They would stay all winter and keep fresh. Cabbages kept this way have a sweet wholesome flavor that you can get no other way, and far exceeds anything you can buy in the supermarket.

And then, of course, there was sauerkraut: cabbage pickled in salt. I also use a little sugar and vinegar. We now put kraut in glass jars, but "back then" we used large churns or crocks or wooden barrels. Our folks would sometimes put the cabbages in the barrel whole, a layer at a time, and cut them up with a shovel. (I have known of people that dried cabbage. I remember watching an old man, when I lived at Dwarf, drying cabbage leaves on his housetop. I never did eat any.)

Beets were cooked and canned in sugar, spice, water, and vinegar; they were eaten no other way. We served them with shucky beans or as a snack. I love to pickle boiled eggs in the liquid where the beets were cooked; the bright red color makes the eggs pretty and gives them a nice flavor. This is a must at Easter for my family.

Tomatoes were thought to be poison by our grandmothers, and were raised only as a flower. We canned the ripe ones to be used in vegetable soup; some added sugar and used it for dessert. Of course, during the summer they were sliced and served with green beans, or added to slaw. Green tomatoes are good sliced, rolled in meal, to which a little salt and pepper is added, and fried in deep fat. My husband likes them sweetened, I don't. There is a small variety which we call "tommy toes." Green tomatoes were also canned in sugar, spice, and vinegar, sometimes by themselves, sometimes with peppers, cabbage, and other vegetables. We also mixed green tomatoes, green pepper, and green cabbage, and pickled them in brine salt water; we called this "pickle lilly" or "chow chow." No matter what you called it—fried in grease and eaten with beans and corn bread—it was good. We ate corn bread for at least two meals each day. Very few people do this anymore. It's easier to use the toaster, I guess.

Next to the beans, I guess more potatoes were used. They were "kelp over" by holing them away. They were "fried, baked, cooked, roasted in the ashes under the grate, added to soup, and boiled with their jackets on." Sometimes we would take them to school with us and boil them in an empty lard bucket, on the coal heating stove. The teacher would help us eat them at recess.

We "bedded" our sweet potatoes in a "hot bed" made from shucks, manure, and dirt, and covered with fodder and an old quilt. After they began sprouting, the fodder and quilt were removed. When large enough, the plants were then transplanted to hills or ridges. Sweet potatoes were baked, roasted, fried in sugar and lard, or cooked with some salt and sugar added. We canned them by cooking them in jars, like the beans. We kept them through the winter in barrels or boxes, each wrapped separately in a piece of paper.

Sweet peppers were eaten raw; stuffed with sausage and other meats; canned in sugar, spice, water and vinegar; mixed with other vegetables to make "pickle lilly" or mixed pickles. Hot pepper or strong pepper was eaten as an additive to other vegetables. We also canned it in vinegar, or strung it up on twine, and allowed it to dry for winter use. Some folks like it added to fresh meat when cooked. We put a few pods of hot pepper on the top of our barrels or churns of salt pickles. It kept the gnats from bothering them, and also gave a good flavor. We added red hot pepper to our paste when we were lining our houses with newspaper and magazines. This kept the mice from eating the paste and ruining the paper. I remember once I had made a large kettle of paste from flour and water, to which I had added a large amount of pepper. I had set it on the back of the stove to cool. One of my boys come in from school, took a large spoonful, thinking it was his supper. It really gave him a hot mouth; I was sorry for him, but I had to laugh. He said he knew why the mice refused to eat it.

Cushaw and "punkins" were planted in the corn, every fourth hill, every fourth row. The small ones were fed to the hogs or cows. The hard-shell cushaws were chopped into small chunks and cooked, then placed in a pan, covered with sugar and spice, and baked. The soft-shell ones were peeled, sliced, cooked and mashed with sugar and spice to make cushaw butter. Some folks added cooked cushaw or pumpkin to their cornmeal dough, and baked it. "Molassie bread" was made this way also. Cushaws are better if molasses is substituted for sugar. And, of course, there were "punkin pies." Many cushaws and pumpkins, along with squashes, were dried. A green pole was hung by strings over the open fireplace. The cushaws were sliced into large circles or rings, then hung on this pole. In a few days they were dried, and more were hung up. This way they could be preserved for winter use, cooked with sugar and lard, or maybe salt pork or hog's jowl—very good. I have seen bushels of dried cushaws and "punkins" hung up in the smokehouse in the winter. By spring, it would have all been eaten.

Asparagus was only grown as a shrub in the yard, never eaten. The full-grown bush, with its green fernlike leaves and bright seed pod, is very beautiful. I have heard the old folks say, "You know, there are folks who eat 'sparegrass' when the sprouts are little." Yet, I never knew of anyone trying it.

Artichokes to us are the potatolike roots of a tall plant that have beautiful yellow flowers that resemble daisies. They were only eaten raw, as a snack.

Cucumbers were sweet-pickled and canned, used with other vegetables for "mixed pickles," pickled in brine salt, eaten raw, sliced and served with green beans or slaw.

Peas were one of the earliest seeds to be planted, sometimes as early as February. We grew a tender-hull kind that could be cooked like string beans, hull and all. We very seldom shelled them. Peas are delicious cooked together with very small young potatoes.

We grew two crops of turnips: a few were planted in ridges for summer use, and then in the fall we planted a larger crop, "broadcasting" the seed over the now empty garden. The tops were cooked for greens; the roots were holed away or put in the cellar. The cold weather does not hurt turnips; they keep growing almost all winter. I like to cook them together—the tops and roots—when the turnips are small.

Rhubarb we called "pie plants." Every garden had a long row, used for pies or dumplings, fried as apples, or mixed with strawberries to make jelly. It "came in" just as most of the winter food was used up, and the new garden was still too young to use. It was supposed to be good for you and help to cure "spring fever."

Some of us grew a few gourds just for the fun of it, but our forefathers grew them to be used. The larger ones would hold lard, salt, soft soap, meal, molasses, or whatever. The small, long-handled ones were water dippers. We called the small round egg-shaped kind "hen foolers," because we used them for nest eggs.

There were many different kinds of onions. Fall and winter onions grew through the winter, and could be eaten green. "Tater onions" got their name for the way the new ones grew in a cluster around the old one; they were kept for the roots. "Spring shallots" were very early and very small.

Onions were eaten as a dish, not an additive. They were fried either while green or after grown, but not as "onion rings," as they are now prepared. To keep for winter, they were pulled while there was still some top remaining, tied in bunches, and hung from nails in the barn or smokehouse. They become better after being allowed to freeze. Onions were used as a medicine, roasted, mashed and made into a "pollus" placed on the chest, to help "break up" a cold. Onion soup was also used for a cold or tonsillitis.

Then there were wild greens or "salet." There are many different kinds; sometimes the same plant was known by a different name by different people. "Plantin" is the one used most, a small thick-leafed green with a very distinct flavor, a little like cabbage. Then for cooking there was "sheep's leg," "groundhog ear," and "speckled dock." Poke salet had to be used very carefully, because it could be poison; it was cooked in one water, washed and cooked again, then fried in a lot of lard. If eaten too often, it can become a laxative. The stalks were also good peeled, rolled in meal, and fried. "Crow's foot," "shoestring," "chicken salet," and "creases" were eaten raw, cut up, sprinkled with salt, and then "killed" by pouring real hot grease over them.

In my father's time hogs were allowed to run wild. Each man had a "mark" so as to tell his own. The pig's ear was either notched or split, some used both, but no two exactly alike. When a sow mothered a "gang" of pigs, if the owner did not catch the small ones and mark them before they were weaned, and they had quit running with the mother, they were then accepted as "wild pigs": anyone who caught them was the owner. He could put his mark on them or butcher them for food. Wild hogs grew very fat on "mast"; nuts and roots they found in the woods. I thought this gave the meat a good flavor, but I have talked with some folks that said this was not so; they were better if brought in and fed corn a few weeks before butchering them. The older generations used more beef and sheep for meat than we did, but chicken and dumplings was counted the best dish of any. I have seen my folks cook as many as sixteen grown hens at one time, in an old-fashioned iron "mink" kettle, when there was a big crowd at a wedding, funeral, or family get-together.

Our folks on Caney, in the past, had plenty of good wholesome food. I don't see how they ever ate all these many barrels, holes, cans, and sacks full of beans, corn, cabbage, and many other fruits and vegetables that they called "sass." But they did. Maybe they knew nothing about vitamins or a balanced diet, but they worked hard to grow and put away food.

My father taught me to love nature's beauty as well as her benefits. I remember how he would listen to the thunder. He would say, "God wouldn't want any of his children to get scared at something He made." I have always loved to listen to the thunder.

He also loved to look at the pretty sunset and rainbows. He often would call me to come outside to enjoy the view with him. The valley would be lit up with bright colors, as the sun set behind the hills. And he would say, "This is the way Eden must have looked before sin entered the world." He would not have known what you meant if you had mentioned any of the masterpieces of paintings. But he enjoyed the pictures painted by the greatest Master of them all. There is nothing more beautiful than a rainbow that seems to form a bridge from one hilltop to the other, or the snow-covered world early in the morning, before man has destroyed it by making paths. The many colors of the autumn leaves remind me of my "crazy quilts," such a blending of colors that the absence of any scheme or pattern makes a beauty or system all its own: a picture you will never forget if you have seen it once.

Loyal Jones

1928–

Loyal Jones was born near the Great Smoky Mountains in Cherokee County, North Carolina, and was reared there and in nearby Clay County. After earning degrees from Berea College (1954) and the University of North Carolina at Chapel Hill (1961), he spent five years directing the Council of the Southern Mountains, a community development organization. From 1970 to 1993 he directed Berea's Appalachian Center, which is named in his honor. Jones helped shape Appalachian literature in the 1960s by advocating for the publication of Appalachian authors such as Gurney Norman and Jim Wayne Miller in the council's periodical *Mountain Life and Work,* making that journal the first to publish specifically Appalachian literature.

First published as a short essay in 1973 in part to counter Jack Weller's negative portrayal of the region in *Yesterday's People* (1964), *Appalachian Values* (1994), excerpted below, is a series of expanded essays about and photographs of the region. The values that Jones sees as particularly Appalachian are love of place, independence, self-reliance, pride, neighborliness, humility and modesty, a sense of beauty, patriotism, religion, personalism, and a sense of humor.

While some have been gently critical of *Appalachian Values's* nonscholarly approach, Jones's work is significant for its repositioning of Appalachian society as positive, valuable, and pride-worthy, making it one of the most beloved books from the region. Jones's book *Faith and Meaning in the Upland South* (1999) develops themes about religion expressed in *Appalachian Values,* presenting his ideas about southern mountain religion relayed through the voices of the people he interviewed. For all his seriousness of purpose, Jones also has a ready sense of humor. In addition to editing the humor section of the *Encyclopedia of Appalachia* (2006), Jones published several collections of humor with Billy Edd Wheeler.

FROM Appalachian Values

Religion

Mountain people are religious. This does not mean that we always go to church regularly, but we are religious in the sense that most of our values and the meaning we find in life spring from the Bible. To understand mountaineers, one must understand our religion.

In the beginning, they were mostly Anglican, Presbyterian or Baptist, with some Bretheren and Lutherans, all rather formally organized churches with confessions of faith and other creedal documents. Presbyterian and Anglican churches did not serve the spiritual needs of all on the frontier, however, and so locally autonomous groups were formed, depending on local resources and leadership. The Methodists rose to prominence in the First Great Awakening of the eighteenth century, stressing the work of the Holy Spirit on human emotions, along with intellectual ideas. The Second Great Awakening, beginning in 1801 in Kentucky, won many Presbyterians and Calvinistic Baptists over to the belief that all who seek the Lord can be saved, not just the limited group that John Calvin said were predestined to be saved. Several churches split over the doctrines of predestination and free-will. Here is a story.

A Free-will Baptist and a Predestinarian Baptist were good friends. One day they went to the courthouse together. As they were coming down stairs from the second floor, the Predestinarian tripped and fell down the stairs, rolling end over end, tearing his suit and bruising himself all over. The Free-Willer rushed down, picked him up, brushed him off and asked how he was.

"Well, I think I'm all right," the man said.

The Free-Willer said, "But I guess you're glad to get that one behind you, aren't you?"

Mountain people in large numbers joined the more optimistic Methodist and Free-Will Baptist churches, churches created to an extent by and for the common people. The members depended on the grace of God to help them through a hard world and to save them in the end, even though they at times were weak and sinful. Eventually, other churches grew up in the mountains to meet the needs of isolated people: Cumberland Presbyterians, Disciples of Christ and Churches of Christ, and the Pentecostal-Holiness movement at the turn of the twentieth century added many others, the last group going beyond the Methodists in stressing holiness and the work of grace from the Holy Spirit.

The home mission boards of the mainline denominations have usually looked on our locally autonomous churches as something that we must be saved from. Thus they have sent many missionaries to us, even if we thought we were already secure in the Lord. Many social reformers have also viewed the local church negatively as a hindrance to social progress, since native Christians sometimes have a dim view of human perfectability. What such outside observers fail to see is that our religion has helped to sustain us and has made life meaningful in grim situations. Religion has shaped our lives, but at the same time we have shaped our religion, since religion and culture are always intertwined. Life in the mountains until recently did not allow for an optimistic social gospel. Hard work did not always bring a sure reward, and so perhaps some of mountain religion is more fatalistic than elsewhere. The point is to get religion—get saved—and try to keep the faith and endure, hoping for a sure reward in the hereafter. The beliefs are more realistic than idealistic, because we know what theologian Reinhold Niebuhr pointed out, that we see clearly what we should be and what we should do, and yet we fail consistently; that is the human tragedy. Someone said that man and woman were made at the end of the week when God was tired. The Good News is that even though we fail, God loves us anyway, and if we believe, we will be saved.

Independence, Self-Reliance, and Pride

Several years ago there came a great snowfall in western North Carolina. The Red Cross came to help people who might be stranded without food or fuel. Two workers heard of an old lady way back in the mountains living alone, and they went to see about her, in a four-wheel drive vehicle. After an arduous trip they finally skidded down into her cove, got out and knocked on the door. When she appeared, one of the men said,

"Howdy, ma'am, we're from the Red Cross," but before he could say anything else, the old lady replied,

"Well, I don't believe I'm a-goin to be able to help you any this year. It's been a right hard winter."

John C. Campbell, in his *The Southern Highlander and His Homeland,* remarked that Americans, Southerners, rural dwellers, and farmers are all independent, and went on to say that since highlanders are all of these things, they have "independence raised to the fourth power." Independence, self-reliance and pride were perhaps the most obvious characteristics of mountain people. Our forebears were independent, else they would not have gone to such trouble and danger to get away from encroachments on their freedom. Independence and self-reliance were traits to be admired on the frontier. People banded together to help one another in communities, but the person who did not or could not look after himself and his family was pitied.

There is a lesson in the mountaineer's all-out search for freedom and independence. We worked so hard for it that many of us eventually lost it. We withdrew from the doings of the larger society, and in ways it passed us by, although not before it bought up most of the natural resources around us. We were hired as "hands" to exploit the timber, coal, gas and oil, and when most of it was shipped out, many of us were let go into circumstance beyond our control, some maimed and damaged beyond healing, and some of us consigned to poverty.

But our belief in independence and self-reliance is still strong whether or not we are truly independent. We still value solitude, whether or not we can always find a place to be alone. We also value self-reliance, to do things for ourselves, whether or not it is practical to do so—like make a dress, a chair, build a house, repair an automobile, or play a banjo, fiddle or guitar. We get satisfaction from that, in this age when people hire others to do work they used to do, even to provide entertainment.

Pride is mostly a feeling of not wanting to be beholding to other people. We are inclined to try to do things for ourselves, find our way without asking directions when we are lost on the road, or suffer through when we are in need. We don't like to ask others for help. The value of independence and self-reliance, and our pride, is often stronger than desire or need. Here is another independence joke:

A Baptist preacher was asked to preach in the Presbyterian church. The Presbyterian minister asked,

"Will you wear a robe?"

"Do I have to wear a robe?"

"Well, no, you don't have to wear a robe."

"Well, all right then," said the Baptist, "I'll wear one."

Familism

Appalachian people are family-centered. Mountain people usually feel an obligation to family members and are more truly themselves when within the family circle. Family loyalty runs deep and wide and may extend to grandparents, uncles, aunts, nephews, nieces, cousins and even in-laws. Family members gather when there is sickness, death, or a disaster. Supervisors in northern industries have been perplexed when employees from Appalachia have been absent from jobs to attend funerals of distant relatives. Families often take in relatives for extended periods, or even raise children of kin when there is death or sickness in the family. One of the biggest problems reported by officials in cities to which Appalachians have migrated for work is overcrowding in apartments when relatives are taken in until they get work and places of their own. In James Still's novel, *River of Earth*, relatives are invited in by the father even though there isn't enough food for everyone. The mother in desperation burns the house down and moves her family into the tiny smokehouse to get rid of those whom her husband could not ask to leave. Blood is thick in Appalachia. Two brothers were talking. One said, "You know, I've come to the conclusion that Uncle Luther is an S.O.B." The other said, "Yeah, he is, but he's our'n."

The Appalachian family is subject to the same stresses and strains that affect all American families, and there is alienation, divorce, and abuse here as everywhere, but there is a strong attachment and commitment to the extended family in Appalachia that is becoming rare in a land where most of us live someplace other than where we were born.

Love of Place

One of the first questions asked in the mountains, after "whose boy/girl are you?" is "Where are you from?" We are oriented around place. We remember our homeplace and many of us go back as often as possible. Some of us think about going back for good, perhaps to the Nolichucky, Big Sandy, Hiwassee, or Oconoluftee, or to Drip Rock, Hanging Dog, Shooting Creek, Decoy, Stinking Creek, Sweetwater, or Sandy Mush. Our place is close on our minds. One fellow said he came from so far back in the mountains, the sun set between his house and the road. Our songs tell of our regard for the land where we were born. Sense of place is one of the unifying values of mountain people, and it makes it hard for us to leave the mountains, and when we do, we long to return.

This fellow died and went to heaven. St. Peter showed him around, and he thought everything was up to expectations—streets of gold, heavenly choirs, harps—and then he heard these people in the corner of heaven raising an awful commotion, quarreling, complaining, and shouting. He went over to investigate and found they were all chained to the wall. He said to St. Peter, "Who are these people?"

"They are Appalachian mountaineers," St. Peter said.

"Why are they chained to the wall?"

St. Peter said, "If we didn't do that they'd go home every week-end."

Harry Middleton
1949–1993

Harry Middleton's life was a rootless one. Born in Frankfurt, Germany, where his father was stationed in the United States Army, Middleton was reared on a series of army bases. After attending college at Louisiana's Northwestern State University (majoring in English) and Louisiana State University (earning an MA in history in 1973), he spent twenty years living in New Orleans, Birmingham, and Denver. He chiefly supported himself by writing for magazines. In addition to this physical rootlessness, Middleton also struggled with depression, which was exacerbated when he was let go by the magazine publishing house for which he had been writing and editing.

Middleton found one natural feature that continued to draw him to Appalachia—the trout stream. During visits to his grandfather's farm in the Ozark Mountains of Arkansas, Middleton learned to fly-fish with his grandfather and his grandfather's Sioux friend. He chronicled these early experiences in his first book, *The Earth Is Enough: Growing Up in a World of Trout and Old Men* (1989). Throughout the 1980s, while living in Birmingham, Middleton traveled regularly to the Great Smoky Mountains and nearby ranges to fly-fish. Out of his experiences in the southern mountains grew his book *On the Spine of Time: An Angler's Love of the Smokies* (1991). The section of this book excerpted below reveals Middleton's belief that spirituality can be found on the trout stream and his concern about the threat posed to that sanctuary by environmental pollution.

FROM On the Spine of Time: An Angler's Love of the Smokies

FROM CHAPTER 4: CROSSROADS OF TIME

The highest peak in the eastern United States, the apex of the ragged Appalachians, is Mount Mitchell. Its summit has the look of a heavy fist, jutting through smoky-blue clouds and perpetual chilly mists. Mitchell, like all great mountains, is a place of wrenching extremes. Its summit makes up the firm belly of the high Appalachians' intriguing, haunting Canadian Zone, a land that is closer in character to parts of China than to North Carolina. Life in this high country, in this land above the clouds, is perpetually pressed by hard times, hard, unforgiving weather. Another mountain paradox: a place that is at once exceptionally fragile and yet doggedly enduring. Like trout in wild mountain streams, what survives above 5,000 feet does so on its own terms, without compromise. The press of civilization, of man's coughing, wheezing, pneumatic world, brings death more than adaptation.

A raw cold wind blows hard atop Mount Mitchell. A constant wind, merciless.

Trees are gnarled, twisted, stunted, bent in grotesque attitudes like galleries of violent sculpture. The summit is a place of harshness, an environment where death is a common resident. For as long as I have been coming to these mountains, the crown of Mount Mitchell has always been marked by dead trees, great stands of them, hard, honest evidence of the vagaries of life above 5,000 feet. They were part of the fabric of the mountains and I paid little attention to them until the winter of 1984 when it struck me that their numbers were growing, that the small stands of dead and dying trees had become a bulging, swelling host. I studied the summit of Mount Mitchell through powerful binoculars and the dead and dying trees piled up before my eyes like massive gray shoals of dust-colored bones. A sweep of the binoculars showed that almost the entire crest of the mountain seemed to have taken on the aspect of a long, rippled, grim scar pinched against the sky.

And the trees, the great stands of spruce and fir on Mount Mitchell, go on dying. The mountain today looks like death's gray land, wearing the despair of a plague's vile kiss. The once thick forest that crowded the ridgeline lies fallen and falling, as though laid down by some sudden killing wind. No matter the month, no matter the press of weather, Mount Mitchell knows only death's touch and its dull gray color.

The death atop Mount Mitchell has fueled argument among scientists and environmentalists for years. The common explanation for the great number of dead trees along the summit was the mountain's severe climate and the sudden appearance in the 1950s of a number of insects, especially the woolly balsam aphid, that feed on the spruce and fir trees. The woolly balsam aphid, it turned out, is a recent immigrant, just another insect that had been accidentally imported into the country. After its arrival, it eventually made its way to the Appalachian Mountains and found there its favorite meal, Fraser firs. Nothing has as yet stopped the aphid. It, too, knows no compromise. It seems as irrepressible as the chestnut blight. But Dr. Robert I. Bruck, a plant pathologist at North Carolina State University in Raleigh, refused to lay all of Mount Mitchell's troubles on a single aphid. There was just too much destruction. He sensed that the mountain's deepening ruin went further than the appetite of the woolly balsam aphid. After all, the aphid ate mostly fir trees, yet the destruction on the mountain swept through all the trees above 5,000 feet. Indeed, in many places the red spruce were dying out even faster than the firs. Bruck believed that something else was killing the trees, or at least contributing to their deaths, and he believed that that something else was airborne pollution and acid rain. He studied the mountain's air, soil, and its water, and his findings portray an atmosphere atop Mount Mitchell that is more toxic than the worst smog-bound summer days over downtown Knoxville, Nashville, Charlotte, Birmingham, and Atlanta combined. Yet another irony: the lure of fresh, invigorating mountain air, the clean winds blowing over the rim of the highest point of stone in eastern North America, when in fact the air swirling about the summit of Mount Mitchell is only slightly less foul than the brown, congestive, ruinous automotive emissions floating stiffly above Los Angeles.

According to the Environmental Protection Agency, concentrations of 120 parts of ozone per billion parts of air at sea level even for an hour a year is cause of serious concern. In 1986 Dr. Bruck measured such alarming ozone levels atop Mount

Mitchell ten times during a single month's worth of readings. Ten times. The summit is literally wrapped in pollution. A gauze of clouds and mist and fog shroud Mount Mitchell more than three hundred days a year. This cloak of moisture, Dr. Bruck has learned, is saturated with toxic substances, whopping doses of heavy metals and acidic moisture. Even more alarming is the mounting evidence that the dire effects of air pollution above 5,000 feet are beginning to show up at lower elevations. Once thought to be the problem solely of the northeastern United States and Canada, the pall of acid rain has now spread over the entire continent, a rain that is an efficient killer, neatly leaching minerals like magnesium and calcium through the leaves of plants and trees, strangling them just as it quietly and efficiently strangles mountain lakes and streams. On the summit of Mount Mitchell the destructive wet cape of acidic moisture is compounded by increasing levels of toxic metals present in the thin soil—traces of cadmium, zinc, lead, mercury, and aluminum. Bruck's studies show that the moisture at the top of Mount Mitchell is from eighty to one hundred times more acidic than that of normal rainfall. It is as if the top of the mountain were daily submerged in a great, sour-smelling sea of pure vinegar. Dr. Bruck, of course, is no soothsayer. He brings neither good news nor bad, only the facts that make such news, one way or the other. Even he remains hesitant to say firmly that pollution alone is killing the Canadian Zone of the high Appalachians. What he does contend is that the high country is under extreme environmental stress caused perhaps by a weave of interconnected causes from insects to airborne pollutants. But he does say, without reservation, that the high country is dying.

I still go to Mount Mitchell, though it is not easy. I hesitate, grapple for excuses to stay away the way I might hesitate about visiting a dying friend because I know that going will seal the truth of things, make me hold death's hand yet again. So I go to the mountain and stare at the dying trees that now cover nearly its entire summit and below, and I understand that even setting aside a wild land, a mountain or a river, any piece of remnant wildness does not guarantee its survival. Against winds heavy with ozone and toxic metals and acid rains, laws that call for protection cannot begin to ensure preservation or survival.

Sometimes as I walk along the bony ridge of Mount Le Conte, I am reminded of Mount Mitchell the way I first saw it more than a decade ago—crowded stands of fir and spruce dripping with tattered wisps of cold mountain clouds, tendrils of fog, sudden icy mists. Often I will taste this cold rain, let it sit for a time on my tongue, waiting for that first bitter metallic taste of acidic rain, while the rain runs off my face and hands and down among the layers of spongy moss that spread among the rocks and fallen trees looking like lush green islands in a vast and bleak gray sea. Still the view of the Smokies from the summit of Mount Le Conte, especially looking north from Cliff Top and east from Myrtle Point, when the daylight is nearly spent and is the old red color of faded roses, is like looking into great sheets of red rain pouring out of the sky and slanting off Clingman's Dome and Thunderhead and the worn hobble-headed crown of Siler's Bald where the headwaters of Hazel Creek gather. The knotted dome of Mount Guyot is clearly visible, too, and beyond the vaporous shapes of the Plott Balsams and Great Balsams, even the rocky thumb of Water Rock Knob.

Enjoying this country's remnant wild places is a touchy issue. The Great Smoky Mountains National Park covers more than 500,000 acres. In the half century since the park's creation, conservationists, state governments, the federal government, lumbermen, and developers have argued about the proper use of the park. In 1988, in a unanimous vote, the House passed a bill that would have permanently set aside 419,000 acres of the Smokies as primitive wilderness area. So far only Senator Jesse Helms of North Carolina has stood in the way of the bill making its way through the Senate.

If the bill does pass it will only more or less validate what has been happening to the park for a long time. There is not enough money or manpower to keep the entire park tidy and groomed, ready to embrace the public at all times. Making most of it wilderness would mean the Park Service could stop spending its time maintaining trails and other facilities that so few people use. Most of the park, and especially the great wild North Carolina sections of the park, is already wild and has been for years.

Let the trails go to hell. Don't improve the roads. Make anyone wanting to expose themselves to the hard beauty of these mountains get a permit. Keep all cars at a distance. Pass laws that will stop anything like a Gatlinburg or Pigeon Forge from happening on the North Carolina side of the mountains. Do all of these things. I am for all of it, and more, selfishly so. These are the kinds of things that will keep the streams open and wild and the trout alive and uncompromising and me trying with fits and starts to hook into them both, hoping they will pull me into the soft, warm cathedral light that comes off mountain streams just at dusk.

I walked the trail down along Slickrock Creek in a hard rain that tasted cold and clean, innocent, free of toxic metals and the sharp taste of acid. Knowing that the creek made a wide bend ahead and that there was a nice pool above a gallery of stones, I stood in a thick grove of sheltering trees, rigged up the Winston rod, and noticed a tiny pool of rainwater gathering in a green fold of my jacket, the drops of rain as firm and regular as cells. On the creek, the light eddied and spilled and rushed with the water and the water took on the moody character of the light until they mingled so completely that I could no longer separate water from light and light from water. Everything drifted in a warm, rainy harmony of motion. I worked the green 4-weight line out through the guides of the willowy rod and tied on a fetching nymph. I cast and watched the small nymph go down in the fast, cold water.

On the sixth cast a small brown took the nymph and ran. I could feel its weight and its anger and its determination as it bent around stones and submerged roots and limbs trying to free itself, to escape line and hook. It spent its energies in a great rush and I pulled it close, bringing the line in with my hands, not even using the reel, and as it rose just out in front of my rod tip I could see its head and eyes—eyes raven black, a blackness as wide as a clear night sky and drenched in wildness, a wildness of trout and creek and rain; everything seemed liquid, a welcome stream that reached for me like a spring tide, flooded around my calves and thighs, pulled at the muscles of my legs and stomach. I felt the full weight of the fish in my hands and arms and I gave it line, not wanting it to die as it fought. Near the surface I saw it still tossing its head violently, folding and unfolding its deep brown body like a coach whip. Its muscled back was mottled with dark blotches of deep red, the red of dried blood, dark and melancholy. Call it Slickrock Red because there is no other name for it, because I have seen it mark no other trout save the big browns of Slickrock Creek. I lifted the fish slightly, just so its back would break the water, and the rain on its back flashed red, ran down its flanks like tiny streams of claret. I held the trout only for an instant, then freed the hood from its lip, let it go, slowly, gently, carefully. For an instant there, knee-deep in the creek with the rain falling and that brown trout's seared-red back disappearing in the deep water, I was absolutely certain of the interconnectedness of all things, the cold touch of time against my chilled skin.

Jason Miller

1939–2001

Born John Anthony Miller in Long Island City, Queens, New York City, playwright and actor Jason Miller had deep connections to the anthracite coalfields of eastern Pennsylvania. The son of Irish American parents and grandson of a coal miner, Miller was reared in the Lackawana Valley. After earning a BA from the University of Scranton and studying theater at the Catholic University of America, Miller lived in New York City to pursue a career in acting and playwriting.

Miller quickly met with success. He staged his first full-length play, *Nobody Hears a Broken Drum* (1970) off Broadway. His second full-length play, *That Championship Season* (1972), won a Pulitzer Prize and a Tony Award and was made into a film, which Miller directed. In 1973, Miller was nominated for an Academy Award for his role as Father Damien Karras in the horror film *The Exorcist*. After a stint in Hollywood, Miller returned to Scranton, where he lived for the rest of his life. His commitment to eastern Pennsylvania and to regional theater was strong.

In *Nobody Hears a Broken Drum,* Miller interweaves three highly political threads: labor unrest in Pennsylvania's anthracite coalfields during the Civil War era; the contemporaneous political unrest in Ireland, which had struggled for centuries to end the oppressive rule of England; and the complexity of ethnic tension, both the discrimination against Irish Americans and, conversely, Irish prejudices against other groups such as African Americans and Jews.

FROM Nobody Hears a Broken Drum

Characters

John O'Hanlin, *an Irish miner*
Jamie O'Hanlin, *his son*
Paul Shayne, *union organizer*
Mary Shayne, *his wife*
George Griffith, *the mine owner*
Mr. Mangan, *Griffith's secretary*
Father Hanley, *a priest*
Pat O'Malley, *a miner who loves words*
Mike Manley, *a miner who loves drink*
Matt McGinty, *an almost toothless miner*
Jim Dyer, *a miner who stutters*
Joe Mack, *an idiot miner*
Tom Reilly, *a pugnacious miner*

William Evans, *a mine foreman*
Recruiting Officer
Young Officer
Mr. Flannelly, *Northern labor leader*
Young Man
Miners

Time

[. . .] The Civil War [. . .]

Place

The southern anthracite region of Pennsylvania.

FROM ACT ONE

MINERS. (*Entering, singing. The lights shift to the entire stage, which represents the entrance to the mine. The time shifts to late February 1862. Pat and Mike join the crowd of miners.*)

So pick up your shovel, Biff Martin.
Take up your pick, you poor bastard, you poor bastard.
Biff Martin, you married a fine girl named Kelly,
Discovered five kids, inside of her belly,
With the roses in your lungs
And supportin' all your sons, all your sons.
So pick up your shovel, Biff Martin.
Take up your pick, you poor bastard, you poor bastard.

(*A long* STEAM WHISTLE BLAST *signals the assembling of the first shift. It is cold; they gather around smudge pots.*)

REILLY. What good is strikin' when it leaves the belly empty?

MCGINTY. I can't face the starvin' eyes o' me little ones with only promises in me pocket.

PAT. (*With newspaper.*) It's safe we are that Griffith didn't send the troops in to force us to work.

REILLY. Up the arse o' that English bastard.

PAT. Coal is important for the war efforts, ya know.

REILLY. Up the arse o' the war effort.

PAT. (*Referring to paper.*) We're in a civil war, ya know. Mr. Lincoln is extortin' us all to greater sacrifices.

DYER. Save the black so he can dig the mines after we're dead an' gone. (*The men agree.*)

REILLY. The ole Jew.

PAT. Who?

REILLY. Lincoln!

PAT. He's not a Jew, ya lug.

REILLY. Abraham Lincoln . . . he's not Irish.

PAT. You're an imbecile, Reilly.

REILLY. Save the union. Jesus, I can hardly save meself. (*John O'Hanlin and his son-in-law, Paul Shayne, join the men. John is a huge man with one arm missing. He is in his sixties. Paul is about thirty, articulate, enthusiastic, the union leader.*) Mornin', John.

(*The rest of the men also greet John but not Paul.*)

PAUL. Have ya got somethin' on your mind, Reilly, that prevents ya from givin' the nod?

REILLY. We gave ya the nod once, an' lost a month's work by it.

PAUL. Griffith broke this strike, but the idea of a union is not a folly of promises.

REILLY. I'm back to work now, an' up the arse o' your union.—

MEN. (*Agreeing.*) Aye, aye, etc.

PAUL. Listen to me here! The next strike will find the North on our side. I promise ya. Griffith won't be able to ship the extra work load up there because they won't take it.

MCGINTY. They're workin' three shifts a day now t' pick up the slack! They'll go where the money is, like everybody else.

PAUL. The North is sendin' a delegation to meet with me tomorrow! After we merge, the owners will have to acquiesce to our demands.

PAT. What was that word again?

REILLY. Shut up, Pat.

PAT. Acquiesce?

REILLY. I can't burn promises in me stove. I'm done strikin'! (*Men agree.*)

PAUL. Believe me, on my faith, the next time we strike we'll bring Griffith to his knees.

JAMIE. (*Entering.*) He'll be right on a level with all of you then, won't he? (*He's drinking from a bottle of whiskey. He's about thirty.*) Such a fine-feathered flock o' doves cooin' again in shy contentment.

MIKE. Christ, here's the earache.

JAMIE. The flock back in the coop. Where's the sound o' marchin' feet an' lusty voices that proclaimed the end of our misery. Pat, give us a little march, will ya now.

PAT. Ya ought to be ashamed o' yourself, makin' sport o' decent hard-workin' men.

JAMIE. Sing the strike song, Mike, an' stir up me heavy heart. Come on now.

MIKE. Take your mockin' somewhere else.

DYER. Sure, it's the likes o' you that spends a life in a bottle that come against us.

PAUL. Jamie, you'll be arrested if you're found on this property again.

JAMIE. You're a good man, Paul, but ya can't lead these dovies with a rosary an' a book of rules.

REILLY. I'll follow him before the likes o' you. Sneakin' through the night burnin' coal cars, shootin' mules. Aye, that's the length o' you.

JAMIE. Reilly, ya sound like ya left your balls home. What's the fancy phrase ya was all shoutin'? Ah, yes, constitutional agitation! Which is polite for gropin' the governor. But, me little flock, you'll never get to his honor's arse because it's tight against the wall when it comes to the question o' the Irish miners. What was it ya said to me at the start o' the strike, Pat?

PAT. I'll acquiesce to that question when I damn well please, Jamie.

JAMIE. Didn't ya say, "We'll fight for our rights like men"? Is this your fightin'? Goin' back down there like o' bunch o' brainless bloody sheep. Down there to where the timbers buckle at the fart of a mule. Down there where a big rat is goin' to slash off your old root, Pat. (*Grabs Pat.*) They tell us, me little pigeons, the world prospered after some savage found fire, an' I'll tell you, we'll have no prosperity here until we use that fire.

(*Evans comes in. He is the foreman—short, ugly, powerfully built.*)

EVANS. Well, the strikers are back. All right, let's line it up. (*The men gather at one side of the stage with their picks, shovels and lunch pails.*) I hope you haven't forgotten how to use your picks after your vacation.

JAMIE. Look at ya, crouchin' an' shufflin' in fear at the arrival of this dried an' decayed piece o' mule shit.

EVANS. You got one minute to get off this property.

JAMIE. Evans, is it true ya bugger the mules?

EVANS. Don't test me, O'Hanlin.

PAUL. You've been warned, Jamie, go!

EVANS. Sleep it off with the pigs, O'Hanlin. You're not fit for the company o' men.

JAMIE. You're a Welch slut, Evans, that sucked the last drop o' sour milk from your dyin' mother's tit.

EVANS. (*Drops his board and grabs a pick from a miner.*) I'm goin' to put a hole in you, you Irish scum.

JAMIE. (*Grabs a pick from Paul.*) Come now, Evans. (*They circle each other, the men move back. As they are about to lunge, John steps between them.*) Get from between us, Da.

EVANS. (*Putting down his pick.*) Don't worry, John, your son is not worth the killin'.

JAMIE. Don't come to the patch, Evans . . . stay away from the shebeen.

EVANS. (*Picking up his board.*) I'll drink where I please and whore where I please. And even in a certain widow's bedroom if I please. (*Reading list—as Jamie jumps for him and the miners restrain him.*) McGinty, Dyer, Kerrigan, Shayne, O'Malley, Mack, Reilly, Manley, McClain . . .

(*The men peel off into the mine as their names are called.*)

JOHN. (*To Jamie.*) Go home.

EVANS. O'Hanlin.

JOHN. Drunk before sunup. You shame me.

EVANS. O'Hanlin!

JAMIE. (*As John starts into the mine.*) See if you can save another mule for us today, Da.

(*Another* LONG WHISTLE BLAST *sounds and the lights shift to the area of the stage that is Griffith's office. Griffith is seated at his desk. He is a tall man in his early forties, an empire builder. Mangan, his secretary, is reading him the monthly report.*)

MANGAN. Pottsville Collery: three mules killed—$75.00. Two men permanently injured. Three men killed. Berwick Colliery: cage repair—$250.00. Six mules killed—$150.00.

GRIFFITH. The Ides of March.

MANGAN. Yes, sir?

GRIFFITH. Just an allusion to March, Mangan, since it seems to be always our worst month. . . . Continue.

MANGAN. Tamaqua Colliery: breaker cable repair—$100.00. Three men injured, none seriously. Two mules shot—$50.00. Three cars of coal burned and entire shipment destroyed—$1,700.00.

GRIFFITH. Tamaqua! Is Evans here yet?

MANGAN. Yes. Mr. Griffith, from what I can gather, your most serious problem at Tamaqua is Evans. He's brutal, unfair, and to a man the men despise him.

GRIFFITH. Bring him in.

(*Mangan exits and returns with Evans.*)

EVANS. Good mornin', Mr. Griffith.

GRIFFITH. Evans, I'm disturbed at the frequency of incidents occurring in Tamaqua. What's the problem there?

EVANS. There's no problem that can't be solved by applyin' some discipline to certain people.

GRIFFITH. Come to the point, man. That tells me nothing.

EVANS. One drunken troublemaker, by the name of O'Hanlin. In my opinion, one good clout on the head would shut him up.

GRIFFITH. Evans, I don't beat my men, is that clear? Violence generally produces an unfavorable reciprocity. . . . That is to say, Evans, a club creates an opposing club.

EVANS. This O'Hanlin is the brother-in-law of Paul Shayne, the unionist, the guy who led the last strike, do ya know that?

GRIFFITH. Is he? Don't touch O'Hanlin until you can prove he committed a crime. And then come to me and I'll handle it. That will be all. . . . By the way, Evans, I will not allow petty ethnic passions to interfere with the operation of my company.

EVANS. Yes, sir. (*He exits.*)

GRIFFITH. That's all we need now: more Irish problems! Burning coal cars, killing mules! (*Pause.*) Have they begun work on the school?

MANGAN. The community voted to build a church on the land instead, sir.

GRIFFITH. A church! A church! God damn it . . . a church!

MANGAN. I learned of the vote only this morning.

GRIFFITH. What in the hell is the matter with those people! I gave them free land, begged, borrowed, and damn near stole the materials to build a school. Not a church!

MANGAN. The vote was unanimous. Under the circumstances . . .

GRIFFITH. Ignorance is unanimous. Superstition is unanimous. It's only through education they'll learn . . . Not unions. Not violence. They need political representation, not religion!

MANGAN. Our only representation is a police sergeant in Pottsville.

GRIFFITH. Exactly. How in Christ's name can your people utilize the vote when they can't read the ballot? Achievement is a struggle, and prayer hasn't advanced the world one God-damn inch.

MANGAN. It takes time to let go of the past. Some things were best left behind in Ireland. . . .

GRIFFITH. Anarchy solves nothing, as exampled by this Civil War. (*Pause.*) You're not shooting mules, burning coal cars, and you're Irish, you're one of these people. Yet we work well together. There is a mutual respect, I might even say friendship. Why aren't there more like you, and less O'Hanlins?

MANGAN. I have less illusions than Mr. O'Hanlin.

GRIFFITH. (*Pause.*) Yes. I'm sure you do. I'm told you have political ambitions.

MANGAN. I understand that's the current rumor being passed about.

GRIFFITH. A splendid evasion! You'll make a superb politician. The Irish could use another O'Connell.

MANGAN. The feeling among the people is we may need a Washington.

GRIFFITH. Merely a soldier, an amateur politician, and now, I'm afraid, a legend. O'Connell, on the other hand, was a brilliant statesman. Something he said I think rather profound: "Equality and freedom are gained by a belief in justice: the well-phrased grievance is more powerful than the cannon." A very timely sentiment.

MANGAN. An excellent sentiment. It's unfortunate that he ended up a defeated man. (*He exits.*)

GRIFFITH. (*Calling after him.*) Telegraph Harrisburg and request a recruiting squad be sent to Tamaqua. Let's get some of these angry Irishmen into the military.

(*Two LONG WHISTLE BLASTS signal the lunch break for the miners; the lights shift to the full stage which is the exterior of the mine again.*)

PAT: Spring is in the wind, I can smell it!

MIKE: Aye, the blackbirds is wheelin' about in the sky, lovely like . . . Look, O'Brian can't put a roof on a church. Hey, O'Brian, put the slate the other way.

PAT: You're an agent o' the devil.

MIKE: Shame on you for making such a filthy gesture from the roof of a church!

MCGINTY. (*Biting into an apple.*) Christ!

MIKE. He's sick again.

PAT. Your face is all outa shape.

MCGINTY. Me tooth is rotted.

MIKE. Let Pat give it a yank, McGinty.

MCGINTY. If he puts his hands in me mouth, I'll die of the plague.

PAT. If I don't, we'll be carryin' ya out of the church.

MIKE. What church? We only got a roof.

PAT. It'll be finished in time for McGinty's funeral.

(*Reilly enters limping.*)

MIKE. Oh God, here's another one.

DYER. What did Father Hanley say?

REILLY. He said he'd talk to Griffith.

MCGINTY. I hope he has a sober tongue in his head when he does.

REILLY. Show respect, McGinty.

MIKE. No wonder your teeth are rotted.

MCGINTY. He's a whiskey priest an' ya all know it!

PAT. Ya shouldn't have kicked the mule while Evans was lookin'.

REILLY. It was standin' on me foot.

MIKE. Ya could have shoved it off, not break its leg.

REILLY. Evans has fired his last Irishman, I'm tellin' you . . . the Welch bastard!

DYER. And your woman is carryin' ya fifth born, isn't she?

REILLY. Aye . . . aye.

(*Suddenly the loud* BOOM *and shrill* BLAST *of a* TRUMPET *and* DRUM *are heard and down the street comes the recruiting officer with a trumpet, flanked by a thin, tubercular soldier, beating a drum. They set themselves on the stage. The noise of the drum and bugle wake up Jamie who has been sleeping in a corner of the stage.*)

PAT. Jesus, he musta lost the rest o' his parade.

RECRUITING OFFICER. "I regret that I have only one life to give to my country."

MIKE. That's nice.

RECRUITING OFFICER. Can any of you tell me who uttered those undying words, my fellow patriots?

MIKE. Brian Boru?

RECRUITING OFFICER. Wrong, my fellow patriot.

PAT. Robert Emmett?

DYER. Wolfe Tone, maybe?

RECRUITING OFFICER. An American patriot and soldier spoke those imperishable words moments before his death. (*Pause.*) He was hung by the English!

PAT. Oh, Jesus, it could be almost anybody then.

RECRUITING OFFICER. Nathan Hale! . . . Nathan Hale!

PAT. Another Jew, Reilly.

RECRUITING OFFICER. Remember that name, cherish that name, love that name. With noose around his neck, Nathan Hale defied the bloody, butchering English by giving to the world that immortal sentence of supreme patriotism. (*DRUM ROLL.*) Do you have a life to spare for your country? In this tragic hour will you give your life to your country?

JAMIE (*Imitation.*) In this time of darkest need, in the season of despair, will you give us your life?

RECRUITING OFFICER. The voice of a true patriot! The republic is in danger of annihilation, the devil hordes from the South threaten the freedom of every man, the black man lies broken on the wheel of slavery . . .

JAMIE. Along with the Irish miner.

RECRUITING OFFICER. If the South wins this war, we'll all die boiled alive in a cotton patch.

JAMIE. If the North wins this war, we'll all die boiled alive in a mine pit.

RECRUITING OFFICER. You're the type we like to draft! And don't forget it's the English who are feeding the South munitions and money. Is there a patriot among you that will unshackle the black man from his iron chain of bondage?

JAMIE. So we can bring the black bugger North to work the mines as cheap as he worked the cotton.

RECRUITING OFFICER. Is there a patriot among you who will stop the Southern aristocracy from pillagin' our great country?

JAMIE. Because the Northern aristocracy's against sharin' the spoils of their pillagin'.

RECRUITING OFFICER. Is there a patriot . . .

JAMIE. No! There's only us mules here.

RECRUITING OFFICER. Is there a patriot . . .

JAMIE. Be off, you silly bastard, before I stuff your trumpet. Go fight your own wars.

RECRUITING OFFICER. $300. Each volunteer will receive upon signing this paper, $300. A gift from his country, a reward for his devotion. You're eligible for your bonus the minute you are accepted.

PAT. Jesus, there's a fortune to be made in killing, Mike.

REILLY. How do you get accepted?

RECRUITING OFFICER. If you are free from tuberculosis, cancer, imbecility, insanity . . .

PAT. You'll never make it, Mike.

RECRUITING OFFICER. Epilepsy, rheumatism, deafness, paralysis, syphilis . . .

MIKE. You're done too, Pat.

RECRUITING OFFICER. Loss of nose, loss of tongue, loss of great toe, loss of sight of right eye, loss of right thumb, loss of testicles . . .

JAMIE. Right or left?

RECRUITING OFFICER. Club foot, rickets, and artificial anus.

MIKE. What's that?

JAMIE. A paper ass!

MIKE. Glory be to God, are they makin' them now? What's next?

RECRUITING OFFICER. Is there a patriot ready to step forth?

REILLY. I got all them things. I'll sign the paper. Do ya have the money with ya now?

RECRUITING OFFICER. You get your money within a month.

REILLY. (*Grabbing his crotch.*) I got your month.

(*The* MEN *laugh and at that moment the* IDIOT *enters.*)

JAMIE. Here, he's got a tongue, eyes, some teeth, a big toe and his original and natural arse.

RECRUITING OFFICER. There's something wrong with him. I can see that!

JAMIE. He's an idiot is all.

[...]

MIKE. (*Stopping the recruiting officer as he starts to exit.*) You could have got us cheap.

PAT. One hundred and fifty dollars.

MIKE. That's for the both of us.

(*A* SINGLE WHISTLE BLAST *signals the return to work. They exit; and the lights shift to Griffith's office. Father Hanley sits waiting for Griffith; he is a young, practical, good man, bewildered by problems that seem beyond solution.*)

GRIFFITH. (*Entering.*) Now, Father, what's this about Reilly?

FATHER HANLEY. His wife is expectin' their fifth child.

GRIFFITH. Tell Reilly if he agrees to work off the cost of the mule, I'll see he's back to work tomorrow.

FATHER HANLEY. I'll talk to him.

GRIFFITH. By the way, Father, I'm more than disappointed at the decision of your people to build a church rather than a school.

FATHER HANLEY. To a man the vote was for the church. They've started the work already.

GRIFFITH. I think it was necessary to lead them into making the proper choice. However, I will respect their decision and not interfere.

FATHER HANLEY. I don't like to come here always with a list of grievances, Mr. Griffith. . . .

GRIFFITH. Don't apologize, Father. I'm always ready to listen.

FATHER HANLEY. The men are claimin' that the pillars in the mine are weak and with the spring thaws comin', cave-ins are a daily danger.

GRIFFITH. They've passed two inspections.

FATHER HANLEY. The men say the inspector is on the company payroll.

GRIFFITH. I can assure you, Father, that is not true.

FATHER HANLEY. Aye. Another thing is that half of them are three months in debt to the company store because o' the last strike.

GRIFFITH. You must remember, you're in an enclave here, surrounded by mostly Welch and English. Overcharge and no credit would be the treatment you'd receive elsewhere.

FATHER HANLEY. Aye, that's true, the poverty is like a plague. Some o' them are forced to perform minor operations on themselves.

GRIFFITH. I've tried, but with the war I simply can't keep enough doctors in the valley.

FATHER HANLEY. I tell ya what really frightens me, Mr. Griffith. In the old country we had a wicked bunch o' murderers, the Molly Maguires. They respected neither God nor man. I pray the spirit of the Mollys never visits us here.

GRIFFITH. That would be unfortunate, Father. When one is slowly gaining headway in a new country, as your people undoubtedly are, an upsurge of violence could seriously alarm certain people.

FATHER HANLEY. Your silence, Mr. Griffith, concernin' the union has left them in an ugly mood.

GRIFFITH. I can no more give public approval to unionism than you can to Anglicanism. As far as I'm concerned, Father, unionism is the first step toward socialism.

FATHER HANLEY. But they had not a chance when you arranged to transfer the extra work load up North during the strike.

GRIFFITH. Let me make this clear, Father, my first loyalty is to my country. A Frenchman by the name of de Tocqueville remarked way back at the beginning of this century that in a hundred years the United States would be one of the two ruling powers in the world. That prophecy is now threatened by this Civil War. The North must win or we will find ourselves living in a divided minor republic. . . .

MANGAN (*Entering with a newspaper which he gives to Griffith and then exits.*) General Grant is preparing to move into Tennessee.

GRIFFITH. Coal will be as valuable as men.

FATHER HANLEY. The times are more to blame than anything, I suppose.

GRIFFITH. The reality of turning a nation into an empire requires immense sacrifice. Why, your church knows this, Father. The world is its domain to conquer for Christ, is it not?

FATHER HANLEY. Conquer is a bit strong a word.

GRIFFITH. Inquisitions, Crusades, Papal armies? They give ample evidence that the sword is as necessary to your church as its sacraments.

FATHER HANLEY. My church has been faced with evil in many disguises.

GRIFFITH. And so has my country. I wonder if your Pope would approve of a union of priests? Well, Father, I hope you'll come again. I'm convinced that it's only through conversations like this that we can even begin to comprehend our mutual problems.

FATHER HANLEY. Yes . . . the buildin' o' the church will be a healthy occupation for their minds.

GRIFFITH. Father, never mind the cost of the mule. Tell Reilly he can go back to work tomorrow.

FATHER HANLEY. Thank you, Mr. Griffith.

(*The lights shift to the O'HANLIN home; evening. There is a table with three stools. JOHN sits at one stool working on the model boat. MARY SHAYNE, daughter of JOHN, is setting the table. She is a quiet, pretty girl.*)

[. . .]

PAUL. (*Entering.*) Enough wood out there to keep the whole valley in flame.

MARY. Better not let Jamie hear ya talkin' like that.

PAUL. True for ya. . . . Potatoes, cabbage, a nice change o' diet. (*John enters.*) John, I'm telling ya, when Griffith meets our demands, we'll have beef roasted and swimmin' in gravy.

JOHN. Aye.

PAUL. What did he say?

MARY. He says he agrees with ya. (*They sit.*)

PAUL. Rafferty, the poet, was not half as eloquent. (*They bless themselves and start to eat.*) Did ya tell your da the news?

MARY. Aye.

JOHN. Aye.

PAUL. Aye. . . . John, you'd talk the milk from a cow.

JOHN. Ya want to be sure she's not handled by the greasy fingers o' them midwives.

PAUL. I'll see it's done proper.

JOHN. Where's the other one?

PAUL. Holdin' court in the shebeen.

JOHN. Aye.

MARY. He can make an empty pocket talk, that Jamie can.

PAUL. If he let go of his anger, there's not a man who would turn a back to him.

JOHN. He's got the mark o' the rope on his neck, an' if he don't stop . . .

MARY. May Christ in his mercy forgive ya, John O'Hanlin, for sayin' such a terrible thing.

PAUL. Mary! He'll right himself, John.

JOHN. I've seen them all in the old country, killin' in the name o' freedom, but killin' just the same.

(*Jamie enters; he is not too drunk.*)

PAUL. Aye, the torchbearer! Come an' sit with us.

JAMIE. Privileged I am to be breakin' bread with the holy family. (*Moves to Mary, and regards her stomach.*) Who did it to ya, ya poor dear?

MARY. Oh, Jamie! He promised me the moon.

JAMIE. Where is the dirty thing?

MARY. (*Pointing to Paul.*) That one, there.

JAMIE. Oh, no. Not him! Not this half lad! Was she asleep or not lookin'?

PAUL. She wasn't lookin'.

JAMIE. (*Taking shawl from under his coat.*) Luck to the three o' ya. Here's something for me nephew, Jamie. (*He gets a fourth stool.*)

MARY. It's beautiful, Jamie! Where did ya get it? (*She sets a fourth bowl on the table.*)

JAMIE. A clothesline. God's green weeds gracin' our table again, I see.

PAUL. And how's the incendiary today?

JAMIE. Flamin'.

PAUL. Very good.

JAMIE. So your meetin' is comin' tomorrow night?

PAUL. Will ye be there with a clear head?

JAMIE. With pity in me heart too.

PAUL. The North is sendin' their top man, Mr. Flannelly, down here to see me.

JAMIE. Words will get ya more words, promises, more promises. . . .

JOHN. Smashin' heads an' reapin' lives will only get ya more o' the same, too.

JAMIE. This country we're crawlin' around in didn't get its freedom by appealin' to the right reason of good King George, did it?

PAUL. We're not at war now, Jamie,

JAMIE. Ya see the hearse at the door as regular as the milk wagon. Is that peace?

PAUL. "Time and preparation will bring progress."

JAMIE. Those words is as stale as this bread. If there's a spike driven into me side am I to wait for time to root it out?

PAUL. Well, how about this one, now: "You'll have to face the chill when makin' the coat"?

JAMIE. Christ, I'm eatin'. Can those words feed the baby growin' in her?

JOHN. Hear the man out. He'll save your thick neck from wearin' a rope.

JAMIE. Never did the shadow o' the rope touch your neck, did it now?

JOHN. Leave us, Mary.

MARY. I'm with me husband.

JOHN. You sport with a man who has peace an' order for our problem. You that are nothing but a drunken disgrace, foolishly and dangerously proclaimin' a doctrine that offends the souls o' civilized men.

JAMIE. An' what have you done since you an' a thousand like ya left your country with a great whine, left her to be chewed like an old bone by that English bitch?

JOHN. The whip o' the famine, not the English, drove us out.

JAMIE. Ya blame everybody from God to the potato, don't ya? Your famine was in here. An' that's the heritage, that's the legacy you're trying to give to me.

JOHN. (*Pause. Very quietly.*) In the old country one night I went with some of your kind, the Whiteboys we called ourselves, an' we was just goin' to chastise a lan'lord, they said. We dragged the poor tremblin' man from his bed an' in the eyes o' his wife and babes, someone took up a shears . . . the tongue was taken from his mouth so quickly that it lay quiverin' in the grass. Then they slit the back o' his ankles. What I saw was no longer a man but a blood-splashed thing that scuttled across the ground, bayin' like some hurt animal. I'll never forget the look on his woman's face, never. It is the greatest sin o' me life that I was among the men that desecrated the sacredness of a human body belongin' to God.

JAMIE. Did ya think o' the bodies bein' desecrated in the mine cave, when ya took only the mule to the surface? Losin' an arm to save a mule. Christ!

JOHN. It was the only thing near me that was alive.

PAUL. Jamie, that's enough.

JAMIE. It's also company policy to take the mule out first, isn't it?

JOHN. It was the only thing that I could save.

JAMIE. You could have let it be, saved ya decency as a man.

JOHN. We're not made to disrespect life.

JAMIE. How much respect had ya for me mother's life when the hope o' this land turned into another kind o' whip and lashed her into an early grave? Where was your respect for her that died with but a bitter taste for life in her mouth? You left more than your arm in that mine.

(*They face each other. John turns and exits.*)

MARY. There's a way o' sayin' things an' not a way o' sayin' things.

JAMIE. I'll tell ya, Paul, there are some o' us that can't stop hearin' the clock tickin' away the minutes o' their lives. I'll keep whistlin' till they hear me. (*He exits.*)

MARY. It's a harsh land that turns a son against his father.

PAUL. I wish I could make Jamie understand that maybe our lives are only a step to a better life, and maybe that's our only meanin'. I used to think the greatest crime was so many of them died before completin' themselves. I used to think the crime was against the dead, but it's not. The pity belongs to the livin', those that are maimed and driven half mad by the truth that perhaps something great, something good is dyin' within them every day.

MARY. You're a good man, Paul Shayne, an' I love you.

PAUL. (*As they clear the table and exit.*) Don't be too hard on Jamie. He's afraid when the famine comes to him he'll not face it with courage.

[. . .]

(*The* LIGHTS SHIFT *to Griffith's office, where Griffith is signing papers.*)

GRIFFITH. You know, Mangan, this country will create someday a man who will feel free and independent. He will not be subject to any authority or principle of conscience, yet he'll be willing to be commanded, to do what is expected, to fit into the machine without friction. This quiet, dependable man will form the spine of a country that will some day lead the world.

MANGAN. By the way, Paul Shayne's meeting with the Northern delegation is set for tomorrow night.

GRIFFITH. Who's coming down from the North?

MANGAN. A Mr. Flannelly.

GRIFFITH. Flannelly. (*Laughing.*) Shayne is in for the surprise of his life.

MANGAN. You know Flannelly?

GRIFFITH. I know of him. You know, I would like to meet with Shayne myself. Sounds like too valuable a man to waste his energy dealing with fanatics.

[. . .]

(*The* LIGHTS FADE out. THREE LONG WHISTLE BLASTS *signal the end of the work shift. The* LIGHTS *come up on the shebeen. All the men wait with rising excitement for the arrival of the Northern delegation. The idiot signals to Mike from the doorway.*)

MIKE. I think they're here.

PAUL. Thank you, Mike. (*A large florid-looking man, impassive and aloof, comes in the shebeen. With him is a thin young man.*) Mr. Flannelly? I'm Paul Shayne and this is . . .

MR. FLANNELLY. Cad na thaobh go bhfuil an sagart annso?

PAUL. Why is he speakin' the Irish?

MAN. Mr. Flannelly asks why is the priest here?

PAUL. None o' us speak the Irish here.

MAN. Mr. Flannelly understands English.

PAUL. The priest is here because he's interested in our cause.

MR. FLANNELLY. Ni bheidh cruinniu ar bith an fhead is go bhfuil sagart i lathair.

MAN. They'll be no meetin' with a priest present.

PAUL. This is not the time to let the quarrels o' the old country prevent us from drawin' together.

MR. FLANNELLY. Nil ga leis an sagart.

MAN. The priest is not needed.

FATHER HANLEY. Never mind, Paul. I'll wait out back. (*He exits.*)

PAUL. Well, now, me words are few. Will you an' the rest o' the North join us in a great strike for human dignity?

MR. FLANNELLY. An mbeidh tusa agus an dream o'n deisceart i n-einfheacht linn san iarracht mhor ar son saoirse an chine danoa?

MAN. Will you an' the Southern bunch be with us in strikin' a great blow for human freedom?

PAUL. Aye, aye, we're with ya to a man,

MR. FLANNELLY. Annsan aontofar an deisceart agus an tuaisceart.

MAN. Then South an' North can become one.

(*Men cheer and congratulate each other.*)

MR. FLANNELLY. An fiu leat Eire Aontaithe?

MAN. Do ya believe in a united Ireland?

PAUL. Aye, I do.

MR. FLANNELLY. Ach an bhfuil tu cinnte, deimhnithe go gcaithfidh Eire bheith saor o daon-smacht Shasana?

MAN. And are you convinced that Ireland must be freed from England's rulin' hand?

PAUL. Aye, but right now I'm worried about the shackles on me own feet. . . . Tell him to speak English if he can.

MAN. Mr. Flannelly has vowed never to utter the sound o' the English language until Ireland is free an' united.

JAMIE. We'll all be speakin' Hindu by the time that comes about.

PAUL. Shut up, Jamie. Listen, we cannot have our feet in the new country, an' our heads in the old.

MR. FLANNELLY. Nilmid dilis d'aon tir ach Eire.

MAN. We have no other country but Ireland,

JAMIE. Sure, we're only here to colonize the United States.

PAUL. Jamie! The old country aside, will ya follow us in strikin' the whole valley?

MR. FLANNELLY. Deanfaimid.

MAN. We will.

(*Men cheer and ad lib their victory.*)

MR. FLANNELLY. Ma thogfaidh tu mionn dilseachta do Bhraithreachas Poblachta-cha na h-Eireann.

MAN. If you'll promise an allegiance to the Irish Republican Brotherhood.

PAUL. I cannot speak for hundreds of men until I know what your organization is about.

MCGINTY. I ain't payin' any dues.

MR. FLANNELLY. Taimid ag ullmhu, arm d'Eireannai tir-ghrach a shluaghadh le dul lsteach ar thalamh bhean-naithe na h-Eireann d'fhonn na Sasanaigh a ruaig-headh aisti.

MAN. We are preparin' to build an army of loyal Irish patriots who, after this war, will invade Ireland and drive the English from her sacred soil.

PAUL. You want me to enlist men in some kind o' liberation army?

MR. FLANNELLY. Sea.

MAN. Yes.

REILLY. We just got here an' this lad wants us to turn around an' go back.

PAUL. Don't ya see, man, I can't do that.

MR. FLANNELLY. Bhfuil tu linn no nar gcoinnibh?

MAN. Are you with us or against us?

PAUL. Will ya get it through that thick skull o' yours that I have not the power to sign men's lives over to some wild dream o' savin' a country that's no longer mine.

MR. FLANNELLY. Ni mor do Ghael aon iobairt ar son a thire.

MAN. There is no sacrifice too great for a true son of Ireland.

REILLY. Bullshit!

PAUL. You're crazed in the head, do ya know that?

MR. FLANNELLY. Raghfaidh an tuaisceart leis fein mar sin.

MAN. The North will go its own way then.

(Father Hanley enters.)

PAUL. It can go to flamin' hell. Is this a trick to hide the fact that you want us to strike alone, so you can make a grand profit by takin' the extra work load?

FATHER HANLEY. Easy, Paul, there must be others in the North with sense.

PAUL. No, this half lad is a little king up there.

MR. FLANNELLY. Sibh-se thios annsin, nil ionnaibh ach bastardai Eireann.

MAN. (Nervously.) You down here are nothin' but Ireland's bastards. (Both exit.)

PAT. Ya dirty soup-drinkers!

PAUL. Me old father said the worst enemy of an Irishman is another Irishman. Da was a prophet.

FATHER HANLEY. Paul . . .

PAUL. The time to strike is now. The war will not last forever. The Polocks will be here, the blacks maybe, at war's end men will beg for work.

MIKE. It's not so bad. You're a foreman now, Paul.

PAUL. Aye, but it's not all to me likin'.

REILLY. Take it, man, it'll keep an Evans out o' there.

PAUL. Aye, it's a bit a power anyway.

PAT. We'll miss ya on the first shift, but you're a fool not to take it.

(Men start to leave, Jamie takes Paul aside.)

JAMIE. It's a damn bitter shame, Paul, but it must be clear to ya now that there's only one way for us to be heard.

PAUL. What would ya do after ya turned the valley into ashes?

JAMIE. I'd burn the ashes. I'd burn and burn till there was nothin' left for them bastards to hide behind.

PAUL. Damned difficult from a jail cell.

JAMIE. Maybe next year you'll be made a mine superintendent.

PAUL. I'll not follow Griffith down that road.

JAMIE. He's already given ya a shove in that direction.

PAUL. Can't ya understand that if ya sow destruction, you'll end up havin' to reap it too.

JAMIE. You even sound like him now.

PAUL. I'm late for work. Are ya walkin'?

JAMIE. No.

PAUL. I'll see ya in the mornin'.

(*Both exit in opposite directions. The* LIGHTS *go to complete blackness. It is the interior of the mine, only the forms and voices of men are distinguishable in the weak light from candles on their hats. The men's quiet chanting of "Biff Martin" is all we hear for a few moments.*)

MAN ONE. Where's Paul Shayne?

PAUL. Over here, man.

MAN ONE. Let's have a piss break.

PAUL. We just had a break!

MAN TWO. Jumpin' Jesus!

PAUL. What, man?

MAN TWO. A rat.

MAN THREE. I need a hand with this slice, Paul Shayne.

PAUL. O'Brian, give Joe a hand.

MAN ONE. I'm pissing.

PAUL. How many bladders do ya have, O'Brian?

MAN ONE. Five! (*Men laugh.*)

MAN TWO. Hey, Shayne, we got a game of rugby against Shenandoah, Saturday.

PAUL. I'll be there. (*Sound of* CREAKING *is heard.*)

MAN FOUR. What's that?

MAN TWO. What?

PAUL. Shut up. (*Pause.*) Do ya feel a sway?

MAN FOUR. I feel it.

MAN ONE. Shayne, there's a shiftin' above me. (*Sound of* TWO LOUD SNAPPINGS *are heard.*)

MAN THREE. Jesus Christ, the pillars is all splittin'!

PAUL. Shut up! Move easily toward the cage . . . no panic.

MAN ONE. Get outa me way.

MAN TWO. Don't grab me! (*Sound of* THREE LOUD SNAPPINGS.)

MAN THREE. Christ help us.

PAUL. CHRIST have mercy!

(CRASH, *then total silence. A* BELL *starts* TOLLING *and the* LIGHTS *come up in silhouette on the stage; men rush in and mill around.*)

PAT. Moran got killed!

MCGINTY. Joe and Dougherty's down there!

DYER. O'Brian got it!

REILLY. Paul Shayne is dead!

JAMIE. (*Enters and pushes and shoves his way among the men during the following lines.*) This country is butcherin' us, butcherin' us on the block of her ambition.

REILLY. Burn the town!

JAMIE. There be no love in silence an' no grief but in revenge!

DYER. Fire the shaft!

REILLY. Burn the town!

JAMIE. If we are to die, let us not die dumbly in a dark pit o' the earth!

MEN. Burn the town! . . . The company store. . . . Fire the shaft!

EVANS. (*Enters with a pick.*) You men go home! Clear the area! Go home! Move! Move! Move!

JAMIE. Let the torch be the voice of our grief. Let it sing a song of deliverance!

EVANS. O'Hanlin, go home!

(*Jamie jumps for Evans. They lock in a struggle with the pick between them. Jamie slowly forces Evans to the ground.*)

DYER. (*Quietly.*) Kill him.

MCGINTY. Kill him.

JAMIE. (*With Evans on the ground, raises the pick in the air.*) You've been feeding us to the earth like stalks to pigs. (*He heaves the pick down into Evans.*)

REILLY. Burn the town!

(*Men exit; stage to black almost immediately.*)

August Wilson
1945–2005

Internationally acclaimed playwright August Wilson was born Frederick August Kittel on "The Hill" in Pittsburgh, Pennsylvania. Son of a German baker and an African American domestic worker, Wilson learned to read at the age of four. After his mother's divorce and remarriage, his stepfather moved the family to a mostly white suburb where they were subjected to hate crimes. Wilson dropped out of school in tenth grade after being falsely accused of plagiarism, choosing instead to spend each day educating himself in Pittsburgh's Carnegie-funded public libraries. Unable to find work, he joined the army in 1963 and successfully sought a discharge one year later.

Wilson turned to playwriting in the early 1970s. *Black Bart and the Sacred Hills* (1977) is considered his debut. He won a Jerome Fellowship for *Jitney* (1979), the first of his American Century Cycle of ten plays designed to capture the African American experience in each decade of the twentieth century. *Ma Rainey's Black Bottom* (1982), a fictional work about the real singer "Ma" Rainey, opened on Broadway in 1984. His first Pulitzer Prize came in 1987 for *Fences* (1985). Wilson won his second Pulitzer for *The Piano Lesson* (1986). The tenth and final play of his cycle was completed just before his death in 2005, the same year that New York's August Wilson Theatre became the first Broadway theater named for an African American.

Wilson's plays address the injustices experienced by African Americans. Known for their poetic, politically charged vernacular, the plays favor humor, surrealism, and empathy over pat polemics. In the poignant one-act play presented below, *The Janitor* (1985), Wilson's protagonist Sam laments the loss of his youth while recognizing his own role in the tragedy.

The Janitor

Characters

Sam
Mr. Collins

Setting

A Hotel Ballroom

(*Sam enters pushing a broom near the lectern. He stops and reads the sign hanging across the ballroom.*)

SAM: National . . . Conference . . . on . . . Youth.

(*He nods his approval and continues sweeping. He gets an idea, stops, and approaches the lectern. He clears his throat and begins to speak. His speech is delivered with the literacy of a janitor. He chooses his ideas carefully. He is a man who has approached life honestly, with both eyes open.)*

SAM: I want to thank you all for inviting me here to speak about youth. See . . . I's fifty-six years old and I knows something about youth. The first thing I knows . . . is that youth is sweet before flight . . . its odor is rife with speculation and its resilience . . . that's its bounce back . . . is remarkable. But it's that sweetness that we victims of. All of us. Its sweetness . . . and its flight. One of them fellows in that Shakespeare stuff said, "I am not what I am." See. He wasn't like Popeye. This fellow had a different understanding. "I am not what I am." Well, neither are you. You are just what you have been . . . whatever you are now. But what you are now ain't what you gonna become . . . even though it is with you now . . . it's inside you now this instant. Time . . . see, this how you get to this . . . Time ain't changed. It's just moved. Or maybe it ain't moved . . . maybe it just changed. It don't matter. We are all victims of the sweetness of youth and the time of its flight. See . . . just like you I forgot who I am. I forgot what happened first. But I know the river I step into now . . . is not the same river I stepped into twenty years ago. See. I know that much. But I have forgotten the name of the river . . . I have forgotten the names of the gods . . . and like everybody else I have tried to fool them with my dancing . . . and guess at their faces. It's the same with everybody. We don't have to mention no names. Ain't nobody innocent. We are all victims of ourselves. We have all had our hand in the soup . . . and made the music play just so. See, now . . . this what I call wrestling with Jacob's angel. You lay down at night and that angel come to wrestle with you. When you wrestling with that angel you bargaining for you future. See. And what you need to bargain with is that sweetness of youth. So . . . to the youth of the United States I says . . . don't spend that sweetness too fast! 'Cause you gonna need it. See. I's fifty-six years old and I done found that out. But it's all the same. It all comes back on you . . . just like reaping and sowing. Down and out ain't nothing but being caught up in the balance of what you put down. If you down and out and things ain't going right for you . . . you can bet you done put a down payment on your troubles. Now you got to pay up on the balance. That's as true as I'm standing here. Sometimes you can't see it like that. The last note on Gabriel's horn always gets lost when you get to realizing you done heard the first. See, it's just like . . .

MR. COLLINS: (*Entering*) Come on, Sam . . . let's quit wasting time and get this floor swept. There's going to be a big important meeting here this afternoon.

SAM: Yessuh, Mr. Collins. Yessuh.

*(Sam goes back to sweeping as the lights go down to——*BLACK*)*

Junebug Productions and Roadside Theater

Junebug/Jack is a joint theatrical production of Junebug Productions of New Orleans and the Roadside Theater of Whitesburg, Kentucky, professional, community-based theaters whose mission is to speak for the historically marginalized and exploited communities in which they are located.

Junebug Productions was founded in 1963 under the name Southern Free Theater as part of the cultural wing of the Student Nonviolent Coordinating Committee (SNCC), the influential civil rights organization. Roadside Theater was founded in 1975 as a component of Appalshop, a media production company in the Kentucky coalfields that was begun as a youth job-training program in film and a way for Appalachian people to take control of their own story. Junebug and Roadside began performing in each other's communities in response to an increase in Ku Klux Klan activity in 1981. The companies have also partnered with grassroots theatrical groups such as Teatro Pregones from the Bronx (1993–2018) and, independently, with traditional artists from Native American communities and theater ensembles from the Czech Republic and elsewhere.

The play *Junebug/Jack* was written by members of the Junebug and Roadside companies. The play explores social, historical, and economic similarities between Appalachian people and African Americans from the Deep South. The central characters of the play are folkloric archetypes. Junebug Jabbo Jones, part ordinary man, part trickster, part divine, was created by SNCC members to represent African American wisdom, enterprise, and history. Jack is a character in a cycle of trickster tales that originated in Europe and was popular in some Appalachian communities.

FROM Junebug/Jack

KENNETH: Hello! I'm Kenneth Raphael. This is John O'Neal and this is Adella Gautier. We're from the Junebug Theater Project which is based in New Orleans, Louisiana.

KIM: This is Nancy Jeffrey Smith, that's Ron Short and I'm Kim Neal. We're a part of the Roadside Theater from the Appalachian Mountains, 'round Kentucky and Virginia.

ADELLA: So what you got here is two groups of hard headed people. Over fifteen years ago out of concern for what was happening in both of our communities, we decided, that whenever we could, we'd get together, share stages and trade audiences. Junebug would play for Roadside audiences in the mountains of Appalachia and Roadside would play for Junebug audiences in the Black Belt South. And we have had some fun. Some more fun than others. Out of these efforts to work together we created tonight's production of *Junebug/Jack*.

RON: What we soon found out was that the people in both our communities have a lot in common, especially music and storytelling. Junebug slash Jack—some people spend a lifetime studying those slashes. Junebug is a mythic African American story-teller invented by young people from SNCC, the Student Non-Violent Coordinating Committee, during the Civil Rights Movement. He represents the collective wisdom of struggling Black people. For mountain people, Jack represents the triumph of the human spirit no matter how hard the times get.

NANCY: And tonight we've all come here together to share some of our songs and stories with you.

ADELLA: See everybody has a story, their own story. (I bet you all got some pretty good stories, too.) But it seems like it has come to the place where people think their stories aren't worth anything anymore.

KENNETH: Trouble is, seems like some people are always wanting to tell our story for us.

KIM: But, we got to tell it ourselves! Otherwise how we gonna know it's us.

JOHN: And if we don't listen to the stories of others how we gonna know who they are?

NANCY: Our ancestors came over to this country on big boats with big sheets on 'em looking for freedom.

KENNETH: Our ancestors came over to this country in the belly of big boats.

NANCY: They got here and lots of them got kindly wild . . .

[. . .]

John Henry hammered on the mountain,
His hammer was ringing fire,
He hammered so hard he broke his poor heart,
He lay down his hammer and he died, *Lord, Lord,*
Lay down his hammer and he died.

Early Monday morning,
When the blue bird begins to sing,
Way up on the mountain top,
You can hear John Henry's hammer ring, *Lord, Lord,*
You can hear John Henry's hammer ring.

You can hear John Henry's hammer ring, *Lord, Lord,*
You can hear John Henry's hammer ring.

ADELLA: John Henry was a Black man. 'Course some people say that John Henry was not a real person at all.

KENNETH: They'll tell you he's just a story—a legend.

ADELLA: There's nothing wrong with telling stories and legends.

KENNETH: 'Course now it depends on who's telling the story and why.

ADELLA: Now here's a fella who hails from South Mississippi and goes by the title of

KENNETH and ADELLA: Junebug Jabbo Jones!

JUNEBUG: I am a storyteller. I say "storyteller" 'stead of liar 'cause there's a heap of difference between a storyteller and a liar. A liar, that's somebody want to cover things over—mainly for his own private benefit. But a STORYTELLER, that's some-body who'll take and UN-cover things so that everybody can get something good out of it. I'm a storyteller, storyteller. Oh, it's a heap of good meanin' to be found in a story if you got the mind to hear. . . . A mind to hear.

I am not the first one to carry the title of "Junebug Jabbo Jones." Neither the onli-est to have that name. The very first Junebug started out life as a Negro slave. From the time that he was big enough to see straight, his Maw took one look at him and said, "Lawd, have mercy, this here's going to be one of them bad boogers!" Booger was so bad as a child he would not take funk from a skunk. Right away his Maw seen it wasn't half a chance for him to make a full grown man 'fore the white folks to kill him.

So when he made seven years old his mother got together with an auntee—who some people say could work root—they took him down to the river and pretended that he got drowned down there.

(HUMMING *from cast begins*) They mourned, had a funeral and everything. Wore black clothes for three weeks! But in actual fact, they snuck around the back way, took him down to the Cypress Swamp, turned him over to Crazy Bill to raise. Now, Bill was so crazy he decided to run off and live in the swamp by hisself rather than to live his life as a slave. That's how crazy Bill was. Bill belonged to what they used to call a "good master."

ADELLA: A good what?

JUNEBUG: A "good master"! Baptist preacher. He taught Bill how to read and everything. He had every intention to make a preacher out of Bill. Bill had to run off one night during a thunderstorm because that Preacher had a fit of rage when Bill showed him where it say in the Bible—"It's a sin 'fore God for a man to own a slave or to be a slave. It's in the Book!"

That preacher got so mad at what Bill showed him in the Bible he went to grab hisself a gun.

Bill took off running in that thunderstorm. That preacher got Bill lined up dead in his sight. About to pop down on him. Bill stopped, seed where that preacher had the drop on him. Stood stark still. Throwed his hands up in the sky, hollered out something loud in African. Well, don't you know, a bolt of lightning come down out of the cloud, hit the barrel of that gun, sealed it up plum shut, knocked that preacher down on his butt and turned every hair on his body from jet black to silver white—right on the spot!

Bill came back over there, looked at that preacher all sniveling up in the mud and the rain, smiled kind of sad like to hisself, and WALKED on down in that swamp. And stayed down there too.

From that night on anytime you'd pass that white haired preacher's house you could see him sitting on the porch with four or five guns beside the one that got sealed shut by that bolt of lightning.

He swore, "I'll kill any man that goes down in my swamp to get Bill before I get ready to go for him." But he ain't never went down there. And he ain't never again stood astride a pulpit nor let his shadow fall across the face of an open Bible.

There's lots of people scared to go down in that swamp. Some said they was haints, but they ain't no haints. It was that first Junebug and crazy Bill. That first Junebug stayed down there with Bill from the time he was seven years old till he became a full grown man. Many nights they sat up all night long reading, studying. Since they didn't have to spend all their time working like all the other slaves had to do they had plenty of time to think. They studied everything that went on around there. They saw everything inside of thirty or forty miles in every direction. They saw that in spite of the terrible conditions most of the colored people were living up under, in most sections it was more of them than there were white folk. If people could have just seen that, there's no telling what could have happened. (Ain't like it is up in here tonight.) Then again there was a whole bunch of white people that might as well to have been slaves for all they could get out of life. They seed that between the colored slaves and the poor white people didn't hardly nothin' get done around there unless they were the one's to do it. They seen where people would make little stories and songs to make their days go faster and make their load seem lighter and they put secret meaning in their stories and songs. But everybody was so busy trying to keep their own heads from getting cracked, that they didn't take the time to stand back and look at the big picture that had everybody in it.

Right there, that first Junebug, and old crazy Bill, seen where there was a job that NEEDED TO BE DONE. It's a job that need to be done. They knowed it was a bunch of people that would have killed them for teaching people how to read or spreading news that they did not want spread. They knowed that. "But they was a job needed to be done. And we got to be the ones do it. We got to do it!"

As soon as that first Junebug got big enough to leave out the swamp on his own, he commenced going from plantation to plantation, living by his wit. He'd listen to what people was saying, watch what they were doing, and then, so people could get a better idea what they could do to help change things, make things better, he would tell these over here what these over here been up to. That way the people that were struggling to make things better would feel support and encouragement. And those who weren't doing all they could, maybe should, would be uncovered, and be made to feel ashamed.

Whenever that first Junebug would find somebody who looked like they might make a pretty good storyteller—he'd help them figure out how they could run away. He'd take them down in the swamp, turn them over to ole crazy Bill. Bill would teach them how to read, make their figures, everything they needed to know to be good storytellers. Before long there were a lot of them going around, watching, listening, and learning and telling stories to whosoever wanted to hear. All of them doing it under the title of . . .

ALL: "Junebug Jabbo Jones"!

KENNETH: Wait, wait, now that's not his real name. It's just a title of a job that need to be did.

JOHN: Yeah, like king.

ADELLA: Or queen.

KENNETH: Yeah! And they all don't have to be Black.

JOHN: And they definitely don't have to be men.

KIM: That's right, Junebug. There's lots of women up in the mountains like to tell stories. Good ones, too. There's one about where I come from. You see, there was this family lived way up on the side of the mountain and they lived like folks lived in that time

NANCY: Which was grubbing out a living

RON: And having younguns to help grub out that living

NANCY: Well, this family sure had a

THE THREE TELLERS: A LOT of younguns.

RON: The first youngun they had they'd named Jack

KIM: A purty good name

NANCY: And after that they just named their young'uns whatever they could

KIM: Well, they got a lot of the names out of the Bible, from Abel to Zebidiah

RON: They went through the Sears Catalogue. Named one Hardware

KENNETH: That's a name to live up to!

NANCY: Then one morning they woke up and Mommy had another little baby with her

RON: Well, for the life of her she couldn't think up a new name for this little youngun

KIM: But they put their heads together and they decided to call him

THE THREE TELLERS: Jack!

NANCY: Reckon by now they'd forgotten that was their first one's name

KIM: And when they figgered out what they'd done it uz too late

RON: So they started callin the oldest boy

NANCY: Big Jack

RON: And they called the youngest boy

KIM: Little Jack

NANCY: Now Little Jack and Big Jack, they really took up with each other

KIM: Little Jack follered Big Jack ever where he went

RON: But then Big Jack went off to work for this rich feller down the road

NANCY: We'll just call him "King"

JOHN: "King Coal"

KIM: "King Cotton"

ALL: always a KING!

KIM: Little Jack wanted to go with Big Jack

NANCY (*as Big Jack*): "No, you got to stay home."

KIM: Now there was plenty brothers and sisters for him to play with but Little Jack missed Big Jack so much

RON: Then, early one morning Little Jack seed Big Jack coming up the mountain

KIM: Little Jack was just about to give him a big bear hug

RON: But they was something bad wrong. Big Jack looked awful. They helped Big Jack back up to the house and put him to bed. But when they took off his shirt they seed

KIM: Three big strops of hide missing out of Big Jack's back!

RON: They doctored him best they could, but he kept on gettin worser. Finally they knowed that Big Jack was gonna have to have some medicine from the doctor if he was going to get well at all

KIM: Course, now they didn't have no money to be goin out buying medicine with, not to buy nothing with

RON: Folks just didn't need money much

THE THREE TELLERS: But doctors sure seemed to!

KIM: Well, one morning Little Jack come down to breakfast with his best little suit of clean clothes on and a little gunny sack with his working overhauls in it

RON (as Mommy): "Just a minute. Just where do you think you're agoin'?"

KIM (as Little Jack): "I'm heading off to work for the KING so to get some money for Big Jack to have some medicine."

RON (as Mommy): "You're too little to be goin off to work."

KIM (as Little Jack): "Well a man has to do what a man has to do, Mommy."

RON: And off he went.

NANCY: It didn't take Jack long to get down to that King's house. Went up and knocked on the door. King come out and Jack says,

KIM (as Little Jack): "Excuse me King, but I was wondering, do you need any work done?"

RON (as King): "Well, you're a mighty scrawny little rooster, but I reckon I can get my money's worth out of you. Pays a dollar a day. You interested?"

KIM: Jack was right in for that

RON (as King): "O, by the way, there's one more little deal . . . Anybody works for me goes by my rules. Whichever one of us makes the other one mad first, gets to throw that one down, take three strips of hide out of his back. See now, if I make you mad, I get three strips of hide out of your back, and I don't have to pay you nothin."

KIM (as Little Jack): "And if I make you mad, King, I get three strips of hide and my wages?"

RON (as King): "Yeah. If you make me mad. I'll tell you what, Jack, I'll throw in a bushel of gold, 'cause you can't make me mad. I'm the King!"

KIM (as Little Jack): "Well, King, we'll see about that."

NANCY: Jack had come a long way and was awful hungry, but he was awful proud too and his Mommy had raised him not to beg, so he says,

KIM (as Little Jack): "Reckon I better wash up before I eat supper."

RON (as King): "Eat! Boy you ain't done nothin to deserve no supper!"

KIM (as Little Jack): "But . . ."

RON (as King): "Why, now, that don't make you mad does it?"

KIM (as Little Jack): "No, I ain't mad. Just hungry."

RON (*as King*): "Oh, good. Now you see that corn crib over there?"

KIM (*as Little Jack*): "That's a corn crib?"

RON (*as King*): "No. That's your hotel for tonight!"

KIM (*as Little Jack*): "Now just a minute, King. I come all the way from Mommy's house, you won't give me nothin' to eat, and now you expect me to sleep THERE?!!"

RON (*as King*): "Um . . . Yeah. It doesn't make you mad, now, does it? You don't mind do ye?"

KIM (*as Little Jack*): "Shucks no. I don't mind."

RON (*as King*): "Oh, good. Now get. You got a hard day's work ahead of you."

NANCY: Next morning Jack went up to the King's house bright and early, but the King met him outside.

KIM (*as Little Jack*): "Uhhh, King. Something smells good! What's for breakfast? I could eat a hog."

RON (*as King*): "Breakfast? You just don't get it do you, boy? You ain't done nothin' to earn no breakfast."

KIM (*as Little Jack*): "Look here, King, I'm getting awful hungry!"

RON (*as King*): "Why, Jack, you ain't gettin mad are you?"

KIM (*as Little Jack*): No, I ain't mad! It's just low blood sugar."

NANCY: The King took Jack out to the barn. Showed him his fine flock of sheep and says,

RON (*as King*): "Jack, take my sheep up to the high meadow. Don't you lose a one of 'em!"

KIM: So Jack took them sheep way up in a high meadow. But he was so weak that he just layed down underneath a shade tree. Felt like his stomach was playing tag with his backbone. When this purty little lamb went skippin by, saying,

NANCY (*as lamb*): "Ba, Ba, Ba . . ."

KIM: But Jack was so hungry it sounded like that little sheep was saying,

NANCY (*as lamb*): "LUNCH, LUNCH, LUNCH . . ."

KIM: Jack banged him on the head, built him up a fire, and had him a fine lunch of roast mutton.

NANCY: That evening he took the rest of the sheep back to the King's house. There was the King counting the sheep.

RON (*as King*): "996, 997, 998, 999 . . . Jack, where's my little prize lamb with the black ears?" (*to audience member*) "Excuse me, have you seen my lamb?"

KIM (*as Little Jack*): "Well, King, you hadn't given me nothin' to eat and I was mighty hungry, so I eat him."

RON (*as King*): "You eat my lamb? That was my little prize lamb I was raising for breeding."

KIM (*as Little Jack*): "Yeah, King, it was a good lamb all right, tasted mighty good."

RON (*as King*): "You good for nothin' . . . "

KIM (*as Little Jack*): "Why, King, are you mad?"

RON (*as King*): "No. I ain't mad."

NANCY: But that night the King fed Jack a real good supper

KIM: And fed him a good breakfast the next morning, too

NANCY: Took Jack out to the field where he had a fine horse hitched up to a plow

RON (*as King*): "Can you plow? I want you to plow up this patch for me. I aim to put in some turnips."

KIM (*as Little Jack*): "Of course, I can plow." So Jack gettyupped that horse and set out plowing these long, straight furrows

NANCY: The King watched him, got satisfied Jack knew what he was doing, went on back to the house

KIM: About that time this old woman come down the road riding this old rickety horse

NANCY (*as horse/woman*): "Rickety, rackety, humpity, bumpity"

KIM: You could hear its bones clanking together, it was that poor. (*As Little Jack*): "Hey, good morning, Moms. That shore is a mighty fine horse you got there."

NANCY (*as woman*): "Why, Jack you ortn't make fun of a ole woman whose got the best she has!"

KIM (*as Jack*): "Now no, I think that is a fine horse. Why, I bet the King wishes he had one like that. I don't suppose you'd be willin' to swap horses with me?"

NANCY (*as woman*): "Hit's a deal." (*Off she gallops.*)

KIM: Jack hitched that old rickety horse to the harness and set in to plowing that field

KIM & NANCY: Just as crooked as a dog's hind leg

NANCY: When the King come back

RON (*as King*): "Hey, Jack, how you doin? Wait a minute! Where's my horse?"

KIM (*as Little Jack*): "Right here, King. That big ole fat horse eat too much so I swapped him for this'n. This'n won't eat much."

RON (*as King*): "You swapped my fine work horse for this bag of bones?"

KIM (*as Little Jack*): "King, you sound mad. You ain't mad, are you?"

RON (*as King*): "No, I ain't mad. Low blood sugar."

NANCY: But the King decided he wasn't gonna let Jack near no more of his animals. The next morning Jack was to pick apples

RON (*as King*): "You do know how to pick apples, don't you?"

KIM (*as Little Jack*): "Sure do."

RON (*as King*): "Well, get to it."

NANCY: The King sent Jack up to the orchard with some bushel baskets and a ladder

KIM: But Jack snuck back down to the house and got a big double bit ax

NANCY: And went to cutting down them big fine apple trees

KIM (*as Jack*): "TIMBER!!!"

NANCY: And then picked the apples off of the limbs once they's down on the ground

KIM: It's the modern way!

NANCY: When the King came out . . .

RON (*as King*): "Hey!! What in the devil are you doing?"

KIM (*as Little Jack*): "Pickin apples."

RON (*as King*): "Boy, you're gonna ruin me, you big dumb hillbilly. Don't you know nothin? You don't chop down the trees. This is how you pick apples."

NANCY: And he took the ladder and set it up against one of the trees, climbed up the ladder, and went to picking apples and putting them in his sack.

KIM (*as Jack*): "Well, that's one way of doin it, all right, King. But what if somebody was to come up to you and do this . . ."

NANCY: And he yanked that ladder out from under the King. The King just had time to latch his arm over a limb

RON (*as King*): "Jack, you let me down. Put that ladder up here this minute!"

KIM (*as Little Jack*): "Uh Uhh. I don't like the way you been treating me, and I don't like the way you treated my brother. But I'll put the ladder back if you'll get your wife, the Queen, to make me a big deep-dish apple pie."

RON (*as King*): "O.K., O. K. Go tell her I said to fix you one."

KIM: So Jack went running down to the house, knocked on the door and the Queen come out

NANCY (*as Queen*): "Yeah, what do you want?"

KIM (*as Little Jack*): "Queen, the King said for you to give me a great big . . . kiss."

NANCY (*as Queen*): "In your dreams, sonny boy."

KIM (*as Little Jack*): "Hey King, she says she won't do it!"

NANCY (*as Queen*): "Am I supposed to do what he says?"

RON (*as King*): "Yes, yes, give him what he wants right now!" (*KISS*)

RON (*King gets out of tree up to house*): "Now you're gonna get it! I'm gonna bust your head wide open!"

KIM (*as Little Jack*): "What's the matter, King. Are you mad?"

RON (*as King*): "You're durn right I'm mad!!"

KIM: Jack threw him down right then and there

NANCY: Cut three big strips of hide off of the King's back

KIM: Collected a bushel of gold and went on back home. He went in to where Big Jack was and seed he was bad off. Family was sure he wouldn't make it till morning. But Jack took them three strips of hide out of his pocket, washed em off real good, and laid them out on Big Jack's back. They fit real good.

NANCY (*as Big Jack*): Next morning Big Jack was up eating breakfast. It wasn't long til he was up and working around the place, feelin fine

KIM: And to this day

NANCY: Big Jack

KIM: Little Jack

NANCY: All their children

KIM: Grandchildren

NANCY: And greats

KIM & NANCY: Are doing well

KIM: And folks still say that that entire family has got

KIM & NANCY: Royal blood in their veins!

Jo Carson

1946–2011

Playwright, fiction writer, poet, and horsewoman Jo Carson was born in Johnson City, Tennessee, where she lived almost all her life. She became interested in theater while studying at East Tennessee State University, where she earned degrees in theater and communications.

Early in her career, Carson worked for Broadside Television, a Johnson City cable series featuring locally made documentaries about the history and folklife of northeastern Tennessee, southwestern Virginia, and western North Carolina. From 1972 to 1992, she worked for the Johnson City–based Road Company, a professional touring theater company for which she wrote two plays and performed in many. Carson frequently took her immediate surroundings and their history as her subject.

In the last decades of her life, Carson worked with community-oriented theater throughout the South, helping local people to collect oral histories from which she developed plays for the community. *Swamp Gravy* (1992), which examines black and white lives in Colquitt, Georgia, has become Georgia's official folklife play.

Carson's *Daytrips* (1988) is based on her experiences caring for her mother, who had Alzheimer's disease. The play employs techniques and themes of the theater of the absurd, such as indeterminacy, nonchronological time, and non sequitur, to explore the real-life absurdity of dementia and old age.

FROM Daytrips

Characters

NARRATOR/PAT—Pat is forty or so. They are the same person and *two people play her.* Pat is caught in these stories. The Narrator has the perspective to tell them and to comment. The Narrator speaks with the audience.

REE/IRENE—They are the same person and one person plays them both. Ree, 60 or so, is a victim of Alzheimers Disease. Irene is younger and healthy. Ree/Irene is the mother of Pat.

ROSE—is old. She is not steady but she does not shake, she stares at things to see but she does not squint. She needs more light, not less. She resists the easy sort of help that is an affront to her dignity. She's hard for the social graces age sometimes strips from people but she is not mean. Rose is the mother of Irene and Helen, the ghost.

> At the open.
> Ree is onstage lost. After a moment, Pat enters holding a jacket.

PAT. Hey, buddy, I got your jacket.

REE. Am I going home, Olivia?

PAT. You are home.

REE. My mother lives at home.

PAT. You live with your husband. Remember good old Price?

REE. I know Price, I married him. And there's a man who says he's Price but he isn't. He's one of the Carter boys but he's not the one I married. It's that other man . . .

PAT. Ree. Don't start.

REE. Price does whatever that other man says, he told Price not to let me have another dog . . .

PAT. We have to put your jacket on.

REE. And he told him not to let me drive and Price won't let me. I can drive. Oh Olivia, you don't know what it's like not to have a car. And he said I couldn't have a dog. He calls Price and Price just goes wherever that other man wants.

PAT. Ree! Your jacket.

REE. Oh.

PAT. OK. Other arm.

REE. Olivia, you've got to help me with my money.

PAT. Your arm buddy.

REE. Price takes it.

PAT. Price does not take your money.

REE. He spends it on that other man and they play golf and they won't take me home. Are you going to take me home?

PAT. Bend your arm! (*Pat gets the jacket on Ree.*) Good. We're going to see your mother.

REE. My mother . . .

PAT. In Kingsport.

REE. My job is to take care of my mother and Price won't let me drive. (*Ree shucks the jacket as if it were connected to "that other man" and leaves it laying in the floor. Punctuate this change.*)

(*Narrator enters. Pat retrieves the jacket and puts it on Ree with no struggle at all.*)

NARRATOR. (*To audience.*) This is Ree. She used to be Irene. Irene was my mother.

REE. (*To Pat.*) I don't have children.

NARRATOR. She has Alzheimers now.

REE. My brain is turning into jelly.

NARRATOR. This is her joke.

REE. Grape.

NARRATOR. This is my grandmother, Rose.

REE. Rose is my mother, I take care of her.

NARRATOR. Rose's mother was Patricia. I am named after Patricia. I am—

NARRATOR and PAT. We are Pat.

ROSE. You are Helen. I know Helen.

PAT. Helen is dead.

REE. This is Olivia.

ROSE. It is not.

NARRATOR and PAT. Pat.

REE. Olivia.

NARRATOR. There is a real Olivia, my great aunt Olivia. Ree confuses me with her. I am gone from Ree's memory but I fit somehow in her memory of Olivia. Tomorrow or next month, I will be somebody else. Ruth, Bernice, Elaine, who knows. Someday she will call me mother because her mother will be all she remembers. (*During the speech, Rose hunts for and finds a box of matches.*)

PAT. What was she like, Grandmother?

ROSE. Who?

PAT. Your mother.

ROSE. She was a mule. All she knew to do was work.

NARRATOR. Old age has fragile flesh that makes it hard to pull on shoes or unlock doors or stand up from sitting or bend over. (*Rose lights a match and looks for an electric socket with it.*) Old age hurts in the joints of bones. Old age cannot see except at a certain distance.

PAT. Grandmother, you light matches to plug the heater in?

ROSE. You have to be so careful of the juice.

NARRATOR. She used to be afraid electricity ran out of sockets if they didn't have something in them. (*Rose is a fire hazard with the match. Pat puts it out, takes the box of matches.*) Old age cannot or will not hear.

ROSE. What'd you say?

REE. Mother, this is Olivia.

ROSE. You mean Helen. What does she want?

PAT. I said you are confused sometimes.

ROSE. Your time's 'a comin'.

PAT. Is this a prophecy?

NARRATOR. She and her husband bought the second model T in Hancock County, Tennessee. She drove it down Clinch Mountain with no brakes but the hand brake. It was the only time she ever drove. They kept their horses to pull it with when it wouldn't start.

ROSE. Or Floyd ran it out of gas.

NARRATOR. She is old enough to have been old already when men landed on the moon.

ROSE. Old enough I shouldn't be livin' alone. Say that and see if it don't stick in your craw, Princess Helen.

❧

PAT. (*To Helen, a ghost she cannot see.*) "Too old to be living alone!" Is this what you hear?

NARRATOR. My aunt Helen has been in her grave 40 years. I speak to her ghost.

PAT. She gave you birth, she held you as you died. Are you back to take care of her? (*Ree sees a ghost.*)

❧❧

NARRATOR. Ree speaks to the ghost of Burkett.

REE. Ohhh. . . . You pulled my ears, I loved you.

NARRATOR. Ree speaks with ghosts every chance she gets. Burkett is a favorite uncle also years dead. He pulled my ears too; said it made more room for brains.

REE. And Margaret! She's not bent. Margaret!

PAT. Where, buddy?

REE. (*Points to a place.*) Margaret, you want to dress up paperdolls? (*A transformation, Ree becomes Irene.*)

❧❧

PAT. Mother?

IRENE. Pat?

PAT. Which jacket do you want?

NARRATOR. Irene, my mother speaks of her favorite jacket.

IRENE. The one that makes me look like Grace Kelly, the one that was much too expensive so I charged it, the one that makes me feel as if I received a Nobel Peace Prize for last week in that library and I am on my way to meet the king of Sweden instead of being on my way to take the queen of East Center Street to the grocery store. (*She has it on. It is the jacket from the opening scene.*) This one. You should try it on sometime. (*A second transformation. Irene to Ree. There are not big physical changes, there is an uncertainty in her bearing and an edge in her voice that turns to panic.*)

NARRATOR. Ree, my patient, speaks of her clothes.

REE. Where did I put . . . I swear people take things. Pat takes my clothes, I used to have good clothes, I had a jacket that I really liked and I now see her with it on like I wasn't even here and she just walks around in it. What have you done with my jacket? Why did you take it? (*Pat shows Ree the jacket she has on, then hugs Ree. A third transformation begins from the hug, Ree wants loose, Pat lets go. Ree struggles with the jacket. There are physical changes. Ree has a tilt, her eyes don't focus. She tries to get the jacket off. Same as the end of the opening scene.*) Olivia . . .

PAT. Leave it on, Buddy, you'll need it. We're going to Kingsport.

❧❧

ROSE. (*She was on this subject last time she spoke.*) I need somebody to live with me. Helen.

PAT. You don't want me, you don't like the way I live, Grandmother.

ROSE. You'll change.

PAT. When I change, I'll come live with you.

ROSE. Lord, just take me home.

PAT. You are home.

ROSE. I want to go back to Kyles Ford. You reckon anybody's still alive?

❧❧

(*Narrator sets chairs back of the sofa to become the back seat of a car. Pat should help Ree and Rose into it. Rose rides in the back seat. If Narrator goes in the car, she is also in the back seat.*)

NARRATOR. This day trip started with a picture Grandmother had had for years.

She never hung it anywhere that I remember but as a child I was allowed an occasional rummage through the closets so I had seen the picture.

PAT. The closets were where I learned about Helen—Helen who haunts us all—

NARRATOR. But that is another story. The picture is a hand tinted photograph of Kyles Ford, Tennessee. It was made by a man who came through with his equipment in the back of a horse drawn wagon. He took the photograph on speculation and sold copies to the residents of Kyles Ford. There weren't many people but most every family bought one. There are two houses in the scene the man chose and the further one is the house where my mother was born.

PAT. I had been there or so I was told.

ROSE. You were just a youngun'. It was when those people came that nobody knew and it turned out they'd come to the wrong reunion. They should have gone to the Kesicks. Cusick is spelled with a C. Cusicks can all read. (*They are in the car.*)

NARRATOR. It was Sunday after Thanksgiving, one of those November gifts, a beautiful, almost warm day.

ROSE. Lord, why on earth do you want to go all the way back there?

PAT. I took the precaution of bringing a map. (*Ree takes the map and looks at it upside down, any way but right.*)

ROSE. What do you need that for? Just start like you was goin' to Rogersville. I'll show you.

NARRATOR. And when we got to Rogersville . . .

ROSE. Turn around, Helen, we've gone too far.

REE. This is Olivia, Mother, Helen is dead.

ROSE. Well, she better turn the car around.

PAT. A mile or so back up the road where the map suggested, I turned off 11-W.

ROSE. This ain't it, ain't no road like this to Kyles Ford.

PAT. Just be patient.

ROSE. I know where I come from.

REE. Maybe we should go back home.

NARRATOR. We came to a crossroads with an arrow that pointed across the mountain to Kyles Ford . . .

ROSE. You're just lucky. They done cut another road. Even a blind hog gets an acorn once in awhile.

PAT. We started up the mountain.

ROSE. Lord, let's turn around. I don't want to do this.

REE. Mother . . .

ROSE. We're a like to die . . . you have to start in the mornin' if you're gonna' get across Clinch Mountain in the daylight and you done took your own time and eat dinner already.

NARRATOR. Once, you probably needed to start in the morning if you were going to get across Clinch Mountain in daylight. Clinch Mountain is one of those ridges with a backbone to it and the gaps are few and far between. It's not much of a gap on the road that runs into Kyles Ford. It's a thirty, forty minute drive and a series of curves that might prove harrowing to the uninitiated.

PAT. We topped the mountain and started down the other side.

ROSE. Robert Wilcox built that house. His wife's family had some money and Robert built him a fancy house with it. George Holms lived in that house yonder. His wife left him and she left his younguns with his mother. Said she'd married the devil and birthed two little devils but she wasn't goin' to raise 'em. Said she walked into Rogersville and caught a ride to Knoxville and took up being one of them street preachers they had down there on Market Square. You believe that? I don't. But that's what they said. Nobody'd pay a woman preacher. Now your daddy's cousin—

NARRATOR. My grandaddy's cousin.

ROSE. —lived there but he wasn't no 'count. Your daddy would of moved in over here if I'd a' let him.

NARRATOR. The road began to follow the Clinch River.

ROSE. Wes Johnson and Charlie Levisay had the ford.

REE. It was a Model T.

ROSE. It was the ford on the river. One of them lived on either side and they run the ferry back and forth. Made a right smart money till the county put the bridge in. They set 'em up a toll booth at the far end of it but the county made 'em take that down. Neither of 'em ever amounted to nothin' after that. There was people that still took the ferry in the winter when the bridge got iced up. Not your daddy.

NARRATOR. We crossed the bridge that put Charlie Levisay and Wes Johnson out of business.

PAT. On the other side was a rock road that turned off the highway and ran along the river.

ROSE. Lord, ain't that a road.

REE. Mother, what?

ROSE. I said ain't that a road.

NARRATOR. I thought she wanted me to turn up it.

PAT. I had to stop the car and back a ways before I could make the turn.

ROSE. What do you think you're doin'?

PAT. Backing up.

NARRATOR. I turned onto the road.

ROSE. Where do you think you're a goin'?

PAT. You said you wanted . . .

ROSE. Stop this car! You stop right this minute!

NARRATOR. I stopped the car.

ROSE. I'm gettin' out. If you go up this road you're goin' without me. (*Rose gets out of the car.*) Now you just go on if you're so dead set on drivin' somewhere! Go on!

PAT. I drove.

NARRATOR. I could see her in the rear view mirror standing in the road with her cane, holding her coat about her with the other hand.

ROSE. Go on! Both of you! Go see for yourselves!

REE. Olivia! I can't be like this . . .

PAT. I put the car in reverse, backed the ten yards and stopped beside her.

ROSE. I'm not goin'.

PAT. There's a law against leaving the likes of you standing in the middle of the road. (*Rose laughs.*)

NARRATOR. I won one, she laughed. And got back in the car.

PAT. Grandmother, what's on this road?

ROSE. You sure do want a lot, don't you?

NARRATOR. How much can you want?

PAT. I want to know what's on this road.

ROSE. Well, yonder's where I was born, and that's the house we moved into after daddy got it built. I didn't live in it very long.

PAT. Why?

ROSE. Just ride on a little.

NARRATOR. On up the road, a quarter of a mile, alone in a field overlooking the river, are the graves of my grandmother's father and the great-grandmother I'm named after.

PAT. I'm going to walk over there.

ROSE. You just sit tight.

PAT. That's Patricia . . .

ROSE. You're not gonna pay respects to a man that was that mean.

PAT. I've never been here.

ROSE. I loved my mother but she lays next to an awful man and she laid with him ever' night that he was home that she was married to him.

PAT. Maybe she loved him.

ROSE. Well, I didn't.

PAT. Maybe she was scared of him.

ROSE. Maybe I'm still scared of him.

NARRATOR. And sitting there in the car, looking at the river across a field she helped to work—

PAT. —she told me how she eloped with the man who was her school teacher.

ROSE. It didn't take no ladder, I just knew where Floyd was waitin' for me and I got in bed and stayed till everybody was asleep and I walked out the door.

NARRATOR. They moved as far as they could afford to go which was a half mile away, down on the main road, to the house in the picture where Helen and my mother were born.

ROSE. I did not go back till he was dying.

PAT. She said two sisters, both younger, came to live with her and Floyd two weeks after they married.

ROSE. He was a bad man. And my husband was a good man. Floyd was good.

PAT. What was so bad about him?

ROSE. Let's just go home.

NARRATOR. I turned the car around and started back out the road.

PAT. Did he beat you?

NARRATOR. We rejoined the main road. It felt like being safe.

ROSE. He beat all of us if somebody didn't do what he wanted.

PAT. What did he want?

ROSE. There are things people don't say to each other, Helen.

REE. Mother, this is Olivia.

(*Rose gets out of the car.*)

NARRATOR. Rose speaks of the man in Ira Cole's tree.

ROSE. I stand here at night and look out and it's the same man every time, it don't matter how cold. He's under Ira Cole's tree. Ira Cole should of cut that tree. Nobody needs a tree that big. But Ira Cole didn't hardly cut his grass. Your daddy cut the hedge. Fifty years. And Ira Cole just let that tree grow. The man lives in it. Don't that beat anything you ever heard? Floyd told me once about a man lived in a tree, could throw mules over a fence. I don't think this is the same man. I think I know this man. He got mad when Irene's Skippy Dog run out in front of him and now he's waiting for your daddy. It was Skippy Dog that died. I wrote him a note and I went over and left it at Ira Cole's tree. Said Floyd Cusick is dead. Leave me alone. I don't know if he can read. I should have put some money in it cause now he's out there every night studying this house. He looks right here at me. He hollers for me to come outside and some night I have to go. (*Rose exits.*)

(*Pat and Ree are still in the car. Ree is looking at things by the side of the road.*)

NARRATOR. Ree and I were on our way to Kingsport in the car.

PAT. I had fastened her seat belt and she didn't like it.

NARRATOR. She never likes it.

PAT. But she had settled down and she was watching things go by.

NARRATOR. Watching things go by is not looking at scenery. Her head moves to try to see specific things by the side of the road.

PAT. Look up, buddy . . .

REE. Don't tell me what to do.

PAT. I found my own thoughts.

NARRATOR. A friend had given me a mess of rhubarb. I love rhubarb and when I remembered it, I thought I might find strawberries.

REE. I haven't had rhubarb in I don't know how long.

NARRATOR. I had not said rhubarb.

PAT. What made you say that?

REE. I got brains I haven't used yet.

NARRATOR. Price, my father, her husband, says she's got brains she hasn't used yet. Ree usually thinks it's funny and laughing sometimes helps her to sit or eat but she was not being funny when she said it.

REE. Rhubarb in the brain and going in the tummy. (*A pause.*)

NARRATOR. We were driving again, again to Kingsport.

PAT. When we are driving together now, we are usually going to Kingsport.

REE. What are you putting in it?

NARRATOR. I planned to buy a quart of oil. I saw myself in K-Mart's parking lot putting oil in my car. She did too. (*A pause.*)

REE. I have to send something.

PAT. What?

REE. I don't remember.

NARRATOR. I did. I had an overdue electric bill ready to mail in my pocketbook.

PAT. I tested her.

NARRATOR. I'd think "dog" and get nothing. I'd think of my dog, a specific dog I could see in my mind.

REE. I pat dogs I like.

NARRATOR. Sometimes it was involuntary on her part. (*A pause.*)

REE. Wash the dishes, wash the dishes! Why do I have to say that?

PAT. How do you know what to say?

REE. What do you think I say?

NARRATOR. She couldn't tell me and she couldn't do it all the time. It happened most when she was sitting in the passenger's seat and the car was in motion.

PAT. Going to Kingsport. (*A pause.*)

REE. You don't like my mother.

PAT. It was a day I didn't want to go to Kingsport.

REE. You're making me fall.

NARRATOR. I see her levels of competency like plateaus. When she comes to an edge, she falls again. She was falling.

PAT. I don't think you're any better, Ree, that's all.

REE. You think I'm stupid.

PAT. I think your memory is bad.

REE. You think I'm worse.

PAT. How do you know that?

REE. You stop it!

PAT. (*To distract Ree.*) Look at the mountains, buddy, look at the sky.

REE. I can't go away just because you want me to.

PAT. Look at the clouds in the sky.

NARRATOR. She did look and the conversation was as lost as my name.

❧❧

NARRATOR. There are the dreams.

PAT. In this dream, we three are at Watauga Lake.

NARRATOR. Watauga is so beautiful, steep and deep and clean. People have been lost in Watuaga, fallen out of a boat never to be found.

PAT. I cut my foot there once, a cut that took stitches to close and I bled into the lake.

NARRATOR. I think of that sometimes when I'm there, that thirty years later, swimming, molecules of my blood may still be there. Mine and other people's, I don't forget them. In my dream, Watauga is the red of the sunset and it makes me think of blood but the day is hot and I wade into the lake.

PAT. Mother and Grandmother are there.

NARRATOR. They don't ever come when I am swimming, playing with friends, but they are there in my dream. They tell me to—

ROSE and IRENE and NARRATOR. —be careful.

NARRATOR. And I say—

PAT and NARRATOR. —I am careful.

NARRATOR. I am careful. I have on plastic shoes so I will not cut my foot again. As I wade into the lake, I say—

PAT. —you come too. (*Irene and Rose begin to take off their shoes.*)

IRENE. We don't have plastic shoes.

PAT. I'll give you one each.

NARRATOR. My shoes would not fit their knotty feet.

IRENE. No, we'll do it anyway.

PAT. And they sit on the shore and take off their shoes and both of them in their afternoon dresses wade into the lake. They hold hands.

NARRATOR. I walk further into the water. My jeans get wet. I call to them.

PAT. Come on!

ROSE. Our dresses will get wet.

PAT. I'm wet, it feels good.

NARRATOR. I am waist deep, I am chest deep, my feet no longer touch the bottom and I kick gently in my plastic shoes to stay afloat.

PAT. Come on.

NARRATOR. And they come. But they do not swim. They walk. Holding hands. They walk past me. I see their heads beneath the surface of the water.

PAT. I told you it feels good . . .

NARRATOR. And they walk. Further than I can see, further than I feel safe to swim and they are gone. I do not call—

PAT. —come back

NARRATOR. I say—

PAT. —good-bye.

NARRATOR. And I swim back to shore and I pick up their shoes—

PAT. —and I bring their shoes home.

PART VIII

Twenty-First-Century Appalachian Literature

Thomas Alan Holmes

Although Appalachia and its authors resist political definition and economic category, one can say that twenty-first-century Appalachian writers attempt to define what changes and what endures in a rapidly globalizing world. As Pulitzer Prize finalist Maurice Manning has noted, at the core of Appalachian literature is a tension between an appreciation of the region and an "anxiety for legitimacy"; this observation reflects the challenges facing authors from a region still often seen as "other" by the broader American culture.

Some Appalachian authors, drawing on older depictions of the region (examples of which can be found in the earlier sections of this anthology), still portray the region as a culture of crisis and poverty, a vision that resonates with certain readers from the region and that, judging from national best-seller lists, has a wide appeal outside the region. Other readers find this recycling of old stereotypes irksome and inaccurate. Many contemporary Appalachian authors have a careful, nuanced view of the region, as they honestly examine Appalachia's social, economic, and environmental problems while at the same time celebrating the region's positive elements.

The iconographic shift from the romanticized, mythic Appalachian moonshiner to the starkly realistic depiction of the Appalachian methamphetamine manufacturer epitomizes the challenges that Appalachian authors face as they struggle to preserve and reconfigure Appalachia, to critique and celebrate the region. See, for example, Ron Rash's exploration of this theme in his short story "The Ascent." Closely related to the methamphetamine problem is the twenty-first-century's opioid crisis, addressed via community theater by Robert Gipe and the Higher Ground Project. Coal mining is another topic that many Appalachian authors grapple with, attempting to reconcile a respect for hard, dangerous work with the environmental and economic realities of an exploitative, nonrenewable, extractive industry, as Ann Pancake does in *Strange as This Weather Has Been*. A third example of the contemporary Appalachian author's challenges is how to produce a nuanced depiction of religious tradition, which, although celebrated by many people in the region, sometimes supports attitudes that authors such as Silas House in *Recruiters* suggest can be repressive.

Some contemporary Appalachian literature explores which traditions are worth preserving and which ones should fall by the wayside. Barbara Kingsolver reflects on the value of cultivating local food in contrast to supporting industrial farming. Other authors consider the importance of regional folkways. In "Affrilachia," for example, Frank X Walker compares his urban culture to rural Appalachian culture by noting "a mutual appreciation / for fresh greens / and cornbread / an almost heroic notion / of family." In "Tipping the Scales," however, Crystal Wilkinson offers a nontraditional story of love's transcending the immediacy of petty gossip and social disapproval. Jesse Graves, in "Digging the Pond," articulates a poignant recognition that a father's knowledge does not necessarily translate into his son's way of life, and in "Jack and the Mad Dog," Tony Earley questions whether traditional folkways are still viable.

Twenty-first-century Appalachian authors also consider how to preserve and expand their Appalachian identity, a process that they sometimes connect with preservation and innovation in literary style. See, for example, Melissa Range's deliberate juxtaposition of Appalachian dialect with Old English, or Robert Gipe's hybrid fiction, which relies on incorporated illustrated panels to expand the story in his more conventional text.

The question arises of just who is Appalachian. In *Loving Mountains, Loving Men*, Jeff Mann recounts the challenges he has faced as an openly gay man in Appalachia, but he takes pride in being one of those "who refuse to dismember themselves in order to assimilate." Mark Powell depicts tender and complex relationships within immigrant families.

In short, many twentieth-century Appalachian authors cultivate in their readers an appreciation of Appalachian perspectives from a self-aware otherness that is sometimes tradition tethered yet is willing to go far beyond received notions about the region.

Sources: Douglas Reichert Powell, *Critical Regionalism: Connecting Politics and Culture in the American Landscape* (2007); Casey Howard Clabough, *Inhabiting Contemporary Southern and Appalachian Literature: Region and Place in the Twenty-First Century* (2012); Amy D. Clark and Nancy M. Hayward, eds., *Talking Appalachian: Voice, Identity, and Community* (2013).

Maggie Anderson

1948–

Maggie Anderson was born in New York City. At thirteen she moved with her family to West Virginia, where her father's family lived. After graduating from West Virginia University, she taught creative writing to the visually impaired in West Virginia and served as poet in residence at area schools, rehabilitation centers, and correctional facilities, putting into practice her belief that poetry should reflect and inform community activism.

Anderson's poetry confronts the hard moments in life. Her subjects include class, war, political protest, cultural identity, the responsibilities of documentary photography, and personal loss. She cites Muriel Rukeyser as the model of an activist poet who motivates readers to examine public or personal issues and then participate in an engaged response. Her belief that activism can inform poetry led her to create a collection of poems commemorating the 1969 shootings at Kent State University, where she taught for two decades. Anderson co-founded the poetry journal *Trellis* with Irene McKinney and Winston Fuller and, while at Kent State, founded and edited the Wick Poetry First Book Series and the Wick Poetry Chapbook Series for Ohio Poets.

Heart Fire

Three months since your young son shot himself
and, of course, no one knows why. It was October.
Maybe he was following the smell of dying leaves
or the warmth of the fire in the heart, so hard
to locate in a country always readying for war.

One afternoon we sat together on your floor, drinking
tea and listening to Brahms on the radio. He would
have liked this music, you told me. He would have liked
everything I like now and what he wouldn't like I don't
like either. He has made the whole world look like him.

Today, driving into Pittsburgh, I see you are right.
The sky is cold blue like a shirt I once saw him
wear and the bare trees are dark, like his hair.
I see how vulnerable the grasses are, pale and flimsy
by the roadsides, trying to stand straight in the wind.

At Canonsburg, all the pink and green and purple houses
have the same slant of roof toward the hill, like toys
because I'm thinking about children, how sometimes
we want to give them up if they seem odd and distant,
yet even if they die before us, we cannot let them go.

I see your son in landscapes as I drive, in a twist
of light behind a barn before the suburbs start,
or under a suburban street light where a tall boy
with a basketball has limbs like those he had just
outgrown. Because I want to think he's not alone

I invent for him a heart fire even the unenlightened
living are sometimes allowed to see. It burns past
the white fluorescence of the city, past the steel mills
working off and on as they tell us we need, or don't
need, heavy industry for fuel, or war. Your son

keeps me company, driving down the last hill into
Pittsburgh, in the tunnel as I push for good position
in the lanes. He is with me as I spot the shiny cables
of the bridge and gear down, as all the lights beyond
the river come on now, across his safe, perfected face.

House and Graveyard, Rowlesburg, West Virginia, 1935

I can't look long at this picture, a Walker Evans photograph
of a West Virginia graveyard in the Great Depression,
interesting for the sharp light it throws
on poverty, intimate for me because it focuses
on my private and familial dead. This is where

my grandparents, my Uncle Adrian and my Aunt Margaret
I am named for are buried. Adrian died at seven, long
before I was born. Margaret died in childbirth in 1929.
The morning sun falls flat against the tombstones
then spreads across Cannon Hill behind them. I see

how beautiful this is even though everyone was poor,
but in Rowlesburg nothing's changed. Everything
is still the same, just grayer. Beside the graveyard
is Fike's house with the rusty bucket, the tattered
trellis and the same rocker Evans liked. Miss Funk,

the school teacher, now retired, and her widowed sister

still live down the road out of the camera's range.
I remember how my Aunt Nita loved that mountain,
how my father told of swinging from the railroad
bridge down into the Cheat. Nita worked

for the Farm Security Administration too, as Evans did.
She checked people's houses for canned goods, to see
how many they had stored, and she walked the road
by here, every day. I can't look long at this picture.
It warps my history into politics, makes art
of my biography through someone else's eyes.
It's a good photograph, but Walker Evans
didn't know my family, nor the distance
his careful composition makes me feel now
from my silent people in their graves.

Frank X Walker

1961–

Frank X Walker is a poet, multidisciplinary artist, and educator from Danville, Kentucky. At the University of Kentucky, where Walker received his BA, he studied with Appalachian author Gurney Norman. He earned an MFA from Spalding University.

With Norman's encouragement and support, Walker published his first collection of poetry, *Affrilachia* (2000), which was well received both critically and publicly. A faculty member in African American and Africana studies and in the Department of English at the University of Kentucky, Walker is founding editor of *Pluck! The Affrilachian Journal of Arts and Culture*. Along with Crystal Wilkinson and Nikky Finney, Walker is a founding member of the Affrilachian Poets, who celebrate as well as challenge Appalachian culture and persistent issues of racism and identity. This anthology presents an assortment of poems from Walker's book *Affrilachia*.

Walker has also addressed historical subjects. *Buffalo Dance: The Journey of York* (2004) imagines the experiences of York, the enslaved African American who participated in the Lewis and Clark Expedition. Walker's fascination with York culminated in the poetry collection *When Winter Come: The Ascension of York* (2008), a sequel to *Buffalo Dance*. Following in the tradition of the York poems, Walker's 2010 poetry collection *Isaac Murphy: I Dedicate This Ride* interprets the life of Isaac Murphy, a nineteenth-century African American and the first jockey to win the Kentucky Derby three times.

A mentor to young artists who feel marginalized, a prominent member of the Kentucky arts and cultural community, and a growing influence in higher education, Frank X Walker, who considers himself an artist activist, merges poetry and politics to encourage the diversification of Appalachian voices.

Affrilachia
(for gurney & anne)

thoroughbred racing
and hee haw
are burdensome images
for kentucky sons
venturing beyond the mason-dixon

anywhere in appalachia
is about as far
as you could get
from our house

in the projects
yet
a mutual appreciation
for fresh greens
and cornbread
an almost heroic notion
of family
and porches
makes us kinfolk
somehow
but having never ridden
bareback
or sidesaddle
and being inexperienced
at cutting
hanging
or chewing tobacco
yet still feeling
complete and proud to say
that some of the bluegrass
is black
enough to know
that being 'colored,' and all
is generally lost
somewhere between
the dukes of hazzard
and the beverly hillbillies
but
if you think
makin' 'shine from corn
is as hard as kentucky coal
imagine being
an Affrilachian
poet

Lil' Kings

what if
the good revren doctah
mlk jr
was just marty
or lil' king
not a pastor
but a little faster
from the streets

quoting gangsta rap
not gandhi

was not dr. king
but king doctah
or ice-k
his peace sign on a gold tooth
or gleaming 14 karat like
from around his neck

what if somebody
screaming 'nigger'
hit 'im in the head
with a brick
and he pulled out a nine
and squeezed off
one or two rounds
not tears
praying
only that he
not miss
sported mlk
on phat brass knuckles
and a left-handed
diamond pinky ring
walked the streets
with his home boyz
spray painting
let freedom ring
and I had a dream
on bus stops
and stop signs

got arrested for
conspiring to incite riots
disturbing the peace
and resisting arrest

didn't preach from
no pulpit
but on a microphone
behind turntables
mixin' and scratchin'
listenin' to dr. dre

wu tang
and the notorious b.i.g.
pants down to his hightops
hat on backwards
eyes on a prized new voice
not no bel
no peace
of nothin'
that just rings
when it's hit
a voice that
hits back

could he still
be king?

Healer

church mother
yoruba high priestess
nandi
to the zulu
pentecostal scripture quotin'
holy water sprinklin'
talkin' in tongues
wearin' white
you studied nursing
to learn to disguise
your own ancient ways
your knowing hands
have prepared birth canals
tied umbilical cords
closed eyelids

you see the storm
before the crickets
your skin crawls
when evil lurks

you closed your fertile gates
long ago
to keep a more vigilant watch
over them that came
over them that were sent

to your shade tree
your front porch
your holy place

I saw you step inside
the weak
inside
the innocent
touch their pain
and shout it out

I saw you
anointed with olive oil
full of the holy spirit
reach down deep
and rebuild backbones
close holes in hearts
rescue lost smiles
and souls

when you said 'go'
I went
when you said
'do the right thing'
I gave the child my name
no questions asked

now you say
read ecclesiastes and weigh
my own struggles
study king solomon
and know real wisdom
you said
'this is just the beginning'
so I'm making room in my hope chest
and saving energy
believing
in your knowing
and praying ways

Pauletta Hansel

1959–

Poet and teacher Pauletta Hansel was born in Richmond, Kentucky, and grew up in several small towns in eastern Kentucky. Hansel began writing poems while still in junior high and was soon published in Appalachian literary journals including *Mountain Review* and *Twigs*. These publications brought her to the attention of the newly formed Southern Appalachian Writers Cooperative (SAWC) and, through that group, to the Southern Appalachian Circuit of Antioch College in Beckley, West Virginia, which recruited her as a student when she was sixteen.

Hansel has been influential in several important collectives of Appalachian poets. While at Antioch College, she founded the politically active group the Soupbean Poets; later, she organized Street Talk, a theater collective, and, since the 1980s, she has worked with SAWC. Hansel has also taught at a feminist creative writing center, Women Writing for (a) Change. In addition to writing, Hansel teaches poetry and memoir in both college and community settings and has served as managing editor of *Pine Mountain Sand & Gravel,* the literary publication of SAWC. As a writer, organizer, and activist, Hansel has made important contributions to Appalachian and women's poetry.

In her poetry, Hansel meditates on the shifting phases of female identity, both universally and personally. Ultimately she acknowledges that she is (and, by extension, other women are) in a liminal timeless space that cannot be defined by the standard tropes of women's maturation and aging.

Writing Lessons (I.)

> *I look for the way*
> *things will turn*
> *out*
>> "Poetics," A. R. Ammons

I am trying to find the shape of things,
to find where words might go
without the prodding of my pen,
left to their own devices:
startled sliding up
as if unnoticed,
nestling in the curve
of *century's* end;
places I have never seen—

Niagara Falls, Lookout Mountain—
sliding down
between the floorboards
of my mother's kitchen, 1962.

I am trying to find the shape of things,
to let them unfold
without my restless hands forever
moving, pressing up or down
into the patterns
so familiar they are all I ever
dare to sew;
to let this life unfold:
a bolt of cloth spilling
from a tall shelf,
haphazard by its own design;
a liar's yarn spinning out
incredulously true.

She

That spring
she let herself go,
uncoiled the cord
and slipped out through
the crack in the window.

She was unleashed.
Even her hair sprung
free of curl.
Her clothes
would not stay put.

She spoke too loudly.
Sentences ran on
ahead of her.
She followed
when she chose.

When people said
they didn't know her
anymore,
she did not
hear them.

Ron Rash

1953–

Poet, short story writer, and novelist Ron Rash was born in Chester, South Carolina, to parents who had moved from the North Carolina mountain counties of Buncombe and Watauga to work in a textile mill. Rash grew up in Boiling Springs, North Carolina, his father an art professor at Gardner-Webb College, where Rash earned his BA. Rash received an MA from Clemson University.

Rash's family retained strong ties to its ancestral communities, instilling in him a love of mountain lands, places, and people. His poetry collection *Eureka Mill* (2001) was named for the Piedmont textile mill where his parents worked. Many of its poems deal with the tensions between manufacturing and agrarian lifestyles as viewed from different speakers' perspectives. In "Spring Fever," the narrator recalls the lure of the farm and the difficult circumstances that drove the men away from the farms in the first place. The poems "1934" and "Black and White" both deal with labor issues. *Eureka Mill* addresses human aspirations for a rewarding, respectful, and joyful life unencumbered by making a living in an economic system beyond an individual's control.

Spring Fever

Each spring you knew when it was planting time.
The men would get more careless on the job
and have that far-away look in their eyes.
You'd know they were behind a mule and plow.

They'd drink a lot more whiskey that time of year,
and take a lot less from their section boss,
who like us wives knew it was the better course
to cut them slack until the fever passed.

But they were just remembering the best,
not the things they'd gladly left behind,
that made them leave. It's easy to love a life
you only have to live the good parts of.

They'd forgotten what a hailstorm does
in fifteen minutes time to six weeks work,
how long it took a hay-filled barn to burn,
when a lantern spilled its flame or lightning struck.

They'd forgotten the loneliness. The days
you wouldn't speak a word from dawn to dusk
except to cows and chickens and felt your tongue
was rusting like a plowshare in the rain.

But maybe deep inside they did remember.
They must have because every March you'd hear
men swear come planting time next spring they'd be
back in the fields. They'd say that every year.

1934

After the union men left town,
Old Man Springs stood by the gate.
He tried to gauge us by our eyes,
unsure whose side we now were on.

As if we knew. It sounded good
what organizers promised us,
a shorter day, a better wage,
a worker getting to boss the boss.

They told us that it was our sweat
that bought the mansion Springs lived in.
The time had come to share the wealth,
they said, we've got them on the run.

But when the other mills laid off,
Springs made sure we had some work.
We'd watch warehouses fill with cloth
we knew there was no market for.

What did we owe him for those jobs?
A tough question, almost as tough
as how on earth we'd feed our kids
if strikers shut Eureka down.

When a flying squadron headed south
and crossed the Chester County line,
we left our shift to walk outside.
We filled our fists to welcome them.

Black and White

One December Colonel Springs dressed down
in overalls himself, his children and wife,
the idea being to create a Christmas card
sure to make his business partners laugh.
The chauffeur drove them to the mill, the photographer
already inside, setting up his camera.

The Colonel placed himself behind a cart
filled up with bobbins, arms taut, brow creased.
His wife stood behind him, her hair tied back
to authenticate the blank look on her face.
The children too pretended they were working,
leaned their lean bodies against a machine.

The photograph turned out a shade too dark
to satisfy the photographer who blamed
a lack of proper lighting, the jolt and jar
of machinery that hurt his concentration.
But Colonel Springs was pleased and always swore
that Lewis Hine could not have done it better.

Diane Gilliam Fisher

1957–

Although Diane Gilliam Fisher's family migrated after World War II from the Appalachian Mountains to Columbus, Ohio, where she was born and reared, they maintained strong ties to Mingo County, West Virginia, and Johnson County, Kentucky. Fisher earned a PhD in Romance languages and literature from Ohio State University and an MFA from Warren Wilson College in Swannanoa, North Carolina, before settling into her professional life as a poet.

Fisher's chapbook, *Recipe for Blackberry Cake* (1999), and her first poetry collection, *One of Everything* (2003), explore her family history in the mountains. *Kettle Bottom* (2004), a departure from her earlier, more personal work, tells the story of the West Virginia Mine Wars of 1920–1921, including the Battle of Blair Mountain, the largest labor uprising in the United States. The fifty-one poems of *Kettle Bottom* have multiple speakers, many of whom are fictional representations of historical people, and explore topics such as workers' rights, labor unions, and mine safety. In "Raven Light," the speaker is trapped in a coal mine after the ceiling collapses. The raven of the title is that of Genesis 8:7, sent from Noah's ark in advance of the dove. Throughout the poem, the speaker sorts through half-remembered scriptural knowledge and his own life as he searches for a saving glimmer of light.

Raven Light

I must of slept, for I dreamed the fire boss
torching the gas up under the roof
as he come toward me down the hall.
Then I seen he had wings
and that torch was the flaming sword
turning every way at the gate
of the Garden, and I look again
and I see his face all black
and grinning—I think it was a dream.
I think I'm awake. Oh, Christ.
Christ, don't let me be in Hell.
Oh, Jesus. Jesus, Jesus.

      ❧

I'd loaded my second ton,
drilled for the third. Took a notion
I was hungry. I took off my coat,
laid it down on the ground

to set on, and opened
my dinner bucket. Fresh sausage meat
fried up and sandwiched in biscuits,
a apple pie, half-gallon of cold water
in the bottom well of the bucket.
But she'd packed the pie in the top tin,
biscuits and sausage in the middle—
she always done it the other way around.
That was when I heard
the rush of rats to the drift mouth.

When I first come in the mine
Daddy told me, *Them rats*
can hear a branch crack
up on top of the mountain.
They hear the earth start to give
when the roof's about to fall.
Them rats makes a run for the drift mouth,
you drop what you're doing, son,
you run.
                    I got so slow
when I heard them. Out in the hall
I seen dust falling thick
about a hundred yards down the way
toward the mouth, I heard beams
start to creak. Dust begin to blow
back where I was, I heard hollering.
I heard praying. I walked back
the other way, into the dark.

      ❧

When I was a boy, I liked the story of Jonah.
He done right, I thought. If God
meant to send him to a evil place,
why shouldn't he get on a boat
and head the other way? I bet Nineveh
was run by folks like Stone Mountain Coal,
men that jokes about using a dago
for a mine post, that figures it's cheaper
to replace a dead miner than
to replace a dead mule. If a whale
swallowed you, at least it wouldn't be
for meanness, nor for money.

      ❧

I feel I could walk a long way,
though I am far past what I know
of the layout of the mine. I left
my dinner and carbide behind
but a man can live
five days if he ain't hurt, taking in
the water he needs through his skin—

for down here, even the air
is mostly water.

           ❧

Pretend.
Pretend it's just you
closing your eyes and not this
god-awful dark.
You're napping by the creek
with Gertie. She's smiling, doing
that thing with the daisy—*he loves me,
he loves me not.* Loves me not.
But it's Jesus I see, instead of her,
plucking petals off that flower
like a boy pulling wings off a fly.
And him not even looking at me
while he makes up his mind.

           ❧

Don't Daddy always come back? I'd say
to Mama when she begin to slam pots
or drop dishes long about shift end.
She got worse when it got down in the fall
and dark come earlier every day—
Like bad news can't wait to get here,
she'd mutter and moan. Then there he'd be,
stomping coal dust off his boots on the porch,
his face blacked and shiny, like it had soaked
up the dark and give it back alive.
He put me in mind of a raven, those times,
and he was beautiful to my eyes.

But it fretted Mama to see him so.
She'd send us to the back room,
he'd set in the washtub, but no matter
how hard we scrubbed he had

them coon eyes, like he was always
looking out from the dark.

❧

Lord, I hope Gertie don't remember
she stacked my dinner bucket wrong.
She'll figure it for bad luck, won't nobody
be able to tell her different.

I ain't afraid in my head—there's a part of me
that's like a kite cut loose, like Noah's raven
that knows it ain't going back—
but when I think on Gertie, my knees buckle,
my whole body's set atremble. Like when
I first come to her and she
let me, oh honey,
and seemed like only my body
knowed what was happening.

❧

I wisht I could sleep
my way to it, but some miles back
I woke to black pressed flat,
smothering agin my face, and screaming—
screaming worse'n a woman birthing
a seven-month baby—
I thought, *Painter!*
and I throwed up my arms to try
and push it off, but I hit air
and cold rock and of a sudden
I knowed them screams
was coming from me.

God almighty, Goddamn.

Our Father who art in heaven,
who maketh me to lie beneath the green pastures,
God the Father, who gave his only begotten son,
Goddamn, what a hell
of a thing to do.

❧

This passage has give out, too low
to walk through, and I ain't fixing
to crawl. Used to be Indians around here

not too awful long ago, and for a minute
I thought I'd found the back end
of one of their caves and this was not
really happening.
That's how simple it would be,
something that'd open.

There is only setting here, now, like Noah
waiting for the storm to pass. He must of pondered
long and hard on how to start over
in a whole new world, not even knowing
who'd be there, or if there'd be trees. Finding out
what it means to not know nothing.

                ❧

Somewhere over top of me now, up on the bald,
is a giant chestnut tree, you can see it
from everywhere in the valley. Mama says
it was already dead when she was a girl.
When I was nine or so, there come
a thunderstorm so wild, lightning
riv'd it right in half—but it's still standing.
Dead as kindling, half a century at least,
and still there. That's got
to mean something, don't it?

When I read the story of Noah,
it was that chestnut tree I pictured
to be the first thing rising up
out of the lowering waters.
First Bible story I ever read on my own—
else I'd never of knowed about the raven,
for Brother Pentecost spoke only of the dove
and the olive branch. That old riven
tree, not what Noah was looking for,
but the raven would of chose the twisted hands
of that old tree, over Noah's solid ground—
if there is any such thing.

                ❧

The cold aches me. My bones
feel like I been stoned, like that woman
in the Bible. What was that for?

I would have a chair, if there was anything

left for me to have. Not a easy
chair but a rocker—back and forth,
back.

·●·

I imagined Gertie, then ordinary dark
to be the last thing I'd see.
Down here once I seen a sheet of rock
pocked with skeletons of ferns, they looked
as dancing in the rock as they must
of looked in the wind. Nothing
like that here, only one of them dripping rocks
that cones down from the roof just
to grow back up from the floor.
Like a hourglass, but moving so slow
you can't see it go. It drips and the top
don't lose nothing, just grows longer
while the bottom gets taller. I wonder
how long till they touch,
till there ain't nothing at all
between what's coming and what's gone.
How long?

·●·

I wisht I had something to write with,
but who could ever read such writing
as I could do in this dark?

·●·

I don't know why I done it. I don't know
why I done it. Come this way.

What I want is to keep seeing Gertie's face
up in the world. I'd give a arm and a leg—
Jesus, I'm laughing and it ain't even funny,
that's a real arm and leg—to of stayed.

I don't know why I come this way.
If we are made in God's image, I bet God
looks something like Henry Burgess. I bet
he could come down here and set his foot
on this rock, prop one elbow on his knee,
lean forward and rub his chin,
like Henry doing a deal on market day,
and say, *Alright, then, son,*

what'll you give me for it? And I'd be dumb
as a little boy again, not one thing
I could tell him worth my life.

So I guess I'll die. I'm dying right now
and I ain't laughing neither. Twenty
years old and crying into my shirt.
I'm glad Gertie can't see me.
But when he seen God
was really gonna make him die, even *Jesus* cried
and tried to change his mind.

I was fifteen when we laid Daddy
in the ground. Uncle Bill and Ted Stanley
and Tom and Woody Hartsell
done for Daddy, though usually the women
washes the body and lays it out. They nailed the lid
on Daddy's box afore me nor Mama either one
got a chance to see him. *It's best,* they told her,
and she let it go. The four of them would set
with Daddy through the night, carry him
up the hill in the morning.
I am aiming to carry Daddy, too, I told Uncle Bill.
He started in, *Now, son. . . .* I stopped him,
I said, *I am aiming to do it.*

Daddy was a big man, and when I hefted
the corner of his box onto my left shoulder
I didn't feel hardly no weight at all but the pine.
Uncle Bill watched me. He set his jaw and looked
straight ahead, so that's what I did. After, them four
was out on the back porch drinking. I went on out,
when I knowed Uncle Bill seen me, I stood
tall as I could. *I reckon I'm a man now,* I told him.
I reckon you are, Nathan, he said.
And we all waited for Woody Hartsell
to speak, for he was the eldest man there.
It was a bad roof fall, he said, twenty,
thirty foot section. Daddy was working
back behind, made a run for it.
When the rocks begun to close in,
he lunged, arms flung forward like diving
for cover. They caught him mid-flight,
crushed everthing below his chest, his head

and shoulders and arms was all they brung out.
Woody reached for the jar, swallowed hard,
Jesus Christ, God Almighty, he swore,
I keep seeing him,
jutting out of the rock
like a baby half-born.

Out of the dark of the drift mouth
they'll be men still coming out. In twos
and threes, holding each other up, dragging
brothers and fathers between them. Only
the carbide lamps show, no faces. I am part
of the dark the lights bob through in little clusters,
wavery constellations that fade into ordinary
men in the daylight. I am far under
the roots of the old chestnut, hid
in the raven light, where the rock
of ages has cleft.

Darnell Arnoult

1955–

Author and educator Darnell Arnoult was born and reared in Henry County, Virginia. After earning a BA in American studies with a concentration in folklore at the University of North Carolina, Chapel Hill, she received an MA from North Carolina State University and an MFA from the University of Memphis. She has released two volumes of poetry, *What Travels with Us: Poems* (2005) and *Galaxie Wagon: Poems* (2016), and a novel, *Sufficient Grace* (2006).

Arnoult is an active presence in the Appalachian literary world not only as an author but as a teacher and mentor. While serving as writer in residence at Lincoln Memorial University, she taught creative writing and co-directed the Mountain Heritage Literary Festival and the Appalachian Young Writers Workshop. She provides both formal training and generous nurturing in her novel-writing workshop. Arnoult is passionate about promoting Appalachian writers.

The speakers in Arnoult's poetry vary, but they all demonstrate an affectionate sense of the personal, as if confiding in readers, as evidenced in the poems below.

Second Shift

They're running Jacquards this week.
I'm a spinner, been spinning for ten years.
Work second and my old man works first.
He tends the kids, three. Better that way
cause he's patient. I aint. Just my nature's
all. No meanness really. Just my nature.
He makes them supper and warms it up for me
when I get home. He feeds me and then we go to bed,
him so he can get up at four in the morning
and me cause I'm tired as a old radio song.
He puts his hands on me and sometimes I want it.
Sometimes I take care to pick the lint from my hair
and tip a little of Rhonda's Shalimar behind my ears
and inside my arms. But one of us is always asleep
before the love comes. Neither of us is disappointed.
Tonight I'll have fried mackerel patties
with cream potatoes and okra stewed with tomatoes.
My old man can really cook.

Photograph in the Hall

Bill leans toward her, hand on the hood, loving her with his eyes.
The woman, head down and eyes up, leans back against the Buick's ribs.
I see this picture and want to be Mae at sixteen, about to be a bride.

They are sharing something private—a joke, lust, full hearts, like minds—
not touching, yet only a hint of separation. They are savoring what is left
    of courtship.
I see this picture and want to be Aunt Mae at sixteen, about to be a bride.

Her hair is swept into soft round waves, a thick roll of dark hair pinned
    behind.
She looks up at Uncle Bill sheepishly, pleasure already on her lips
and Bill presses toward her, hand on his new Buick's hood, loving her with
    just his eyes.

Bill and Mae came to visit this evening. Out for a little Sunday ride.
Him with his hardening arteries and her straining against arthritis in her
    back and hips.
I see this picture and want to see Aunt Mae at sixteen, about to be a bride.

Bill saw her working a tobacco field and right there decided.
He offered her a new dress, but she chose the freedom of vows in her own
    old shift.
Bill leans toward her, hand on the Buick's hood, loving her eye to eye.

Today they move slow. Hold hands to hold up. Stop to rest. Hard to believe
    back when there was no rest to be had, he watched her old shift slide
    like water across her breasts and hips and pool at her feet.
I want to be the young girl I never knew, sheepishly urgent. Ready to be a
    bride.
Her handsome man leaning toward her, hand on the hood, loving her with
    ready eyes.

Spoons

Two tarnished spoons,
we lie in the dark
drawer mirroring one
another—cupped
in perfect silver-plated
fit, the curves

of our backs, the flats
of our feet, breath
to neck. How much
sugar we've shared.
The intimate sound
of sip. We fit
snug and slick,
loving and waiting
on morning
on creamer
on the strong rich
work of coffee
and first light.

doris davenport

1949–

doris davenport, born and reared in northeast Georgia, continues to identify as an Appalachian despite living and working outside the region. She holds degrees from Paine College (BA), the State University of New York at Buffalo (MA), and the University of Southern California (PhD) and teaches at Stillman College in Tuscaloosa, Alabama.

Although davenport acknowledges the influence of Appalachian writers such as Lee Smith and Nikki Giovanni as well as others such as Toni Morrison and Zora Neale Hurston, her work defies easy categorization. Her independent voice initially caused her difficulty in the publishing world, even among the more liberal alternative presses. Yet it is that undiluted voice—haunted and haunting, Appalachian and African American, lesbian and anti-essentialist—that has established her reputation as an artist.

The poems in davenport's collection *Madness Like Morning Glories* (2005) examine what Frank X Walker termed "Affrilachian" experiences. Additionally, her "Ceremony for 103 Soque Street" brings Native American identity into the mix, recognizing the narrator's black community as a type of reservation on what is rightfully Cherokee land. "Miz Clio Savant" conveys the voice of a spirit medium, whose own voice in turn disintegrates into that of a gaggle of gossiping locals. Davenport's poetry channels the views of a diverse community, effectively bridging the gap between her own unique persona and the larger world of Appalachia.

Ceremony for 103 Soque Street

Soque is a Cherokee word turned Black on the Hill
across the railroad track, in Appalachian foothills where
madness like morning glories took over everyone trying to be
insane and acceptable all the time and all the while, hainted.
Two rows of houses along the railroad track
Mr. Oscar Wise, the Peanut Man, and his family
still there in the air and honeysuckles, hainted.
Mack, our cousin, said he saw a casket roll down Soque,
stop in front of 103 and roll back up the hill again.

Mr. Miller's wife, and that's all the name she had, been dead
for years but we saw her pale, pale face surrounded by wild
colored-Indian black hair pressed against the window pane. At
103 Soque, in the bedroom where 10 people slept, a square

hole in the ceiling. From that hole, one night, a man in white
floated down, ate the lightbulb, floated back up. Anthony and
Jeff, 20 years later, saw the lightbulb dance up and down.
Instantly sober they split. Some of this ain't acceptable.
Some of it *wasn't* acceptable. But we got a permit.
Now.

Fish said the man Jimmy saw, sitting over the middle of the well,
with no head was his great-granddaddy. He got his head cut off.

Near no ocean, just Russell Lake, the other side of and down
a steep mountain. Nothing to cause this fog. Thick, wet
blinding fog when fall softened the already quiet hill leaves
fell muffled & slow in animated fog. In that fog

they dream silence dreaming each other. In that fog, one
walked out alone at night, never told what she saw
but Miz Clio knew the fog in the trees, in & out the leaves,
winds with wordless voices, distinct, endless. The red dirt
hums, pine trees chant the background calling.
Red dirt reaches up, the trees down
meet in people's minds
in the same dream. Dreaming they are real.

Outsiders and foreigners from Atlanta claim disbelief.
Laugh at a big red apple for a downtown monument; say no
highways come near us so we don't exist to them who can't
touch a belief that recreates each other, each day and in sleep,
dream the same dreams.
Red dirt inflected pine trees scented dreams.

We shared dreams & short memories. dreams, memories and
amnesia. At the end of school we always "went somewhere"
a bus full of excited children in May headed to the
Indian Reservation in North Carolina
each time like the first time, except a few jaded ones
("Oh shoot! The Indians *again?*") but

WE   were a
reservation, on Cherokee land. On a beautiful hill of
apartheid, reserved for "the coloreds" and though
many of us honestly had Indian blood
we had short memories, dreams and amnesia.

The Cherokee *could* have traveled to Northeast Georgia
to see *us* making, not beads and moccasins, no Touristy
Attractive stuff, just inventing each other repeatedly on Soque
Street with names like Wolf. Drunk Dessa. Mr. Rat. Mr.
"Poppa" Doc. Mr. Jim Smith.
"The Elephant Killer," Miz Zelma. Miz Clio. To see our
ritual stompdowns you'd find Sally's Lunchroom,
Fred's Tavern or another juke joint way, way back
in the woods with permission (and a guide)
and then . . .

Miz Clio Savant

(1883–present)

It seemed like I was "chained and bound"
like that song says. Oh I listen to this
blues stuff if nobody is around.
Alone, I listen.

What *you* know about it? Nothing.

> By the time we got to Banks County, it
> was hard enough. Bad enough,
> leaving Charleston. But Jehru—
> my brother—had to leave for messing with
> the wrong man's daughter.
> And I was *some* tired riding, riding, riding that wagon up
> into pine trees, hills, mountains and a few funny
> talking people by the time we got to that
> hill in Cornelia,
> I told Jehru this was the place.
> If he'd do like I say this was it.

> Hot-hot that day, playing out
> back with my five sisters
> half naked too young to cover what
> we didn't have. And that raggedy doll two of my
> sisters fighting over, so hot it almost
> melt, I laughing, don't want that doll
> noway except to bury it maybe
> poke sticks in glassy no-color eyes
> another sister singing
> one just yelling like any other

summer day
but then I see
our momma sister, Aunt Zese
quiet-quiet in too much white
clothes she always wear
stand there, stare us silent;
silent too, my momma with her.
Aunt Zese point slow, raise her arm
her finger at me, "She the one."
I start crying
saying Momma it not me. It
them—making fight over ugly doll,
making noise, NOT me!

"Shhh," Momma say. "Come on in the house."
She look at my aunt—aunt look back
at her; nod. I go.
I go to Aunt Zese house and I—what I know—
almost ten. From that day,
that heat still on me now,
I live with my Aunt Zese, in her house, on her
island off Charleston.

When the moon full up we do certain thing.
Moon gone, sky dark-dark I
do other things
Aunt Zese tell me sometimes know
what to do without her.
I do what she say, and don't. I grow.
They say in town
Clio the one. She see she talk with
the Spirits.

Other full moons we dance. Aunt Zese
make the movements
my body follow words, chants
drums, not many
years later I am what
my Aunt Zese said. I was the one.
I am the one.

The men came, after the boys. They came,
when my aunt said and after
she gone, I stayed. The men came, with

drums, with words—
how I don't need no mo'
power except what I got
all over Charleston they wait for the
day I boat over to
see Momma, to market,
all the men wait &
watch me walk—women too.
They knew. I was the one.

And I could see, knew how I looked, coming and going
rich black skin, deep-set eyes full
lips; long, long arms and legs smooth walk so
there *were* men, on my island.
For the work, for the Spirits,
they came. They left but
Dina stayed.

Another hot-*hot* this one day I
had done all the things
fixed all and sent them home
so evening, night. I
listened to tree frogs talk to lightning bugs,
small waves slap
my porch; plenty stars but new moon, dark-dark
like I like it. I take a
deep breath and get comfortable to
set a spell when I
hear soft boat sounds, steady coming.
Who *now* I think, aggravated, who *now*
giving birth, bleeding to death, wanting
love fixed and a soft voice

"Clio?"
the way she said my name
asking, but telling me too.
I know her voice, her eyes, her thighs. She
dance the Spirits in too. Honey-sweet, her voice.
She came, soft, on my porch
stood quiet, look a question and answer
at me we neither one spoke I
stood. Went to her. Took Dina's hand.
Went in my cabin.

I was the one. She stayed and
we stayed like that for a long, long
time until she died. I would still
be there. Except for my brother, Jehru

was the reason I left. He, the only son,
after six girl-wimmin. He, with no
power except what little Momma had
left after us.
He claimed he was a seventh
son but he was not (I was the one). He
was just baby boy to us, and he stayed a
boy, a baby to me and because he
was a baby, and because I was the one, I
was the one got on
that wagon to save his trifling life.

Don't even remember why we headed for North Georgia
except it had to be a ways from
the two-headed doctor's daughter
and I had to go to
save his life. And brought the
Spirits saw this red dirt and mixed in.
Mixed me in with it. But I

was some tired, halfway
evil at first. This little no-sidewalk place
people in shacks and no conjure womon, except
one back in the woods, power shriveled up
but I paid my respects.
We live in the big yellow
house at the crossroads
of Second and Soque.

And I work them all. Got us all
dreaming the same dream like
Dina in my blood.
All I felt for my Dina, they feel for each other, and
other things I never felt for nobody. I fixed us
and anybody else come through here, too.

"Deacon J," my brother became and all anybody

said, except maybe Zelma and
two more, I was just "Deacon's sister."

My walk was the same
even if I went not much further
than church and back. My feet remembered
the drums, the ocean. There even was a few women
walked smooth like me—even
little girls—but no Dina. I talked to
the Spirits and haints all up on the hill.

It *looked* like I was bound, and chained.
My spirit, it was free.

*. . . and you are to hear these all speaking at once like somebody opened a tightly sealed
jar of peach preserves gone bad or a jar of wasps*

I always knowed Miz Clio was a bull dyke / uh huh, knowed she was funny / y'all
make me *tired.* just cause she didn't want nunna the sorry men y'all had / lot of nerve
she got! / it ain't her bizness to tell nothing / she ain't even *from* Cornelia / ANY of y'all
from Cornelia? man, you ain't nothing but a apple knocker, no way / and you just
a sooner, y'self. / if she just *got* to say something, I wish she'd tell / y'all just jealous.
always was. / me? me?! I could whup her ass right now she ain't nothing to me / Jealous? Jealous? What she got for us to be jealous of? / Well, she /

Anne Shelby

1948–

Teacher, activist, poet, and singer/songwriter Anne Shelby was born in Berea, Kentucky. Throughout her life, she has defined herself by her connection to home—and against that connection as well. Though she acknowledges the beauty of her rural Kentucky farmhouse and the historical roots that characterize her home, she does not shy away from writing about Appalachia's problems, past and present, including methamphetamine use, divisive politics, endemic poverty, and mountaintop removal coal mining.

Shelby has written children's books, plays, essays, and a collection of newspaper columns entitled *Can a Democrat Get into Heaven? Politics, Religion, and Other Things You Ain't Supposed to Talk About* (2006), a humorous account of life as part of a liberal minority in Clay County, Kentucky. Her collection of original children's tales, *The Adventures of Molly Whuppie* (2007), based on traditional eastern Kentucky folktales, received the Aesop Accolade from the American Folklore Society. For *Songs for the Mountaintop* (2006), a CD produced by Kentuckians for the Commonwealth to help fight mountaintop removal coal mining, Shelby composed "All That We Have." Through many mediums, Shelby asks her audiences to take an honest look at Appalachia, and to take action with her.

Shelby's poetry collection *Appalachian Studies* (2006), from which these poems are taken, includes detailed, perceptive descriptions of Kentucky people and landscapes. Her poems illustrate a love of Appalachia that celebrates homeplace and abides in the face of mountaintop removal coal mining and seismic cultural shifts. Shelby weaves the personal with the political, paralleling a grudging admiration of her own changing, aging body with the changing landscape and culture.

Appalachian Studies

What we propose to implement
is a large-scale multi-faceted
data-intensive resource-exhaustive
longitudinal interdisciplinary assessment
based on the utilization of
existing and non-existing data banks
for the identification of cultural,
environmental, socioeconomic and historico-political
factors that in conjunction tended to contribute
to a deviant oil to water ratio
on Teges Creek, Kentucky, in February 1983.

Well what it was
they was drilling up at Virgil's
and the well blew up.
And the creek turned yaller.
And a big lot of oil men swarmed in here
and give out a lot of red caps that said
SOMETHING OR OTHER PETROLEUM.
And if you can find one minner
in that creek, I will eat it.

Clyde Hacker Talks about Hog Meat

Now you can talk till you're blue in the face, drive
up and down this road ninety miles an hour,
shoot ever stop sign and cuss everbody
from here to the county seat.
It will not do you one bit of good.
They have got us right about where they want us.

I look at it this way.
Say you've got a hog out here you're fattening up to kill. First good
little cold snap, you're going to shoot that hog and kill it. Now are
you going to look that hog in the *eye*? Are you going to wonder
how the *hog* feels about it? No. For that would take all the enjoyment right out of eating hog meat. You've got to look at that hog
and see breakfast in the early stages. You've got to believe that a
hog is nothing in this world but lazy, nasty, dumb as a post or a
bucket of coal, and deserves just exactly what it gets.

Now I'm not saying we're a hog, boys,
but we been skinned a time or two.

Maurice Manning

1966–

A native of Danville, Kentucky, poet Maurice Manning connected early and deeply with the stories of rural life in eastern Kentucky that his grandfather shared with him. With degrees from Earlham College (BA), the University of Kentucky (MA), and the University of Alabama (MFA), Manning has taught in the creative writing programs at Indiana University, Warren Wilson College, and Transylvania University.

Manning's poems manifest a concern with nature and spirituality. In *Bucolics* (2007), which draws on the pastoral tradition in literature, the speaker, a shepherd, talks to "Boss," or God, about his place in the natural world. Additionally, Manning cites Whitman and Wordsworth as influences on his sense of the importance of the earthy and the everyday. His respect for the past is indicated not only by poems about historical figures but also by his use of old-fashioned terms, playfully illustrated in "That Durned Ole Via Negativa."

Manning is concerned with line and meter in poetry. The poems in *Bucolics,* for example, move from rough to smooth as the speaker becomes more attuned to the Boss. Manning has also devised a poetic form that he calls "honky tanka," a humorous reference to a traditional form of Japanese poetry.

IX

are you ever sorry Boss ever
have a problem ever get
shamefaced stuff your hands
in your big boss pockets
it's never easy is it Boss never
Boss ever get a slow start ever
feel like you're at the end
of the line the end of your rope
have you ever had it up to here
wherever that is on you I know
it's high up to your neck Boss
the top of your head you must
be tall to take it all the way
you do taller than the top
of the moon Boss O I wonder
what you see when you look up

XIII

are you ever in my chest Boss
are you ever in there with a hammer
tapping on my rib cage as if
you want to make a hum drum
right where I can feel it how big
is that little hammer anyway
does it have a silver head Boss
does it spark against my ribs
I know they're made of iron
I've got a heap of horseshoes
nested in my chest like heavy birds
Boss you make them sing you tap
away is one arm bigger than the other
from all that hammering you do
I wonder if you're knocking for
a reason are you just fooling Boss
or have you found a little door
O if it's really you I wish
you'd whistle through the keyhole Boss
I wish you'd lift my little latch

That Durned Ole Via Negativa

You ever say a word like *naw,*
that *n, a, double-u* instead

of *no?* Let's try it, *naw.* You feel
your jaw drop farther down and hang;

you say it slower, don't you, as if
a *naw* weighs twice as much as *no.*

It's also sadder sounding than
a *no.* Yore Daddy still alive?

a friend you haven't seen might ask.
If you say *naw,* it means you still

cannot get over him. But would
you want to? *Naw.* Did you hear it then,

that affirmation? You can't say *naw*
without the trickle of a smile.

The eggheads call that wistful, now—
O sad desire, O boiling pot

of melancholy pitch! Down in
that gloomy sadness always is

a hope. You gittin' any strange?
That always gets a *naw,* and a laugh.

I've had that asked of me. It's sad
to contemplate sometimes, but kind

of funny, too. It makes me think
of *git* and who came up with that,

and the last burdened letter hitched
to *naw,* that team of *you*s and yoked

together—the you you are for now
and the you you might become if you

said yeah, to feel the sag of doubt
when only one of you is left

to pull the load of living. My,
but we're in lonesome country now.

I wonder if we ever leave it?
We could say yeah, but wouldn't we

be wiser if we stuck it out
with naw, and know the weight of what

we know is dragging right behind us,
the squeak and buck of gear along

with us, O mournful plea, O song
we know, by heart, by God, by heart.

Jesse Graves

1973–

Jesse Graves grew up in Sharps Chapel, a rural community north of Knoxville, Tennessee, on land his family, of German heritage, had lived on for more than two centuries. Graves sees himself as belonging to perhaps the last generation of Appalachians still able to touch the region's rural heritage directly, and his poetry frequently explores the geography, history, and culture of the region.

Despite Graves's awareness of a changing mountain culture and landscape, his poems eschew nostalgia and overtly Appalachian tropes. They question what elements of Appalachian culture it may be productive to leave behind and what should be held on to while embracing the contemporary world. Graves identifies Walt Whitman and Robert Morgan as his literary influences, firmly grounding his poetry in the quotidian world.

Graves earned his BA and PhD from the University of Tennessee, Knoxville, and an MFA from Cornell University, where he studied with Robert Morgan. Recognition of Graves's work came early; he won the Weatherford Award in Appalachian poetry, given annually by Berea College and the Appalachian Studies Association, for his first book, *Tennessee Landscape with Blighted Pine* (2011). Graves became the first poet to win the Weatherford Award twice when his second book of poetry, *Basin Ghosts* (2014), was honored in 2015. Graves teaches English and is poet in residence at East Tennessee State University in Johnson City.

Digging the Pond

The vision must have come after rain,
a picture of water standing so deep
a house could hide under it.
He pushed and dug and cut through
scrub pines like they were tall blades of grass,
dragged orange clay from under the topsoil.

At thirteen, I mostly stood back and waited
for rocks to lug into the nearest gulley,
sinking my hands under the cool mud
so long buried, the runoff from two ridges—
we found an arrowhead the first day
and envisioned bone shards and lead slugs.

For years a hard rain would spill its banks,

and pond lilies would sheen it with yellow
through the warm months, before the drought
years and turtles did their work, and its water
looked like something caught in a rusted bucket.

When my father stands on the bank and talks
over what to do with the farm, he looks up
toward the ridge-line and down at cracked dirt.
He can name every species of tree, wild root,
the compounds of the soil in every field,
and knows that I stood off to the side too often
to learn what he was born knowing.
The doing and the undoing.
I can find in his face what he reads
about the future in the tea-colored water,
his eyes and mine trying to avoid it.

Mother's Milk

A couple of things she gave me:
powdered formula mixed with water
heated on a stove but held very near
her heart, she said, while I drank it;
the certainty that Jimmy Carter
should have been president for life
and that a yellow dog would be better
for poor people than Ronald Reagan.

By the time I was born, we had moved
back to Sharps Chapel and taken over
my great-grandfather's old house.
My mother directed the small ensemble
of our family: her kind sister, alone
with three kids in a falling-down house;
her uncle, speaking mostly to relatives
already dead; an aunt across the ridge
whose husband tried to shoot my brother.
My older brother and sister, crashing and
dreaming their way through high school.
My father parked his rig one day a week
to clear fields or fix the ancient tractor.
And me, the youngest by eleven years,
born in the vacuum of her father's early death.

I stepped out of the airport in Syracuse

into the first darts of a swirling snow
the whole western skyline dropping fast
back in lake effect country
$38 in my wallet
alone and wishing for home
Sunday after Thanksgiving

Once I tripped over a barbed wire fence,
both legs tangled between the strands,
six years old, struck down by the first
mountain 1 thought I could climb.
She carried me home, my shins wrapped
in a t-shirt and my ear close against her pulse,
tears starting to dry on both our faces.

A few other things she gave me:

an ear for slightly off-pitch singing
notes left lingering in throats
from Loretta Lynn to Lucinda Williams—

unwavering loyalty to women who wear
choppy haircuts and just-visible tattoos
and who pay half-interested attention to me—

an avalanche of love and kindness
the best preparation a man
can get for this world's embrace.

Ricardo Nazario y Colón

1967–

Writer, educator, environmental activist, and diversity coordinator Ricardo Nazario y Colón was born in the Bronx and raised in Puerto Rico and New York City. He received his undergraduate education at Fordham University and the University of Kentucky, graduating from the latter in 1992 after serving in the US Marine Corps. In 1996 he earned an MS from Pace University.

Nazario y Colón was a co-founder of the Affrilachian Poets. Although the term "Affrilachia" was initially coined by poet Frank X Walker to refer to African Americans in Appalachia, the word also describes a cultural space inhabited by people of many backgrounds living in the geographic region.

Nazario y Colón encourages readers to see connections between Puerto Rico and Appalachia, and many of his topics echo those found in much Appalachian writing—family, poverty, discrimination, and the beauty of the mountains. Since, furthermore, many Hispanics have immigrated to Appalachian communities such as Dalton, Georgia, Nazario y Colón's poetry underscores Appalachia's connectedness to the global community.

The following poems come from *Of Jíbaros and Hillbillies* (2010). The Puerto Rican word "jíbaro" originally referred to mountain dwellers; like words used to describe mountaineers in the United States, the term has had both negative and positive connotations. Nazario y Colón is active in the fight against mountaintop removal, and in 2011 he was appointed to Kentucky's Native American Heritage Commission.

In the Beginning

No matter how deeply you pick to the bone,
she is the color of copper.
Her distinguishing features are rugged,
tall and craggy.

Hers is a story written in sediment layers,
in circles beneath the bark of trees
and by the smoothing power of water.

She was there when the almighty sat down
to rest at Lebanon Valley, flattening her,
watched Mounts Washington and Mitchell
wear down to stumps prior to the passing
of the dinosaurs.

Opened up her streams for the brook trout
to escape the great freeze,
said hello to the Himalayas before
they were a whisper and bequeathed
Chomolungma the sky.

She watched animals become men
with erect backs and spines
and then built a great wall
to keep one another apart.

Before Persia swept across the Middle East
expanse and the Romans created a continent,
she stood watch over the Taíno, Olmec and Maya.

Before the Cherokee scratched her face,
her veins pulsed with coal.

Tujcalusa

In the west side of Tujcalusa,
country boys still say howdy and ma'am
and they tip their cowboy hats
to salute a lady.

This morning their daily ritual
was interrupted by a subtle nod
from a vaquero with his family.

The Copenhagen smiles disappeared
and memories of the running of the bull
across the deep South decades ago,
brought about a chill at the country store
we call K-Mart.

Alabama sounds Spanish to me
and Tujcalusa reminds me of Yabucoa,
Humacao and other aboriginal names
in Puerto Rico. The familiarity of these names
beckons me.

But this is the Deep South
and no matter how thirsty you are
or how warm it is outside,
it can be a cold place to take a drink of water.

Dalton

Carpet capital of the world, a growing community.
Small enough for the people to still be friendly.

With only one chapter of the council of concerned citizens,
a 21st century evolution of the Knights of the Ku Klux Klan.

A family oriented town filled with parks;
a lot of the charm left over from the good old days.

Along old Highway 41, a red-stenciled billboard
declares that, *uncontrolled immigration has raised taxes,*
crowded schools, lowered wages and working conditions.
Congress sold us for cheap labor.

A laid back town not too overpopulated,
with the right share of churches for any religion.

A place where the work ethic of America
is being reborn in the hands of southerners
who happen to speak Spanish.

With little snow and 85 degree summers,
close to everything including major cities.

This not so Pleasantville is being transformed
by Latinos who dared to live the dreams advertised
by the same people professing no dogs
and no Mexicans allowed.

Melissa Range
1973–

Poet and educator Melissa Range was born in 1973 and reared in Elizabethton, Tennessee. Range identifies as Appalachian but is pulled away from the region as well.

Among her degrees, Range has a master's in theological studies from Emory University, so her meditations on the qualities of faith carry as much depth of consideration as her musings on language and heritage. As she is not a member of an organized faith, her outsider's perspective permits her a certain latitude. Despite the pugnacity of "Ofermod," Range questions how people—mainly men—rationalize pursuit of spiritual ideals through warfare.

Stylistically, Range's poetry is a tour de force. The influence of Gerard Manley Hopkins shows not only in the careful craft of her lines but also in the playful and respectful ear she has for dialects, as shown in "Ofermod," which addresses, among other things, the nuances of Appalachian speech.

Scriptorium, from which "Ofermod" is taken, was a winner of the 2015 National Poetry Series. Range teaches creative writing and American literature at Lawrence University in Wisconsin.

Ofermod

"Now, tell me one difference," my sister says,
"between Old English and New English."

Well, Old English has a word for our kind
of people: *ofermod,* literally

"overmind," or "overheart,"
or "overspirit," often translated

"overproud." When the warrior Byrhtnoth,
overfool, invited the Vikings

across the ford at Maldon to fight
his smaller troop at closer range,

his overpride proved deadlier
than the gold-hilted and file-hard

swords the poet gleefully describes—
and aren't we like that, high-strung

and *ofermod* as our daddy and granddaddies
and everybody else

in our stiff-necked mountain town,
always with something stupid to prove,

doing 80 all the way to the head of the holler,
weaving through the double lines;

splinting a door-slammed finger
with popsicle sticks and electrical tape;

not filling out the forms for food stamps
though we know we qualify.

Sister, I've seen you cuss rivals,
teachers, doctors, bill collectors,

lawyers, cousins, strangers
at the red light or the Walmart;

you start it, you finish it,
you everything-in-between-it,

whether it's with your fists,
or a two-by-four, or a car door,

and it doesn't matter that your foe's
stronger, taller, better armed.

I don't tell a soul when I'm down
to flour and tuna and a half-bag of beans,

so you've not seen me do without
just to do without, just for spite

at them who told us,
"It's a sin to be beholden."

If you're Byrhtnoth
lying gutted on the ground,

speechifying at the troops he's doomed,
then I'm the idiot campaigner

fighting beside his hacked-up lord
instead of turning tail,

insisting, "Mind must be the harder,
heart the keener, spirit the greater,

as our strength lessens."
Now, don't that sound familiar?

We've bought it all our lives
as it's been sold by drunkards,

bruisers, goaders, soldiers,
braggers with a single code:

you might be undermined, girl,
but don't you never be *undermod*.

Rose McLarney

1982–

Rose McLarney was reared near Asheville, North Carolina. From an early age, she had a keen love for the mountains, which she credits in part for her decision to attend Warren Wilson College for both her BA and MFA degrees, where she has also taught. McLarney is a professor of creative writing at Auburn University. She has published two collections of poems, *The Always Broken Plates of Mountains* (2012) and *Its Day Being Gone* (2014), the latter of which won the 2013 National Poetry Series award.

Much of McLarney's poetry examines power, displacement, and change in Appalachia. Sometimes difficult, rough, and raw—but always rewarding—the poems suggest that these problems are not just Appalachian but global. Far from providing easy answers about the role of Appalachian insiders and outsiders, McLarney asks how readers themselves—even Appalachian people—might be complicit in exploitation. Furthermore, as evidenced in "Cakewalk," which appears below, McLarney's poetry addresses a panoply of issues that affect people in the mountains and beyond.

Cakewalk

Pound, foam, sponge, sheet, chiffon, velvet,
devil, angel, gold, lightening—
so many kinds of cake.

Layered, jelly-rolled, spring-formed, Bundt-shaped,
petit-four-sized, liqueur-soaked, baked upside down.

Imagine them all ringed around one room.
    ✦

And a cakewalk commencing in it.

How long the walk would be.
If the size of the circle were to encompass
all the exhibits of how people have kept on

sifting and separating, whisking and folding—
such fuss—to raise something fine up
on a cake stand, no crumbs
on the frosted surface.
    ✦

My elementary school held cakewalks.
People orbited the gymnasium,
over red goal lines, under pink crepe paper,
accompanied by fiddle.

If I had gotten to play, I would have
moved across that floor praying
for a very particular fate.

But my mother didn't want me to have too much
sugar. She wanted better. We single
our ones out. And so I stood on the sidelines,
separate, wanting.

I wanted the cake from Crystal's mother.
She decorated cakes at the grocery store.
She obscured cakes under piles of icing
that became full skirts into which
she inserted princesses' plastic torsos.

The icing was sugar whipped stiff
with lard.

At the grocery store today, I watched as a boy
bit only the icing off the top of a cupcake.
Then with his blue-dyed mouth he said,
"I don't eat the bread."

In the beginning one may make such claims,
believe it possible to live on cloudy stuff
floating above lack.

Above a mother's cart,
its half-price loaf.

Sometimes, Crystal would bring cake for lunch.

A decadent diet, I thought,
believing, then, in choice.

It was after weddings were called off
or expectations for a holiday were too high
that she'd come with her cake.

She didn't share.

Sometimes, she didn't bring a thing.

&

Once, when my mother wasn't watching,
my grandfather poured syrup on my pancakes,
in the proportions he saw fitting. He flooded
the plate. I drank from the lip.

The maple was artificial, I'm sure.
But the feelings in me were real—the realization
afterward, of excess, sickening.

&

At the cakewalk of all the kinds,
when the music stops

some would be in the position
to receive layers overrun with ganache and filled
with cream between, a three-tiered tower,
or a torte topped with fondant flowers.

Some would find themselves stuck
at milkless cake, eggless cake, or butterless—
a cake defined by what it lacks.

&

Somebody sent a stack cake
to the school. A country recipe,
cooked over wood, in cast iron,
served with sorghum—unrefined sweetener
poor families wrung from their own cane
once. The most unpopular contribution ever.

Nobody made the mistake
of bringing journey cake, a cornmeal round hard
as the travel it was made to bear
with the Shawnee, or some say Cherokee,
or some say slaves. The history is uncertain.

&

What is known for sure is that cakewalks come from
plantations, performances slaves were forced to put on,
parading in front of their masters.

So how is it cakewalks are held at schools
and kids are brought to them, happily?

    ❥

So many things, you aren't told for a while.
Parents put candles on birthday cakes
for a while. No matter if wishes can be.

No matter the trailer from which they may come,
to which classmates will have to go
if there is a party.

Trailer they make fun of for years after.
Your daddy fixed that hole in the wall yet,
or does he like looking at you?

    ❥

Crystal never attended a party.
Neither should she ride

with her daddy, she told the bus driver,
when he was waiting for her after school in his truck.

But she went somewhere with somebody.
I saw one "Missing" notice,
and never her again.

    ❥

"Some kinds, you can't help,"
my grandfather would say
when my mother gave me cans
for the food drive, coins for some raffle.

How harsh he used to talk
of others not light as white cake
and himself, and at least as rich.
How hard was his voice, the slam of his hand
on the table where grandmother served him.

In his 90s, mostly he keeps quiet.
Or he compliments my mother and me.

We cannot help but love him
and make square cakes he prefers.

    ❥

My favorite birthday cake ever
was one that cracked.
I placed toy animals careening
into crevasses, called it earthquake cake.

It was run through with faults,
but I didn't know to see it that way.

That particular day, my mother
wanted me have a celebration,
and I did.

    ☙

Some cooks don't give up their efforts,
though their good is of the smallest sort.

Crazy cake, depression cake, war cake—
these arose from food shortages
(no milk, no eggs, no butter),
as fortunes and bombs fell.

    ☙

We bake him square cakes because
the most icing can be applied to that shape.

And because the old tongue unlearns tastes,
becomes simple. Sweet is all
grandfather can sense now,
palate turned back to a child's.

Which does not mean anything will ever be easy
for him again, or hasn't been worse for others,

or that it would be better if we did not
want to cut for our kin, for our closest,
the caramel-coated slices from all four corners.

Crystal Wilkinson

1962–

Reared by her grandparents on their farm in the Indian Creek community of Casey County, Kentucky, Crystal Wilkinson writes fiction, poetry, and essays about the rural and small-town experiences of African Americans in the late twentieth and early twenty-first centuries. Wilkinson's exploration of this overlooked element of the contemporary African American experience places her in a group of Kentucky artists associated with the Affrilachian Poets, of which Wilkinson was a founding member. Inspired by poet Frank X Walker's concept of "Affrilachia," an acknowledgment of the African American presence in and influence on Appalachia, Wilkinson and her colleagues have explored African American connections to rural and small-town places, families, and communities. Wilkinson's work includes two volumes of short stories—*Blackberries, Blackberries* (2000) and *Water Street* (2002)—and a novel, *The Birds of Opulence* (2015).

Wilkinson's artistic endeavors complement her teaching of creative writing, a mainstay of her professional life that has underpinned her career in public relations and literacy promotion. Trained as a journalist, Wilkinson graduated from Eastern Kentucky University in 1985. In 2003, she completed an MFA at Spalding University, allowing her to expand her teaching from the public schools to college classrooms. Wilkinson has served as the Appalachian writer in residence at Berea College, taught writing and literature at Spalding University, and operates Wild Fig Books and Coffee in Lexington, Kentucky.

Tipping the Scales

Josephine Childs was a big woman. She stood up around five foot eleven and weighed round two hundred and fifty pounds. She wasn't sloppy fat though, just big, solid. Anybody who thinks big women can't get no man just needs to sit down and chat with Josephine. She's sure had her hands full in the men department most all her life. Josephine came into this world on the edge of a storm and them rain clouds followed her round for years. And all Josephine's children was brought in the world pretty much under the same circumstances that she was born into. Miss Ethel Childs, Josephine's mama, was sneaking round with Edgar Walls, a mortician that traveled handling the black folks' dead kin in about three or four little towns clumped together, when she came up with the bun in the oven what turned out to be Josephine. Edgar was already married and had three full grown children back over in a town called Middleburg when Miss Ethel gave him the news. He built Miss Ethel a house right outside of Stanford, where she lived for her to raise Josephine in as long as she never said a word about him being the daddy.

Now in them times having a baby outta wedlock carried more seriousness than it does today. The whole town bout tipped over with everybody traveling to the edge of it to see what Ethel Childs was a-doing. Lotta folks went to they grave worrying and fretting cause they couldn't crack into Miss Ethel's business. Course Edgar snuck in and out of that house for years seeing Miss Ethel and Josephine on up until he died without a soul knowing it. Even said he loved them but just never had the with-it-all to leave his wife. Miss Ethel died when Josephine was twenty-five and she set up housekeeping just like her mama.

Josephine started having babies to have something for herself. Her mama always belonged to her daddy and her daddy was somebody else's husband and somebody else's daddy most of the time, which didn't leave much for her. Now as far as why she was hell bent on having men that always belonged to somebody else, I guess that's all she had ever known or maybe all she thought she deserved.

Her first child, Clifford, was by a man down in Calvary who was engaged to be married. His name was Cleavon, I think, well don't matter too much what his name is now. He met Josephine down at The Brown Diner, that's where she's worked all these years as a waitress, from six in the morning to two in the evening most every week day. Cleavon, or whatever his name was, was in town with the state people, building the new highway. He and the rest of the highway makers came into The Brown bout everyday for lunch for a month. Josephine was eyeing him so he started eyeing her back. They had made waitress to customer conversation, you know the kind all waitresses make just to make sure they get a tip. So Josephine already knew most of the man's business. She knew he was from up Calvary. Knew he was engaged and how much he loved his wife-to-be. But she just kept on making eyes at him and then toward the end of the month when they was getting ready to finish off the high-way, she wore a real low-cut dress to The Brown, not exactly the kinda outfit that a woman should be waitressing in but Josephine knew what she was doing. When she practically laid her big double-D breasts out on the man's plate it was more than he could handle, wife-to-be and all. So Josephine scribbled her address on a napkin and Cleavon made his way to the edge of town for a visit. Now I'm sure it sounds strange to you but Josephine was twenty-five and her mama had just died and she hadn't never had no man. She tried to tell Cleavon that when he mounted hisself up on top of her, slurping, hungry for them big double-Ds he had seen a peek of. But he had left all his tenderness back in Calvary with his wife-to-be and wallered all over her real rough-like. I guess like a man who's told a woman he's engaged to be married and she keeps on after him anyway. Josephine cried at the pain in her body and the pain in her heart. Cleavon went on out the door, packed his bags and left even before the highway was made. He had made enough in Stanford, I guess. All that wallering, mean-style, had made Clifford. When Josephine got her belly full, the town bout tipped over again with all the folks bending their ear toward her door to try and find out her business. Didn't nobody know nothing but the highway makers and by the time Clifford was bout to come they was long gone. Word through the town was that she was her mama made over. The Browns what owned the diner didn't fire her though. They knowed she needed the money with a brand new baby. Josephine kept on waitressing til she couldn't stand no more, had the baby and came on back to work in four or five weeks just as soon as she got her baby with a sitter.

Josephine's milk barely had time to dry fore she was back at it again. Same story. She hooked herself up with some businessman in a suit that grounded hisself for a week on his way to Tennessee. Couldn't even tell you his name, cause I couldn't pronounce it when he was here. He sure was a good-looking something though. A flashy man glittering and flittering round like gold. Rings on most his fingers. Always running his hand through his slickered back hair. Didn't look like no black man we'd ever saw, though he claimed he was. By Wednesday of the week he stayed, he had moved on in with Josephine. He was a gentle lover and although he didn't have no love in his heart for the woman, he didn't want to leave no woman he had breezed through on this earth to ever say he didn't do nothing for em. To him, love making was an art. Josephine's body was a canvas and he was the brush, painting her up one side and down the other til she fell off to sleep. Now why Josephine got all teary eyed when he left, I don't know, cause she knew he was just passing through on his way from here to there, but she shed tears anyway. He took her into town on Saturday night, draped across his arm. They danced to the juke box in The Brown in front of everybody. He kissed her full on the lips and all the women in the restaurant sucked in air. He took her home, painted his most breathtaking picture and come morning he was a breeze in the wind. That breeze left behind Goldean nine months later, a beautiful girl child indeed.

Don't get me wrong, now. Mixed round among all this cavorting, Josephine was a good mama. She always had them babies shining—took them to church, even with all the stares—and hurried home to them every night after she got off at The Brown.

After the one's name I can't pronounce, Josephine settled down a bit. Men would shoot her feisty looks and she wouldn't take them up and all kinds of men came through The Brown traveling down the new highway but she didn't give none of them the time of day. I guess it was two or three years til she got up with Jewell Barker and started shaking his tree behind a closed door.

Jewell Barker was a married man and to make things worse he lived right in Stanford. Josephine saw him and his wife, Maylene, every Sunday in church. She eyed them often, not cause she was after Jewell, but because she was envious of the love they seemed to share. He always had his hand at his wife's waist or she would notice Maylene pat his knee. But all that changed when Josephine's washer went out. Mrs Brown down at the diner told her to call Jewell Barker cause he owned a fix-it business and could fix most anything. And I guess he could. He went up to Josephine's house three times with four different parts for that washer and by the fourth time he had fixed it all, including Josephine. At first Josephine wasn't paying Jewell no mind at all. She hummed herself through her evening chores, cooking supper, reading a bedtime story and putting the kids to bed. Every night, after she put the kids to bed was her time, she let her hair fall down round her shoulders and put on a long purple housecoat that come down to the floor. The first night Jewell had seen her in the doorway, her hair all down hitting against that purple, he was hooked. It just took her a little longer to get hooked on him. In fact, she thought Jewell wasn't much a man at all to look at. He was a lot shorter than her, a small man, and talked real quiet and stuffy-nosed like. The only thing she saw in him was his gentleness with his wife.

"Josephine, I'm sorry to have to bother you again, but I'm gone have to come back tomorrow evening with another part," he said his voice a whining and wheezing. That was on the third day.

"Seems like I ain't never gonna get to wash up all these clothes. Now is this thing gonna work again or not Jewell, am I gonna have to get another one? How much is this costing me?" she snapped back, her hands on her hips.

"Don't worry Josephine," he said back, "I promise you I won't charge you anymore for the labor just the parts."

After he got her mind at ease bout the finance of it all, he got to working on her steady.

"All of us at the church was real sorry to see Miss Ethel go a few years back."

Josephine knew he was lying cause didn't nobody in town like her mama, but just that he was trying softened her heart a little.

"Yeah, I still miss mama like it was yesterday. Have some coffee, Jewell?"

They sat awhile at the kitchen table, her getting a chance that she didn't get too often to talk about the goodness of her mama, him soaking in all the joy she had in her that she don't show to nobody. They talked way up til the morning. Jewell rubbed his hand cross her face and left. He told Maylene that he got an emergency call over in the next county and had been up all night, fixing a furnace trying to keep somebody's young-uns from freezing to death.

The next time Jewell came through Josephine's door the spare part sat on top the washer and they talked some more. He even played with Clifford and Goldean before they was put down for bed. After the kids was asleep, Jewell worked his way from his side of the couch down to Josephine's, before she knew it, like men do. He ran his hand through her hair and around the back of her neck and pulled her down to him. She didn't even attempt to resist. He kissed her long and slow, a soft kiss, til they was both in the world they had made. He kissed her neck and put his arms around her as far as they could reach. "Jewell don't you think you need to be heading on home," formed in her brain to say but the words got lost in the kindness of Jewell Barker's eyes. She tried to think bout all them things she knew to be true. He's married. He's short and little. His voice always sounds like he's full a cold. But before too long she had grabbed Jewell by the hand and led him down the hall to her bedroom. When they laid longways so the right parts were meeting, Jewell's head rested right at Josephine's breasts and his feet hit at somewhere up round her shins but none of that mattered. Jewell kissed her breasts like they were her lips and Josephine moved Jewell around on top of her where she wanted him to go. It felt nice to her to be in charge of a man, even under these circumstances. Jewell kept lying to his wife, coming by Josephine's, fixing things two or three times a week, Josephine a throwing him all over that bed, and they both getting just what they needed out of it. I guess it took two or three months fore Josephine's monthly stopped again. Jewell quit coming by in the late months but started back up again after Steve Edward was born. Things wasn't the same at first but soon they fell into a pattern. Jewell came by on Mondays and Wednesdays and dropped off a little money and stayed a little while. Just long enough for the kids to get to sleep and to let Josephine throw him around on the bed, if she wanted to.

Josephine was still working at The Brown but the Browns like everybody else in town was starting to look at her even more funny. They let her stay though cause she needed the money. Three kids now by three different daddies. Two of them a mystery and a third by a breeze in the wind that had a name couldn't nobody pronounce. Things was getting kinda rough for Josephine with four mouths to feed now including her own. The money that Jewell was dropping off and her wages at The Brown together wasn't enough to keep up with the bills. Course her house was paid off, her daddy had took care of that, but there was still the lights, water and gas and all not counting the phone, groceries and her climbing day-care bill. So when George Elvis started sniffing round The Brown after her, flashing wads a money he done won shooting craps, it wasn't hard deciding what to do. Josephine took up with George Elvis quick. He was tall, taller than her. Stood about six-four, slim, a light-skinned man. Bits of gray sprinkled all through his hair, even though he was round the same age as her. George was the kind of man that took up a whole room when he walked in it no matter how big it was. And when he walked in The Brown flashing money and set his sights on Josephine, he swept her on up with the rest of the room without anyone knowing but just them two. George Elvis was known in town as a ladies' man. Was all time juggling two, three women at a time and Josephine knew it. But in no time he was out at her house ringing her doorbell at midnight after his Friday night crap shooting. First time he came wasn't no games played. He walked straight on in her house like he owned it, laid two hundred dollars out on the table in a fan and said to her with matter-of-fact in his voice, "Here is some money for you and your babies like I promised, now how bout showing some appreciation to ole George Elvis." He walked round Josephine like a cougar stalking deer meat and came up on her from behind rubbing all he had up next to her. She could smell beer and cigarettes stale on his breath but it was nice to have a take-charge man again. And charge he took. Josephine was so used to Jewell's kind of loving that when George Elvis flipped her cross the bed she was kind of shook up at first til she felt his tongue moving, beer, cigarettes and all, round in her mouth. George Elvis made love to her strong and good and would never stop for nothing til she said his name.

Mondays and Wednesdays still belonged to Jewell and Fridays was George Elvis's. They all three had an agreement. George Elvis agreed to do whatever the hell he wanted and come see her on Friday nights after his crap shoot. She kept her Fridays clear and he kept the money coming in. He didn't even know that Jewell Barker was the other man and really didn't care. He had more women than enough. And Jewell Barker agreed that long as he dropped by twice a week or so and let Josephine throw him around on the bed, the way she had when they was making her third child, then he didn't have to worry about his wife, Maylene, finding out or make no real child support payments. Josephine just agreed to do whatever it took to keep both her men happy and be able to feed her children, pay her bills and grab a piece of happiness for herself now and then.

The problem with all this was that Josephine's pieces of happiness was getting smaller and smaller all the time. Her kids were getting older and she wanted to give them something sides a Monday/Wednesday daddy. And she wanted more than a Monday/Wednesday/Friday man. She would see Jewell and Maylene in church every Sunday and long for what they had. Course he played Maylene like a fiddle, but she wasn't talking bout that part. Jewell didn't hold her at the waist like he did Maylene. Not that she wanted Jewell to be the one doing the holding. It's that she wanted somebody to really love her all out in the open like that. Most time now when Jewell made his trip over, Josephine would just sit and stare at the floor. Jewell would motion his head toward the bedroom and she would shake her head, no, and he would go on home to Maylene. And George Elvis was one of them men that didn't see love in no woman. Just saw a contest. Saw making love kinda like setting a record. He worked and sweated and poked, kissed, prodded, rubbed . . . whatever he had to do to please a woman and when he got done and she called out his name, he was ready to go find the next one. Josephine got to the point where she got to moaning and groaning on George Elvis soon as he got started, just to get him out the door quick.

She went to spending more time with her kids. She let 'em stay up later cause there wasn't no need in rushing them off to bed. Sometimes they was all up playing when George Elvis would come over on Friday nights. He would leave and Josephine was glad that he did. Only thing that bothered her was the money part and she figured she'd find a way.

Jewell started just coming by on just Mondays and when he came, he'd come early and spend most all his time playing with the kids, specially Steve Edward.

Josephine started working overtime at The Brown on weekends to try and make ends. And I guess it was a good thing cause if she didn't, she never would have met Ashe Yerby. Ashe Yerby was a broad-chested, stout, long, brown-skinned man with a voice so deep a body could fall right in it. He worked for the sewing factory and had got transferred from way down in Alabama to the Stanford plant. He came by bus one Saturday morning and stopped at The Brown for a bite of breakfast. Josephine served Ashe without a notice, filling his coffee cup, giving him some more eggs and gathering up her tip when he left. Ashe returned for lunch and set at the same table. He asked Josephine directions to an apartment he'd called about. Words danced out his mouth like thunder and Josephine didn't even notice. She scribbled directions on a wet napkin and kept on going.

"Ashe Yerby, I'm moving here to y'alls town," he says extending his hand out toward Josephine. "I'm new to round here. New to Kentucky."

"JosephineChildsWelcometoStanfordWelcometoKentuckyWannahearthespecials?" she said shifting from one of her hips to the other trying to get some relief down to her feet. She ignored his outstretched hand.

"Okay, let's hear em," Ashe said, trying to smile through Josephine's sadness.

"Yourchoicefriedchickenordeepfriedshrimpwithcoleslawfrenchfriescornbreaddessertanddrinkfourninetyfive," Josephine said like a menu-machine. No smile, no nothing.

Ashe ordered the special and watched Josephine work.

He moved in his new apartment so he got to cooking for hisself and didn't go to The Brown no more, but most every weekend he could see Josephine coming and going to work right past his window. He'd never seen a big woman move so smooth, like she floated by his window and he wanted to know more about her. But he tried to put her out his mind. She was so dry, hateful almost, and he came here for a job not no woman.

All the women round town, single and married, was a buzzing bout this new man from Alabama that done moved to Stanford. All kind of women got to strutting back and forth down the street right up in Ashe's window but he didn't pay them much mind. Josephine didn't pay them much mind either. She was either too tired from working overtime at The Brown or just too tired period to put another man in her mind.

The next time Ashe laid eyes on Josephine it was at church. Josephine came in with her children, each of them in a straight line following behind their mama like they had proper home training. They were all a sight to see.

Josephine settled herself and her young-uns in the pew. She looked straight ahead toward the pulpit when Jewell and Maylene walked in. It wasn't til the deacon called on visitors did Josephine really hear Ashe's voice for the first time. She was rested and peaceful in church with her ears wide open. Ashe stood up in the back of the church when visitors was called on and all the women in the church turned to look. Ashe's voice moved cross the church like a note in a jazz song.

"Just glad to be a member of this community and to be in the house of the Lord with you all here today. Thank you for having me." That's all he said but a feeling went out over the women in the crowd like ain't nobody ever seen. Josephine heard him loud and clear.

After church every woman alive was gathered round Ashe Yerby offering to bring him casseroles, cakes and cobblers, offering to help him with whatever he needed. And I'm sure each of them was serious as cancer bout what they was saying.

Ashe searched the crowd for Josephine but looked out and saw her and her children walking hand-in-hand away from him. "Miss Josephine," he hollered breaking away from the mob of church women. "Miss Josephine, wait." His voice, cool as water, bounced off Josephine's ears like springtime. She turned round and saw the whole women's congregation behind Ashe with their hands on their hips. "I just wanted to compliment you on the sight that you and your children are. They are the most well-behaved children, to be so little, I think I've ever seen and you are quite a vision, too."

"Thank you, Mr Yerby," Josephine said and kept on stepping, relishing the fact that he remembered her name. Ashe headed in the other direction, relishing the same feeling.

Ashe started hanging out at The Brown regular when Josephine was working. He'd sit at the counter and talk to her for hours between customers. He'd talk til his throat was dry then she'd bring him some ice tea or lemonade over and they'd talk some more. Jewell and George Elvis both noticed but couldn't neither one of them say a word. All them women in need of a man took notice too.

Wasn't too long til Ashe was picking up Josephine and the kids for long drives out in the country and taking her to work or walking her to work, depending on the weather. Two or three months went by fore Josephine really invited Ashe to her house. He came over for dinner, ate with her and the kids, helped her put them all down for bed and went home.

One night, fore things got too far down the road, Josephine sat Ashe down and told him bout her whole life. Told him bout her mama and daddy . . . all her babies' daddies, including Jewell Barker . . . Jewell's visits to see Steve Edward . . . George Elvis . . . and everything else there was to tell.

She expected to see his backside headed out the door after that long story but he pulled her close to him. Josephine opened her mouth for a kiss cause she knew he wanted to get some of her after hearing bout what everybody else done got but he just pulled her close and held her tight. "Damn, woman you been dragged down the river and back again, ain't you? Well, long as I'm living you won't go that way no more," was all he said. Josephine let loose of bout ten years of tears on Ashe that night. He held her and wiped her face and whispered cool words in her ear like a mama comforting a sick child. When she fell off to sleep, he stretched her out on the couch and covered her up. When Josephine woke up with panic in her eyes, Ashe had already got the kids dressed, gave them some breakfast and had her waitressing uniform pressed and ready.

On Monday nights, Ashe greeted Jewell Barker at the door, invited him in and told him that Steve Edward was waiting on him in the kitchen. Jewell was in some kinda shock but he visited with his son and left without a word to Josephine except, hello.

Guess six months had passed before Ashe really took Josephine in his arms. But when he did, they both was more than ready. He kissed her in tiny, soft kisses and long hard kisses, stopping to ask if she liked this or that. She did the same for him. They explored each other, stopping to check if each other was all right. He made love to Josephine like a man in love and that was something she had never had. They laid in a heap as high as love would stack up and when morning creeped in, Ashe had nowhere and nobody to run off to and they made love all over again before the kids got up.

Ashe and Josephine began to go everywhere together. They went to church, the grocery store and to each other's work, always with his hand at her waist. They sat in church and she patted him lovingly on the knee or held his hand. Every woman in all of Stanford went wild. It just didn't make no sense to them at all. So they would corner Ashe when he was by hisself and try to tell him some of Josephine's business, what little they knew. But he always knew bout what they was telling him and more so he'd shut them up quick.

Come the next spring, Ashe and Josephine got married at the church. The whole town turned out for the wedding just to see if it was true, some fine, hard-working man all out in the open with Josephine Childs and marrying her to boot.

Josephine was a vision sure nuff with her hair all down round her shoulders, joy pouring out her face and a great, long lavender dress touching the floor. She had both

Jewell Barker and George Elvis wanting to reach out to her, cause they was remembering old times, but they couldn't. And Ashe all dressed in white, a smile cross his face a mile long, his voice booming out vows to love Josephine forever. All three of her kids stood up with her, a sight to see. And the whole town bout tipped over with everybody traveling to the edge, bending their ears to the door.

Dorothy Allison

1949–

Dorothy Allison was born in Greenville, South Carolina, grew up in a working-class family, and was the first in her family to graduate from high school. At Florida Presbyterian College, she became involved in the women's movement and credits this political activism with her urge to become a writer. During the 1970s and early 1980s in New York City, where she had moved for graduate study in anthropology, Allison wrote for and edited feminist and gay and lesbian publications.

Allison's childhood experiences of poverty and sexual abuse, along with her commitment to feminism and the LGBTQ community, have informed her writing. *Trash* (1988), Allison's first collection of short stories, was awarded a Lambda Literary Award for Best Lesbian Fiction. Her first novel, the semi-autobiographical *Bastard out of Carolina* (1992), which earned her critical acclaim and was a finalist for the National Book Award, recounts the childhood of a girl who grows up in a dysfunctional family with an abusive stepfather. "Nice," the story included in this anthology, is a reminder that Florida is a destination for Appalachian out-migration.

Allison's staunch commitment to communicating hard truths and her position on sexuality put her at odds early on with some feminists and anti-pornography advocates. Nonetheless, she has remained devoted to feminism and asserts that her political beliefs are integral to her need to speak and write about her sexuality and upbringing.

A resident of northern California for many years, Allison has served as a board member of the Fellowship of Southern Writers.

Nice

I spent my teenage years in Central Florida, making fun of tourists and, whenever possible, profiting by their naivety and willingness to spend money on things we found laughably easy to provide. This mostly meant that while sitting with my homework, waiting for my mother to finish up her waitress job, I would happily give directions to wayward Yankees who had stopped in at the lunch counter to thirstily guzzle iced tea and try to read maps spread out precariously on damp tabletops.

"How far is it to Cocoa Beach?" a man with a bright pink bald spot would ask me.

"You can get there in an hour," I'd tell him. "Just take the expressway past the airport straight on till you hit the ocean." If he hadn't been quite so bleary-eyed, he would have seen the answer with one glance at the map. Orlando, Florida, was dead center in the flat pan of the state, and there were only two major highways, one running north and south from Tallahassee to Miami and the other criss-crossing from Tampa and St. Petersburg to Cocoa or Daytona Beach.

"Is it nice?" his wife would ask.

"It's very nice," I'd say politely though I was never sure quite what they meant by that question. Nice? Cocoa was a swampy bird sanctuary and desultory beach town, noted mostly for its proximity to Cape Kennedy where astronauts could be seen eating fried eggs served by women who looked and behaved just like my mother. It wasn't nice or not nice, it was just another place like Orlando where too many people had to make their living being nice to strangers with money.

Be nice, my mother would say.

"Nice" was a word my mother used just like the lady tourists, so I also knew there was another question they were asking. They wanted to know how clean and respectable the place was. Could you go there and not get robbed blind just for being from out of state? Would people treat you kindly? Were the motels the kind of place you could take your children and not have them catch some hideous disease from the water in the pool? Probably so, I'd think remembering when we'd gone to the beach with a cousin. Tourist traps were tourist traps. To keep pulling those flies in, the web had to meet a certain standard of benign hospitality. Nice was hospitable. Nice was what you wanted.

Telling tourists just what they wanted to hear meant that the "nice" lady or the pink-faced man would happily give me a quarter or buy me a counter soda—exactly what I hoped. If I had warned them that the motels' sheets were full of sand and that small armies of teenagers from Orlando regularly rented those rooms to drink too much Southern Comfort and throw up in the pool—well, they wouldn't have been so cheerful or generous.

It was best to be "nice" and reassuring, and smile gratefully when handed a little change.

"I'd like to do that some time," my mother would say when the tourists headed for their car and she collected her big old purse for our drive home. "Just take off and go. Drink iced tea at a lunch counter and decide what to do as I went along."

"Be a tourist?" I grinned at her.

"Not work, not worry. Vacation."

Vacation. It was a magic word, not a real possibility. My stepfather was a truck driver, a man who delivered uniforms and rugs to small businesses all over Central Florida. He was good at his job, but short tempered and prone to suddenly becoming unemployed. That meant we moved often and never had any savings. My mother was good at her job too, a hardworking handsome woman, who never expected much and knew how to make do when her expectations proved correct. She had worked as a waitress since she was fourteen years old, now and then taking off to be a cook or a fruit packer once we moved to Florida from South Carolina. She had never had the kind of job where you actually got to take a real vacation. Not working for my mother was a period of not earning money. Being laid off or out sick meant counting coins until she could get work again.

We were good people, nice in our own way, but we were not people who vacationed. I knew the difference even at eleven, twelve or thirteen. We were people who bought lottery tickets and dreamed of vacationing. We played "what-if?" without really expecting our fantasies to ever be made real. What if Mama hit big on Jai Lai? What if our uncle had another car accident and came to stay with us after he got his settlement check? What if some tourist fell in love with our mother's smile and left a fortune as a tip when he drove away in his little sports car?

"I'd go somewhere," my mother always said. "I'd do what everyone does. I'd pay some bills, but I'd use the money to do what I've always wanted to do. I'd be the one that someone else served a plate of steak and eggs. I'd sleep late, and let someone else make the bed. I'd sit in the shade and read paperback novels. I'd drink those fizzy drinks with the umbrella sticking out over the lip of the glass."

"You'd gamble," I'd tease her. "You would bet on race horses or play roulette." I was not sure just how you played roulette. My familiarity with that game derived entirely from James Bond novels, where he played baccarat and won thousands of dollars on the turn of a card. But I didn't know how to pronounce baccarat, so I said roulette and watched my mother smile.

"I would," she'd admit. Then she'd walk down the side of the highway to the liquor store where she could buy another lottery ticket and a dream.

When I was thirteen years old, my mother's bowling team won the Panhandle Bowling tournament. The prize was a fancy matching bowling shirt for the team members, and a four-day passage for all on a cruise ship to the Bahamas.

"You're going on a vacation!" my sisters and I shouted when Mama called home to tell us the news.

"I am," she said into the phone. Her voice sounded thin and high and excited. "I'm going to be a tourist just like we always said."

Mama came home with brochures that showed the ship, gleaming white and black and layered as a wedding cake. Photos showed beaming couples sitting at big white tables with shining glasses raised to toast the captain who had stopped to welcome them aboard. The picture of the room our mother and stepfather would have was a marvel of grained wood and built-in storage spaces.

"It looks like the inside of Uncle Jack's RV," my little sister said.

"Think of it as a hotel room with an ocean view," Mama told us. "You look out that little round window and you can watch flying fish passing by."

We sat open-mouthed imagining our mother's prize. Flying fish and waiters in white tailored jackets, meals served twenty-four hours a day, deck chairs where she could lie back and sip something sweet and wonderful while reading her favorite book or just watching the sun travel across the sky. Our mother never just sat, never just laid back. She read her favorite novels at the kitchen table with a cup of coffee and bills spread out before her. She worked fourteen-hour days and got up early the next morning to make us lunches of pimento cheese sandwiches while smoking a cigarette and worrying about those same omnipresent bills.

I took the brochure to bed and dreamed of my mother dancing with the captain of the ship. He would fall in love with her of course, and steal her away from our stepfather to live on the ship and travel the oceans the rest of her life. She would come back only to collect us and install us in our own cabins right next to hers. We would take classes from tourist teachers and learn to eat Baked Alaska as if it were an everyday dessert like Jell-O or cake-mix cupcakes. What-if dreams comforted me all night long, and all the days till our parents left us with our cousin Bobbie while they went off to Fort Lauderdale to meet the ship. What-if dreams distracted me the long weekend while my mother did what she had never done—nothing at all that she did not want to do.

My mother came back pink-cheeked and quiet. My stepfather complained that their room had been so tiny, he couldn't turn around if Mama was standing up at the same time. The food was only so-so, and the Bahamas were full of people he wouldn't trust to serve him a cup of coffee. But Mama didn't complain. She had souvenirs for us, little dolls constructed entirely of shells just like the ones the tourists could buy at the gift shop just down from the diner where she worked. But these had been made in the Bahamas. A little sticker under the belled skirt said so, and the doll faces were honey-gold and dark-eyed unlike the blue-eyed dolls you got in Orlando.

"Was it wonderful?" I asked her early in the morning, as she was getting ready to go to work. I was sure it had to have been but I wanted to hear her say it. "Did you dance with the captain? Did you play roulette? Did you eat Baked Alaska?"

My mother put her arm around me and pulled me in close to her neck. Her whisper came down through my thick dark hair and seemed to reach right down into my insides. "I did everything you think," she said. "Everything."

She squeezed me tightly, so tight I knew to wait. She breathed in and out for a moment, her rough fingers warm on my arms.

"When you grow up," she began. But she stopped.

I tilted my head back to look into my mother's face. The sunburn on her cheeks burned in the bright kitchen light. She had pressed her lips so tightly together, her mouth was a strange flat line. Her eyes were looking out the curtains to the backyard, to the blue pan of sky where the sun was already burning.

"Mama?" I said softly.

It took her several moments to come back, to look down at me, to relax her mouth and shake her head and kiss my forehead before letting me go.

"You ever get to do something like that, you do it. You go anywhere you can. You see stuff. You do stuff. You be a tourist. You go on vacations." She nodded her head as if she were thumping her chin on the future.

"You go do it and see what it's like, you hear me?"

I nodded in reply and watched her tuck her cigarettes in her purse, stuff half the bills in there as well and take a final drink of coffee. The day was begun, we had to stop looking into space or talking or playing what-if. There was work to be done and no time to waste. There was barely a word till she was heading out the door to the Pontiac and another day of work. There she gave me one more quick embrace and reminded me sternly not to let my sisters out of sight till we were all safely on school grounds.

"Yes."

Her hand smoothed my hair and she smiled. "I saw a fish," she said. "I saw a fish flying past the little window. It was silvery and good luck. I knew it meant good luck, so I played blackjack with a real dealer who told me he could see the luck in my face. And I won, mostly."

She laughed then, a quick short laugh before I could ask anything.

"It was nice," she said. "It was really really nice."

Charles Frazier

1950–

Born in Asheville, North Carolina, Charles Frazier grew up in Franklin and Andrews, North Carolina, with two younger siblings, the children of educators. An avid reader, Frazier studied English and taught at the university level before devoting himself full time to fiction writing.

Frazier's first novel, *Cold Mountain* (1997), emerged from his intense research of his family's connections to western North Carolina, his own relationship to the mountain South, and the history and culture of the region. The novel quickly rose to the top of the *New York Times* best-seller list, won the 1997 National Book Award for fiction, and was adapted into a movie in 2003.

In 2006, Frazier published *Thirteen Moons: A Novel,* which is loosely based on the life of William Holland Thomas, a white friend of the Cherokee during the nineteenth century. In the excerpt below, Will Cooper, a white man who as a youth is adopted into the Cherokee Nation, is reluctantly forced to help round up Cherokee who have refused to comply with the US government's orders to leave their traditional homelands and move to Indian Territory in Oklahoma in 1838 and 1839 on the Trail of Tears.

The Cherokee Literature Initiative of the Museum of the Cherokee Indians in Cherokee, North Carolina, sponsored a translation of *Thirteen Moons* into the Cherokee syllabary by Myrtle Driver Johnson of the Eastern Band of the Cherokee. The initiative was established with grant funding from Frazier.

FROM Thirteen Moons

CHAPTER THREE

We left the horses tied a half mile down the river and moved up as quietly as we could through the thick ground layer of frosted leaves. Smith lay behind a blown-down hickory trunk glassing the camp. The other three boys were farther back in the woods, sitting with their muskets beside them. Two of them started loading pipes, tamping tobacco with their thumbs like filling a posthole. I looked at the final few leaves on the trees to see the way the wind moved, and then I looked at Smith, who kept his scope to his eye and made no attempt to keep the boys from lighting up, so I motioned back to them with both hands like pushing something down to the ground and they stopped.

Charley and his people had camped on a piece of land where two rivers joined together. It was a configuration of terrain that had an old appeal to the Cherokee and to the people before them. In the old days, they had usually built their mounds and villages in such places, both for practical reasons of defense and agriculture and flat ground for dances and ball games, and also because watercourses held spiritual import for them. I always thought it a sign of their generosity that they found water spiritual even in a land so wet that water is more often a nuisance than anything else.

An old hemlock grew on the highest part of this piece of land. Its stout trunk was still six feet through at head height, and the ground underneath would be soft, hundreds of years deep with a bed of its needles and the loose black earth into which the needles decay. Charley's people had built insubstantial shelters under the tree, a tentative-looking pole shed and an arbor, both lashed together with vines and roofed with brush and leaves and pine boughs. Provisional structures that would fall apart and melt into the ground in a few seasons. A dying fire sent up white smoke from its bed of ashes, and Smith said he could see muskets propped against the hemlock trunk nearby. Everyone in camp still seemed to lie abed, though the sun had been up for nearly an hour.

That worried Smith. He thought it was a ruse, and he began whispering about ambush and his plans to avoid it, all of which were unnecessarily complicated and impractical and based on the assumption that these baffled and powerless people—whose country had, as if by conjuration, dissolved beneath them and been reconstituted far off on some blank western territory—would put up a fight. I rose from behind the hickory trunk and started walking into camp, and as I went Smith was saying something to me in a hissing whisper inflected like he thought he was issuing orders. I looked back, and a vigorous plume of vapor puffed from Smith's mouth.

I went on and walked into camp and got between the people and their guns. I collected the two muskets, old worn trade pieces, where they lay propped against the hemlock trunk. They were loaded and cocked. I took out the caps and put the hammers down. I went and sat by one of the fires with the muskets on the ground beside me. There was a woodpile, and I stoked the fire and motioned for Smith and the boys to come on in.

They jingled and crashed and thumped their way into camp and everyone in the two shelters woke up and rose fully dressed. Charley walked partway to the fire and stopped.

—Hey, Charley, I said. Sit down here where it's warm.

Charley looked at the muskets on the ground and grinned and said, Hey, Will. He came over and sat down.

—I don't expect we're going to have any trouble here today, I said.

—No trouble.

The soldiers stood spaced out. They had their muskets aimed generally at the bunched people. I didn't know all the names. Just Charley and Nancy and their grown boys, Nantayale Jake and Lowan. And the boy Wasseton and the married daughter Ancih, and a few other women. There were several children, all wakening and hungry and crying. The women drew them together and the younger children stood behind the women and leaned out to look from behind the barrier of calico skirts that were thin and pale from long wear. Smith went and looked in the shelters for weapons and found none. He came back out and sent two of the boys off to fetch the horses.

I didn't see Ancih's husband and said so to Charley.

He said, George is out hunting. Gone two days.

—With anyone else?

—Maybe some others. Maybe alone.

I told Smith what Charley had said, and Smith said, We'll wait awhile and see if some more come in.

—They are not likely to come in if they see us, I said.

—They either will or they won't. We'll sit here today and start walking them out in the morning. And by the way, don't ever ignore my orders again.

I was fairly furious at his high-handed manner and the assumptions he was making about how the lines of authority ran within our little party. I started to remind Smith that I was not under his command and had not taken a cent in pay from the Government and would do as I pleased and call my own orders. I managed to hold my tongue but resolved within myself that all Smith had to do was utter one more word and I'd mount up and ride away and they could discover their own route out of the mazy mountains and wave hand signals in the air to communicate with their captives.

But Smith looked tired and white-eyed with fatigue and the nervous strain of this woods duty, which had been confusing and frightening to him. His fatigue made him look every bit as young as he was, maybe younger, and I remembered that he was so fresh out of school he still remembered how to read a little bit of Greek. I thought about the previous weeks of travel and camping, how Smith didn't sleep well in the mountains, jumping at every sound of falling leaf and foraging possum. Every morning he awoke twisted in his blankets, more exhausted than when he went to bed. I had once been like that myself. As a boy alone in the world, I slept best after the first grey of dawn began rising and dissipating the fear that collected in the dark. Now I found the woods narcotic. The blacker and noisier the better. Bear's old lessons in fearlessness and my own experiments in nightwalking had brought about the transformation.

I decided to exercise a certain amount of sympathy for Smith's nervousness and said, A day of cooking and eating and resting by the fire wouldn't hurt any of us. And then, in the casual tone of bidding good morning to a stranger you pass on the roadway, I said, Do not fear the universe, young lieutenant.

Smith did not have a response, and when the boys returned leading the horses, I turned my attention to the food. Smith and his boys had the inevitable potatoes and bacon, a partial sack of flour with little yellowish miller-moth grubs working in it, and a few bruised cabbages. I had a pannier full of my own stores, not caring much for army victuals. Cured ham, lard, salted butter, white cornmeal, dried beans, grits, dried apples and peaches, porridge oats, dark sugar, cinnamon, black tea, green coffee beans, and a small hand mill to grind them. Also a tin of ginger candies and a bottle of good Tennessee whiskey. And Havana cigars wrapped carefully in oilcloth.

I put Perry to work helping cook while the other two stood watch at the edge of camp. Smith sat looking at the fire in a daze. Charley's people went back into the shelters and talked among themselves, and then Charley and Lowan and Jake came and squatted by the fire. I roasted coffee beans and directed Perry in the assembly of a big pot of porridge with dried peaches minced in it and flavored with a profligate amount of cinnamon and dark sugar and butter. The children ate it and became all big-eyed with wonder at the taste, and the soldier boys, including the lieutenant, were not far behind in their appreciation. I took just a little of it in a tin cup, and mostly sat drinking coffee and enjoyed watching the people eat. All in all, it was a companionable breakfast. Charley and I talked and Smith sat listening as if he expected to catch a word now and then.

Charley said, Where we going?

—Where the Nation is going, I said. You live on the Nation.

Charley said, I'm abiding by the old lines.

—You've got to quit thinking that way, I said.

—Then where we going?

—Going west, I said. A long way.

Charley made an exhaling noise between his teeth and lips like a long string of F's.

Later in the afternoon, the soldier boys squatted on the ground, gambling penny stakes on tic-tac-toe, the grids scratched in the dirt with the point of a knife. Perry did not have a firm grasp on the logic of the game; otherwise no money would have changed hands as every game would end in a draw. As it was, he played as if the outcome were as random as casting dice or flipping a coin. He, of course, lost steadily and seemed to think the other two possessed enormous luck. After a while, I went over and said, Look, son. Put your marks where I say.

After a few games, with me whispering, Top left, bottom middle, Perry saw what he'd been missing. Goddamn, he said. There's nothing to it at all.

The Charleston boy looked at me and wiped the last grid away with a sweep of his palm and said, Hell, I could have won tobacco money off him from now on out, but you've boogered that all up.

Smith, of course, wanted to assign watches through the night. But I told him that he had not the least worry that any of Charley's people would make trouble, and besides, I'd about rather have Lowan or George cut my throat in mid-dream than sit awake in the long hours between midnight and dawn. So Smith assigned me the first watch, from just after sundown to bedtime, as if that had been his plan all along and my objecting to the watches had nothing to do with it. And Smith would take the last watch, from around four to sunup, which left those three boys to stand the worst of it. Smith reckoned to keep them awake two at a time, letting one always sleep, spelling one another every couple of hours.

Supper that night was beans and bacon and cornmeal mush fried crisp in lard. Charley's bunch mostly took their food to the brush arbors to eat, and maybe it was just the food but they seemed unaccountably happy. They talked and laughed and seemed able to let their larger circumstances not weigh on their thoughts for now. Content to let worrying wait for later.

The soldier boys ate their supper and then tried to get in an hour or two of sleep, but they just rolled around in their blankets and muttered to one another. Smith and I sat studying the fire and Smith had almost nothing to say. I left him and gathered a fist of cigars and the bottle of whiskey from my packs and went to Charley's fire.

They were telling tales, and I nodded at them to keep on with what they were doing. Sometime when no one was looking, George had slipped back into camp to share the fate of his wife and children. I passed out cigars to the men, and we lit them with a twig caught alight in the fire and passed the bottle around. Charley was doing most of the talking, telling a hunting story from the days of elk and bison, neither of which anyone in attendance but Charley had ever seen. He made them epic animals in his story, inhabitants of an old better world not to come round again. He then told about his lost farmstead at the old mound village of Cowee, before one of many disastrous treaties had driven him and his family west to Nantayale. At Cowee, he had been noted for his success with apple trees, which over the years he had planted at the spots where his outhouses had stood. Apples grew on his trees huge as dreams of apples. That Cowee house was old, from the time when they still buried dead loved ones in the dirt floor, but Charley could not remember exactly whose bones had rested near as a lover beneath his low sleeping platform. Then, without transition, Charley told how Nancy tailored his pants. She would have him lie down on his back on a smooth patch of bare dirt outside their door. She would take a stick and trace the outline of his lower body as children trace their hands. When she was done marking, Charley got up carefully, and Nancy would scribe lines to show his waist and the bottoms of his pantlegs. Then she'd lay out pieces of rough wool or linen she had loomed herself and scissor two pieces to match the pattern on the ground and stitch them together. In Charley's telling, it was a miraculous process, at the end of which he suddenly had new pants.

And then Charley told a new story from the past month, another hunting tale. He had been out alone under a low sky, moving up a narrow cove north of here into a deep closed landscape, a cut in earth so sharp he sometimes had to walk the creek like it was a trail because the cove walls narrowed and rose straight from the lapping water of the creek edge. He had a sort of lidded forage basket or creel woven from oak splits on a strap across his shoulder, and when he came to a place where the cove widened and there was a flat woods floor for a stretch, he looked about at the dry stalks and frost-burnt leaves of low-growing plants. He stopped and got down on his knees and dug in the black ground with a stick and then with the tines of his stubby and spatulate fingers, the knuckles swollen like galls in a blackberry cane. He didn't use the broad-bladed knife or the hatchet that hung in leather scabbards from his pantwaist, though they would have made the job easier. They were each sharpened keen enough to shave his forearm bare, but he would rather damage his hands than his tools.

He dug elbow-deep in the dirt and then came out with a root, pulling it from the ground as if he were a fisherman with his hands plunged in muddy water grabbling out a heavy and reluctant catfish. His catch went into the creel with its fellow roots, and Charley closed the lid as if they might otherwise escape. Some would be for eating. Some for making tea. Some for medicine.

He stopped at midday and struck up a small fire from pine shavings and oak sticks. He boiled creek water in a kettle and set it off the fire and steeped rounds cut from a piece of ginseng root. When it had made tea, he drank it out of a tin cup he kept tied to his rope belt with a smaller loop of rope. That was his dinner.

Charley sat by the fire a long time thinking about food. The trees were nearly empty. The thorny chestnut husks had fallen and the nuts had been eaten every way there was to eat them. Raw and roasted in the fire and made into bread. The leaves of the poplars and maples and chestnuts lay on the ground, and at night the bare limbs cast jagged moon shadows across the rocks of the river. Just the oaks held out against the cold with a few yellow-brown leaves left rattling in the wind. Wasseton had darted all the squirrels within a mile of the camp with his blowgun. Their slim charred bones and tiny skulls were mixed with the white ashes of the fire pit. Also the long column of spine and the many curved keen ribs of a big rattler that Wasseton had hit right in the soft underside of its head as it rose up in striking posture and then finished off with thrown rocks until it lay twisting, head crushed, in the leaves. There seemed to be few turkey or quail or even songbirds left in the woods. No hares or coons. The horses were long gone—traded to Axe, first one and then the other— during late summer and early fall. All they had brought in the trade was a puzzlingly small quantity of beans and cornmeal and a few pumpkins and cabbages. At this precise moment of the fall, since the beginning of known time, passenger pigeons had arrived in great clouds, their masses like a dark river flowing southward down the sky, settling into the bright-colored woods for a few days like a dense grey fog of bird meat. And in the past, Wasseton would dart them out of the trees with his long blowgun until the muscles of his diaphragm and stomach became weak from the effort of deep and sharp exhalations, and his six hickory darts became heavy and dark with blood all the way to the thistledown fletching. He could reliably drive a dart through a pigeon's head at nearly the distance he could throw a rock. But this year the pigeons came only in ones and twos, and then after a few days they were suddenly gone altogether. All Wasseton could provide for the group was one feast of birds roasted over coals. For the children, one little leg apiece like upside-down water drops of meat. Small split breasts and bony backs for everyone else. Then, only a day later, nothing but watery grey soup of feet and necks and gizzards. The woods refused sustenance. One day, all anyone had to eat was a clear broth made from a single goldfinch, so dilute you could have gotten as much flavor from dropping a stone into the water.

Though Lowan and Jake and George hunted daily, they had failed to kill a deer for the better part of a month. All the meat left now was a little venison jerky, just tag ends and scraps that served no purpose beyond flavoring a pot of cornmeal soup. Charley remembered that last deer, a fat buck. Half of him they'd eaten fresh, and half of him had been shaved into thin strips and hung from drying frames to jerk near the fire. Charley had gone out of camp to piss one night, and as he came back the hanging meat with the firelight coming through looked like bloody curtains. Before sunrise three mornings earlier, Lowan had killed a possum with a pouchful of babies. They stewed her and roasted the little ones on sharpened sticks over the fire, and the little ones were hardly a mouthful apiece. And that to feed a dozen people. The women and children had no energy and they hardly spoke. They spent most of the days sleeping under the brush arbors or sitting wordless by the fire. Winter was falling soon, and they would need more shelter. If they were this hungry now, just after the fall of leaves, what would it be when the Bone Moon came? Beyond looking for a cave, Charley had no plan for winter. The days of the year were too evasive for planning. They fled shapeless before him. The future held no hope. And he had already abandoned fearfulness. All he could do was exercise an attitude of still acceptance.

Charley's fire would have fit in his pair of hands, and when it began dying he covered it with dirt, for it is a bad and unbalancing thing to put out fires with water. He walked away from the creek and began climbing a dry ridge to cross over to another cove whose creek he figured to descend toward the river and the camp. As he walked, he scuffed his feet in the deep leaves just for the companionship of the rustling sound. The poplars, simplified by having shed their broad palmate leaves, stood as bright vertical slashes against the brown hillsides. Charley curved around a cropping of rock and climbed steep to the crest of the ridge and then pitched down the sharp slope toward the next creek. There was a joy in descent, in suddenly finding the pull of the earth acting consonant with your needs. He barely took note that the sky was closing down over him, becoming a grey press of moisture.

It began raining hard, straight down, as if the air had turned to water. All he could do was squat under a stand of rhododendron with his blanket over his head and wait. For a while the long glossy leaves turned water away from him, and then suddenly they did not. Water fell in runnels from the leaves onto the chalky ground litter under the shelter of the rhododendron and pooled at his feet. Charley's blanket and clothes became heavy and sodden. Then, at the point when he became wet to the skin, the rain tapered away to nothing but dense fog.

Charley rose from under the rhododendron and twisted the water out of his blanket and set out again downhill through the foggy dripping woods. He walked at a smart pace, and before long came to the creek and turned downstream. This was not his home country, and he did not yet know it well, but he reckoned he could reach camp and the heat of the fire long before dark.

Deep woods are haunted places in the fog. Light comes from everywhere at once, shapes shift, and sounds are muffled and magnified unpredictably. As Charley walked, he began to feel a presence in the woods, a sense of being watched from out of the fog. He spun and looked behind him and saw the blurred black shape of what might be bear at the edge of vision. If so, it stood square to the ground looking his way, motionless. It was probably a tree stump or a wet rock.

Charley started walking downhill again, and the fog thickened as he descended into it. He was partly blinded. The big trees were visible only halfway up their wet trunks, and the creek was a muffled rush off to his left. He could not even see the far bank, just a ribbon of dark water and the mossy rocks rising from it. All color was damped down to shades of grey. The passway lay narrow and slick underfoot, and his best idea for navigation was to keep the creek within hearing to his left and not climb any ridges to the right. By doing so, even a blind man would strike the river eventually.

He walked on down the winding creek, passing a white cascade and a deep black pool. But the thought kept weighing on him that a bear would be awfully good eating about now. A bear with yellow fat lying three fingers deep over the red muscles from a long autumn of gorging on chestnuts, hickory nuts, acorns, and huckleberries. Tasting sweet and dark like a rendering of the forest. Meat to last into the next moon. Cooking grease for the entire winter. A heavy fur for the children to sleep beneath when snow comes. Long curved claws the color of charcoal for his grandchildren to auger holes through and string into necklaces and keep as relics to remember Charley, evidence of his existence long after he was gone. He could see them showing the claws to their own grandchildren and telling the story of the day he came walking into camp bloody to the elbows, bent from the weight he packed over his shoulder, a great bear haunch in a black bundle made from its skin. And then how the women started cooking the meat and the men all followed Charley back up the mountain to finish butchering the bear, and then how they all sat about the cook fire for days, eating until their bellies hurt.

Charley stopped and turned back around and saw a motionless square shape, a dark interruption in the luminous fog. He took out his hand axe and knife and felt their heft and looked at their edges, honed bright with spit and a flat river rock. Charley reckoned his tools might suffice to kill this bear. Men had done such things before, or at least people told stories of killing bear in close combat. He had never actually seen it done. But in the stories, the men had always first wounded the animal with bow or gun and then let it bleed awhile to weaken.

The famous Bear Drowning Him, now mostly just called Bear, was said to have gotten his name when he was still a boy by killing the master bear of all this territory, wounding it first with an arrow to the lungs and then fighting it with a knife in his fist until they both streamed blood. They brawled down a hillside and then to the river's edge and then onward until they were waist-deep in the water. They closed awkwardly together, neither finding much purchase against the round slick stones of the riverbed. But the boy drove a blade deep in the bear's vitals. And then the bear lurched forward and pressed the boy down under the water with his full weight. All that remained visible was the muscled hump of the bear's back breaking the dark surface of the river. But at the last moment of Bear Drowning Him's strength, the bear died. It went still and lay with the water flowing around the bulk of it in a pair of smooth curves. The boy came up and slung the water out of his hair, and he still had the knife in his fist, the blade shining and clean from the water.

The bear was claimed to have measured a full arms' span across at the ass. Even deducting for decades of exaggeration, that was still a big bear. Even now, when Bear wanted to cut a dash for children, he sometimes exhibited the parallel welted scars across his back and ribs where the claws had scored him to the bone in their last embrace. Bear had narrated the story to Charley's children several years ago when, on a hunting trip, he had spent a rainy night in their cabin. Bear loomed over them at his lean excessive height and told the story, and the children looked up and listened in amazement. And then at the climactic moment, Bear turned to a quartering position and pulled up the tail of his long hunting shirt, and the skin was becoming creped and hanging loose over the bones, but the scars were bright as ropes of rubbed silver, relics of an accomplishment that could be taken to the grave and perhaps beyond.

There was a slight shift of wind from up the creek, and it carried an odor like wet dog. Charley began walking back toward the dark shape. He talked to it in a low voice.

He said, Come to me. Come to me. And then he sang the bear hunter's song: I want to lay them low on the ground. Low on the ground.

He reckoned that taking nothing but a cup of bitter tea without honey for the entire day was about the same as the hunter's fast of the old times. He had the hatchet in his right hand and the knife in his left hand with the edge up for good ripping after a deep belly stab. He said again, Come to me. And then he said the last prayer before the kill: Let the leaves be covered with clotted blood, and may it never cease to be so.

Through the fog, Charley could see the bear's ears and tan muzzle. It made a bouncing motion with its front end. Charley took it that the bear was willing to fight. Without thinking much about it, he took two running steps forward and let fly the hatchet. It was a deep throw, all the strength in his old stout body expressed in a flow of movements calibrated so that the hatchet would make two revolutions in air before burying its blade in the bear with great force.

There was the sound of a solid blow struck, but he could not see what he had hit. The bear did not charge but made a single plosive utterance, a huff. It wheeled and ran uphill at amazing speed, crashing through a stand of laurel and disappearing into the fog. Charley stood and listened to the cracking of limbs and imagined the working of the massive hams and buttocks. Big muscles that would make good eating. He sheathed the knife and went and retrieved the bloody hatchet where it lay on the ground and took off running hard.

Charley was like the bear in his squat build, his power all settled in his ass and thighs, and he ran lumbering but strong, and his short legs were good for climbing. For a while he could take his direction by stopping for a second and listening to the bear moving ahead of him through the leaves. But when Charley grew short of breath and slowed to a walk, the bear soon outdistanced him. He stopped to listen, and there was silence, even when he opened his mouth wide to aid his hearing. But he could follow the trail of disturbed leaves and broken branches and blood, and when there was no sign, he chose his forward path only by guessing how the bear would react to the flow of terrain and the way the forest plants might serve as obstacle or cover. At intervals he found gouts of blood on the forest floor and broad smears against tree bark to confirm the correct working of his imagination. He moved in the bear's wake all afternoon, climbing without letup. The blood led on, but thinned down. Bleeding out or healing up.

Gouts became drops. Drops became rare as garnets cupped in fallen leaves. Step by step, footprints lay lighter on the earth, fainter and fainter as if the bear were slowly elevating into the sky.

Charley went at a near trot, bent double to look for fading sign. He climbed out of the coves where colored leaves still hung on the trees, through a region where ferns and vines had grown fountainous through the summer and were now melancholy and dying as far as the eye could see, and then along the dry ridges, and by dusk he was rising through a forest of bare trees grey as winter toward the ominous balsam forests draped black across the highest ridges, a world of shadow and hush, where every step fell muffled by the soft foot-bed of old brown needles. He hoped he would not have to cross that boundary, for the only time he had done so a giant owl had glided silent and big-headed right past him in the half dark that was day under the balsams. The owl's face as big as his own and pale as the moon. A bad sign. Not the word you wanted spoken to you out alone in the high mountains.

Charley went on upward, one red drop at a time until the sign died entirely before him. He went casting forward until that direction became hopeless, and then he backtracked to the last drop of blood and began circling, making wider and wider rounds without success. He looked up into the trees and the sky beyond, for it seemed as if at some point the bear had spread wings and taken flight. He followed a rill of water no wider than his hand back to its source, for it is widely known that certain springs offer entrance into the world underneath the world, a refuge. But there was no sign of bear along the rill. Charley kept searching until it was so dark he could not tell one kind of fallen leaf from another. He sat with his back against a tree and looked up through the bare winter woods toward the highest peaks and sent out a prayer to the bear and all his animal brethren, speaking aloud without hope or despair. Saying that since the beginning of time, animals have willingly sacrificed themselves to the needs of people, have given us their pain and blood as a gift along with their fat and meat. Don't stop now.

He waited by the tree until dawn for the outcome to his prayer. Ready with knife and hand axe in case a dark shape separated itself from the night and came to him, offering him its life.

When Charley returned to camp the next day, it was with neither a bloody haunch over his shoulder nor a heroic story to tell. He had only his creel of withered roots. He set about peeling and slicing them and brewing a pot of bitter tea the color of strong urine.

Charley concluded his hunting story by saying that until this night by the camp-fire with the tobacco smoke and brown whiskey, he had not spoken a word about his lost bear to any of his descendants but only whispered about it to Nancy the night of his return as they lay on their bed of hemlock boughs, and she held him and brushed his face with the big knuckles of her fingers and told him that he had tried but failed and sometimes that is all the victory we are allotted.

Ann Pancake

1963–

Novelist, short story writer, and essayist Ann Pancake was born in Richmond, Virginia. Her upbringing in Romney and Summerville, West Virginia—an area sometimes referred to as "the heart of coal country"—lies at the heart of her fiction. But that experience is also filtered through her education at West Virginia University (BA), the University of North Carolina at Chapel Hill (MA), and the University of Washington (PhD), as well as her experience teaching English in American Samoa, Japan, and Thailand. Her fiction examines class, Appalachian otherness, environmental and social justice, and ecology.

Pancake's first novel, *Strange as This Weather Has Been* (2007), which won a Weatherford Award, is the story of a rural West Virginia family struggling with the economic, cultural, psychological, and health effects of encroaching mountaintop-removal coal mining. Between the passionate anti-mountaintop-removal activism of main character Lace and the pragmatic reserve of Jimmy Make, her husband, lie their four children—Bant, Dane, Corey, and Tommy—who are growing up in a traumatized land and community. The family is not alone; others experience this same devastation. The novel is based, in part, on interviews Pancake helped her sister, documentary filmmaker Catherine Pancake, conduct for Catherine's film *Black Diamonds: Mountaintop Removal & the Fight for Coalfield Justice* (2006).

Pancake is also the author of a prizewinning collection of short stories, *Given Ground* (2001), and a collection of novellas and short stories, *Me and My Daddy Listen to Bob Marley* (2015).

FROM Strange as This Weather Has Been

Lace

A month after we came home, I got on at the Dairy Queen. Jimmy Make wouldn't take a job like that, and I knew it was my fault we'd come home, so I got on. Still, I believed if Jimmy Make would just lower himself to do something regular along with me, we'd get by okay, it was a whole lot easier to be poor up Yellowroot than in Raleigh, North Carolina. But, no. If he couldn't find a "real job," he had to "work for himself," so he started cutting grass and doing handyman jobs. Problem was, most people around here know how to fix their own stuff and couldn't afford a handyman even if they needed one. I didn't say much, though. Didn't feel I could, not then, not yet.

Even though I was working thirty-five, thirty-seven hours a week, I tried to get up into the woods that summer as much as I could, and I made sure to take with me what kids would go. City'd made me understand again how little else I had to give them, but city'd also made me see how woods were almost enough. Tommy was old enough to go by then, and Dane'd come most of the time. I'd leave Bant to look after Corey, Corey never took much interest in woods for woods' sake, and Bant, going on fourteen, wouldn't do anything with me anymore unless I made her. The boys and me'd blackberry some, but mostly we just walked, or sat and listened, or played in the Ricker Run. And it was only in the woods I felt less lonesomeness for Mom. I tried to feel her in the cemetery, but there it never came, I felt her only in the woods, so I'd lead the boys to certain places without telling them why. Feel Mom's seat on logs where she'd rest. Lay my hand on trees where I knew Mom'd laid hers. But I stuck to Cherryboy during those roamings, I almost never took the boys up on Yellowroot or even up Yellowroot Creek. That's how I knew later that I knew then, I just had to keep it still a secret from myself,

I was already hearing a few things at the Dairy Queen, though. And in truth, I was already seeing it in the creek. I tried to fool myself about that too, said, *well, maybe you just remember the water as clearer than it really was, memory does that kind of thing.* But nothing could cover that day in August Corey and Tommy brought back two of those big margarine tubs full of rotting crawdads. Or the afternoon a week later when I looked out the back window and saw what Tommy had in his hands.

I was rushing around getting ready for work and arguing with Jimmy Make at the same time—"Me working a full shift, and you can't take twenty minutes to pick up this place?" "I'm working, too! Just because I'm not out there cutting grass don't mean I'm not working, I'm working just as hard drumming up business, it's an investment, what I'm doing now"—when something caught my eye out a window I was passing. Tommy standing in the creek in nothing but a pair of shorts, mud smeared over his belly, and studying something he held in each hand. I stopped and squinted. It was full-sized dead fish that he held.

"Drop em!" I heard myself scream.

His face snapped up towards the window in surprise, and he did, the fish sliding out of his hands. Then I was rushing out, I was jerking him up over the bank to the outside spigot, and then I was scrubbing his hands, "Bant!" I heard me hollering. "Get me some soap!" Then Bant was there, handing me the dishwashing stuff off the sink and saying, "What's wrong, Mom? They're just dead fish."

I couldn't help telling my work friend Rhondell about it as soon as I clocked in. She was busy refilling the soft serve machine, on her tippy-toes hefting the sloppy mix bag over the machine's mouth—"Well, my god. My god. Uh-uh-uh. Uh-uh-uh"—I wasn't real sure how close Rhondell was even listening. Then all of a sudden there came a voice right behind me: "Poisons in the runoff got em."

I wheeled around, and here of all people, it was Dunky talking. This girl no more than nineteen, came from farther than anybody else to work, from clear over in Boone County. And I'd tried to be friendly with her at the beginning, but Dunky always acted real nervous, so I gave up. Now I looked at her behind her big purplish glasses, and said, "What poisons?"

"Mercury." Dunky took one finger and pushed her glasses back up her nose. "Lead, arsenic, cadmium, copper, selenium, chromium, nickel." She stopped and swallowed, got this look on her face like she'd just realized we might think she was showing off, and that's not what she meant at all. "At least that's what's in the slurry," she said kind of apologetically. "Do you know what's over top you-all?"

Rhondell actually busted out laughing. I just stared at Dunky, her round cheeks under her cheek-shaped glasses, her skin completely without lines, unlived, I'd thought that skin said, but now I saw I was wrong. I'd never even heard the word "selenium" before. "How do you know?"

"My mother-in-law learned about it." She looked down at her feet now. "You should see what all they're doing back in where we live at."

Now we all knew who Dunky's mother-in-law was. Loretta Hughes, the woman Rhondell was convinced was having an affair with Charlie Blizzard. Sometimes Dunky drove herself to work, but often Loretta dropped her off, and usually during those drop-offs, Loretta and Charlie Blizzard would hole up in a hard red booth in the corner farthest from the counter, kind of behind the trash cans, each of them nursing a small black coffee or maybe nothing at all. They'd crouch forward there towards each other, talking furious and shoving papers back and forth, Loretta sometimes getting so worked up she'd throw her hands around, but always, always, keeping it low enough that you couldn't exactly hear her words. Rhondell had it in her head it was an affair, and up to that day Dunky spoke, I'd played along, it helped to pass the time. Even though I knew it was no affair, not with Dunky right there watching and the way Loretta and Charlie would get so mad, but not at each other.

The next day when Loretta came in, I watched her and Charlie in a different way. I even made a point to empty the trash can near them, and although I couldn't tell exactly what they were up to, I thought I overheard Loretta saying something about blasting. The time after that, I thought about getting Dunky to introduce us, but part of me still didn't really want yet to know. A week later, though, I asked Dunky, and she said sure.

We walked up to them during my break. I saw they were working with a magnifying glass on something that looked like newspaper classifieds. Charlie was on the far side of the table facing us, but we could see only Loretta's back, and as we got close, he glanced up, nodded sharp and quick, then brought his arm around the paper to shield what was there. Then Loretta swung her head around, and Dunky said, "She's the one's just got the fish kill behind her house," and when Dunky said that, Loretta Hughes's face sprung wide open. I saw Loretta's face wasn't scared of nothing.

"Well, you just set right down here, buddy," Loretta said, "you just set yourself down." She scooted over and slapped the seat beside her. "What's going on up above you all?"

After that, I learned fast. Loretta and Charlie had educated themselves, they were two of the first, but there were other people too, like Patty McComas, and Jim Corbin and his wife Mavis, and Jeannie Thurst. They were ahead of people like me because their places were already being destroyed, and the Dairy Queen was their main gathering place. Most other restaurants around had closed except for Fox's, and Fox's didn't allow that kind of talk. It was a permit they'd been studying that day I first met them, they'd learned how to interpret them, and they'd taught themselves chemistry, geology, hydrology, biology, politics, law. It was amazing what all they'd taught themselves, Loretta with nothing but a high school diploma and Charlie without even that, but when I mentioned it once to Charlie, he just grunted, "You'd be surprised how quick you can learn about something that's on the verge of killing you."

At first I didn't believe everything they said—how nearly a thousand miles of streams had been filled with the rock and dirt that used to be mountaintops, and how the fill had killed everything there. How what soil was left on the flattened tops was compacted so hard that if anything ever came back besides the grasses and shrubs the company sprayed on, it wouldn't be for at least several hundred more years. How over fifty percent of the electricity in the United States came from coal. But Loretta would bring in newspaper articles to back up what she said, and materials she'd picked up from the environmental group just starting over in her county, and she had a computer, too, she'd print stuff off the Internet. Charlie would sit there and quote statistics without a shadow of emotion crossing his face, and I knew Charlie was too practical to exaggerate.

I couldn't help but come home talking about it, and there at the beginning Jimmy Make didn't say much when I did. The little bit of trying Jimmy Make'd done with me in North Carolina had vanished the day we moved home, and after only a week or two, my smallness faded. I was my whole self again. Now we were back to how it'd been before. I can't say, though, that I gave it a whole lot of attention. Things'd been neutral or worse for so long I didn't expect any better, and besides, I was so busy with working and learning and looking after the kids, Jimmy Make was more an annoyance than anything else. Something in your family you just have to put up with, like a surly teenage kid who gets on your nerves but doesn't do real harm. The phone had hardly rung all summer for his "business," and now that we were getting into fall, it was going to ring even less. But instead of looking for a regular job, Jimmy Make started talking about buying a snowplow for his truck. Although he half tried to hide it from me, he wasn't doing much of anything but watching TV, not only in the evenings, but in the daytime, too, even though with the old satellite dish scrambled, we picked up only that one channel we'd gotten when I was a kid. I'd walk in in the middle of the afternoon, from work or from the store, and there Jimmy Make'd be flopped out on that sagging sofa with his shoes off and his sock bottoms black, putting away Dr Peppers and Mountain Dews. I'd go so far as to open my mouth, but then I'd make myself shut it. I was the one made us come home. I still didn't feel I could say anything yet.

Charlie took a lot longer than Loretta to warm up to me, and those first couple of weeks, he'd often just go quiet after I came around. Eventually, though, he opened a crack. Loretta, she knew the facts, but she'd also talk about exactly what was going on behind her house and how that made her feel. Charlie would mostly talk information. Talking to Loretta was like reading a story, while Charlie was a newspaper article. I gathered that he lived over in Tout, a little town at the other end of the county I'd only visited once in my life, and somehow his home had been badly damaged, too, but I couldn't yet tell how. The first time Charlie talked to me by himself was an evening in October, and it wasn't his own troubles he was worried about.

I clocked out about nine and stepped outside for a cigarette while I waited for Connie to let Rhondell off, too. Rhondell was my ride home. It was just starting to get honestly cold, and I hadn't brought a heavy enough coat, so I sheltered between the Dumpsters, turning to the wall to keep the lighter lit. Then I heard the door open, and I looked and saw Charlie bowlegging out. But instead of heading for his car, he surprised me by coming my way.

"Hi, Charlie," I said, kind of soft so not to scare him. He mumbled back. He had this full shock of white hair like a bowl upside down on his head, and that head only came to about my shoulder. His ears, his nose, his eyes, them small, too, like a shrunken Santa Claus with no beard and no joy. He eased in between the Dumpsters and stood there looking out on the dark hill behind us, not facing me.

"I finally got into some records, Lace," he said. Then he stopped.

"Yeah?" Right away, a badness coiled up in my stomach.

"Couldn't figure out what's killing your fish, but I found out something else." He went still again.

"What?" I said.

"They've got the permit for Yellowroot Mountain."

A boot heel in my chest. "You're sure?"

He nodded. "Yeah. I saw the permit myself."

I took a deep drag on my cigarette, and that's when I felt how my hands were trembling. Filter jogging against my lip. "Who is it?" I said, steadying my voice.

"Lyon. An extension of Bitex 4. Started all the way over at Slatybank a couple years ago." He shook his head. "They must have already blasted to bits every ridge between there and you-all." He took one hand out of his pocket. And although I'd never seen Charlie touch a soul, right then he touched my arm. "I'm real sorry, Lace. You-all be careful."

I got off the next day around three, I remember. The older kids weren't quite home from school, and Jimmy Make was watching Tommy. I walked up on Yellowroot that time. Right up the creek behind the house, facing it head-on after a summer of fooling myself. Past the places where me and Daddy used to fish, past the pools where you used to could drink, and I felt nothing but numb as I passed them. Almost as high as the Hemlock Hole I went, but before I reached that, I veered away from the creek to the high steep bank, going all the way down on my hands and knees to climb it. And then, maybe how low to the ground I got, maybe the hurt of the rocks under my bare hands, the numb dropped away. It cracked off, and my mind and my heart were working hard as my body, and this is why, mind was thinking, heart was knowing, this is why we feel for it like we do—the long, long loss of it. This is why. Its gradual being taken away for the past hundred years, by timber, by coal, and now, outright killed, and the little you have left, mind thinking, heart knowing, a constant reminder of what you've lost and are about to lose. So you never get a chance to heal. Then I heaved myself on up to the bench, and I dropped down onto a log, and *Mom*, I heard myself say in my head. "Mom." I said it out loud. I looked up, towards Yellowroot's top, through limb and falling leaf and, past those, crisscrossed sky. I didn't hear nothing back.

Not a month later, I was in Dunky's husband Nathan's old Blazer, bumping up the road back to their place. "Wanna see what you-all got to look forward to, huh?" Nathan had said when he picked me and Dunky up. We pulled a slow mile, following the creek, crossing it twice on low-water bridges, wiggling along between close wooded hills, when the road finally breathed out into a big open clearing.

Many times Loretta told me how beautiful it had been, and I saw now that it used to be. Three houses tucked quiet in a broad cleared hollow, the pastured hills mounding behind them, and I could imagine it in May, when the ground would be a soft bright almost glowy green, and from a distance, all you'd want to do was to lay your cheek against it. Up against one hill was the white frame house that Loretta'd told me had started as a log cabin, and her husband's family had lived in that place for a hundred and fifty years. Against the opposite hill set the modular home where I knew Loretta's older son, Tike, and his wife Janie and son lived, then a little below it, Nathan and Dunky's trailer, all of the places prettily kept with shrubs around them.

But now it was a beautiful painting that had been ripped in two. Between the white house and the others slashed a clawed-out gulch choked with big rocks, that gulch about as deep as Dunky was tall and wide across as a riverbed, the rocks thrown out all around it even farther, eating up the yard, and at the upper end of the slash, you could see a barn caving down into it. "And I'd always thought they couldn't steal the land right out from under you," Loretta'd said the first time she told me about it. "But turns out they can rob you that way, too." You couldn't any longer pull a car all the way to the white house because of the gash in the ground, so Nathan parked at his trailer, and when I got out and looked towards the house, Loretta was leaning over the railing. "Hey, buddy!" she called. "Welcome to our mess!"

"Yeah, we felt the blasting, of course, but we didn't understand exactly what was going on—couldn't get up there, you know, the guards and gates and all—until that '96 summer flood." That was Tike talking, him and Loretta leading me up the rim of the gash to where I could get a good view of the fill. "Dad's family's been right here since the mid-1800s, and there ain't never, ever, been water through here like came that day." We had to pick our way careful over the rocks and logs, and now that we were getting closer to the barn, I saw how the flood had just plowed the ground out from under half of it. "And now we've got it three times since."

"So after the water went down that first time," Loretta said, "me and Tike took his four-wheeler back in there, snuck past the guards to see it." She took my elbow and guided me around the safe side of the sucked-down barn, and then we were standing behind it where we could see how the gulch ran clear up the hollow. "But that was two years ago, and you don't have to go far now."

There it was. This monster gray plateau, not a landscape ever had or ever would belong in our mountains, it was like it had been dropped out of the sky from some other place on earth, and running down off it, these lord-god-huge gullies cut vertically all across the face of it, and I understood, the force of the water to have carved such canyons in it. We all three stood quiet then, even Loretta stopped talking, and a November wind was stinging down that gorge. I pulled my coat tighter to me. My ears were ringing, but the ringing had nothing to do with the wind. I recalled what I'd said to Loretta when she'd told me about it back at the Dairy Queen, how naive I'd been just a month before. I'd said, "What'd the DEP say when you complained about the damage?"

Loretta snorted. "Act of God. Normal weather event. Mining didn't contribute at all."

I still stood hypnotized when Loretta was turning away, Tike behind, and they'd gone ahead several feet before I jerked my eyes loose and brought up the rear. Single-file we went along the rim, silent this time, and Loretta slipped once on a sharp-sided rock, caught herself before Tike got her arm. The wind was at my back now, pushing my coat ahead of me. Then I noticed what must have been the goat pen. Part of the fence still standing, part shredded in the rock. I knew Loretta hadn't pointed it out coming up, Dunky had told me this months ago, because the goats were the single thing Loretta couldn't bring herself to speak about. How when that first big flood hit, the nanny and her kids had been latched in their pen. And with the water crashing down so quick, no warning, by the time they knew what was happening, the current was too strong for anybody to rescue them, although Nathan tried, and nearly drowned himself doing it. As we passed the pen, I couldn't help touching one upright fence post. I rubbed my scarf across my eyes, then dropped it and jammed my hands back in my pockets, scolding myself, how much easier it is to cry for goats, why is it easier to cry for goats? And then I understood it was because a goat death was possible to imagine. It was possible to imagine a goat dying that way.

Then we were warming up in Loretta's living room, pumpkin bread and coffee, Loretta's husband, who they all called "Dad" and who looked fifteen years older than Loretta, laid up in a recliner wrapped in a blanket from the waist down. Tike and Janie's four-year-old, Zeke, was bumping up against Tike's knees—I already knew they were holding off on having another one and Dunky and Nathan were waiting on their first until they got a better grip on their future here—and Tike was showing me a spiral notebook where they'd recorded all their incidents since the first flood. The blasts, and the smaller floods, and the dead fish, and the fly rock, the number of times they'd had to pressure-wash the blasting dirt off their house, the outbuildings they'd lost, all of it written neat in marker, date and description of event, and Loretta was saying, "Did you know the explosives they use are exactly the same as the ones Tim McVeigh used in Oklahoma City? Only most of the blasts here are ten times stronger than what blew up that building."

"Oh, yeah, we'll get real large shakes," Tike went on, "see how that ceiling's cracked? I could show you all over the house. The walls are splitting off from the floors."

And me, so full up by then it was like listening from under water, and over top it all, over top all they were telling me, *this can't be, can't be, can't be, us.* Me sitting there on the edge of the couch, the coffee going cold in my hands, nodding at what they said and reading and rereading, reading and rereading, the needlepoint hanging on the opposite wall. "They're out of their minds," Nathan was saying. "You don't shit where you get your water. Any animal knows that." "Watch your language," said

Dunky, nodding at Zeke, and that needlepoint, "In His hands are the deep places of the earth. The strength of the hills are His also. Psalm 95:4." "And all of em scared they'll lose their jobs, and I say, lose jobs? Lose jobs?" Loretta talking, "Why should a few people, most of em from out-of-state, get $60,000 a year while the rest of us got nothing but dust and floods and stress and poison and never knowing when that water's gonna take your house with it?"

Then all of a sudden, although he hadn't made a sound past his "good to meet you," Dad cleared his throat. I heard the phlegm in it. When he did, everybody shut up quick and turned to the recliner in surprise. Dad sat forward a little bit, and when he spoke, it started in a croak but then it ran clear. "It's like having a gun held on you with the hammer back." He raised his hand, he pointed at his head. "And not knowing when the man's gonna pull the trigger."

I wrote my first letters shortly after that, to Jay Rockefeller and Senator Robert Byrd. I'd never had any use for politicians before, around here you learn very young where a West Virginia politician's loyalties lay, but Loretta and Charlie and the others said we had to speak our piece. I listened even harder to the people who had already educated themselves, I stayed late at work, came early, to do it, and I learned fierce. It hurt to learn it, it did. It was easier to half-ignore it, pretend it wasn't that bad anyway, or if it was, couldn't do nothing about it so why get worked up, that's how a lot of people lived. But I realized to at least know part of what was going on made you feel like you had a particle of control instead of none at all.

By spring of '99, when the dozers first went up the creek to dig the sediment ponds, I'd started making phone calls to agencies. Loretta had given me the job of combing the Beckley classifieds for permit applications. The companies tried to slip those past you and wrote them in such a way you couldn't understand them unless you were trained. Charlie trained me. I even went to a permit hearing, and although I was too backwards then to speak at the mike, I was there.

Jimmy Make'd spent the winter of '98–'99 looking for any deep mine or construction outfit that might be hiring, but nobody was. He acted like he wouldn't work for a mountain top job, but truth was, even if he'd wanted to, he couldn't have gotten on, most of them passed over workers with union experience, and, besides, the skills you needed on those operations were different from what you learned underground. When I got home, I still told Jimmy some of what I'd learned, I had to tell somebody, but while he'd asked a few questions back at the beginning, now he said nothing at all. And I could feel it start to grind in him. I was familiar with that in him, the way he could push back without actually opening his mouth. In April, when a few days were getting warmer, he spried up and started tinkering with his lawnmower and weed-eater. He made flyers by hand for his "business" and went to the Madison library to photocopy them, then he drove all over the county putting them up, he even put an ad in the paper, now that wasn't cheap. And with all that, the cockiness came back in him, the swagger in his limp. Then he did start talking back.

"Nothing to do but get used to it or move," he shrugged, not taking his eyes off the TV to prove how deep he didn't care. "Why'd you think I wanted to stay in North Carolina?"

I knew he knew that'd make me mad, and I wanted to ignore it, but I couldn't leave it be. "This is my homeplace, Jimmy Make," I said. "What about the kids? What do they got to look forward to if we don't fight?"

"Fight?" he snorted, and then he turned from the screen to face me, this know-it-all how-stupid-can-you-be look. "Honey, you won't never beat coal. It's who has the money, the rich people always win, that's how it's always been, especially in the state of West Virginia. That's why the smart people get out."

Then after we ran through that tired give-and-take for about a month, I finally said, kind of quiet and calm, "Well, some people are fighting."

I said it to test Jimmy Make a little, see what he'd do, although I mostly figured he wouldn't even know what I was talking about. So I was surprised when I saw he right away did.

"You stay out of it, hear me?" He sat up and swung his feet to the floor, and I saw his eyes lit live for a change. "You stay clear of the shit-stirrers."

"I'll do what I damn well please, just like I've always done."

Jimmy Make swallowed, he ran his tongue inside his mouth to wet it, and I saw he'd gone past mad to scared, and that surprised me a second time. It even scared me a little. "You keep the hell away from the shit-stirrers." He said it snaky, between his teeth. Then he stopped and dropped his voice even lower, Tommy and Corey coming up on the porch. "You can't do a thing about this here, and you'll just turn people against us. End up making it even worse for me and the kids."

By July of our second summer back, we were hearing the blasting, still distant, not enough to shake the house, but there it was. And by August, it was clear Jimmy Make wasn't going to get any more "handyman" work this summer than he had the summer before. I blamed that on him. He blamed it on me. He still wouldn't apply for what few minimum wage jobs there were, even though that would have doubled our income and been easier on his back. We were in a terrible tight for money, I worried about it just all the time, and going into that fall, I couldn't even get the kids school clothes, it was all we could do to eat, and a lot of that we did on credit. Thank god the house was paid off. Tommy turned five that year, and in August he started kindergarten. It was just a couple weeks after that I got the visit from Bell Kerwin.

Late morning, nobody home but Jimmy Make and me, and I remember I was out back hanging laundry when I heard Bell calling from the front of the house. I went around and there she stood, her hands balled down into the single pocket of the apron she wore, grinding. A friendly and calm type of person she'd been when I was a kid, but that was before her middle boy'd got bad into drugs, and since then—it'd been years by now—Bell'd moved deep into herself. But today she looked even more nervous than she usually did, those half-hidden hands kneading, her not meeting my eye. I invited her in, but she said no, she didn't have time to sit and visit, she'd just had to come up and tell me, at the head of the hollow like we were.

"Tell me what?" I said.

She pulled her hands out of her pockets then. She had a watch on, and she went to turning it back and forth on her wrist, her still looking at the ground. "Ralph heard it at work. Now, Lace, you know there's so many rumors going around anymore I don't know if it's true or not, but up here like you all are, I had to tell you." She finally stopped her hands then, and she looked directly at me. "Ralph heard they're putting in a slurry impoundment at the top of Yellowroot Creek."

Ron Rash

1953–

For biographical information on Ron Rash, see the headnote that accompanies his poetry in this anthology. In "The Ascent," from *Burning Bright* (2010), Rash explores how methamphetamine addiction has damaged individuals, families, and mountain communities.

The Ascent

Jared had never been this far before, over Sawmill Ridge and across a creek glazed with ice, then past the triangular metal sign that said SMOKY MOUNTAINS NATIONAL PARK. If it had still been snowing and his tracks were being covered up, he'd have turned back. People had gotten lost in this park. Children wandered off from family picnics, hikers strayed off trails. Sometimes it took days to find them. But today the sun was out, the sky deep and blue. No more snow would fall, so it would be easy to retrace his tracks. Jared heard a helicopter hovering somewhere to the west, which meant they still hadn't found the airplane. They'd been searching all the way from Bryson City to the Tennessee line, or so he'd heard at school.

The land slanted downward and the sound of the helicopter disappeared. In the steepest places, Jared leaned sideways and held on to trees to keep from slipping. As he made his way into the denser woods, he wasn't thinking of the lost airplane or if he would get the mountain bike he'd asked for as his Christmas present. Not thinking about his parents either, though they were the main reason he was spending his first day of Christmas vacation out here—better to be outside on a cold day than in the house where everything, the rickety chairs and sagging couch, the gaps where the TV and microwave had been, felt sad.

He thought instead of Lyndee Starnes, the girl who sat in front of him in fifth grade homeroom. Jared made believe that she was walking beside him and he was showing her the tracks in the snow, telling her which markings were squirrel and which rabbit and which deer. Imagining a bear track too, and telling Lyndee that he wasn't afraid of bears and Lyndee telling him she was so he'd have to protect her.

Jared stopped walking. He hadn't seen any human tracks, but he looked behind him to be sure no one was around. He took out the pocketknife and raised it, making believe that the pocketknife was a hunting knife and that Lyndee was beside him. If a bear comes, I'll take care of you, he said out loud. Jared imagined Lyndee reaching out and taking his free arm. He kept the knife out as he walked up another ridge, one whose name he didn't know. He imagined Lyndee still grasping his arm, and as they walked up the ridge Lyndee saying how sorry she was that at school she'd told him he and his clothes smelled bad.

At the ridgetop, Jared pretended a bear suddenly raised up, baring its teeth and growling. He slashed at the bear with the knife and the bear ran away. Jared held the knife before him as he descended the ridge. Sometimes they'll come back, he said aloud.

He was halfway down the ridge when the knife blade caught the midday sun and the steel flashed. Another flash came from below, as if it was answering. At first Jared saw only a glimmer of metal in the dull green of rhododendron, but as he came nearer he saw more, a crumpled silver propeller and white tailfin and part of a shattered wing.

For a few moments Jared thought about turning around, but then told himself that an eleven-year-old who'd just fought a bear shouldn't be afraid to get close to a crashed airplane. He made his way down the ridge, snapping rhododendron branches to clear a path. When he finally made it to the plane, he couldn't see much because snow and ice covered the windows. He turned the passenger side's outside handle, but the door didn't budge until Jared wedged in the pocketknife's blade. The door made a sucking sound as it opened.

A woman was in the passenger seat, her body bent forward like a horseshoe. Long brown hair fell over her face. The hair had frozen and looked as if it would snap off like icicles. She wore blue jeans and a yellow sweater. Her left arm was flung out before her and on one finger was a ring. The man across from her leaned toward the pilot window, his head cocked against the glass. Blood stains reddened the window and his face was not covered like the woman's. There was a seat in the back, empty. Jared placed the knife in his pocket and climbed into the backseat and closed the passenger door. Because it's so cold, that's why they don't smell much, he thought.

For a while he sat and listened to how quiet and still the world was. He couldn't hear the helicopter or even the chatter of a gray squirrel or caw of a crow. Here between the ridges not even the sound of the wind. Jared tried not to move or breathe hard to make it even quieter, quiet as the man and woman up front. The plane was snug and cozy. After a while he heard something, just the slightest sound, coming from the man's side. Jared listened harder, then knew what it was. He leaned forward between the front seats. The man's right forearm rested against a knee. Jared pulled back the man's shirt sleeve and saw the watch. He checked the time, almost four o'clock. He'd been sitting in the backseat two hours, though it seemed only a few minutes. The light that would let him follow the tracks back home would be gone soon.

As he got out of the backseat, Jared saw the woman's ring. Even in the cabin's muted light it shone. He took the ring off the woman's finger and placed it in his jean pocket. He closed the passenger door and followed his boot prints back the way he came. Jared tried to step into his earlier tracks, pretending that he needed to confuse a wolf following him.

It took longer than he'd thought, the sun almost down when he crossed the park boundary. As he came down the last ridge, Jared saw that the pickup was parked in the yard, the lights on in the front room. He remembered it was Saturday and his father had gotten his paycheck. When Jared opened the door, the small red glass pipe was on the coffee table, an empty baggie beside it. His father kneeled before the fireplace, meticulously arranging and rearranging kindling around an oak log. A dozen crushed beer cans lay amid the kindling, balanced on the log itself three red-and-white fishing bobbers. His mother sat on the couch, her eyes glazed as she told Jared's father how to arrange the cans. In her lap lay a roll of tinfoil she was cutting into foot-long strips.

"Look what we're making," she said, smiling at Jared. "It's going to be our Christmas tree."

When he didn't speak, his mother's smile quivered.

"Don't you like it, honey?"

His mother got up, strips of tinfoil in her left hand. She kneeled beside the hearth and carefully draped them on the oak log and kindling.

Jared walked into the kitchen and took the milk from the refrigerator. He washed a bowl and spoon left in the sink and poured some cereal. After he ate Jared went into his bedroom and closed the door. He sat on his bed and took the ring from his pocket and set it in his palm. He placed the ring under the lamp's bulb and swayed his hand slowly back and forth so the stone's different colors flashed and merged. He'd give it to Lyndee when they were on the playground, on the first sunny day after Christmas vacation so she could see how pretty the ring's colors were. Once he gave it to her, Lyndee would finally like him, and it would be for real.

Jared didn't hear his father until the door swung open.

"Your mother wants you to help light the tree."

The ring fell onto the wooden floor. Jared picked it up and closed his hand.

"What's that?" his father asked.

"Nothing," Jared said. "Just something I found in the woods."

"Let me see."

Jared opened his hand. His father stepped closer and took the ring. He pressed the ring with his thumb and finger.

"That's surely a fake diamond, but the ring looks to be real gold."

His father tapped it against the bedpost as if the sound could confirm its authenticity. His father called his mother and she came into the room.

"Look what Jared found," he said, and handed her the ring. "It's gold."

His mother set the ring in her palm, held it out before her so they all three could see it.

"Where'd you find it, honey?"

"In the woods," Jared said.

"I didn't know you could find rings in the woods," his mother said dreamily. "But isn't it wonderful that you can."

"That diamond can't be real, can it?" his father asked.

His mother stepped close to the lamp. She cupped her hand and slowly rocked it back and forth, watching the different colors flash inside the stone.

"It might be," his mother said.

"Can I have it back?" Jared asked.

"Not until we find out if it's real, son," his father said.

His father took the ring from his mother's palm and placed it in his pants pocket. Then he went into the other bedroom and got his coat.

"I'm going down to Bryson City and find out if it's real or not."

"But you're not going to sell it," Jared said.

"I'm just going to have a jeweler look at it," his father said, already putting on his coat. "We need to know what it's worth, don't we? We might have to insure it. You and your momma go ahead and light our Christmas tree. I'll be back in just a few minutes."

"It's not a Christmas tree," Jared said.

"Sure it is, son," his father replied. "It's just one that's chopped up, is all."

He wanted to stay awake until his father returned, so he helped his mother spread the last strips of tinfoil on the wood. His mother struck a match and told him it was time to light the tree. The kindling caught and the foil and cans withered and blackened, the fishing bobbers melting. His mother kept adding kindling to the fire, telling Jared if he watched closely he'd see angel wings folding and unfolding inside the flames. Angels come down the chimney sometimes, just like Santa Claus, she told him. Midnight came and his father still wasn't back. Jared went to his room. I'll lay down just for a few minutes, he told himself, but when he opened his eyes it was light outside.

He smelled the methamphetamine as soon as he opened his bedroom door, thicker than he could ever remember. His parents had not gone to bed. He could tell that as soon as he came into the front room. The fire was still going, kindling piled around the hearth. His mother sat where she'd been last night, wearing the same clothes. She was tearing pages out of a magazine one at a time, using scissors to make ragged stars she stuck on the walls with Scotch tape. His father sat beside her, watching intently.

The glass pipe lay on the coffee table, beside it four baggies, two with powder still in them. There'd never been more than one before.

His father grinned at him.

"I got you some of that cereal you like," he said, and pointed to a box with a green leprechaun on its front.

"Where's the ring?" Jared asked.

"The sheriff took it," his father said. "When I showed it to the jeweler, he said the sheriff had been in there just yesterday. A woman had reported it missing. I knew you'd be disappointed, that's why I bought you that cereal. Got something else for you too."

His father nodded toward the front door where a mountain bike was propped against the wall. Jared walked over to it. He could tell it wasn't new, some of the blue paint chipped away, one of the rubber handle grips missing, but the tires didn't sag and the handlebars were straight.

"It didn't seem right for you to have to wait till Christmas to have it," his father said. "Too bad there's snow on the ground, but it'll soon enough melt and you'll be able to ride it."

Jared's mother looked up.

"Wasn't that nice of your daddy," she said, her eyes bright and gleaming. "Go ahead and eat your cereal, son. A growing boy needs his breakfast."

"What about you and Daddy?" Jared asked.

"We'll eat later."

Jared ate as his parents sat in the front room, passing the pipe back and forth. He looked out the window and saw the sky held nothing but blue, not even a few white clouds. He thought about going back to the plane, but as soon as he laid his bowl in the sink his father announced that the three of them were going to go find a real Christmas tree.

"The best Christmas tree ever," his mother told Jared.

They put on their coats and walked up the ridge, his father carrying a rusty saw. Near the ridgetop, they found Fraser firs and white pines.

"Which one do you like best, son?" his father asked.

Jared looked over the trees, then picked a Fraser fir no taller than himself.

"You don't want a bigger one?" his father asked.

When Jared shook his head no, his father kneeled before the tree. The saw's teeth were dull but his father finally broke the bark and worked the saw through. They dragged the tree down the ridge and propped it in the corner by the fireplace. His parents smoked the pipe again and then his father went out to the shed and got a hammer and nails and two boards. While his father built the makeshift tree stand, Jared's mother cut more stars from the newspaper.

"I think I'll go outside a while," Jared said.

"But you can't," his mother replied. "You've got to help me tape the stars to the tree."

By the time they'd finished, the sun was falling behind Sawmill Ridge. I'll go tomorrow, he told himself.

On Sunday morning the baggies were empty and his parents were sick. His mother sat on the couch wrapped in a quilt, shivering. She hadn't bathed since Friday and her hair was stringy and greasy. His father looked little better, his blue eyes receding deep into his skull, his lips chapped and bleeding.

"Your momma, she's sick," his father said, "and your old daddy ain't doing too well himself."

"The doctor can't help her, can he?" Jared asked.

"No," his father said. "I don't think he can."

Jared watched his mother all morning. She'd never been this bad before. After a while she lit the pipe and sucked deeply for what residue might remain. His father crossed his arms, rubbing his biceps as he looked around the room, as if expecting to see something he'd not seen moments earlier. The fire had gone out, the cold causing his mother to shake more violently.

"You got to go see Brady," she told Jared's father.

"We got no money left," he answered.

Jared watched them, waiting for the sweep of his father's eyes to stop beside the front door where the mountain bike was. But his father's eyes went past it without the slightest pause. The kerosene heater in the kitchen was on, but its heat hardly radiated into the front room.

His mother looked up at Jared.

"Can you fix us a fire, honey?"

He went out to the back porch and gathered an armload of kindling, then placed a thick log on the andirons as well. Beneath it he wedged newspaper left over from the star cutting. He lit the newspaper and watched the fire slowly take hold, then watched the flames a while longer before turning to his parents.

"You can take the bike down to Bryson City and sell it," he said.

"No, son," his mother said. "That's your Christmas present."

"We'll be all right," his father said. "Your momma and me just did too much partying yesterday is all."

But as the morning passed, they got no better. At noon Jared went to his room and got his coat.

"Where you going, honey?" his mother asked as he walked toward the door.

"To get more firewood."

Jared walked into the shed but did not gather wood. Instead, he took a length of dusty rope off the shed's back wall and wrapped it around his waist and then knotted it. He left the shed and followed his own tracks west into the park. The snow had become harder, and it crunched beneath his boots. The sky was gray, darker clouds farther west. More snow would soon come, maybe by afternoon. Jared made believe he was on a rescue mission. He was in Alaska, the rope tied around him dragging a sled filled with food and medicine. The footprints weren't his but those of the people he'd been sent to find.

When he got to the airplane, Jared pretended to unpack the supplies and give the man and woman something to eat and drink. He told them they were too hurt to walk back with him and he'd have to go and get more help. Jared took the watch off the man's wrist. He set it in his palm, face upward. I've got to take your compass, he told the man. A blizzard's coming, and I may need it.

Jared slipped the watch into his pocket. He got out of the plane and walked back up the ridge. The clouds were hard and granite-looking now, and the first flurries were falling. Jared pulled out the watch every few minutes, pointed the hour hand east as he followed his tracks back to the house.

The truck was still out front, and through the window Jared saw the mountain bike. He could see his parents as well, huddled together on the couch. For a few moments Jared simply stared through the window at them.

When he went inside, the fire was out and the room was cold enough to see his breath. His mother looked up anxiously from the couch.

"You shouldn't go off that long without telling us where you're going, honey."

Jared lifted the watch from his pocket.

"Here," he said, and gave it to his father.

His father studied it a few moments, then broke into a wide grin.

"This watch is a Rolex," his father said.

"Thank you, Jared," his mother said, looking as if she might cry. "You're the best son anybody could have, ain't he, Daddy?"

"The very best," his father said.

"How much can we get for it?" his mother asked

"I bet a couple of hundred at least," his father answered.

His father clamped the watch onto his wrist and got up. Jared's mother rose as well.

"I'm going with you. I need something quick as I can get it." She turned to Jared. "You stay here, honey. We'll be back in just a little while. We'll bring you back a hamburger and a Co-Cola, some more of that cereal too."

Jared watched as they drove down the road. When the truck had vanished, he sat down on the couch and rested a few minutes. He hadn't taken his coat off. He checked to make sure the fire was out and then went to his room and emptied his backpack of school books. He went out to the shed and picked up a wrench and a hammer and placed them in the backpack. The flurries were thicker now, already beginning to fill in his tracks. He crossed over Sawmill Ridge, the tools clanking in his backpack. More weight to carry, he thought, but at least he wouldn't have to carry them back.

When he got to the plane, he didn't open the door, not at first. Instead, he took the tools from the backpack and laid them before him. He studied the plane's crushed nose and propeller, the broken right wing. The wrench was best to tighten the propeller, he decided. He'd straighten out the wing with the hammer.

As he switched tools and moved around the plane, the snow fell harder. Jared looked behind him and on up the ridge and saw his footprints were growing fainter. He chipped the snow and ice off the windshields with the hammer's claw. Finished, he said, and dropped the hammer on the ground. He opened the passenger door and got in.

"I fixed it so it'll fly now," he told the man.

He sat in the backseat and waited. The work and walk had warmed him but he quickly grew cold. He watched the snow cover the plane's front window with a darkening whiteness. After a while he began to shiver but after a longer while he was no longer cold. Jared looked out the side window and saw the whiteness was not only in front of him but below. He knew then that they had taken off and risen so high that they were enveloped inside a cloud, but still he looked down, waiting for the clouds to clear so he might look for the pickup as it followed the winding road toward Bryson City.

Pamela Duncan

1961–

Pamela Duncan was born in Asheville, North Carolina, and reared in Black Mountain and Shelby, North Carolina. She holds a BA from the University of North Carolina at Chapel Hill and an MA from North Carolina State University, where she studied with Appalachian author Lee Smith. She teaches creative writing at Western Carolina University.

Duncan's novels focus on working-class southern characters, often but not exclusively women. Her first novel, *Moon Women* (2001), follows three generations of women in a rural North Carolina family. *Plant Life* (2003), Duncan's second novel, also takes a multigenerational approach to examine the lives of women working in a textile mill. In *The Big Beautiful* (2007), Duncan's protagonist leaves the mountains for the coast of North Carolina.

Duncan's importance to Appalachian literature extends beyond her own well-received fiction, for she has mentored and influenced many writers, both at Western Carolina and at various regional workshops and festivals.

On the Inside Looking Out

After supper, Daddy goes back to work and I sit at the table reading *Little Women* in my lap so Mama won't see. It's the fourth time I've read it, and it just gets better. The baby won't quit crying, so Mama slaps her a little bit to let her know she means business. But Sarah just cries louder. Uncle Jim says, oh yeah, real smart Linda, so Mama slaps him too. He slaps her back, just playing, and then he starts whooping and laughing when she grabs the greasy skillet and chases him out the back door. Uncle Jim's supposed to be helping Daddy in the barns, but Mama said she needed help washing windows. They still look dirty to me.

I can see Mama's laughing now. That Uncle Jim, he's got her on the ground tickling her. He don't know that if you tickle Mama too long she wets her pants. But I'm glad to see her laughing for a change. She's been in a real bad mood for a while.

I take the baby to the front room and change her diaper, then set her on my lap to watch a rerun of *Hogan's Heroes*. She just laughs whenever Colonel Klink comes on. I think she likes him cause he looks like Pappaw, except Pappaw wears an American uniform. He's shell shocked and crazy as a loon. He sits over in his chair all day and talks to himself. He probably used to talk to Mama and Granny, but Granny's dead and Mama don't listen no more. I'll listen to him when I get the time, but it don't never make sense. There's a rat in my foxhole, he'll say, or my ears are full of blood and so are my boots, Captain.

Diane comes in with her stupid boyfriend Earl Coggins. Sarah looks up and says, Di-AN-a, Di-AN-a.

"Elaine, I told you to quit teaching her to call me that. My name is Diane. Get it? Di-ane."

"But Diana's so much more musical, like Anne of Green Gables' best friend."

"Well, you ain't Anne of Green Gables and I ain't your best friend, so shut up!" And she thumps me upside the head real hard with one of her long old fingernails. Then her and Earl laugh and go upstairs to her room to play records. If I wasn't so nice, I'd tell Earl them are Lee Press-On Nails, and that Diane has been talking to another boy on the phone for a week. When she talks to Earl, she yawns a lot, but with the new boy, she giggles and says, oh Larry, you're so funny!

I like to call my sister Diana because she has a small imagination and can't get expanded enough to see she could be a Diana if she wanted to. All she has to do is believe it hard enough. Like me. I'm sometimes Anne Shirley and live on Prince Edward Island, or P.E.I., as it says on the map of Canada at school. Then again, sometimes I'm Jo March of *Little Women,* eating apples and writing stories in my garret, or what I call the attic. I'm also fond of Joan of Arc, except for the burning at the stake part, which I think she could've got out of with a little imagination.

But my dearest favorite is Helen Keller. She suffered so, but she didn't let it get her down. I used to give myself a choice: if I could be deaf or blind or mute, which would I choose? Of course, I can't even bear the idea of blindness for more than a few minutes. When I tried walking around the house blindfolded, I got scared of the dark. Last year I said mute, because I never talk much anyway. But now I believe I would have to go with deaf. To be deaf might be magical, all silent and hushed and still, watching people's mouths moving and nothing coming out. Mama would hate for me to be deaf cause then I couldn't hear her hollering for me to feed the baby or clean out the bathtub or some such.

Even though I'd love to learn something as mysterious and secret as sign language, I'd miss some things terribly if I was deaf. I'd miss the crickets singing in the evening, like now, all chirpy and joyful. I'd miss the gold and browny-blue sound of songs from Daddy's guitar, all about railroads and rivers and roads out into the world, lonesome and also full of the truth. I'd miss the sound of my own voice when I sing harmony with him, and we sound better than Kenny and Dolly even. I always sing the high part. I'd even miss the sound of baby Sarah's voice saying Di-AN-a, Di-AN-a.

"Elaine, get your little self in here and wash these dishes now!" Mama's back to her old self again.

I put the baby in her bed and give her a toy. Laney, she says and holds her fat little arms up. She can't say my name right yet. If she didn't always smile at me so sweet, I might get mad at her for being such a burden. But she's too pretty to be mad at, like Diane, like Mama. Nobody ever stays mad at them for long, cause they ain't near as pretty when they're mad. Sometimes I can't help but regret that I take after Daddy, because the Moseley looks don't suit a girl. Granny used to say I was lucky to be plain cause people would be attracted to me for the right reasons, but Diane says I'm a ugly little troll Mama and Daddy found under a stump. I don't get mad no more, though, not since I read *Jane Eyre* last year. I just think of her and Mr. Rochester and I feel better.

The kitchen is empty by the time I get there and I'm glad. After I stack the dishes and fill up the sink with bubbles and warm water, I turn off the kitchen light. I want to watch the sun set over behind the tobacco barns, and then the stars come out on the horizon and get brighter and brighter like the sparkles in the snow on a sunny day. I'm the only one I know can get dishes clean in the dark. It's easy. When the sandy-feeling cornbread and dried up pinto juice is washed off, I run my fingers across the plates and they're smooth and slick as a wet window pane.

The pinky-yellow sky fires up to glowing red-orange and then down to purple-black while I'm rinsing the glasses. I wish I could have those colors in my room all the time. When I look at them, the feeling makes a tight fist in my chest so I can't hardly breathe or even feel myself no more. Once I broke a glass watching the sunset, and my hand bled in the sink. Mama whipped me over that glass, but I didn't care. I'll always have the little scar on my thumb to remind me of that glory feeling.

The cold air outside makes everything sharp and clear, so if I squint, I believe I could almost see France. Joan of Arc lived in France, and I plan to visit there some day and write about what I feel in places like Paris and Orleans. I'll travel to P.E.I. to see Anne Shirley's White Way of Delight with my own eyes, and I'll stand in the cold night winds on the moors of England and imagine a powerful black horse and rider pounding toward me. Diane says I live in a dream world. Maybe she'll believe me if I send postcards.

Daddy's home early. He don't usually come back till way past bedtime. Granny couldn't never go to sleep till she heard him come in, and now I can't neither. Daddy's headlights swing around the driveway and he gets out and kicks the tire when the truck backfires. He's not drunk, but he's mad. That's good. I can stand him to be one or the other, but both together spell trouble. My hands slip around the sink and pick up the forks to wash. You have to pull the rag in between all the little fingers on the forks to get the food out. Mama's eye is still purply from when Daddy found dried-up egg on his fork. I don't think that's really what the fight was about though.

He goes to the barn first. He's got him a bottle of something hid out there, cause Granny didn't let him drink in the house, and even though she's been dead nearly a year, he still won't. But she allowed him to be drunk in the house, so I say, why don't he bring it on in and save himself some trouble? But maybe he likes having a secret about something.

If I hurry, I can finish the dishes in time to go to my hideout before bedtime. It's in the oak tree next to the back of the house. Daddy nailed some boards to the trunk so I could reach the low limbs and climb into the tree. It's my favorite thing he ever done for me. He called me out back that day and said, look here Elaine, you been wanting to climb that tree, well go at it. When I got to the top, the little branches would just hold me, and I could see bout all of Jones County from up there. I can't go that high no more, though, cause I weigh sixty-two now.

Granny used to always tell me I'd dry up and blow away if I didn't eat. But I'm just naturally petite, Mama says, like her. She told Granny to mind her own damn business and quit trying to boss somebody else's children. But Granny didn't mean to boss me.

It makes me sad to have to sleep all alone in our room. Granny was so fat and soft and warm, and she'd always tickle my back and tell me about her girlhood days in the mountains when there was panthers and bears running loose. I think they come in my room now Granny ain't there. I see shadows and hear creaky things I never noticed before. Mama says they've been there all along and nothing ever happened to me, so I should hush and go to sleep.

I turn the kitchen light on again so Daddy can see to get to the house, then I put on my coat and step outside. When I suck the air deep in my nose, it burns cold all through my head, and I know there's no cleaner smell in the world than January. I climb to my favorite arm of the tree, which is wide and the perfect size for me, and lay on my back. The stars I see through the dark black limbs wink at me, and sometimes seem to move.

I think about secrets. Diane has told me one, and she says if I tell Mama or Daddy, she'll scoop out my eyeballs with a tablespoon and feed em to the goats. The goats'll eat em too; they'll eat anything. Diane's secret is that she's going to have a baby. It'll come in July. She says she loves Earl Coggins and wants to marry him.

I will never fall in love if it makes people act such a fool. Diane always says, oh yes you will, and giggles like a monkey. She says when you meet a boy you like, you'll do anything for him. The way she says anything makes me sick.

I think Diane's taste is all in her mouth if she'd do anything for Earl Coggins. I don't like that boy. He has a bunch of faults, but the worst is he's cruel to animals. Once he put a firecracker in his own dog's butt and lit it. And he used to pop toads with his BB gun just to see them explode. Old Earl Coggins will get what's due him, though. When Daddy finds out Diane's pregnant, he's gonna set fire to Earl's backside with some buckshot.

I bet they're in Diane's room having sex right now. That's why the tape player's so loud, I know, to cover up Diane moaning and groaning like Lucinda when she had her calf. I don't like that music they play, that Bon Jovi. He's way too loud. Me and Granny and Pappaw always used to listen to Big Band. That's cause Granny and Pappaw met at the Crystal Ballroom in Goldsboro during the war. They danced the night away, and in the morning they got married. Then Pappaw had to go off to war. Granny said about the time the doctors took Daddy out of her, the Germans was bombing all of Pappaw's sense out of him. I don't think Pappaw likes listening to his records now Granny's gone. He used to get real quiet, but now he hollers so you can't hear the music. I miss Glenn Miller myself, especially "Pardon Me Boy, Is That the Chattanooga ChooChoo?"

Mama's bedroom light comes on, and I know it's time for me to go on in. Daddy's room looks dark, so he must still be in the barn. I sit up to shake the cold out of my legs so I can climb down when I see Uncle Jim in Mama's room. She never pulls the shade down like a lady, even though there ain't no neighbors to see her naked. She's almost naked now, except for her panties and her bra. I know I should quit watching and go to my room, but my legs feel too wiggly.

Uncle Jim grins at Mama over the record player. He plugs it in and puts an album on, and then he wraps his arms around her. "Moonlight Serenade" fills up the air around us all while they laugh and twirl. Granny and Pappaw fell in love dancing to that song. I think Uncle Jim must be in love with Mama, cause he's kissing her like Daddy used to before Granny died, before baby Sarah was born, I guess even way back before Uncle Jim come to live with us.

I squeeze my eyes shut hard, then open em again. Mama and Uncle Jim are still kissing. I hear the screen door slam and I know Daddy's in the house. I think I can hear Pappaw hollering something about bombs, and then the light in Daddy's room comes on, and I watch his shadow move around behind the shade. After a few minutes, his light goes out again. Daddy's going to bed.

My breath whooshes out in a big foggy cloud, and I let go of the little tree limb I must've broken off. It drops to the ground, and I can just see it there on top of the pile of leaves below me. There's no moon tonight, only stars and the light from Mama's room.

When I look up to Mama's window again, Daddy is there too. His shotgun looks long and dark, like one of the limbs of my oak tree. Uncle Jim is hollering something. His arms are waving and I can see his mouth moving, but I can't hear what he's saying over the music, "Pennsylvania 6-5000," Daddy's favorite song when he was a little boy. I hear Pappaw screaming, but I can't make out the words, and now Mama's lips are moving too.

Here is the best part of the song. The singers shout Pennsylvania 6-5-oh-oh-oh, but this time the oh's sound louder than they're supposed to.

Something's wrong. There's smoke around Daddy, and I can't see Mama or Uncle Jim anymore. All I see is Daddy looking right at me. He's crying just like the night we went to see Granny at the funeral home.

The cold has got inside my coat because I'm shivering hard. If I'm not careful, I'll shake myself right out of this tree. I lay back on my limb and look at the stars some more. I decide to think about another girl just like me on one of those stars, and what she might be thinking about. Does she have books to read? Does she know about Anne of Green Gables and Joan of Arc and Jane Eyre? I would like to discuss Helen Keller with that girl. I would like to ask her would she choose deaf or blind or mute? I would like to tell her I think Helen Keller was lucky because she didn't have to choose.

Blake M. Hausman

1976–

Blake Hausman, an author, professor, and citizen of the Cherokee Nation of Oklahoma, was born in Michigan and grew up in North Carolina and Georgia. His mother is Cherokee and his father is Jewish. After earning a BA from the University of Georgia, Hausman earned an MA at Western Washington University and a PhD at the University of California–Berkeley, where he studied creative writing and Native American literatures.

During the Trail of Tears (1838–1839), the US Army forcibly relocated Native Americans from the South—including the Cherokee from their homeland in Southern Appalachia—to present-day Oklahoma to open their lands for white settlement. Hausman's satirical science fiction novel *Riding the Trail of Tears* (2011) presents a fictitious enterprise called the Tsalagi Removal Exodus Point Park (TREPP), which promises to provide tourists with a virtual Trail of Tears experience. Theoretically, the TREPP experience is tailored to specific audiences, ranging from minimal violence to full violence, or "authentic"; however, when the virtual Cherokee characters seek to develop a new ending for themselves, they take a tour group led by a Cherokee named Tallulah into dangerous and uncharted territory.

The novel questions who controls Native American narratives, how Native American history is recorded and performed, and in what ways Native American culture is appropriated and exploited in the modern world. To write the book Hausman not only consulted historical sources but retraced the Trail of Tears in reverse. Hausman's own ancestors were from the present-day town of Rome, Georgia, and were relocated during the Trail of Tears.

FROM Riding the Trail of Tears

CHAPTER 11

Naturally, Tour Group 5709 obeys the soldiers without much resistance at first. Given the situation—with Corn Grinder's house tightly surrounded by a circle of soldiers, with Deer Cooker's arms tied behind his back and a flurry of bayonets pointed at his head, with their dogs sliced open and bleeding profusely, and with the soldiers running eager fingers through the women's hair—resistance is pointless. The shock-and-awe method proves effective once again.

As the Removal gets under way, Tallulah speaks calmly, instructing her tourists to do as they're told and follow the soldiers' orders. She promises that nothing is out of the ordinary, that everything will be all right as long as they cooperate with the army. She tells the tourists in no uncertain terms—don't fight back.

Spencer Donald almost fights back. Tallulah watches Spencer's eyes fix upon a soldier's weapon for too long, but she halts his insurrection with body language. Her head twitches and shakes, motioning toward the ground. She directs him with her eyes. The others see this interaction and they quietly fall in line, for now.

The tourists in 5709 have lived relatively comfortable lives in the real world, so they are unaccustomed to the intricacies of being captured by an invading army. Even Bob Rosenberg isn't sure what to do. 5709 clings together and keeps their eyes on Tallulah. As long as they can see her, they have something solid to hold onto.

But Tallulah is now certain that something is very wrong. Of course, the house-storming always happens, even on a Level One tour, but the dogs should never be butchered like that in front of young children. Those sorts of graphics are reserved for Level Three or above. Someone is going to have to explain all of this, Tallulah thinks. And they better not expect me to do it, at least not all of it. True, I violated my own protocol by leaving the First Cabin before the customers, but the degree of graphic violence was beyond my control. Tallulah eyes Nikki and Willa, concerned about their impressionable young memories. Still, the Johnson twins are handling themselves much better than the Athenians, who are acting as if they've never seen blood before.

Given the circumstances, Tallulah defaults to passivity. It is always the course of least resistance. Tallulah is a professional victim. She leads by example. She keeps a brisk pace, never falling too far out of line and never speaking too loudly. The Corn Grinder family walks with similar stoicism. They are professionals too.

In the early days detailing the initial roundup and concentration at the stockades proved to be the most difficult part of writing the program. Very little clearly documented evidence exists regarding these events and their facts. The writers had very little to go on, one of the many reasons why the TREPP dazzled Tallulah with recruitment funds. They needed real Cherokee people to sift through the data, to figure out what really happened, to find the true aboriginal connections, to wade through gruesome and dislocated material in search of a coherent narrative that the actual victims did not want to remember. In college Tallulah consumed every document she could find about the roundup and the stockades, and they all said the same things. The same five statements appeared in every text she consulted. These statements were often written in quotations, but the texts attributed the quotes to different sources. Tallulah concluded that the Trail was intentionally undocumented and that the quotations were anonymously concocted post-Removal by writers who melded shards of memory in the fires of nostalgia.

Each document in the university library that discusses the actual roundup reads like a restatement of the Removal chapter in the James Mooney book. Even the official tribal information from the Cherokee Heritage Center in Tahlequah reads like a collection of excerpts from the Mooney book. Tallulah read the same three "eyewitness" accounts of soldiers' actions in some sixty different texts.

One account always stands out in her memory—the killing of a pregnant mother and her fetus. Apparently, soldiers struck the woman and stabbed her with bayonets because she walked too slowly. Then they sliced the unborn baby out of her stomach and shot it multiple times—with their rifles—a decisive crowd-control tactic, just to let the Cherokees know who ran the show.

The story seemed so tragically believable that, after telling it to the first two or three hundred tour groups that she led through the trail, Tallulah began to question it. Why was it so easy to believe? What larger purpose did this story serve? She wanted hard data, but there was none to have. Only stories. She wondered how often this sort of mother-fetus double homicide actually occurred. Did it happen only once, leaving such a vivid impression on everyone that so many survivors mentioned it to the nineteenth-century anthropologists? Or did it happen repeatedly, becoming a pastime for bored officers? Or was it actually a grand fiction? Perhaps it was invented in the late nineteenth century by a proto-pro-lifer who was eager to demonstrate the sinful nature of humanity. Perhaps it was like George Washington's cherry tree—a story that stuck because it served a larger national mythology, not because it was actually true.

When early American ethnohistorians—those Reconstruction-era scholars who wanted to collect authentic details about the Cherokee Removal before the survivors' generation died out—when those founding fathers of American social science asked old Cherokee people for memorable stories about the Trail of Tears, how many people described that dead pregnant woman and her mutilated fetus? And how many of those people had only heard about the story, but never actually saw what happened? How did they even know for sure that it happened? Did they find it easier to recycle the mother-fetus killing story than to tell the real stories of their parents, or their children, who actually died in their arms? For all Tallulah knew, that fetus could have been killed five hundred times, or it could have been killed zero times. The texts didn't say, and the texts never seemed to change.

At first, this dearth of historical detail created a massive dilemma for TREPP programmers—the dilemma of knowing what *really* happened. What truly happened between May 1838 and July 1839? And more importantly for the TREPP, how could it be transformed into a user-friendly, consumer-driven ride? The programmers ultimately concluded that the only workable answers involved identity and chance.

At the TREPP you pay for your identity, but you take chances with your actions and reactions. For example, during the initial roundup, how does the machine determine if a pregnant tourist is merely stabbed, or fully gutted, or plainly shot and left for dead? Of course, being pregnant in real life does not mean that a customer needs to be pregnant on the trail. Many pregnant women have ridden the trail simply to enjoy a few hours without swollen ankles, widening thighs, and persistent back pain. One column in the Atlanta paper actually suggested the Trail of Tears as virtual therapy for aching pregnant bodies. Furthermore, many women who have difficulties getting pregnant have requested a pregnant persona on the Trail. They often claim it gives them a truer sense of purpose, a tangible reason to live and believe. And it's not uncommon for male customers to request a pregnant female persona. For those men who resent the fact that they can never feel their child's heartbeat inside their own bodies, the Trail of Tears experience can be full of revelations. However, this being Georgia, personal details regarding gender and pregnancy are altered only for tourists who make specific requests.

Though the tourists choose their identities, choice alone does not determine one's fate upon the Trail of Tears. Chance is perhaps the most important element of survival. Though a hundred-dollar customer is not expected to fight off soldiers—especially since most soldiers held a certain reverence for such noble and wealthy Cherokees—there is always the chance that a hundred-dollar player might grab a gun and aim for a soldier's head, which invariably ushers the customer off to see the Old Medicine Man. There is also the constant chance that, with good behavior and a stoically silent disposition, a five-dollar player could walk from Corn Grinder's cabin to a Georgia stockade to the big stockade in Ross's Landing without catching the tip of a single bayonet.

As chance would have it, Tour Group 5709 would not go gently.

As chance would have it, the previous night's discussions of Jeep Cherokees and Volkswagen Touaregs led to a lapse in Tallulah's memory. Caught up in the ironies of vehicle names, Tallulah Wilson forgot to remind her customers to bring something that anyone walking a thousand miles must absolutely remember to bring—shoes.

Though timid and willing during the initial shock and awe, 5709 begins to rumble with resistance as they march barefoot into the hot, dewy north Georgia morning. The trouble begins as the tourists gather outside the cabin, where they realize that they are barefoot. No one is expected to sleep in Corn Grinder's house with their shoes on, but neither should anyone have to walk the Trail of Tears without footwear. If the tourists were more self-reliant, perhaps they would have remembered their shoes without prompting. But they're novices. They have no frame of reference, regardless of how much their own ancestors suffered. They have no reason to instinctively reach for their footwear when their peaceful rest is ransacked at dawn. Perhaps they should have known, but it was Tallulah's job to remind them, and Tallulah forgot to do her job.

She blames herself. She was so busy getting the young people riled up about automobile names that she forgot to remind them about the shoes. How terribly self-indulgent, she thinks.

The Johnson twins cry. Not only are they being forced to walk the Trail of Tears without any shoes, but these soldiers are particularly scary.

Tallulah senses a new problem in the system, one she cannot see. But the offness is everywhere. Something is out of joint. Things are too fast. The soldiers' faces wear too many shadows. Is it only her imagination? Is she projecting her guilt? Maybe. They have the same weapons as always. No, no—they turn corners with fast cuts. Little things are moving faster than they should. Everyone is too anxious. The action is way too edgy for a Level One tour. It's clear the shoes aren't her only problem. Someone else has done something much worse. She knew this was a problem from the beginning, and no one listened to her. Ramsey checked his console and said there wasn't a problem. Why didn't they take her more seriously? Maybe she didn't press her concerns hard enough. Maybe she was focused on something else. Tallulah feels strangely panicked by the presence of Tour Group 5709. Everything is too close.

Things degenerate rapidly when the soldiers issue instructions. The soldiers are unflattering caricatures who spit and grunt. They are archetypal antagonists, and Carmen Davis stands up to them. She defies the power of their vulgarity.

"I'm sorry," she proclaims. "But how can I take your orders seriously when you don't have a single woman in your army?"

The lead soldier, a boy of barely twenty-two, approaches Carmen and stares cold into her eyes. His jaw hangs sideways. His teeth seethe rage. Carmen plants her feet and puffs her chest in defiance, as if to tempt the inevitable.

Spencer's feet begin to tremble, and Tallulah sees bulges forming in the Athenian's face and throat as he watches the young soldier move upon the woman he wants to love.

In one fluid motion the soldier swirls his bayonet in a looping arc and swings the knifed tip into Carmen's leg. She falls, hard upon the calf of the injured leg. Her knee twists out.

Tallulah stretches her arms to hold back the other tourists. She appreciates Carmen's spunk—few people have the guts to stand so boldly. But nothing can save Carmen Davis now, not even Corn Grinder's well-timed distraction. The soldier raises a long knife, craning his head and pointing the blade to the sky.

He announces, "Let this be a lesson to y'all!"

He shifts his weight and prepares to strike Carmen. But just then, Corn Grinder makes a wailing dash for her cabin.

Now, if the scene were truly authentic, she would scream in Cherokee. But translation is critical to customer satisfaction in such pivotal moments of the Removal, so Corn Grinder screams in English. She wails about her pots and pans, she wails about her blankets and baskets, she wails about the mortar and pestle that her own grandmother gave her on her wedding day. Running to the doors of her house, Corn Grinder is shot dead in the back. She falls, instantly limp. Her double braids bounce upon the red earth. Her brown skin skids along the ground as her lifeless body stiffens and rolls still. Her blood drinks the dirt.

The Rosenbergs freeze. The Johnsons scream. Mandy bawls. Deer Cooker bawls louder, throwing his big hands toward the sky, sobbing hysterically, this time in Cherokee.

Tallulah, naturally, is unfazed by the death of Corn Grinder. But Deer Cooker is programmed to grieve. Traumatized and suddenly weary, Deer Cooker plays the role of a model American Indian—he does not fight back, he does not harbor lasting resentment toward the soldier who killed his wife, and he does not protest when another soldier grabs his arm and hoists him back onto the Trail.

"You fucking piece of shit!" cries Carmen. "You cracker-ass bastard piece of shit!"

"Carmen, shut up!" screams Spencer, but the young feminist is on a roll. Broken, but unflinching in her drive to speak truth to the illusion of power, Carmen Davis struggles to stand.

Tallulah eyes Carmen's feet. Already swollen. She wonders if a nice pair of boots or moccasins would have made Carmen comfortable enough to endure the soldiers' misogynist commands. Maybe one of Corn Grinder's extra mocs, the ones she keeps near the fireplace.

"You fucking hurt me!" Carmen screams. "Fuck!" Her legs buckle and bend as she tries to stand. As the other tourists are huddled into a crooked line, prodded, walking methodically and stoically with the bayonet tips at their heels, Tallulah sees the chipped bone protruding from Carmen's twisted knee. Carmen can no longer put her weight on the earth. By all practical standards, she is already useless on the Trail of Tears. She will become unnecessary mass for the wagons if she isn't killed now. And for thirty-dollar tourists, the wagons don't appear until after Fort Dahlonega.

Spencer sees the protruding bone. His eyes well up. Spencer reaches for Carmen, but a subordinate soldier pokes his arm with a bayonet. His arm bleeds a slow, thin line. He cries. Carmen refuses to cry, but her broken body can barely hobble.

"Hey," calls Rachel. "Kill me too!" Michael echoes her, but their pleas go unacknowledged.

"How come it's so easy for her to get it?" Michael mutters to his wife.

Tallulah glances at the young Rosenbergs, then at the Johnsons. Nell is shielding the children with her clothes. The kids are crying, terrified. Tallulah reaches for the water beetle [a communication device in the game]. She is not supposed to contact TC while tourists are dying, but this is an extraordinary tour.

Wallace answers her call. He has information, though it makes no sense. The tour has switched to Level Four.

"Level Four!"

"Let me call you right back." He hangs up. TC has never hung up on Tallulah, until now.

"We never finished our lesson from before," says the lead soldier, loud and brash. He likes being in command. He abruptly turns and shoots Carmen in the face. Carmen falls upon the hot ground. The soldier turns around and never looks back.

A knot twists in Tallulah's stomach. She suddenly finds it painful to stand, but she forces herself upright. She tells the surviving tourists not to worry. Carmen is happier now. She has gone to see the Wise Old Medicine Man, where she can get the kind of authentic spiritual information that anthropology students yearn for.

Tallulah gazes at the sight of Carmen Davis's busty twenty-year-old body as it lies lifeless next to Corn Grinder's. It will be burned by looters within minutes. For a Level Four tour there is nothing unusual about Carmen's death, nothing to suggest that she hadn't gone to visit the Old Man. She is a good dead imaginary Indian.

Tallulah contemplates the significance of having young children on a Level Four tour. This has never happened before, to her or anyone else. So much for the potential middle-school field trip, she thinks. Malfunctions are, as she well knows, inevitable. Yet they aren't usually so drastic. Tallulah begins to feel that she is being observed. Not just by TC, but by something larger. When they hung up on her, they must have had Homeland Security nearby. She wonders if Tour Group 5709 contains an insurgent customer, someone who has brought a virus into the system. How deeply am I being infiltrated? She didn't know about the Great Flushing, of course, but her imagination was always active. Tallulah pictures Carmen Davis, a double agent. Maybe the anthropology class was an elaborate scam. Tallulah dials TC; no one answers. She imagines Ramsey talking to Homeland Security. Ramsey the half-Iranian transplant techie—in what dark corners would they interrogate him if they thought he was dangerous? Tallulah watches the Johnson kids hold their mother as they walk.

Spencer sidles up next to Tallulah. "This is fucked up," he whispers harshly.

"It's okay," she says. "This is the Trail of Tears. Bad shit happens."

Silas House

1971–

Silas House was born in Lily, Kentucky, and was reared in Leslie County, Kentucky, the basis for his fictional Crow County and the setting of his first three novels. His first novel, *Clay's Quilt* (2001), appeared on the *New York Times* best-seller list, and is the first in a series of three novels—including *A Parchment of Leaves* (2002) and *The Coal Tattoo* (2004)—that recounts the lives of three generations of a Kentucky family. In addition to novels, House has written plays and young-adult fiction and has co-edited collections of essays protesting mountaintop removal coal-mining practices. Additionally, he completed *Chinaberry*, James Still's unfinished novel, published posthumously in 2011.

House's keen sense of home is a catalyst for both his activism and his writing, which he uses to redefine Appalachia. His richly developed characters, often members of the rural working class, also want to be seen as real people, not romanticized abstractions. They worry about the responsibility of carrying on traditions and memories in the face of a changing economy and landscape.

These issues are evident in "Recruiters," which was inspired by Sue Massek's song "Brennen's Ballad." Though the story is a pointed commentary on the ethics and methods of military recruiting in poor regions, it is also a celebration of acceptance and love in modern Appalachia.

Recruiters

> *Recruiters come round to our small mountain towns*
> *With money and glory to tempt them.*
>
> Sue Massek, "Brennen's Ballad"

When she come and told me, I begged her not to go. But she wouldn't listen.

"It's awful good money, though," she said. She wrapped my hand up in both of hers. I felt my lip trembling as I pictured all them reports on the news. "And it'll get me out of here. You know this ain't no place for somebody like me."

Rock of Ages never had fit Brennen the way it did my boys, who always had a smooth ride, not a bit of trouble being a part of anything or anybody. But not Brennen.

Brennen lived her life the way I had wanted to when I was a girl. She depended on herself, looked out for herself. Didn't need no man. When I was young, nobody ever told me that was even possible, so soon as I got old enough, I thought I had to get married and have a big gang of children. That's just the way it was. I was twenty-one years old with three kids of my own before I figured out that I didn't have to stay in that little blue trailer and let Robert treat me like a dog for the rest of my life, even though my own mother encouraged me otherwise.

"It's just our lot in life," my mother told me. I can still see the blue veins on the tops of her hands. I always loved her so, without knowing why. "Just accept it and go on."

So I tried to accept it. For a time.

But my Brennen always knowed who she was. And I guess I'm the only person living in this world who understood her. I knowed from the time she was real little that she was different. She used to rock so hard in that old red rocking chair on the front porch that it leaned all the way back, so close to tipping over that it scared me to death, but she just laughed that big laugh of hers. She wasn't scared of anything, buddy.

Brennen always was a tomboy, tearing right along with her brothers, climbing mountains and trees, getting into fist-fights and ending up the winner against boys twice her age. All the girls in our holler rode four-wheelers, but not like Brennen. She rode a four-wheeler like she was taming it: hunched over the handlebars, her shoulders squared like flat rocks, her eyes squinted against the dust. Always wanted to dress just like my boys, always wanted to wear that hat she loved better than anything.

A mother knows, and even though my mother would say, "Oh, she'll grow out of that," I knowed she wouldn't. I knowed my daughter.

When she finally told me she was funny, when she was seventeen, I said, "Honey, I know." She was kneeled down on the floor in front of me as I sat on the couch and I could hear the *nit-nit-nit* of the big plastic Home Interior clock on the wall above my head. I'll never forget the way she was looking up at me, waiting for something. I didn't know what at first, but then, I did. So, I said: "It's alright. It don't matter."

And then she crumbled down on my lap like a little girl, just shaking with tears, her hat tumbling off into the floor. I watched it land, upside down. It had been my daddy's, the only other person besides me that ever just took Brennen for who she was. "My fedora," he always called it, like that was a pet-name. It liked to killed me and Brennen both when the black lung finally took him. Coughed to death.

Brennen laid there a long time, just shuddering with tears, and I run my hand along her hair from the top of her head all the way down her back. It was always so long and shiny, so clean. You could lift it up to your face in one big cold sheet and draw in its scent. Her hair always smelled like summer leaves.

I loved her more right then and there than I ever had before. All my life I had heard people go on about how funny people are evil and have been turned over to a reprobate mind and all that but my Brennen never had an evil bone in her body.

I tell you what now: I never did go to church much but I've sure enough read that Bible and any fool living in this world can tell you that not every single thing in there is meant to be took exactly as it is wrote. Seems like to me that most of these people around here just pick the parts they want and leave out the other parts. I say if you are going to go on like it is all the law then go by every bit of it instead of just what's convenient for you. Either that or use your mind. Because I believe the Lord intends for us to study on things and work them out in our brains instead of just taking everything word for word.

These people that announce the loudest that they're Christians, they make me sick, acting like they know the mind of God. Why, that's blasphemy, if you ask me, to go on like you know what God intended. And why would anybody choose to be that way, when being that way makes your life such a hell?

She was my child. That's all that mattered. I don't understand people getting all worked up over people loving. What they ought to be hollering about is people hating.

When finally Brennen looked up at me her eyes was red as beets, but happy, and she said "Thank you, Mommy." She hadn't called me Mommy in a long time, although the boys—both of them older than her—always did. Before that she had took to calling me by my first name. "Yes, *Justine*," she'd say when she was about thirteen and a devil like girls are at that age, handling my name like it was something hot in her mouth she had to spit out.

And so that is what *I* felt like doing when she come and told me she had signed up for the Army: putting my head in her lap and crying like all was lost, the way she had that day two years before.

Both the boys was gone by then—Christopher was studying to be an English teacher at Berea College, and Marcus was married to goody-goody Markeeta (who said their names was her first tip-off that they should be together) who was trying to make him into a holy-roller preacher like her crazy-ass daddy, Oscar Bowling, who handled snakes and drunk poison to prove he was holier than anybody else. I told Marcus the apples on the trees was holier than one hair on that man's head, and he didn't come around much after that. He had took up with them Bowlings and made them his family. So it was pretty much just me and Brennen.

I was off from work at the prison that day, so I cooked us a big supper that night: soup beans, neck bones, fried taters, kraut and wieners, macaroni and maters, a big skillet of cornbread, crusty on the outside and soft on the inside. Her favorite meal. Me and Brennen had eat until we had just about foundered and shook ourselves out of feeling so big and heavy by singing and dancing while we washed the dishes and straightened up the kitchen. We always was good at working together like that, like separate parts on the same machine.

We had it on the good radio station, the one that plays an oldie in between the newer songs, which are not much account, if you ask me. Why, they don't even sound like country music. But every once in a while there is a *real* country song that comes on. I recall that that night me and Brennen had had a big time in particular when Loretta Lynn come on to sing "Your Squaw Is On the Warpath." Now Loretta is *real* country, no doubt about it. So we danced and sung as loud as we could and I throwed soap suds in her face and then she sprayed me with the sink sprayer. We always did have a good time together except for that rough patch when she was in junior high and starting to get her period and hated everybody, especially me.

It was that time of year when everything feels all wrong because the time has just fell back. So it was getting dark way too early and the night moved in like a big terrible thunderstorm that never did amount to anything, creeping in black and low. Indian summer was behind us and already the cold breathed at the door, so it was an evening when you feel real good to be sitting in your own little home. The house was warm and close with the smell of the cornbread still hanging in the air.

I had just set down to watch the evening news when Brennen come in, standing right in front of the television. They was talking about Iraq on the television and I tried to look around her but she moved so she'd be blocking my view. Then I could see that her face was white and blank like a sheet of writing paper.

"Don't freak out, now," she said, before I could ask what was wrong. Something come over me and I knowed what she was about to say, so I put my hand up as if to say "Hush." There was an understanding between us that probably didn't last much more than a couple seconds but in that space of time I memorized everything about her. Them big brown eyes, so good and kind. The way the fedora cast that little shadow over them eyes, somehow making them even prettier. The set of her shoulders, the way she shoved her hands into her pockets anytime she was standing still. Her ironed shirt. She was always so neat and clean, never a hair out of place. I could see the little scar on her chin where she had fell in the creek when she was ten. Didn't even cry, and it cut right to the bone. I thought to myself: don't forget this moment right here. You never will have it back again.

"Brennen, surely to God you ain't—"

"I've joined the service," she said.

That summer Brennen wouldn't hush until I went over to the Black Gold Festival in Hazard with her. Now I don't know why in the name of God I had let her talk me into going to that foolishness but Brennen wasn't the kind of person you could say no to. "Oh please, Mommy," she'd said, making her eyes wide and putting out her bottom lip like she was eight again, and I fell for it every single time. As soon as she seen she had her way, she'd let out that big boyish laugh, a big har har har laugh that come from way down in her neck. You could feel that joy in her throat; it was a real thing.

The Black Gold Festival is the biggest thing to happen around here every year although it is a pure-D mess if you ask me. People come from all over and most them are the worst old riff-raff you ever seen. People will come out of the woodworks for a carnival. And that's what it was: a carnival, made up of rides that was just flat-out throwed together by convicts; booths lining Main Street that sold chicken dumplings and roach clips and everything in between; every awful old country band you could think of; some poor pitiful men in white shirts and white boots trying to sing bluegrass and failing real bad at it; that sort of thing. Every once in a while there'd be some good music, but not much. But Lord, people just think it is the biggest thing in the world and that if you don't go you've plumb missed out.

So off we went.

Town was packed tight with people and as we squeezed down Main Street trying to look at the booths I thought about how much happier I'd been back at home drinking me a pot of coffee and reading me a Harlequin but then Brennen reached behind her and grabbed hold of my hand, making sure we didn't get separated. She glanced back over her shoulder and give me a little smile and I tell you what now they is nothing much better than when your grown child lets you know they love you. So I squeezed her hand once and held on.

We looked at all the old tacky crafts and Brennen made me try on a hat that looked like it was made out of pot leaves—she threw her head back and let out that good strong laugh and took a picture of me on her cell phone—and then she bought us a funnel cake and we set on the curb and ate it out of a Styrofoam plate while we people-watched. I never had seen so many people in my life.

Over behind us was a tall, golden-skinned girl who was playing the banjo and singing real mountain music, not that old fake stuff. She could sing just about as good as Patty Loveless, who is the flat-out best one besides Loretta, if you ask me. So when we finished our funnel cake we went over there and watched her awhile.

The singer sung with her eyes closed. She sung:

> *She went upstairs to make her bed*
> *And not one word to her mama said*
> *Her mama she went upstairs, too*
> *Says, "Daughter, O Daughter, what troubles you?"*

Lord have mercy, the way she played that banjo. Her big hands with their big round knuckles, her middle finger swinging wild and free above the strings, her head moving around to the music like she felt every bit of it flowing through her. Brennen was watching her awful hard, and I could see why. She was so strong and could play that banjo so good that I'd be after her too if I'd liked girls.

I studied Brennen while she studied the banjo-player and she made me happy all over.

When the banjo player finished her song she looked right up and her eyes lit right on Brennen and then I knowed she was the whole reason we had come to the Black Gold Festival, period.

"That's Sue," Brennen said. "What do you think?"

"I like her," I said.

When the song was finished she joined us and we strolled on down to the rest of the booths. We ambled along, just taking our time. It was a fine, black-skyed night with a big old silver moon and the warm air moved in off the mountain and settled over Hazard until everything felt just right. There was a few people who stared because it was plain as day that Brennen and Sue was funny, and it seemed like it was made way more plain when you put both them side by side with Brennen's fedora and Sue's big old square-toed boots. But I didn't care. I felt like I had knowed Sue all my life and I had just met her. They was already in love and I had been without that in my life so long that it made me want to bust out laughing, just to be close to it.

We was having a real good time but then at the end of the booths there was a big black van set up with US ARMY painted on its side. It was all souped up, sharp as a tack. The back doors of the van had been opened to reveal a great big television that set back there. There was a long line of children in front of the TV, all waiting to play a video game. Army recruiters was working the line, giving the controller over to a new child, handing out pencils and erasers and shiny brochures. I had seen those

Army recruiters before because they come up Rock of Ages a lot. Them recruiters always go where the poor people live, to get them some more soldiers.

Brennen had always been interested in the Service. Some people are just not cut out for school, no matter what, so she knowed college wasn't for her. Brennen's daddy never came around her much after I quit him, but when he did, he was all the time talking about his adventures in Vietnam. He never told the bad parts of it to anybody, but I had slept with him for enough years to know that the war lived in his dreams. Sometimes it lived in his eyes, too. The war ain't why he was mean—he just *was*—but is sure didn't help his temper any. Even when she was little, Brennen had liked to play with them little green plastic Army men, and act out War and Hostages and all that. But I was real surprised when she wanted to watch the video game because it made me sick.

I listened to one of the recruiters explain the game. 'The point is to kill the insurgents without hitting the civilians,' he announced. When one of the children shot the insurgents *or* the normal people running down the video-game street—it didn't matter which—blood went everywhere and there was a sound like mush hitting the ground, then the next character come on-screen to get shot and it was just like nothing had happened at all to that bunch lined up there. Sometimes when one of the characters would get shot, some of the children would holler, excited and happy, and they'd egg on whoever was playing. And all them kids had parents standing there who was cheering them on, too.

"This ain't right," I told Brennen.

"It's just a video game, Mommy," she said.

"But war ain't no video game, Brennen. And that's what they're making it out to be." I grabbed hold of her arm. "Come on now. This is sickening."

Them recruiters wasn't doing a thing but trying to get them little children to join up and go over to Iraq and Afghanistan or wherever else Bush was going to have them shipped off to. I never will forgive myself for not saying something to them. I ought to have. I should have gone over there and told them what they's doing was wrong.

Lord have mercy, if I had only knowed then what I know now, why, it's untelling what I'd have done.

I thought about that game all the way home as we drove past the black mountains and the yellow windows of every little house setting near the Parkway. Sue had insisted on me riding up front with Brennen so she leaned on the back of my seat and talked to Brennen but I never paid neither one of them no mind. I thought about it after Brennen had took Sue for a midnight walk along the creek. I thought of that game and them parents and the way they had stood there and cheered for their children to kill people. And I thought about them recruiters. I know they was just doing their job, but there's a right way and there's a wrong way.

And I thought about all of that when Brennen left. When it was just me, standing there watching her bus disappear around the curve in the road. When it was just me, setting in that house at night watching the news and trying to see Brennen in the crowds of soldiers they showed on there, or washing dishes alone with the radio turned off, or eating with nothing but the silver sound of fork against plate. I thought about it when Sue would come over to keep me company and we'd set on the front porch to watch the night roll up the holler.

When I was working at the prison, all day long, I didn't think of anything except my daughter, fighting overseas. And them recruiters who wouldn't quit coming to the house or showing up at festivals or ball games, or wherever kids from around there went all the time. I thought about them recruiters a great big lot every single day Brennen was gone to Iraq. I thought about them when I knelt down by my bed every night and prayed for Brennen. And I tell you what, I prayed for them recruiters, too. And every one of them people who stood there while their kids played that old video game. Because it's just like what Christ said when he was hanging on the cross: they didn't know what they was doing.

I called Sue as soon as I got off the phone with the Army people, who told me they was taking Brennen to that Army hospital in Washington DC. I guess I ought to have called my boys, but instead of comforting me Marcus would have just come over to convince me that I wasn't saved, that nobody, in fact, was saved except for him and Markeeta and Oscar Bowling. And there wasn't a bit of use in upsetting Christopher with him doing so good in his classes up at Berea. And to tell the truth I guess the main reason I wanted Sue is because I knowed that Brennen loved her, and so I wanted her closeby.

She got there quick as she could and cried into her big hands, her callused finger laid aside her nose to hide her grief. We set on the porch for awhile, trying to figure out what to do and how to do it.

Just two days before I had seen on the news about that Walter Reed hospital. How it was nasty and eat up with rats and roaches even though it was slick-full of soldiers from Iraq and Afghanistan. They showed pictures of it and there was great big holes in the walls and mold growing in the bathrooms. And that's where they had put my baby. They was still taking soldiers there even though everybody knowed it should have been condemned.

It was bad enough that she had gone over there and fought in that war and got her mind destroyed but now they was putting her in with the roaches and rats. I had been waiting all this time for them to bring her home and this is what they were doing.

"We can leave tonight, Justine," Sue said. "You just say the word."

"I need to do this by myself, Sue," I told her. "I appreciate you. But you stay here and get everything fixed for her."

"But I want to go."

"I know you do. But you'll do her more good by getting everything set up."

Sue nodded. I knowed she wanted to go, and I guess it was real selfish of me, but I wanted to go by myself, and I knowed she would obey my wishes. It's what Brennen had told her to do in case anything happened to her.

What happened to her is that she had been too close when a car exploded. The blow knocked her back so hard that she was unconscious for two days. But the main thing was that she couldn't get over what she had seen. The little children's bodies blown to pieces, the man tore plumb in half and somehow still alive, his eyes darting around in his head, his chest taking great big heaves of breath, the women crying in the road, the soldier with his leg and groin gone.

Brennen was gone, too, in some way. And no matter what they done, they couldn't get her back.

But I could. I would.

I never had been nowhere in my life. Furthest I'd ever been away from home was to Gatlinburg a couple of times, when I'd took Brennen down there to Dollywood. Never had no need to go nowhere. Everything I needed was right there in Rock of Ages. But now I was driving to Washington DC. Sue had made me five or six CDs to listen to on my drive but I hadn't even thought of them until I had drove all the way across West Virginia. I had drove that whole way with silence, not thinking of anything but my baby. Brennen, Brennen, Brennen, I kept thinking. I don't remember anything about that drive but her name.

I found out I was pretty good at reading maps. Sue had printed me out directions from the computer and I had a big old atlas that spread out over the whole passenger seat. Lots of people blowed their horns at me and one woman even give me the finger, but I didn't care. I barely noticed them. I was real surprised to see that that part of Washington DC wasn't that different from back home, with kudzu and a big rolling creek and trees all over the place. I just followed the directions and made every single turn and before I knowed it I was setting right in front of Building 18 of the Walter Reed Army Hospital and it looked just like it had on the news. This part of the hospital used to be a hotel and still looked like one to me, except way worse.

I pulled my car right up on the curb—I wouldn't be there long enough to park—and took a big deep breath and strutted right in there. I was so mad before I even got to the door that I was shaking all over. Not from nerves, but from anger.

The receptionist was on the telephone and looking at something on her computer at the same time. Her fingernail click click clicked on the computer mouse.

"No, I totally left without saying anything," the receptionist squealed into the phone, then started laughing amongst her words. "I did! I totally did!"

She didn't even look up at me, so I slammed my hand down on the counter. "Hey! I need some help here," I said.

She looked at me like she could kill me. Her eye shadow was the color of grapefruit meat. She gave a little tilt of her head and blinked her eyes in a big exaggerated way that said: "What?"

"I need to know what room Brennen Bright is in."

"Hold on a sec," she said into the phone, then just held it out from her head on her palm. "And who are you?" she said.

I could tell right then she was useless as the tits on a boar-hog, so I just breezed right on past her. I hollered out Brennen's name with the girl standing behind me yelling for me to stop, that I couldn't go back there, that she was going to call security.

"I own this place," I shouted over my shoulder to her, my words coming out like four big rocks I could hurl through the air.

I poked my head into the first room, where a boy laid propped up in a bed looking out a nasty window while "The Price Is Right" played on a TV stuck to the wall. I hollered out for Brennen without realizing it, and he didn't even turn his head. The room was shadowy and smothering.

On down the hall. "Brennen! Brennen?"

Dark room after dark room. Boys in beds, looking at me, looking at nothing, their eyes like coins. More televisions, playing soap operas and game shows and talk shows. Either that or total silence, nothing. Each room with its own dank smell. A black woman was mopping the hallway and smiled at me. Next room, this time an older man. His head was bandaged up.

"I'm sorry," I said when I realized Brennen wasn't in the room. He put out both arms, hands grasping for me. "Joanna!" he hollered.

In my head, like a heartbeat gone wild: Brennen Brennen Brennen Brennen Brennen Brennen Brennen Brennen Brennen Brennen Brennen Brennen Brennen.

There was a stairway at the end of the hall, just like there would be in any old cheap hotel. I bound up the stairs, conscious in the back of my mind of a commotion at the end of the hall. The phone-girl must have finally got security.

Rushing down the hall now Brennen poking my head in every room Brennen Brennen Brennen seeing faces of the wounded and the gone and all of them just flatout gone, shadows of themselves, ghosts of themselves, Brennen Brennen Brennen.

Room 201 and 203 and 205.

And there she was. I cried out her name and tears popped out of my eyes, instantly. They had been there, waiting without knowing. I sang her name. I savored it in my mouth, my daughter, my baby, my child, my little darling.

She was worse than I had expected. Her head propped back, her eyes looking at the ceiling, but seeing nothing. She was blinking far more than normal and each blink was a trembling of her eyelashes coming together. She breathed hard.

I kissed her whole entire face. There wasn't a place on her anywhere that I could see, not one bruise or anything at all to let on that she had been hurt. I couldn't stop saying her name, as if saying it enough would make her come back to me.

But there wasn't time to grieve. I wanted her out of this place. There was an IV in her arm and I was careful but quick in taking the needle out. I had seen it done plenty of times when Daddy was dying. I hustled her out of the bed and was surprised that she could stand on her own. She leaned on me, all of her weight on me, but she was standing.

"Walk, baby," I whispered, positioning her arm around my neck. Even in the ripe, stinking room her scent washed over me and it was like being back home, walking the hills in August. I breathed her in as deep as I could. The little hospital gown they had on her was thin as paper and I could feel the heat of her body right through it. I knowed her back was probably all bruised and tore but I had no other choice but to steer her out of there. "Walk, walk."

There was no way I could get her down them stairs, but I found a little elevator with nasty carpet that took us down to the first floor and as soon as the door opened there was the receptionist and a big man in an Army uniform standing like a wall. I just breezed right on by them.

"Stop, ma'am," he said. "You can't take her out of here."

I kept walking, struggling to keep Brennen on her feet. There wasn't a thing they could do to make her stay there and I knowed it.

By the time I made it to the door she couldn't go any further. She fell against me like a little sapling coming to rest against a bigger tree and I knowed she couldn't go a step further. She was so little now but still bigger than me. She always had been a big old gangly girl with them long legs and arms. But I didn't think twice about it. I picked her up in my arms.

And I carried her out of there.

She still ain't spoke a word. But I know she's listening. She keeps her head back, chin pointed up, eyes rolled back like they're searching the ceiling for something, one hand drawn up to her shoulder. What I hate worse than anything is that she can't wear her fedora anymore—it always falls off because of the way she keeps her head back.

I've quit work at the prison so I can stay with her. We get by all right.

Marcus come over a few times but all he wanted to do was pray and preach to us and I finally run him off when he said this was a punishment for Brennen being funny. I went wild on him. I run him all the way to his car, slapping at him. I won't allow nobody to say that about her. I won't. And she don't need the likes of him praying for her. Brennen is in there somewhere and I know that she can pray for her own self. She never did like for nobody else to do anything for her.

I guess I am bad to run people off for I did the same to my mother. Soon as I got Brennen back, here she come, running that mouth, saying I need to put Brennen in a home. I got so mad that I drawed my hand back. Almost slapped my own mommy. So, to keep from it, I told her to never darken my door again. I won't have anybody saying Brennen needs put away somewhere.

Christopher come home from school for the summer and every evening he reads whole chapters of *The Dollmaker* to us as the plastic clock nit-nits the time away. It is the saddest old book ever was but there is something comforting about the kind of sadness in it. It's a beauty I can't rightly describe.

Sometimes Sue comes up and sings and plays the banjo for us. I believe that when Brennen comes back, it'll be on account of the music. She always stirs a little bit when Sue plays that banjo. Last week I could've swore on the Bible that she patted her foot but nobody else seen her. When I started hollering about it Christopher and Sue both looked at each other like I was crazy, but I know that I'm not.

My favorite time of the day is after the supper dishes have been washed and the house smells like cornbread and lemon Joy and the cool of the day settles in over the holler and all down the creek there's nothing but katydids hollering and crickets singing and the pink smoothing itself out over the top of the mountain.

I don't watch the news anymore. Instead, I watch Brennen.

Sometimes, on evenings like that, we help her out onto the front porch and settle her in the old red rocker she always loved so good. I brush out her hair and Sue sings real quiet, so as not to disturb the twilight:

> *Redbird sittin' on my sill*
> *Wonderin' if you love me still*

The setting sun casts its light on Brennen's skin and she is the most beautiful thing I've ever seen in my life with her hair shining on her shoulders. She looks like a mountain queen. If I look straight ahead and just feel her beside me it is like old times. One of these days she will say "Mommy" right out of the blue, and it might be a long hard road but eventually someday I know that I am going to hear that big strong laugh again. And she will have come back to me.

Tony Earley

1961–

Tony Earley was born in San Antonio, Texas, and grew up in North Carolina near the Blue Ridge Mountains. He graduated from Warren Wilson College in 1983 and earned an MFA in creative writing from the University of Alabama. Since 1997 he has taught writing at Vanderbilt University.

Earley's fiction is often set in the mountains of North Carolina. Although his sentence structures have been compared to Hemingway's, Earley cites William Faulkner as the primary inspiration for his style. Earley self-identifies as Appalachian, and says that he strives to articulate universal concerns through the lens of locale. Earley has written novels, short story collections, and novellas.

Some of Earley's fiction, including *Jack and the Mad Dog,* has affinities with folklore and the supernatural as well as the weird tale as practiced by twentieth-century authors such as Manly Wade Wellman, who also uses an Appalachian setting. The protagonist of *Jack and the Mad Dog* is the trickster-hero of the traditional Jack tales. An example of a traditional Jack tale appears in part V of this anthology.

FROM Jack and the Mad Dog

Jack, *that* Jack, the giant-killer of the stories, spent the better part of the evening squatting in the blackberry briars opposite the house of a farmer's wife who would—for four dollars, but with no particular enthusiasm—lean over her husband's plow and let a boy have a go. She was to step into her yard and fling a rock across the road when her husband went to sleep; Jack was to meet her behind the barn, money in hand. This farmer's wife was widely known to possess both a strong arm and noteworthy accuracy, and, to the rabble who frequented the briar patch, her flung invitations often seemed more punitive than hospitable. So Jack waited in the briars, the black shapes of the berries plain against the less black sky, the berries not quite ripe, on a spot in the dirt worn bare by waiting farm boys, the summer air as close and fetid as the breath of a cat. He tried not to think about the whore-flung, judgment-seeking meteorite that might at any moment drop out of the sky and render him senseless. He waited and drank odd-tasting white liquor out of an indifferently washed Mason jar until he came into a cloudy, metallic, buzzy-headed drunk.

The liquor had been a welcome if, as it turned out, not entirely pleasant surprise. He had found it sitting upright in the middle of the road, the lid of the jar screwed on tight, as he had set out on his carnal errand. Jack had often found along the road the things he needed most in his travels, so he assumed he needed the moonshine as well. It had smelled all right enough, just a little off, overcooked maybe, and he took a drink. When he did not die or get carted off by witches he took another. Now he squatted and waited and drank, sucked on the sour berries, flinching beneath his hat every time he thought about the rock with his name on it, until both feet went to sleep and the mosquitoes found him in his unlikely lair, thinking: I'm Jack, *that* Jack, the giant-killer of the stories, and my life has come down to *this*.

And still the farmer's wife did not sling her stone: her husband, the farmer, did not grow sleepy. Jack watched the man smoking on the front porch; the red eye of his homemade cigarette stared out toward the blackberry briars from which Jack stared back with increasing agitation. The farmer's shape was distinct, the outline of his hat sad and plain, lit by that single, small flare, which—the more Jack drank—began to leave fire trails in the darkness as the farmer moved the cigarette between his mouth and the spot where he rested his hand on the arm of his chair. The farmer smoked, one cigarette after another, until the hour grew late and the night grew long, until the katydids tired of their chanting and the crickets tuned down, until all hope passed away from the world, until Jack's hooch and patience dripped away, until that, finally, was that. Jack drained the last of the liquor out of the jar, grimaced, retched, swallowed bile, bad liquor, and a gutful of green blackberries. He stood up, the briars ripping at his clothes, and with a great shout of what he meant to be a curse (but came out instead as an animal blare that made no sense at all, not even to him) he threw the empty jar across the road toward the farmhouse, where it landed in the yard without even breaking.

Jack cocked an ear, listened, waited for the man on the porch to curse back, to yell "Who's out there?" to fire his shotgun into the darkness, to storm down off the porch spoiling to fight the man who had come sneaking onto his property to buy a four-dollar piece of his wife. But the farmer did not make a sound, did not move, sat instead smoking on his porch, placid as a steer, shallow as a mud hole, as if strangers shouting from the briars and Mason jars falling from the sky were every-night occurrences. Jack thought about killing the man—for in the stories he had occasionally killed regular men, but those men had been robbers and millers and the like and had therefore needed killing. He had never killed a farmer, and the one parked on the porch offered Jack no real excuse to start now. He didn't stand up, didn't speak, didn't flick his cigarette into the yard, nothing.

Son of a bitch, Jack thought, he's sitting over there chewing his cud. It was more than Jack could bear. "Cud chewer!" he yelled.

"Go on home, Jack," the farmer said from the porch.

"How do you know it's me?" Jack called. At the time he considered this a clever question.

No response came from the porch.

"How about I come over there with a silver ax and chop your head off?"

"You ain't gonna do no such a thing, Jack. Go on home and get in the bed."

"How about I send my magic beating stick over there to beat you about the ears until you run off down the road and nobody never hears from you again? Then you'll be sorry!"

"Jack," the farmer said patiently, "everybody knows you ain't got no magic beating stick no more. You ain't had one since I don't know when. Now, head on out."

"I'll . . ." Jack said, considering as he spoke an unexpectedly depleted list of options. "I'll come over there and play a trick on you! I'm still smarter than you are!"

"Not tonight, you ain't. I'm on to you and your sneaking *that* Jack ways. There ain't gonna be no Jack tale around here tonight."

"Ha!" Jack hollered. "There already is! And you're in it! It just ain't a very good one!"

"I'll grant you that," said the farmer.

Jack stood quietly for a moment. "Oh, come on," he pleaded. "Just one little slice. All you have to do is go to sleep. It's late. Ain't you got milking and plowing to do in the morning? Ain't that rooster gonna flap up on the fence post and crow before you know it?"

"Jack . . ." the farmer chided sadly.

"What?"

"Don't beg. You used to be somebody."

Disappointed in more ways than he could count, drunk but not pleasantly so, both legs asleep all the way up to his hipbones, Jack climbed from the briars and set out. He was not, so far as he knew, setting out to find a job of work, or a maiden to seduce, or new ground to clear. He was not even leading a cow. He did not expect that he would, at the end of this setting out—sordid though it was—encounter an imbecilic king, inexplicably enraged at the sight of Jack whistling down the road; or a giant greedily clutching a gold-shitting goose in an improbably suspended castle; or a coven of witches yowling from a derelict mill in a fury of feline estrus. He did not, to be honest, even feel like fooling with kings and giants, each of whose slayings—despite the inevitable mental and physical challenges such killings called for—still amounted to nothing more than a job of work, but thought it might be okay to taunt and kill some witches once he sobered up, especially if they were good-looking, although he could not remember the last time he had seen a witch, good-looking or not. The witches had gone off somewhere, along with the silver axes and his magic beating stick and the geese and the giants and the swaying beantrees; along with the kings and their bejeweled, creamy daughters and glittering hoards of gold. Tonight all he had was the setting out itself. So he set out.

He trudged along, intent on forgetting his lust for the doughy expanse of the farm wife's lunar bottom, his squatting in the briars like a stray dog waiting to steal a scrap, his rising black hatred of farmers and all things agricultural, until he stepped unexpectedly into a compensatory truth: he could see in the dark. In a single miraculous moment the road beneath his feet, virtually invisible the moment before, unspooled into the distance before him, silvery and faintly glowing, a still river lit by stars or the thinnest sliver of moon. Yet the sky contained neither stars nor moon, just the low black night pushing down.

"Huh," Jack said.

He could see the tall corn on both sides of the road attentively pressing in; he could see not only the wooded ridges which bordered the fields but the thick summer foliage, billowed and full, blooming on the ridges' steep sides; he could see the ancient, giant-trod mountains in the distance beyond the ridges, separated from the black of the sky by faint bands of light which shimmered and held colors Jack could not name, colors that vanished if he looked at them directly—angels or ghosts or shy, pale brides undressing in darkened rooms. The light wasn't dawn, or even the idea preceding dawn, which still lay hours away, but something Jack had never seen before, something he was sure no one else had ever seen, either, something that only he could see: the world itself was lit from within. The ridges glimmered, the corn in the fields, the road, the mountains, everything he could see gave off a secret light. When he held his hand in front of his face, it, too, shimmered, and he studied it, his good right hand, a fine thing, well-shaped and strong, a hand as adept at caressing a virgin as plunging a silver sword into the disbelieving eye of a giant. All around his raised hand, wherever he looked, the world revealed itself the way Creation must have revealed itself to God, everything part of the greater light, and it was good, and he stood there dazzled and proud and happy, once again Jack the giant-killer, the best man in the world.

So he whistled along, twirling his Saturday hat on his finger, hoping now for a taller tale, until he reached a good-sized creek spanned by a narrow bridge. As he stepped onto the planking he savored for a moment a breath of vestigial excitement, the anticipation he had once felt every time he crossed a bridge. Perhaps this first step would presage not only a pedestrian traveling from here to there but a crossing over from this into that, a passing into a proper story. He hoped briefly for a troll to flummox, but remembered that trolls were now extinct, save for a non-breeding pair locked up in a zoo in Romania.

Jack was halfway across the creek when a large black dog rose up out of the bridge, simply squeezed itself into being out of the bridge's black wood. Jack pulled up fast. He wasn't afraid—startled a little, maybe, at the dog's sudden appearance, but not afraid. Over the years he had learned that nothing really bad ever happened to him, that he was impervious to injury, if not embarrassment, no matter how formidable the adversary or unexpected its appearance. Learning that he didn't have to be afraid had, however, in an almost tragic irony, also robbed him of the corollary excitement. Why, the last time he had rousted out a giant—however long ago that had been—it was all he could do to make himself run.

"Grr," said the dog.

"Howdy," said Jack. (It was his experience that sometimes animals could talk, and sometimes they couldn't, but that it always paid to find out.) He could see the dog's white teeth as it snarled, could see its slobber-lapping, lengthy red tongue.

"Hello, Jack." The dog had a low voice and spoke wetly, deep in its throat.

"So tell me," Jack said, noting that the dog knew his name, but still wanting to get on with things, "why are you impeding my progress across this here bridge?"

"Because that is my solitary calling."

"Where'd you come from?"

"I'm not sure. It was elsewhere or about, but that is all I can know."

Jack nodded. "Limited omniscient narrator," he said. "My point of view."

"Don't rub it in."

The two spent an expectant moment in silence, as if they were actors strutting and fretting, each thinking that the other had forgotten the next line. Jack finally clamped his hat on top of his head.

"Well, Skippy, or whatever your name is," he said, "this has been interesting and all, but why don't you step to one side and let me pass so I can get along with my setting out?"

"I'm afraid I can't do that."

A flicker of impatience flared distantly behind Jack's eyeballs. He remembered that he was still drunk, but not pleasantly so; that the farmer, simpleton though he was, had smoked him out of dipping his wick; that the summer night was still chokingly close and humid. A liquorous headache began to mold itself into something that felt like a thumb, and to jab repeatedly against the backside of his forehead bone.

"Look," he said, pinching the bridge of his nose, "I don't know what kind of story you think this is, but I can see in the dark, and I was enjoying it, even though I'm drunk but not pleasantly so, and I don't want to fool with no talking dog."

"You don't have any choice," the dog said.

"What do you mean, I ain't got a choice? By God, I'm *Jack*. I've always got a choice."

"Not tonight you don't. I'm going to bite you before you get off this bridge. That's how this story goes."

"Shit," said Jack. "You ain't going to bite me."

The dog sank into a crouch. "Jack, I was put on this earth to bite you."

"Whoa, now," Jack said, spitting out a laugh as if it tasted bad. "You ain't supposed to *bite* me. There ain't never been nobody to *bite* me, not ever, in lo all these many years."

"Grr," the dog said.

"Wait a minute," Jack said. "Just hold what you got and let me think." His setting out had arrived at an arrival he was unprepared to ponder. He hadn't met an old man on the road to tell him he would meet a dog on a bridge and give him a silver sword or magic words with which to kill it. (Jack had always counted on the utilitarian, if narratively implausible, appearance of the old man bearing implements and instruction, but somewhere along the way the old man had disappeared, too.) He was by himself in the middle of a bridge in the middle of the night, beset with tiredness and discouragement. His mind was lightly fogged by odd-tasting liquor, and he struggled to think of a way to outsmart a talking dog. He looked around. There wasn't even a non-magical stick lying about, nor a tree to climb in the corn bottoms. Still, in his younger days this problem wouldn't have given him pause. Come on, Jack, he thought, you're *Jack*. Think of something.

"This is the last Jack tale," the dog said, inching closer. "The end of the story."

Jack backed up a step. "Just hold on there, Spot. Before you bite me, I need to know something. Are you mad?"

The dog stopped. "Angry? Somewhat, I suppose."

"No," Jack said. "I mean rabid."

"Hmm," said the dog. "I think so, yeah. I feel a little hindered in the hindquarters."

"So once you bite me I'll die a slow and excruciatingly painful death."

"That seems to be the idea."

Jack frantically searched through his overalls but found only four dollars. He didn't even have a pocketknife.

Without further warning the dog scrabbled forward and leapt at Jack, who managed to take a step backward as it leapt and wrap his hands around its neck mid-leap and keep it at arm's length; he fell down on top of it, pinning the dog's head and chest to the bridge.

"Ow," said the dog.

As the dog jockeyed with its back legs, trying to find purchase, Jack squeezed its neck as hard as he could. Each of his fingers sought its correspondent on the other hand and interlocked as if playing the child's game of building a church. (Here's the people, Jack thought.) He felt the dog gathering its front legs underneath its body, testing Jack's weight. Jack soon realized he could neither choke the dog to death nor hold it for very long. It was one big dog.

"Damn you, dog," Jack panted. "You should *not* have done that." He felt the dog calmly push up against his chest, preparatory to bucking him off.

"You're done," the dog said. "Once I stand up, it's all over."

"I am not *done*," Jack said. "For the last time, I am JACK!"

"Which means nothing."

"I'm important to people."

"Not anymore. Not in any substantive way. The day is soon coming when your stories will be told only by faux mountaineers in new overalls to ill-informed tourists at storytelling festivals."

"Well, what's wrong with that?"

"It's *ersatz*, Jack."

"I don't even know what that means."

"It means you're dead already and you don't even know it."

When the dog pushed itself to its feet, Jack grabbed a fistful of fur in each hand. He spun in a tight circle, lifted the dog off the ground by its head, and with a great shout he threw it off the bridge.

Then Jack ran.

By the time he heard the dog crash into the tangled hell of laurel on the creek bank he had already left the bridge behind. Jack didn't know where he was going, only that going seemed to be a good idea, that his setting out needed to be speeded up. Hiding seemed advisable. He ran a few steps down the road, angling toward the creek bottom, gaining speed with each stride, and leapt from the road, over the gully, his legs running through the air, his arms waving in a vain search for flight; he landed on both feet in the sandy soil of the bottom, and with another step crashed into the thick corn. Behind him, he knew, the dog would soon struggle up through the matted underbrush along the creek bank and set itself on his trail.

The corn was fully tasseled, six and eight feet tall, its ears hardening, two hot weeks away from coming ripe. It reached out and grabbed Jack as he fought through it; it struck at him with its thin, pointed fists; it slid its thick stalks and ropy roots beneath his feet to trip him; it became a congregation of angry Baptists—preachers and deacons and teetotalers and desiccated spinsters and dentists and disaffected, undipped Methodists, rattling with judgment and contempt as he fought through it.

Jack, the corn called in multitudinous chorus, *you're a fornicator and a murderer and a thief!*

"Let me go, corn!" Jack spat. He lowered his head and struck back wildly with his arms.

And you're a ne'er-do-well and a swindler and a liar!

"I am *not* a swindler!"

The truth is not in you, Jack! For shame! Why, you swindled your own brothers!

"They had it coming."

You disappointed your mother.

"Don't you talk about Mama."

Repent! cried the corn. *Repent!*

"Go shuck yourself," snarled Jack.

Behind him he could hear—or thought he could hear, imagined he could hear—the dog huffing with deadly inevitability, bulling after him in a rabid straight line.

Jack fled and fought and cursed with the rage of the unredeemed and the panic of the pursued. He struggled through miles and hours and years and lifetimes of corn and space break and the exposition implied therein, and imagined with each step the rabid fangs of the black dog inches from his hamstrings. After an age and a day he crashed suddenly and unexpectedly out of the corn and sprawled headlong into a prairie of golden wheat. For a long moment he lay facedown on the ground, his nose filled with the rich, anesthetic smells of earth and grain, and considered falling simply into sleep, dog or no dog. He had come a long way. But as soon as he thought about the death that awaited him should the dog catch him—or any death at all, for that matter—he climbed wearily to his feet and stared toward the horizon, where he could at least make out a tree line, no more than a smudge between the field and the sky, who knew how many miles distant, but a destination to aim for nonetheless, a place to flee *to.* He took a first leaden step toward the trees, and a young girl, maiden age, sprang with a yelp from the wheat in front of him and lit out across the field. Before Jack could even cry out, the wheat around him exploded with girls—hundreds, thousands, multitudes of girls—flushed like succulent quail, bounding toward the distant trees. They cried out, "Help me! Somebody help me!" as they leapt gracefully through the wheat.

"Maidens!" Jack thought, breaking unconsciously into a jog. "Look at all the maidens!"

Maidens with glowing complexions of peach and cream and alabaster and ivory, clad uniformly in simple country dresses of virginal white, each dress cut perhaps a size too small and a smidge too short; maidens whose firm flanks fetchingly swayed and flounced, their downy bosoms heaving and swelling; maidens whose flaxen and wheat and chestnut and mahogany and ebony and sable and scarlet and crimson hair billowed and flowed and streamed out behind them; maidens whose panted exhalations were sweet and soft and breathy and catching; maidens whose mysterious and dark and depthless and cerulean and emerald eyes were flashing and shining. In other words, lots and lots of maidens. Tired no longer, Jack vaulted youthfully into full pursuit. He loved nothing more than maidens. He crazily wondered if it were possible to herd all of the girls into one place, like a pasture, or a feedlot. "Hey!" he called, "Come back!"

Jack soon gained ground and fell in behind a pair of twins whose fair hair cascaded behind them in fragrant waves. The girls capered and frisked in step; their silken hair undulated in hypnotic unison. Jack watched their hair for some distance—the girls seemed to have no idea that he was there—but the moment his eyes strayed below their narrow waists the girls stopped and whirled on him so quickly that he almost crashed into them. He managed to bring himself to a teetering, arm-waving halt.

"What do you think you're doing?" asked one.

"Doing?" Jack panted. "I'm running away from a rabid black dog that can talk. What do you think I'm doing?"

"That's not what she meant," said the other. "What she meant was, 'What do you think you're looking at?'"

"Looking at?" Jack said, averting his eyes. "I'm not looking at anything."

"Liar," said the first.

"You were looking at our fair nether parts," said the second.

"Asses," said her sister.

"I was not."

"You were, too."

"Then tell me *this*," Jack said shrewdly. "If you were running *away* from me, how can you *know* I was looking at your fair nether asses?"

"Because we know, Jack. We *know*."

"You think we don't know, but we know."

"Girls always know."

"Hmm," Jack said. "I guess I knew that."

"Next you're going to look at our breasts," the first said.

"I am not."

"You are, too," said the second.

The twins stared at Jack until he blinked. Then he looked at their chests. He tried not to, but he did. And there they were, maiden bosoms. Downy. Tumescent. Firm. The ripe pomegranates of the Old Testament. The top buttons of the girls' dresses strained nobly to restrain them.

Jack thought, *Dah-um.* He thought, *God Almighty,* italics his. He felt his manhood stirring. Or his loins. He could never tell them apart.

"See?" said one.

"Told you," said the other.

Jack smiled what he hoped was an old-fashioned Jack smile. "Do I know you?" he asked.

"Do you know us," said one, shaking her head sadly. "Do you know us."

"Oh, you know us," said the other. "The first time we set eyes on you, you came whistling down the road, looking for a job of work, after your setting out."

"You had the dinner your poor old mama made for you slung over your shoulder on a pole. But the dust on the road had made you powerful thirsty and you had not a drop to drink."

"Mama never remembered to send along water," Jack said. "It was a shortcoming."

"You came upon me first. I was sitting by the roadside, weaving a basket of golden straw for to carry eggs to the market. You asked me to draw you a dipper of water from the well."

"And *I* was sitting in the doorway of our daddy's sturdy cabin, churning a bait of butter for to bake a cake. Then you asked *me* to draw you a cup of water from the well."

"You sure did drink a lot of water."

"Was your daddy a farmer?" Jack asked.

"Miller," said both.

"Ah," Jack said. For one sweet moment he sensed more than remembered the rhythmic rumble of a turning wheel, the gentle *shush shush shush* of water splashing, a slant of silver moonlight, an intake of breath as soft as the noise made by the wings of a moth, but he couldn't conjure the face of a girl. So many maidens, so many mills. Twins, though. He thought he would've remembered twins.

"That night at supper, while our daddy was eating his vittles and eyeballing his shooting-gun leaning by the doorstop, you tricked him into giving you his silver sword and ten bags of gold."

"We still don't know how you pulled that one off."

"Then you slipped him a sleeping draught that made him snore so that the door joggled and the roof shook and nobody never heard the like, then or now."

"You met me in the mill when the black cat mewled, and lay with me in the moonlight on the tow sacks of meal our daddy had ground by day."

"Then you lay with *me* on the same tow sacks when the old owl hooted three times in the sweet gum tree."

Jack tasted a whiff of the bad liquor he had drunk. He felt another stirring, not of loin but of remorse. The feeling was unfamiliar, and he did not care for it. What was wrong with him? If the three of them managed to get away from this dog, why couldn't he lie with them again? He was Jack, after all, *that* Jack. But instead he swallowed. He said, "Forgive me, but I'm not . . ."

". . . sure you remember us?"

"I, I'm sorry, no, I . . ." He leaned forward and looked intently into the eyes of one girl and then the eyes of the other.

"They're not limpid pools of amber, Jack," said the first.

"They're light brown."

"And they're not shining or flashing or burning with passion."

"They're just eyes."

Jack glanced back and forth between their lovely faces with increasing consternation. Why couldn't he remember?

"It's just as well you don't recollect us."

"We were fifteen, Jack. *Fifteen.*"

"I know," he said. "I mean, were you? I mean, I guess I know that now because you just told me."

The girls stared at him, their brows slowly lowering.

"It was wrong, what happened," he said, "wasn't it?"

"It was wrong, Jack."

"It was wrong before you even stepped forward into that particular setting out."

The liquor roiled in Jack's stomach. Inside his head he felt himself stepping off down an unfamiliar road. No good lay at its end. The way was dark and cold and he was alone and growing older with each step. He couldn't find his shoes. Jagged stones bruised and cut his feet.

"What happened after I left?" he asked, his voice falling so that he could barely hear it. "Tell me what happened next."

One girl blinked into a frown. "Why, nothing happened, Jack. You took the narrator with you. Daddy never woke up from the sleeping draught you gave him. He kept snoring so the door joggled and the roof shook and nobody never heard the like. Except us. We were the only people about the settlement once you left. Eventually the mill rotted down and the dam gave way and the great wheel tipped and toppled into the ivy, where it lays till this day."

"But what happened to *you?*" Jack whispered.

"Me? I just sat by the side of the road weaving a basket of golden straw for to take eggs to the market."

"And *I* sat in the doorway churning a bait of butter for to bake a cake."

"And nobody else came down the road."

"Not ever."

"For ages and ages."

"Till the day I looked up and saw a big black dog a-standin' on the hilltop. At first I was thrilled with joy because we'd been sitting there a hundred years waiting for a new story, and his appearance set us free, but then I realized he meant us no good, so I grabbed up my sister and off we ran down the road."

"And after an age and a day of running down the road and over the creek and fighting through the corn, here we are," the other girl said, sweeping her arm around the wheat field. "Here we are. We found you, and we found us a narrator."

Jack looked nervously over his shoulder. A few more girls, stragglers, splashed out of the corn. They looked haggard, their simple country dresses soiled and torn. They hurtled by beat and bored and glared at him as they passed. He saw in their eyes that they recognized him, but nobody smiled and nobody waved and nobody stopped. Nobody asked for his help. He forgot to look at their fair nether parts as they ran away. Jack turned to the twins.

He said, "All these girls, I—"

"Yep."

"Some of 'em twice."

"Are any of 'em, well, you know—?"

"You'd have to ask them."

"Are you proud of yourself, Jack?"

"That's what we want to know, Jack *that* Jack. Tell us, are you proud?"

Jack was ashamed of what he had done—maybe for the first time in his life—but still, in his most secret heart, he wished that he had counted as the girls ran away. "Well," he admitted. "Maybe a mite."

"Then what are their names?" demanded one.

"Names?" Jack said.

"You heard her. Their names."

Jack realized he had never known any of their names. They had all been farmers' daughters and millers' daughters and kings' daughters.

"Uh," he said, thinking hard. "Susan?"

"No, Jack. None of us never *got* names."

"The same way none of us never got more than the one white dress to wear, and it too tight, not even after you saw to it we needed a different color."

"You never saw fit to ask us."

"Not even after you lay with us."

Jack remembered then—as clearly as if he were there—the rhythmic screech of a turning wheel, a dagger of hard moonlight, a girl lying back on a stack of sacked cornmeal, her white dress pushed above her waist. She said, I don't know, Jack. I don't know. But what had that meant, the "I don't know"? He dug the heels of his hands into eyes. What he wanted most right then was to forget that he had ever set foot in that mill, that he had ever set out down the road that led to that mill, but he could smell the corn dust, hear the wheel, the water, a soft gasp of breath.

"You have put thoughts in my head I find troublesome," Jack said. "Please make it stop."

"It ain't gonna stop, Jack."

"You drank the seeing juice."

"The what?"

"The seeing juice. You drank it all up."

"Out of the jar we put in the road."

"That's why you can see in the dark."

"Oh, no!" Jack wailed. "I shoulda known. Y'all are witches. I thought all the witches was gone! Y'all done went and gave me a potion!"

"We're not witches, Jack. And not maidens. We're just girls."

"We got the seeing juice from the old man beside the road. He said it was something you needed."

"What prodigious perfidy!" Jack said.

"We put out it in the middle of the road so you would find it on your setting out."

"But why?" Jack said. "Why would you do that to me?" But he knew even as he asked the question that its answer was obvious.

"Because we wanted you to see."

"So you would know."

"And now you see."

"And now you know."

"But I don't want to see," Jack said. "And I don't want to know. I just want to set out. I want the sky to be new and the wind fresh on my cheek. I want to feel the warm red dust scrouging up between my toes. I want to whistle off down the road with the lunch my mama made slung over a pole and meet an old man who'll say, 'Howdy, Jack. Today you're going to meet a giant with two heads, here's two silver hatchets.'"

"That ain't going to happen no more, Jack."

"The black dog is going to get us all. He's eating all the stories up from the inside."

"So enjoy it while you can."

"It's almost like living, this knowing."

Jack grabbed the twins by their hands and tried to pull them with him through the wheat.

"It's no use, Jack. Just let us go."

"No," Jack said, squeezing their hands so tightly he was afraid he might hurt them. "I ain't gonna turn you loose."

"It's fine like this, Jack," said one. "It's fine."

"It's not fine," he said.

"We're lucky in a way," said the other. "We got to be in another story. Even if it was with you."

"We're not weaving baskets and churning butter when nobody never comes. This is better."

"But the way it ends . . ." Jack said.

"Is the way it ends. The black dog's gonna catch us and say what it is he has to say and he'll bite us and we'll scream and that'll be that."

"Come with me," Jack pleaded, not knowing if their coming with him was even a narrative option. He had always traveled alone. "I'll get us a farm. How about that? I'll get us a farm and clear some new ground and sow some seeds and grow some corn and a few tomatoes and I won't set out no more. I won't be in any more stories. I'll try to be a regular man. Come with me and I'll marry one of you and won't lay a finger on the other one, I promise. We can grow us up a barnload of kids and live happily ever after. We can live happily ever after."

"Oh, Jack," one chided. "You don't *do* happily ever after."

"I do, too," protested Jack. "I've done happily ever after lots of times."

"But then the page turns."

"The page turns and off you go again."

"Shut *up*," Jack said. "Just shut *up* and come *on*."

He tried to jerk the girls after him. Their hands were sweaty, almost hot to the touch, calloused from weaving and churning. When they pulled back against him he squeezed harder and felt their delicate bones rubbing together underneath their skin.

"Ow!" said the girl he clutched with his left hand. "You're hurting me!"

"You let her go!" cried the girl on his right just as she clouted him upside the head. "Don't you hurt her no more!"

Jack dropped the hands of both girls and rubbed his ringing ear. He said, "What the hell'd you do that for? I'm just trying to save you!" But when he looked up the girls were gone, just gone, vanished as completely as if they had been imagined along the side of a road, and just as quickly forgotten.

Robert Gipe

1963–

Robert Gipe was reared in Kingsport, Tennessee. After earning a BA from Wake Forest University and an MA from the University of Massachusetts–Amherst, Gipe worked in marketing and educational outreach at Appalshop, a grassroots media production company in Whitesburg, Kentucky, a position that foreshadowed the synthesis of community outreach and the arts that has characterized his career. Beginning in 1997, Gipe served as the director of the Appalachian Program at Southeast Kentucky Community and Technical College in Harlan County.

Gipe is committed to working with his community to address problems besetting Appalachia's coalfields, including poverty, drug addiction, out-migration, and discrimination based on race, gender, or sexual orientation. Gipe's community activism has taken a number of forms. For more on Gipe's extensive work in the community, see the headnote for the Higher Ground Project in this anthology.

In 2006, Gipe began attending the annual Appalachian Writers Workshop at Hindman Settlement School in Hindman, Kentucky; subsequently, he became active in Lincoln Memorial University's Mountain Heritage Literary Festival and, in 2010–2011, participated in Darnell Arnount's novel-writing workshop, in which he developed the novel *Trampoline* (2015). Its sequel, *Weedeater*, appeared in 2018; a third is planned. Gipe's fiction is hybrid, with elements of the graphic novel, the illustrated novel, and the traditional text-only novel. In Gipe's novels, the illustration panels, drawn by him, are an essential part of the narrative. The novels grapple with the same community issues that Gipe addresses in his work as an educator and community activist.

FROM Trampoline: An Illustrated Novel

CHAPTER ONE: DRIVING LESSON

Mamaw stared through the gray-gold wood smoke curling from a pile of burning brush in the front yard. I set a glass of chocolate milk at her elbow and sat down next to her on the porch glider.

"That's where they're going to strip," she said, nodding at the crest of Blue Bear Mountain. "They'll start mining on the Drop Creek side. But they'll be on this side before you graduate." She sipped her chocolate milk. "You watch."

Mamaw linked her lean arm through mine and told me about growing up on Blue Bear Mountain. Her stories smelled of sassafras and rang with gunfire, and the sound of her voice was warm as railroad gravel in the summer sun, but the stories flitted through my mind and never lit. I was fifteen.

That August, Mamaw signed her name to a piece of paper, a lands-unsuit-able-for-mining-petition, the state calls it. The petition stopped a coal company from strip mining on Blue Bear Mountain. The coal companies told everybody Mamaw's petition would be the end of coal mining. Halloween, Mamaw got her radio antenna broken off her car. We never even had a trick-or-treater.

Mamaw didn't get her antenna fixed until the Saturday before Thanksgiving. That afternoon Mamaw came in my room. I was eating M&M's straight out of a pound bag, about to make myself sick. They weren't normal M&M's. They were the color of the characters in a cartoon movie that hadn't done any good and the bags ended up at Big Lots, large and cheap and just this side of safe to eat.

"Put them down if you want to go driving," Mamaw said.

I took off running for the carport. I was strapped into Mamaw's Escort a long time before Mamaw came out. She got in the car and turned to me, the keys closed in her hand.

"Put your seat belt on," she said.

"It is on, Mamaw."

"You know you got to keep your eyes moving when you're driving."

"Yes, Mamaw."

A pickup truck covered in Bondo pulled up and spit out Momma.

"Going for a driving lesson?" Momma's cigarette bounced in her mouth.

Neither one of us said anything. Momma jumped in the backseat. I closed my eyes and wished her gone. She was still there in the rearview when I opened my eyes. I started the Escort and backed onto the ridge road.

I WENT THROUGH THE CURVE TOO QUICK.

My cousin Curtis come flying the other way on his four-wheeler. Mamaw's Escort side-swiped the wall of rock on the high side of the road. The sound of the scraping metal felt like my own hide tearing off.

"Daggone," Momma said. "You're worser than me."

"Hush, Patricia," Mamaw said. "Dawn, are you all right?"

"Yeah," I said, my hands shaking.

"Get on home, then," Mamaw said.

When I pulled into the carport and shut off the motor, Mamaw and Momma got out and looked at the side of the car.

"'Whoo-eee," Momma said.

They went in the house, left me sitting there breathing hard, all flustered. I turned on the radio. It was tuned to a station Mamaw liked. Most of the time they played old country music, but that night they had some kind of rock show on. "I'm about to have a nervous breakdown," a boy sang. "My head really hurts." The guitars sounded like power tools being run too hard. I'd never heard such before. I turned it up til the speakers buzzed. The next song was a country song, all slow and twangy. I was about to turn it off when the singer sang, "My head really hurts." The country song had the same words as the one before. At the end of the song, there was the sound of a throat clearing. The voice that spoke sounded like spent brake pads.

"That was Whiskeytown doing the Black Flag song 'Nervous Breakdown.' Before that we had the Black Flag original. You're listening to Bilson Mountain Community Radio. I'm Willett Bilson. This here next one is another record I got from my brother Kenny, by the band Mission of Burma."

Willett Bilson sounded about my age. He sounded like someone I would like to talk to. The power tool guitars started again. Willett played five angry, reckless songs in a row. My head got light. I started the engine and slipped the shift into reverse. The bands came on one right after another, rough and mad, and they carried me through curve after curve. It felt good, like riding a truck inner tube down a snowy hill curled up in my dad's lap. When I pulled into Mamaw's, rain pecked the carport roof, bending the last of the mint beside the patio. Inside, Momma was gone, and Mamaw set a bowl of vegetable soup in front of me. She didn't say anything about me taking the car back out.

The next day after school, Mamaw asked me if I wanted to ride with her to Drop Creek, the place where she grew up, to look at a man's house. I ran out of the house and started the Escort.

"You aint ready to drive to Drop Creek," she said. "You need more practice."

"Well then, I aint going."

"Yes, you are. Scoot over."

The house we went to had vinyl siding and set on blocks. The yard was neat and the gravel thick on the driveway. A little boy with a head like a toasted marshmallow bounced a pink rubber ball against the wall under the carport. When he saw us he hollered in the house. A stout silver-haired man came out.

"How yall doing?" he said. He told me how tall I was getting like everybody does.

"Want a piece of pound cake?" People always fix pound cake when Mamaw comes to talk about their troubles with the coal company. We went inside. It was quiet and neat in there too.

"Look at that Christmas cactus," Mamaw said. "So beautiful."

"Thank you," the man's wife said. "It likes that spot."

The wife had a northern accent. She moved through the room making things straight. Mamaw and the silver-haired man set down at a table in the kitchen next to the wall. I stood at Mamaw's shoulder. The man showed Mamaw pictures he pulled from a drugstore one-hour photo folder.

"These was done before they started blasting." The man pointed at a picture of the block at the base of the house. "I took these the other day." He showed Mamaw a picture of a crack running up through the same block. Then he showed her a closeup picture with a thumb stuck up in the crack.

Mamaw said, "Did the state inspect?"

"Yeah," the man said, "they did."

"What did they say?"

"I keep notebooks where I write down when the blasts happen and how long they last. They looked at them said they'd look into it."

"That all they said?"

The man's wife set down a plate of sliced pound cake, a bowl of strawberries, and a tub of Cool Whip. Mamaw looked at the pound cake, then she looked into the man's eyes.

"They said subsidence was natural, could have caused those cracks," the man said.

"Oh, bullshit," Mamaw said. "When was this house built?" Mamaw put a piece of pound cake on a paper napkin, took a big bite out of it.

"Daddy built it with Granddaddy. Right after him and Mommy got married. Finished it a year before they went to Michigan. So, 1958, 1959. Something like that."

"And you aint never had no cracks before, have you?"

"No ma'am," the man said. "Not that I know of."

"Pure sorry," Mamaw said, spooning out strawberries and Cool Whip into a bowl. She crumbled the rest of her pound cake down on top of the strawberries and Cool Whip and mashed it all up with a spoon. Then Mamaw said, "What do you want to do about it, Duane?"

"Well," the man said, "I hate to see people get run over."

"You coming to the meeting Tuesday?"

"Yeah," he said, "I got a doctor's appointment in Corbin. But I should be back."

"Well," Mamaw said, "we could use you. You coming tonight to the planning meeting?"

"I'll be there," Duane said.

I went outside. Marshmallow boy threw his ball into a pile of leaves. A little black dog leapt in the leaves and disappeared. The rustling leaves looked like Bugs Bunny moving underground.

Mamaw and the boy's daddy come outside, and the man showed Mamaw the cracks.

"The blast shook the whole house, throwed her china plates out on the floor," the man said. "They was stood up in a cabinet and they busted all over the place." The man shook his head.

Mamaw toed a weed in the gravel. The little dog ran up to me and the boy, dropped the ball, and backed off, its tail wagging. Mamaw told the man to thank his wife for the pound cake, that it was real good. Mamaw drove us back to Long Ridge.

The state scheduled a meeting the Tuesday before Thanksgiving for people to come and give their testimony about whether or not the company's permit to mine should be approved. Monday night Mamaw's group had a meeting in town at the library to talk about what they were going to say at the meeting on Tuesday. That's the way it was that fall. Meetings about meetings, and then a meeting on top of that. Again she made me go, and again she wouldn't let me drive.

I sat at the back of the room in the basement of the public library and looked at pictures of the USS *Canard County* in a glass case. It was a navy ship that hauled tanks and trucks to Haiti and the Persian Gulf and Argentina til the navy sold it to Spain.

The organizers that the statewide group sent came in carrying rolled-up maps and armloads of flyers and information sheets. The one named April wore a home-made sweater of purple yarn that hung big on her. The one named Portia had leather patches across the shoulders of her sweater, like she was on a submarine. They both had big wild hair. Mamaw said they looked like woolyboogers.

April and Portia talked awhile, and then different ones in the group said things. A man with a receding hairline stood up and said that they would use the same explosives on that strip job that blew up the building in Oklahoma City. A woman with short hair and a sticky-faced little boy said they used to eat fish out of the creek.

"You see what it is now," the woman said. "Yellow mud." She put spit on her thumb and used it to wipe her boy's face.

Mamaw said, "Duane, why don't you say what happened to yall."

Duane told what had happened to him, to his house.

April told them they had to practice what they were going to say, have their facts straight, if their petition was to stop any new strip mines on Blue Bear Mountain. They had to have goals, April said. She put paper on the glass case that held the sugar-cube battleship and made people make a list of goals. Portia put big maps on the case and showed them what lands would be protected.

When they took a break, a woman with a gray ponytail and trembling hands out smoking said the dust from the coal trucks was so bad she couldn't let her grandbabies play outside. April tried to get her to say she would talk at the meeting.

On the way home, Mamaw stopped at the Kolonel Krispy dairy bar and got a double fudge shake with brownies swirled up in it. We sat in the parking lot and watched the red light, and Mamaw said all strip mining ought to be outlawed. I asked her if I could drive home. She said I needed to practice more.

When we got home, Mamaw looked at a pile of mail on the kitchen counter. "Where's my check?" she said. Three of Momma's cigarettes were in the ashtray. Mamaw called my uncle Hubert's house and asked where Momma was. They said she'd gone to Walmart. When Mamaw caught up to Momma in the Walmart parking lot, Mamaw's face was solid red.

"You come here," Mamaw said, hard as a broomstick to the back of the legs.

Momma kept walking towards the store. I guess Momma didn't think Mamaw would do anything in the Walmart parking lot.

Mamaw caught up to Momma and got her by the arm and smacked her in the face. She stuck her hand in Momma's front pocket and pulled out a wad of money.

"You don't do me that way," Momma yelled.

"Watch me," Mamaw said.

Then they both went to yelling at the same time. I went in the store, looked dead in the eye of the people coming out, the ones who didn't know yet Cora Redding and her wasted daughter were having it out in the yellow stripes of the crossing zone. I went back to jewelry and asked my dad's niece who worked there to take me home. She said it would be an hour. I wandered through the store, through the Christmas candy and blow-up snowmen and stupid dancing Santas playing the electric slide and stupid reindeer socks. My cousin took me to the snack bar and bought me everything I wanted to eat. Pizza sticks. Two slushies. Then we went to the Chinese restaurant. I ate every fried egg noodle they had in there.

When my cousin dropped me off at Mamaw's, Momma and Mamaw sat at the kitchen table, hundreds of envelopes and flyers saying write the governor to protect Blue Bear on the table between them. Momma helped Mamaw stuff the envelopes like nothing had happened. I was so sick on cookies and pop and hot dogs and Chinese food.

But I didn't. I went to my bed panting like a black dog in August and swore to the ceiling I wouldn't never have a child. When I slept, I dreamed I was playing music on the radio with Willett the DJ.

The next day in biology, a girl from up the river sat behind me and talked to her cousin the whole class about whose chicken nuggets had better crust. "They got too much pepper on theirs." "Them others is too mushy." I was ready to kill her. I turned around and said, "There's more to life than chicken nuggets, you know." She looked at me like I wasn't there.

I told my friend Evie about the chicken nugget girl when we were out in the parking lot drinking beer at lunchtime.

"I whipped that girl one time," Evie said. "It wasn't fun at all."

I asked her why not.

"She's too stupid," Evie said. "It was like stomping a baby bird."

I told Evie about the band that played the nervous breakdown song. Black Flag. She said she never heard of them. She only listened to what was new. I told Evie about the radio station on Bilson Mountain. She said only old people and hippies listened to that station.

Mamaw picked me up after school. "I need to stop by Duane's," Mamaw said.

The sun peeped over the ridgeline and lifted steam off Duane's roof. In the shadows there was still frost on the yard. A dark pile of something lay in the carport. I thought it was a wadded-up shirt. It was the little black dog frozen solid. Mamaw knocked at the kitchen door and went in before anyone answered. I stood in the carport looking at the dead dog. It was going flat. Its tongue was out. There was no sign of the boy. The pink ball was up against the back wheel of Duane's truck. Mamaw came out of the house. "Let's go," she said.

"What happened, Mamaw?"

"Duane aint coming to the meeting."

"Why not?"

"Somebody fed his dog broken glass mashed up in hamburger."

The meeting was in a stone community building the VISTAs built on Blue Bear Creek back in the sixties. There must have been two hundred people there. Where Blue Bear had the state's highest peak on it, people all over were excited about protecting it. It wasn't just an ordinary mountain with ordinary people living on it. It belonged to the whole state.

Three people from the state—two men and a woman—sat in front of the stage at a table. Their powder-blue shirts had button-down collars and an embroidered patch of the state seal on the sleeve. Hair striped the top of one man's head. The other had a thick bronze helmet of hair. The woman's eyes were wide behind clear-framed glasses, cheap like they gave us for free at school. The three of them sat behind their table. They stacked and restacked their papers, took folders out of file boxes and then put them back in.

People filed in in clots of three and four. There were painted signs saying stuff like: "SAVE BLUE BEAR," and "COAL KEEPS THE LIGHTS ON" strung out along the walls of the community center. People settled in, talking low to them they came with, leaning forward and greeting the people on their side with pats on the back and handshakes, smiling.

IT WAS LIKE A CARNIVAL, LIKE A CHICKEN FIGHT.

When time came to start, the man with the bronze helmet of hair leaned forward into a microphone. "Good evening everyone. This hearing is required by law, and pertains to mine 848-1080, amendment 3, a surface-mining permit application in the Drop Creek and Little Drop Creek watersheds in Canard County, Kentucky. Everyone who wishes to speak should have already signed up. All speakers will be limited to three minutes. If anyone has more to say, they may wait until everyone who has signed up to speak has spoken, and then we will go around again. I would remind everyone no decision will be made tonight. Everything said will go into the file and will be taken into consideration as the cabinet makes its decision. We will begin in three minutes."

After three minutes, they called the name of the first woman signed up to speak. The state woman brought her a wireless microphone. The first woman said she was proud of her husband, that she had married him because she wanted to be a coal miner's wife. She said she would not be ashamed of what he did and would not allow her children to be ashamed of what he did.

The second person to speak was also a woman. She said the state should consider all the trash that was in the creeks, how terrible a shape the road was in. All the dust from the coal trucks flying up and down the road was terrible. She couldn't even hang her clothes out on the line, she said, and when she said something to one of the drivers he was just rude.

The third speaker he talked about the ozone layer, how there was holes in it and how we couldn't go on burning coal forever, that we needed to think about the future, about what we were leaving behind for our children. He talked for a while longer, and the man from the state had to tell him his time was up. The speaker said he had more to say, and the state man said he could give his paper to him and he would attach it to what all else he had.

Then the man from the state said he wanted to remind everybody that they was only there to consider testimony pertaining to mine permit 848-1080 amendment 3 and that of course people could use their minutes any way they wanted to but that that particular permit application was what they were there for.

Mamaw sat stone still in her folding chair, and the speeches went on and on. Every speaker tried to talk people into believing what they themselves believed.

The fluorescent lights flickered. Four different ones needed changing. Out the high windows, the lights of coal trucks streaked past. The state people sat like prizes at a carnival game, eyes wide and blank, stuffed pink monkeys, green hippopotamuses piled too close together. Every once in a while they would take a note, but not that often.

A woman I'd seen at Mamaw's meetings called the coal company out by name, said they'd told her mother they weren't going to strip mine her land, that they was just going to build a coal haul road across it and that they wouldn't be out there even a month. She said they'd promised to build a road out to her family's cemetery—widen it. And then when her mother signed her rights away they'd strip mined the shit out of it—that's what the woman said—and they'd mined right up to the cemetery and probably would've mined right through it if she—the daughter—hadn't come back from Georgia. There wadn't no way, that woman said, that company ought to be allowed to mine coal period, much less on Blue Bear. They ought to be put in jail, that woman said, everyone of them, and especially you, she said, and pointed to a man with a wire-brush moustache standing in the back spitting into a plastic pop bottle, his arms folded across his chest.

"Especially you, Mickey Mills that lived right here in this community and lied to my mother. You're a sorry excuse for a man," that woman said, and started towards him before her husband stopped her.

Then a woman stood up and said "You aint taking my husband to jail. You're just a busybody. You don't live here no more and don't deserve no say in what goes on here."

The man from the state got on the microphone. "All right. Order. Please."

The next speaker was a man in a sweater vest and a green plaid shirt I didn't know. He talked about the Indiana bats and the Turk's cap lilies and other plants and animals that only lived in Kentucky near the top of Blue Bear Mountain. I didn't know what difference that would make to anybody. Mamaw told me it did.

A thick coal company office man stood up and told how many jobs the company made, about their participation in the youth baseball leagues and their big ads in the high school gymnasium. Another company man talked about how that if they didn't approve these permits that it would likely mean the end of coal mining in Canard County and maybe all of Kentucky. He said people didn't know how the coal industry could fall apart at any minute, and then where would Canard County be? When he asked that question he spread out his arms and turned to the crowd, and it seemed to me that that was who he was talking to anyway. He finished up by saying that the state should approve the permit and get out of the company's way and let the good working people of Canard County do what they do best—do better than anyone in America—run coal. When he said that there was all kinds of cheering and whistling as he sat down.

The next person to speak was the woman with the pulled-back hair who had been at Mamaw's meeting, the one I'd swore would never have spoke. She was on the other side of Mamaw from me, her paper shaking in her hands. She put her other hand on the back of the folding chair in front of her, barely able to see over the frosted blonde head of the miner's wife sitting in front of her.

"My name is Agnes Therapin. I live on Little Drop Creek." Her back straightened when she said the name of the creek. "I am against this here permit. They's people that lives beneath these strip jobs. It aint out in a desert somewheres. It's up the creek from me. This here is the third time you have let them add on to this strip job. I wish you'd never let them start, but I don't know why you didn't just let them mine the whole thing to begin with. Then we wouldn't always have been a-hoping that maybe we might have a decent place to stay." Her hands beat restlessly on the back of the chair in front of her. The miner's wife leaned forward, turned to look at Agnes. "My mommy lives with us," Agnes went on. "She has a bad leg, and this dynamite has knocked her out of bed more than once. We thought you fellers—you come up here from Frankfort or wherever—and I guess I thought you was there to protect us. To protect our homes and our property. I thought that was what the law was supposed to be there for. To keep the peace. Well, you fellers need to know, and I don't know if you all have been up there or not, but let me tell you. There aint no peace on Little Drop Creek."

Agnes's neck was stiff. She arched her back like it hurt.

She stared at the state people. People were quiet, but the seconds passed and people started to rustle.

"Thank you, Ms. Therapin." The state man said her name wrong.

"You are supposed to protect us," Agnes shouted. "Surely they's laws against blowing up people's houses. People aint setting off dynamite at your house are they? Don't reckon they come blowing your people up do they? Where do you live?"

"Thank you, ma'am," the state man said.

"Where's your house at?" The state woman came to take the microphone from Agnes. Agnes jerked it away.

"Sit down, Ms. Therapin," the state man said.

"Maybe we ought to come set a couple shots off at your place." Agnes's neck was red as blood. "See how you like it."

"Agnes," Mamaw said, and covered Agnes's hand on the back of the chair with her own. Agnes sat down. Another woman across the room with "I heart coal" on her T-shirt stood up and faced Mamaw.

"Cora Redding, this wouldn't be happening if you weren't stirring everybody up. You don't live on Drop Creek. You moved to town. You wouldn't have no business, you wouldn't be sitting on your little pile of money, if it wasn't for the working people around here, people mining coal. You need to mind your own damn business."

"Anyone who cannot remain civil," the state man said, "will be removed from the meeting."

The woman stuck her finger out at Mamaw. "You need to keep your big fat nose out of things don't concern you."

I stood up. I pointed back at the woman.

I said, "You don't need to be telling my mamaw what her business is. You don't know my mamaw. You aint got no right to talk to my mamaw."

"Young lady," the state man said, "you are speaking out of turn."

I wadn't done. "What do you want us to say? 'Go ahead and tear up the world. We'll just get out of the way while you destroy ever thing our friends ever had? Here, take my house; I'll just live here in this hole in the ground. Yeah, go ahead and set that big yellow rock on our heads. We'll be fine.'"

"If I could ask the deputy sheriff—" the state man started.

"Dawn, sit down," Mamaw said. "Sir, she don't mean it . . ."

I sat down. A buzzing in my head kept me from hearing what was said after that. I wished I hadn't spoken. I wished I hadn't said a word.

Someone held up a jar of dirty water. Somebody brought in a bunch of kids carrying a banner. I'm not sure what side they were on. When it was over Mamaw had to shake me to get me to move. I dreaded walking out. I wasn't invisible anymore.

Wiley Cash

1977–

Born in Fayetteville, North Carolina, Wiley Cash grew up in Gastonia, North Carolina. He earned a BA from the University of North Carolina at Asheville, an MA from the University of North Carolina at Greensboro, and a PhD from the University of Louisiana at Lafayette. At Louisiana, he studied with Ernest Gaines, an influence on his thinking about the importance of place in fiction. Cash identifies early twentieth-century Appalachian author Thomas Wolfe and southern authors William Faulkner, Flannery O'Connor, and Bobbie Ann Mason as other sources of his interest in place.

Cash's first novel, *A Land More Kind Than Home* (2012), was a critical and popular success, as was his second, *This Dark Road to Mercy* (2014). Cash's third novel, *The Last Ballad* (2017), is a historical novel set amid the labor strife in Gastonia in 1929. The protagonist, Ella May Wiggins, was a labor organizer whose song "Mill Mother's Lament" appears elsewhere in this anthology. "Verchel Park," the short story below, features characters from *The Last Ballad*.

In all his novels, Cash offers sympathetic depictions of people in many different walks of life. He is sensitive to economic injustice, the plight of women, and discrimination.

Cash currently is writer in residence at the University of North Carolina at Asheville and teaches in the Mountainview Low-Residency MFA program at Southern New Hampshire University.

Verchel Park

By the time he met his wife, Verchel Park was forty-eight years old and had lost the use of his right hand after getting it caught up in the spinner belt at the Cowpens Manufacturing Company. He'd spent most of his time since the accident convalescing in his brother's front room and using his good hand to spoon cornbread and buttermilk into the mouths of his twin niece and nephew when he wasn't yanking up weeds from the patch of garden out behind his brother's house. What little bit of time he'd had left he'd spent at the Baptist church out on the highway toward Spartanburg, singing hymns, watching old Pastor Olyphant save a few souls, and praying for his ruined hand to come back to life right there in his lap. He hadn't had a drink in the almost eight months since the accident, and he needed something to prove he was doing right in the eyes of God. He didn't know what kind of proof he needed, but he figured getting married to the preacher's widowed daughter was about the best proof of God's hand in one's life that he could hope for.

At forty-eight herself, Myra Olyphant née Stebbins had been widowed for just one week when she moved to Cowpens, South Carolina, from somewhere outside Atlanta. Verchel had first heard that her dead husband had owned a feedstore out in the country south of the city, and then Verchel heard it was a whole entire farm and that his business alone is what kept the feedstore going. And then he heard folks whispering that Mr. Stebbins might've just used that farm and the money it charged at the feedstore to hide the fact that he was running liquor between Atlanta and New Orleans and keeping women in just about every town in-between.

But one look at Miss Myra Olyphant née Stebbins and Verchel had her figured for a merchant's wife; she didn't look earthy enough to live too distant from a town like a farmer's wife would, and she sure didn't look like somebody who'd put up with a husband who ran liquor and dabbled in loose women. Fairly put, she looked like a preacher's daughter, even if she was an older woman. And that's what she was after all: an older woman and a preacher's daughter.

Verchel didn't know how long her husband had been dead, and at first he didn't know if that was why Miss Myra always wore black. But he figured out soon enough that black suited her better than any other color ever could have. The first day she appeared at church she wore a long black dress and a black hat and sat right up front in the first pew of the little church. The windows were open on both sides to let the air circulate to put down some of the heat, and Verchel watched from his pew as the light moved across the right side of the room and began to illuminate the black cloth of Myra's dress. He wondered how she wasn't burning up in all that thick wool, the rest of the women wearing thin cotton shirts and long skirts, most of the men in overalls and collars, nothing denoting the holiness of the day except the grease they'd used to slick down their cowlicks and the whiskers missing from their ruddy cheeks.

This was a church built for farmers. Folks who worked at the mill or in one of the little businesses in town went to Spartan Baptist where old man Haney could keep an eye on the people who worked at the mill. After the accident and before Miss Myra compelled him to hold his head high and throw his chest out and go back to Mr. Haney for work, Verchel just didn't feel right sitting in that church in town, his limp right hand in his lap, his dry, thirsty throat swallowing at something that wasn't there. He felt more at ease out here off the highway with the people who made their livings from the earth. These were the kind of people who always asked how you were doing but never asked how you were doing it, and Verchel knew there wasn't too much room for gossip among men and women and children who spent their days working hard and their evenings resting up so they could do it again the next day.

Pastor Olyphant seemed like the right man to lead such a group as the one he found when he made his way northeast to Cowpens from Greenville in 1910, which had only been seven years earlier but seemed like ages and ages to the people who'd witnessed his sermons each Sunday in the years since his arrival. His favorite subjects were iniquity, a word he used in all of its variations instead of the word "sin," and lechery, a word he used to describe every kind of wanton act or wanton thing a person could imagine, be it of the flesh or otherwise.

His appearance hadn't changed a bit either; he still had the wide-eyed, crazed look of the recent convert who the day before had been a wild sinner and was taking that very moment to impress a Lord God who was always watching. What hair he had left around his ears was white and long enough to brush his collar, and his eyes were a chestnut brown that in another face could be construed as threatening. His shoulders were stooped and he seemed to strain when raising his face to the faces of his congregants, but no one knew whether the stoop was due to hard work, old age, or a genuine inability to acknowledge the gaunt faces of the people he saw each Sunday but whose names he rarely remembered.

But even though he appeared disinterested in learning about his congregants' lives, Pastor Olyphant did seem intent on letting his congregation know a little about his own. That's how they'd all come to know who the woman was in the dark black dress and hat sitting in the front pew on that first Sunday morning of June in 1917, the day Verchel Park had first laid eyes on Miss Myra Olyphant née Stebbins, the woman who'd become his wife by the end of the summer.

At the close of the service, just after he'd finished the altar call, Pastor Olyphant stood up as straight as he was able and looked out over the faces before him. His eyes came to rest on the matronly middle-aged woman sitting bolt upright in the middle of the first pew. "Brothers and sisters," he said, "I'd much appreciate it if y'all'd welcome my only child: my daughter, Miss Myra Stebbins."

Miss Myra turned in the pew and looked over her left shoulder first, her gaze slowly sweeping that side of the room. Verchel could tell whose eyes she was looking into because that man or woman or child would nod his or her head whenever Miss Myra's eye fell upon them. And then she turned the other way and looked over her right shoulder, and Verchel experienced the warm blood-rush of exaltation. He'd felt the spirit move before. He'd made a public proclamation of faith. He'd waded out into the creek that ran on the other side of the field across the road from the church where Pastor Olyphant had been waiting, his arms outstretched and his mouth already praying the prayer of Verchel's baptismal moment. He could recall what it was to live a secular life in pursuit of earthly pleasures. But he'd never felt something stir his soul the way the gaze of Miss Myra stirred it that morning.

Although Verchel considered himself new to the congregation and still didn't know the names of most of the church members, he'd somehow come to learn his own story as it was perceived through their eyes: he was a nice, quiet man who'd been injured in the mill and was getting his spiritual life in order while his body healed. There seemed to be no mention of his past or his life back in town, no suspicion of why he waited until the age of forty-seven to step out into those baptismal waters, no rumors swirling about the circumstances of his injury or the reasons the mill hadn't cared for him after the accident or visited his brother's home or made any entreaty to welcome him back once he had healed as much as he ever would.

So Verchel figured that that was all Miss Myra had come to know about him by the time he found himself face-to-face with her the next week once the Sunday service ended. Verchel usually kept his seat and busied himself by thumbing through his Bible while the church cleared, and that's what he did on this particular morning. But as soon as he stepped out into the bright sunlight the first face he saw was that of

Miss Myra. She looked up at him and smiled and excused herself from the two old farmers' wives she was talking to, and she walked right up to Verchel before he even had the chance to lift his foot off the last step and onto the dry patch of dirt out in front of the church. Miss Myra gathered herself as if she were about to make a speech or deliver some kind of warning.

"Mr. Park," she said. She nodded her head slightly while keeping her eyes locked on his. "I was hoping you'd be able to accompany me home. My father has a few things to attend to and won't be joining me."

"Why, yes. Sure," Verchel said. "I reckon so."

And so the two of them set out on the red dirt road that led east away from the church and farther away from town. Verchel had no idea where Pastor Olyphant lived or how long it would take to get there, and he felt as if Miss Myra were leading him to some destination she already had fixed in her mind, which was fine with him because Verchel found himself unable to think clearly. The afternoon air lay humid and heavy upon him, and the scuffs of their feet along the road seemed to take years to reach his ears. He wondered if he would faint from the heat or the mild exertion of the walk, and he thought back over the long months of sitting in his brother's dark front room while his brother and his sister-in-law worked at the mill. Those hours and days and weeks and months had softened him, and he found it difficult to walk along the road and both listen to and talk to Miss Myra, so it was convenient that she seemed to want to do all the talking.

"I'm not living with my father because I can't shift for myself," she said. "I'm living with my father because it's improper for a woman of my age and means to be living alone, especially in a county as wild and depraved as this one seems to be." She cocked her head as if she were looking out over the field off on the left side of the road where the glossy green expanse appeared to have erupted in bright red strawberries overnight, but even in his stupor Verchel perceived this attempt to steal a glance at him, to somehow appraise his reaction to a word like "depraved" in reference to the county he'd always called home.

"Aw, it ain't such a bad place," Verchel said. "You'll see."

"Perhaps," Miss Myra said. "But that's only if I stay." She looked out at the road before them as if she considered having to walk the full length of it until it came to some conclusion in the indeterminate future. "You may not know this, Mr. Park, but it's a hard life for a single woman. It can cause you to wonder how a person can make it alone in this world without the help of a friend."

And in that very moment Verchel understood why he'd been asked to come along on this walk with Miss Myra, but that wasn't the only thing he understood. Everything came together for him: the accident, his months of dark solitude at his brother's house, his seeking the Lord, and now the Lord delivering this new life unto him.

They were married exactly one month later after church had ended on an already too-hot July afternoon, two days before Independence Day. Verchel didn't think to invite anyone who wouldn't already be there; he hadn't even thought to tell his brother. The whole thing had come about so quickly that he didn't half-believe it until he arrived at the church that morning and found that instead of her customary black dress and hat Miss Myra had worn a white cotton dress of her own design and making. He hadn't done anything differently except worn a thin black tie just in case this Sunday was any different than any Sunday that had come before.

The church members were caught unawares as well. Right after the closing prayer Pastor Olyphant launched right into his marriage sermon, and Miss Myra turned her head and looked at Verchel where he always sat in the last pew. She smiled as if her smile could raise him to his feet, and maybe it did, because the next thing Verchel knew he held Miss Myra's hands in both of his, and the two of them were standing in front of her father. The congregants didn't even have time to stand and stretch before the ceremony, much less leave their seats and process down the aisles toward the doors to escape into the white-hot light of the afternoon.

But somebody in the church must've known something about the wedding, because as soon as Pastor Olyphant announced Verchel and Miss Myra as husband and wife and the couple had shared their first kiss, two young women appeared and began serving slices from a pound cake and pouring tea into glass cups. The roomful of bodies and voices and smiles that belonged to people he'd hardly ever spoken to but somehow knew well enough to share his wedding day with caused Verchel to lose his breath with all the backslapping and handshaking that was heaped upon him.

"You look a little pale, dear," Miss Myra said, taking her new husband's hand and leading him to a seat on the first pew, the very place she'd been sitting the first time Verchel had laid eyes on her. She pulled Verchel's handkerchief from his breast pocket and dabbed at his brow as if it were clotted with sweat, which it probably was. Miss Myra bent at the knees and looked up into Verchel's face, and then she lifted her hand and for just the briefest of moments she cradled his cheek like a mother who's just found her baby scared over something that he and he alone believed to be terrifying. "It's okay, darling," she said. "We've just given ourselves over to one another. Something like that can take it out of a body on a hot day like this one." Verchel's mind didn't register her absence until she returned with a piece of pound cake in a cloth napkin and a glass of iced tea. "Here you go, darling," she said. "Happy wedding day."

And that was Verchel's wedding day; he sat there in the pew wearing the one black tie he'd ever owned, taking small bites from a piece of pound cake so small and dry it reminded him of a communion wafer. But of everything that happened that day what Verchel knew he'd remember the most clearly were the quick sips of iced tea from the cold, sweat-beaded glass and his silent offering of thanks that it wasn't rotgut whiskey, but that didn't keep his tongue from turning it over in his mouth and wishing it were.

Mark Powell

1976–

Mark Powell was born and reared in Walhalla, South Carolina, in the foothills of the Blue Ridge Mountains. He earned a BA in English from the Citadel, an MFA from the University of South Carolina, and studied theology at the Yale Divinity School. After teaching at Florida's Stetson University and other colleges, Powell came to the mountains to teach creative writing at Appalachian State University.

Powell's five novels evidence his diverse background, not only in terms of geographic setting (including the South Carolina foothills and Florida) but also in the issues his work addresses. Powell's theological interests impact the moral weight of his writing, and he challenges readers to think carefully about contemporary issues. *The Sheltering* (2014), for example, examines the ethical implications of modern warfare through such characters as a drone pilot and a returning combatant from the war in the Middle East. "A Woman with a Torch" (2018) explores the contemporary controversy over immigration.

A Woman with a Torch

Nayma's abuelo was up before the sun, the dim necessary light of his dressing bleeding through the beach towel hung to partition the room, pin-pricks dotting a seascape of balloon-eyed sharks and smiling flounder. Nayma kept her face in her pillow and waited. She knew her abuela was up, too, out on the stoop with a heating pad on her knees. She would be sitting in her chair, extension cord run under the screen, rubbing the nubs of her rosary and saying her prayers. Through the pasteboard walls of the Walhalla Motel, Nayma could hear the human moaning that filled the gaps of whatever cartoon was playing. But it was their fingernails that got to her.

Bullshit starts early, Nayma thought. Or maybe bullshit never stops.

The sound was like a dog scratching itself bald, trying to scratch out its own guts, but was, in fact, the couple next door—the early twenties man and woman and their ghost-like wisp of a daughter, all three brown-toothed and frail—the daughter haunted by malnutrition, the mother and father ravaged by the meth mites crawling in and out of their bones, an itch that signaled the impossible distance from one government check to another.

By the time Nayma got up and left her "bedroom"—you had to think of it like that when a worn-out Little Mermaid towel formed the limit of your privacy—both her grandparents were off to work for the Greaves family and she was left alone in the kitchen to eat her Cocoa Pebbles and finish the last of her homework for Dr. Agnew's English IV. She was seventeen and currently first in her senior class. They were reading *The Grapes of Wrath* and no, the irony wasn't lost on her. Very little was—with the exception of eight hours of sleep and little more than a passing engagement with the four food groups.

She showered and ate breakfast in the kitchenette: an alcove with a mini-fridge, microwave, and the hot plate they had to keep hidden from the motel's owner and her crazy son, an Iraq vet who twitched with the same intensity as the couple next door. She spooned cereal and flipped pages. It was quiet next door—the methheads having fallen into some catatonic stupor—and she was grateful for the silence. A few minutes to collect herself before the walk down to the bus stop where she'd ride with two dozen kids half her age, the lone high schooler in a sea of white faces because what kind of senior doesn't have a car? What kind of senior isn't riding with her girl-friends or boyfriend or somebody, right?

This kind, she had thought, in the months past when she used to try to riddle out the why of her days.

One cheek against the cool glass while outside grainy darkness gave way to the gathering daylight, back pressed against the torn pleather seat while they rolled past the Hardee's and the First Methodist Church, and Nayma just sitting there, books in her lap, trying to hear that small still voice that was all: how do you put up with this shit? I mean seriously.

There were other places she could be. Her parents were at home in Irapuato, but home was a tenuous concept. She was born in Florida, a U.S. citizen—her parents and grandfather were not—and had spent far more of her life in the States than in Mexico. Her parents came and went, blowing on the wind of whatever work visa allowed them entry. But for the last two years they had been working at a garment plant in Guanajuato State. It was good work (relatively speaking), at a fair wage (again, in relative terms), and Nayma had the sense that her parents were finished with their cross-border migrations. No more queuing at the U.S. consulate. The forms in tripli-cate. The hassles from ICE. The rhetoric of hate—*build a wall! build a wall!*—spouted by the same folks paying you three dollars an hour to pick their tomatoes or change their babies. When she had last visited her parents—last summer it had been, two weeks of mosquitoes and long days watching telenovelas wherein she experienced the sort of cosmic boredom that would later haunt her with the sort of guilt you smelled in your hair—when she had last visited, she had detected a certain relief in her parents' eyes, a sort of bounce that glided them around the edges of Nayma's life. They were done with *el Norte*.

That her grandmother was a housekeeper and her grandfather a gardener, that they had ascended to these positions from the indentured servitude of migrant labor, that they were meant to be grateful for the condescension and hand-me-down clothes. That her parents had been rounded up by the federal government, held for a week on Red Cross cots in the city gym after INS raided Piedmont Quilting, and subsequently deported with the rest of the three hundred workers Piedmont Quilt-ing had recruited to come in the first place. That she had said goodbye to her parents through a scattering of holes punched in a plexiglass visitation window at the county detention center, that both her mother and father had contorted their bodies in such a way as to hide the zip-ties binding their wrists. All this, *all this, mija,* would burn off in the fire of her success.

As a U.S. citizen, as a brilliant minority student—relatively brilliant, Nayma thought again, glancing now from the graying milk of her Cocoa Pebbles to the papered wall behind which slept the methheads—she would receive some sort of generous scholarship to some sort of prestigious university and from there she would go to law school or medical school. She would spend the rest of her life in New York or Washington D.C.—the capital of the universe—and make money in such ridiculous amounts as to assuage the decades of humiliations suffered by her family. That was her parents' plan at least. Their daughter would become rich, she would become a *blanco* by the sheer aggregated weight of her bank account, and there would be no better revenge.

But first she had to get to school.

She rinsed her bowl and brushed her teeth, put her phone along with the Joads in her backpack, and stepped into the morning. The night's thunderstorm seemed to have blown out the last of summer, and in the skin-prickling cool it was disturbing to see so many children shivering in short sleeves and shorts. There were ten or so that lived at the Walhalla Motel with their mothers or grandmothers or aunts or some elderly female they may or may not have been related to, and they clustered at the edges of body morphology, either fat on Mountain Dew and pixie sticks or emaciated with need, lean as the Hondurans she remembered doing the stoop work in the strawberry fields outside Tampa. That they were cold, that their noses ran, that their hair had been shaved to their skulls (the boys, at least) or matted around forgotten Elsa barrettes or Princess Sophia hair clips (the girls, especially the younger ones) seemed most days like the results of a referendum on human negligence, something to fill her with anger at the world's injustice. But today it just made her sad.

She stood on the concrete stoop, the motel L-shaped, the rooms opening onto an apron of parking lot. Down by the highway a sign read SOFT BEDS COLOR TV WEEKLY RATES.

"Hey, girl!" she heard a voice call.

The motel office was at her far left, a block building with a pitched roof and a neon vacancy sign, a window A/C and a cupped satellite dish. It was from that direction that the voice came, and she didn't have to bother looking to see who it was. D.C. was the son of the hateful old woman who owned the motel. He cut the strip of browning grass along the filled-in swimming pool and on two occasions had unclogged their toilet when the septic tank backed up. He was of some indeterminate age—somewhere between thirty and fifty was her best guess—and possibly he was a decent guy trying to do right by his mother and the world and possibly he was an embryonic serial killer running on Zoloft and cognitive behavioral therapy at the V.A. The brim of his Braves ball cap was pulled low and his arms and throat were inked with assault rifles and an unsettlingly precise map of the greater Middle East, complete (she had noted one day as he ran the weed-eater) with a legend denoting capitals, troop movements, and sites of major U.S. battles.

She started across the parking lot toward the bus stop and a moment later the pickup sidled up beside her, rattling and clunking. This was D.C. on his way to work or maybe on his way to get his mamma a gravy biscuit from the Dairy Queen or on his way to any number of the errands and jobs that occupied his days.

"Hey, little girl, you want a ride?"

"No."

"Why not?"

"Because I'm riding the bus." She didn't look at him. She didn't stop moving. That was her theory: no eye contact and no hesitations. He maintained the grounds at the high school—cut the grass, marked the athletic fields—and his offer of a ride was a near daily occurrence. Without so much as a glance she knew he was hanging from the open window like a happily sloppy dog, meaty arm on the door-panel.

"Well, I'm headed to the same place. You know that don't you?"

She motioned in the direction of the children gathered ahead of her.

"Why don't you offer *them* a ride?" she said.

"Can't do it. Liability."

"That's bullshit."

"Maybe," he conceded. "It's mamma keeps track of the legal stuff."

"Whatever."

"What's that?"

"I said whatever."

He seemed to consider this for a moment.

"You know I ain't offering a ride cause I like you," he said finally.

"Wow. How flattering."

"I'm asking cause you a human being."

"I know why you're asking."

"Because you a human being and you too old to ride the bus like some ten-year-old."

"Go away."

"I mean unless you like the bus. Eighteen wheels and a dozen roses, right?"

"You're a creep."

He gave the engine a small rev. "You got too much grit in your shit, girl. You know that? Turning your nose up at people trying to be kind."

She started to tell him a third time to go away, but then looked up and realized that he already had.

She tried to read on the bus, if only to prove she wasn't lonely. But it was loud and somewhere ahead of her the window was down and a stream of air kept rattling the pages. Finally, she put the book away. She was ahead anyway—there was no rush. What there was, was a bus ride that took seventy-five minutes to cover the four miles to the school. That would be four miles via the direct route, but Nayma guessed they covered a good twenty of back road, stopping at every trailer park or block monolith of Section Eight housing where poor children clustered sleepily by mailboxes and stop signs with their backpacks and dogs. Bullwinkle to Thompson to Tribble—back and forth over the bridges that spanned the wiggle of Cane Creek—East Broad to

Sangamo to Torrington Road. The occasional watchful adult, a grandmother behind the screen door, a mother smoking on the stoop. The old men sat in plastic chairs and stared or took great care not to stare, depending, she often thought, on their experiences with the South Carolina Department of Corrections. The bus stopped first at the elementary school where the children bounced off, awake now, and then the middle school where they navigated blindly, faces fixed to the screens of their phones. When the bus pulled out of the middle school parking lot there was no one left but the driver and Nayma.

The driver, for his part, seemed to have not the slightest notion she was there. He parked the bus and walked away without a word, earbuds plugged into his head as he lumbered toward his car, pushed the door open and crossed from the bus ranks toward the school. She was up near the main doors, and down the gentle slope that eased toward the football stadium she could see people loitering around their cars, talking and flirting and ensuring their collective tardiness. Someone was playing Taylor Swift. Someone was playing Eminem. Her classmates were already self-segregating into their American lives. There were jacked-up pickups with fog lights and boys in Carhartt pants. The girls in Browning jackets of pink camouflage. There were stickers that read MAKE AMERICA GREAT AGAIN and WE HUNT JUST LIKE YOU—ONLY PRETTIER! and FFA jackets from the thrift shop—no one was actually in the FFA— and trucker hats from the rack at the Metromont (MY HUSBAND THINKS FOREPLAY IS TWENTY MINUTES OF BEGGING). Beside them were seven or eight vintage Ford Mustangs—the Stang Gang with their bad skin and BOSE speakers, the bass dropped to some heart-altering thump. They looked underfed and in need of haircuts and she could practically see the crushed Ritalin edging their nostrils. Beside them were the athletes, few in number but easily identifiable by the swish of their warm-up suits. The school's dozen black kids in football jerseys and Under Armor. Bulky red-headed lineman with arm zits and man-boobs. Cheerleaders with their fuck-me eyes. The rich kids—the lake kids—were in Polos and second-hand Benzes. It was a mark of late teen sophistication: the '90s German engineering, the chatter about diesel versus gas.

There were no brown kids. Or very few, at least.

It hadn't always been like that. There had been a moment, brief as it was, right before the great INS raid when sixty or seventy kids made a little Mexico out of the right quadrant of the parking lot. They were mostly older than Nayma, and she had watched them congregate and laugh and play the same pop you heard in the D.F. She had watched them go, too, all but a handful deported with their parents, and when they were gone, they were gone. And so too was the world they had made. There was no more gathering. The dozen or so who, like Nayma, stayed in the States had drifted to the edges of existence, a few quietly dropping out, a few quietly graduating or returning to Mexico. All governed by an abiding sense of bereavement, a mourning so softly realized it hadn't been realized at all. Nayma hadn't been part of it, but she felt it then, and felt it still. Even knowing what she knew, knowing what she was—the smart girl, the girl with a future—didn't help. Knowing didn't make her happy.

That was the thing, maybe.

She could watch them—her classmates, she meant—classify them, dissect them, in her secret heart—her real heart, the one she kept tucked behind what she considered her public heart—she could mock their choices and dismiss their lives as sleepwalking clichés (like her analysis was anything more than an '80s movie replayed on TBS—you could find sharper insight on Wikipedia; these groups had their own sociological studies and trends, they had their own Tumblrs, for god's sake). She recognized their inherent ridiculousness. But crossing toward the main doors of the school she was also forced to recognize their happiness.

She entered the great stacked, rocked cathedral of the school's foyer with its trophy case and barely noticeable metal detectors.

Most days that galled her. Most days it sent her into fantasies of returning to Mexico, but never Mexico as it was. What she dreamed about was some idealized homeland, some creamy rainbow's end without the roof dogs and fireworks and the women holding posters showing their disappeared sons. In her dreams there were no cartels. There were no beggars or bag ladies with deformed feet or children dehydrating and lost somewhere south of Nogales and then not dehydrating and lost but dehydrated and dead, past tense. There was no room for that. But then there didn't seem to be any room in her dreams for Nayma either. She was always some ethereal floating thing, a gauze of veils hovering just beyond imagination's reach, watching.

The bell sounded and the languor of the hall began to fray, kisses, goodbyes, speed-walking to first period. Nayma moved forward at the same inexorable speed. She was the senior assistant to Dr. Agnew's sophomore English course and that was where she was headed.

Bullshit started early, she thought.

But also, more accurately: bullshit never stopped.

And here was the worst of it: Dr. Agnew had scooched her desk right up against his, like she was his junior partner, his little frizzy-haired sidekick, and together they could survey the vast sea of indifference that was English II at 8:15 in the morning. Maybe that was the worst thing—though admittedly her choices here were legion. For Nayma there was a hierarchy of embarrassment, a sort of great chain of humiliation that she would sometimes finger when Dr. Agnew went on a particularly long and tangential rant about Keats or Sylvia Plath or white shoes after labor day or the way gentlemen no longer wore hats *and why is that, Nayma? I'll tell you, my dear, I'll give you a hint, it is linked—is it not?—to the decline of moderate political beliefs in the tradition of western enlightenment philosophy which has hitherto stretched from Copernicus and Francis Bacon to LBJ's Great Society and you, Connie Cayley, I don't know what you're laughing about, my dear, no ma'am, I don't, why, if I found myself giggling in peach culottes with a sixty-four quiz average and an apparent inability to comprehend the mere definition of allegory in the work of George Orwell I believe I might be inclined to seek if not sartorial at least ecclesiastical intervention, don't you agree, Nayma?*

She did not. But that didn't mean she didn't love the man.

He was the local community college's lone humanities professor until the local community college lost state funding and evolved into a start-up incubator slash pet-grooming salon with two tanning beds in the back. Now Dr. Agnew was the over-educated, overweight chair of the high school English department. A long-suffering, put-upon Log Cabin Republican who was sarcastic and erudite and slowly losing a war with his diabetes. He was overweight and, though Nayma had never seen him in anything other than a suit and a vintage NIXON '72 straw boater worn, perhaps, out of a sense of irony so overdeveloped it had become sincere, quite slovenly: shirt untucked, hair a mess, somehow barely avoiding tripping over his untied Keds as he lumbered into the room leaning on his four-stoppered cane, sighing contentedly, as if the only necessary supplement to truth and beauty was a charge account at Ken's Thrifty Pharmacy and Medical Supply.

Have you seen this year's line of Rascal scooters, Nayma? My Lord, they are sleek creations, compact and carbon-neutral. I imagine them conjured in some modernist fever dream of glass and brushed steel, let us say the aerospace industry, headquartered in Orange County, circa 1953, whisking Baptists through the aisles of Walmart, baskets laden with Chinese manufacturing. Why, it almost tempts a man to eat his weight in organ meat and simply be done with this bogus charade we collectively describe as walking.

Today they were discussing, or Dr. Agnew was free-associating on, Emma Lazarus's "The New Colossus": "A poem, my children. A sonnet. Fourteen lines following a strict rhyme scheme and structure. Sing it with me. Give me your tired, your poor. Come on, children, we all know it. Your huddled masses yearning to breathe free." He cupped his ear. "I know you know it, my sweets."

But if they knew it they were offering no sign. That much was evident from Nayma's perch at the front of the room. Equally evident was the deep dislike radiating off the face of Stinson Wood, a dislike that appeared on the verge of crackling like sparked dryer-lint into full-blown hate. He was one of the rich lake kids and, as if to prove it, had the shaggy salon-dyed blond locks generally associated with Orlando-based boy bands. In a class of tenth graders he was the lone senior, not stupid so much as lazy, entitled into a catatonic stupor he broke only to thumb indifferently through his Facebook newsfeed. But today he was alert, today he was all smirk, all dismissive superiority and all of it aimed at Nayma. She got this, she did because:

> A. in case anyone had failed to notice, she was decidedly brown in a decidedly white world, and Stinson Wood—who appeared to be of Swedish extraction, or perhaps of something even whiter (an Icelandic Republican from, say, Tennessee?), should something whiter exist—didn't exactly come across as someone with what might be referred to by Dr. Agnew as an open mind bound to an open heart,

And:

> B. she was ostensibly Stinson's peer, yet here she was seated at the front of the room, occasionally called upon by Dr. Agnew to provide the right answer after Stinson Wood supplied the wrong, or more likely no, answer.

It was surely both A and B, and just as surely didn't matter. What mattered was that he was staring at her, staring with a freakish intensity that would have implied amphetamines were it not for his sociological preference for designer drugs filched from his mother's purse.

Dr. Agnew seemed to catch it too.

"Why Mr. Wood," he said, "and top of the morning to you, good sir. What a pleasure to find you both diurnal and present. To what do we owe this rare convergence of the twain? Were you, perhaps, musing on the possibility of encountering a mighty woman with a torch? Because I am here to assure you, my son, that the likelihood of such is something just short of none, though I grant you that with some focus and persistence on your part it may yet approach not at all."

"What?"

"What? A Swedish diphthong and an interesting one—its interest is beyond refute. Though perhaps not terribly illuminative as to our current state."

"I'm just watching her," Stinson said.

"And to whom, my child, might you be referring?"

"Her," he said, and thrust his chin at Nayma. "Chiquita Banana there."

"You mean Nayma?"

"Whatever her name is."

"Her name is Nayma. Child, are you slow? Are you of addled mind? Did, perhaps, your mother pass to you some derivative of the coca plant, smoked, perchance, in a glass pipe, while you nestled in her womb? Mr. Wood? Dear Mr. Wood?"

But Stinson Wood said nothing. He just stared at Nayma with his lopsided grin, nodding so imperceptibly it was possible she was only imagining it. But she knew she wasn't. He was entitled. He was privileged. He was exactly the sort of person who hated people like Nayma. The non-white, non-male, non-southern, non-straight, non-whatever it was that Stinson Wood had been declared by the accident of his birth—it still went on, the hate, the bigotry, only it was softer now, it was subtle. It was patronizing and—the look on his face told her—it was smug.

Dr. Agnew was off discussing the poem again. "A woman with a torch," he was saying, "let's talk about this image, let's talk about this French woman standing in the harbor with her copper robe and patrician nose . . ."

Stinson had gone back to his phone, but every so often he would look at Nayma and wait for her to look back. Then he would smile that smug smile and look away, like he couldn't believe how ridiculous she was there at the front of the room with her obese mentor (was that what he was?) rambling on about the world's most irrelevant shit.

She went back to the poem. *I lift my lamp beside the golden door!* it finished, and she imagined that golden door, that place at which she might finally arrive. Did it exist? The cynical side of her said it did not. But the truth was, she believed in it. By the standards of Walhalla she appeared as un-American as you could get. But she was more American than all of them put together. She was more American than all of them by dint of her belief, and by dint of her arrival, by dint of her parents' sacrifice. By dint of—

She sensed Stinson's head snap up with a reptilian quickness. He had the sort of green eyes and pale skin that made her imagine him as cold-blooded in the actual biological sense. He was looking up now, but not at her. He was looking across the room at Lana Rogers, a freshman in sophomore English (whereas Stinson was a senior in sophomore English).

The girl looked up, Lana Rogers. She was cute and brunette and appeared just barely old enough to gain entry to the high school. She sat legs crossed in her tennis skirt, a worried look clouding her face. She had her phone in her lap and her eyes dropped to it: Stinson was texting her. She put the eraser of her pencil in her mouth and slowly lowered one hand to her lap where the phone was hidden. Not that it needed hiding. Dr. Agnew was holding forth at maximum velocity, sweeping hands, grand declarations. The girl texted back. Stinson texted again. The girl looked even more worried.

Then Lana's phone actually rang.

Dr. Agnew snapped around from the board where he had been busy diagramming the Roman street where Keats had died, but now, but now . . .

"A cellular call! My, my," he declared, "who is it that is calling? Who is it that fancies himself or herself so wondrously and spectacularly important to call during a discussion of the world's unacknowledged legislators?"

Then Nayma realized it wasn't Lana's phone, but her phone, the cheap Wal-Mart Asus with its fifteen-dollar SIM card and factory-direct ringtone. She hadn't bothered silencing it because why should she? No one ever called. But now someone was.

"Nayma?" Dr. Agnew looked as hurt as surprised.

"I'm sorry."

"Why I don't—"

She was up out of her desk now, the phone pressed to her stomach as if not so much to mute the sound as to cradle some wound. "Excuse me. Sorry, Dr. Agnew."

She hurried into the empty hall and flipped open the phone—yes, God, it was a flip-phone—to find her abuela yammering in a Spanish so frantic Nayma could barely understand her. Then, finally, she did: it was the Greaves woman, the grandmother. She was in the basement. She had fallen. There was blood.

Was she alive?

"Call the ambulance," Nayma said. Then she realized she would have to call. She got the address and hung up just as Dr. Agnew lumbered into the hall.

"Nayma," he was saying, "this is highly peculiar. I think perhaps—"

He stopped when he heard the voice on other end.

"9-1-1, what's your emergency?"

"Oh Lord!" said Dr. Agnew and pirouetted on his four-stoppered cane.

It was like an elephant dancing and Nayma might have applauded had she not been reciting the address. The voice of the operator carried up the block hall.

"Is she breathing?"

("Breathing!" cried Dr. Agnew.)

"Yes."

"Is she conscious?"

("Conscious! Oh Lord!")

"I don't know."

"Please stay on the line, ma'am. Ma'am?"

But she had already slapped the phone shut, louder than she had intended.

"Oh Lord!" Dr. Agnew said, "Child—"

But she cut him off with a look.

"Dr. Agnew," she said, "I need to borrow your car."

Nayma piloted Dr. Agnew's Oldsmobile into the parking lot of Oconee Memorial Hospital, her body hung over a giant steering wheel the size of a manhole cover, her butt slid forward over the beaded seat-cover as rough as the corrugated motel roof where she would occasionally hide in plain sight. It was a little like driving a boat—not that she'd ever driven a boat, she had never even been on a boat—but that didn't stop her from imagining the car as a great yacht that rocked lightly as she turned at the traffic signal and eased nimbly around corners. She was going too fast and couldn't get the cassette of the Statler Brothers to cut off, but then she was going too slow and accelerated until she could feel the car bouncing on its shocks. She had driven before—she could certainly drive—but never in something this big and never over forty-five miles an hour.

She glided into the parking lot, fairly sailing over a speed bump while the dashboard hula dancer bobbed wildly and across the bench leather. Dr. Agnew's papers and books fluttered and slipped. John Donne. Geoffrey Hill. Some ancient coffee table atlas of Olde England. She shoved them all to the side and made for the main entrance, the glass doors sliding open onto the chilly foyer with its potted palms and new carpet. The walls were lined with Purell dispensers and signs explaining the importance of sanitized hands in English and Spanish. She took the elevator to the fifth floor ICU, more or less bouncing on her heels and wringing her bacteria-free hands.

When the doors opened the smell hit her: not so much the sharp of antiseptic as something heavier and more frightening: it smelled here, she realized, like death. Up until that moment she had worried solely about her abuelos, but at that moment she felt her heart lurch for the Greaves woman, alone here with the tubes and wheeled machines and that smell she was starting to recognize as the aftertaste of human shit. She was in her nineties but somehow lived alone. But not anymore, Nayma thought. Not after today.

She found her grandparents in the waiting room, a couple of aged nervous children who fluttered to their feet when they saw Nayma. Her abuela had virtually no English, which made her, a woman who was otherwise a workhorse of devotion and faith, pathetically helpless. Her abuelo was fluent in English, educated, smart and sarcastic. Or had been once. He'd been expelled from the tomato fields of Immokalee, Florida, after attempting to organize what were effectively indentured servants. But the process of kicking him out—she suspected it had been more than simply driving her grandparents to the city limits and telling them to beat it—had cracked something in him, or widened a crack that already existed so that these days he was mostly silent. There were no more jokes, no more laughing. He worked. He smoked. He drank one Budweiser every evening in a plastic chair on the indoor-outdoor carpet of the motel stoop.

He had never told her much about Immokalee, but she knew enough to imagine the circumstances of his life there. The town, to the extent that it was anything beyond an encampment of trailers and processing centers, was the hub of the tomato fields, the place from which migrant workers began the trek north, harvesting tomatoes in South Florida and then strawberries in the irrigated fields along the Gulf and then peaches and apples in the Carolinas. It was an eight-month odyssey of endless indentured work. Slave work, if you got down to it. Coyotes slipped the workers through the Sonora Desert on foot and into Florida in the backs of U-Hauls. When they got out they owed fifteen hundred dollars for the transport and went to work paying it back, earning two or three dollars a day while living ten to a trailer in the windless fog of mosquitos and heat and the powdered residue of insecticides so harsh they burned the skin.

Of course you paid for that too, the privilege of the trailer costing, say, ten dollars a week, and transportation to the fields—that was another two bucks. Then, of course, you might one day decide to eat something and there was yet another cost. In the end, it meant not only could you never pay off your debt, you actually wound up in greater debt. Which meant you could very easily spend the rest of your relatively short life never venturing a half-mile beyond the fields. There were periodic raids by ICE or the Department of Justice but none of it added up to anything like justice. At best, you were deported and what was waiting for you there? Work in a textile mill if you were lucky in the way her parents were lucky: making sixty pesos for ten hours of work, sewing collars and fostering arthritis. More likely you would exist at the whim of the cartel. You might be a runner, a look out, a mule. Until, of course, you weren't. Until, of course, a bullet placed neatly behind your right ear pierced the growing tumor the insecticides had started years prior.

So he drank his beer.

After that, he lay in bed, hands crossed on his chest as if by arranging himself for death he would save a few dollars on the undertaker. Whether he actually slept or not she never knew. She didn't think he prayed. It was her abuela who prayed. Her abuela who kneeled on her swollen knees before the candle of the Virgin Nayma had gotten her from the "Ethnic" aisle at Ingles. Her abuela who took Nayma to mass at La Luz del Mundo behind Hardee's.

But now they were both standing, silent, tragic.

She started to speak but something in their faces stopped her. They weren't staring at her, but past her, and Nayma turned to see Mrs. Greaves carted past, all wires and tubes, somebody's idea of an art project, or maybe just a bad joke.

It was the end of lunch by the time Nayma had dropped her grandparents off at the Greaves' house and made her way back to school. Nayma had fairly dragged abuela to the elevator. By the time they got to Dr. Agnew's car her abuela was in tears and Nayma had only gotten a sidelong glance at the Greaves woman—it was all she would allow herself—but even in passing it looked bad. Her tiny self a tent of bones pitched beneath a tangle of tubes and monitors. It didn't seem fair that she would die like that. But it surely didn't seem fair to have to go on living.

She parked the Oldsmobile and headed for the front doors. You could sneak out of the school but you couldn't sneak in. The building was a well-concealed fortress of alarmed doors and hidden metal detectors and the only way in was through the entrance where, surely, someone would be waiting on her. They would suspend her, they would express their utter bafflement and complete disappointment in her and she could try to explain but, honestly, how? and why? The college applications had all been submitted, the essays written, the recommendations sent. In a few months she would leave Walhalla and never come back. When the time came—when the money came—she would send for her grandparents. She would send for her parents, too, if they would come. The money would make them untouchable. Her U.S. citizenship and a bank account in the high six-digits. That wasn't wealth—that was protection. That was stability.

It was what she couldn't explain to the people who would question her in another sixty seconds when she walked through the front doors and confessed to having stolen Dr. Agnew's car (if she said he had freely handed her the keys he would likely be fired and she wasn't about to let that happen). *Why did you go, Nayma? If there was a family problem, why didn't you come to us? Why didn't you let us help you?* As if by the mere comingling of their white skin and good intentions they could unravel the tangle of her life. As if skin pigment and evangelical hope would solve her problems. *Not a handout, Nayma.* (How satisfied they would appear across their shiny desks or behind the ovals of their rimless eyewear.) Not a handout, but a hand up.

Why didn't you let me help you, Nayma?

Because you can't, she wanted to say.

Because how could you solve something you couldn't begin to understand?

Her life was a construction of wildly misaligned but nevertheless moving parts that were labeled individually as money, language, citizenship—or the lack of all three—and to tinker with one, to attempt to explain one, was to risk the others, and at this point, so close to her exit, so close to the end of her sentence at the Walhalla Motel, so near the end of the next door meth mites clawing their open sores, so near the end the creepy D.C. trying to lure her into his pickup, so near the end of so much the last thing she was going to do was take chances.

She put her hand on the front door and took a moment to study herself in the reflection. But it wasn't her own face that caught her attention, but the face beyond the glass. It was turning. The school receptionist was walking away from the reception desk and into the warren of hallways and offices behind her, and what Nayma realized was that she was being given a chance.

She didn't delay.

She pulled open the door and shot through, past the metal detector and the sliding second door that was—thank you!—unlocked before the door could even chime her arrival. Behind her she sensed the woman returning—excuse me?—but Nayma was already in the main hall crowded with lunch traffic.

She walked as fast as possible without running. The woman was still behind her. "Excuse me? Miss? Stop please." But she wasn't stopping, not now and not ever. She rounded the corner and ducked into the girls' bathroom—okay, she was stopping now, but this was strategic. She went to the farthest stall, locked the door, and crouched on the closed toilet seat so that her feet wouldn't show.

She waited and then came down, took a moment to collect herself at the bathroom sink. Splash her face, smooth her clothes. She put her phone on vibrate and took Dr. Agnew's keys from her pocket. That was all that was left: to return his keys, get to her next class, get through her next class, her next day, week, and so on until she could walk. Where didn't matter. Just not here.

Middle hall was less crowded. She passed the band room and the art rooms and turned right toward the English wing. A few couples were pressed along the walls, blowing little bubbles of privacy out of the otherwise public. Girls with their shampooed hair against the walls, showing their vulnerable throats. The guys were all lean. Elbows and knuckles and bristled hair. Eighteen-year-olds in letterman jackets kissing girls in cheerleading skirts. Resting their sweaty hands on hip bones. No one looked at her. She heard the guys whisper and the girls giggle as she walked past. Giggling in such a way as to let her know how different she was. Giggling to make certain she was cognizant of how ugly and brown and plain. That there was nothing of the strawberry to her, she knew this. No strawberry-blonde hair. No strawberry sun-kissed skin. Never the right shoes or jacket or skirt, never the eyeliner that was oh my God so on point. But there was something that made them giggle: the remarkable extent to which she didn't belong.

Even if she did.

You're a woman with a torch, Nayma.

She tried not to walk faster.

You can do this, Nayma.

She tried to keep her head level, her eyes straight ahead. She rounded the corner—she was near the gym now, past the groping and giggling—and then heard something. Whispers. But not whispers directed at her. These were people oblivious to her presence. They were arguing. She could tell that much. Two people—a boy and girl. She peeked around the corner.

The hall here was long and dim and off-limits. Along one side were framed portraits of Walhalla athletes who had gone on to play college sports. Point guards and goalies and fast-pitch catchers in jerseys that read Warriors and Tigers and Chanticleers. Along the other side was fencing behind which were large wheeled bins full of everything from shoulder pads to orange traffic cones. The voices, the arguing—it wasn't louder now so much as more intense—was coming from there.

She shouldn't stop.

She knew she shouldn't stop. This was a wholly unnecessary detour yet some part of her—there was no use not admitting it—really did believe she was a woman with a torch. Someone put in the world to light the way, to take care of others, be it her parents, grandparents, whoever it was now tucked back among the portable soccer goals and arguing very volubly.

"Stop, please. Please don't, Stinson."

Stinson?

Then she knew why she had stopped: because she recognized the voice.

Two quiet steps forward and she recognized the faces. It was Stinson Wood and Lana Rogers, both from English II. Stinson had Lana backed up against the wall just like all the other boys. But unlike all the other girls Lana wasn't kissing his throat or idly fingering whatever faux-gold chain he hung around his neck. She was pushing her fingers into his smug handsome face. She was begging him to stop.

Nayma had her hands on his jacket before she realized she was even moving. It was the white heat they talked about in books, rage, supernatural strength. The sort of thing that allowed mothers to lift wrecked automobiles off their trapped children. Except it wasn't a car she was lifting but what turned out to be a kite-thin boy who was mostly hair gel and lip—"Fucking bitch!"—and a cloying cloud of Axe Body spray. She pushed him behind her where he arranged himself, smoothed his hair, his clothes, all the while repeating to her what a fucking bitch she was.

But Nayma registered it as no more than noise.

She had one hand on Lana Rogers' shoulder, the other extended toward Stinson Wood, palm raised like a crossing guard arresting traffic.

"Are you okay?" Nayma asked.

The girl nodded but said nothing.

Then Stinson grabbed Nayma's hand and knocked it aside.

"This has nothing to do with you, Chiquita Banana."

"Leave her alone," Nayma said.

"Fucking make me, how 'bout it?"

"Touch her again," Nayma said, "and I will." And with that she watched something terrifying take place: she watched his face morph from normal human rage to something approaching a mask of smug—that word again—comprehension. It was a look that said he was suddenly realizing this wasn't a joke, this fucking Mexican bitch was serious. That she didn't get it. Yet who the hell was she to interfere with him? Did she not know how this game worked? Then the bafflement was replaced by the sort of cruelty that only comes in very deliberate calibrations.

"I will have your daddy's ass on the banana boat back to fucking taco-time by sundown," he said. "You understand that?"

"Don't touch her again."

"She wants me to touch her," he said then, a strange tactic in argument. "Don't you, Lana?"

They both looked at the girl who said nothing.

"Don't you?" Stinson said again, but Nayma cut him off.

"Let her speak for herself."

She couldn't, or wouldn't, and this seemed to fuel something deeper in Stinson, some tertiary rage that had thus far remained buried.

"Fuck you both," he said, straightened his jacket a last time, zipped his open fly, and started down the dark hall. Halfway down he stopped and turned. "When you're ready to apologize you know where to find me, Lana," he called. "And you, you fucking illegal bitch. You will suffer for this. I promise you that."

And then he was gone.

Nayma turned to Lana and was about to speak but then she was gone too, rushing past her, all unsteady legs and bed-headed hair.

Gone up the hall.

Gone around the bend.

Gone, Nayma could only hope, anywhere but back to him.

Dr. Agnew's door was open and thankfully he was not at his desk. She put his keys by a paperweight bust of Evelyn Waugh (where on earth did you buy something like this?) and had started for the cafeteria when she heard him.

"Nayma, my dear."

It found her like a spotlight, his voice. One of those cartoon moments where the searchlight settles on the bandit escaping prison.

"Dr. Agnew," she said. "Your keys."

"Yes?"

"Thank you. I'm sorry about that. They're on your desk, right there by Mr. Waugh."

"Mr. Waugh, my dear. As in War."

"Right there by Mr. War."

"All right, dear," he said. "Thank you."

She was by the door when he spoke again.

"Excuse me, Nayma."

She stopped but didn't turn.

"If you ever want to talk about it," he said, "I've told been told I'm a good listener."

She said nothing.

"I know what it is to need a good listener," he said. "I also know what it is to be a stranger in a strange land. If that's not too saccharine a thing to admit. Realizing fully that perhaps it is."

She stood silent and still. He was moving, walking, but not toward her. He had exited through the backdoor into the materials room and she realized she was alone, and then she realized she was crying and couldn't stop. Crying for her mother and father and grandparents. For the scared girl in middle hall. Crying for creepy D.C., who was back from the war and lonely. Crying for Dr. Agnew who was simply lonely. And crying for herself. These endless tears. These stupid, stupid tears she felt running down the copper of her robe, beneath her torch, past her book, and over her sandaled feet, these tears gathering in the vast harbor she suddenly realized surrounded her life.

Sandor Ellix Katz

1962–

Cookbook writer, fermentation guru, and gay activist Sandor Katz is representative of the new demographic that has made Appalachia home since the back-to-the-land movement of the 1970s. Katz was born and reared in New York City and attended Brown University before moving in 1993 to Short Mountain, an intentional community on the western Cumberland Plateau of Tennessee in Cannon County.

Short Mountain is a self-designated radical faerie sanctuary designed to provide LGBTQ members with a sense of home and community. As in many intentional communities, gardening and food preparation are important to the residents. Katz also has a vested interest in wholesome food: he is HIV-positive. Searching for ways to improve his health, Katz came to believe that among the most healthy foods are those that have been fermented, such as sauerkraut, yogurt, and kefir. He has written three books about fermentation and given numerous workshops on the topic.

Fermentation was traditionally practiced by many Appalachian homemakers, and Katz's interests in food preservation, gardening, and other back-to-the-land skills have helped him connect with his Tennessee neighbors, breaking down barriers between Short Mountain community members and others. This desire to blend older traditions with new lifestyles is evident in the following excerpt from Katz's first book, *Wild Fermentation* (2003), a collection of essays, meditations, and recipes. His subsequent book, *The Art of Fermentation* (2013), won the James Beard Award and has cemented Katz's reputation in the Appalachian food community.

FROM Wild Fermentation: The Flavor, Nutrition, and Craft of Live-Culture Foods

CHAPTER 13: CULTURAL REINCARNATION: FERMENTATION IN THE CYCLES OF LIFE, SOIL FERTILITY, AND SOCIAL CHANGE

Fermentation is a lot bigger than its food-transforming aspect. Fermentation also describes the process by which microorganisms digest dead animal and plant tissue into elements that can nourish plants. As the early microbiologist Jacob Lippman eloquently stated it in his 1908 *Bacteria in Relation to Country Life,* microorganisms

> are the connecting link between the world of the living and the world of the dead. They are the great scavengers intrusted [*sic*] with restoring to circulation the carbon, nitrogen, hydrogen, sulphur, and other elements held fast in the dead bodies of plants and animals. Without them, dead bodies

would accumulate, and the kingdom of the living would be replaced by the kingdom of the dead.

This image helps me to accept death and decay. It is clear evidence on the physical plane that life is a cyclical process, with death as an indispensable part. It makes the harshest reality of life more understandable, more acceptable.

During this same past decade that I have developed my fascination with fermentation, I have spent a fair share of my fantasy life pondering my own decay and death. How could I not imagine it after receiving the HIV-antibody test death-prophecy? Nobody has said this more eloquently than the late poet Audre Lorde:

> Living a self-conscious life, under the pressure of time, I work with the consciousness of death at my shoulder, not constantly, but often enough to leave a mark upon all of my life's decisions and actions. And it does not matter whether this death comes next week or thirty years from now; this consciousness gives my life another breadth. It helps shape the words I speak, the ways I love, my politic of action, the strength of my vision and purpose, the depth of my appreciation of living.

I wonder: Can thinking about illness and death make them manifest? Diagnostic medical testing, like the HIV-antibody test, is often promoted as unambiguously good information technology, assuming that more information will simply help you and your medical providers make better decisions. On the basis of my experience of the slow transition from HIV-positive "asymptomatic" to the onset of AIDS symptoms, I question whether it really is helpful for a seemingly healthy person to receive a diagnosis of inevitable illness. Ignorance can definitely be bliss.

As I wrote this book, I turned forty. My age-group peers talk about mid-life. It does not seem implausible to me that I could be at the mid-point of my life, and that I will celebrate my eightieth birthday in the year 2042. I love life and I believe in the infinity of possibility. But I am a student of observation and realism and probability, and frankly forty more years seems extremely unlikely. The medicines that supposedly keep me alive are probably not sustainable over decades; they are toxic and take a heavy toll over time. Though people with AIDS are living longer, friends keep dying of it. I have had ample opportunity to get used to the idea that my body is in its decline, that this is the latter period of my life. I wonder: Is this resignation? Is this the loss of will to survive?

I feel there is wisdom in making peace with death. It will come. All I can do is embrace life as best I can, and when I die, I know, I believe, I have faith, that all that is me will continue to be part of the cycle of life, fermenting and nourishing and becoming myriad other life forms. My fermentation practice is a daily affirmation of this faith.

Getting Acquainted with Death

Our society distances us from death. We have created impersonal institutions to handle the transition. What are we so afraid of? I feel lucky to have been present with my mother, at home, when she died. She had been unconscious for about a week, at the end of a long struggle with cervical cancer; edema (fluid accumulation) bloated her legs and slowly rose higher on her body. Her breathing grew labored as her lungs filled with fluid. Our family gathered around her in a death watch. Her breaths became shallower and spasmodic, until one involuntary muscle contraction was the last. We sat with her for a while and cried, trying to grasp the enormity of the event. The men who came to our apartment for her body in the middle of the night were right out of central casting, pale and grim. They lifted my mother's bloated body into a bag on a stretcher and rolled it to the elevator. To get it into the elevator they had to stand it up, and my mother's body fell like a lead weight. Death was graphic and real.

Since then I have spent time with two other bodies post-mortem. One was Lynda Kubek, a friend who died of breast cancer. In the period before she died I was part of her caretaking team. What I remember most vividly about caretaking Lynda is applying clay compresses to a baseball-size tumor protruding from her armpit. Cancer is such an abstract concept, so internal and hidden and shrouded in euphemism, yet that tumor was so very concrete.

When Lynda died, her body was left on her bed for twenty-four hours before her home burial. By the time we arrived from Short Mountain the morning after her passing, friends and family had created a shrine around her, with flowers and incense and photos and fabrics. It was truly beautiful, and felt like an appropriate transition between life and burial. We sat with Lynda's body for a while. It was a very peaceful time. Afterward we went swimming in a nearby pond, and when I came up from diving in, there was a snake skin floating on the surface of the water. It was a powerful affirmation for me of the idea that death is part of the process of life, nothing to fear.

Tennessee is one of the few states that allow home burial, and Lynda's nephews spent the day digging her grave; a carpenter friend built a simple pine casket. Late that afternoon, her assembled friends and family processed with songs and drums and chants to her gravesite and laid her to rest. It felt so good that no commercial establishments—the cemetery, the funeral home, the crematorium—were involved. It was people taking care of their own.

The other dead body I spent time with was Russell Morgan. Russell is a friend who died at the age of twenty-eight of AIDS, actually Kaposi's sarcoma lesions in his lungs. I was visiting him at the time of his death. He had been in and out of the hospital. His breathing became uncomfortably difficult, and he decided to go back to the hospital. I helped carry him down the front steps and into the car. He never returned home. I was in the corridor outside his hospital room when he died. He was with his lover Leopard, and his family. I knew he had died because I heard Leopard wailing. Russell had been connected to oxygen, and still his breathing became more and more labored. As the scene was recounted to me, Russell removed the respirator mask, threw it to the floor, said "Fuck this!" and dived bravely into the unknown beyond. I admire his courage. The hospital staff let us spend some time in the room with Russell's body. I helped Leopard erect a shrine around Russell in the hospital bed, trying to create a ritual of transition in that denatured environment.

These experiences have given me a vision for how I would like my own death to be handled. I'll be happy to live a good long time; but I have given death plenty of thought. I would like my body to be given a transition period as Lynda's was. I want my friends and family to be able to be with me during this in-between period, to touch my clammy skin and say good-bye to my lifeless form and have death demystified a little bit. Then I want to be returned to the earth without resort to the impersonal industries of death. A huge funeral pyre would be lovely; if that's too much to bear, just place me in a hole in the ground, no casket please, and let me compost fast.

Compost Happens

I love to watch the compost decompose. Recognizable forms with histories, such as onion skins from last night's soup, gradually melt back into the all-oneness of the Earth. I find the process itself so beautiful: poetry. Walt Whitman found inspiration in compost, too:

> The summer growth is innocent and disdainful above all those strata of
>   sour dead.
> What chemistry!
> That the winds are really not infectious.
> . . . .
> That all is clean forever and forever,
> That the cool drink from the well tastes so good,
> That blackberries are so flavorous and juicy,
> That the fruits of the apple-orchard and the orange-orchard, that melons,
>   grapes, peaches, plums, will none of them poison me,
> That when I recline on the grass I do not catch any disease,
> Though probably every spear of grass rises out of what was once catching
>   disease.
> Now I am terrified at the Earth, it is that calm and patient,
> It grows such sweet things out of such corruptions,
> It turns harmless and stainless on its axis, with such endless succession of
>   diseas'd corpses,
> It distills such exquisite winds out of such infused fetor,
> It renews with such unwitting looks its prodigal, annual, sumptuous crops,
> It gives such divine materials to men, and accepts such leavings from them
>   at last.

I use the term *compost* broadly, to describe the piles of kitchen scraps, the piles of weeds and prunings, the piles of goat "muck" (their excrement mixed with bedding straw), and the piles of our own human feces from our outhouse, mixed with toilet paper, sawdust, and ash. After a year or two, each of these piles looks the same. They are all broken down into simpler forms by microorganisms in the act of fermentation. Composting is a fermentation process.

There are many different ideas about the best composting methods. Gardeners are a passionate bunch, with strong opinions about the best ways to do things.

Rodale's *Complete Book of Composting* describes gardeners who "spend years running from method to method, charting secret figures, constructing weird bins, boxes, ventilating pipes and watering systems, and carefully measuring each bit of material which is placed just right on the heap." Certainly you can manipulate conditions to encourage compost fermentation to proceed faster, or hotter, or more odor-free. But even if you do nothing and let the food scraps just accumulate in your kitchen, compost happens. There is nothing you can do to stop it. Fermentation makes organic compounds decompose. It is this process, the breaking down of fallen leaves, animal feces and carcasses, dead trees and other plants, and any other organic matter, that regenerates the soil. Fermentation is the basis of soil fertility.

In chapter 2, I referred to a nineteenth-century German chemist named Justus von Liebig, who staunchly opposed the idea that fermentation is a biological process. This same misguided man pioneered the idea of fertilizing soil with manufactured chemicals. "We have now examined the action of the animal or natural manures upon plants but it is evident that if artificial manures contain the same constituents, they will exert a similar action upon the plants to which they are applied." Von Liebig's 1845 monograph *Chemistry and Its Application to Agriculture and Physiology* laid the groundwork for the chemical agricultural methods that have become standard practice and that are rapidly depleting soils everywhere. Fermentation is a natural, biological, self-generating process of decomposition that builds soil fertility and nurtures plant life. Chemical fertilization may be effective in terms of short-term yields, but it impairs the function of the soil as a self-regulating, biodiverse ecological system.

Thinking about mass food production makes me sad and angry. Chemical monocrop agriculture. Genetic engineering of the most basic food crops. Ugly, inhumane factory animal breeding. Ultraprocessed foods full of preservative chemicals, industrial byproducts, and packaging. Food production is just one realm among many in which ever more concentrated corporate units extract profits from the Earth and the mass of humanity.

Historically, food has been our most direct and tangible ongoing connection to the Earth. Increasingly, though, food has become a collection of mass-produced and aggressively marketed commodities. This is the song of progress: We have supposedly been freed, by technology and mass social organization, from the burdens of growing or procuring our own food. Just going to the supermarket and putting the food into the microwave is burden enough. Most people do not know or care where their food comes from.

Social Change

The astute reader will have noticed by now that my outlook can be rather bleak. Many current trends, not only mass food production, but war, global warming, accelerating species extinctions, the growing class divide, the persistence of racism, the incredible number of people in prisons, high-tech militarization and social control, consumerism as patriotic duty, and ever more insipid television programming, contribute to my pessimism.

What gives me hope is the simple notion that current trends do not necessarily have to continue. It seems to me that they cannot possibly. The revolutionary spirit of liberation and hope always and everywhere remains, even dormant or confined to dreams, like a seed culture, ready anytime to multiply, thrive, and transform, given the right conditions.

Social change is another form of fermentation. Ideas ferment, as they spread and mutate and inspire movements for change. The *Oxford English Dictionary* offers as the second definition of ferment: "The state of being excited by emotion or passion, agitation, excitement . . . a state of agitation tending to bring about a purer, more wholesome, or more stable condition of things." The word "ferment" derives from the Latin *fervere,* "to boil." "Fervor" and "fervent" are other words from the same root. Fermenting liquids bubble just like boiling liquids. Excited people can channel the same intensity, and use it to create change.

Though fermentation is a phenomenon of transformation, the change it renders tends to be gentle, slow, and steady. Contrast fermentation with another transformative natural phenomenon: fire. As I wrote this book the awesome drama of fire seared itself into my consciousness in three separate events. The first was the one we all witnessed via images that we are destined to be reminded of frequently for the rest of our lives. I am referring to the great balls of fire that resulted from the impact of the jet planes hitting the World Trade Center, melting the steel structures and toppling the towers. Whatever other meanings we ascribe to the infamous events of September 11, 2001, we collectively witnessed the sudden collapse of one of the great feats of modern engineering, by the sheer indomitable force of fire.

Two months later, I found myself in the middle of a forest fire, when I visited my friends at Moonshadow. Approaching their place from miles away, I could see and smell smoke. The fires had been started by kids as Halloween pranks or possibly arson. They had burned along the forest floor for more than a week, reached Moonshadow's land, and threatened to burn their buildings and gardens. The fire itself was a line of flame hundreds of feet long, moving slowly downhill (uphill, I'm told, it would have traveled faster), leaving in its wake an eerie landscape of ash and burning tree trunks. My Moonshadow friends had been days without sleep, raking and digging to create firebreaks to contain the fire. The breaks were in place by the time we got there, but wind could easily blow embers across them and continue the spread of the fire. The imperative was to monitor the firebreaks so any stray embers could be put out or at least contained.

Living trees were surviving the fire, but many pine trees, dead from infestations of the southern pine beetle, were falling. We wore helmets near the fire, but as trees fell at frequent intervals, I wondered what good the helmet would do if fate dropped an eighty-foot tree on me. We slept near the firebreak that night, on call in case the fire jumped and hands were needed to contain it. I woke up a lot during the night, hearing falling trees, observing the flames move downhill, relieved that it was following the predicted course and not jumping the firebreak. By morning, the fire had reached the creek and died out, leaving a forest full of smoking ash and embers, and a grateful group of people, humbled by the fire's uncontrollable, transformative power.

Then, another two months later, during a January cold snap, our nearest neighbors on Short Mountain had a fire in the middle of the night. Embers fell from their woodstove undetected, and built into a sizeable fire before the sound of bottles bursting in the kitchen woke the guests sleeping in the next room. By the time they awoke, the smoke was thick. Their water line was frozen, so there was no quantity of water at hand. Luckily, with a fire extinguisher, blankets, rugs, and buckets of snow, they were able to put out the fire. Had they awakened a few moments later, or panicked in the confusion, their house would have been ashes. The fire was another humbling reminder, and a fire safety wake-up call for the rest of us heating with wood and reading by candlelight. Fire can change everything, in an instant.

In the realm of social change, fire is the revolutionary moment of upheaval; romantic and longed for, or dreaded and guarded against, depending upon your perspective. Fire spreads, destroying whatever lies in its path, and its path is unpredictable. Fermentation is not so dramatic. It bubbles rather than burns, and its transformative mode is gentle and slow. Steady, too. Fermentation is a force that cannot be stopped. It recycles life, renews hope, and goes on and on.

Your life and my life and everyone's lives and deaths are part of the endless biological cycle of life and death and fermentation. Wild fermentation is going on everywhere, always. Embrace it. Work with the material resources and life processes that are close at hand. As microorganisms work their transformative magic and you witness the miracles of fermentation, envision yourself as an agent for change, creating agitation, releasing bubbles of transformation into the social order. Use your fermented goodies to nourish your family and friends and allies. The life-affirming power of these basic foods contrasts sharply with the lifeless, industrially processed foods that fill supermarket shelves. Draw inspiration from the action of bacteria and yeast, and make your life a transformative process.

Wendell Berry
1934–

Although Wendell Berry is often thought of as Appalachian, he comes from western Kentucky. He has written about Appalachia, however, and his importance to the region is great.

Berry was born in 1934 in Henry County in western Kentucky. He earned degrees in English at the University of Kentucky and studied creative writing with Wallace Stegner at Stanford University. After teaching at New York University's Bronx campus, he moved back to Kentucky with his wife and children, and in 1965 began farming in Henry County. For many years he taught creative writing at the University of Kentucky.

Berry's farming practices and his understanding of the environment are those of ecologists and organic farmers whose concern for the long-term health of the soil leads them to eschew chemical fertilizers, pesticides, and herbicides. Berry's commitment to organic, sustainable farming has led him to such practices as working his land with draft horses instead of tractors. Berry's work comes out of the early-to mid-twentieth-century organic farming lineage of the British botanist Sir Albert Howard, J. I. and Robert Rodale of eastern Pennsylvania, and the New Englanders Scott and Helen Nearing.

Berry has been an inspiration to environmentalists and organic and sustainable farmers throughout the United States both for his farming practices and for the philosophical awareness articulated in his writings. He has written nonfiction, fiction, and poetry. In the essay below, Berry discusses the problems generated by extractive industries from the point of view of an environmentalist and a sustainable agriculturalist.

FROM Missing Mountains: We Went to the Mountaintop but It Wasn't There

AFTERWORD

At the end of a book attempting to deal with an enormity so staggering as the human destruction of the Earth, it is difficult to resist the temptation to write out a "vision of the future" that would offer something better. Even so, I intend to resist. I resist, not only because such visions run a large risk of error, but also out of courtesy. A person of my age who dabbles in visions of the future is necessarily dabbling in a future that belongs mostly to other people.

What I would like to do, instead, if I can, is help to correct the vision we Kentuckians have of ourselves in the present. In our present vision of ourselves, we seem to be a people with a history that is acceptable, even praiseworthy, a history that we are privileged to inherit uncritically and with little attempt at rectification. But by the measures that are most important to whatever future the state is to have, ours is a history of damage and of loss.

In a little more than two centuries—a little more than three lifetimes such as mine—we have sold cheaply or squandered or given away or merely lost much of the original wealth and health of our land. It is a history too largely told in the statistics of soil erosion, increasing pollution, waste and degradation of forests, desecration of streams, urban sprawl, impoverishment and miseducation of people, misuse of money, and, finally, the entire and permanent destruction of whole landscapes.

Eastern Kentucky, in its natural endowments of timber and minerals, is the wealthiest region of our state, and it has now experienced more than a century of intense corporate "free enterprise," with the result that it is more impoverished and has suffered more ecological damage than any other region. The worst inflicter of poverty and ecological damage has been the coal industry, which has taken from the region a wealth probably incalculable, and has imposed the highest and most burdening "costs of production" upon the land and the people. Many of these costs are, in the nature of things, not repayable. Some were paid by people now dead and beyond the reach of compensation. Some are scars on the land that will not be healed in any length of time imaginable by humans.

The only limits so far honored by this industry have been technological. What its machines have enabled it to do, it has done. And now, for the sake of the coal under them, it is destroying whole mountains with their forests, water courses, and human homeplaces. The resulting rubble of soils and blasted rocks is then shoved indiscriminately into the valleys. This is a history by any measure deplorable, and a commentary sufficiently devastating upon the intelligence of our politics and our system of education. That Kentuckians and their politicians have shut their eyes to this history as it was being made is an indelible disgrace. That they now permit this history to be justified by its increase of the acreage of "flat land" in the mountains signifies an indifference virtually suicidal.

So ingrained is our state's submissiveness to its exploiters that I recently heard one of our prominent politicians defend the destructive practices of the coal companies on the ground that we need the coal to "tide us over" to better sources of energy. He thus was offering the people and the region, which he represented and was entrusted to protect, as a sacrifice to what I assume he was thinking of as "the greater good" of the United States. But this idea, which he apparently believed to be new, was exactly our century-old policy for the mountain coalfields: the land and the people would be sacrificed for the greater good of the United States—and, only incidentally, of course, for the greater good of the coal corporations.

The response that is called for, it seems to me, is not a vision of "a better future," which would be easy and probably useless, but instead an increase of consciousness and critical judgment in the present. That would be harder, but it would be right. We know too well what to expect of people who do not see what is happening or who lack the means of judging what they see. What we may expect from them is what we will see if we look: devastation of the land and impoverishment of the people. And so let us ask: What might we expect of people who have consciousness and critical judgment, which is to say real presence of mind?

We might expect, first of all, that such people would take good care of what they have. They would know that the most precious things they have are the things they have been given: air, water, land, fertile soil, the plants and animals, one another—in short, the means of life, health, and joy. They would realize the value of those gifts. They would know better than to squander or destroy them for any monetary profit, however great.

Coal is undoubtedly something of value. And it is, at present, something we need—though we must hope we will not always need it, for we will not always have it. But coal, like the other fossil fuels, is a peculiar commodity. It is valuable to us only if we burn it. Once burned, it is no longer a commodity but only a problem, a source of energy that has become a source of pollution. And the source of the coal itself is not renewable. When the coal is gone, it will be gone forever, and the coal economy will be gone with it.

The natural resources of permanent value to the so-called coalfields of Eastern Kentucky are the topsoils and the forests and the streams. These are valuable, not, like coal, on the condition of their destruction, but on the opposite condition: that they should be properly cared for. And so we need, right now, to start thinking better than we ever have before about topsoils and forests and streams. We must think about all three at once, for it is a violation of their nature to think about any one of them alone.

The mixed mesophytic forest of the Cumberland Plateau was a great wonder and a great wealth before it was almost entirely cut down in the first half of the last century. Its regrowth could become a great wonder and a great wealth again; it could become the basis of a great regional economy—but only if it is properly cared for. Knowing that the native forest is the one permanent and abundant economic resource of the region ought to force us to see the need for proper care, and the realization of that need ought to force us to see the difference between a forest ecosystem and a coal mine. Proper care can begin only with the knowledge of that difference. A forest ecosystem, respected and preserved as such, can be used generation after generation without diminishment—or it can be regarded merely as an economic bonanza, cut down, and used up. The difference is a little like that between using a milk cow, and her daughters and granddaughters after her, for a daily supply of milk, renewable every year—or killing her for one year's supply of beef.

And there is yet a further difference, one that is even more important, and that is the difference in comprehensibility. A coal mine, like any other industrial-technological system, is a human product, and therefore entirely comprehensible by humans. But a forest ecosystem is a creature, not a product. It is, as part of its definition, a community of living plants and animals whose relationships with one another and with their place and climate are only partly comprehensible by humans, and, in spite of much ongoing research, they are likely to remain so. A forest ecosystem, then, is a human property only within very narrow limits, for it belongs also to the mystery that everywhere surrounds us. It comes from that mystery; we did not make it. And so proper care has to do, inescapably, with a proper humility.

But that only begins our accounting of what we are permitting the coal companies to destroy, for the forest is not a forest in and of itself. It is a forest, it can be a forest, *only* because it comes from, stands upon, shelters, and slowly builds a fertile soil. A fertile soil is not, as some people apparently suppose, an aggregate of inert materials, but it is a community of living creatures vastly more complex than that of the forest above it. In attempting to talk about the value of fertile soil, we are again dealing immediately with the unknown. Partly, as with the complexity and integrity of a forest ecosystem, this is the unknown of mystery. But partly, also, it is an unknown attributable to human indifference, for "the money and vision expended on probing the secrets of Mars . . . vastly exceed what has been spent exploring the earth beneath our feet." I am quoting from Yvonne Baskin's sorely needed new book, *Under Ground,* which is a survey of the progress so far of "soil science," which is still in its infancy. I can think of no better way to give a sense of what a fertile soil is, what it does, and what it is worth than to continue to quote from Ms. Baskin's book:

> . . . a spade of rich garden soil may harbor more species than the entire Amazon nurtures above ground . . . the bacteria in an acre of soil can outweigh a cow or two grazing above them.
>
> Together [the tiny creatures living underground] form the foundation for the earth's food webs, break down organic matter, store and recycle nutrients vital to plant growth, generate soil, renew soil fertility, filter and purify water, degrade and detoxify pollutants, control plant pests and pathogens, yield up our most important antibiotics, and help determine the fate of carbon and greenhouse gases and thus, the state of the earth's atmosphere and climate.
>
> By some estimates, more than 40 percent of the earth's plant-covered lands . . . have been degraded over the past half-century by direct human uses . . .
>
> The process of soil formation is so slow relative to the human lifespan that it seems unrealistic to consider soil a renewable resource. By one estimate it takes 200 to 1,000 years to regenerate an inch of lost topsoil.

And so on any still-intact slope of Eastern Kentucky, we have two intricately living and interdependent natural communities: that of the forest and that of the topsoil beneath the forest. Between them, moreover, the forest and the soil are carrying on a transaction with water that, in its way, also is intricate and wonderful. The two communities, of course, cannot live without rain, but the rain does not fall upon the forest as upon a pavement; it does not just splatter down. Its fall is slowed and gentled by the canopy of the forest, which thus protects the soil. The soil, in turn, acts as a sponge that absorbs the water, stores it, releases it slowly, and in the process filters and purifies it. The streams of the watershed—if the human dwellers downstream meet their responsibility—thus receive a flow of water that is continuous and clean.

Thus, and not until now, it is possible to say that the people of the watersheds may themselves be a permanent economic resource, but only and precisely to the extent that they take good care of what they have. If Kentuckians, upstream and down, ever fulfill their responsibilities to the precious things they have been given—the forests, the soils, and the streams—they will do so because they will have accepted a truth that they are going to find hard: the forests, the soils, and the streams are worth far more than the coal for which they are now being destroyed.

Before hearing the inevitable objections to that statement, I would remind the objectors that we are not talking here about the preservation of "the American way of life." We are talking about the preservation of life itself. And in this conversation, people of sense do not put secondary things ahead of primary things. That precious creatures (or resources, if you insist) that are infinitely renewable can be destroyed for the sake of a resource that to be used must be forever destroyed, is not just a freak of short-term accounting and the externalizing of cost—it is an inversion of our sense of what is good. It is madness.

And so I return to my opening theme: it is not a vision of the future that we need. We need consciousness, judgment, presence of mind. If we truly know what we have, we will change what we do.

Jeff Mann
1959–

Jeff Mann chafes against a world that would pigeonhole people into mutually exclusive categories. Mann was born in Clifton Forge, Virginia, and reared in Covington, Virginia, and Hinton, West Virginia. He earned undergraduate degrees in English and forestry, along with an MA in English, from West Virginia University. Mann lived briefly in Washington, DC, and since 1989 has taught Appalachian literature, LGBTQ literature, and creative writing at Virginia Tech.

Mann writes poetry, fiction, memoir, and essays, sometimes combining genres in a single text. Early in his career, he addressed Appalachian and gay issues in separate works, but he fused the two in later works. His subjects range from elderly relatives and Appalachian foodways to the gay "bear" lifestyle. Some of his work, such as *A History of Barbed Wire* (2006) and *Cub* (2014), is openly homoerotic. Mann insists that erotica should be viewed as a legitimate literary genre.

Throughout his writing, Mann is concerned with the discrimination and harassment that queer people have traditionally faced in Appalachia, as the selection from *Loving Mountains, Loving Men* (2005) included in this anthology indicates. Yet, according to Mann, the gay world can have its own biases. Its bicoastal orientation suggests that gay lifestyles flower in large cities such as Washington, New York, or San Francisco, not in the rural areas that lie between, and Mann has sometimes experienced anti-Appalachian prejudice from gay friends and acquaintances.

Mann is a pioneering activist in Appalachia's gay community and an important role model for young people negotiating LGBTQ Appalachian identities. The excellence of his writing, simultaneously critical and celebratory, invites all readers, straight and LGBTQ, to meditate on Appalachia, otherness, and the human capacity for love.

FROM Loving Mountains, Loving Men

PREFACE: CONSTRUCTING HEAVEN

> Do I contradict myself?
> Very well then I contradict myself,
> (I am large, I contain multitudes.)
> —*"Song of Myself,"* Walt Whitman

I dress quietly, not wanting to wake my partner, John. Leaving the cabin, I head for the guest house, ready for some coffee and some time alone to write. Along the path, across the fence, the horses stand, enjoying the cool of the morning, the absence of biting flies. Dew drips from the pine needles, and thistles edge the pasture, small explosions of lavender, reminding me of Scotland, where my mother's family came from: beautiful, prickly blooms. Stubborn, able to survive the harshest landscapes. An endurance I admire.

In the downstairs breakfast room, I pour coffee, listening to the music in the kitchen, where the guest house owners are preparing a big country breakfast, what smells like pancakes and sausage. Out on the upstairs screened-in porch, there is no music, only the sound of a crow, the hum of pool machinery. From this perspective, I can watch mist rise from the coves of the Potomac Highlands, hear a flicker rapping somewhere, watch a hummingbird fly by. Here I can muse on heaven.

In *Storming Heaven* by Denise Giardina, one of my favorite authors, the character Carrie Bishop states, "Heaven is where everyone you love is all in one place." I think of that quotation when John and I take one of our too-infrequent trips back to my hometown of Hinton, West Virginia, and find ourselves sitting around the Sunday breakfast table with my sister and my father, tucking into fresh-baked biscuits, bacon, and scrambled eggs. I think of that quotation here, too, spending the weekend at Lost River, this gay-owned bed and breakfast in the hills of Hardy County, West Virginia.

An earthly heaven can be difficult to construct when your loves seem irreconcilable. For gays and lesbians in Appalachia who want to live full lives, who want to embrace both their gay and their mountain identities, who refuse to dismember themselves in order to assimilate, it can be very difficult to find some compromise between love of the same sex and love of home. If a gay man flees to the city, he is often encouraged to drop "that funny accent" and "those country ways," to feel ashamed of his mountain culture. If a lesbian stays in the mountains, she might face bigotry and abuse, especially from intolerant fundamentalist Christians; she might feel obliged to stay in the closet; she might suffer from the relative lack of social and romantic opportunities.

My compromise has been to live in university towns in Appalachia: Morgantown, West Virginia, for thirteen years, and now Blacksburg, Virginia, for the last fifteen. In such towns, I can feel safe in a liberal, intellectual atmosphere. As an academic, I can even combine my seemingly contradictory passions and teach both gay and lesbian literature and Appalachian studies. And I can stay in the mountains, close to what remains of my family, for, as Loyal Jones so eloquently points out in his famous essay "Appalachian Values," we hill folk are powerfully attached to our native places and our kin.

Lost River achieves a heaven that admits both a love for mountains and a love for men. In Hinton, as much as I cherish my family and the landscape of Summers County, I will never feel entirely welcome, entirely safe. It is a small town, full of folks who would more than object to the kind of man I am, and I have spent years arming myself with the emotional equivalent of a thistle's thorns against that kind of hatred. I have too many unpleasant high school memories to forgive that town: a split lip, a note pasted to my back stating "Kick Me, I'm Queer."

Here at Lost River, however, an entire gay enclave has grown up. It's one thing, after years of loneliness and romantic debacles, to finally find a lover and together to develop a protective circle of like-minded queer friends with whom to socialize. It's another thing entirely to find an active and open gay and lesbian community in Appalachia. Lost River is unique in this respect, at least in my experience. It is true that most of the members of this community are urban transplants—Lost River is only an hour or two from Washington, DC—but I still delight in being able to stay at a gay bed and breakfast or dine at a gay-owned restaurant without having to leave the mountains, without having to make the trip to Key West or Provincetown, New Orleans or Dupont Circle, Greenwich Village or the Castro. As much as I love those places, as often as I might want to escape to them for brief vacations, they are not Appalachia. I could never live there. They are not home.

☙❧

The pancakes and sausage are tasty, the gay camaraderie about the breakfast table boisterous and witty. This morning I'm wearing one of my Ajaxx 63 T-shirts, with "Butch County Forest Service" blazoned across my chest, a slogan many straight folks won't get. It combines those apparent antipodes, gay culture and rural life, and harkens back to my undergraduate days at West Virginia University, where I tried to satisfy contrary halves of my intellect by majoring in both English and forestry. Later, by the pool, I'll be reading *Rebel Yell 2,* a collection of short stories about gay men in the South. I am, in other words, immersing myself this Lost River weekend in All Things Queer, which is a delicious relief when one spends one's life entirely surrounded by straight, mainstream culture.

The sunny afternoon goes too quickly, as vacation time always does. Phil, Dan, John, and I vacillate among the hot tub, the chilly waters of the pool, Manhattans in plastic cups, and a few chapters in our magazines or books. For dinner, the four of us end up at the nearby Lost River Grill. Everything in the restaurant reflects the dual nature of this valley, the unusual combination of urban gay culture and native Appalachian ways. The owner is a handsome, well-built gay man who lives part of the week in Baltimore; the waitress is a local high school girl whose West Virginia accent and small-town friendliness immediately make me feel at home. The menu ranges from fairly exotic Mexican options to meat loaf, fried chicken, and other down-home specialties I grew up on, including—to my gourmand delight—a case full of homemade pies, including apple, peach, and coconut cream. The customers are either middle-aged and elderly Hardy County natives, usually heterosexual couples, or gay men and lesbians enjoying one another's company. Everyone seems to get along.

This peace was not instantly achieved, the owner tells us, as we gobble down our tortillas and rib eyes. When he and his lover first bought the business, the local ministers encouraged their flocks to boycott the place. This unpleasant state of affairs lasted only a month, until the pious realized that the Lost River Grill was the only place in the valley to eat out. For once, the calorie-covetous flesh won out over the narrow-minded spirit. Appetite conquered prejudice.

Last summer at Lost River, I experienced prejudice of a different sort, reminding me of what an odd creature I am, cultural amphibian insisting on both worlds, Appalachian and queer. John and I were enjoying barbecue at another gay-owned establishment and chatting with a male couple from DC, when one of them said, "Well, you two can't be from West Virginia. You seem too literate." I smiled stiffly and raised my hand. "West Virginia here. I'm from Summers County. I teach Appalachian studies at Virginia Tech." He had enough grace to be at least mildly embarrassed.

Alone with John later, I dropped my polite mask to snarl like any rural dweller, "Why the hell do these big-city folks come out here if they're just going to mock us? Why don't they just go home?" My resentment of such Appalachian stereotypes is only slightly less strong than my detestation for those country fundamentalists whose religious attitudes make life for many gays and lesbians miserable, full of loneliness, self-doubt, and fear.

Divided loyalties, perhaps. Still, I refuse to relinquish either world. I insist on it all. The late-summer pastures full of ironweed and goldenrod. Muscular, hairy, goateed men—just my type—marching in the West Virginia Gay Pride Parade. My father's gardens, the buckets of tomatoes and cucumbers he proudly brings home, the jars of spaghetti sauce and chowchow and corn relish he and my sister put up. Harness-strap boots, my black-leather motorcycle jacket, my leather-flag baseball cap. Listening to Tim McGraw, Brooks and Dunn, Melissa Etheridge, Joni Mitchell, Kathy Mattea as I drive my dusty pickup truck down winding West Virginia back roads. Harpers Ferry, Helvetia; San Francisco, Key West. Leather bars like Charleston's Tap Room or the Baltimore Eagle. "Poor Wayfaring Stranger," one of my few specialties on the lap dulcimer. Lobster and paté, brown beans and cornbread. *The Journal of Appalachian Studies*, *The Gay and Lesbian Review*. In my life, at least, these contradictions coexist. They cannot be separated.

❧

For many, the desire might be to separate these poems, to set them apart, to tug out the references to mustaches and chest hair and stick to cornfields, ramps, and tomato stakes. As defiantly as I cling to both mountain and queer heritage, such segregation would be my first tendency, and, in the past, in the few volumes of poetry I've published, that has been my decision: "hillbilly" poems here, "queer" poems there. They seem incongruous, not to be mixed, like sodium and chlorine, chemicals that explode when combined.

Similarly, up to now I have published poetry *or* memoir, not a combination of the two. Indeed, some readers might prefer that I stick to one genre, not blend the two as I do in this book. Mixed-genre books are a rarity, an odd hybrid most agents and publishers would eye askance. No one knows quite what to do with them. Like gay Appalachians, such books resist simple labeling, simple pigeonholing.

Here, however, I have chosen to mix not only regional identity with sexual identity, but also poetry with prose, and these amalgams are a relief. It has been a difficult process, the work of decades, my attempts to make sense of the many complex and often contradictory facets of my personality. The hard-won integration resulting from that process is reflected not only in the content but in the form of this book. Mixed genre allows for many voices: the melancholy, romantic reflection, and solemnity of my poetry; the sharp humor, anger, political reflection, and storytelling of my prose; the necessary density of poetry; the roomier space of creative nonfiction. In order to more clearly meld the book's disparate elements, I have often borrowed phrases from related poems to title the segments of memoir, and hopefully the two genres here complement each other, memoir making more understandable the poems, poems lending greater depth to the memoir.

Thus, this collection is an attempt to reconcile my loves in my work as I have in my life. It is my attempt to construct the heaven that Carrie Bishop imagines, in which my passions—for the beauty of mountains and the beauty of men—may intertwine and, even in their tensions, achieve some kind of integrity, some tenuous wholeness. What I want is unity, however briefly achieved, like that cool morning at Lost River, drowsy horses standing in the mist, September dawn dripping from the trees, and the thistles, hardy as Highland warriors, enduring what they must, stoking their lavender fires, brandishing their swords, fusing in one stalk loveliness and ferocity.

Emory and Henry

It was the year America turned two hundred, the summer of freedom celebrations and especially grand Fourth of July parties. When I think of 1976, however, what I remember is not so much bicentennial excitement as a small college in southwest Virginia and my first vivid taste of homophobia. Even in America, I was to discover, living freely and honestly has its risks. Even in America, I realized, I do not wholly belong.

That spring—it was my junior year at Hinton High School—Jo Davison had lent me that momentous novel *The Front Runner,* and I'd realized that I was gay. College was still over a year away, but meanwhile there was a briefer escape in the offing. Davison was a biology teacher, an excellent one, in whose class I'd excelled, and she encouraged me to apply for a National Science Foundation (NSF) biology honors program at Emory and Henry College.

I was accepted, to my delight. In early June of 1976 my parents drove me the few hours through dramatically mountainous countryside to the college, dropped me off at the boys' dorm, Armbrister House, and soon departed. I sat in the porch swing and watched them drive off, both excited and a little frightened to be on my own for the first time, far from family, friends, and home. That evening, after orienting myself with a campus stroll, I met my roommates—Jim, from New York, and Kenny, from Narrows, Virginia—then began to unpack.

At an introductory meeting the next morning, all the students met Dr. Jones, a biology teacher at Emory and Henry, who had organized the NSF program and who would teach most of the classes. It would last for six weeks, and twenty students would participate. Along with daily classes in botany, microbiology, forestry, and other branches of the life sciences, Dr. Jones had scheduled trips to many local spots of cultural and biological interest: Abram's Falls, Mount Rogers, Saltville's strip mines, Abingdon's Barter Theater, and Lake Norris, Tennessee, where we would have a week's worth of study.

There was just enough spare time for me to feel headily independent. I rose early some mornings to jog around the misty track, thinking of my *Front Runner* hero Billy Sive. I wandered around the picturesque campus, admiring its huge old trees, its stream, its columned brick buildings. One evening I attended an organ recital in the campus chapel, sitting alone in the balcony, where early mornings and late nights of study caught up with me and I fell asleep on the pew. After meals in the cafeteria, I'd head down to the pond to visit Luther, an ill-tempered white swan, who would dutifully bite my boot when I thrust my foot within range of his vicious beak. One evening, straddling a wall near the pond, feeling a little homesick, I looked down to discover, scratched in the stone, the name of an ecology club friend of mine from back home, a girl who'd attended the very same program two summers before. The serendipity was comforting.

Having spent my entire life in Appalachia, I found it very stimulating to meet students from other areas of the country. All five kids from New York were Jewish, and this I found especially interesting. For me, Jews were an exotic breed, since I'd rarely encountered them in small-town West Virginia, and the same intellectual curiosity I applied to my class work drove me to ask many questions about their culture and religion. One girl in particular I grew fond of, Sue, from Syosset, on Long Island. She had long black hair and a big smile. Around her neck she wore a *chi*, a Hebrew letter whose significance she was to explain, along with many other details of Jewish history.

Sue and I were quite simpatico. What a luxury it was to spend time with someone so intelligent. One evening we inadvertently caused a thrill of gossip to run through the group. After a long talk in the lounge of the girls' dorm, we stretched out at opposite ends of a couch, covered by the same blanket, listening to Chicago's "Color My World" in candlelight. Drowsing, we heard a door creak. An eavesdropper, apparently, for soon the word was that Sue and I were dating.

It was no wonder that Sue and I were suspected of a romantic or erotic entanglement, for, within the first few weeks of the NSF program, with the tide of flirtation waxing high, several of the boys and girls in the group of twenty had coupled off. We were living in a hothouse environment, certainly. Pumped full of the hormones of late adolescence to begin with, we were living together, eating together, studying together, going to classes together, traveling together: circumstances conducive to dangerously intense feelings.

I wasn't interested in using Sue as a cover for my homosexuality, however. Instead, fairly early in the six-week program, I'd come out both to her and to Lisa, a pretty, big-breasted girl from Aliquippa, Pennsylvania, whom I was to nickname "Sweetums" for her perpetually sunny personality. The other girls, unaware of my queer inclinations, must have regarded me as possible dating material. I assume this only because Sue reported one day that the girls had all methodically rated the guys and come to the conclusion that, since I had the hairiest legs, I must also have the biggest "bird." I had just enough adolescent macho pride to be pleased at this report, though I wasn't interested in presenting my bird to any of my female classmates.

In fact, I wasn't all that interested in my male classmates, or very many other boys my age. Instead, my lust focused on older men, on several of the college students who were attending summer school at Emory and Henry. Some evenings after studying, I'd head down to the tennis courts and sit in the bleachers to watch sweaty young men bound about in the humid twilight. At some point in the failing light, lamps would switch on, about which the summer moths would crazily congregate. Occasionally, a few of the athletes would strip to the waist, and I, feigning interest in the game, would move a little closer to study the fur on their chests and bellies, the stubble on their cheeks, the way the muscles in their backs and shoulders moved. Instead of taking such beautiful flesh into my mouth, I was consigned by age and shyness to fantasy, to metaphor: the hard curves of their biceps were river-smoothed stones, their moist body hair was dark orchard grass, mosses, fern fronds, the spring-soft needles of larch. I had never touched a man before, not in the way I wanted to, and sitting there in the dark, stiff beneath my denim shorts, I would try to imagine how they tasted, how they smelled. I had no idea how to approach them, what to say that might encourage their interest, their consent.

One college student in particular grabbed my interest that summer. He much resembled the way I envisioned Billy Sive from *The Front Runner:* tanned, lithe, with a head of golden-brown curls and long, fine-muscled legs glistening with golden hair. Several of the girls in our NSF group clustered about him when they could, usually after lunch in the cafeteria, and I envied them their femaleness, only because it licensed them to flirt with desirable men. I had grown up around enough intolerant straight men to guess how he was likely to receive my lusty admiration, so I kept it to myself.

He was strikingly handsome and he knew it, showing off his body as often as possible in skimpy tank tops and tiny running shorts. One especially hot afternoon, when I strolled down to the duck pond to offer my boot to the savage swan's snapping beak, my idol was lounging in the shade beneath an oak with another coterie of undergrad girls. He had nothing on but blue nylon swim trunks. At sixteen, out barely four months, I was already a chest man. I walked past with exaggerated slowness, thankful for the way that sunglasses conceal a randy stare, and devoured him with the only sense I could. His nipples were glossy and nut brown, his tanned torso hairless except for the trail to happiness, as I had already learned to call it, the ridge of golden fur that bisected his lean belly and disappeared into the top of his nicely packed shorts.

The next time I saw him, several days later, was in the cafeteria, sitting a few tables down with more admirers. In the first of what has proven to be twenty-five years' worth of wicked techniques for spying on men's bodies, I deliberately dropped my fork on the floor, then bent beneath the table to fetch it. There they were, a few yards away, those long, delicious runner's legs. For a minute I thought of dropping to the floor myself, crawling through the forest of calves, and running my tongue up his thigh before tugging his revealing shorts down with my teeth. Needless to say, I thought better of it. Still, as I returned to my lunch, I regretted living in a world in which such libidinous acts occur not at all often, a world in which I would not discover how such a man might feel as he stripped us both and then lay on top of me naked.

While I wrestled with my hormones, occasionally finding solitary relief in the shower, I was also experiencing many novelties, the presence of which makes most youthful years seem effervescent and many adulthoods fall a bit flat. Along with classes in genetics and ecology, we enjoyed regular jaunts off campus. In Saltville, Virginia, we drove about a strip-mined site and learned about the deleterious environmental effects of coal mining. We climbed Mount Rogers, the highest mountain in Virginia, and in the process I discovered how gullible city kids are. They were ridiculously afraid of a herd of cows we passed in a field on our way to the top, and when they pointed to cow pies and asked what they were, I took the opportunity to explain that the French use such soft and fragrant fungi in sauces and salads. I recommended that they do the same upon their return home, though where in downtown Manhattan they might find such ripe produce I did not know.

One day in class Dr. Jones passed out tickets, and later that afternoon he and his assistants drove us to Abingdon, Virginia, for a play at the Barter Theater, so called because during the Depression, when it was founded, the poor would pay for tickets with homegrown vegetables. After a tour of the quaint town and a glimpse of the elegant Martha Washington Inn, we settled into our seats in the theater. The performance that evening was a series of dramatic readings from *Transformations,* Anne Sexton's sardonic take on the Brothers Grimm, accompanied by Walter Carlos's *Sonic Seasonings.* My first taste of both modern poetry and electronic music. I was entranced. The world was beginning to widen. And I knew, even more vividly than before, that the small town where I had grown up could never satisfy me, could never give my mind or my body what they craved.

Another afternoon in late June we all hiked to Abram's Falls. After a walk along a path through thick woods, a good opportunity to learn some of the native plant species, we came to an overlook. Below, across a shady dell, creek water poured dramatically over a rocky lip, smashing into foam on rocks below. Several hippie hikers who'd gotten there before us had climbed onto a ledge behind the waterfall's translucent veil. One of them, in the dim emerald light, stripped off his soaked T-shirt, pulled off his boots, and, clad now only in faded denim shorts, stepped forward into the cascade. Laughing and gasping, he backed out of the pounding water, then stepped in again, his long brown hair plastered to his shoulders, the creek running its clear fingers down his chest and back. He was the image of a forest god, a satyr, and I wanted to join him in his freedom and his ecstasy. A shaggy kid with straggling teenaged beard and thick glasses, I wanted to strip and enter the waterfall, become someone else, someone equally desirable, make love to him on carpets of moss.

A week later, the big day came, America's birthday, and we all were invited over to Dr. Jones's house for a cookout. One of the girls, Charlotte, arrived wearing a T-shirt that brazenly announced, "Fuck the Bicentennial." I found this disconcerting, for my mother had long forbade me to use that word in public, much less let it grace an article of clothing. But, inspired by this naughty example, several of us, over hot dogs and pop, shared lyrics to vulgar songs when Dr. Jones's back was turned: "Gonna tell you all a story 'bout a man named Jed. He raped Ellie May and he threw her on the bed." Afterward, a few of us, on a dare, wandered tentatively through a nearby cemetery in the misty, firefly-haunted dark. When I returned to my dorm room alone, I stretched out on the bed and listened to the radio. The Carpenters sang "I Know

I Need to Be in Love." Pulling off my shirt in the summer heat, I stood in the dark before the mirror, running my fingers over a chest still a stranger to hair or gym workouts, wondering when and how I would lose my hated virginity.

I was to discover, like most queer youth, the pains of being gay long before the pleasures, however. Having realized the nature of my sexuality only months before, I took to Emory and Henry's library in the first weeks of the NSF program to track down information on homosexuality. Emboldened by ignorance, youthful optimism, and a blithe disregard for the world's disapproval, I didn't go to any great efforts to conceal my reading material. Surely I would be safe from prejudice on the campus of such a bastion of learning.

One evening as I returned from such a library raid, I ran into Tonia, a tall, pretty classmate with long red hair, a spoiled air, and a sharp sense of humor. "What are you reading?" she asked, eyeing my armful of books. I showed her. She wrinkled her nose, then headed off with a piece of news destined to dwarf any other gossip our group had eagerly tossed about that summer.

It took less than twenty-four hours. After a class on microbes the next afternoon, our group dispersed. Most headed out to relax before dinner, but a few lingered in the hall of the biology building. I was talking to Lisa about the next assignment when another classmate, Steve, wandered up. I hadn't gotten to know him very well, but I had noticed, during an afternoon of water volleyball in the campus pool, that he had a fine body, pale, smooth and lightly muscled; that he thus looked almost as appealing as an adult in his form-fitting swimsuit; and that he was a skilled, almost poetic, diver.

"So, Jeff, I hear you're having a gay old time at the library this summer," Steve said snidely. "What's it like to like boys?"

I flushed with shock and stood speechless. Lisa, however, was far from paralyzed. Rustling up some of the odd insults of her Pennsylvanian hometown, she spat, "That's none of your business, is it? And how'd you like to kiss my ass, you hoopie, you numnard, you heeneyhocker!" Steve instantly retreated before this linguistic barrage, this indignant buxom amazon. He turned tail, scuttling down the stairwell and out the door. It was not the first time, nor the last, that men would cause me pain and women would take my part.

I was too young to know what to expect. Had I known, I might have hidden my library books more carefully, despite all my high-flown nonconformist principles. What I got was not violence, or even the threat of violence—we were all too scholarly and well brought up for that—but avoidance, whispers, averted eyes. Never again anything as crudely blunt as Steve's comment. Rather, all the body language that makes one aware of one's status as a pariah.

In the difficult days that followed, Sue and Lisa stood by me, of course, very deliberately sitting with me in the cafeteria and in classes. Katie, from Knoxville, a girl with big glasses and bobbed hair, and Lauren, from Silver Spring, a good-looking athletic girl with long Scandinavian braids, also seemed supportive. Of all the boys, only Travis seemed not to care about the rumors. An awkward, skinny, bookish boy with a big Adam's apple and nerd glasses, he'd grown up in the tiny community of

Meadows of Dan, Virginia, where he'd probably endured enough ribbing to make him sympathetic to any outcast's plight.

My greatest nemesis was Ira, an unattractive kid from New York with an annoying accent and a sense of entitlement. He never said anything to me directly, probably because I had a bigger build than he did. However, my female friends reported that, in my absence, he was the most insulting of the crew, a baby homophobe. I thought of infant copperheads, whose venom is virulent and ready for the using as soon as they hatch. I hated Ira. I wanted to break his arms and feed him to Luther, who would hold him under the pond's scummy waters with his beautiful white wings till the bubbling stopped and the pond's surface was smooth again.

My roommates Jim and Kenny were the greatest martyrs in the midst of this mess, for they had to share their room with an apparent monster. They began dressing, both morning and evening, in the bathroom down the hall, rather than allowing me glimpses of their skinny, hollow-chested, adolescent bodies—glimpses that, they must have imagined, would madden me as a matador might a bull. With no other place to sleep, they must have lain in bed staring at the ceiling, only yards from the dozing dragon. Did they think that I might descend on them as soon as they'd drifted off, to suck their blood, their breath?

This unpleasant situation built to a head pretty quickly. One evening, as I was stretched out on my bed reading, Travis came by and whispered that there was a meeting about to begin downstairs, a meeting Ira called, a meeting to which I had not been invited. When Travis hurried out, I lay back, stared at the maple leaves filling the windows, and listened to dorm-room doors slam and footsteps descend the stairs. Travis, Ira, Jim, Kenny, Steve, Jeremy.

A long time passed. I gave up any pretense of reading. Though I didn't really expect violence, it did occur to me that I had never struck anyone before in my life, that it was a long drop from my windowsill to the ground. I was too young, too ignorant of history, to realize how ironic it was that Ira, a Jew, was spearheading this persecution. He would have popped me into a concentration camp in a heartbeat.

Then footsteps ascended the stairs. One set of footsteps, surely a good sign. Would whoever it was be brandishing a torch, a crucifix, or, in Ira's case, a Star of David? If only I had a vampire's fangs. At this point, I'd use them not to drain vital juices but, like any cornered beast, to rend.

It was Dr. Jones's assistant, Chris, who served as the boys' RA. On his shoulders had fallen this uncomfortable duty. The NSF program and its intense togetherness would be continuing for another three weeks. He couldn't dismiss me, because I'd done nothing but check out library books, like any good student. Somehow he had to make peace.

He did so by ignoring the truth and encouraging everyone in the program to do the same. Denial. It does save lives. The boys were concerned, they'd come to him, he gently explained. "But I can't believe that you're a homosexual choosing to make your presence known," Chris stated flatly. Perhaps he thought I would have to be effeminate, crinoline clad, to be truly queer. Perhaps only a rigorous routine of mincing and tittering would convince him. Or perhaps he realized that I was indeed gay and that the best thing to do under the circumstances was to encourage me to officially renounce an identity that had proven dangerous. I felt like Galileo: Yes, the earth is flat. Chris was asking me to lie to make life easier for all of us.

I wouldn't lie and claim to be straight, but I wouldn't insist on my homosexuality either. He'd given us both an out, an early version of "Don't ask, don't tell." I was sixteen years old, I was frightened, I was not a career activist, I was far away from supportive queer friends. So I said nothing. I gave him the silence he needed to smooth things over.

Chris left briefly, only to herd up my two roommates Jim and Kenny. "Now, shake hands and let's forget this misunderstanding," Chris insisted. As Jim stepped forward and gingerly gripped my hand, our eyes met. His face was flushed, his stare was full of fear. I couldn't believe it. He was terrified of me. I, who was not yet bitter, angry, and irritable, as I am at forty-five. Still the sixteen-year-old Jeff, I was a nonviolent idealist, a shy intellectual, a southern boy who tried to be polite and kind in every situation. It would take me many years to realize that such fear, in different degrees and different circumstances, is the sort that sometimes kills.

Everyone seemed grateful to escape this unpleasantness, and, in the remaining weeks of the program, the topic surfaced only rarely. Tonia, the gossip queen whose loose tongue had started the semiscandal, attempted suicide for no reason the rest of us were ever to learn, and within days she was sent home.

We remaining students spent a week at a biology field station near Norris Lake, Tennessee, studying limnology with a local expert who discoursed on lake microorganisms and aquatic plants. One day, to my amazement, I discovered a dead scorpion on the floor of the lab. Recalling my father's stories of his World War II days in the Sahara and such creatures' penchant for dark sleeping places, I idly wondered if I could coax one into Ira's shoe the next time he took a nap. Then, as now, I have a crippling inability to forgive.

One morning, Sally, a quiet classmate, did a sudden cartwheel as she, Sue, and I strolled through a clearing toward the classroom. Her shirt briefly slipped up, exposing bare breasts. How much simpler life must be, I mused, for those boys who would find that sight arousing. That afternoon, as we all floated about the lake in a pontoon boat, a sudden thunderstorm broke loose. I sat on the deck in my swimsuit, cross-legged, head thrown back, welcoming the passionate violence of the sky, surges of rain crashing over me like the foamy cascades of Abram's Falls. Laughing and shivering, I knew what I felt was ecstasy, a taste of things to come.

On the drive back to the field station, a crescent moon rose with silver certainty over a tobacco barn's silhouette. One more night there, time to enjoy a bonfire, songs, marshmallows, to listen to crickets and watch fireflies flicker. Then back to the campus of Emory and Henry for a few more days of class. Our time together was almost up.

The afternoon we returned from Norris Lake, I sat on the porch swing reading Hermann Hesse's novel *Demien*. Kenny joined me on the swing with a book of his own. A few minutes passed in studious silence. Then, stretching, I rested my arm across the back of the swing. Kenny looked around nervously. Did he think that, blind with desire, I was trying surreptitiously to work my arm around him in order to slip my hand down his shirt? "Oh, for God's sake!" I snarled. "Sorry," he blushed, moving to the opposite end of the swing, and then, by slow degrees, with studied casualness, onto the porch steps and so out into the shade of the nearest tree. No use taking a chance when the possibility of infection might be present.

The last evening of the NSF program, in an old cabin on the campus, we shared a farewell dinner, during which tongue-in-cheek awards were given out. I received "The Gayest," which Ira announced before passing over the mock certificate. Every-one laughed nervously. I smiled good-naturedly, thinking of Luther, the truly vicious killer swan, the churning pond waters, the shrieks subsiding to silence. I would never have to see these kids again.

But a few I would heartily miss, after six intense weeks together. At the dinner's end, Knoxville Katie hugged me hard and whispered, "You're cool, don't you forget it," before heading off to pack. The next morning Sue and Lisa left early, and I saw them off. As she stepped into her mother's car, Sue took off her *chi* necklace and put it around my neck. I watched the cars disappear, then sat alone on the steps of the biology building in the thick fog of a summer dawn and cried.

◆-◆

For several years I corresponded with my Emory and Henry favorites, before our lives sped up in college and we eventually lost touch. In one letter Katie confessed to me that she had recently realized that she was bisexual and thanked me for enduring what I had that summer, for it had helped her come to terms with her own sexual-ity. Sue told me of a minireunion in New York in 1978, a car ride during which Ira had discussed me contemptuously and a drunken Lauren, from the back seat, had growled, "So what's so wrong with homosexuality?" thus effectively shutting him up. I like to think that flaxen-haired amazon has delighted many a lesbian since I last saw her, and Ira, though lucky enough to have escaped Luther's voracity, has long ago fallen prey to a snapping piranha swarm of predatory drag queens.

In March of 1999 I attended the Appalachian Studies Association Conference in Abingdon, Virginia, the first time I'd been back to that part of the state since 1976. When I presented my paper on gay life in Appalachia, I was applauded stren-uously by an audience composed of many gays and lesbians. Their enthusiasm was, I suspect, less a comment on the paper's quality than it was evidence that there are many mountain queers who are desperately eager to read material on a topic so little acknowledged or discussed. Afterward, my lover John and I spent the night at the luxurious Martha Washington Inn, last seen when I was sixteen. That evening we attended a performance at the Barter Theater, and I thought of that teenager hearing for the first time the work of Anne Sexton, a writer who would teach him how effec-tively a poet can use pain.

On the way home, John and I drove through the campus of Emory and Henry. The layout of the buildings came back to me in a rush: the boys' dorm, the biol-ogy building, the library brimful of dangerous books, the chapel, cafeteria, and duck pond. No sign of Luther in the gray wintry drizzle, no bare-chested boys lunging about on the tennis courts, no *Front Runner* look-alike. He's probably plump, balding, and married like myself. Perhaps his son is now as old as he was the day I saw him shirtless, lounging in the hot shade beneath the oak trees

This November, at a friend's invitation, I will be reading poetry at Emory and Henry, almost twenty-five years after my memorable summer there. I will wear Sue's *chi* beneath a suitably academic dress shirt and blazer. When I look over the audience, I will remember their faces, the ones who knew me for six weeks in 1976, when I was still a sheltered boy, the ones who treated me with kindness. I will try to imagine, in one empty seat (for there are always those at poetry readings), that boy himself, shaggy, sparsely bearded, frightened into silence. When he looks up at me and smiles, I will begin to speak.

Barbara Kingsolver

1955–

Barbara Kingsolver grew up in Carlisle, Kentucky, on the border between the Bluegrass and the mountains. She earned her undergraduate degree in biology at DePauw University in Indiana before settling in Arizona, where she lived for two decades and earned an MA in ecology and evolutionary biology at the University of Arizona. Kingsolver's writing and life are inextricably linked. Her work has typically focused on the various landscapes where she has lived: the Southwest (*The Bean Trees* [1988] and other works); Africa (*The Poisonwood Bible* [1998]); and Southern Appalachia (*Prodigal Summer* [2002], *Animal, Vegetable, Miracle* [2007], a large section of *The Lacuna* [2009], and *Flight Behavior* [2012]).

Kingsolver's writing unabashedly embraces political themes and places a heavy emphasis on social and biological communities, both human and nonhuman. Often she explores women's lives, infusing a feminist sensibility into traditional female roles of homemaking and motherhood. Her concern for social justice issues has also led her to write about Native Americans, Africans, and LGBTQ people. To stimulate and support socially aware writing, which she feels is marginalized in the mainstream literary world, Kingsolver established the Bellwether Prize, which is given to a first, unpublished novel demonstrating literary excellence in politically involved fiction.

On their farm in southwestern Virginia, Kingsolver and her family conducted a yearlong experiment in eating only locally grown foods, an experience she recounts in the nonfiction book *Animal, Vegetable, Miracle: A Year of Food Life* (2008), which she co-authored with husband Steven Hopp and daughter Camille Kingsolver.

FROM Animal, Vegetable, Miracle: A Year of Food Life

CHAPTER 13: LIFE IN A RED STATE

August

I've kept a journal for most of the years I've been gardening. I'm a habitual scribbler, jotting down the triumphs and flops of each season that I always feel pretty sure I'd remember anyway: that the Collective Farm Woman melons were surprisingly prissy; that the Dolly Partons produced such whopping tomatoes, the plants fell over. Who could forget any of that? Me, as it turns out. Come winter when it's time to order seeds again, I always need to go back and check the record. The journal lying open beside my bed also offers a handy incentive at each day's end for making a few notes about the weather, seasonal shifts in bloom and fruiting times, big family events, the day's harvest, or just the minutiae that keep me entertained. The power inside the pea-sized brain of a hummingbird, for example, that repeatedly built her nest near our kitchen door: despite her migrations across continents and the storms of life, her return date every spring was the same, give or take no more than twenty-four hours.

Over years, trends like that show up. Another one is that however jaded I may have become, winter knocks down the hollow stem of my worldliness and I'll start each summer again with expectations as simple as a child's. The first tomato of the season brings me to my knees. Its vital stats are recorded in my journal with the care of a birth announcement: It's an Early Girl! Four ounces! June 16! Blessed event, we've waited so long. Over the next few weeks I note the number, size, and quality of the different tomato varieties as they begin to come in: two Green Zebras, four gorgeous Jaune Flammés, one single half-pound Russian Black. I note that the latter wins our summer's first comparative taste test—a good balance of tart and sweet with strong spicy notes. I describe it in my journal the way an oenophile takes notes on a new wine discovery. On the same day, I report that our neighbor wants to give away all her Russian Blacks on the grounds they are "too ugly to eat." I actually let her give me a couple.

As supply rises, value depreciates. Three weeks after the **First Tomato!** entry in my journal, I've dropped the Blessed Event language and am just putting them down for the count: "10 Romas today, 8 Celebrity, 30 Juliet." I continue keeping track so we'll know eventually which varieties performed best, but by early August I've shifted from numbers to pounds. We bring in each day's harvest in plastic grocery sacks that we heave onto a butcher's scale in our kitchen, jotting down the number on a notepad before moving on to processing.

At this point in the year, we had officially moved beyond hobby scale. My records would show eventually whether we were earning more than minimum wage, but for certain we would answer the question that was largely the point of this exercise: what does it take, literally, to keep a family fed? Organizing the spring planting had been tricky. How many pumpkins does a family eat in a year? How many jars of pickles? My one area of confidence was tomatoes: we couldn't have too many. We loved them fresh, sliced, in soups and salads, as pasta sauces, chutneys, and salsa. I'd put in fifty plants.

In July, all seemed to be going according to plan when we hauled in just over 50 pounds of tomatoes. In August the figure jumped to 302 pounds. In the middle of that month, our neighbor came over while I was canning. I narrowed my eyes and asked her, "Did I let you *give me some tomatoes* a few weeks ago?"

She laughed. She didn't want them back, either.

Just because we're overwhelmed doesn't mean we don't still love them, even after the first thrill wears off. I assure my kids of this, when they point out a similar trend in their baby books: dozens of photos of the first smile, first bath, first steps . . . followed by little evidence that years two and three occurred at all. Tomatoes (like children) never achieve the villainous status of squash—they're too good to wear out their welcome, and if they *nearly* do, our in-town friends are always happy to take them. Fresh garden tomatoes are so unbelievably tasty, they ruin us utterly and forever on the insipid imports available in the grocery. In defiance of my childhood training, I cannot clean my salad plate in a restaurant when it contains one of those anemic wedges that taste like slightly sour water with a mealy texture. I'm amazed those things keep moving through the market, but the world apparently has tomato-eaters for whom "kinda reddish" is qualification enough. A taste for better stuff is cultivated only through experience.

Drowning in good tomatoes is the exclusive privilege of the gardener and farm-market shopper. The domain of excess is rarely the lot of country people, so we'll take this one when we get it. From winter I always look back on a season of bountiful garden tomatoes and never regret having eaten a single one.

At what point did we realize we were headed for a family tomato harvest of 20 percent of a *ton?* We had a clue when they began to occupy every horizontal surface in our kitchen. By mid-August tomatoes covered the countertops end to end, from the front edge to the backsplash. No place to set down a dirty dish, forget it, and no place to wash it, either. The sink stayed full of red orbs, bobbing in their wash water. The stove top stayed covered with baking sheets of halved tomatoes waiting for their turn in the oven. The cutting board stayed full, the knives kept slicing.

August is all about the tomatoes, every year. That's nothing new. For a serious gardener, the end of summer is when you walk into the kitchen and see red. We roast them in a slow oven, especially the sweet orange Jaune Flammés, which are just the right size to slice in half, sprinkle with salt and thyme, and bake for several hours until they resemble cow flops (the recipe says "shoes," if you prefer). Their slow-roasted, caramelized flavor is great in pizzas and panini, so we freeze hundreds of them in plastic bags. We also slice and slide them into the drawers of the food dryer, which runs 24-7. ("Sun-dried" sounds classy, but Virginia's sun can't compete with our southern humidity; a low-voltage dryer renders an identical product.) We make sauce in huge quantity, packed and processed in canning jars. By season's end our pantry shelves are lined with quarts of whole tomatoes, tomato juice, spaghetti sauce, chutney, several kinds of salsa, and our favorite sweet-sour sauce based on our tomatoes, onions, and apples.

August brings on a surplus of nearly every vegetable we grow, along with the soft summer fruits. Squash are vegetable rabbits in terms of reproductive excess, but right behind them are the green beans, which in high season must be picked every day. They're best when young, slender, and super-fresh, sautéed and served with a dash of balsamic vinegar, but they don't stay young and slender for long. We've found or invented a fair number of disappearing-bean recipes; best is a pureed, bright green dip or spread that's a huge crowd pleaser until you announce that it's green bean paté. It keeps and freezes well, but needs a more cunning title. Our best effort so far is "frijole guacamole," Holy Mole for short.

We process and put up almost every kind of fruit and vegetable in late summer, but somehow it's the tomatoes, with their sunny flavor and short shelf life, that demand the most attention. We wish for them at leisure, and repent in haste. Rare is the August evening when I'm not slicing, canning, roasting, and drying tomatoes—often all at the same time. Tomatoes take over our life. When Lily was too young to help, she had to sit out some of the season at the kitchen table with her crayons while she watched me work. The summer she was five, she wrote and illustrated a small book entitled "Mama the Tomato Queen," which fully exhausted the red spectrum of her Crayola box.

Some moment of every summer finds me all out of canning jars. So I go to town and stand in line at the hardware store carrying one or two boxes of canning jars and lids, renewing my membership in a secret society. Elderly women and some men, too, will smile their approval or ask outright, "What are you canning?" These folks must see me as an anomaly of my generation, an earnest holdout, while the younger clientele see me as a primordial nerdhead, if they even notice. I suppose I'm both. If I even notice.

But canning doesn't deserve its reputation as an archaic enterprise murderous to women's freedom and sanity. It's straightforward, and for tomato and fruit products doesn't require much special equipment. Botulism—the famously deadly bacterium that grows in airless, sealed containers and thus can spoil canned goods—can't grow in a low-pH environment. That means acidic tomatoes, grapes, and tree fruits can safely be canned in a simple boiling water bath. All other vegetables must be processed in a pressure canner that exposes them to higher-than-boiling temperatures; it takes at least 240°F to kill botulism spores. The USDA advises that pH 4.6 is the botulism-safe divide between these two methods. Since 1990, test kitchens have found that some low-acid tomato varieties sit right on the fence, so tomato-canning instructions published years ago may not be safe. Modern recipes advise adding lemon juice or citric acid to water-bath-canned tomatoes. Botulism is one of the most potent neurotoxins on our planet, and not a visitor you want to mess with.

Acidity is the key to safety so all kinds of pickles preserved in vinegar are fair game. In various parts of the world, pickling is a preservation method of choice for everything from asparagus to zucchini chutney; I have an Indian recipe for cinnamon-spiced pickled peaches. But our Appalachian standard for the noncucumber pickle is the Dilly Bean, essentially dill pickles made of green beans. This year when I was canning them on a July Saturday, Lily and a friend came indoors from playing and marched into the kitchen holding their noses, wanting to know why the whole house smelled like cider vinegar. I pointed my spoon at the cauldron bubbling on the stove and explained I was making pickles. I do wonder what my kids' friends go home to tell their parents about us. This one dubiously surveyed the kitchen: me in my apron, the steaming kettle, the mountain of beans I was trimming to fit into the jars, the corners where my witch's broom might lurk. "I didn't know you could make pickles from beans," she countered. I assured her you could make almost anything into pickles. She came back an hour later when I was cleaning up and my finished jars were cooling on the counter, their mix of green, purple, and yellow beans standing inside like little soldiers in an integrated army. She held her eyes very close to one of the jars and announced, "Nope! They didn't turn into pickles!"

Every year I think about buying a pressure canner and learning to use it, so I could can our beans as beans, but I still haven't. Squash, beans, peas, okra, corn, and basil pesto are easy enough to steam-blanch and put into the freezer in meal-sized bags. But since tomato products represent about half the bulk of our stored garden produce, I'd rather have them on the shelf than using up electricity to stay frozen. (We would also have to buy a bigger freezer.) And besides, all those gorgeous, red-filled jars lining the pantry shelf in September make me happy. They look like early valentines, and they are, for a working mom. I rely on their convenience. I'm not the world's only mother, I'm sure, who frequently plans dinner in the half-hour between work and dinnertime. Thawing takes time. If I think ahead, I can dump bags of frozen or dried vegetables into the Crock-Pot with a frozen block of our chicken or turkey stock, and have a great soup by evening. But if I *didn't* think ahead, a jar of spaghetti sauce, a box of pasta, and a grate of cheese will save us. So will a pint of sweet-and-sour sauce baked over chicken breasts, and a bowl of rice. I think of my canning as fast food, paid for in time up front.

That price isn't the drudgery that many people think. In high season I give over a few Saturdays to canning with family or friends. A steamy canning kitchen full of women discussing our stuff is not so different from your average book group, except that we end up with jars of future meals. Canning is not just for farmers and gardeners, either. Putting up summer produce is a useful option for anyone who can buy local produce from markets, as a way to get these vegetables into a year-round diet. It is also a kindness to the farmers who will have to support their families in December on whatever they sell in August. They can't put their unsold tomatoes in the bank. Buying them now, in quantity, improves the odds of these farmers returning with more next summer.

If canning seems like too much of a stretch, there are other ways to save vegetables purchased in season, in bulk. Twenty pounds of tomatoes will cook down into a pot of tomato sauce that fits into five one-quart freezer boxes, good for one family meal each. (Be warned, the fragrance of your kitchen will cause innocent bystanders to want to marry you.) Tomatoes can even be frozen whole, individually on trays set in the freezer; once they've hardened, you can dump them together into large bags (they'll knock against each other, sounding like croquet balls), and later withdraw a few at a time for winter soups and stews. Having gone nowhere in the interim, they will still be local in February.

❧·❧

In some supermarket chains in Virginia, North Carolina, and Tennessee, shoppers can find seasonal organic vegetables in packages labeled "Appalachian Harvest." The letters of the brand name arch over a sunny, stylized portrait of plowed fields, a clear blue stream, and the assurance: "Healthy Food, Healthy Farms, Close to Home."

Labels can lie, I am perfectly aware. Plenty of corporations use logo trickery to imply their confined meat or poultry are grown on green pastures, or that their tomatoes are handpicked by happy landowners instead of immigrants earning one cent per pound. But the Appalachian Harvest vegetables really do come from healthy farms, I happen to know, because they're close to *my* home. Brand recognition in mainstream supermarkets is an exciting development for farmers here, in a region that has struggled with chronic environmental problems, double-digit unemployment, and a steady drain of our communities' young people from the farming economy.

But getting some of Appalachia's harvest into those packages has not been simple. Every cellophane-wrapped, organically bar-coded packet of organic produce contains a world of work and specific promises to the consumer. To back them up, farmers need special training, organic certification, reliable markets, and a packaging plant. A model nonprofit called Appalachian Sustainable Development provides all of these in support of profitable, ecologically sound farming enterprises in a ten-county region of Virginia and Tennessee. In 2005, ten years after the program began, participating family farms collectively sold $236,000 worth of organic produce to regional retailers and supermarkets, which those markets, in turn, sold to consumers for nearly $0.3 million.

The Appalachian Harvest packing house lies in a mountain valley near the Virginia-Tennessee border that's every bit as gorgeous as the storybook farm on the product label. In its first year, the resourceful group used a converted wing of an old tobacco barn for its headquarters, using a donated walk-in cooler to hold produce until it could be graded and trucked out to stores. Now the packing plant occupies the whole barn space, complete with truck bays, commercial coolers, and conveyor belts to help wash and grade the produce. Tomatoes are the cash cow of this enterprise, but they are also its prima donnas, losing their flavor in standard refrigeration, but quick to spoil in the sultry heat, so the newest major addition at the packing house is a 100-by-14-foot tomato room where the temperature is held at 56 degrees.

Participating farmers bring vegetables here by the truckload, in special boxes that have never been used for conventional produce. Likewise, the packing facility's equipment is used for organic produce only. Most of the growers have just an acre or two of organic vegetables, among other crops grown conventionally. Those who stick with the program may expand their acreage of organic vegetables, but rarely to more than five, since they're extremely labor-intensive. After planting, weeding, and keeping the crop pest-free all season without chemicals, the final step of picking often begins before dawn. Some farmers have to travel an hour or more to the packing house. In high season they may make three or more trips a week. The largest grower of the group, with fifteen acres in production, last year delivered 200 boxes of peppers and 400 of tomatoes in a single day. Twenty-three crops are now sold under the Appalachian Harvest label, including melons, cucumbers, eggplants, squash, peas, lettuces, and many varieties of tomatoes and peppers.

The packing house manager labels each box as it arrives so the grower's identity will follow the vegetables through washing, grading, and packaging, all the way to their point of wholesale purchase. Farmers are paid after the supermarket issues its check; Appalachian Harvest takes a 25 percent commission, revenue that helps pay for organic training, packing expenses, and organic certification. Cooperating farmers can sell their produce under the umbrella of a group certification, saving them hundreds of dollars in fees and complex bookkeeping, but they still would need individual certification to sell anywhere other than through the Appalachian Harvest label (e.g., a farmers' market). The project's sales have increased dramatically, gaining a few more committed growers each year, even though farmers are notoriously cautious. Many are still on the fence at this point, watching their neighbors to see whether this enormous commitment to new methods will be salvation or disaster. The term "high-value crop" is relative to a dirt-cheap commodity grain like corn; in season, even high quality organic tomatoes will bring the farmer only about 50 to 75 cents per pound. (The lower end, for conventional, is 18 cents.) But that can translate into a cautious living. Participants find the project compelling for many reasons. After learning to grow vegetables organically, many families have been motivated to make their entire farms organic, including hay fields.

The Appalachian Harvest collective pays a full-time marketer named Robin who spends much of her life on the phone, in her vehicle, or pounding the grocery-store pavements, arranging every sale with the supermarkets, one vegetable and one week at a time. As a farmer herself, she knows the stakes. Also on the payroll here are the manager and summer workers who transform truckloads of field-picked vegetables into the clam-shelled or cellophane-wrapped items that ultimately reach the supermarket after produce has been washed and sorted for size and ripeness.

On a midsummer day in the packing house, vegetables roll through the processing line in a quantity that makes the work in my own kitchen look small indeed. Tomatoes bounce down a sorting conveyor, several bushels per minute, dropping through different-sized holes in a vibrating belt. Workers on both sides of the line collect them, check for flaws and ripeness, and package the tomatoes as quickly as their hands can move, finally pressing on the "certified organic" sticker. Watching the operation, I kept thinking of people I know who can hardly even stand to hear that word, because of how *organic* is personified for them. "I'm always afraid I'm going to get the Mr. Natural lecture," one friend confessed to me. "You know, from the slow-moving person with ugly hair, doing back-and-leg stretches while they talk to you . . ." I laughed because, earnest though I am about food, I know this guy too: dreadlocked, Birkenstocked, standing at the checkout with his bottle of Intestinal-Joy Brand wheatgrass juice, edging closer to peer in my cart, reeking faintly of garlic and a keenness to save me from some food-karma error.

For the record, this is what Appalachian Harvest organics look like at the source: Red Wing work boots, barbershop haircuts, Levi's with a little mud on the cuffs, men and women who probably go to church on Sunday but keep their religion to themselves as they bring a day's work to this packing house inside a former tobacco barn. If sanctimony is an additive in their product, it gets added elsewhere.

The tomato room offered a 56-degree respite from the July swelter, but it was all business in there too: full boxes piled on pallets, in columns nearly reaching the ceiling. The stacks on one end of the room were waiting to be processed, while at the other they waited to be trucked out to nearby groceries. Just enough space remained in the center for workers to maneuver, carting out pallets for grading, sorting, and then slapping one of those tedious stickers on every one of the thousands of individual tomatoes that pass through here each day—along with every pepper, cabbage, cucumber, and melon. That's how the cashier ultimately knows which produce is organic.

Supermarkets only accept properly packaged, coded, and labeled produce that conforms to certain standards of color, size, and shape. Melons can have no stem attached, cucumbers must be no less than six inches long, no more than eight. Crooked eggplants need not apply. Every crop yields a significant proportion of perfectly edible but small or oddly shaped vegetables that are "trash" by market standards.

It takes as much work to grow a crooked vegetable as a straight one, and the nutritional properties are identical. Workers at the packing house were as distressed as the farmers to see boxes of these rejects piling up into mountains of wasted food. Poverty and hunger are not abstractions in our part of the world; throwing away good food makes no sense. With the help of several church and social justice groups, Appalachian Harvest arranged to deliver "factory second" vegetables all summer to low-income families. Fresh organic produce entered some of their diets for the first time.

❦-❧

I grew up among farmers. In my school system we were all born to our rank, as inescapably as Hindus, the castes being only two: "farm" and "town." Though my father worked in town, we did not live there, and so by the numinous but unyielding rules of high school, I was "farmer." It might seem astonishing that a rural-urban distinction like this could be made in a county that boasted, in its entirety, exactly two stoplights, one hardware store, no beer joints (the county was dry), and fewer residents than an average Caribbean cruise ship. After I went away to school, I remained in more or less constant marvel over the fact that my so-called small liberal arts college, with an enrollment of about 2,000, was 25 percent larger than my hometown.

And yet, even in a community as rural as that, we still had our self-identified bourgeoisie, categorically distinguished from our rustics. We of the latter tribe could be identified by our shoes (sometimes muddy, if we had to cover rough country to get to the school bus), our clothes (less frequently updated), or just the bare fact of a Rural Free Delivery mailing address. I spent my childhood in awe of the storybook addresses of some of my classmates, like "14 Locust Street." In retrospect I'm unsure of how fact-based the distinction really was: most of us "farm" kids were well-scrubbed and occasionally even stylish. Nevertheless, the line of apartheid was unimpeachably drawn. Little socializing across this line was allowed except during special events forced on us by adults, such as the French Club Dinner, and mixed-caste dating was unthinkable except to the tragic romantics.

Why should this have been? How did the leafy, sidewalked blocks behind the newspaper office confer on their residents a different sense of self than did the homes couched among cow pastures and tobacco fields? The townie shine would have dimmed quickly (I now realize) if the merchants' confident offspring were catapulted suddenly into Philadelphia or Louisville. "Urban" is relative. But the bottom line is that it matters. The antipathy in our culture between the urban and nonurban is so durable, it has its own vocabulary: (A) city slicker, tenderfoot; (B) hick, redneck, hayseed, bumpkin, rube, yokel, clodhopper, hoecake, hillbilly, Dogpatch, Daisy Mae, farmer's daughter, from the provinces, something out of *Deliverance*. Maybe you see where I'm going with this. The list is lopsided. I don't think there's much doubt, on either side, as to which class is winning the culture wars.

Most rural people of my acquaintance would not gladly give up their status. Like other minorities, we've managed to turn several of the aforementioned slurs into celebrated cultural identifiers (for use by insiders only). In my own life I've had ample opportunity to reinvent myself as a city person—to pass, as it were—but I've remained tacitly rural-identified in my psyche, even while living in some of the world's major cities. It's probably this dual citizenship that has sensitized me to my nation's urban-rural antipathy, and how it affects people in both camps. Rural concerns are less covered by the mainstream media, and often considered intrinsically comic. Corruption in city governments is reported as grim news everywhere; from small towns (or Tennessee) it is fodder for talk-show jokes. Thomas Hardy wrote about the sort of people who milked cows, but writers who do so in the modern era will be dismissed as marginal. The policy of our nation is made in cities, controlled largely by urban voters who aren't well informed about the changes on the face of our land, and the men and women who work it.

Those changes can be mapped on worry lines: as the years have gone by, as farms have gone out of business, America has given an ever-smaller cut of each food dollar (now less than 19 percent) to its farmers. The psychic divide between rural and urban people is surely a part of the problem. "Eaters must understand," Wendell Berry writes, "that eating takes place inescapably in the world, that it is inescapably an agricultural act, and that how we eat determines, to a considerable extent, how the world is used." Eaters *must,* he claims, but it sure looks like most eaters *don't.* If they did, how would we frame the sentence suggested by today's food-buying habits, directed toward today's farmers? "Let them eat dirt" is hardly overstating it. The urban U.S. middle class appears more specifically concerned about exploited Asian factory workers.

Symptomatic of this rural-urban identity crisis is our eager embrace of a recently imposed divide: the Red States and the Blue States. That color map comes to us with the suggestion that both coasts are populated by educated civil libertarians, while the vast middle and south are crisscrossed with the studded tracks of ATVs leaving a trail of flying beer cans and rebel yells. Okay, I'm exaggerating a little. But I certainly sense a bit of that when urban friends ask me how I can stand living here, "*so far from everything?*" (When I hear this question over the phone, I'm usually looking out the window at a forest, a running creek, and a vegetable garden, thinking: Define *everything.*) Otherwise sensitive coastal-dwelling folk may refer to the whole chunk of our continent lying between the Cascades and the Hudson River as "the Interior." I gather this is now a common designation. It's hard for me to see the usefulness of lumping Minneapolis, Atlanta, my little hometown in Kentucky, Yellowstone Park, and so forth, into a single category that does not include New York and California. "Going into the Interior" sounds like an endeavor that might require machetes to hack through the tangled vines.

In fact, the politics of rural regions are no more predictable than those in cities. "Conservative" is a reasonable position for a farmer who can lose home and livelihood all in one year by taking a risk on a new crop. But that's *conservative* as in, "eager to conserve what we have, reluctant to change the rules overnight," and unrelated to how the term is currently (often incomprehensibly) applied in party politics. The farm county where I grew up had so few Republicans, they all registered Democrat so they could vote in the only local primary. My earliest understanding of radical, class-conscious politics came from miners' strikes in one of the most rural parts of my state, and of our nation.

The only useful generalization I'd hazard about rural politics is that they tend to break on the line of "insider" vs. "outsider." When my country neighbors sit down with a new social group, the first question they ask one another is not "What do you do?" but rather, "Who are your people?" Commonly we will spend more than the first ten minutes of a new acquaintance tracing how our families might be related. If not by blood, then by marriage. Failing that, by identifying someone significant we have known in common. Only after this ritual of familial placing does the conversation comfortably move on to other subjects. I am blessed with an ancestor who was the physician in this county from about 1910 into the 1940s. From older people I'll often hear of some memorably dire birth or farm accident to which my great-uncle was called; lucky for me he was skilled and Hippocratic. But even a criminal ancestor will get you insider status, among the forgiving. Not so lucky are those who move here with no identifiable family ties. Such a dark horse is likely to remain "the new fellow" for the rest of his natural life, even if he arrived in his prime and lives to be a hundred.

The country tradition of mistrusting outsiders may be unfairly applied, but it's not hard to understand. For much of U.S. history, rural regions have been treated essentially as colonial property of the cities. The carpetbaggers of the reconstruction era were not the first or the last opportunists to capitalize on an extractive economy. When urban-headquartered companies come to the country with a big plan—whether their game is coal, timber, or industrial agriculture—the plan is to take out the good stuff, ship it to the population centers, make a fortune, and leave behind a mess.

Given this history, one might expect the so-called Red States to vote consistently for candidates supporting working-class values. In fact, our nation in almost every region is divided in a near dead heat between two parties that apparently don't distinguish themselves clearly along class lines. If every state were visually represented with the exact blend of red and blue it earned in recent elections, we'd have ourselves a big purple country. The tidy divide is a media just-so story.

Our uneasy relationship between heartland and coasts, farm and factory, country and town, is certainly real. But it is both more rudimentary and more subtle than most political analysts make it out to be. It's about loyalties, perceived communities, and the things each side understands to be important because of the ground, literally, upon which we stand. Wendell Berry summed it up much better than "blue and red" in one line of dialogue from his novel *Jayber Crow,* which is peopled by farmers struggling to survive on what the modern, mostly urban market will pay for food. After watching nearly all the farms in the county go bankrupt, one of these men comments: "I've wished sometimes that the sons of bitches would starve. And now I'm getting afraid they actually will."

❧

In high summer, about the time I was seeing red in my kitchen, the same thing was happening to some of our county's tomato farmers. They had learned organic methods, put away the chemicals, and done everything right to grow a product consumers claimed to want. They'd waited the three years for certification. They'd watered, weeded, and picked, they'd sorted the round from the misshapen, producing the perfect organic tomatoes ordered by grocery chains. And then suddenly, when the farmers were finally bringing in these tomatoes by the truckload and hoping for a decent payout, some grocery buyers backtracked. "Not this week," one store offered without warning, and then another. Not the next week either, nor the next. A tomato is not a thing that can be put on hold. Mountains of ripe fruits piled up behind the packing house and turned to orange sludge, swarming with clouds of fruit flies.

These tomatoes were perfect, and buyers were hungry. Agreements had been made. But pallets of organic tomatoes from California had begun coming in just a few dollars cheaper. It's hard to believe, given the amount of truck fuel involved, but transportation is tax-deductible for the corporations, so we taxpayers paid for that shipping. The California growers only needed the economics of scale on their side, a cheap army of pickers, and customers who would reliably opt for the lower price.

As simply as that, a year of planning and family labor turned to red mush.

Our growers had been warned that this could happen—market buyers generally don't sign a binding contract. So the farmers took a risk, and took a loss. Some of them will try again next year, though they will likely hedge their bets with Delicata squash and peas as well. Courage, practicality, and making the best of a bad situation are much of what farming is about. Before the tomatoes all rotted away, Appalachian Harvest found a way to donate and distribute the enormous excess of unpurchased produce to needy families. The poor of our county were rich in tomatoes that summer.

"We were glad we could give it away," one of the farmers told me. "We like to be generous and help others, that's fine, that's who we are. But a lot of us are barely making ends meet, ourselves. It seems like it's always the people that have the least who end up giving the most. Why is that?"

In Charlottesville, Asheville, Roanoke, and Knoxville, supermarket shoppers had no way of knowing how much heartache and betrayal might be wrapped up in those cellophane two-packs of California tomatoes. Maybe they noticed the other tomatoes were missing this week, those local ones with the "Healthy Farms, Close to Home" label. Or maybe they just saw "organic tomatoes," picked them up, and dropped them into their carts on top of the cereal boxes and paper towels. *Eaters must understand, how we eat determines how the world is used.*

They will or they won't. And the happy grocery store music plays on.

Shannon Hayes

1974–

Writer and farmer Shannon Hayes lives with three generations of her family on Sap Bush Hollow Farm in West Fulton, New York, a rural community at the northernmost tip of Appalachia. Like many of her peers, Hayes left the region after high school. However, after receiving a BA in creative writing from Binghamton University and an MA and PhD in sustainable agriculture and community development from Cornell, she returned to the farm where she was reared and became what she calls a radical homemaker: a woman or man who focuses on a sustainable domestic life without rejecting feminist ideals. In making this choice, Hayes is part of a larger group of people who are rejuvenating communities while growing and consuming more local food.

Hayes explains her ideas in *Radical Homemakers* (2010), which emerged from more than two hundred interviews with other homemakers. In the excerpt below, Hayes explains how and why she traded the life of a professional career woman for that of a farmer and homemaker. Hayes maintains a daily blog and has written six books, including *Long Way on a Little: An Earth Lover's Guide to Enjoying Meat, Pinching Pennies, and Living Deliciously* (2012), published by Left to Write Press, which she and her husband co-founded.

FROM Radical Homemakers: Reclaiming Domesticity from a Consumer Culture

INTRODUCTION: RADICAL HOMEMAKING— POLITICS, ECOLOGY AND DOMESTIC ARTS

I never intended to write this book. My mother's generation fought for the right to go to work, to achieve personal fulfillment through professional accomplishments. I charged through high school and college at full throttle, ravenously ambitious, eager to start my own career as soon as possible. At age sixteen, I attended high school during the day and I took college courses at night. My first college paper was about the psychological benefits of enrolling children and babies in day care. Full-time. I completed college before I was of legal drinking age, spent a year working overseas, another year administering a housing rehabilitation program for flood victims, then enrolled in Cornell University and had a PhD by the time I was twenty-seven. I was ready to conquer the world in a big way.

My ambition was probably fueled by the fact that my primary and secondary schooling took place in a town on the rural-suburban fringe, in Cobleskill, New York, the only town in our county with not one but *two* exits along the newly built interstate. It seemed Cobleskill students were cultivated to gaze longingly at those highway on-ramps, to dream of the day they would lead us away from an otherwise backward rural county. The trouble was, in my heart, I never wanted to leave home. My family's farm was just barely inside the district lines. We didn't actually live in Cobleskill, but in the next town over, with *no* interstate to be seen. West Fulton was far above the valley floor, at the northern edge of the Appalachian mountain chain, and the Appalachian agrarian culture was still very much alive throughout my childhood. During the week I worked to get straight A's in town. On the weekends and summers, I worked in the hills on a neighboring farm, where the inhabitants lived very well on only a few thousand dollars per year.

Ruth, the farm matron, kept chickens and a garden. She put up her vegetables for winter, sewed her clothes, and made pies and jams from berries picked on the field edges. Sanford, her octogenarian boarder, took care of the beef herd that supplied their winter meat, and kept the house, outbuildings, tractor and car in good repair. I loved every minute I spent with them, repairing fences, shoveling manure, cutting their grass, stacking firewood, raking leaves, and most especially, collecting my wages, which came in the form of midday feasts. I loved being on my family farm as well. I took great joy in spending time with my folks, spent endless days roaming the hills, and countless summer nights sleeping out under the stars.

Nevertheless, I faithfully adhered to my career track. But in an effort to find a path back to my own community, I studied subjects that I thought would help me get a job there, that would make me an asset to the local agricultural college or county government—rural sociology, sustainable agriculture, community and rural development, adult and extension education. So committed was I to finding a way home that Bob (my soon-to-be husband) and I took out a mortgage and bought a small cabin on fifteen acres even deeper into the hills, just seven miles from the family farm. Two weeks later he was fired from work. I never even got a job interview. The writing seemed to be on the wall. Sell the house, find jobs someplace else, leave town.

Bob and I were heartbroken. Our dream had been to help my family on the farm, to enjoy Ruth's and Sanford's friendship until the end of their days, to start a family in the place where I grew up, surrounded by a supportive community. Instead, we faced the same future that seemed inevitable for so many American couples—leave home to find work, fracture the extended family into nuclear units, and hope for ample salaries that would pay for the day care and assistance that loving relatives and neighbors could have offered at home.

My education had prepared me to accept this inevitability. But Ruth, Sanford and my family had, rather unwittingly, prepared me to reject it. Unlike so many people my age (I'm thirty-five), basic homemaking and self-reliance skills were part of my childhood foundational knowledge. My community and family practiced subsistence farming, food preservation, barter and frugal living as a matter of course. I had been taught in school to plan for a six-figure income in a dual-earning family. But I learned growing up that there was an arsenal of resources available that could offer a happy alternative lifestyle. Bob and I did the math. We could move away, take on dual careers, get a new house, own two cars to get to work. By the time we subtracted out what we'd pay for commuting, a new house, professional wardrobes, taxes, and buying rather than growing our food, we were only $10,000 ahead in annual income than where we would be if we stayed home and put our hearts and minds to work on our grassy hillsides. That was before we had figured in the costs for day care. Thus, Bob and I officially joined my parents on the family farm, I wrote cookbooks about sustainable food, we started a family, and we became homemakers.

The trick that Ruth and Sanford had taught us was simple. Mainstream American culture views the household as a unit of consumption. By this conventional standard, the household consumes food, clothing, household technologies, repair and debt services, electricity, entertainment, health-care services, and environmental resources. In order to be a "successful" unit of consumption, the household must have money. Ruth's and Sanford's household was not a unit of consumption. By growing their own food, living within their means, providing much of their own health care, and relying on community, family and barter for meeting their remaining needs, their household was essentially a unit of *production* (just not by the standards of a market economy). Thus, their *income* wasn't critical to their *well-being*. In fact, over the course of her life, Ruth even amassed considerable financial savings.

This was the model that Bob and I, together with my parents, adopted for our own lifestyle. Admittedly, there are some modern twists and indulgences on Ruth and Sanford's ways. We are not the sort of folks who would willingly don sackcloth. The month of May will find me out in the fields with my father during lambing season, while Bob watches the girls and Mom prepares the gardens. By the end of the month, our farmers' market season is in full swing, and Bob and I are selling Sap Bush Hollow meats every Saturday. Our daughters come to the market to meet their friends, or stay at the farm with Grammie and Pop Pop. During the week, the kids join me as I help move fence, milk the family cow, and do chores. On chicken processing days, Bob heads down to the farm, and the girls and I stay home to go for hikes, visit the neighbors, or explore the woods in search of fairies. The entire family labors throughout the season, tending livestock, cutting meat, making sausages, keeping records and weeding gardens, but there is ample time for us to take turns with vacations, canoe trips, afternoon swims and naps, and evening cocktails. As late summer rolls around, like Ruth, I pull out my canning gear and work 'round the clock to put up peaches, pears, plums, green beans, beets, tomato sauce and even some homemade stews. A giant crock fills first with sour dill pickles, then myriad fermenting mixtures of summer vegetables, then finally, at the season's end, with cabbages for a winter's supply of sauerkraut. Before mid-October, we team with friends to press cider; Mom pulls mountains of bright orange, yellow and deep green squashes out of the garden, which we stow away in our coldest rooms; I render pork and beef fat for lard and tallow for soaps and cooking; a fellow farmer swaps us a supply of storage onions and potatoes in exchange for meat; and the farmers' market closes for the season. We harvest the turkeys for Thanksgiving, and then begin our winter's rest . . . and play. Where Ruth and Sanford lived most of their lives in the confines of Schoharie County, during the winter months we take a different path. Our incomes and ecological concerns don't allow for cheeky weekends in Paris, but they do, every few years, allow for some pretty extraordinary extended travels . . . Those trips have included renting a home for three months in rural France (where cheeky weekends in Paris *were* doable), a winter in Argentina researching a book, or extended trips across the country by train. The years that don't find us boarding planes or trains during our resting months are still full of fun. We take the girls to area museums or on short mini-vacations for homeschool study to learn about the pilgrims, our colonial history, witch trials, Native Americans, or to hear some live music. We do science experiments at our kitchen table, read long novels aloud at night, play music and sing by the fire, enjoy cider and popcorn while playing games (or fighting over toys), or pile up on the couch to watch a movie. Sunny wintery days find us out for walks, hiking through the woods on snowshoes, or sledding down the road.

My family has always understood that the key to success as farmers wasn't necessarily how much money we made, but how much money we didn't have to spend. What's good for farming is also good for homemaking. There are, admittedly, some things we do without. We limit restaurant visits, take advantage of local thrift stores, wear our clothes until they are threadbare, have only one car in our family, and we forego health insurance, both from inadequate finances and a conscientious objection to corporate health care (this will be discussed in further detail later in the book). We pay cash, make use of sliding scales and barter for the health-care services we require. We celebrate birthdays and holidays with verve, but Bob and I do not exchange gifts (although we do find or make a few things for our daughters). We make very heavy use of our library, and commit to keeping our car off the road at least one day each week during the growing season and two to four days a week during the winter. Because we produce so much of our own food, grocery shopping only needs to happen every other month. Using such tricks and accepting a few limitations, Bob, the girls and I have lived very, very well on less than $45,000 per year.

Along this path, naturally, I became a local-food advocate. After writing two cookbooks about working with sustainably raised meats, I found myself taking on the role of a spokesperson for the integration of ecologically sound, humane animal production into a sustainable diet. (I felt like the dairy princess for the grass-fed meat movement.) As a result, in 2007, I was invited to speak at the national conference of the American Dietetic Association. My charge was to explain to several hundred dieticians what *exactly* this grass-fed meat movement was, why the darn thing wouldn't go away, and to justify why Americans should be willing to spend money on food that was so much more expensive than what could be found in the grocery store.

As I tooled away on my presentation, the final requirement was the most troubling. I could come up with lots and lots of reasons *why* we should be willing to pay more for our food. Social justice. Ecological benefits. Stronger local economies. Superior nutrition. Animal welfare. Saving farmland. Reversing global warming. Reducing our reliance on fossil fuels. But I realized then, that *why* was never going to matter if Americans couldn't figure out *how* to afford it. Up until then, the grass-fed movement had been pegged as a niche farming vocation that appealed to the wealthy folks who were in search of higher-quality foods. It was not regarded as an option for the rest of America.

But truth be told, when I crunched the numbers, a farmers' market meal made of a roasted local pasture-raised chicken, baked potatoes and steamed broccoli cost less than four meals at Burger King, even when two of the meals came off the kiddie menu. The Burger King meal had negligible nutritional value and was damaging to our health and planet. The farmers' market menu cost less, healed the earth, helped the local economy, was a source of bountiful nutrients for a family of four, and would leave ample leftovers for both a chicken salad and a rich chicken stock, which could then be the base for a wonderful soup. But when push came to shove, I knew that Burger King would win out. The reason? Many people don't even know how to roast a chicken, let alone make a chicken salad from the leftovers or use the carcass to make a stock. Mainstream Americans have lost the simple domestic skills that would enable them to live an ecologically sensible life with a modest or low income.

Ordinarily a calm public speaker, my hands shook when I stood in September of 2007 before an audience of 600 professional registered dieticians, many of whom were women. I had a painful message to deliver, one that I considered leaving out every time I rehearsed my speech. Eating local, organic, sustainably raised, nutrient-dense food was possible for every American, not just for wealthy gourmets or self-reliant organic farmers. But to do it, *we needed to bring back the homemaker.* As I made this claim, my toes curled in the tips of my shoes. The room was completely still. And then, before I could continue on, the crowd burst into spontaneous applause. I learned in conversations afterward that I had called attention to the elephant in the room, a simple truth that was felt by so many dieticians who were trying to help families reclaim good nutrition and a balanced life.

As I looked more closely at the role homemaking could play in revitalizing our local food system, I saw that the position was a linchpin for more than just making use of garden produce and chicken carcasses. Individuals who had taken this path in life were building a great bridge from our existing **extractive economy**—where corporate wealth was regarded as the foundation of economic health, where mining our earth's resources and exploiting our international neighbors was accepted as simply the cost of doing business—to a **life-serving economy,** where the goal is, in the words of David Korten, to generate a living for all, rather than a killing for a few, where our resources are sustained, our waters are kept clean, our air pure, and families can lead meaningful and joyful lives.

More than simply soccer moms, Radical Homemakers are men and women who have chosen to make family, community, social justice and the health of the planet the governing principles of their lives. They reject any form of labor or the expenditure of any resource that does not honor these tenets. For about five thousand years, our culture has been hostage to a form of organization by domination that fails to honor our living systems, where "he who holds the gold makes the rules." By contrast, Radical Homemakers use life skills and relationships as a replacement for gold, on the premise that he or she who doesn't *need* the gold can *change* the rules. The greater our domestic skills, be they to plant a garden, grow tomatoes on an apartment balcony, mend a shirt, repair an appliance, provide for our own entertainment, cook and preserve a local harvest or care for our children and loved ones, the less dependent we are on the gold.

These thoughts led me to wonder if salvation from our global woes—the rampant social injustices, climate change, peak oil—was going to be dependent upon the women, upon questioning all the hard-fought battles of both the first and second waves of feminism that have swept this country. Women, after all, have been the homemakers since the beginning of time. Or so I thought.

Upon further investigation, I learned that the household did not become the "woman's sphere" until the industrial revolution. A search for the origin of the word *housewife* traces it back to the thirteenth century as the feudal period was coming to an end in Europe and the first signs of a middle class were popping up. Historian Ruth Schwartz Cowan explains that housewives were wedded to *husbands,* whose name came from *hus,* an old spelling of *house,* and *bonded. Husbands* were bonded to houses, rather than to lords. Housewives and husbands were free people who owned their own homes and lived off their land. While there was a division of labor among the sexes in these early households, there was also an equal distribution of domestic work. Once the industrial revolution happened, however, things changed. Men left the household to work for wages, which were then used to purchase the goods and services that they no longer were home to provide. Indeed, the men were the first to lose their domestic skills as their successive generations forgot how to butcher the family hog, how to sew leather, how to chop firewood.

As the industrial revolution forged on and crossed the ocean to America, men and women eventually stopped working together to provide for their household sustenance. They developed their separate spheres—man in the factory, woman in the home. The more a man worked outside the home, the more the household would have to buy in order to have the needs met. Soon the factories were able to fabricate products to supplant the housewives' duties as well. As subsequent chapters in this book reveal, her primary function ultimately became chauffeur and consumer. The household was no longer a unit of production. It was a unit of consumption.

The effect on the American housewife was devastating. In 1963, Betty Friedan published *The Feminine Mystique,* documenting for the first time "the problem that has no name," *housewife's syndrome,* where American girls grew up fantasizing about finding their husbands, buying their dream homes and dream appliances, popping out babies, and living happily ever after. In truth, pointed out Friedan, happily-ever-after never came. Countless women suffered from depression and nervous breakdowns as they faced the endless meaningless tasks of shopping and driving children hither and yon. They never had opportunities to fulfill their highest potential, to challenge themselves, to feel as though they were truly contributing to society beyond wielding the credit card to keep the consumer culture humming. Friedan's book sent women to work in droves. And corporate America seized upon a golden opportunity to secure a cheaper workforce and offer countless products to use up their paychecks.

Before long, the second family income was no longer an option. In the minds of many, it was a necessity. Homemaking, like eating organic foods, seemed a luxury to be enjoyed only by those wives whose husbands garnered substantial earnings, enabling them to drive their children to school every day rather than putting them on the bus, enroll them in endless enrichment activities, oversee their educational careers, and prepare them for entry into elite colleges, and to win a leg-up in a competitive workforce. At the other extreme, homemaking was seen as a realm of the ultra-religious, where women accepted the role of Biblical "help meets" to their husbands. They cooked, cleaned, toiled, served and remained silent and powerless. Bob and I fell into neither category. And I suspected there were more like us.

I was looking for a different type of homemaker—someone who wasn't ruled by our consumer culture, who embodied a strong ecological ethic, who held genuine power in the household, who was living a full, creative, challenging and socially contributory life. For lack of a better word, I wanted to find folks who were more . . . *radical*. I began writing and speaking more on the subject, and in November of 2007 I posted a call on my Web site, seeking such homemakers:

> If you have learned to live on less in order to take the time to nourish your family and the planet through home cooking, engaged citizenship, responsible consumption and creative living, whether you are male, female, or two people sharing the role, with or without children, full or part-time, please drop me a line and tell me your story.

With the help of a full page story that appeared in *The New York Times* and a few other magazines, blogs and newspapers, my inbox filled up with over two hundred letters. Unable to fully document the lives of all these people, I selected twenty homemakers to interview, seeking a balance of young and old, rural, urban and suburban, single and married, male and female, with children and without. I wanted to know who these people were, how they chose their life paths, how they were faring in our American economy. I wanted to see their domestic lives with my own eyes, to gauge the balance of power in their relationships, to gain insights about their impact on their local communities. I wanted to know if they were able to thwart the chronic depression that Betty Friedan wrote about, and if so, how they did it. I wanted to understand their tactics for both surviving and thriving. I packed up my family whenever we could squeeze away from the farm, and we eventually worked our way across the country, from Maine to Los Angeles.

As I got to know each of these families, I learned that most Radical Homemakers do not have conventional jobs. They simply refuse to work to make the rich richer. They do have some form of income that comes into their lives. But they were not the privileged set by any means. Most of the families that I interviewed were living with a sense of abundance at about 200 percent of the Federal Poverty Level. That's a little over $40,000 for a family of four, about 37 percent below the national median family income and 45 percent below the median income for married couple families. Some lived on considerably less, few had appreciably more. Not surprisingly, those with the lowest incomes had mastered the most domestic skills and had developed the most innovative approaches to living.

I learned that Radical Homemaking is a domestic choice made by all the adults in a household. It is true that a man may work outside at a job that honors the four tenets of ecological sustainability, social justice, family and community, while the woman stays home. But the reverse may also be true. Sometimes neither partner works outside the home. As we'll see later on, this is in no way a throwback to the 1950s household. Nor can it be confused with some form of ultra-conservative religious sect. Radical Homemakers draw on historical traditions to craft a more ecologically viable existence, but their life's work is to create a new, pleasurable, sustainable and socially just society, different than any we have known in the last 5,000 years. While they learn from history, they do not seek to recreate it in all forms. Women are not second-class citizens. The governing tenet of social justice precludes treating any member of the family as subservient.

Some of the Radical Homemakers I came to know professed a strong spiritual faith. Others did not. If there was one unifying belief among them, it was to question all the assumptions in our consumer culture that have us convinced that a family cannot survive without a dual income. They were fluent at the mental exercise of rethinking the "givens" of our society and coming to the following conclusions: nobody (who matters) cares what (or if) you drive; housing does not have to cost more than a single moderate income can afford (and can even cost less); it is okay to accept help from family and friends; to let go of the perceived ideal of independence and strive instead for interdependence; health can be achieved without making monthly payments to an insurance company; child care is not a fixed cost; education can be acquired for free—it does not have to be bought; and retirement is possible, regardless of income.

As for domestic skills, the range of talents held by these households was as varied as the day is long. Many kept gardens, but not all. Some gardened on city rooftops, some on country acres, some in suburban yards. Some were wizards at car and appliance repairs. Others could sew. Some could build and fix houses; some kept livestock. Others crafted furniture, played music or wrote. All could cook. (Really well, as my waistline will attest.) None of them could do *everything*. No one was completely self-sufficient, an independent island separate from the rest of the world. Thus the universal skills that they all possessed were far more complex than simply knowing how to can green beans or build a root cellar. In order to make it as homemakers, these people had to be wizards at nurturing relationships and working with family and community. They needed an intimate understanding of the life-serving economy, where a paycheck is not always exchanged for all services rendered. They needed to be their own teachers—to pursue their educations throughout life, forever learning new ways to do more, create more, give more.

In addition, the happiest among them were successful at setting realistic expectations for themselves. They did not live in impeccably clean houses on manicured estates. They saw their homes as living systems and accepted the flux, flow, dirt and chaos that are a natural part of that. They were masters at redefining pleasure not as something that should be bought in the consumer marketplace, but as something that could be created, no matter how much or how little money they had in their pockets. And above all, they were fearless. They did not let themselves be bullied by the conventional ideals regarding money, status, or material possessions. These families did not see their homes as a refuge from the world. Rather, each home was the center for social change, the starting point from which a better life would ripple out for everyone.

Home is where the great change will begin. It is not where it ends. Once we feel sufficiently proficient with our domestic skills, few of us will be content to simply practice them to the end of our days. Many of us will strive for more, to bring more beauty to the world, to bring about greater social change, to make life better for our neighbors, to contribute our creative powers to the building of a new, brighter, sustainable and happier future. That is precisely the great work we should all be tackling. If we start by focusing our energies on our domestic lives, we will do more than reduce our ecological impact and help create a living for all. We will craft a safe, nurturing place from which this great creative work can happen.

Dana Wildsmith

1952–

As the daughter of an itinerant Methodist preacher and as a navy wife, poet and essayist Dana Wildsmith has changed addresses many times in her life. During these frequent transitions, Wildsmith rooted herself through her writing, publishing four collections of poetry. After her husband retired in 1999, Wildsmith moved with him to the farm in the Georgia mountains that her mother and father bought in 1972.

Barrow County, where Wildsmith's farm is located, has seen a recent influx of Mexican, Colombian, and Cambodian immigrants and is the twelfth fastest-growing county in the United States. In response to this shifting physical and cultural landscape, and in reaction to her own experiences on the farm, Wildsmith wrote a collection of poems titled *One Good Hand* (2005) followed by a series of essays collected in *Back to Abnormal: Surviving with an Old Farm in the New South* (2010).

Although Wildsmith seeks to protect her farm from encroaching sprawl, she acknowledges that it is part of a complex history and cultural landscape. Moreover, she refuses to romanticize nature and wildness which, after all, include both forests and snakebites. How, then, do these various cultural and physical worlds live side by side? What is the responsibility of a woman, an environmentalist, a person in modern Appalachia? These are the questions Wildsmith poses.

FROM Back to Abnormal: Surviving with an Old Farm in the New South

KEEPING A LIST

> "I have grown further and further from my muse, and closer and closer to my posthole digger."
>
> —E. B. White

Mama's tough. She and Daddy had been living here almost twenty years when Daddy began to die from liver cancer. Daddy wanted no part of hospitals after it became clear hospitals couldn't cure him, so Mama took care of him at home for years. He didn't want Hospice to come and take away his privacy, so Mama provided his hospice care. The night he died in his own bed we called the Sheriff and the County Coroner, as the law requires of home deaths. Their soft rap on Mama's front door at two a.m. sounded apologetic and courteous. "Evenin', Miss Grace," was Sheriff John Robert's greeting, as if he had dropped by for coffee on a Sunday afternoon. And in fact he did accept a cup when Mama offered. I remember the two men drinking coffee in Mama's living room, not getting down to their business just yet, allowing her a last space of time with Daddy. Since that night, when conversations turn in the direction of how best to die, I tell everyone to try and die at home in the country. I tell them their family will be treated with graciousness and care.

Dying in a rural home may be gently handled but living a rural life can get pretty rough. After Daddy died, their neighbor Richard died, too, and local crack dealers claimed squatters' rights to his single-wide on the ten-acre swath of woods adjoining ours. That self-same sheriff who had honored my newly-dead father through gentlemanly benevolence toward my just-widowed mother claimed he couldn't do a thing about clearing criminals off the property next to hers without violating private property rights. Many nights my seventy-year-old mother had to go to bed alone in an old creaky house while drug deals were being transacted twenty yards away. These unsanctioned sales events did not get Mama's goat as much as the fact that the crackheads plowed down a length of her split-rail fence and stole a bird bath Daddy had bought her and no one would own up to being able to do a thing about it. Tornadoes, half-butchered deer tossed out by poachers and, once, human remains on the side of the road were among the other delights of country living Mama dealt with during her widow years. Life after she married Mac and gained a helper and an ally must have seemed to her like a waltz.

So when Don and I announced our intention to come back to the farm, she probably wondered why in the world she needed grown children moving in with their needs and their opinions? My hunch is that she agreed to our move almost wholly for my and Don's benefit, with not a thought that the situation might turn good for her somehow.

As our family arrangement has settled in over the last few years, it has become obvious to me that Mama could, in fact, survive without us here, but she enjoys life a lot more with us. And I, with her. There can be no greater treasure for a writer than to live within easy stepping distance of a mother who constantly says things worth writing down, the sorts of things I wish I had said myself, except that they work better on paper coming from someone else's mouth.

Mama said this morning that she and my step-dad, Mac, both of them eighty-somethings, have reached an awkward stage in their lives: their sofa is wearing out, but they're not sure it's worth investing in a new one. This is the same woman who, when she was just a few years older than I am now, bought a worn-out farm in rural north Georgia as the place for her and my daddy to live out their retirement years. Half the outbuildings here then were falling to their knees with rot. The house's only bathroom stood twenty steps out the back door. A fuse box installed for the powering of five overhead bare bulbs had been optimistically laden with wiring for a stove, a refrigerator and sundry small appliances, the not surprising result being that unless my parents turned off a light, any light, before plugging in the toaster, they'd blow a fuse. The house's only phone was tied in to a twelve-party phone line (not exaggerating here) which eleven other parties treated as a '70s version of an Internet chat room. Then there was a certain neighbor from down the road who passed by every week or two pushing his wheelbarrow laden with bags of sugar and copper tubing. Hmmm. And our farm's former owner was weekly digging up and hauling away the flowerbeds. So why would my mama, a woman who willingly took on this sort of challenge, now be asking me if buying a new sofa might be chancy?

I've got her pegged. This is just her Old-Age Excuse for not going shopping. Mama's current sofa has no visibly exposed stuffing and only the slightest sag in the cushion where she reads by lamp light with a cat on her lap. Adopting a foreign sofa into her home would mean first considering a headache of choices—Solid? Print? Two-cushion style, with its built-in fault line for any middle sitter? Or three-cushion, with its air of parlor manners?—and second, having to live through the courtship period inherent to life with new furniture. Bringing home a new sofa makes a living room feel about as comfortable as if you'd seated a tax auditor in there. You can't shake the uneasy feeling that the new sofa knows you're capable of major indiscretions involving ketchup or wine. Better to stick with furniture that knows your eating habits. As far as Mama is concerned, Emily Dickinson had it wrong. It is after purchases, not after death, that "a formal feeling comes."

One of the dearest delights of living on a tired-out farm is the comfortable broken-down-ness of everything. Our log smokehouse had been easing to its haunches quite a spell before Mama and Daddy's tenancy began, which fact allowed them and now me the grace of open-ended repair time. Jacking up the smokehouse must not be a priority seeing as how the last family never got around to it, so just *Put it on the list,* we say. The act of updating a list functions as a sort of hour of prayer in the home-repair world. By giving name to a need, we acknowledge its existence and claim responsibility for its ultimate resolution—but not right away. Having given the job over to the list, a bright benevolence of time lightens our days.

Every afternoon this week has been more sunny than not, warming to the high sixties. Whenever I've had an hour, I've been out clearing winter debris from the azalea bed nearest the smokehouse. All winter long I've passed this bed a hundred thousand times without noticing how it had filled up with blackberry brambles, honeysuckle, last year's daylily stalks and cussed catbrier, but on Monday I suddenly saw the true state of the bed: brown and choked. It makes sense to me that I couldn't see the weeds until that soft March day came, because the job of weeding flowerbeds had not yet risen to visibility on the job list. The most alluring reason for keeping a job list is just this—any task added to the list comes to our attention only in its season. It's a kind of compassionate magic, allowing our burn pile to stay a blind spot in our collective vision until the first windless dry day. It gently nudges us toward use of Mama's side and back doors only, until there's time and money enough to jack up the front sills and re-hang the front door. And it stiffens the spine of that leaning dead pine back of the garden until we can get the chainsaw sharpened.

This week these weeds revealed themselves, came into their season, so I'm bound by the covenant of the list to weed them. Mama comes out and sits on the tool shed stoop to talk with me while I weed my bloody way (briers, remember?) from the bottom round of the bed's stone border to the tall Ligustrum hugging the smokehouse wall. "You want to cut that Ligustrum back, go ahead," Mama tells me. "It used to be a perfect shape, but it's not been the same since your brother cut it down." "Why'd he do that?" "I don't know. There's no stopping a man with a chainsaw in his hands."

I'm for letting the shrub continue in its imperfection, so I bend back to clearing the quartz rock border, which oddly stops just short of closing into a full circle.

My guess is that the rock border never got finished because for all the years Lona Bell lived here before my family came, she kept her own list. Tomorrow I'll bring six more rocks from the creek and finish that circular border, she'd tell herself, noticing it from the kitchen window while she dried her hands after supper dishwashing. Then she'd get busy putting away the beans she'd canned and the rock border would go invisible again. As years passed, the border took pity on this lady trying to keep up a farm by herself and resolved to remove itself from her sight. It tried to think heavier-than-normal rock thoughts, willed itself to sink below dirt, sent out gravelly whispers to nearby reindeer moss to *Grow more this way; cover me over.* And the stones were covered up and stayed covered until this past Monday when a sharp edge of quartz poked itself up, caught the sun, and glinted like a wink at me: *Scratch this dirt away, honey. It's time.*

While I'm scratching dirt with my trowel, John Henry, Mama's tailless orange cat, swishes over to inspect my work. Mama watches him lie down where I'd been about to clear next, says she shouldn't be taking up my time when I'm working. *I'm not working, Mama. I'm just putting things right.* I've always found a Puritan-like satisfaction in cleaning up big messes. Pulling up weeds, cleaning out a closet, even changing diapers—I like the sort of job where you can see what you've done. I like the process of walking through disorder to its other side.

I think this love of process may be a dying perception. As an English as a Second Language teacher, I recently attended an educator's conference. The keynote speaker, Georgia's current Commissioner for the Department of Technical and Adult Education, told us that eighty percent of Georgians no longer make things. We think, we design, we plan, we purchase. We do not make. We are not involved in process. And, yes, inherent to any process is the actual labor, but an equally vital tool is time, time given over to thinking about the next step.

The value of apparently empty time seems to be going missing as we whizz along into the 21st Century. If you walk into any high school in the United States you'll likely be horrified by what appears to be a chaotic lack of respect for the teachers. Kids talk, run around, generally do not pay attention, or at least not to the degree that students once sat still in class, but I don't think we can dismiss this as simple disobedience. It may be, instead, a learned inability to wait.

Almost every visual and aural contact in the lives of most Americans today emphasizes result, not process. Many of us live our lives never seeing a farm or the inside of a factory or a loom or a forge, but we can't drive a mile without passing a store. Hardly anyone writes letters (blessings on you, Fred, Lois, Joe, my faithful pen pals). E-mailing and Texting and Instant Messaging require no touching of paper, no folding of paper, no licking of flaps, no stamp, no walking to the mailbox, no waiting and rethinking what you wrote and wondering if you said too much and how the person you wrote to will take what you said and what they'll say back. A cell phone in your purse means never having to sit home by a phone waiting for a call, with all that is implied by your willingness to sit there giving up time you might have spent somewhere else. Things change while waiting is going on. Sometimes the changes are as we'd hoped but sometimes they knock our thinking sideways.

The need for change seems to be an intrinsic one, but people who have never learned to wait can bring about change only through capturing and presenting one result after another. Kids running around like crazy during a high school play rehearsal are working to fill their current space with noise, with action, with interaction—all of which they have learned to regard as valid products of passing from one moment to the next. The kids aren't being unruly—they are trying to make something. They just haven't learned how.

Had I been born to some other mother, I might not have learned how to wait, and so might not be a writer. Waiting is integral to the writing life. The writer Erma Bombeck once invited her daughter to participate in "Take Your Daughter to Work Day" with her. The daughter countered, "That would be the job where you sit and stare into space for hours at a stretch? No thanks, Mom." My mother has always told me that daydreaming isn't wasted time, it's time when the work you're doing hasn't yet started to show on the outside. Once when pressed to name a favorite Bible verse, Mama said she guessed she'd have to say "Be still and know that I am God." Being still is not, as I have learned from her, a cessation of activity, but a time of transitioning to a higher level of creative activity.

While Mama's been sitting here supposedly keeping me from working, what she's actually done is give me more tools for my toolbox. I'm still weeding, but now my brain has clicked into gear. Now I'm thinking about how later I'll write the story of my brother running amuck with a chainsaw during his twenties and ruining the lines of a perfect shrub. I'm not wasting time; I'm earning my spot among the twenty percent of Georgians who make things.

I'm also earning my residency on a tired brown farm. It takes a certain kind of character to live where nothing is new or shiny or plumb. The great majority of my working hours are geared toward keeping things the same. We replace rotten boards with equally weathered boards salvaged from one of the barns that had to come down. Someday we'll jack the smokehouse level so that after a fifty-year rest, it looks ready again for hanging a hog. And Mama and I keep weeding Lona Bell's flowerbeds and unearthing rocks she laid in order to maintain the flowerbeds pretty much the way they looked in 1959 or 1921.

Now that I've weeded this flowerbed down to poison ivy roots Mama, John Henry and I walk to the house together, looking back to admire how cleaned the bed looks, how tidy. We don't look at honeysuckle choking the hearts-a-busting bush or at siding gone mushy with rot under Mama's kitchen window. We don't even see these. We don't hear that high yowl which sounds distressingly like yet another puppy dumped in the woods. None of these worries have risen to their season on the job list yet. They're there, but waiting, and we needn't pay them any mind today.

Mama looks again at the smokehouse and says, "Maybe I should hold off buying a new sofa until we see how much it's going to cost to fix the smokehouse." I nod, we walk on, and behind us a small noise of shifting begins, a tiny creaking as of something stretching awake after sleeping long and deep. Spring is coming on.

Karen Salyer McElmurray

1956–

Born in Topeka, Kansas, where her father was serving in the air force, Karen Salyer McElmurray has deep Kentucky roots, with family connections to Floyd and Johnson Counties. The first person in her family to attend college, McElmurray earned a BA from Berea College, an MFA from the University of Virginia, an MA from Hollins University, and a PhD from the University of Georgia. McElmurray left a tenure-track position at a university—an uncommon step for an academic—to teach writing in more varied settings and to pursue a career as an author of fiction and nonfiction and as an anthologist.

McElmurray's work examines the hard choices people make in their personal lives and the long-term consequences of those choices. She examined her own life in this way in her nonfiction. Her memoir, *The Surrendered Child: A Birth Mother's Journey* (2004), recounts her experience of giving up a child for adoption when she was fifteen. In the excerpt from the longer essay "Trip around the World" that appears below, the author wrestles with her conflicting perceptions of herself as an Appalachian person.

FROM Trip around the World

Harlan. For some the word means coal mine disasters and union wars and some of the worst poverty in the United States. I remember seeing a family of thirteen children walk up the road mornings to school past our trailer park. *The Esteps.* My mother spoke disdainfully of this family, talked about how black their faces and hands and nails were from coal dust, the same dust she feared contaminated the walls and floors of our trailer. I went to the same grade school, Lynch Elementary, that the Esteps did, and my memories of that place are of oiled board floors and turkey and gravy lunches from Meals on Wheels. At singing circle, a mop-headed boy sang the theme from *The Beverly Hillbillies* and I remember, with a funny taste in my mouth, how the teacher would get him up front, give him a toy guitar, and let him lead us in verse after verse. *A poor mountaineer, barely kept his family fed.*

We weren't exactly poor, but we were trailer park people nonetheless. My mother and father and I lived in Cumberland, a tiny town one over from Lynch, where there was a lot on a back street my mother liked as well as she'd like anywhere not her own parents' home, in Floyd County. High school teaching salaries were low, low enough that my father signed us up for commodity cheese and peanut butter and his mother kept me clothed all the years up to high school with homemade dresses and hand-me-downs.

My father taught at Lynch East Main, a high school smack dab in the middle of Harlan. My father's stories today are about names of people in Lynch, changed from Italian or Polish or Czechoslovakian, names made Smith-and-Jones simple for the lines for coal scrip or welfare. He still tells a story about a boy, his favorite trigonometry student, who got blown up at the face of a mine his first day on the job after he graduated. He urged his students to want more. Applications to University of Kentucky. Football scholarships. Jobs in the big city of Lexington. I remember my father's slashed tires in the driveway one morning. *The Esteps*, my mother said.

Some late Friday afternoons after my father finished teaching, we drove north, home to Floyd County. We passed towns like Middlesboro, Pineville, Whitesburg. We took back roads, Highway 119 or 23 and one stretch called Straight Creek, an unusual section of highway that ran along a creek as straight as a chalk line for thirty-five miles. On one ride home, rain cascaded down as our car snaked up and around the mountains and we stopped for soda crackers to ease my stomach. *Reckon it'll let up any?* The store's owner cut slices for us from a round of deep yellow cheddar and offered us tomatoes so ripe they glistened. My mother, fearing stains on our clothes and stray crumbs and dirt of any variety at all, vetoed those tomatoes, and later my parents' angry voices collided as we eventually straddled the top of Pine Mountain, 2,500 feet of it. Rain fell more quietly as we stopped beside the road and my father held the back of my head as I vomited into a paper bag. We looked down past a trash-strewn hill and into a valley so deep and wet-green and far away, I shivered.

You come by it honest, my Granny Baisden, my mother's mother, would say. My love of all things spiritual. When I was a child, I tried to read the Bible cover to cover, checked out *Fox's Book of Martyrs* from the public library. I read about as many women saints as I could. By high school, I was drawn to the meditations of Thomas Merton, the prison diaries of Dietrich Bonhoeffer. I loved Frazer's *Golden Bough* and the studies of sacred places by Mircea Eliade. To this day I'm drawn to anything that describes power of the transcendent variety. Rudolph Otto, in a book called *The Idea of the Holy*, describes mysterium tremendum—awe, ecstacy, revelation—and in my teaching, over the years, I have been fascinated with how to impart this very experience to the creative writing classes I teach. I've read them essays about the power of love and the human heart. We've listened to Nusrat Fateh Al-Khan and written about our pasts. We've sat on a dock on an October night and tried to describe the moonlight. *Transcendence*, I tell them, *must reach for that moonlight and make it as ordinary as the work of our hands.*

Eastern Kentucky *was* a hardscrabble existence, one that my mother escaped when she married my father, the air force man who bought her an engagement ring in Morocco, married her, took her away from Home. *Kansas. Lexington. Harlan County.* We moved from place to place, then finally to a subdivision house in Frankfort, the state capitol, where my father worked for the Kentucky Department of Education.

When we made visits east, my father would bring us to Dwale while he took off for the next county to visit his own mother and father, a visit and a house to which my mother preferred not to accompany him.

During visits to Dwale, I still remember my mother's distaste as she tiptoed down the hill, in and out of the dirt ruts and stones of the path that led to the outhouse. At home, our floors were so pristine, neither my father nor I had ever walked on them in our outdoor shoes. We had to shower in the garage to keep the bathtub clean. I still remember the feel of my mother's hand at night, the gloves thick with lotions she wore to bed to try to heal her hands, so chapped from housework they bled. *Don't touch anything in there*, she'd say when we visited the outhouse in Dwale. She'd stand by me while I looked down into a hole that led to lime and decomposition, to all the vile things she preferred to forget from her own childhood. I loved standing there, listening to magpies in the stone pear tree in the bottom land.

Her father, my grandfather called Pa, worked in the mines in Martin and David, tiny towns in the next county, up until I was much older and he filed for black lung benefits. He'd head out with a dinner pail before daylight, leaving us to days of visiting with my granny and my mother's two sisters. It's my Granny Baisden I remember most. She raised or canned or made everything the family ate, and I remember her, in a cotton sunbonnet, hoeing one more row of potatoes or beans in the hot sun in the bottom down from the house. Mornings she'd wake me and my mother where we slept in the bed in the front room. *Morning this morning, fine morning,* she'd say, her face all creased and toothless, her teeth in a canning jar in the kitchen where she'd next go to make us all homemade biscuits and sugar syrup I'd stir up with butter on a plate. I'd watch her hands folding that light dough, up and over, watch her make pie crusts with meringues that could float all the way up to heaven. I'd sit out in the side yard, afternoons, and watch her maneuver work shirts and overalls through the tight rollers on the wringer washing machine. Her hands were strong and freckled from the sun, palms orangey from sulfur water from the well as she reached in, took the clothes back out, put them through again.

Evenings, I'd sit with her on the front porch that overlooked the bottom land, and she'd take down her long, braided hair, let me play with her combs and pins. She'd show me how to pretend the white porch chairs were cars. I planned all the places I'd go, the roads I'd someday take to foreign places in the world she'd never see. Who'd have thought of Thailand, Nepal, India, all those places I'd someday go, ones that meant nothing then, next to the bottom land and the pear tree and that house in Dwale, all the world both of us then knew.

It was my father who took me to church on Sundays on those trips home. Lick Fork Missionary Baptist Church sat on the side of a road I'd jog on, twenty years later, on visits to Eastern Kentucky. It was a small, whitewashed building full of benches and the preacher's voice. He was red-faced and short-sleeved and sweating as he held his hand against his ear and told-sang-shouted his sermon for the day with an almost sexual frenzy, words about hell and devotion to Jesus Christ Our Lord and doing good with our neighbors. Men and women knelt in the front below the preacher and prayed, all together. People ran circles around the church's insides, shouting—

Oh Hallajamondia, Hallajamondia—waving their ecstatic arms to God. *Praise Jesus. Praise Him.* And sometimes someone would fall out in front of the pulpit, her body quivering with the power of God. Hands fell on this person, that one, anyone visited by the power of the Spirit, the power of the Holy Ghost.

Later, outside, the brothers and sisters gathered around chairs set out here and there on top of the hill near the church. There was a wash basin, an aluminum one like the one my Granny Baisden washed dishes in. This one or that one, Brother Clifford or Brother Howard, took a seat and untied his boots, peeled off his socks, waited his turn for the metal pan. I remember the thick-nailed toes, the rough heels. Hands reaching into cool water, touching those feet, their calloused and yellow hides. *Foot washing.* A sign of humbleness. Loving one's neighbor like one's self.

At home, feet were dirty things, laden with grime and toil and stench. At home, we took our shoes off and barely touched the floors on our prescribed paths to television, to bed, to the door out. At Lick Fork, I watched towels dry the feet of strangers. Small, remembered acts of devotion.

A few weeks into my Prose Forms class, I meet with all my students, one by one. I've had some of them already in nonfiction writing workshops, so we talk about both essays on their writing lives for Prose Forms class, and about their nonfiction in general. One student is writing about his cross-country journey, a Hunter S. Thompsonesque van ride through the small towns and valleys of the South. Another is writing about both her decision to leave a job in finance and her fascination with Prader-Willi syndrome, a genetic disorder causing constant feelings of hunger. I am holding some of my conferences in a local Tex-Mex restaurant, and I'm sitting there nibbling at a burrito when the student from upstate New York comes in, orders her own taco salad, and takes a seat.

The student and I, since the first night of class, have been experiencing some unease. She smiles tightly in class when I talk about "the writing life," and has more than once referred to such a topic of class discussion as "simplistic." I've been, I admit, inwardly cringing, for weeks, about her first-night comments about hardscrabble lives, and about transcendence itself. I've heard it rumored that she calls me "the leader of a school of transcendence." And all that stuff about art. Art, she maintains, is like any other trade. Why not, she asks us in class, speak of the transcendent value of plumbing, the transcendent value of drywall?

She divides the lettuce and cheese in her salad. "I don't think that's it," she begins. "I'll be honest," she says. "My problem is the topic itself."

"What do you mean?"

"Why I write." She leans forward into the table, peers at me. "I'm just a student," she says. "Not an artist. How am I supposed to know anything about the writing life? About why I write?"

Not to mention, she goes on, all this business about human hearts and transcendence. She wants the nuts and bolts. She wants to get in there and unravel stories, rip them apart.

"I'm here to learn about craft."

My face feels warm, salty-warm. I am somewhere between shame and anger. We sit quietly.

"I've worked with someone like you before," she says. "A mountain writer, when I was at college. She likes the same things you do."

We eat and I now feel unaccountably sad. What things do I like? And maybe she's right. What, I wonder, *is* all this business about transcendence anyway?

In grade school when we lived in Frankfort, we were studying a chapter on genealogy. We had to tell the class about our families, and there was a paper to fill out with questions. *Our mother's maiden name. The story we heard repeated most often at the dinner table.* Dinner table stories? We fought there, over who got the fattiest ham slice, over who my father flirted with at the office. I raised my hand and asked permission to come up front, tell my teacher privately what my mother's peculiar name was. *Pearlie Lee Baisden.* A good mountain name, but one I was sure my peers would laugh at, just as I knew they laughed at my odd-turned way of speaking, the long i's of mountain-speak that I still had, from when we lived in Harlan. *Night. White. Bright.* A nasal, long *i* that I held in on my tongue, sour as communion crackers and grape juice. I was ashamed. Of the names we still held for things, at home. *Rack.* Meaning coat hanger. *Smelled of.* Meaning had a scent. *Gommed.* Meaning tangled up.

By the time high school came, I was ashamed of my dresses, the homemade ones with rickrack and lace, fresh-made by my father's mother, my Granny Salyer. I was ashamed of the clothes I had to wear to school, hand-me-downs from my own mother's high school days, back in Floyd County. I was ashamed of the way my mother stayed home all the time, hiding from the world out there, the clean, middle-class world of Frankfort, so desirable, yet jarringly different from the one she'd grown up with in Eastern Kentucky. She never went to church, hid when the church ladies from Graefenburg, my father's Baptist church, came calling. I was ashamed of the way, on Sunday mornings, when I accompanied my father to church, he nervously clipped his nails, cleared his throat, of the way, on Sunday afternoons, we stayed away from my mother, hiding out at his office. [. . .] During church services I heard echoes of Lick Fork in my head. *Praise Him. Praise Jesus.* I was ashamed, of thinking of how tame the church world was now with its sculpted lines of pews, its carpeted floors, its smart sermons. At night once, I believed I heard the voice of God, coming through my bedroom window, just for me. *Daughter, I have need of you.* His voice was long-voweled with Eastern Kentucky-speak, just like my own.

I grew up, moved away to other towns, states, countries. But shame, some variety or other of it, followed me like a shadow, like a drift of coal dust. At Berea, where I went to college, I was in my element, in some ways. Berea is a school "for mountain youth" where education is paid for by student labor. At my job in Crafts and Weaving, I sewed stuffed animals and wove placemats. Our crafts industry, along with Berea's pottery and broom-making and Appalachian heritage museum, was a tourists' hot spot. We were hillbillies. Poor mountaineers. I sat there, furious and ashamed, when a group came through the crafts shop one day. *Do you children really not have shoes?* a woman asked me.

In graduate school, at the University of Virginia, I felt totally out of my element. I'd earned my points at Berea, but could not now adequately apply theoretical language to the books that had been my salvation, back in my parents' house. In my first creative writing workshop, I began to write stories that hinted at both my childhood and Eastern Kentucky. *I appreciate this quaint story,* a peer wrote, *about a little mountain hamlet.* When, at last, I won a fellowship for my stories, I received many congratulations from the other writers. *It's good that this went to someone who really needed the money,* one person said. I continued to write stories about baptisms and fortune tellers and quilts with names like "Trip Around the World." *What you're writing,* one person said in my workshop. *It isn't fiction yet.*

That was true. I was in-between worlds. *Fiction. Nonfiction. Childhood and now.* I was somewhere between the mountains that often hurt in my memory and the life I was now living. I was translating my life into stories that did not yet possess a soul.

After graduate school, I spent some months in England and France, but found myself most alive as my traveling companion and I traveled east, first to Greece, where I was thrilled mornings by the sounds of the muezzin's call to prayer. *Thailand. Nepal. Malaysia. India.* Oils and curries. Funeral pyres and sadhus. We traveled north and south. *Kashmir. Jaipur. Rajasthan.* The hot months before the monsoon season left us sleepless and exhausted. I ate water-thin dal and picked bits of filth from my rice. I loved the feel of my own sharp hips and ribs.

Soon I was reduced to something thin and brittle. I had visions so palpable I could hold them in the palm of my hand. A leper with his fingers eaten away. A sadhu with a swollen scrotum, ringing a bell in a marketplace. A blind man at a train station who told me he'd seen God and time and that he could give me both. An ear cleaner on the steps of a temple assured I'd hear like before if I sampled his skills. And in the deserts of Rajasthan, heat so keen I watched it shine on the desert sands at night. Here, I told my friend, everything is real. *Unconcealed.*

At night, as we slept in hostels and cheap and good guest houses with the blood of street junkies on the walls, I dreamed often of Eastern Kentucky. I dreamed of praying in the church at Lick Fork. I dreamed once of a bridge spanning a creek and on its other side, my grandmother's house and on the porch, my Granny Baisden and my mother. They beckoned to me.

In order to go home again, I heard a voice tell me, I had to learn how to pray.

Praying, is, in fact, something I haven't done very much of in years. Not really.

I've prayed for this or that outcome. *Please, oh please, let this turn out this way.* There've been the aphorisms from my childhood that I sometimes say, like prayers, at sunset. *Red at night, sailor's delight.* There are always mealtime blessings at my father and stepmother's new home in Shelbyville, Kentucky, prayers of thanks during which we hold hands. *Thank you, Lord, for bringing us this food today.* And at my mother's, now that she is living alone, back in Eastern Kentucky, there are bitter charms, stays against disaster. *You can't trust love, not one bit of it.* And if there are other prayers, times I travel back to Eastern Kentucky, they are ones said over the dinner table at my aunt and uncle's trailer, up Mining Hollow. *Forgive us, Lord, for our sins. Teach us, Lord, to live in the loving ways.* Out the window of that trailer, you can see the grave of their son in the family cemetery.

And yet it is via Eastern Kentucky, or the Appalachian mountains themselves, that I have at last learned to genuinely listen those times I tilt my head up to the sky and wait. In the fall of 2006, I taught a class in Appalachian Literature as a corollary to the classes I teach in the creative writing program. I arranged films, photos, food, oral history projects. I picked a range of books—novels, stories, poetry—and I called upon all the names I love from prominent Appalachian writers. *Denise Giardina. Lee Smith. John Ehle.* In short, I began to summon my own past and to tell my students stories of my own childhood. I remembered again the coal tipples at Martin, the ones we'd drive by on trips home to Floyd County. I remembered the particular taste of wild greens. *Cressy. Mustard. Poor man's bacon.* I took out the quilts I'd inherited from my father's mother and I touched this square of cloth, that one, pieces from junk stores she'd visited, pieces from my grandfather's shirts, ones cut from the dresses made for me when I was child. The names of those quilts stirred my heart. *Cathedral Window. Trip Around the World.*

The heart, says Deborah McCauley in a book called *Appalachian Mountain Religion,* is "one of the most significant and telling recurrent themes in mountain preaching." It is the heart, "broken . . . tender . . . a heart not hardened to the Spirit," that is important in mountain faiths. And, most significant for me, McCauley says that, for mountain faiths, "rational belief alone . . . what makes sense to the head, is woefully inadequate." There I was again. Back in Lick Fork, at church. Back in other church houses I'd been to in the mountains, ones that were tender. Soft as the laying on of hands. But fierce and unabashed, full of visions of angels and Spirit. I remembered when my great-grandfather died, and the funeral they had for him. A service at some church house, maybe in Dwale. All the windows were open to the sound of bees and wind and summertime. And inside, rapturous voices called up to God. *Lordy. Lordy.* Hands waved. My great-aunt Essie ran up and back, mourning and weeping, then threw herself across the body of her daddy. *Lord,* she cried. *Take me. Take me.* As I read now about tender hearts and hands, about the faith of the mountains, I feel again how I felt that long-ago day. As if the dark arms could reach down, scoop me up, make me disappear.

And yet, when it comes to matters of the heart, how to convey that in the classroom, in the study of the text, the manuscript itself, without some sense of shame? If I teach from the heart, will I hear what I've sometimes heard before in the halls of academia? My colleagues hint that matters of the heart are precious, touchy-feely, of less consequence than intellect and analysis. Deborah McCauley, again in her text *Appalachian Mountain Religion,* confirms just that schism. Mountain people, who base their faith on the heart, on grace, on inspiration of the Holy Spirit, met an influx of missionaries and revivalists during the Great Awakening of the mid-1800s. Visions and tongues and the Holy Spirit began to seem barbaric. Emphasis on grace and knowledge of the heart took a back seat to social action, individual achievement, and rational interpretations of religious experience.

Patricia Foster, in an essay called "The Intelligent Heart," writes that "the heart is the source, the goods, the first principle from which everything else is made." It is that heart, spirit, source, goods, first principle that I long for both when I lead workshops and when I read drafts of my students' stories. For me, it is by far not enough to discuss characterization, setting, plot. It is not nearly enough to write a story or a poem or an essay with the publisher, the magazine, even the audience in mind. I want my students, first, to locate the intentions of their writing. The story must have "an about," a purpose that begins with understanding "heart," both of writer and act of writing, of story and story's *why*. A story must understand itself and language must translate that understanding—a process that, on my best of days, this is what I mean by transcend. "Story," says Foster, "must act as a catalyst for thinking and feeling [and] the congruence of both elevates the story to the status of art." Division of heart and mind translates into a schism of spirit and language.

"I'm trying to sort it out," Foster wrote me recently. "Exactly what's happened with my students of late. The ones who don't seem interested in the darker conflicts of the human spirit, the emotional range of familial and cultural incidents, the hard work of trying to forgive self and other. I do hope to write about this determined resistance to the inner life of story, to the inner life of either self or another." I, like my friend, am finding this true, this perplexity about interest in the human spirit, no less a larger world. Transcendence, my Prose Form and Theory student told me toward the end of that particular class. She'd tried it, and it just didn't work. *Transcendence.* Is it something we try? Or is it a gift, an unexpected wonder that lies at the heart of the best of our words and, I hope, the best of what we have to teach. Is true poverty, as Heather Sellers says in her essay in [*An Angle of Vision: Women Writers on Their Poor and Working-Class Roots*], one of imagination? Or of spirit and heart?

One fall, a few years back, I traveled with a friend to Atlanta to hear a reading by poet Robert Bly and to see a performance by Sufi dancers. On the drive, I kept hearing lines of Bly's—ones about mystery—that haunted me. *The toe of the shoe pivots in the dust . . . the man in the black coat turns.* We were late as we took our seats in the upper tier of a darkened auditorium at the Emory Center for the Performing Arts, and we'd missed the poet. What we saw was light on a stage and a circle of trousered men in long white and gold coats—the Sufi dancers. Their long coats swayed and the dance was silent except for the whoosh of cloth and that dizzying circling, over, over, faster and faster until their coats belled out. I remembered the way women danced in the church houses I'd visited when I was a child. *The dizzying circle of those women as they summoned the spirit.* The six men turned and turned in dance, and something—a translation of memory I'm still waiting to understand—traveled out and settled in the palms of my hands.

bell hooks

1952–

Writer, educator, and feminist bell hooks was born Gloria Jean Watkins in Hopkins-ville, Kentucky. After initially attending segregated schools, hooks, who is African American, graduated from an integrated high school. She earned a BA from Stanford University, an MA from the University of Wisconsin, Madison, and a PhD from the University of California, Santa Cruz. hooks adopted her pen name from the name of her maternal great-grandmother, Bell Blair Hooks, a woman known for her bold speech.

In the 1980s, hooks was one of the people who brought into feminist theory and activism a concern for minority voices, which the mainstream feminist move-ment had tended to overlook. Her first major work, *Ain't I a Woman? Black Women and Feminism* (1981), articulated this critique. Since then, hooks has published more than thirty books of prose and poetry.

Hooks has taught at several universities, including the University of Southern California, San Francisco State University, Yale University, Oberlin College, and the City College of New York. In 2014 she founded the bell hooks Institute at Berea College.

Returning to Kentucky to work at Berea College, hooks has focused on her rural Kentucky heritage and her feeling of solidarity with African Americans in rural Appalachia. The following essay is the introduction to her 2012 collection of poems *Appalachian Elegy: Poetry and Place.*

On Reflection and Lamentation

Sublime silence surrounds me. I have walked to the top of the hill, plopped myself down to watch the world around me. I have no fear here, in this world of trees, weeds, and growing things. This is the world I was born into: a world of wild things. In it the wilderness in me speaks. I am wild. I hear my elders caution mama, tell-ing her that she is making a mistake, letting me "run wild," letting me run with my brother as though no gender separates us. We are making our childhood together in the Kentucky hills, experiencing the freedom that comes from living away from civ-ilization. Even as a child I knew that to be raised in the country, to come from the backwoods, left one without meaning or presence. Growing up we did not use terms like "hillbilly." Country folk lived on isolated farms away from the city; backwoods folks lived in remote areas, in the hills and hollers.

To be from the backwoods was to be part of the wild. Where we lived, black folks were as much a part of the wild, living in a natural way on the earth, as white folks. All backwoods folks were poor by material standards; they knew how to make do.

They were not wanting to tame the wildness, in themselves or nature. Living in the Kentucky hills was where I first learned the importance of being wild.

Later, attending college on the West Coast, I would come to associate the passion for freedom and the wildness I had experienced as a child with anarchy, with the belief in the power of the individual to be self-determining. Writing about the connection between environments, nature, and creativity in the introduction to *A Place in Space*, Gary Snyder states: "Ethics and aesthetics are deeply intertwined. Art, beauty, and craft have always drawn on the self-organizing 'wild' side of language and mind. Human ideas of place and space, our contemporary focus on watersheds, become both models and metaphors. Our hope would be to see the interacting realms, learn where we are, and thereby move towards a style of planetary and ecological cosmopolitanism." Snyder calls this approach the "practice of the wild," urging us to live "in the self-disciplined elegance of 'wild' mind." By their own practice of living in harmony with nature, with simple abundance, Kentucky black folks who lived in the backwoods were deeply engaged with an ecological cosmopolitanism. They fished; hunted; raised chickens; planted what we would now call organic gardens; made homemade spirits, wine, and whiskey; and grew flowers. Their religion was interior and private. Mama's mama, Baba, refused to attend church after someone made fun of the clothes she was wearing. She reminded us that God could be worshipped everyday, anywhere. No matter that they lived according to Appalachian values, they did not talk about themselves as coming from Appalachia. They did not divide Kentucky into East and West. They saw themselves as renegades and rebels, folks who did not want to be hemmed in by rules and laws, folks that wanted to remain independent. Even when circumstances forced them out of the country into the city, they were still wanting to live free.

As there were individual black folks who explored the regions of this nation before slavery, the first black Appalachians being fully engaged with the Cherokee, the lives of most early black Kentuckians were shaped by a mixture of free sensibility and slave mentality. When slavery ended in Kentucky, life was hard for the vast majority of black people as white supremacy and racist domination did not end. But those folks who managed to own land, especially land in isolated country sites or hills (sometimes inherited from white folks for whom they had worked for generations, or sometimes purchased), were content to be self-defining and self-determining even if it meant living with less. No distinctions were made between those of us who dwelled in the hills of eastern or western Kentucky. Our relatives from eastern Kentucky did not talk about themselves as Appalachians, and in western Kentucky we did not use the term; even if one lived in the hills where the close neighbors were white and hillbilly, black people did not see themselves as united with these folk, even though our habits of being and ways of thinking were more like these strangers than those of other black folks who lived in the city—especially black folks who had money and urban ways. In small cities and towns, the life of a black coal miner in western Kentucky was more similar to the life of an Eastern counterpart than different. Just as the lives of hillbilly black folks were the same whether they lived in the hills of eastern or western Kentucky.

In the Kentucky black subcultures, folks were united with our extended kin, and our identities were more defined by labels like "country" and "backwoods." It was not until I went away to college that I was questioned about Appalachia, about hillbilly culture, and it was always assumed by these faraway outsiders that only poor white people lived in the backwoods and in the hills. No wonder then that black folks who cherish our past, the independence that characterized our backwoods ancestors, seek to recover and restore their history, their legacy. Early on in my life I learned from those Kentucky backwoods elders, the folks whom we might now label "Appalachian," a set of values rooted in the belief that above all else one must be self-determining. It is the foundation that is the root of my radical critical consciousness. Folks from the backwoods were certain about two things: that every human soul needed to be free and that the responsibility of being free required one to be a person of integrity, a person who lived in such a way that there would always be congruency between what one thinks, says, and does.

These ancestors had no interest in conforming to social norms and manners that made lying and cheating acceptable. More often than not, they believed themselves to be above the law whenever the rules of so-called civilized culture made no sense. They farmed, fished, hunted, and made their way in the world. Sentimental nostalgia does not call me to remember the worlds they invented. It is just a simple fact that without their early continued support for dissident thinking and living, I would not have been able to hold my own in college and beyond when conformity promised to provide me with a sense of safety and greater regard. Their "Appalachian values," imprinted on my consciousness as core truths I must live by, provided and continue to provide me with the tools I needed and need to survive whole in a postmodern world.

Living by those values, living with integrity, I am able to return to my native place, to an Appalachia that is no longer silent about its diversity or about the broad sweep of its influence. While I do not claim an identity as Appalachian, I do claim a solidarity, a sense of belonging, that makes me one with the Appalachian past of my ancestors: black, Native American, white, all "people of one blood" who made home-place in isolated landscapes where they could invent themselves, where they could savor a taste of freedom.

In my latest collection of essays, *Writing Beyond Race,* I meditate for page after page on the issue of where it is black folk may go to be free of the category of race. Ironically, the segregated world of my Kentucky childhood was the place where I lived beyond race. Living my early childhood in the isolated hills of Kentucky, I made a place for myself in nature there—roaming the hills, walking the fields hidden in hollows where my sharecropper grandfather Daddy Gus planted neat rows of growing crops. Without evoking a naïve naturalism that would suggest a world of innocence, I deem it an act of counterhegemonic resistance for black folks to talk openly of our experiences growing up in a southern world where we felt ourselves living in harmony with the natural world.

To be raised in a world where crops grown by the hands of loved ones is to experience an intimacy with earth and home that is lost when everything is out there, somewhere away from home, waiting to be purchased. Since much sociological focus on black experience has centered on urban life—lives created in cities—little is shared about the agrarian lives of black folk. Until Isabel Wilkerson published her awesome book *The Warmth of Other Suns*, which documents the stories of black folks leaving agrarian lives to migrate to cities, there was little attention paid to the black experience of folks living on the land. Just as the work of the amazing naturalist George Washington Carver is often forgotten when lists are made of great black men. We forget our rural black folks, black farmers, folks who long ago made their homes in the hills of Appalachia.

All my people come from the hills, from the backwoods, even the ones who ran away from this heritage refusing to look back. No one wanted to talk about the black farmers who lost land to white supremacist violence. No one wanted to talk about the extent to which that racialized terrorism created a turning point in the lives of black folks wherein nature, once seen as a freeing place, became a fearful place. That silence has kept us from knowing the ecohistories of black folks. It has kept folk from claiming an identity and a heritage that is so often forgotten or erased.

It is no wonder, then, that when I returned to my native state of Kentucky after more than thirty years of living elsewhere, memories of life in the hills flooded my mind and heart. And I could see the link between the desecration of the land as it was lived on by red and black folk and the current exploitation and destruction of our environment. Coming home to Kentucky hills was, for me, a way to declare allegiance to environment struggles aimed at restoring proper stewardship to the land. It has allowed me to give public expression to the ecofeminism that has been an organic part of my social action on behalf of peace and justice.

In *Longing For Running Water: Ecofeminism and Liberation*, theologian Ivone Gebara contends: "The ecofeminist movement does not look at the connection between the domination of women and nature solely from the perspective of cultural ideology and social structures; it seeks to introduce new ways of thinking that are more at the service of ecojustice." In keeping with this intent, in the preface to *Belonging: A Culture of Place*, where I make a space for the ecofeminist within me to speak, I conclude with this statement: "I pay tribute to the past as a resource that can serve as a foundation for us to revision and renew our commitment to the present, to making a world where all people can live fully and well, where everyone can belong."

The joyous sense of homecoming that I experience from living in Kentucky does not change the reality that it has been difficult for black rural Kentuckians to find voice, to speak our belonging. Most important, it has been difficult to speak about past exploitation and oppression of people and land, to give our sorrow words. Those of us who dare to talk about the pain inflicted on red and black folks in this country, connecting that historical reality to the pain inflicted on our natural world, are often no longer silenced; we are simply ignored. It is the recognition of that pain that causes a constant mourning

My cries of lamentation faintly echo the cries of freedom fighter Sojourner Truth, who often journeyed deep into the forest to loudly lament the pain of slavery, the pain of having no voice. Truth spoke to the trees, telling them, "when I cried out with a mother's grief none but Jesus heard." When I first walked on the hills belonging to me, I felt an overwhelming sense of triumph. I felt that I could reclaim a place in this Kentucky landscape in the name of all the displaced Native Americans, African Americans, and all the black Indians (who cannot "prove" on paper that they are who they really are). Chanting with a diverse group of ecofeminist friends, we called forth the ancestors, urging them to celebrate return migration with us. We spread sage, planted trees, and dug holes for blossoming rose bushes in the name of our mother Rosa Bell. I wanted to give her a place to rest in these hills, a place where I can commune with her spirit.

The essays in *Belonging: A Culture of Place* give voice to the collective past of black folks in Kentucky. They include family values that cover the ethics of life in the backwoods and hills of Kentucky. If psychologists are right and there is a core identity imprinted on our souls in her childhood, my soul is a witness to this Kentucky; so it was when I was a child and so it is in my womanhood. My essays are almost always written in clear polemical prose, nothing abstract, nothing mysterious. When poetry stirs in my imagination it is almost always from an indirect place, where language is abstract, where the mood and energy is evocative of submerged emotional intelligence and experience.

Poetry is a useful place for lamentation. Not only the forest Sojourner found solace in, poems are a place where we can cry out. *Appalachian Elegy* is a collection of poems that extend the process of lamentation. Dirge-like at times, the poems repeat sorrow sounds, connecting the pain of a historical Kentucky landscape ravaged by war and all human conditions that are like war. Nowadays we can hear tell of black jockeys, the ones who became famous. But where are the stories of all enslaved black servants who worked with horses, who wanted to mount and ride away from endless servitude? Those stories are silenced. Psychohistory and the power of ways of knowing beyond human will and human reason allow us to re-create, to reimagine. Poems of lamentation allow the melancholic loss that never truly disappears to be given voice. Like a slow solemn musical refrain played again and again, they call us to remember and mourn, to know again that as we work for change our struggle is also a struggle of memory against forgetting.

Denise Giardina
1951–

Born in Bluefield, West Virginia, Denise Giardina experienced the uncertainties of life in a coal camp firsthand. Her grandfather and two uncles were coal miners, her father was a bookkeeper for the coal company, and her mother was a nurse. When Giardina was twelve, her father was laid off and the family moved to Charleston, West Virginia. After graduating from West Virginia Wesleyan College in 1973, Giardina earned a master's of divinity from Virginia Theological Seminary in 1979 and taught at West Virginia State University. She is an activist for environmental and social justice, an ordained deacon in the Episcopal Church, and a former third-party candidate for governor of West Virginia.

Giardina has written numerous historical novels, including two set in Appalachia, *Storming Heaven* (1987) and *The Unquiet Earth* (1992), which deal with West Virginia from 1890 to 1990. Giardina's West Virginia novels explore the transition of land from local control to absentee ownership; the rise of some families at the expense of the decline of others; the struggle for union representation in the coalfields; the environmental effects of strip mining; and the legacies these things had on individuals, families, and communities.

The following is from a memoir on which Giardina is currently working.

Candy

My mother and father suffered a contentious marriage. I now see Candy as an emblem of their fractures. Candy was an auburn cocker spaniel, my father's dog before he married my mother. To understand my dad, I have to understand his love for Candy.

My father was born in the United States but returned to Sicily with his family when he was still an infant. My grandfather Sam was lured to West Virginia to work in the coal mines. He came from a poor village on the north coast of Sicily, San Giorgio near Patti, and he wanted out. The coal company would pay his passage and he would come to America, where he would certainly become rich.

Instead he dug coal, one of the most backbreaking and dangerous jobs possible, for little pay. He met Rosarin Peruzzi, called Sara, a young woman from another immigrant Sicilian family, in their McDowell County coal camp. She had memories of cooking for a well-to-do family in Palermo. Hard, in West Virginia, to come by artichokes, pungent olives and decent olive oil, calamari, baccala. And vino. She, too, had come down in the world. Sam and Sara married and produced several children. My father was the youngest. Then they went back home.

According to Homer, Scylla was a monster that dwelt in the narrow strait between the Italian boot and Sicily, a monster who was also a cliff. Charybdis was a monster, and a whirlpool, closer to Sicily. Any attempt by a ship to avoid one would lead to destruction by the other. Between Scylla and Charybdis was the Sicilian dilemma, what Appalachian culture would call between a rock and a hard place.

It is a myth that everyone who came to this country in search of a better life was happy with what they found. It is a myth that everyone thought, *This place, wonderful America, is far better than where I came from.* Sam and Sara did not think so. Somehow, and it must have cost them dearly, they were able to come up with the means to return to Sicily. They stayed ten years.

They named my father, born in West Virginia but raised in Sicily, Tindaro. I only learned why decades after his death. They had longed to return to Patti, a town that sprung up after an earlier, ancient settlement going back to the Greeks was abandoned because of the encroaching ocean. The ancient Greek town was Tyndaris. At some point a statue of Madonna and child arrived from Africa and was lodged inside a church. The church, fortunately located on higher ground, survived the loss of Tyndaris to the sea, and still stands. It houses the statue, the ancient statue, of a black Madonna and child. Madonna Tindari, the name enduring. She was a saint; she was a Madonna, a conflation. She was perhaps originally from Ethiopia, she is black, and she holds her black Jesus proudly in front of her. A Latin inscription in gold fronts her: NIGRA SUM SED FORMOSA. I am black but beautiful. The "but" rather than "and" a sign of defensiveness, but pride nevertheless.

Pilgrims prayed to her statue. One local legend both calls out and rebukes racism: a pilgrim who arrived refused to pray to the Madonna after realizing she was black. As the pilgrim was leaving she accidentally dropped her baby into the encroaching ocean. Madonna Tindari caused the land to rise to form a lagoon and save the baby. People have since named their children after her, Tindari for girls, Tindaro for boys. Thus my father's name. In America, the name was officially changed to Dennis, as all Tindaris and Tindaros lost their names to forced American translation, and for some reason Dennis was preferred for the Tindaros. Though my father's family continued to call him Tindaro when referring to him affectionately.

The name is ironic for me, because my young-woman clashes with my father were often based upon my perception of his racism. I know now my father's name was meant to hold his family close again to Sicily, to little Patti, and to Africans. But his family could not survive there.

So my grandparents left the brutal certainty of a Sicilian tenant farm to return to the brutal uncertainty of a West Virginia coal camp. I could never ask them about the decision because they spoke little English. And my father's experiences in a West Virginia coal camp, where the races were segregated but still lived cheek by jowl, wiped away Tindaro and allowed Dennis to enter. Dennis, the Italian now in America, was often pitted against black boys in his coal camp, each facing discrimination and fighting for second place. Neither could have been to blame, but he carried some bad memories of fistfights that he never disclosed. No trace of his connection to Africa was passed on to his children in those days. Perhaps he had forgotten it himself, or chose to forget.

Nona Sara always seemed difficult to me. It was not just because her English was poor. She was a force, and my Nono Sammie seemed almost a child beside her. Though my cousin, who is older than me, tells me that they had once had magnificent fights, Nono Sammie had surrendered and chosen the path of least resistance. I wondered if the decision to return to West Virginia had been hers. Perhaps there were clashes with in-laws in Sicily. Perhaps she missed her relatives still here in the coal camps, or thought her children would have more opportunity here. Perhaps they were, in fact, starving in that poor Sicilian village. In any event, they left Sicily for good. The only memory of that time I could coax from my father, who always had difficulty expressing deep emotions in English, was he'd had to abandon a beloved donkey in Sicily, and that had broken his heart.

At age ten my father, who spoke no English, found himself in a first-grade class in Welch, West Virginia. His teacher, Mrs. Sutcliffe, saw something in him. I met her years later when I was in high school, after she'd retired and moved to Charleston, where my family had also relocated. She said she'd called upon my dad as an enforcer. She was not a particularly good disciplinarian. But my father was twice as big as the other boys, so when the class got out of hand, Mrs. Sutcliffe would have him stand, fold his arms, and walk around the room glaring at the troublemakers. The class of six-year-olds would fall silent. Mrs. Sutcliffe spent extra time outside of class tutoring my father in English. He always spoke her name as though invoking a saint, and many years later he wept when she died, the only time I saw him cry.

We never knew my dad's exact birthdate—his family had not taken particular note when he arrived on the scene. So we celebrated his birthday on New Year's Day, and based on the memory of an older brother estimated the year to be 1911, eleven years before my mother. Though my father insisted he had been born in 1919. That was perhaps the year that he had actually arrived back in the United States. He might have been trying to lessen the distance from my mother, which seemed far enough as it was, and would grow as the years passed. Perhaps he saw his return as a new birth.

My father came of age in rough times. Much of the country was booming after the war, spending freely and partying despite Prohibition, as oblivious to the coming Depression as a late-night carouser aboard the *Titanic*. But not so in West Virginia, which has never been in synch with whatever time in which it exists. After years of postwar turmoil, socialism was still popular in West Virginia, the miners' union was broken, wages continued low and safety conditions poor. Massive mine explosions claimed scores of lives. Italians faced discrimination, and taunts of "wop" and "dago."

For my father and his siblings, choices must be made. The two oldest boys, Giuseppe (Joe) and Francisco (Frank), were teenagers who spoke no English, and sending them to school seemed unpromising. Besides, their income was needed. So they went into the mines with Sammie. Joe worked for many years, but after years of facing the danger, he fled to Detroit to work in a factory, then on to Los Angeles, where he opened a red-sauce pasta restaurant in the San Fernando Valley. The oldest sister, Josie, escaped to Detroit as well. The next son, Francisco, continued in the mines, because someone must help support the family, and he didn't know what else to do. Decades later, his black lungs clogged with coal dust, he would literally drown in his hospital bed.

For my father, both choices seemed impossible. Scylla and Charybdis again. He didn't want to leave West Virginia. But he knew the dangers of coal mining, and he was claustrophobic. When, during my childhood, we took a vacation that led us to a guided tour of an underground limestone cavern, he could not bring himself to go inside. He waited in the car, nervously smoking a cigarette, and was very quiet after we returned, as though relieved we had survived. Had he tried to enter a coal mine, he thought he might die of a heart attack.

Again his beloved first-grade teacher, Mrs. Sutcliffe, came to the rescue after his high school graduation. Her husband was a mining executive who arranged for my father to attend a two-year business program in Bowling Green, Kentucky, at what later became Western Kentucky University, paid for by the coal company if he would return to West Virginia and work for that company as an accountant. My father was good with numbers. He could control numbers. He did not have to use either Sicilian dialect or English to communicate with numbers. He is the only person I've ever known who enjoyed doing his income taxes each year. He gladly accepted her offer.

As was his father before him, my father was a lady's man. I have seen pictures of him when he was young. He was athletic, and played on the high school basketball team. (When my brother and I were young, we did not believe our short, tubby father had played on a high school team, despite the photograph he showed us. My father had a basketball goal built in the backyard. When it was done, he walked around, dribbling a ball on the grass, sinking shot after shot. Then, we believed.) He was sloe-eyed, with a round face and curly black hair. My mother later claimed he had dated, and slept with, half the women in the county. She met him on a blind date, just before Pearl Harbor. She was from another world, rural eastern Kentucky, where there were very few Italians and those only in a handful of towns. My mother had never eaten pasta. Though they had one thing in common. He'd mourned his childhood donkey; she'd lost a beloved mule, sold during the Depression when her family was desperate for money.

Because of the Depression, my mother's family moved from their Kentucky farm to West Virginia, where my grandfather took a job managing a coal company store. My mother was in her early twenties, not long out of nursing school, and my father was already well into his thirties. She proudly claimed she refused his sexual overtures, and she seemed to think that had intrigued him enough to propose. (This reasoning did not impress me.) Then the war came and they separated. My father served on the European front, my mother as a nurse in the Philippines.

My mother occasionally reminisced about nursing POWs returned from the Japanese prison camps, and dating a variety of soldiers. I included some of her memories in my novel *The Unquiet Earth*. My father was posted to the Signal Corps in North Africa, and after the invasion of Sicily he was used as an interpreter. Because the British Army was short on Italians, he was loaned to General Montgomery, who later gave him a medal of thanks. A number of his fellow interpreters, mostly immigrants who had landed in large cities like New York and Chicago, became lifelong friends.

My father loved going back to Sicily during the war, so much so that though it was a war, and a terrible one, it seemed like a time he cherished. Indeed, it was an exciting time, a period of growth and exploration, for both my parents, the great adventure of their lives. That was what I gathered as a child. When I later came across accounts of the horrors of Iwo Jima, Bataan, Monte Cassino, Auschwitz, I was shocked. World War II had not been fun after all.

As soon as the war was over, my father acquired a dog, Candy the cocker spaniel. In the 1940s, cockers were the most popular dogs in America. My father had helped win a world war; once-despised Italians, because of their sheer numbers and their cultural contributions, had finally been accepted. (Look now—Joe DiMaggio and Frank Sinatra and Dean Martin! Although my father would adamantly refuse to change his name from the Italian as Dino "Martin," nee Crocetti, had done, shamefully to my father's mind. I often think of that, gratefully, even as I am forced for the hundred-thousandth time to spell out my name for people. And even though a high school teacher once called me a "wop," I was proud of being half-Italian and proud that my father was proud.)

My father reclaimed a coal company job that would place him solidly in the middle class. He loved animals, and he deserved America's most popular dog. Candy came first, and then he married my mother. They moved to the coal camp of Black Wolf in McDowell County, West Virginia.

I never really understood how they got back together. They bumped into each other by accident, but why did they bond again? Was it because the war was over and the available mates who had survived were being snapped up, right and left? What about all those soldiers my mother claimed she dated in the Philippines? Somehow, they hadn't panned out. She did admit to particularly pining for an Irishman named O'Sullivan from New Orleans. Apparently he pledged undying love, but when he returned home, she never heard from him again. So she accepted my father, the blind date she'd met before the war. My mother used to claim that the men in her family, and the neighbor boys she knew back in Kentucky, begged her not to marry "that Eye-talian." She claimed the young men of Feds Creek offered themselves as substitutes, to save her honor. I never quite believed that, for she obviously accepted none of them, if they were available. But I did believe that her family was not happy with her choice of husband. For several reasons, most, but not all of them, based on ethnic prejudice.

And my father? She might have fascinated him because she was old family Appalachian, the place he identified with but did not quite belong to despite his love for hillbilly and gospel music. Her family was large and close, and I always sensed he admired them greatly, wanted to belong.

But my parents had very little in common that would have seemed to draw them together. Perhaps my mother was rebelling against all those men and boys back home who wanted to dictate and limit her future; stubbornness and rebelliousness were her most endearing and enduring qualities. Perhaps she sensed that my father, despite his shortcomings, had one great advantage—unlike many men, he would never try to run her life or hold her back. I never once saw my dad try to bully my mom, never try to block any of her plans or dreams.

Perhaps my mother's relationship with her own family was more problematic than she later let on. She tried to paint a picture to me of nostalgic times on the Homeplace in Pike County, Kentucky, which they lost to the Depression, though as I grew older I began to doubt it was all so rosy. Perhaps after serving in the Philippines, she saw herself as worldly and adventurous, ready to engage with someone so very different from what she'd known. Perhaps she just wanted to try pasta for the first time. Anyway, my mother married, not in a formal wedding gown, but in a prim white suit, with a reception of punch and cookies in the basement of a coal camp Methodist church. Certainly my father's family would have preferred a traditional Catholic ceremony, but such things were not important to my father in those days. So in 1946, flush with money from a new coal company job, he whisked my mother off to New York City (which he discovered during the war and fell in love with) for their honeymoon, neon lights and that first taste of pasta.

I arrived after five years, a bit late. My mother was desperate that I should arrive at once, and claimed she never once tried any sort of birth control. But nothing happened. She made fruitless trips to the doctor. One suggestion was that my father had a low sperm count. Finally she resigned herself to adoption. Suddenly, I appeared. I seemed to go a good ways toward mending the rift with her family.

My mother always made clear to me the wonder of my birth, after all those years of trying, those scarce sperm seeking in vain to penetrate her egg. Perhaps that warped my sense of myself, that I was somehow special in the scheme of things. Mom said that when the first television arrived in our house, while I was still an infant, I resented it. When my mother stared at the screen, I grabbed her chin and tried to direct her gaze to me.

Despite my father's position as bookkeeper, we lived in a coal camp house in Black Wolf with four rooms, just like those of the miners. Kitchen, two bedrooms, and living room, with a closet-sized add-on for the coal furnace that heated the radiators and a bathtub and toilet in the enclosure next to that. The only room for a wringer washing machine was the front porch.

And there was Candy. By the time I entered grade school, Candy was old, fat and smelly. Her teats, which were hardened, especially disgusted me, peeling scabs that I disdained to touch. Candy was cranky, and she ignored children. She didn't like to play or have adventures like the dogs on television, Rin-Tin-Tin and Lassie. I couldn't imagine Candy rescuing anyone like those dogs did. And as long as Candy lived, we could never have a real dog. My dad wouldn't allow the competition; he said it would upset Candy, who he adored.

My mother hated the cocker spaniel. Candy spread fleas, which got on all of us, because she slept in the house and there was no treatment for fleas that we knew of. I can recall my angry mother picking fleas off of us and crushing them between her fingernails before we settled into bed, and upending carpets to hoover up white clots of flea eggs. She had been raised on an eastern Kentucky farm. There, cats lived in the barn, to prey on vermin, and dogs stayed under the house or on the porch. Animals never came indoors with people. Candy's presence was a shock to her.

I believe mom might have been jealous as well. I never saw my father embrace my mother, never saw him kiss her. But Candy spent the evenings sprawled on the couch beside my dad while he read the newspaper or watched TV. He rubbed Candy's ears, scratched her scabby belly. Mom ignored them both and concentrated on me.

Still my mother also loved animals and was determined her children would have pets. She was partial to cats and other animals. With our orange tabby Tiger dead, failure there, my mom bought a parakeet at the local Murphy's five-and-dime. Petey had a cage where he spent his days, but at night, after the house was shut up tight, he was allowed out to fly about. He loved to fly to the bathroom and perch on the shower curtain rod while my mother bathed me and my brother, who had arrived three years later as unexpectedly as I had. I suspect, knowing now Petey was a bird meant for the tropics and not West Virginia winters in a drafty coal camp house, he enjoyed the steamy heat of the tiny bathroom.

But one evening he left the curtain rod for the floor, and we weren't paying attention. Candy was. After a search we found Petey beside the commode, bloody circles in his blue-feathered chest where Candy had bitten into him. From then on, I hated Candy as much as my mother did.

Higher Ground Project

The power of community is at the center of a series of musical plays created by the Higher Ground Project, which is composed of students at Southeast Kentucky Community and Technical College and residents of Harlan County, Kentucky, and is spearheaded by Robert Gipe, director of the college's Appalachian Program. The plays begin with oral histories gathered by Appalachian studies students and other Harlan County community members as part of grants awarded by the Rockefeller Foundation and the Appalachian Regional Commission; from these interviews, Higher Ground participants create musical theater. Playwright Jo Carson worked with the project for its first play.

The first *Higher Ground*, which examines prescription drug abuse, negative public health, and family trauma, was highly successful and prompted two more community dramas. *Playing with Fire* (2009) extended the conversation about drug abuse and incorporated stories from coal miners. *Talkin' Dirt* (2012) explored the choices young people in economically hard-hit Harlan County face and honored African American history in the area. In addition to three more theatrical productions, the Higher Ground group and Robert Gipe have completed mural projects and produced an annual arts festival called Crawdad.

FROM Higher Ground 2: Playing with Fire

FIRE: GONE

(SIREN SOUND. *Much running about. Through the running, a young woman enters, slowly, deliberately. The* FIRE *frenzy freezes. A child and her grandmother, the mother of this woman, watch this. This woman's sister watches too; others, call them neighbors, are the chorus.*)

LUCY. My house burned down. Why? Cause an idiot tried to refill a kerosene heater without turning it off. This particular idiot knew better than to try to refill the heater when it was still burning. I knew better, but I wasn't thinking. I wouldn't have needed the heater, but the power company cut off my juice. I've been torn up ever since I broke up with my boyfriend. He was supposed to pay the juice bill.

Instead, she feels like an idiot. What did I lose?

So let me name some of what is lost. Start with the contents of my pocket book. About 40 dollars cash, my driver's license, my favorite sunglasses. The keys to the pickup. And a lipstick Max Factor doesn't make that color of anymore.

CHORUS. Gone.

LUCY. My clothes. Good thing I had my coat on. My shoes are gone. My underwear is gone. My sexy nightgown is gone. My new-last-year robe.

CHORUS. Gone.

LUCY. Where's my daughter? With Mama. Tiffany was not in the house, thank God, because Mama had come for her when she found out I'd bought some vodka. My daughter told her. It was an arrangement they had that made me furious, but if I bought liquor, she was to call her grandmother to come and get her. Just a bit of vodka. I swear. Big deal outta nothing. The vodka is . . .

CHORUS. Gone.

LUCY. and just little bit down my throat.

CHORUS. Gone anyway.

LUCY. The house was my grandmother's house.

CHORUS. Gone.

LUCY. My Tiffany and me had been living there because I couldn't afford anything else. Mama still owned it because it is so far back in the woods, nobody ever wanted to buy it. And the fire department couldn't hardly get to it.

CHORUS. Gone.

LUCY. The bed Mama was born in, and the bed I slept in . . .

CHORUS. Gone.

LUCY. The quilts grandmother made . . .

CHORUS. Gone.

LUCY. The coffee pot, the good skillet, the washing machine, the refrigerator, the smoked trout my big sister Kayla gave me . . .

CHORUS. Gone.

LUCY. It is really smoked now. So what do I do without all the stuff of a life around me? Who am I now? I don't think I know.

CHORUS. She doesn't know.

LUCY. I'm not ready for this. I don't think I can handle this.

RED PEDAL, GREEN PEDAL

KAYLA: Let me tell you a story. Mama got me a go-kart for my birthday when I was 12. At first, I was kind of scared of it. I didn't know how to drive and dad had to paint the brake pedal red and the gas pedal green so I'd know which was which. Red for stop, green for go. And Lucy and I were riding the go-kart up and down the road. Lucy was four, and she was always wanting to do stuff she shouldn't and she just kept on at me, "let me drive let me drive let me drive" and I said "No. You're too little, you couldn't reach the brake." So she kind of huffed and sat there. Next thing I know she was on me, and she grabbed the steering wheel and turned really fast and I panicked. I forgot which pedal was the brake—red—and I hit the gas—green—and we took off towards this cliff and we went airborne over a big ditch on the way. We jumped the ditch and we hit the mountain and keep on going cause I had my foot on the *gas* all the way because I thought I was standing on the brake. *Green for "go."* Lucy had fallen out of the go-kart right after the ditch. I was going through all this brush and weeds and didn't realize she had fallen out. I even ran over Lucy. Green to the floor. Finally I got hung in some mud and the go-kart stalled out. I heard Mama and everybody panicking because they seen me run over Lucy and they thought she was dead except she was screaming so she wasn't dead. They picked Lucy up and she had sticks and thorns and weeds sticking out of her hair and little burrs all over her clothes. And you know what Lucy said when she stopped screaming? "That was fun! Let's do it again!" And you know what the rest of 'em did? Hugged her and kissed her and told her how cute she was. And she is cute. If you don't believe me, ask her.

EDUCATION PAYS

CARL. Use your head, not your back. That's what I heard growing up. Use your head, not your back. And there were men in my family sitting around the dinner table that had used their backs and they just about didn't have a back to use anymore. My father hurt all the time. So they were proud of me when I got my degree. A man with a family already, going back to college, got an associate, then a bachelor's, then a master's. And they backed me up while I was applying for every job coming and going. But let me tell you about jobs. The education you get in school now is not necessarily going to get you a job that pays very well. Not even a master's. Not around here. One day I was at the employment office, or should I say the unemployment office, and I saw my buddy who'd quit teaching to go back in the mines. I asked him why he'd done that. Said he got a master's and a job making 28,000 a year. First year underground, he made 52,000. Fixing to move up, too. So I asked what he did. He said a little bit of everything. Ran a continuous miner. A scoop. Ran roof bolters. He said everybody starts shoveling at the beltline, mucking the belt. If you do ok, you move up. Said they were hiring, he'd put a word in for me. I looked again at the wall in the unemployment office—nothing close to 52,000. So I'm a man with a master's degree and a family mucking the beltline in a coal mine. It is a back job if ever there was one. My wife worries from the time I leave in the morning till the time I get back in the door because it is a dangerous job. But it *is* a thinking job. I'm thinking about what I could do that might earn 52,000 doing something that doesn't ruin your back and leave tears in your wife's eyes every morning. (*Lights Fade.*)

FIRE: BATTLE

(*This scene starts on fire and gets hotter.* LUCY *is in her own place—speaking her words flat out, and not to* MAMA, *who relates the story in past tense.* KAYLA *witnesses, behind* MAMA.)

MAMA. I had a rough time with Lucy. She wasn't taking care of herself, and she looked bad. I was afraid it was maybe drugs.

LUCY. I don't have to listen to you!

MAMA. She had got hanging around with people that I knew were on the drugs, and so I worked up the courage. I asked was she on something . . .

LUCY. No. You just never like my friends. They're my friends, not yours.

MAMA. But my fears wouldn't go away . . . and I saw the signs.

LUCY. How would you know?

MAMA. It hit me the night I came home from bible study and the TV was missing.

LUCY. Why do you always think it's me? Never Kayla. Not "Little Miss Perfect."

MAMA. I went down to the pawn shop. I told them her name and they said yeah she brought it in.

LUCY. So you believe him and not me, your own daughter? You listen to him over family? He's just trying to make a dollar.

MAMA. I told them I was her mother and she stole that TV from me. I went by the bank, I paid the hock ticket, and I carried my TV home. So I figured she was on oxys, but it is one thing to be on them and another to be stealing like that and I come home and I threw her out. I told her "if you want to do your drugs then you do it somewhere else, but you're not going to do it here in my house. You are not going to make me watch you die."

LUCY. Whatever.

MAMA. I said I don't want to look at you until you are off those things. I said there was a rehab in Corbin.

LUCY. I don't need that. I'm not no addict.

MAMA. Then I said, "Here's $500, and the keys to the pick-up. Take it. Just don't come back."

LUCY. (*Catches the keys.*) Whatever. (*A look, a thought, and she's outta there. Pause.*)

KAYLA. Mama?

MAMA. What? (*A silence*)

KAYLA. That's the pick-up truck I drive. I'm still here.

MAMA. She can't leave without something to leave in.

KAYLA. I'm still here.

MAMA. Oh, I know, Kayla darling. You're always here.

JOINED TOGETHER

(*Onstage are two men taped together, with industrial strength tape. They can't talk—their mouths are taped or gagged. They probably can and should grunt. They desperately want to be free. What they do manage to do in their taped together state is fall down and roll into the middle of what becomes a road.*)

BOB. Well, they finally got you two, did they?

TAPED MEN. (*The men do make some noises in response to what he says, and if their mouths weren't gagged, they would mostly say things like cut me loose!*)

BOB. I figured it was coming. You put a snake in a man's lunch pail, that's beyond what fellows want to tolerate. Nobody wants a live snake in the hole.

TAPED MEN. (*Noise. One of them protests. More of this throughout.*)

BOB. (*To the men.*) Yeah, I know, it was a blacksnake and it wasn't gonna hurt anybody, but it didn't look like a blacksnake to me slithering out of that bucket. Looked about like my worst nightmare. (*To the audience.*) These two . . . they've been a problem. They went to different high schools, but this was seven, eight years ago, and they played on opposing football teams, and this one (*One of the men*) will tell you that this one (*The second of the men*) kneed him every time he got a chance in a place that ain't supposed to be talked about. I don't know whether it was true or not. But this fellow (*the first*) won't shut up about it. So this fellow (*the second*) walked up and kneed him when he didn't have any of that football gear on, and 'bout bent him double. And then, things started showing up in lunch pails. This one's lunch covered with Tabasco. Little things looked like chocolate cookies made out of cow piles in this one's bucket. A dead catfish. And this goes on. About the time you get to the dead fish, this ain't very funny anymore, and these guys aren't just leaving it in the lunch pail. I mean, they're doing things to one another. And it'd be one thing if it was only them at risk, but it ain't. We're all in it together. And then, there was the live black-snake in the lunch bucket. And nobody wants to eat lunch with a snake. At the time, we didn't know for sure it was a blacksnake. Looked like a copperhead to me, down there in the dark. So I ain't surprised somebody taped 'em. That there's *strong* tape. You can do a lot and nobody'll get on you for it, and folks are rough on one another sometimes, but that was everybody with that snake loose down there. (*To the two men, he starts moving them, rolling them to the side of the road . . .*) I ain't cutting you loose. They'd tape me up with you. That's the rule: only them that tapes can set you free. Once two are joined together, let no man cut asunder. (*Laughs quietly, he's moved them, he gets back on his machine . . .*) You boys, you'll do well to lie there and figure out how to kiss and make up.

BLACK DAMP

HANK. It was just a regular normal day. Got up and fooled around the house a little while. I worked third shift so I did a little yard work that day. Always laid down for about an hour before I'd go to work. Got up. Got ready. My wife kissed me. Told me she loved me. Told me she'd see me in the morning and she made some promises, you know . . .

CHORUS B. White damp,

CHORUS C. Fire damp,

CHORUS D. Stink damp,

CHORUS A. Black damp.

HANK. Got to work. Outside, you put your lights and stuff on, boots and every-thing. Jump around, play . . . Now, this is bigger than it sounds like. Your life can depend on your co-workers underground, and that horsing around, well, that hors-ing around can save you. We started the shift, everything was fine, we went in and started the man trip, went down to the coal face and started working, everything was going good all day.

CHORUS C. White damp,

CHORUS D. Fire damp,

CHORUS A. Stink damp,

CHORUS B. Black damp.

HANK. We all stopped at lunchtime, got together and we were talking like we always did. Somebody was missing a sandwich and nobody would fess up to having eaten it. We knew who it was likely to be. My wife, she knows about that business, and she packs me a lot in my bucket, so I usually have a sandwich I can give somebody. It was that liver loaf and cheese and I caught some guff about the liver loaf, but I like it fine. It ain't Alpo, I said. But it don't get stolen like ham or roast beef. They can cut me all the guff they want to about my liver loaf, I've always got something to eat.

CHORUS D. White damp,

CHORUS A. Fire damp,

CHORUS B. Stink damp,

CHORUS C. Black damp.

HANK. When we were back at the face after lunch, I was cutting coal, and it was too soft. Felt too soft. The machine was eating it too fast. And I told my friends, these men I work with, these men I care about and depend on, those that were with me, I said "This is awful soft coal."

CHORUS A. White damp,

CHORUS B. Fire damp,

CHORUS C. Stink damp,

CHORUS D. Black damp.

HANK. Then the biting edge of that machine went through the wall. Went right through to an old abandoned mine that wasn't in the right place on the map.

CHORUS D. White damp,

CHORUS A. Fire damp,

CHORUS B. Stink damp,

CHORUS C. Black damp.

HANK. The air that was coming out of it. It felt like it was a big ocean of water coming through on us. You could take a breath, but you got no oxygen so you might as well have been breathing water. Nitrogen and carbon dioxide.

CHORUS C. White damp,

CHORUS D. Fire damp,

CHORUS A. Stink damp,

CHORUS B. Black damp.

HANK. We ran for our lives. We ran. It was trapped air from an abandoned mine that was supposed to be 500 feet above us, and it pushed black damp in on us, I had cut into black damp. And I was breathing it. I run maybe 300 foot out of the section to gather the men, my friends, these men that don't like liver loaf and leave my lunch alone, I'm not sure how, I got no good air. I was trying to get them together. There was terrible danger behind me and coming. Fast.

CHORUS B. Black damp

CHORUS C. Coming,

CHORUS D & A. Coming.

CHORUS (ALL). Coming.

HANK. When we got to the man trip, I knew there were two still back there. Then the boss said

BOSS. I've got to go back.

HANK. And I'm struggling to breathe, but I was trying my best to get him to stay in the man trip but he wouldn't do it—

BOSS. I gotta get 'em. I gotta. We can ride the belt out. Keep it running . . . Now you all! Get out!

CHORUS C. Coming,

CHORUS D. Coming,

CHORUS A. Coming,

CHORUS B. Coming . . .

HANK. He went back towards where we'd come from, and that was the last time we seen him. I got out and then me and the repairmen had got in to the black damp bad, so we had to get to the hospital, they gave us oxygen and I didn't know what was going on back at the mine so I told them at the hospital I had to go back. I'm trained for rescue, I had to go back. They didn't want to release me, but I wanted to go. And we went back into that mine with gas masks and oxygen, and all three of them were dead so we got them on the man trip and brought the bodies out.

CHORUS A. White damp,

CHORUS B. Fire damp,

CHORUS C. Stink damp,

CHORUS D. Black damp . . .

BERT. Nobody said nothing much. Not at first. I'd been friends with them forever. Me and Roy we went to grade school all the way through high school. Graduated high school together. All of us worked together there. Worked at other mines together. It gets to be about like you are brothers when you're coal miners. See them more almost than you do your own family. Listen, it tore me to pieces. Three of my *brothers* died. Black damn damp. But I wanna say this: that boss, he was all right. He might steal your sandwich, but that was horsing around. When push came to shove, that man stood up. He was the good shepherd, the one that goes back out after the sheep that's lost. I count that man maybe the most honorable I've ever known. Wish to hell he was still here to steal every one of my roast beef sandwiches.

CHORUS A. White damp,

CHORUS B. Fire damp,

CHORUS C. Stink damp,

CHORUS D. Black damp . . .

HANK. Just once, I wish we'd rescue somebody living instead of just recovering a body. I think that's why I keep doing the rescue stuff. I think I got to do it until I bring somebody out alive.

THINGS TO SAY—THE NINETY-NINE

(*As this monologue unfolds, people gather and light candles.*)

BOSS. (*We see him cutting lunch buckets—looking through several for the best snack. Toward the end he finds what he's looking for. Is he alive, or a ghost?*) You get in a cave-in or a damp or something. Running out of air, and you know it, and you search your pockets for anything, a store receipt, anything to write on, and then maybe all you've got to write with is your own blood, so you say "I love you" in blood cause that's all you got room for. Well, I've been thinking about that. And I've got more to say. Elizabeth, my wife, you have been the making and the breaking and the breaking and the making of me. Time and again. I love you beyond what I can say. This language isn't big enough to say love. My sons, James and Paul, my daughter Melinda, I see myself in all three of you, my graces and my failings. You are the very wheel of time as it turns for me. You are my life ongoing. Can a man love something better than his own life? Yes, he can. Our home, my work, those things I do, my can of beer, the Corvette I've spent a small fortune trying to make run right, I love them too. Not in the same way, but I love them too. Let me say this: I love this life that is my life. Might as well say it. I would like to die an old man in a comfortable bed. However I go, I'm gonna be a little afraid when that time comes, I guess everyone is, but I don't want fear and regret to be the only things I'm feeling. I want to say this now. I have been blessed beyond what I can name or understand. I have loved and I have been loved, and I have *been amazed. I have been amazed. (He takes a big bite.)*

FIRE: RESCUE

(*LUCY and KAYLA in a car. KAYLA is driving. It is dark, the conversation is slow. LUCY clutches a burnt piece of wood.*)

KAYLA. You ready for something to eat? (*Pause*) Wanna stop for that burger?

LUCY. Not yet.

KAYLA: You mad at me?

LUCY. No. (*But she is some.*)

KAYLA. You know why I couldn't let you come in?

LUCY. Yes. (*But she doesn't yet feel it's fair or just.*)

KAYLA. I want you to make it. (*LUCY is silent.*) It would be nice if you did. (*Sighs.*)

LUCY. (*A silence, then LUCY speaks. Not to KAYLA but in an aside to the audience. KAYLA does not hear this.*) What I want to say but I can't say it out loud, not yet. Can't, cause I don't know whether it's true or not—I want it to be true—but . . . I don't know. Well, here it is: Kayla was right to do that. I hate her for it, but I'm glad she did it. Or I will be. I'm going to be glad I'm in this car. I am not the same person who burnt down the house. You'd think burning down the house would be enough for me to get the message. Maybe. But here's the thing. What happens changes us, but what changes in *me* depends on how I tell *myself* the story. This could be a poor me story: "those kerosene heaters are so dangerous, you are flirting with a house fire just using one of those things." Not my fault. "That SOB boyfriend drove me to it, if it hadn't been for him, I would never even have bought that stuff and I wouldn't have had any trouble with the heater . . ." Lots and lots of NOT MY FAULT versions of this story. Which means, if I tell myself one of those versions, I can do it again. But there is no poor me here. It was MY fault. I got high, ran out of money, and burnt down the house. That was something I did. I own this (*the piece of burnt wood*). It is mine. And I had great good fortune in that fire: all I lost was things. Tiffany is alive. I am alive. That means something. My Mama opened her door, in spite of everything. That means something. My sister just threw me a lifeline. (*Pause.*) And my life has a big new story in it. Once, I was a big enough idiot that I burnt my house down. (*Sighs.*) It's a long way to Corbin. And a long way back. And I can't say any of that yet. Maybe I never will be able to say it. (*To* KAYLA) Kayla?

KAYLA. Yeah?

LUCY. Thanks.

Acknowledgments

This project began in a conversation between Katherine Ledford and Theresa Lloyd at the 30th Annual Appalachian Studies Conference at Maryville College in Maryville, Tennessee, in 2007. Katherine was teaching Appalachian literature for the first time and was frustrated by the lack of a single, comprehensive text for course adoption; Theresa was researching the writings of nineteenth-century Appalachian women. The outcome of our conversation is the text you are now reading.

Several years into the project, we asked Rebecca Stephens to join us as associate editor. Rebecca worked diligently and brought a fresh perspective on contemporary Appalachian writers. Subsequently, Richard Parmer joined the team, tackling the permissions problems with vigor.

On a project of this size, scope, and duration, we have accumulated many debts. First, we thank our editors at the University Press of Kentucky. Their enthusiasm and unwavering support for this anthology has kept us going. They believed in this project from day one and have assisted us with good cheer at every turn.

We also thank our colleagues who generously gave of their time to write some of the section introductions in this anthology: Kevin E. O'Donnell, Katherine Hoffman, Jesse Graves, and Thomas Alan Holmes.

Additionally, we thank the Department of Literature and Language, the Department of Appalachian Studies, the Archives of Appalachia, and the Sherrod Library Interlibrary Loan at East Tennessee State University, Theresa's academic home; and the Center for Appalachian Studies, the Appalachian Studies Program, and the William Leonard Eury Appalachian Collection at Appalachian State University, Katherine's academic home. The undergraduate and graduate students in our Appalachian literature and Appalachian studies courses shaped this book through the questions they asked, the frustrations they expressed, and the curiosity they exhibited. We are also grateful to the authors, editors, agents, and artists who helped us obtain permissions.

The following people have also been integral to the success of this project: Sandra Ballard, Patricia Beaver, George Brosi, Robin DuBlanc, Grace Toney Edwards, Stephen Fox, Alexandra Frank, Chan Gordon, Chris Green, William A. Hart Jr., Jean Haskell, Roberta Herrin, Katherine Hoffman, Mary Jackson, Carl Lindahl, Erica Abrams Locklear, Michael Montgomery, Ted Olson, Diana Qualls, Ron Roach, Carmen Rueda, Randy Sanders, Emily Satterwhite, Judith Slagle, Laura Smith, Catherine Strain, and Katherine Weiss.

Katherine Ledford thanks the Cratis D. Williams School of Graduate Studies at Appalachian State University for a Graduate Research Associate Mentoring Program award, which allowed her to mentor a graduate student, Kris Dearmin, through collaborative work on this research project. She also thanks the following graduate research assistants: Marc Bentley, Melanie Harsha, Brittany Hicks, Takahiro Omori, Karen Russo, Robyn Seamon, Rachel Simon, KaLeigh Underwood, and Leigh Walters. With special gratitude, she acknowledges the support, patience, and love of her husband, Brian McKinney, and their children, Ada Ledford McKinney and Zebulon Ledford McKinney, who grew up alongside this book in the Appalachian Mountains they all love.

Theresa Lloyd acknowledges the support of the Small Grants Program at East Tennessee State University and a non-instructional leave of absence from the university to work on the anthology. She is grateful for the help of her graduate research assistants Dusty Brice, Julie Hale, Kari Keeling, and Robert Kottage. Tess also thanks her father, Eldridge Lloyd, whose undergraduate honors thesis on Mitchell County, North Carolina, and work as a seasonal ranger on the Blue Ridge Parkway got her to the mountains; her mother, Evelyn Lloyd, who first put a book in her hands; and her husband, Dan Kleeman, who has supported all her endeavors.

Rebecca Stephens acknowledges all of her friends and colleagues who generously listened to and debated questions about Appalachia and its literature, especially Nate Freeman. She is grateful to her children, Lilah Catron, Liberty Lucas, and Tristan Lucas, for sharing her with this project and growing in the love of the mountains alongside her.

Richard Parmer thanks his parents, Ricky and Rita Parmer, as well as Theresa Lloyd, Katherine Ledford, and Rebecca Stephens, who brought him on board the anthology project, and Marion Rust, his dissertation director.

Bibliography and Permissions

Akers, Robert. "What a Time We're Living In." Recorded August 20, 1978, in Galax, Virginia. In *Children of the Heav'nly King: Religious Expression in the Central Blue Ridge.* Library of Congress AFS L69/70 (1973); Rounder 1506/07 (1988). Reprinted by permission of Rev. Robert Akers.

Allison, Dorothy. "Nice." Previously unpublished story, 2004.

Alther, Lisa. "Walking the Knife's Edge, or Blue Balls in Bibleland." In *Kinflicks.* Knopf, 1976. Reprinted by permission of Lisa Alther.

Anderson, Maggie. "House and Graveyard, Rowelsburg, West Virginia, 1935" and "Heartfire." In *Windfall: New and Selected Poems.* University of Pittsburgh Press, 2000. © 2000. Reprinted by permission of the University of Pittsburgh Press.

Armstrong, Anne Wetzell. "The Branner House." *Yale Review* 27 (1938). Permission *Yale Review.*

Arnoult, Darnell. "Second Shift" and "Photographs in the Hall." In *What Travels with Us: Poems.* Louisiana State University Press, 2005. © 2005. Reprinted by permission of Louisiana State University Press.

———. "Spoons." In *Galaxie Wagon: Poems.* Louisiana State University Press, 2016. © 2016. Reprinted by permission of Louisiana State University Press.

Arnow, Harriette Simpson. "The Un-American Activities of Miss Prink." In *The Collected Short Stories of Harriette Simpson Arnow,* edited by Sandra L. Ballard and Haeja K. Chung. Michigan State University Press, 2005. Reprinted by permission of Thomas L. Arnow.

Awiakta, Marilou. "Genesis," "An Indian Walks in Me," "Marriage," "Smoky Mountain Woman," and "Where Mountain and Atom Meet." In *Abiding Appalachia: Where Mountain and Atom Meet.* St. Luke's Press, 1978. Reprint, Pocahontas Press, 2006. We used the author's hand-corrected version of this edition. Reprinted by permission of Marilou Awiakta.

Bartram, William. *Travels through North and South Carolina, Georgia, East and West Florida, the Cherokee Country, etc.* 1791. Reprint, J. Moore, W. Jones, R. McAllister, and J. Rice, 1793.

Bell, Thomas. *Out of This Furnace.* Little, Brown, 1941. Copyright © 1941; 1976 by W. H. Auden, renewed. Reprinted by permission of Curtis Brown, Ltd.

Berry, Wendell. Afterword to *Missing Mountains: We Went to the Mountaintop but It Wasn't There,* edited by Kristin Johannsen, Bobbie Ann Mason, and Mary Ann Taylor-Hall. Wind Publications, 2005. Reprinted by permission of Wind Publications.

Boudinot, Elias [Gallegina "Buck" Watie]. *An Address to the Whites Delivered in the First Presbyterian Church, on the 26th of May, 1826.* W. F. Geddes, 1826.

Broome, Harvey. "Formative Years." In *Out Under the Sky of the Great Smokies: A Personal Journey.* University of Tennessee Press, 1975. Reprint, University of Tennessee Press, 2001. Reprinted by permission of University of Tennessee Press.

Byer, Kathryn Stripling. "Full Moon." In *Black Shawl.* Louisiana State University Press, 1998. Reprinted by permission of Louisiana State University Press.

———. "The Still Here and Now." In *Coming to Rest.* Louisiana State University Press, 2006. Reprinted by permission of Louisiana State University Press.

Campbell, Olive Dame. *Appalachian Travels: The Diary of Olive Dame Campbell.* Edited by Elizabeth McCutchen Williams. University Press of Kentucky, 2012. Reprinted by permission of University Press of Kentucky.

Carson, Jo. *Daytrips.* Dramatists Play Service, 1998. Reprinted by permission of Lisa Mount.

Cash, Wiley. "Verchel Park." *Idaho Review* 16 (December 2015). Copyright © 2015 by Wiley Cash. Reprinted by permission of Wiley Cash.

Caudill, Harry. "O, Appalachia!" Originally published in *Intellectual Digest,* April 1973. Reprinted in *Voices from the Hills: Selected Readings of Southern Appalachia,* edited by Robert J. Higgs and Ambrose N. Manning. Frederick Ungar Publishing Company, 1975. Reprinted by permission of Anne Caudill.

Chandler, Lloyd. "Remember and Do Pray for Me (A Conversation with Death)." 1915. *Journal of Folklore Research* 41, no. 2 (May–August 2004). Copyright 2003 by Estate of Lloyd Chandler. Reprinted with permission of Brenda Chandler.

Chappell, Fred. *I Am One of You Forever.* Louisiana State University Press, 1985. Reprinted by permission of Louisiana State University Press.

———. "My Grandmother Washes Her Vessels." In *Midquest: A Poem.* Louisiana State University Press, 1981. Reprinted by permission of Louisiana State University.

Cooper, James Fenimore. *The Pioneers, or The Sources of the Susquehanna; a Descriptive Tale,* vol. 2. Charles Wiley, 1823.

Couch, Jim (pseud.). "Mat Layson." In *Up Cutshin and Down Greasy: Folkways of a Kentucky Mountain Family,* by Leonard W. Roberts. University Press of Kentucky, 1959. Reprinted by permission of Lynneda J. Denny on behalf of the four daughters of Dr. Leonard Roberts

"The Daemon Lover." Child 243. Sung by Sarah Buckner at Black Mountain, North Carolina. In *English Folk Songs from the Southern Appalachians,* edited by Cecil J. Sharpe and Olive Dame Campbell. G. P. Putnam's Sons, 1917.

davenport, doris. "Ceremony for 103 Soque Street" and "Miz Clio Savant." In *Madness Like Morning Glories.* Louisiana State University Press, 2005. © 2005. Reprinted by permission of Louisiana State University Press.

Davis, Rebecca Harding. "The Yares of the Black Mountains: A True Story." 1875. In *Silhouettes of American Life.* Charles Scribner's Sons, 1892.

Delany, Martin Robison. *The Condition, Elevation, Emigration, and Destiny of the Colored People of the United States.* Published by the author, 1852.

Drew, Benjamin. [James Adams narrative in] *A North-Side View of Slavery. The Refugee: or the Narratives of Fugitive Slaves in Canada.* J. P. Jewett, 1856.

Duncan, Pamela. "On the Inside Looking Out." *Still: The Journal,* Summer 2010. Reprinted by permission of Pamela Duncan.

Dykeman, Wilma. *Return the Innocent Earth.* Holt, Rinehart and Winston, 1973. Originally published by Wakestone Books, 1973. Reprinted by permission of Dykeman Stokely.

Earley, Tony. "Jack and the Mad Dog." In *Mr. Tall: A Novella and Stories.* Backwater Bay/

Little Brown, 2012. Copyright © 2014, 2015. Reprinted by permission of Little, Brown and Co., an imprint of Hachette Book Group, Inc.

Embree, Elihu. *The Emancipator,* April 30, June 30, 1820.

Fain, Fannie A. Diary, 1863–1865. Archives of Appalachia, East Tennessee State University. Johnson City, Tennessee. Reprinted with permission from Archives of Appalachia.

"Father Grumble." Sung by Mrs. Charles B. Cannaday, Morgantown, West Virginia. In *Folk-Songs of the South: Collected under the Auspices of the West Virginia Folk-Lore Society,* edited by John Harrington Cox. Harvard University Press, 1925.

Fisher, Diane Gilliam. "Raven Light." In *Kettle Bottom.* Perugia Press, 2004. Reprinted by permission of Diane Gilliam Fisher.

Fox, John, Jr. "The Pardon of Becky Day." In *Christmas Eve on Lonesome and Other Stories.* Charles Scribner's Sons, 1904.

"Frankie Silver." Version a. Sung by M. I. Pickens. In *The Frank C. Brown Collection of North Carolina Folklore,* edited by Newman Ivey White, vol. 2, *Folk Ballads from North Carolina,* edited by Henry M. Belden and Arthur P. Hudson. Duke University Press, 1952. Copyright 1952, Duke University Press. All rights reserved. Republished by permission of the copyright holder. www.dukeupress.edu.

Frazier, Charles. *Thirteen Moons.* Random House, 2006. Reprinted by permission of Charles Frazier.

Frost, William Goodell. "Our Contemporary Ancestors in the Southern Mountains." *Atlantic Monthly,* January 1, 1899.

Furman, Lucy. *Sight to the Blind: A Story.* Macmillan, 1914.

Giardina, Denise. "Candy." Originally printed in *Appalachian Heritage* 44, no. 4 (Fall 2016). Reprinted by permission of Denise Giardina.

Giovanni, Nikki. "Knoxville, Tennessee." 1979. In *The Collected Poetry of Nikki Giovanni.* William Morrow, 2003. Reprinted by permission of Nikki Giovanni.

Gipe, Robert. *Trampoline: An Illustrated Novel.* Ohio University Press, 2015. Copyright © 2015 by Robert Gipe. This material is used by permission of Ohio University Press, www.ohioswallow.com.

Goodrich, Frances Louisa. "The Three Gray Women." In *Mountain Homespun.* Yale University Press and Oxford University Press, 1931.

Graves, Jesse. "Digging the Pond" and "Mother's Milk." In *Tennessee Landscape with Blighted Pine.* Texas Review Press, 2011. © 2011. Reprinted by permission of Jesse Graves.

Hansel, Pauletta. "She" and "Writing Lessons (I.)" In *Divining.* WovenWord, 2001. Reprinted by permission of Pauletta Hansel.

Harlan Miners Speak: Report on Terrorism in the Kentucky Coal Fields. Edited by Members of the National Committee for the Defense of Political Prisoners (Dreiser Committee). Harcourt, Brace, 1932.

Harris, George Washington. "Parson John Bullen's Lizards." In *Sut Lovingood. Yarns Spun by a "Nat'ral Born Durn'd Fool." Warped and Wove for Public Wear.* Dick and Fitzgerald, 1867.

Haun, Mildred. "The Piece of Silver." In *The Hawk's Done Gone, and Other Stories,* edited by Herschel Gower. Vanderbilt University Press, 1968. Reprinted by permission of Vanderbilt University Press.

Hausman, Blake M. *Riding the Trail of Tears: A Novel.* University of Nebraska Press, 2011.

Reproduced by permission of the University of Nebraska Press. Copyright © 2011 by the Board of Regents of the University of Nebraska.

Hayes, Shannon. Introduction to *Radical Homemakers: Reclaiming Domesticity from a Consumer Culture*. Left to Write Press, 2010. Reprinted by permission of Shannon Hayes.

Higher Ground Project. *Higher Ground 2: Playing with Fire*. Southeast Kentucky Community and Technical College, 2009. Reprinted by permission of Robert Gipe, Higher Ground Executive Director.

hooks, bell. "On Reflection and Lamentation." In *Appalachian Elegy: Poetry and Place*. University Press of Kentucky, 2012. Copyright © 2012 by bell hooks. Reprinted by permission of the University Press of Kentucky.

House, Silas. *Recruiters*. Larkspur, 2010. Originally published in the *Anthology of Appalachian Writers* 2 (2010) by Shepherd University. Reprinted by permission of Silas House.

Jackson, Aunt Molly. "Hard Times in Coleman's Mine." From Lomax and Barnacle's 1937 oral history session. Courtesy of Jack Wright, *Music of Coal: Mining Songs from the Appalachian Coalfields*, 2007.

Jefferson, Thomas. *Notes on the State of Virginia* (1785, 1787). In *The Writings of Thomas Jefferson*, vol. 1, edited by Albert Ellery Bergh. Thomas Jefferson Memorial Association, 1907.

"John Henry." Version e. Sung by G. S. Robinson, Asheville, North Carolina. In *The Frank C. Brown Collection of North Carolina Folklore*, edited by Newman Ivey White, vol. 2, *Folk Ballads from North Carolina*, edited by Henry M. Belden and Arthur P. Hudson. Duke University Press, 1952. Copyright 1952, Duke University Press. All rights reserved. Republished by permission of the copyright holder. www.dukeupress.edu.

Johnson, Don. "And the River Gathered around Us," "1946," and "Raymond Pierce's Vietnamese Wife." In *Watauga Drawdown*. Overmountain, 1990. Reprinted by permission of Don Johnson.

Jones, Loyal. "Familism," "Independence, Self-Reliance, and Pride," "Love of Place," and "Religion." In *Appalachian Values*. 1973. Reprint, Jesse Stuart Foundation, 1994. Reprinted by permission of Loyal Jones.

Jones, Mary Harris "Mother." *Autobiography of Mother Jones*. Edited by Mary Field Parton. Charles H. Kerr, 1925.

Katz, Sandor Ellix. *Wild Fermentation: The Flavor, Nutrition, and Craft of Live-Culture Foods*. Chelsea Green, 2003. Copyright © 2003 by Sandor Katz, used with permission from Chelsea Green Publishing (www.chelseagreen.com).

Kephart, Horace. *Our Southern Highlanders: A Narrative of Adventure in the Southern Appalachians and a Study of Life among the Mountaineers*. 1913. Reprint, Macmillan, 1922.

Kingsolver, Barbara, with Steven L. Hopp and Camille Kingsolver. "Life in a Red State" [pp. 196–211 excluding sidebar by Steven Hopp] from *Animal, Vegetable, Miracle: A Year of Food Life*. HarperCollins, 2007. Copyright © 2007 by Barbara Kingsolver, Steven Hopp, and Camille Kingsolver. Reprinted by permission of HarperCollins Publishers.

Kyofski, Bonelyn Lugg. "Grandma Hess's Story about Jack, Bill, and Tom." From *Jack in Two Worlds: Contemporary North American Tales and Their Tellers*, edited by William Bernard McCarthy. University of North Carolina Press, 1994. Copyright ©1994 by the University of North Carolina Press. Used by permission of the publisher. www.unc.press.org.

Lyon, George Ella. *With a Hammer for My Heart*. DK Publishing, 1997. Reprinted by permission of George Ella Lyon.

Mann, Jeff. *Loving Mountains, Loving Men*. Ohio University Press, 2005. Copyright © 2005 by Ohio University Press. This material is used by permission of Ohio University Press, www.ohioswallow.com, and Jeff Mann.

Manning, Maurice. "IX" and "XIII." In *Bucolics*. Harcourt, 2007. Copyright © 2007 by Maurice Manning. Reprinted by permission of Houghton Mifflin Harcourt Publishing Company. All rights reserved.

———. "That Durned Ole Via Negativa." In *The Common Man: Poems*. Houghton Mifflin Harcourt, 2010. Copyright © 2010 by Maurice Manning. Reprinted by permission of Houghton Mifflin Harcourt Publishing Company. All rights reserved.

Marion, Jeff Daniel. "Ebbing and Flowing Spring." In *Vigils: Selected Poems*. Appalachian Consortium, 1990. Originally published in *Out in the Country, Back Home* by Jackpine Press, 1976. Reprinted by permission of Jeff Daniel Marion.

———. "The Man Who Loved Hummingbirds." In *Lost and Found: Poems*. Sow's Ear, 1994. Reprinted by permission of Jeff Daniel Marion.

McElmurray, Karen Salyer. "Trip around the World." In *An Angle of Vision: Women Writers on Their Poor and Working Class Roots,* edited by Lorraine M. Lopez. University of Michigan Press, 2009. Reprinted by permission of the University of Michigan Press.

McGhee, Brownie. "Pawn Shop." BMI WORK #1159057. Reprinted by permission of Pru Music and Lori Cadena.

McKinney, Irene. "Twilight in West Virginia: Six O'Clock Mine Report." In *Six O'Clock Mine Report*. University of Pittsburgh Press, 1989. © 1989. Reprinted by permission of the University of Pittsburgh Press.

McLarney, Rose. "Cakewalk." *Town Creek Poetry,* Spring 2017, Tenth Anniversary Issue. Reprinted by permission of Rose McLarney.

McNeill, Louise. "Cassandra," "Genesis," "Of Fitness to Survive," "Potherbs," and "The New Corbies." In *Paradox Hill: From Appalachia to Lunar Shore*. West Virginia University Library, 1972. Reprinted by permission of West Virginia University Library.

———. "Katchie Verner's Harvest" and "Oil Field." In *Gauley Mountain*. Harcourt, Brace, 1939. Reprinted by permission of Pocahontas Communications Cooperative Corporation dba Allegheny Mountain Radio.

Middleton, Harry. *On the Spine of Time: An Angler's Love of the Smokies*. Simon & Schuster, 1991. Originally published by Pruett Publishing, 1991. Reprinted by permission of Queen Literary Agency.

Miles, Emma Bell. *The Spirit of the Mountains*. James Pott, 1905.

Miller, Jason. *Nobody Hears a Broken Drum*. Samuel French, 1970. Reprinted by permission of Stephen Breimer and Jason Patric.

Miller, Jim Wayne. "Brier Sermon—'You Must Be Born Again.'" In *The Brier Poems*. 1980. Reprint, Gnomon, 1997. Reprinted by permission of Gnomon Press.

Mooney, James. *Myths of the Cherokee* (1900). Government Printing Office, 1902.

Morgan, Robert. "Audubon's Flute," "Double Springs," "High Wallow," and "Paradise's Fool."

In *Green River: New and Selected Poems.* Wesleyan University Press, 1991. Reprinted by permission of the author.

———. "Mountain Bride." In *Groundwork.* Gnomon, 1979. Reprinted by permission of Gnomon Press.

Murfree, Mary Noailles. "The Star in the Valley." In *In the Tennessee Mountains.* Houghton Mifflin, 1884.

Nazario y Colón, Ricardo. "Dalton," "In the Beginning," and "Tujcalusa." In *Of Jíbaros and Hillbillies.* Plain View, 2011. Reprinted by permission of the author.

Norman, Gurney. *Divine Right's Trip: A Novel of the Counterculture,* 1971. 2nd edition, Gnomon, 1972. Reprinted by permission of Gnomon Press.

O'Neal, John, Ron Short, and Donna Porterfield. Excerpt from the play *Junebug/Jack,* co-created by Junebug Productions and Roadside Theater; co-written by John O'Neal, Ron Short, and Donna Porterfield with original music composed by Michael Keck, Ron Short, and John O'Neal. *Junebug/Jack* was directed by Dudley Cocke and Steve Kent; it premiered October 4, 1990, Atlanta, Georgia, and toured nationally 1990–2000. Reprinted by permission of Donna Porterfield and Theresa Holden for John O'Neal.

Pancake, Ann. *Strange as This Weather Has Been: A Novel.* Shoemaker & Hoard, 2007. Copyright © 2007 by Ann Pancake. Reprinted by permission of Counterpoint Press.

Pancake, Breece D'J. "First Day of Winter." In *The Stories of Breece D'J Pancake.* Little, Brown, 1983. Copyright © 1977, 1978, 1979, 1981, 1982, 1983 by Helen Pancake. By permission of Little, Brown and Company. All rights reserved.

Phillips, Jayne Anne. "Souvenir." In *Black Tickets.* Delta Trade Paperbacks, 1979. Reprinted by permission of the author.

Pittman, R. H. "Daniel Smith Webb" and "Mrs. Temesia Ann Hardy." In *Biographical History of Primitive or Old School Baptist Ministers of the United States: Including [. . .] Brief Sketches of a Few of Our Talented and Spiritually-Minded Sisters and "Mothers in Israel."* Herald, 1909.

Powell, Lynn. "At Ninety-Eight" and "Raising Jesus." In *Old and New Testaments.* University of Wisconsin Press, 1995. © 1995 by the Board of Regents of the University of Wisconsin System. Reprinted by permission of The University of Wisconsin Press.

Powell, Mark. "A Woman with a Torch." *Witness* 31, no. 1 (Spring 2018). Reprinted by permission of the author.

Range, Melissa. "Ofermod." In *Scriptorium: Poems.* Beacon, 2016. Copyright © 2016 by Melissa Range. Reprinted by permission of Beacon Press, Boston.

Rash, Ron. "The Ascent." In *Burning Bright.* HarperCollins, 2010. Copyright © 2010 by Ron Rash. Reprinted by permission of HarperCollins Publishers.

———. "Black and White," "1934," and "Spring Fever." In *Eureka Mill.* Hub City Writers Project, 2001. Reprinted by permission of the author.

Reece, Florence. "Which Side Are You On?" 1931. Originally published by Stormking Music Inc., 1947. Reprinted by permission of Sanga Music Group.

Ritchie, Jean. "The L&N Don't Stop Here Anymore." 1965. ASCAP WORK ID: 420192090. Reprinted by permission of Geordie Music Publishing.

Royall, Anne Newport. *Sketches of History, Life, and Manners, in the United States, by a Traveller.* Printed by the author, 1826.

Rukeyser, Muriel. "Absalom." From *The Book of the Dead* [originally published in *U.S. 1* (1938)] in *The Collected Poems of Muriel Rukeyser,* edited by Janet E. Kaufman and Anne F. Herzog with Jan Heller Levi. University of Pittsburgh Press, 2005. Reprinted by permission of ICM Partners, Inc. Copyright © [2005] by Muriel Rukeyser.

Sexton, Earl. "But Thank God That Light: A Sermon." Delivered July 17, 1977, in West Jefferson, North Carolina, and transcribed by Howard Dorgan. In *Giving Glory to God in Appalachia: Worship Practices of Six Baptist Subdenominations,* by Howard Dorgan. University of Tennessee Press, 1987. Copyright © 1987 by The University of Tennessee Press. Reprinted by permission.

Shelby, Anne. "Appalachian Studies" and "Clyde Hacker Talks about Hog Meat." In *Appalachian Studies.* Wind Publications, 2006. © 2006. Reprinted by permission of the author.

Slone, Verna Mae. *What My Heart Wants to Tell.* University Press of Kentucky, 1987. Reprinted by permission of Milburn Slone.

Smith, Effie Waller. "Answer to Verses Addressed to Me by Peter Clay." In *Songs of the Months.* Broadway, 1904.

———. "The 'Bachelor Girl.'" In *Rhymes from the Cumberland.* Broadway, 1909.

Smith, Lee. "Folk Art." In *Mrs. Darcy and the Blue-Eyed Stranger: New and Selected Stories.* Algonquin Books of Chapel Hill, 2010. Reprinted by permission of Lee Smith.

Still, James. "The Nest" (1948). In *The Hills Remember: The Complete Short Stories of James Still,* edited by Ted Olson. University Press of Kentucky, 2012. Reprinted by permission of the University Press of Kentucky.

———. "Of the Wild Man" (1978), "Rain on the Cumberlands" (1936), and "Wolfpen Creek" (1954). Originally published by Berea College Press, 1976. Also reprinted in *From the Mountain, from the Valley: New and Collected Poems,* edited by Ted Olson. University Press of Kentucky, 2001. Reprinted by permission of Loyal Jones Appalachian Center.

———. "Spring" (1937). In *From the Mountain, from the Valley: New and Collected Poems,* edited by Ted Olson. University Press of Kentucky, 2001. Reprinted by permission of the University Press of Kentucky.

Stuart, Jesse. "406." In *Man with a Bull-Tongue Plow.* E. P. Dutton, 1934. Reprinted by permission of Marian Reiner.

———. "Men of the Mountains." In *Men of the Mountains.* 1941. Reprint, University Press of Kentucky, 1979. Reprinted by permission of Marian Reiner.

Taliaferro, Hardin E. ("Skitt"). "Uncle Davy Lane." In *Fisher's River (North Carolina) Scenes and Characters.* Harper & Brothers, 1859.

"The Two Sisters." Child 10. Sung by Louisa Chisholm at Woodridge, Virginia. *In English Folk Songs from the Southern Appalachians,* edited by Cecil J. Sharpe and Olive Dame Campbell. G. P. Putnam's Sons, 1917.

Walker, Frank X. "Affrilachia," "Healer," and "Lil' Kings." In *Affrilachia.* Old Cove, 2000. Reprinted by permission of the author.

Washington, Booker T. *Up from Slavery: An Autobiography.* Doubleday, 1901.

West, Don. "No Lonesome Road." In *Clods of Southern Earth.* Boni and Gaer, 1946. Permission granted by Linda McCarthy.

———. "Symbols," "Toil and Hunger," and "What Shall a Poet Sing?" In *Toil and Hunger: Poems.* Hagglund, 1940. Permission granted by Linda McCarthy.

Wheeler, Billy Edd. "They Can't Put It Back." 1966. Originally published by Quartet Music, Inc. & Bexhill Music Corp. Reprinted by permission of Billy Edd Wheeler.

"Whipping a Catamount." In *The Crockett Almanac: Containing Adventures, Exploits, Sprees & Scrapes in the West, & Life and Manners in the Backwoods.* Ben Hardin, 1839.

Wideman, John Edgar. "Lizabeth: The Caterpillar Story." In *Damballah.* Avon, 1981. Reprinted in *The Homewood Books.* University of Pittsburgh Press, 1992. Copyright © 1981 by John Edgar Wideman, used by permission of the Wylie Agency LLC.

Wiggins, Ella May. "The Mill Mother's Song." *Labor Defender,* October 1929.

Wildsmith, Dana. *Back to Abnormal: Surviving with an Old Farm in the New South.* Motes Books, 2010. Reprinted by permission of Dana Wildsmith.

Wilkinson, Crystal. "Tipping the Scales." In *Blackberries, Blackberries.* Toby, 2000. Reprinted by permission of Crystal Wilkinson.

Williams, Jonathan. "Aubade," "The Chameleon," "The Epitaph on Uncle Nick Grindstaff's Grave on the Iron Mountain above Shady Valley, Tennessee," "Jeff Brooks, Wagon-Master of Andrews, en Route to Franklin through the Nantahalas," "Paint Sign on a Rough Rock Yonside of Boone Side of Shady Valley," and "To Charles Oscar." In *An Ear in Bartram's Tree: Selected Poems, 1957–1967.* University of North Carolina Press, 1969. Copyright © 1969 by Jonathan Williams. Used by permission of the University of North Carolina Press. www.uncpress.org.

Wilson, August. *The Janitor.* In *Short Pieces from the New Dramatists,* edited by Stan Chervin. Broadway Play, 1985. Reprinted by permission of Constanza Romero.

Wolfe, Thomas. *The Lost Boy: A Novella.* Edited by James W. Clark Jr. University of North Carolina Press, 1992. Copyright © 1992. Used by permission of the publisher. www.uncpress.org.

Wright, Charles. "Appalachian Farewell" and "Morning Occurrence at Xanadu." In *The Wrong End of the Rainbow.* Sarabande Books, 2005. Reprinted by permission of Charles Wright and Sarabande Books.

Wright, James. "Autumn Begins in Martins Ferry, Ohio," "In Response to a Rumor That the Oldest Whorehouse in Wheeling, West Virginia, Has Been Condemned," and "Lament for My Brother on a Hayrake." In *Collected Poems.* Wesleyan University Press, 1971. © 1971 by James Wright. Used by permission of Wesleyan University Press.

Author and Title Index